MANAGEMENT

MANAGEMENT:
Concepts and Practices

R. WAYNE MONDY
East Texas State University

ROBERT E. HOLMES
Southwest Texas State University

EDWIN B. FLIPPO
The University of Arizona

ALLYN AND BACON, INC. *Boston · London · Sydney · Toronto*

Managing Editor: Michael E. Meehan
Series Editor: Jack B. Rochester
Production Editor: Charleen Akullian
Cover Designer: Christy Rosso
Preparation Buyer: Patricia Hart

Library of Congress Cataloging in Publication Data

Mondy, R Wayne, 1940–
Management, concepts and practices.

  Includes index.
  1. Management.   I. Holmes, Robert E., 1941–
joint author.   II. Flippo, Edwin B., joint
author.   III. Title.
HD31.M616   658.4   79-26367
ISBN 0-205-06859-6

Printed in the United States of America.

To Frank and Alvora Edens whose friendship, patience,
and understanding have been invaluable   R.W.M.

To Martha C. Holmes for her love, support,
and encouragement   R.E.H.

To my family   E.B.F.

Mother,
You do mean so much
to me and have throughout
the years. Thanks for
being so kind, loving and
supportive of me and my work.
Love "Bob"
5/17/80

Contents

Preface

This book was written for an audience that desires management theory to be linked with actual management practice. Although it is essentially pragmatic in approach, the text is balanced throughout with current management theory. A common theme—a "real-world" approach to management—exists throughout the book. Each of the managerial functions—planning, organizing, directing, and controlling—is discussed from the standpoint of how each function interrelates to become the management process. The book puts the student in touch with reality through the use of numerous illustrations, quotes from company executives, and company material that depicts how management is being practiced in today's organizations.

Included in the text are several chapters the authors believe deserve special emphasis. Among these are—

- **Management by Objectives: An Approach to Planning.** This chapter presents the importance of and the basic concepts relating to management by objectives in an understandable format. A comprehensive example is presented to illustrate the application of MBO in a large, diverse organization. In addition, the chapter provides extensive coverage of the strengths and weaknesses of MBO.
- **Staffing the Organization.** The authors present a thorough discussion of a human resources system and the staffing process. The chapter contains a model of the staffing process, and a section on the special considerations that must be taken in selecting managerial personnel is included.
- **Production and Operations Management I and II.** Two complete chapters are provided to expose students to production and operations management tools and techniques. Both traditional and current approaches are discussed. Each technique is described from the viewpoint of how it is currently used in industry and what knowledge a manager would need to possess in order to use the technique. After studying the chapters, students should have a better understanding of how these techniques are actually being used by managers in today's organizations.
- **Managing Small Businesses.** This chapter is full of useful information for those students who are contemplating entering business for

themselves. It contains a thorough discussion of the potential problems that may be encountered in starting and managing a small business. In addition, information on how to deal with the problems in managing small businesses is provided along with suggestions for obtaining financial and managerial assistance.

- **Managing the Multinational Enterprise.** This chapter utilizes a tremendous amount of company material and quotes from executives of multinational firms to provide students with a realistic understanding of the significance of the operations of multinational companies. The chapter illustrates how different environments can affect the operations of the multinational.

- **Corporate Social Responsibility and Business Ethics.** When the chairman of the board of a major corporation states that the company's business practices have been deficient in the past and then presents a program that has been developed to ensure that it does not occur again, students can appreciate the need for this chapter. The chapter provides a clear distinction between ethics, social responsibility, and illegal activities.

And, in the appendices—

- **Careers in Management.** In this appendix, the student is provided with meaningful information about careers in management and career development. The authors stress the need for a thorough self-assessment and an identification of career objectives before beginning the initial job search. A unique feature of this appendix is its coverage of the initial job threats a person should be aware of when a new position has been secured.

We have included the following features to promote both the readability of and practice in important management theory:

- Learning objectives are listed at the beginning of each chapter to provide students with a general overview of the purpose and the key concepts of the chapter.
- Key terms appear at the beginning of each chapter. Each key term is also presented in bold print the first time it is defined or described in the chapter, as well as highlighted in the margin for easy and quick reference.
- Career profiles of successful managers are included to show students that corporate executives are "real people."
- Insights to success by key executives from a wide variety of firms are provided. The comments from these managers are interesting and

informative and should give additional emphasis to the real-world approach of the text.

- A large number of easy to read figures and tables are provided in each chapter to help describe the various concepts.
- Illustrations are provided to make specific points about selected topics.
- Review questions are provided at the end of each chapter to test the student's understanding of the material.
- Experiential exercises are provided at the end of each chapter to permit students to become involved in the various concepts that have been discussed in the text.
- A comprehensive list of references is provided to permit students to conduct additional in-depth study of selected topics.
- True-to-life case studies are provided at the conclusion of each chapter.

All of the features mentioned are designed to enhance student interest and to provide students with an enjoyable learning experience. Numerous real-life situations were used as models in writing the text. We believe that certain managerial topics are easier to explain if the writers have had "firing-line" managerial experience. The managerial experience of the authors hopefully has added a touch of realism to the book. Our sincere desire is that the reader be stimulated by the book and choose to go into one of the most challenging and rewarding careers—MANAGEMENT!

Acknowledgments

The writing of a book cannot be accomplished without the assistance of many people. It was especially true in this instance. Although it would be impossible to list each person who assisted in this project, the authors feel that certain people must be credited due to the magnitude of their contributions.

Frank N. Edens of Louisiana Tech University and James R. Young of East Texas State University, dear and close friends of ours, provided the inspiration and moral support to see the project through to completion. A sincere note of appreciation goes to the faculty and staff of the College of Business at East Texas State University for their support and encouragement throughout the preparation of the text. Graham M. Johnson, Dean Emeritus, Kenton E. Ross, Dean, Trezzie A. Pressley, Head, Department of Marketing and Management, and Professors Robert M. Noe, III, Harry N. Mills, Randal D. Lewis, Jerry M. DeHay, and Suzanne H. McCall all offered valuable suggestions and moral support during the process. Professor Mildred Golden Pryor, Chairman, Management and Marketing Department at Stephen F. Austin State University and Dean Ed D. Roach, School of Business Administration of Southwest Texas State University deserve special recognition for their continued support. Dean John Owen, Professors Robert D. Hay and Franklin S. Williams, all of the College of Business Administration, University of Arkansas, also deserve special recognition for their encouragement. The work of Gordon R. Thomas of East Texas State University provided valuable assistance in preparing the art work for the manuscript. Kathie B. Wells, our typist for the manuscript, not only did an excellent job, but stayed of sound mind and spirit as the manuscript progressed through the various revisions.

We would also like to thank our wives for their patience, understanding, and encouragement. Without their support, the project would not have been completed. They willingly made a number of sacrifices during the long process of the preparation of the manuscript.

Because of the pragmatic nature of the book, it was necessary to secure the assistance of many corporate executives to assist in its development. We sincerely thank the following firms for providing us with valuable input which significantly aided in bringing realism to a book on management:

AMF Incorporated
Abbott International, Ltd.
American Broadcasting Companies, Inc.
American Hospital Supply Corporation
American Management Association
Applied Management Services
Armco Inc.
Arthur Young and Company
Armstrong Rubber Co.
Avon Products, Inc.
Ball Corporation
Bausch & Lomb Inc.
Baxter Travenol Laboratories Inc.
Baylor University Medical Center
Beech Aircraft Corp.
Bell & Howell Company
Bendix Corporation
Burlington Northern Incorporated
Burroughs Corporation
Carrier Corporation
Champion Spark Plug Co.
Chicago Bridge and Iron Co.
Chrysler Corporation
Citizens Insurance Company of America
Colgate-Palmolive Co.
Commercial Metals Co.
Continental Air Lines, Inc.
Copperweld Corporation
Corning Glass Works
Crown Zellerbach Corporation
Dallas Cowboys Football Club
The Dallas Morning News
Dallas Southwest Media Corporation
Daniel International Corp.
Deere & Company
Digital Equipment Corp.
Direct Lumber, Incorporated
Dow Chemical Co.
E-Systems, Inc.
Equifax Inc.
Fisher Controls Company, Inc.
Formfit Rogers, Incorporated
Fruehauf Corp.
GAF Corp.
General Electric Co.
General Foods Corp.
Georgia-Pacific Corp.
Gifford-Hill & Company, Inc.

Graniteville Co.
Gulf Oil Corp.
Hewlett-Packard Co.
Geo. A. Hormel & Co.
Howard Johnson Co.
Hughes Tool Company
The E. F. Hutton Group Inc.
Illinois Tool Works Inc.
Inland Container Corp.
Inland Steel Co.
Institute of Certified Professional Managers
Internal Revenue Service
Jack Eckerd Corporation
Jones & Laughlin Steel Corp.
Kaiser Aluminum & Chemical Corp.
Kaiser Steel Corp.
Kellogg Co.
Kemper Corporation
Kimberly-Clark Corp.
Lear Siegler, Inc.
Leaseway Transportation Corp.
Mallinckrodt Inc.
Maremont Corp.
Maytag Co.
J. Ray McDermott & Co.
McDonnel Douglas Corp.
Memorex Corp.
Michigan General Corp.
Minnesota Mining & Mfg. Co.
Monsanto Company
Morrison-Knudsen Co., Inc.
Murphy Oil Corp.
NCR Corp.
A. C. Nielsen Co.
Occidental Petroleum Corp.
Oscar Mayer & Company
PROBE, Incorporated
Pay 'N Save Corporation
Pioneer Corp.
Proctor & Gamble Co.
Raytheon Co.
Rockwell International Corp.
SCM Corp.
The Seven-Up Company
Sherwin-Williams Co.
The Signal Companies, Inc.
Signode Corp.
Spencer Foods Inc.

Southern Railway Company
Southland Corp.
Southwestern Public Service Co.
A. E. Staley Mfg. Co.
Texas Instruments Incorporated
Textron Inc.
Time Inc.
U. S. Eaton Corporation
United Telecommunications, Inc.
Univar Corporation
University Computing Co.
Wal-Mart Stores, Inc.
Washington Post
The Washington Post Company
Wyly Corp.

MANAGEMENT

INTRODUCTION

The foundation for studying the various management topics included in this book is provided in Part 1. Introductory comments related to planning, organizing, directing, and controlling are presented here. Managerial skills necessary to accomplish these functions are also described. A main purpose for this part is to show there is no one best approach to management that meets the needs of all organizations.

Chapter 1

Management

LEARNING OBJECTIVES

After completing this chapter you should be able to

1. State the importance of management to all types of organizations.
2. Define management and describe the work of managers.
3. Identify and describe the management functions of planning, organizing, directing, and controlling.
4. Explain the important managerial skills—technical, communications, human, analytical, decision-making, and conceptual.
5. Distinguish between the classical and behavioral schools of management.
6. Relate the importance of situational management—that there is no one best approach to management that meets the needs of all organizations.

As president of Centrex Corporation, a large real estate development firm, Paula Johnson is responsible for the overall success of the firm. In the five years since Paula became president of Centrex, her attitude toward managing the organization has changed considerably. Initially, she believed that if things were going to get accomplished properly, she had to make all of the decisions. It was keeping her busy seemingly twelve hours a day, seven days a week. Things have changed now. She now has five vice-presidents who report directly to her. Paula works with these vice-presidents in directing the firm toward its objectives. She thinks to herself, "At first, I was not really a manager. I was trying to do all the work myself. After I began considering myself a manager who gets the work done through other people, my job became much easier."

As office manager for Commercial Manufacturing Corporation, Wayne Thompson is responsible for supervising twelve clerks and typists. He has earned a reputation for being an excellent manager and his work group has consistently been able to process large volumes of paper work with a high degree of accuracy. When Wayne was asked the reasons for his department's efficiency, his reply was, "My employees do an excellent job. All I have to do is to let each person know what is expected of him or her and work with them to see that each job is accomplished efficiently and effectively."

Steve Carmen recently has been elected president of S.A.M. (Society for the Advancement of Management) at State University and he is busily reviewing what must be accomplished for the Fall semester. He is honored to have been elected to the position but is slightly frightened. The last president nearly flunked out of school due to spending so much time with S.A.M. The faculty advisor to S.A.M. offered Steve the following advice, "Steve, if you're going to be a successful president, you must involve other S.A.M. members in performing much of the work. Your job is to tell them what needs to be done and ensure that the work is accomplished. I don't want your grades to suffer like the former president's did."

Did you realize that 50 percent of all new businesses fail within the first two years of operation, and 70 percent fail within five years? In over 90 percent of the cases, the cause of failure can be attributed to ineffective management. The costs of poor management to individuals and to society are great. Not only are financial and physical resources wasted, but individuals often suffer psychological damage from a business failure. It's not fun to say you've failed! Many business failures can be avoided through good management practices. This is why management is a subject of increasing importance today.

We live in a society of large and small organizations. In these organizations people work together to accomplish goals that are too complex or large in number to be achieved by a single individual. Throughout life we have experiences with a variety of organizations—hospitals, schools, churches, the military, businesses, colleges, government agencies, and other types of institutions. More and more, it is being recognized that the most significant factor in determining the quality of performance and success of any organization is the success of its management.

The three examples above all involve managers. Paula, Wayne, and Steve are concerned with accomplishing a job through the efforts of other people. Why are some managers successful while others are not? The reasons for the success of managers in today's organizations are as diverse as individual personalities. Perhaps the comments of Elton H. Rule, president of American Broadcasting Companies, Inc., when he was asked the reasons for his success as a manager, best summarize the reason for success of many managers,

> Intelligence, integrity, imagination and energy: these are qualities essential to any manager anywhere. Here, though, two other qualities are equally important. A successful manager must be responsive; we serve many communities, not least among them the public at large. A manager too devoted to a single community or a single approach will rapidly become unable to function effectively. And a successful manager must be people-oriented, because human judgment and creativity are by a wide margin the most productive assets of our industry.

As the comments of Mr. Rule indicate, managers must work through others to achieve success. In this book we are concerned with providing you with more knowledge about the fundamental concepts and techniques used by effective managers. Throughout the text, we will present ideas, concepts, and practices to show how important effective management is to the successful operation of all organizations. The material will be presented from the standpoint that *there is no one best way to manage.* In order to accomplish this goal, "real world" examples of how management is actually being practiced today will be presented. While our primary focus will be on the management of business organizations, most concepts and principles also apply to nonbusiness organizations such as hospitals, churches, government agencies, and schools or universities.

WHAT IS MANAGEMENT?

It is likely you will be employed by some type of organization, and, as a result, be working in a "managed environment." Therefore, an understanding of the organization and basic management concepts will be

MR. TEXAS E. (TEX) SCHRAMM

President and General Manager
Dallas Cowboys Football Club

Texas E. (Tex) Schramm is President and General Manager of the Dallas Cowboys Football Club. While there are certainly people to argue the point, many knowledgeable sports enthusiasts believe the Dallas Cowboys to be the best organized and managed team in the League. Their success as a football power has been attained, to a great extent, because of the leadership and management ability of Tex Schramm.

When Tex graduated from the University of Texas in 1947 with a degree in journalism, little did he suspect that he would eventually become president of a highly successful football club. After working for a short time as the sports editor for the Austin American Statesman, he accepted the position of publicity director for the Los Angeles Rams Football Club. Before he left the Rams in 1957, he had progressed to the position of general manager. Tex next became assistant director of sports for Columbia Broadcasting System from 1957 to 1960. He joined the Cowboys in 1960 and has watched the team steadily progress from a weak expansion club to a power in the League.

Tex is, in the truest sense of the word, a manager. He says he performs the same role as any chief executive officer in that he attempts to create the proper climate within the organization so that the individuals who are specialists in their fields can perform to their maximum ability. He views his job as one of providing the resources—facilities, tools, and support—to permit his staff to perform at their maximum ability. Tex believes that the success of every organization depends upon the selection and development of quality personnel.

Tex further states that an organization should be measured on the basis of how consistently they are successful rather than, for instance, if they make it to the Super Bowl for one year. The Cowboys have certainly achieved this goal and many teams are fearful that this trend may continue.

★

INSIGHTS TO SUCCESS

Expect to work damn hard. Expect that the competition gets keener as time goes on. Demonstrate dedication, integrity, loyalty, curiosity, humility. Don't be afraid to express ideas for change because change certainly needs to happen—but remember always that things are the way they are because there was some good reason at some point in time. Expect that the supervision will recognize competency, desire for growth, aggressiveness, with appropriate humility, and will reward achievement. Don't be too impatient, and think twice before declining potential assignments. Don't expect (at least in a company like Dow) to become a key officer of the company within the first 5–10 years, and for the individual fortunate enough to achieve that position, don't expect that the hard work, the pressure, the decisions will all of a sudden ease at that point—rather they tend to accelerate.

H. H. Lyon, Vice-President—Administration, The Dow Chemical Company

beneficial to your success. Many of you will become managers and those who are not managers will be professional and technical personnel such as engineers, salespersons, systems analysts, accountants, market researchers, or computer programmers. But, what is management?

There are almost as many definitions of management as there are books on the subject. Most definitions of management do share a common

management idea—**management** is concerned with the *accomplishment of objectives through the efforts of other people.* Objectives, or goals, are the final results expected. For example, your immediate objective may be to pass this course while your long-term goals may be to graduate from college and obtain a good job. The goals of most business firms are to provide products and/or services for which they earn a profit. In order to accomplish their objectives it is necessary for managers to do the following:

planning
- Determine what is to be achieved **(planning).**
- Allocate resources and establish the means to accomplish the plans
organizing **(organizing).**
directing
- Motivate and lead personnel **(directing).**
controlling
- Compare results achieved to the planned goals **(controlling).**

Thus, management may be defined as the process of planning, organizing, directing, and controlling to accomplish organizational goals through the coordinated use of human and material resources.

MRS. OLIVE ANN BEECH

Chairman of the Board
Beech Aircraft Corporation

 Climbing the ladder from secretary and bookkeeper to president and then chairman of the board is only a dream for many people. Most people would not be capable of adapting to the many different situations that Mrs. Beech has confronted. However, it has been a reality for Mrs. Olive Ann Beech, who is now chairman of Beech Aircraft Corporation. Mrs. Beech is today one of the most outstanding individuals in business in the world. A few of her many accomplishments are noted below.

1943 Selected by the *New York Times* as one of the 12 most distinguished women in America, speaking on nationwide radio broadcast (April).

1951 Selected as "Woman of the Year in Aviation" by Women's National Aeronautical Association.

1956 Selected by *Business Week* magazine to appear on the cover of its February 25, 1956 issue, along with an accompanying feature article.

1959 Named "Man (Woman) of the Month" by the National Aviation Club in recognition of her leadership and achievement in a highly competitive field. Also named honorary Army Aviator and received Master Army aviator wings.

1962 Named chairman of the Utility Airplane Council of the Aerospace Industries Association of America.

1965 Chosen by Who's Who of American Women as "Outstanding Woman in the Field of Business."

1967 Appointed by President Johnson to serve on the President's Commission on White House Fellows.

1970 Selected by the nation's business and financial editors as one of America's 10 most successful businesswomen.

1971 Appointed as the first woman member of Flight Safety Foundation awards board for selection of the Aviation Week and Space Technology "Distinguished Service Award."

1973 Selected as one of "The Ten Highest-Ranking Women in Big Business" by *Fortune Magazine.*

1976 Selected one of the 10 best chief executives of companies with sales under $1 billion. Selection was made January 9, 1976, by Gallaghers President's Reports.

Selected by *Business Week* magazine as one of America's 100 Top Corporate Women.

Featured in *Life Magazine's* Special Report on "Remarkable American Women."

1978 Selected as one of "The Top Women in Big Business" by *Fortune Magazine.*

In 1924, the young and aspiring Olive Ann Mellor tied her future to the young but rapidly developing aviation industry. When she joined the Travel Air Manufacturing Company of Wichita, Kansas, she was the only female among its 12 employees. One of the 12 employees was pioneer aviator Walter H. Beech, who later became president and general manager of the company. With an opportunity to learn the airplane manufacturing business from the ground up, and showing an unusual business and financial perceptiveness, she advanced rapidly, becoming office manager and secretary to the president. By 1929, Travel Air Manufacturing Company was the world's largest producer of commercial aircraft.

She and Walter Beech were married in 1930 and became residents of New York City where Mr. Beech headed up the Curtiss-Wright Airplane Company, after selling his interests in Travel Air. Two years later they returned to Wichita to co-found Beech Aircraft Company. Mrs. Beech was secretary-treasurer and the financial guiding hand of the company.

From this unheralded beginning, with a handful of employees and a couple of lean years, the company created two new airplanes. These planes brought wide recognition and served as the backbone of the company for many years. They ultimately led to the establishment of the Beech Aircraft Corporation— now recognized as a major designer and producer of high-performance private, commercial and military airplanes.

The company's directors elected Mrs. Beech president and chairman of the board in 1950, following the death of Walter Beech. Under her guidance, Beech Aircraft continued to progress, expanding into diversified, aviation-related fields and growing steadily in the production of business and corporate aircraft. In the middle 1950s, she led the corporation to the establishment of a research and development division to become a pioneer in the science of super-cold—cryogenics. From this activity have come vital systems and assemblies for the successful Gemini, Apollo, Skylab, and Apollo–Soyuz Test Project which will be employed in future Space Shuttle programs. Today, Beech Aircraft Corporation reports over $525 million in annual sales, and has 10,000 employees, located at six plants in Wichita, Salina, and Liberal, Kansas and Boulder, Colorado, and twelve company-owned marketing operations.

Mrs. Beech relinquished the role of president in 1968 to a veteran executive of the company, retaining the position of chairman of the board, and chief executive officer. Widely acclaimed as a philanthropist, patron of the arts, and strong supporter of youth, Mrs. Beech also has earned the highest respect from her peers in aviation and business through awards, recognition, and appointments to high-ranking positions locally and throughout the state and nation.

WHO IS A MANAGER AND WHAT DOES A MANAGER DO?

In a sense, each of us is a manager. We manage ourselves by planning, organizing, directing, and controlling our skills, talents, time, and activities. Parents manage their jobs, households, and children; children manage their allowances; and students manage their time if they expect to be successful in various subjects in school or college. Take the example of Sally Smith, an accounting major at a university. Sally's objective is a career in the public accounting field. In order to accomplish her goal, she must first complete her degree in accounting with good grades. The completion of her degree in accounting requires that she be a "good manager" of herself and her time. She must plan her course schedule, organize her time and financial resources, direct her energies toward her goal, and evaluate or control her own performance to maintain her grades.

We sometimes think of managers only in terms of top-level positions within large organizations. But actually, managers operate at various levels within every type of firm, large and small, business and nonbusiness. As shown in Figure 1.1, there are three basic levels of management.

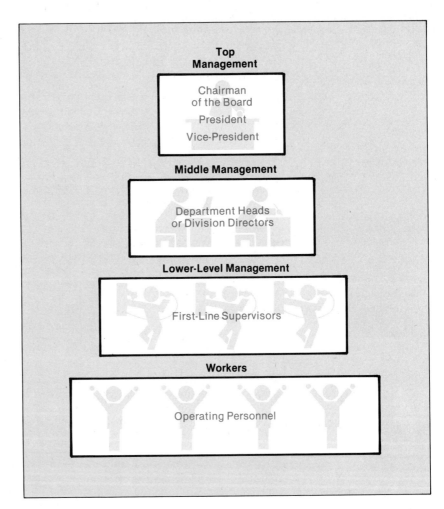

FIGURE 1.1
Managerial Levels

lower-level managers

middle managers

top management

Lower-level managers, usually referred to as supervisors, are responsible for managing employees in the performance of the daily operations. **Middle managers,** such as department heads, are concerned primarily with the coordination of programs and activities that are necessary to achieve the overall goals of the organization as identified by top management. Finally, **top management,** referred to by such titles as president, chief executive officer (CEO), vice-president or executive director, are responsible for providing the overall direction of the firm. In later discussions within the text, reference will be made to operating managers. Included within this category are lower- and middle-level managers.

In the final analysis, *a manager is anyone, at any level of the organization, who directs the efforts of other people in accomplishing goals.* Wherever you have a group of people working together to achieve results, a manager is present. School principals, meat market supervisors, and service station operators are managers, just as the presidents of General Motors, Gulf Oil, and General Electric are managers. The President of the United States is a manager, too, as are government agency heads or college deans.

A manager is the person who is responsible for making decisions concerning the use of a firm's resources to achieve results. *A manager is the catalyst that makes things happen!* He or she establishes goals, plans operations, organizes various resources—personnel, materials, equipment, capital—leads and motivates people to perform, evaluates actual results against the goals, and develops people for the organization.

The manager is the catalyst that makes things happen.

Sadly enough, in many organizations, the success of a particular manager is judged exclusively on *short-run* output. In other words, a manager may be said to be *effective* if his or her unit is earning a profit, or reducing costs, or increasing the market share for the company's products, or other such measurable results. Naturally, these accomplishments are very important to a business organization. However, a major challenge and indeed obligation of any manager, is the development of people under his or her direction, and in doing this, long-term goals may be more effectively achieved. Developing competent and well-trained people who can be promoted to more responsible jobs is a very significant part of a manager's responsibilities. This is an excellent *long-run* indicator or measure of the effectiveness of a manager and also contributes significantly to the growth and success of the firm.

THE MANAGEMENT FUNCTIONS

In every organization, managers perform certain functions for the purpose of achieving goals. The work done by managers is concerned with performing the functions of planning, organizing, directing, and controlling to achieve the objectives of the firm. Managers perform these functions within the boundaries established by the external environment, and must consider the interests of such diverse groups as the customers, stockholders, government, unions, suppliers, and the public. Although a separate section of this text will be devoted to each management function, a brief discussion of the four basic functions will be presented here.

PLANNING

Planning, the first function of management, is concerned with determining the goals the firm has and the means for achieving the goals. It is not enough to say that the goal of the company is to be the leader in the industry. The plan must be specific and provide the means for the goals to be achieved. For example, two of the primary goals of a major brewing company might be to attain a 20 percent share of the U. S. beer market and a 15 percent rate of return on investment. In order to accomplish these goals, the firm would develop specific plans for producing and marketing their products. We will discuss the planning process further in chapters 2–4.

ORGANIZING

An organization must be created to accomplish the goals and plans. Human and economic resources are allocated to various work areas within the firm. Relationships are established among the various units within the company. The management function of organizing is concerned with developing a framework that relates all personnel, work assignments, and physical resources to each other. The framework is usually termed the organization structure and is designed to facilitate the accomplishment of the objectives. For example, a university's organization structure would be quite different from that required by a firm engaged in producing steel. The organizing function of management will be discussed in detail in chapters 5–7.

DIRECTING

The third basic management function is directing, which is concerned with stimulating members of the organization to undertake action consistent with the plans. The directing function involves creating a climate with good communication, and one that is conducive to the effective motivation and leadership of people. Topics relating to directing will be presented in chapters 8–11.

CONTROLLING

The final function of management is controlling. The purpose of establishing controls is to assure proper performance in accordance with the plans. Through the establishment of controls, management is able to compare actual performance with the predetermined plan. In the event of unsatisfactory performance, corrective action can be taken. For instance, if a company's costs for producing a product are higher than planned, management must have some means to recognize the problem and take the appropriate action to correct the situation. The controlling function will be discussed in chapter 12.

MANAGEMENT FUNCTIONS AT VARIOUS MANAGERIAL LEVELS

As illustrated in Figure 1.2, the basic functions of planning, organizing, directing, and controlling are performed by managers at every level within an organization. However, the amount of time and effort devoted to each function will likely depend on the level of a manager within the organization. As shown in the figure, the amount of time that lower-level managers spend on planning is much less than top-level ones. The first-line supervisor must devote considerable time and effort in directing and controlling the work of others—accomplishing routine tasks and

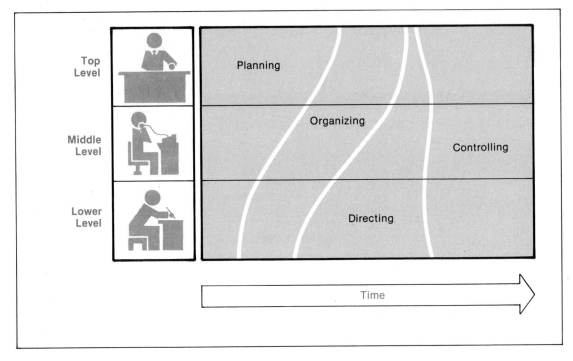

FIGURE 1.2
Management Functions at Various Managerial Levels

putting out daily fires. As managers move to higher levels in the organization, a greater percentage of their time is devoted to planning and less to directing. The amount of time spent on the controlling function is fairly consistent at all levels of management except for the very top executive level positions such as president or chief executive officer. At this high level, the chief executive is concerned with overall control of resources essential to the very survival of the firm. Finally, the amount of time devoted to the organizing functions is fairly consistent at all levels of management.

MANAGERIAL SKILLS

In order to be effective, a manager must possess and continually develop several essential skills. Figure 1.3 illustrates several skills that are important to a manager's overall effectiveness. As can be seen, the relative significance of each skill varies according to the level of management an individual manager occupies within an organization.

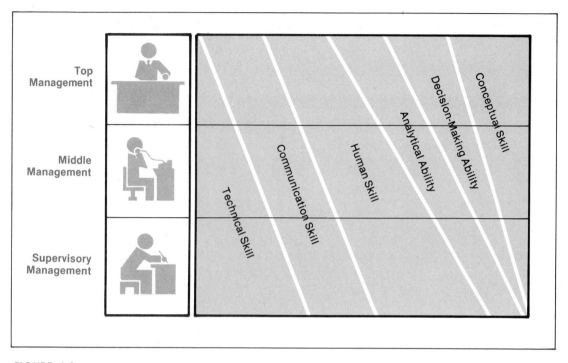

FIGURE 1.3
Essential Skills Necessary at Various Levels of Management in
an Organization

TECHNICAL SKILL

technical skill

The ability to use specific knowledge, methods, or techniques in performing work is referred to as technical skill. **Technical skill** is considered to be very crucial to the effectiveness of lower-level managers and supervisors because these individuals have direct contact with employees

INSIGHTS TO SUCCESS

Recognize that the best management training is experience and be patient with the process of acquiring that experience. Training or academic courses are effective primarily when they accompany an opportunity to use the training.

Ernest S. Robson, Jr., Vice-President, Energy and Materials Management, Monsanto Company

performing work activities within the firm. The first-line supervisor must provide technical assistance and support to personnel within the work unit. For example, a supervisor of keypunch machine operators must possess specific knowledge of the methods and techniques of operating the keypunch machines so that he or she may train newly hired operators and answer technical questions of the operators. As one moves to higher levels of management within the organization, the importance of technical skills usually diminishes because the manager has less direct contact with day to day problems and activities.

COMMUNICATIONS SKILL

communication skill

The ability to provide information orally and in written form to others in the organization for the purpose of achieving desired results is referred to as **communications skill.** It is a skill that is vital to the success of every-one, but most especially managers who must achieve results through the efforts of others. Communications skills are equally important at each level within the organization. Because of the importance of communications, chapter 11 of this text is devoted to the process of communications and methods to improve managerial effectiveness.

HUMAN SKILL

human skill

The ability of a manager to understand, work with, and get along with other people is referred to as **human skill.** This skill is essential at every level of management within the organization, but it is particularly significant at lower levels of management where the supervisor has frequent and direct contact with operating personnel. Managers have "human skill" if they are able to create a climate for effective motivation and leadership. In chapters 8–10 the importance of human skill and the ways to develop the skill are discussed in detail.

ANALYTICAL SKILL

analytical skill

Analytical skill is the ability of the manager to use logical and scientific approaches or techniques in the analyses of problems and business opportunities. Although important at all levels of the organization, analytical skill tends to be relatively more significant at the upper levels of management. Lower-level managers tend to operate in a fairly stable or predictable environment with specific guidelines for their performance. By contrast, upper-level managers must function in an environment that is subject to considerable complexities and uncertainties. Some of the quantitative techniques available to assist managers in coping with a dynamic environment are discussed in chapters 13 and 14.

DECISION-MAKING ABILITY

decision-making ability

The manager's skill in selecting a course of action designed to solve a specific problem or set of problems is known as **decision-making ability.** Decision-making skills are essential to managers for effective planning. Effective decision making is an important skill for managers at all levels within a firm, but it is relatively more important to upper-level managers than to lower-level supervisors. Corporation presidents have indicated that decision making was the most important skill needed for successful performance. Upper management's primary responsibility is to make effective decisions, whereas lower levels of management are required to execute or implement decisions made by higher management. In chapter 4 we discuss the decision-making process.

CONCEPTUAL SKILL

conceptual skill

Conceptual skill is the ability of the manager to understand the complexities of the overall organization and how each department or unit fits into the organization. This skill is extremely crucial to the success of top-level executives for they must be concerned with the *big picture*— assessing opportunities in the environment and determining overall objectives, plans, and strategies of operation. These managers must have the ability to see how each part of the organization interrelates and contributes to the primary goals of the firm. As one moves down the managerial hierarchy, conceptual skill becomes less important because other skills are more important to the success of the lower-level managers and supervisors. For instance, first-level supervisors are able to refer to operating manuals to discover the capabilities of a particular piece of equipment whereas top-level managers must use their conceptual skills to determine what products will be produced with the equipment.

Professional managers recognize that they must develop and practice each of the managerial skills to be effective in accomplishing organizational and personal goals. A manager cannot concentrate his or her efforts on one or only a few of these skills. It is the blending of the skills in the proper proportion based on the particular level occupied by the manager that is important.

MAKING MANAGEMENT WORK: THE SYSTEMS AND SITUATIONAL APPROACHES

A primary goal throughout this book is to show you how the various management concepts interrelate. This can be accomplished through the use of the systems and situational approaches. These approaches provide a way of thinking that all managers can use to improve their performance.

THE BUSINESS SYSTEM

One cannot consider each function of management as being separate and distinct. All organizations must be viewed as a dynamic, ongoing process. A firm may be objectively studied through the systems approach. A **system** is an arrangement of interrelated parts designed to achieve objectives. Through the **systems approach,** the functions of management are interrelated and coordinated to accomplish the goals of the organization.

system
systems approach

Successful managers have found the systems approach aids significantly in managing organizations. In any organization, management's job is to use resources (inputs) in an efficient manner to produce or achieve desirable products and/or services (outputs). Although the systems approach is useful in managing any type of organization, our illustration of its usage is applied specifically to a business firm. The basic business system components are graphically illustrated in Figure 1.4 and discussed below.

Resources

As may be seen from the illustration, a business enterprise uses certain inputs that are processed into outputs (products and/or services). Just as we cannot live long without food and water, a dynamic business system cannot survive without substances (resources) that keep it alive. These items may be human (employees to run the plant) or nonhuman energies (fuel for the factory), supplies, and information. The **inputs** or **resources** needed by the system vary according to the objectives or goals of the firm. If, for example, a watch manufacturer has the objective of making high quality watches, the inputs needed are likely to be highly trained crafts-persons and quality equipment and materials. On the other hand, a manufacturer of lower quality watches may need different inputs, such as equipment capable of mass production and less skilled employees.

inputs, resources

FIGURE 1.4
The Business System

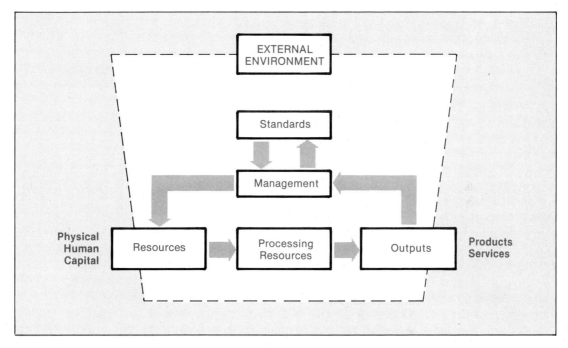

Source Adapted from Edwin B. Flippo and Gary M. Munsinger, *Management*, 4th ed. (Boston: Allyn and Bacon, Inc., 1978), p. 7.

Processing Resources

Resources or inputs are next processed within the organization to create desired outputs in the form of products or services. This processing includes every aspect of the firm with the exception of managerial talent. It would contain the necessary equipment, employees, and structure needed to convert resources into outputs. The processor for a university would include the faculty, the nonmanagerial staff, and the buildings required to maintain the university. The president, vice-presidents, deans, department heads, and other managerial personnel would not be considered as part of the processor. The desired outputs of the processor vary with the objectives of the firm. The Ford Motor Company takes steel, aluminum, and glass and converts it into automobiles. The hospital changes sick patients into healthy ones; the school changes uninformed students into knowledgeable ones; and the retail store transforms products on the shelves into values of satisfaction in the home.

Outputs

outputs

The products and services are the end result of the conversion process. These **outputs** should conform to the objectives and goals of the firm (to be discussed in greater detail in chapter 2). The output of General Motors is automobiles while the output of an electric utility firm would be energy. A different system may be required for both firms to reflect their goals and the output required.

Management and Standards

standards

Viewing the business system still further, one notices the information feedback to management (noted by the arrow from outputs to management). The manager uses this information to ensure that the outputs are being produced according to standard. **Standards** provide management with basic guidelines for desired performance. If standards are not being achieved, management must make changes to correct the deviation. The cause of the deviation may be due to incorrect inputs (e.g., defective parts). The processor itself may be the cause of the problem (low morale has caused production to drop). Whatever the cause, it is the task of management to identify the deviation and make corrections in line with company objectives.

All of the components of any firm—resources, processor, output, management, and standards—operate as a system. The systems approach provides management with a means of viewing different interrelationships within a firm as they are directed toward the accomplishment of organizational goals.

THE SITUATIONAL APPROACH

situational approach

A student of management begins to recognize the many interrelationships that exist within all organizations through the use of the systems approach. Another concept—the situational approach—builds upon the systems approach and provides the manager with a broader appreciation of the management process. The **situational approach** is defined as management's ability to adapt to meet particular circumstances and constraints that a firm may encounter. It is not a totally new concept; in 1512, Nicolo Machiavelli wrote,

> Therefore, you ought to know that there are two ways to fight: by using laws, and by using force. The former is characteristic of man; the latter, of animals. . . . Therefore, since a prince must perfect his knowledge of how to use animal attributes, those he must select are the fox and the lion. Since

the lion is powerless against snares and the fox is powerless against wolves, one must be a fox to recognize snares and a lion to frighten away wolves.[1]

By this statement Machiavelli was attempting to tell his Prince that he must be capable of making decisions based on the demands of a particular situation; nothing is consistently either yes or no. The manager who utilizes the situational approach recognizes the many different types of businesses that can exist and adapts to meet them.

Although there are an unlimited number of specific factors a manager may encounter, they can be reduced to six major categories (see Figure 1.5). Not only must the manager recognize that these factors exist, he or

FIGURE 1.5
The Situational Approach: Major Factors

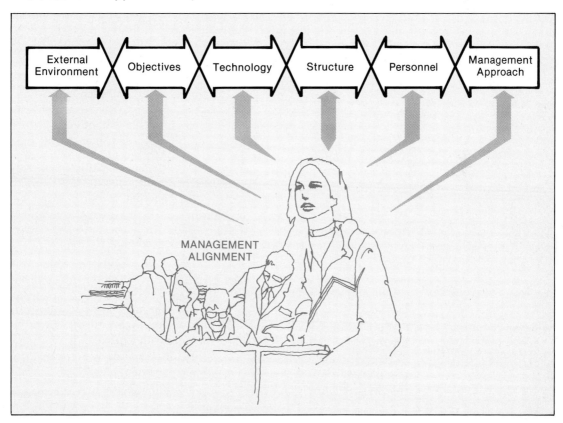

External Environment — Objectives — Technology — Structure — Personnel — Management Approach

MANAGEMENT ALIGNMENT

Source Adapted from Edwin B. Flippo and Gary M. Munsinger, *Management*, 4th ed. (Boston: Allyn and Bacon, Inc., 1978), p. 25.

1. Nicolo Machiavelli, *The Prince*, 1512.

she must be capable of aligning or synchronizing them through the help of the systems approach to achieve the best results. The situationally oriented manager must be constantly aware of these factors and the manner in which they interact. Managers should also recognize there is no *one* best approach to management that meets the needs of all organizations.

External Environment

external environment

The **external environment** of a firm consists of anything outside the organization (legal, sociological, political, and economic) that can affect the firm. As may be seen in Figure 1.6, many factors may be involved. For instance, the external factors may be competitors, customers, suppliers, labor unions, and government. Knowledge of the external environment is quite important in the management process. The speed of making decisions may be critical in an uncertain environment as opposed to a certain environment. For instance, technology is rapidly changing in the computer industry. Information must be available to enable top management to make decisions as quickly as possible to cope with the rapidly changing environment. A firm may have the best product and be out of business tomorrow because a competitor has developed a new and better product. Failure to react fast can easily mean the difference between success and failure of an organization. On the other hand, a firm that exists within an environment that changes slowly, such as a producer of aluminum cans or table matches, may place greater emphasis on decisions being made high in the organization.

Objectives

objective

An **objective** describes the end result a firm desires to accomplish. Appropriate objectives in one firm may prove disastrous in another. These objectives may be severely affected by the external environment that may cause a firm to alter or even completely change their direction. For instance, during the oil shortage of 1979, many plastic manufacturing firms could not obtain sufficient petroleum to maintain their operation. This caused some firms to modify their objectives and to diversify to produce products that did not have a petroleum base. In highly uncertain environments, the objectives may be subject to rapid change. In more stable and predictable environments management is able to establish more specific and steady objectives. As environmental requirements change, the objectives of a firm that desires to survive and prosper must also change.

Technology

technology

Technology takes into consideration all the skills, knowledge, methods, and equipment required to convert resources into desired products and/or

FIGURE 1.6
External Environment Factors

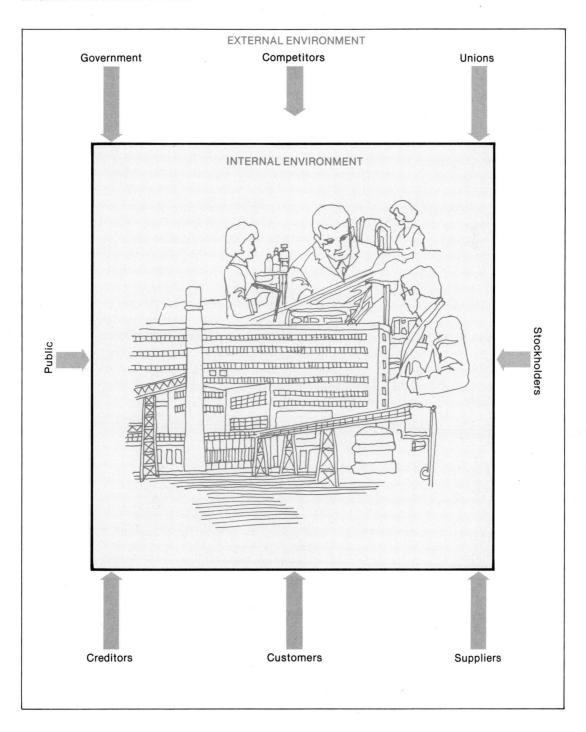

services. In terms of the situational approach to management, technology can be characterized on the basis of the *state of the art.* If the technology is well worked out and we know what we are doing, a routine can be developed and applied on a uniform basis. If the technology is quite complex and uncertain, the organization is more dependent on people for effective accomplishment. The technology for manufacturing an automobile is better worked out than that for teaching college students. In turn, the technology for teaching is better developed than the technology for curing mental illness.

Structure

structure

As used here, **structure** means the manner in which the internal environment of the firm is organized or arranged. If most major decisions are made primarily by top-level executives, the organization is *centralized.* If lower-level supervisors and managers are permitted to make significant decisions, the structure is more *decentralized.*

Personnel

personnel

Hire good people and let them do their thing is the general philosophy toward **personnel** held by many effective managers. But because we are all different in varying amounts in our goals, aspirations, background, experiences, and personalities, some employees are a better *match* with one organization than another. It has been found that employees tend to move toward a firm that possesses an environment closely compatible to their needs. If a firm has a need for individuals with skills that are different from those presently within the organization, changes may have to be made.

Managerial Approaches

managerial
approaches

There are two fundamental **managerial approaches:** (1) the more auto-cratic approach and (2) the more participative style. Situational theory accepts *both* approaches as being workable under certain conditions. Management has discovered that participation by workers in the deci-sion-making process provides greater acceptance of the decision. But, there are times when participation in the decision-making process is not in the best interest of the firm. If a firm is in a fight for its survival, a more direct or autocratic approach may prove superior. Thus, situations often call for varying mixtures of managerial style.

BALANCING THE SITUATIONAL FACTORS

Thus far we have discussed the systems and situational approaches as if they were separate and distinct. This is not really the case since the systems approach provides the manager with the ability to balance the situational factors. It is how these factors interact, rather than any one factor taken separately, that is significant.

Thus, both concepts must be interrelated if a person is to be an effective manager. As seen in Figure 1.7, the organizational system must take into consideration the situational factors. These factors must be balanced if good results are to be achieved. As the situational factors change, it may be necessary for the system to be modified. For instance, if the goals of the firm are altered (the firm decides to diversify because of a high depend-ence on foreign oil), the situational factors will likely be out of balance. There may be a requirement for new technologies to comply with the new objectives. New workers will likely be needed in the labor force. If the structure is not one that can accommodate these new employees or if the firm finds that it is having difficulty recruiting the type of people necessary to bring about these changes, the situational factors will likely require realignment. As they are altered, the system must change to adapt to the restructuring of the situational factors.

A manager must be capable of recognizing when the situational factors are out of balance and bring them back into line by making changes in the system. Any of the six situational factors may require the other factors to be modified. Thus, maintaining proper alignment of the situational factors ensures that the firm is operating with the best system to meet the objectives of the organization.

FIGURE 1.7
Management from a Systems and Situational Viewpoint

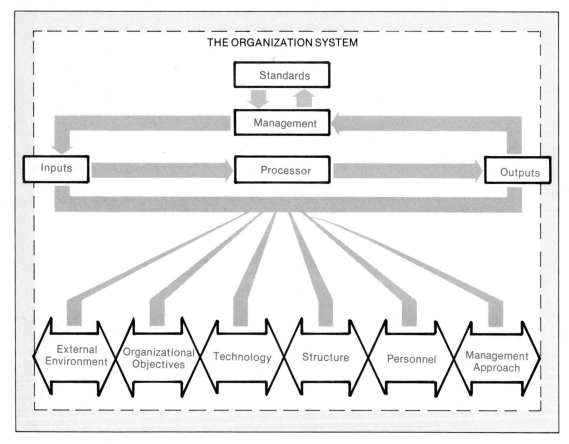

For instance, Underwood, the leading producer of typewriters many years ago, failed to recognize the changing trends toward mechanization of the office environment. These changes were conducive to the development and sales of electric typewriters that would later become standard equipment in virtually every office. Underwood failed to recognize a change in the external environment and continued to produce manual typewriters under the assumptions of the *old* base condition. On the other hand, IBM recognized the trends and brought their base conditions into alignment with the environment. IBM adapted their organizational objectives, technology, structure, personnel, and management approach to meet the needs of a changing environment. The situational factors were in alignment with the base conditions as Underwood perceived them. However, the external environment had changed and this was not recognized by Underwood.

Since this time, IBM has become the leading manufacturer of electric typewriters and office products. Underwood (which merged with Olivetti in 1966 to become Underwood-Olivetti) ultimately recognized the changing market conditions and entered the electric typewriter business, but has been unable to reestablish their dominant position in the typewriter industry.

With situational management, the trick is to balance the various factors in the most effective manner with the assistance of the systems approach. One can also argue the necessity for a situational approach to management by contrasting different types of organizations. It would be inappropriate to try to manage a college or university as one does a large manufacturing corporation. Though the management functions are the same in all types of organizations, their performance depends on the situation. Both the systems and situational approaches provide the general theme for studying the process of management throughout the rest of the text.

BASIC SCHOOLS OF MANAGEMENT THOUGHT

While we can agree that every organization requires management, there is considerable disagreement about the most effective way to manage. As we have stated previously, there is no single, unified theory of management that is universally applicable to all situations.

In order to improve our understanding of current management concepts it is helpful to discuss the historical development of management thought. Most of today's management practice is based on management theory developed in this century. A look at the history of management thought is important because we must know where we have been before we can determine where we are or want to go in the future.

Historically, two basic but substantially different schools of thought have developed. These have been referred to as the classical and behavioral schools of management.

THE CLASSICAL SCHOOL OF MANAGEMENT

classical school of
management

Although various philosophical approaches to management have been developed over the years, the oldest and perhaps most widely accepted among practitioners has been called the **classical,** or traditional, **school of management.** The classification of the four functions of management—planning, organizing, directing, and controlling—is derived from this school. The primary focus of the classical school is on the manager as he or she establishes plans and directs effort toward the accomplishment of organizational goals.

As a result of the industrial revolution, people were brought together to work in factories. This was in marked contrast to the handicraft system where people worked separately in small shops or in their own homes. Thus, industrialization created a need for the effective management of people and other resources in the emerging organizations. In other words, there was a need for the efficient planning, organizing, directing, and controlling of work activities performed by specialized labor.

Scientific Management

In response to the changing conditions in the late nineteenth century and during the early part of the twentieth century, there was an intensified and dedicated interest in management as a process and as a science. It was apparent to many, especially Frederick Taylor, H. E. Emerson, H. L. Gantt, Frank Gilbreth, Henri Fayol, Lyndal Urwick, and Chester Barnard, that management could be made more effective and efficient.

scientific management   Taylor, Gantt, and Gilbreth were primarily interested in developing a *scientific* basis for management of work. The interest and research efforts of these men gave rise to **scientific management.** Frederick Taylor, who is generally recognized as the father of scientific management, was convinced that management was a process in which the scientific method should be used. The scientific method provides a logical framework for the analysis of problems. It basically consists of: defining the problem, gathering data, analyzing the data, developing alternatives, and selecting the best alternative. Taylor, Emerson, Gantt, Gilbreth, and others believed that following the scientific method would provide a means to determine the most efficient way to perform work. Instead of abdicating responsibility for establishing standards, for example, management would scientifically study all facets of an operation and carefully set a logical and rational standard. Instead of guessing or relying solely on trial and error, management would go through the time-consuming process of logical study and scientific research to develop answers to business problems. Taylor's philosophy can be summarized in the following four principles:

1. The development and use of the scientific method in the practice of management (finding the "one best way" to perform work)
2. Using scientific approaches to select employees who were best suited to perform a given job
3. Providing the employee with scientific education, training, and development
4. Encouraging friendly interaction and cooperation between management and employees, but there was to exist a separation of duties between managers and workers

Taylor stated many times that scientific management would require a *revolution* in thinking on the part of both the manager and the subordinate. His motives were not confined solely to advancing the interests of the manager and the enterprise. He believed sincerely that scientific management practices were for the mutual benefit of the employee and the employer through the creation of a larger productive surplus. Thus, the organization would achieve higher output and the worker would receive a greater income.

The greater part of Taylor's work was oriented toward improving management of production operations. The classic case of the pig-iron experiment at the Bethlehem Steel Company illustrates his approach.[2] The task was simple, so much so that most managers would tend to ignore it. Laborers would pick up 92 lb. pigs from a storage yard, walk up a plank onto a railroad car, and drop them at the end of the car. In a group of seventy-five laborers, the average output was about 12.5 tons per man per day. In applying the scientific method of study to this problem of getting work done through others, Taylor developed

1. An improved method of work (motion study)
2. A prescribed amount of rest on the job (fatigue study and rest periods)
3. A specific standard of output (time study)
4. Payment by the unit of output (incentive wages)

Using this approach, the average per man per day output rose from 12.5 tons to 48 tons. Under the incentive system, the daily pay rose from $1.15 to $1.85, an amount substantially higher than the going rate in the community.

Taylor's dedication to the systematic planning and study of processes pervaded his entire life. With a specially designed tennis racket, he became part of the National Doubles Tennis Championship team. When he played golf, he used uniquely designed clubs for any predictable type of lie. When he used a particular putter, his friends refused to play because of its accuracy. A famed novelist reported that Taylor died of pneumonia in a hospital with his stopwatch in his hand.

Other pioneers of scientific management were Frank and Lillian Gilbreth, who concentrated on motion analysis to develop *the one best way* and H. L. Gantt, who developed a control chart that is used to this day in production operations. Harrington Emerson developed a set of twelve principles of efficiency. Emerson's principles state that a manager should

---

2. Frederick W. Taylor, *The Principles of Scientific Management* (New York: Harper and Bros., 1911), pp. 41–47.

carefully define objectives; use the scientific method of analysis; develop and use standardized procedures and methods; and reward employees for good work.

General Management Theory

Henri Fayol and C. I. Barnard, in contrast to Taylor, Emerson, Gantt, and the Gilbreths, attempted to develop a broader theory, concerned with general management. Fayol's thesis was that the fundamental functions of any manager consisted of planning, organizing, commanding, coordinating, and controlling. He attempted to evolve empirically a number of general principles that, if followed, would improve the practice of general management. Barnard's ideas expressed in his classic book, *The Functions of the Executive*,[3] have significantly influenced the development of the theory and practice of management. Barnard was a practicing manager as president of New Jersey Bell Telephone. Although Barnard made numerous contributions in the development of management thought, his concept that the most important function of a manager is to provide the basis for cooperative effort, directed toward goals of the organization was highly significant. Barnard believed that the degree of cooperation depends upon effective communications and a balance between rewards an employee receives and contributions made by employees.

The classical school attempted to provide a rational and scientific basis to the management of organizations. The primary contributions of the classical school of management include the following:

1. The application of the scientific method to management
2. The classification of the basic management functions—planning, organizing, directing, and controlling
3. The development and application of specific principles of management

In essence, classical management concepts have significantly improved the practice of management and have led to substantial improvements in performance within organizations.

THE BEHAVIORAL SCHOOL OF MANAGEMENT

In the 1920s and 1930s, there were some observers of business management who became concerned with what they felt was a shortsightedness

3. Chester I. Barnard, *The Functions of the Executive* (Cambridge, Mass.: Harvard University Press, 1938).

and incompleteness in the scientific management approach. In particular, Elton Mayo and F. J. Roethlisberger began to point out that the approaches advanced by scientific management were not necessarily the most efficient, nor did they always work as intended. The essentially human character of business organizations had been largely ignored. The field of human relations emerged from the work of Elton Mayo who has become recognized as the father of the human relations movement, and, thus, the **behavioral school of management** was developed.

behavioral school of
management

The Human Relations Movement

The project that had the most to do with the beginning of the concern for human relations in business was the Hawthorne experiments conducted in the Western Electric Company between 1927 and 1932. In these experiments, researchers attempted to prove the validity of generally accepted principles of management. Several experiments to determine the relationship between working conditions and productivity were conducted by varying working conditions within the plant.

In one experiment, the researchers established *test groups* where changes in lighting, frequency of rest periods, and working hours occurred, and *control groups* where no changes were made. When rest periods and other improvements in working conditions were introduced to the *test group* productivity increased as expected. However, the researchers were surprised when output continued to increase when the various improvements in working conditions that had been introduced, such as rest periods, were removed. As a result of these changes, the scientists expected a decrease in productivity. Contrary to these expectations, production still continued to improve in most instances. Obviously, everything had not been controlled in the experiment; the human mind was still free and uncontrolled.

The results of these experiments prompted Mayo and his fellow researchers to conclude that when employees are given special attention by management, output is likely to increase regardless of the actual changes in the working conditions. This has become known as the *Hawthorne Effect.* To gain a more indepth understanding, Mayo and Roethlisberger followed up the experiments at the Hawthorne plant with an intensive interviewing program and an investigation of informal cliques, groupings, and relationships initiated by the members of the organization. The basic conclusion emerging from the intensive interviewing program was that the needs of the individual and the role of the informal group have a significant impact on the performance of the work group.

Some have conceived of a total overlapping of interests between the organization and its members and contend that the objectives of both classical and behavioral approaches are identical. Much behavioral research does support the thesis that reasonable satisfaction of the needs and desires of those people who work within and contribute to the enterprise will lead to greater output. A management approach that ignores or deemphasizes the human element will often result in only partly accomplished objectives, reduced creativity, and general dissatisfaction.

Modern Behavioral Management Science

behavioral
management science

Since the early experiments of Mayo and Roethlisberger at the Hawthorne plant, there has been an increased interest in and application of behavioral science in management. The human relations approach has evolved into **behavioral management science.** In recent years, considerable research has been conducted for the purpose of developing techniques to more effectively utilize people in organizations. The contributions—theories and research applications—of such well-known behavioral scientists as Abraham Maslow, Douglas McGregor, Chris Argyris, Frederick Herzberg, and Rensis Likert have provided considerable insight into approaches for increased managerial effectiveness.

While we will discuss in considerable detail the specific contributions of each of the above behavioral scientists in chapters 8 and 9 on Motivation and Leadership, a brief mention of the basic concepts of behavioral management science will be discussed here.

Behavioral scientists have, in general, criticized classical management and organization theory as not being responsive enough to the needs of the employees. In essence, the behaviorists' specific criticisms include the following:

- Jobs have been overly specialized.
- People are underutilized.
- Management has exercised too much control and has prevented employees from making decisions of which they are capable.
- Organizations and management have shown too little concern about a person's needs for recognition and self-fulfillment.

Behavioral scientists argue that the design of work has not changed enough to keep pace with changes in the needs of today's employees and the working environment they confront. In today's complex, affluent, and rapidly changing society, employees cannot be treated as *interchangeable parts* within the organization. Today's worker has a higher level of education and tends to possess higher expectations for improvements in the working environment along with a desire for more diverse and challenging work. This has placed increased pressure on management to be responsive to these changes and to provide an environment designed to meet these needs.

WHY STUDY THIS MANAGEMENT TEXT?

Effective management is essential to the success of every organization. Management influences the lives of all of us as members of an organized society. For individuals, knowledge of management is valuable as evidenced by the fact that organizations actively recruit students who have a concentration in management. It is vital for each of us to gain a better understanding of and appreciation for management if we are to more effectively function in an organization.

In this text, our study of management will provide you with the following:

- A greater knowledge of and insight into the responsibilities of managing people and other resources
- A better understanding of the problems of operating a business organization
- An opportunity to learn the skills essential to effective managerial decision making
- An understanding of basic principles of management
- Increased knowledge about production and operations management techniques
- The ability to identify and cope with internal and external forces in the environment that affect performance
- The skills and attitudes to continue your professional development

In order to accomplish these objectives this book is organized into seven sections as illustrated in Figure 1.8. Our intent is to present fundamental management concepts and principles in a readable and interesting format.

SUMMARY

We live in a society dominated by large organizations in which people must work together effectively to accomplish goals. The degree of success of all organizations—business and nonbusiness—is determined to a great extent by the quality and overall effectiveness of management. But what is management? Who is a manager? What do managers do? What skills are needed for good management? In answering these questions, it is important to realize that there is no *one* best approach to management that is effective in every situation. This is a theme that we stress throughout the text.

Management is the process of planning, organizing, directing, and controlling to accomplish organizational goals through the coordinated use

FIGURE 1.8
Organization of the Book

of human and material resources. A manager is anyone, regardless of level within a firm, who directs the efforts of other people in accomplishing goals. A manager is the catalyst that makes things happen by *planning* what is to be achieved, *organizing* personnel and other resources to achieve the plan, *motivating* or *directing* people, and comparing results achieved to the planned performance (*controlling*). In order to be effective, managers need to possess and develop several essential skills including the following: technical, communication, human, analytical, decision-making, and conceptual. These skills must be mixed in the proper proportion based on the particular level occupied by the manager.

Various management theories and concepts are interrelated through the use of the systems and situational approaches. The systems and situational approaches to management provide a framework for thinking. All of the components of any organization—resources, processor, output, management, and standards—operate as a system. In using the situational approach the manager not only must recognize the major external and internal factors, but also must be capable of aligning them to achieve the best results. The six situational factors—external environment, organizational objectives, technology, structure, personnel, and management approach—are important considerations for a manager.

While we can agree that every organization requires good management, there is considerable disagreement as to the most effective way to manage. Historically, two basic but different schools or approaches to management have developed. The classical school, including the work of Frederick Taylor, Henri Fayol, C. I. Barnard and others, attempted to provide a rational and scientific basis to management. Major contributions of scientific management include the application of scientific method to management and the classification of the basic management functions.

The behavioral school of management is concerned with the human element in the organization. The early "human relations" era, which resulted primarily from the Hawthorne experiments in the late 1920s and early 1930s, evolved into behavioral management science. Behavioral scientists have criticized classical management theory as not being responsive to the needs of its employees, that jobs are overly specialized, people are underutilized, and overmanaged, and that management has shown too little concern about a person's need for recognition and self-fulfillment. In today's world, management has little choice but to be more responsive to the needs of employees if improved performance is to be achieved.

Review Questions

1. Define management. Who is a manager and what does a manager do?

2. List some factors that may account for the success and effectiveness of a manager.

3. Why is the study of management important?

4. Briefly describe/summarize the profile of chief executives presented in FIGURE 1.1.

5. List and briefly describe six skills important to managerial effectiveness. How are these skills related to managers operating at different levels in the organization?

6. What is the Classical School of Management? Identify the basic contributions of this school of management.

7. Frederick Taylor is known as the father of "scientific management." Why? What is scientific management and Taylor's philosophy?

8. Identify briefly the major contributions of the following:
   a. Henri Fayol
   b. C. I. Barnard
   c. H. L. Gantt
   d. Harrington Emerson

9. Discuss the Behavioral School of Management. How and why did the movement originate?

10. What specific criticisms did behavioral scientists have of traditional or classical organizations?

11. "There is no *one* best approach to management that meets the needs of all organizations." Comment and explain.

Exercises

1. Interview three managers from different types of organizations (for example, talk to managers in a bank, retail store, manufacturer, or college/university). Have a list of prepared questions including, but not limited to, the following:
   a. How did you become a manager?
   b. What does your job as a manager entail? Describe your major functions.
   c. Why are you a manager?
   d. What skills are necessary for success as a manager?
   e. What advice would you give a person interested in a career in management?
   f. Is management a profession?
   g. Can one learn to be a better manager? If so, how?

2. Some critics believe that management cannot be taught in a classroom. As the basis for small group discussions, each student should go to the library and find two articles supporting this view and two articles in opposition. Summarize the arguments of each and formulate conclusions. Next, the instructor should divide the class into five discussion groups and have each group discuss the criticisms for thirty minutes.

After the issue has been discussed within each group, a spokesperson from each group should present the conclusion arrived at in the group. "Can management be taught?"

3. Review the employment classified ads in the *Wall Street Journal* and a Sunday edition of a large city newspaper. Make a list of the types of managerial jobs, the companies offering employment, and the qualifications needed to obtain the positions. What is your basic conclusion after this review in terms of the availability of managerial positions and the necessary qualifications for obtaining a position?

REFERENCES

Barnett, Rosalind and Taguiri, Renato. "What Young People Think About Management." *Harvard Business Review,* May/June 1973, pp. 106–118.

Bennis, Warren. *Changing Organizations.* New York: McGraw-Hill, 1966.

Drucker, Peter F. *Management: Tasks, Responsibilities and Practices.* New York: Harper & Row, 1974.

Fayol, Henri. *General and Industrial Management.* New York: Pitman Publishing Company, 1949.

George, Claude, Jr. *The History of Management Thought.* Englewood Cliffs, N.J.: Prentice-Hall, Inc., 1972.

Greenwood, William. "Future of Management Theory." *Academy of Management Journal* 17 (1974): 503–513.

McGregor, Douglas. *The Professional Manager.* New York: McGraw-Hill, 1967.

Mintzberg, Henry. "The Manager's Job: Folklore and Fact." *Harvard Business Review,* July/August 1975, pp. 49–61.

Mintzberg, Henry. *The Nature of Managerial Work.* New York: Harper & Row, 1973.

Newman, William H., ed. *Managers For The Year 2000.* Englewood Cliffs, N.J.: Prentice-Hall, Inc., 1978.

Roethlisberger, F. J., and Dickson, W. J. *Management and the Worker: An Account of a Research Program Conducted by the Western Electric Company Hawthorne Works, Chicago.* Cambridge: Harvard University Press, 1939.

Case Study **PROMOTION OF AN ENGINEER TO A MANAGER**

Jack Freemont had recently received a promotion to the position of Manager of Engineering within the California Manufacturing Company, a medium-sized firm producing numerous household products. Jack had an electrical engineering degree and had been with the company for nine years since graduating from the University of California—Berkeley.

Jack's record as a design engineer was excellent. He had developed three new products that had been marketed around the world and was widely respected for his many innovative contributions to a department recognized for its reputation as the industry leader in new product research and development. Not only was Jack an effective engineer, he also was popular with almost everyone in the company. Throughout his nine years with California Manufacturing, Jack had kept "up-to-date" in his field by reading engineering journals and by attending continuing education workshops. Because of his technical/engineering experience with the company and his ability to get along with people, top management felt very confident in promoting Jack to the position of Manager of Engineering.

Jack's early experience in supervising the eighteen engineers in the department proved to be a real challenge. He experienced considerable difficulties with being a manager as compared to an engineer. He continued to be very involved with research and product design and worked very long hours (sometimes up to twelve hours a day) in order to "keep up" his design engineering. As a result of this situation, Jack did not provide the overall direction and coordination of the department that top management believed was necessary in order to achieve maximum effectiveness.

Jack also began to feel pressure from some of the engineers who likewise believed he was overly involved in performing "routine engineering" and not "managing" the department.

Since Jack wanted to improve as a manager, he decided to discuss the problems with his boss.

Questions

1. What is the basic problem confronting Jack Freemont as a manager? What is the cause(s)?
2. How does being a manager differ from being an engineer? Be specific.
3. Did top management make a mistake in promoting Jack to the position of engineering manager?
4. What skills are important for Jack as the manager? Why?
5. Does being a good engineer guarantee success as a manager? Why or why not?

Case Study

THE NEW PRESIDENT

The day has finally come; Garrick Phillips is to assume the position of president of Metro Manufacturing. Metro is a widely respected producer of high quality control mechanisms. When the previous president retired, Garrick was identified as the likely choice for assuming the post. He was respected for his competence in the field and for his ability to work with employees at all levels of operations. Garrick arrived at work early this morning, not so much to work but to think. As he sits behind his new executive desk, drinking a cup of coffee, his thoughts go back to his early days with Metro.

Twenty years ago Garrick was just a young man right out of college with no business experience and a degree in industrial management. He was hired as an assistant foreman and was placed immediately on the production line. "Oh, those were the days," he thought. "Seems like there was a problem that required solving every minute. Thank goodness for the standard operating procedures manuals (SOP's) and for a foreman who was patient enough to answer my questions. Didn't have to make too many critical decisions then but I sure was putting out a lot of daily fires."

As the nostalgia influence continues, Garrick thinks back to the time when he was taken off the production line and promoted into middle management. "Things sure did change then," he thought. As production manager, he had to think further into the future. As a foreman, Garrick was primarily concerned with meeting daily production requirements. Now he had to plan weeks and even months in advance. The human and communication problems remained although it seems like the reports he had to write were longer. But, as he remembers, the major changes occurred because he had to do more creative thinking. Laughing to himself he thought about the time he went to the files to pull out an SOP for an unusual problem he had confronted and there was none. He was frustrated because he had to handle the problem with little assistance. But, as his analytical, decision-making, and conceptual ability increased, he found himself using his technical skills less and less.

Another cup of coffee provided the stimulus to think about the special promotion he made to vice-president of planning five years ago. It was a major hurdle in his life because he had been in heavy competition with five well-qualified managers. He had heard through the grapevine that he had received the position because he was able to think for himself. But, even his past training did not fully prepare Garrick for the demands of the job; he had to learn much of it on his own. Rather than think months into the future, he now was required to envision years. Grinning, he remembered that at first he did not realize that there were so many people outside of production that he had to coordinate activities with. Marketing and finance had to be tied together with production. His conceptual and decision-making skills continued to increase. A long time ago, the benefits of the "good old" SOP's lost their value.

But now, as Garrick looks at his desk plate which says "President," new thoughts run through his mind. A whole new world opens to him now. He wonders what new requirements will be placed on him. A twinge of fear moves through his body as the thoughts of the new job take hold. What skills will he now need to be successful?

Questions

1. As the president of Metro Manufacturing, what specific skills will Garrick need to be effective? Reference to FIGURE 1.3 will provide insight into this question.

2. How do the demands of different levels of responsibility change as a manager progresses up the hierarchy of an organization?

3. What general recommendations would you offer for Garrick Phillips?

THE
PLANNING
FUNCTION

2

In Part 2 we look at the importance of planning to management. First, objectives and plans are viewed from the standpoint that all managers, no matter what level in the organization they are at, must carefully plan for their objectives if they are to be achieved. Then, a discussion of management by objectives as a means of assisting the planner follows. Part 2 concludes with a discussion of managerial decision making.

Chapter 2

KEY TERMS

planning

objectives

reactive planning

strategic planning

forecasting

operating planning

standing plans

policy

procedure

rule

standard

performance results standards

process standards

reactive planning

Objectives and Plans

LEARNING OBJECTIVES

After completing this chapter you should be able to

1. Describe the goal setting and planning sequence.
2. Discuss the types of objectives a firm must consider.
3. Relate the goal complexities which management confronts.
4. Explain the importance of planning for both upper and lower level management.
5. Describe the concept of reactive planning and its importance to a businessperson.
6. Recognize the various types of standards which may be established.
7. State why plans are not successful.

As production foreman for Stoner Manufacturing, Mike Richards is responsible for ensuring that the scheduled weekly production quota he receives every Monday morning is successfully accomplished. In order to ensure that each item on the quota sheet is completed, Mike must carefully schedule the activities of each of his workers for the entire week. Failure to properly plan the weekly activities can result in overproduction or underproduction of the weekly schedule.

As president of Duran Electronics, Rodney Odom is responsible for implementing the objectives of the organization. He recognizes that if the firm is to achieve its goal of being a leader in the industry, many projects must be planned now if they are to be implemented in the future. Today he is working on the plans for a new plant which will not go into production for five years.

When asked what his career goals were, Bobby Jones stated that he wanted to become a production manager for a large manufacturing firm. In order to accomplish this objective, Bobby planned to enter a university that had the reputation for providing an excellent education in production and operations management. His plan consisted of maintaining good grades and being active in campus organizations so as to have the opportunity to interview and be selected by the company of his choice.

As with Mike, Rodney, and Bobby, all individuals and businesses have similar needs—to establish goals and develop effective plans to achieve these goals. The product or service provided by an organization may be different from the goals of an individual, but the need for goal setting and proper planning remains. In this chapter, the planning process is discussed first. Next, we'll show the importance of clearly defined objectives which is followed by a presentation of the strategic and operating planning process. Next, we will discuss policies, procedures, rules, and standards. The intent of the chapter is to provide the student with an appreciation of the importance of effective planning, regardless of whether the planner is a company president, a first-line supervisor, or a manager of a small business.

INSIGHTS TO SUCCESS

Unless an individual has a logical, formal technique for problem solving, he will flounder in wheel-spinning.

MARVIN F. GADE, Executive Vice-President, Kimberly-Clark Corporation

THE PLANNING PROCESS

planning

objectives

reactive planning

The process of determining objectives and the courses of action needed to obtain these goals is referred to as **planning.** The planning process presented in Figure 2.1 serves as a guide for the entire chapter. This model is appropriate whether planning is done by upper or operating (lower-level) management. As can be seen in Figure 2.1, **objectives** or goals which serve as the desired end results should be established first. Then, plans are developed to specify the manner in which objectives are to be accomplished. Appropriate policies, procedures, and rules are then created to specify in greater detail the manner by which the plan will be achieved. Standards are developed to determine if the various aspects of the plan have been attained. Yet, the successful planner does not operate in a vacuum and must be flexible enough to respond to changing external and internal conditions. This can be referred to as **reactive planning** and must be designed into the system. Thus, the planning process is dynamic and plans should be constantly evaluated and modified to conform to the current and anticipated situations.

Tex Schramm, president and general manager of the Dallas Cowboys, provides an excellent illustration of a manager who recognizes the value of planning. He states, "My team's objective is to win, and win consistently." His long-range plan involves creating an environment to accomplish this objective. Management stability is emphasized as part of the plan. Apparently this approach has worked; the Cowboys have consistently been in the National Football League playoffs, and since their beginning in 1960, there has been but one coach, Tom Landry. The player personnel director and many of the assistant coaches also have been with the team for a long period. Tex says about the Cowboys, "It is our policy to allow people to work in their area of expertise and use their initiative to gain not only team and organizational success, but individual recognition." Coach Landry provides each player with a team play book which covers in detail offensive and defensive formations as well as individual assignments. All phases of the planning process relate to the objective of winning consistently.

ORGANIZATIONAL OBJECTIVES

As described by Tex Schramm in the illustration provided above, his primary objective is to develop a team that wins consistently. This goal establishes the end result that management desires. After watching a successful team play an average team on Sunday, one sometimes wonders if the objectives of both teams are the same.

JIM WATSON

President
Direct Lumber, Incorporated

 "A good business planner will beat out a nonplanner time and time again" is the philosophy of Jim Watson, president of Direct Lumber, Incorporated, a manufacturer and wholesaler of forest products. Jim attributes much of his success to his knowledge and understanding of planning and his

career shows what people can accomplish when they know what they want to accomplish.

Jim credits hard work and a dedication to accomplishment of a personal goal for his success. He began selling newspapers when he was six years old and worked in various part-time sales jobs until he obtained his B.A. in Marketing in 1962. Upon graduation from college he took a position as a sales representative with a building products company. Although Jim achieved a highly successful "track record" he realized that additional education would help him achieve his career objective of progressing to a top-level position in management. In 1967, Jim quit his job and went back to college, receiving his M.B.A. from Louisiana Tech University in 1968. After graduation he took a position with a building hardboard company and one year later was promoted to sales manager. In 1973, he accepted the position of product manager for three hardboard plants.

Jim went to work for Direct Lumber, Incorporated in 1975, a firm with $50 million annual sales. He progressed rapidly from Sales Manager to General Manager to President. Jim attributes much of his success to establishing his goals and then determining the means for them to be accomplished. He says that his return to graduate school to obtain an M.B.A. provided him with the tools and techniques which have been invaluable in progressing to higher level managerial positions.

Jim expressed his view of the planning process very concisely when he said, "Planning is examining where you have been, where you are today, where you want to go, and what you must do to get there." He believes that too many businesspersons get so wrapped up in day-to-day operations that they forget their end objective. The successful businessperson is one who has a clear picture of what must be accomplished and then reacts to changing business conditions to accomplish his or her goals.

FIGURE 2.1
The Planning Process

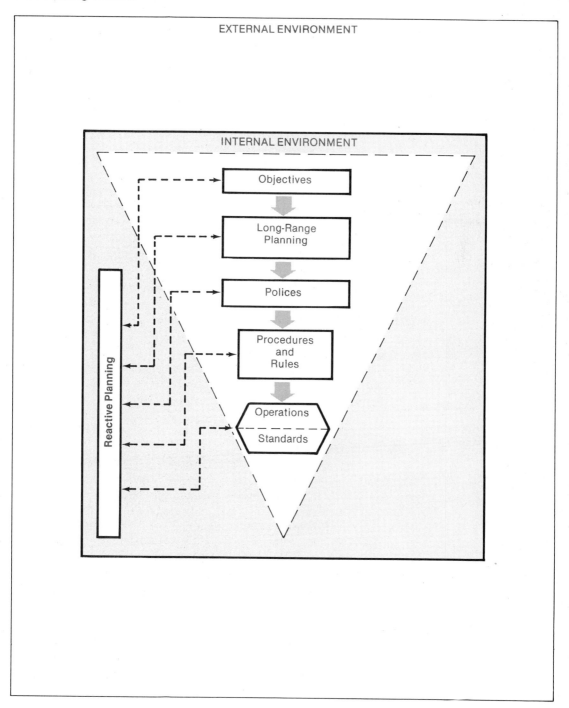

Objectives affect the size, shape, and design of the organization, and are important in motivating and directing personnel. In order to appreciate the importance of objectives in an organization, the types of objectives that a firm may consider will next be discussed. This will be followed by a presentation of the process of establishing objectives and goal complexities that a firm must consider.

TYPES OF OBJECTIVES

The creation of specific organizational objectives is no simple task. As we discussed in chapter 1, there are numerous external factors that exert their influence on a firm. Some of these external considerations include competition, stockholders, customers, unions, suppliers, creditors, the public, and the government. Because of these external factors, an organization usually has more than one objective and the emphasis may change depending on the impact of a particular environmental factor or group of factors that is present. At least three main types of objectives can be identified for the business firm in our society

- Economic objectives—survival, profit, and growth
- Service objectives—creation of economic value for society
- Personal objectives—goals of individuals and groups within the organization

Economic Objectives

The desire to survive is a basic objective of all organizations. It is the one goal common to all firms. Whether an organization is producing a desired economic value or not seems to take second place to just staying alive. It is difficult for a firm to take into account higher societal objectives when it is not known whether the next payroll can be met. As an anonymous statesman once said, "It is extremely difficult to think that your initial objective was to drain the swamp when you are up to your neck in alligators."

In order to survive, a firm must at least *break even*—that is, it must generate enough revenues to at least cover costs. But, business firms want more than mere survival—they are in business to make a profit. Profit provides a vital incentive for the continued, successful operation of the business enterprise. "What is an adequate profit?" This primarily depends on the industry and the specific needs of an organization.

Growth may also be a major objective of a firm. Growth may ensure survival in the long run. In an effort to avoid failure, a company may seek unrestricted growth and sometimes this growth can become an end in itself. When this happens, the company may become blind to the goal of economic service. There are, of course, certain economic advantages that come with size, and many companies see growth as a way of competing more effectively in the marketplace. But, if the products manufactured cannot fulfill an economic value, the growth will eventually prove to be useless.

Service Objectives

Profit alone is often viewed as the primary motive for being in business. While it is true a firm cannot survive for long without making a profit, the old question, "Which comes first, the chicken or the egg?" may have meaning when discussing the profit versus the service objective. If a firm cannot consistently create economic value for society, it will not stay in business long enough to make a profit. Many firms have gone out of existence when they ceased to produce goods and services that were desired by society. For instance, of the largest 100 companies in the U. S. in 1900, only two are still in business today. To accomplish the economic objective, a firm must produce goods the consumer wants. The creation of economic value constitutes the major goal of organizations within our economic system.

Personal Objectives

Organizations are made up of people who have different personalities, backgrounds, experiences, and goals. Most likely, their personal goals are not always identical to the objectives of the organization. If the difference in goals is significant, the employee may choose to withdraw from the firm. However, withdrawal does not necessarily mean departure from the organization. For instance, an employee may not feel that he or she can financially afford to leave the firm. A major difference between the employee's goals and the organization's goals can result in minimum work effort, absenteeism, and even sabotage. Employees are not the only ones whose goals, when they differ from those of the organization, can affect that organization. For instance, a stockholder can cease to provide support for the organization, but keep his or her stock.

If the organization is to survive, grow, and earn a profit, it must attempt to provide a match between its goals and the goals of groups who have contact with the firm. Therefore, achievement of members' personal goals should become an organizational objective (some differences in member goals may be seen in Table 2.1). It is not unusual for particular groups or members to feel their personal goals are in conflict with the goals of other individuals related to the organization. For instance, some customers may

TABLE 2.1
Differences in Organizational Member Goals

Internal Environment	Member Goals	External Environment	Member Goals
Management	Salaries, bonuses, etc.	Materials suppliers	Profitable prices
Employees	Wages and bonuses	Customers	Quality, low-cost products
		Labor unions	Influence, justice, improved working conditions
		Creditors	Interest on investment
		Stockholders	Profit and dividends
		Public	Protection and enhancement of human and environmental resources
		Government	Taxes, socially usable resources, etc.

Source Edwin B. Flippo and Gary M. Munsinger, *Management*, 4th ed. (Boston: Allyn and Bacon, Inc., 1978), p. 78.

believe that higher wages will make the prices of products higher, while the government may believe that stockholders' profits are too high. Management has the difficult task of reconciling these conflicts, whether or not they are real.

ESTABLISHING OBJECTIVES

It is the organizational members who provide the strength of a firm and these members are the ones who establish objectives. However, because of the wide diversity of personalities, backgrounds, experiences, and the personal goals that exist among individuals, objectives of firms may differ, even though a similar product is produced. Sometimes, it is forgotten that people, as opposed to some unknown organizational force, create these goals.

The person or persons charged with the responsibility of establishing corporate objectives vary from business to business. At times, the president or chairman of the board provides the major thrust in goal creation.

INSIGHTS TO SUCCESS

Be patient. Work hard. *Be a doer!* Always look for things to improve—*then improve them.* Don't sit back and wait to be told to do everything. At the end of the work day ask yourself—"What did I do today to help the company become more competitive?" Granted—the answer at times is "nothing," BUT IT WORKS.

DALE R. MCCRACKEN, Vice-President—Manufacturing, Champion Spark Plug Company

Planning is important at all levels in the organization.

At other times, a group of top-level executives are consulted in the creation of corporate goals. Whatever the source, these objectives provide the course toward which future energies of the firm will be directed.

Objectives should be well thought out and concisely stated. They should not constrain lower management to the degree that no further decision making is possible. An objective permits the greatest possible freedom for lower-level management while still providing direction to achieve a specified end result.

Effective goal creation also requires priorities that may not be altered too frequently. Obviously, major decisions have far-reaching and drastic effects on areas such as the type of personnel required, the style of management, and the type of organizational structure. For instance, a firm dedicated to maintaining a high quality product needs to recruit individuals capable of achieving the goal of quality. Also, a more participative structure may be required to keep skilled employees. Thus, once a corporate objective has been stated, the effects of the decision will be felt throughout the organization for a long time.

PROBLEMS ENCOUNTERED IN ESTABLISHING OBJECTIVES

Numerous difficulties can arise when creating objectives. Here are three types of conflict.

Real versus Stated Objectives

The *real* goals of any organization may be at odds with the *stated* goals. Objectives are often the result of power plays and pressures that come from circumstances in the marketplace or from internal tensions. The personal goals of the board of directors, outside creditors, lower managers, employees, stockholders, and labor unions are bound to be different. Because of these differences, the stated goals are at times different from the actual goals of the organizations. Goals are often significantly altered by individuals and groups who seek to adapt the organization to their narrower purposes.

To determine the real goals of an organization, one must look at the actual decisions and actions that occur day-to-day. A manager's actions speak louder than words. What functions or groups actually receive the major share of the resources? What type of behavior is accorded the greatest rewards by management? If the administration of a prison, for example, specifies its major goal as rehabilitation of prisoners, but has only two counselors on its payroll while it employs five hundred guards, the facts go against the stated goal.

Multiple Objectives

At times, an organization may have multiple and sometimes conflicting real goals that must be recognized by management. For instance, what is the major service goal of a university? Is the primary objective of the university to provide education of students, or to conduct research to advance the state of knowledge, or to provide community service? In some universities, research is given the first priority in money, personnel, and privilege. In others, the teaching goal is dominant. In still others, an attempt is made *to be all things to all people*. However, given limited funds, priorities must be established in most cases. One can debate the priority of goals for such institutions as a mental hospital (therapy or confinement); a church (religion or social relationships); a prison (rehabilitation or confinement); a vocational high school (skill development, general education, or keeping young people off the streets); a medical school (training medical students for clinical practice, basic research, or academic medicine); and an aerospace firm (research information or usable hardware). At some point, choices must be made.

Goal Distortion

The more quantitative the goal, the greater the attention and pressure for its accomplishment. Production managers must meet specific quotas and schedules; personnel managers often have more subjective goals, and consequently, less pressure. If the most important goal is also the most measurable, as with the goal of winning with a professional sports team, then little distortion will take place. If the reverse is true, the organization is likely to be pushed in the direction of more quantitative, but perhaps less important, goals. In universities, research and publication are far easier to measure precisely than excellence in teaching. The primary goal of excellence in education may be replaced with the research emphasis.

PLANNING

Many businesspersons are not good planners. They are often active, energetic individuals who have become accustomed to making rapid decisions and putting out daily fires. Because of this, they often find it difficult to force themselves to think far into the future. But, planning is a task that every manager, whether a top-level executive or a lower-level supervisor, should perform. Jim Watson, in the career profile at the beginning of the chapter, summarized the need for planning when he said, "A good business planner will beat out a nonplanner time and time again." In this section, strategic plans will be discussed followed by a discussion of operating plans.

STRATEGIC PLANNING

strategic planning

The determination of how the organizational objectives will be achieved is referred to as **strategic planning.** In essence, there are two basic stages of strategic planning—determining the strategy and developing the specific plans to implement the strategy. Long-range strategic planning has been said to cover a time frame typically extending five years or more into the future. Of course, this can vary depending on the purpose of the organization and the technology of the industry. For instance, it may be unrealistic for a professional football team to plan five years into the future. Too many factors can change: a star player can be sidelined by injury or a player may develop much faster than expected. A long-range plan for two or three years may be more realistic.

On the other hand, long-range strategic planning for some manufacturing firms may be in excess of ten years and for the forestry products industry, some thirty or forty years. Thus, long-range planning depends, to a large extent, on how far the organization can look into the future with a reasonable expectation of being accurate. What should be the strategic plan of Dr Pepper, since they have a goal of being number one in the soft drink industry? Should they diversify into other soft drinks, add new product lines other than soft drinks, add new plants, and/or expand into international markets?

Logic suggests that the firm that establishes an overall long-range strategic plan will be more effective than one that does not develop such a plan. This tends to be supported by the tendency for long-range planning to receive increased emphasis among business firms. For example, Stewart Hall, president of PROBE, Incorporated, an executive search firm, states, "More and more clients are coming to me with a priority requirement that the top-level executives they are seeking must have a strong background in strategic planning and forecasting." Another significant trend that illustrates the importance of strategic planning is the fact that numerous companies have established formal planning departments for the purpose of developing three-, five-, and ten-year plans for their organizations. In fact, over 100 of the top 500 U. S. firms in sales have actually specified a position of vice-president of planning. Many of the remaining companies have top-level executives with titles relating to corporate planning and development.

The specific tasks to be accomplished in strategic planning are determined by corporate objectives and the type of business in which the firm is engaged. Gary R. Miller, director of corporate planning for Morrison–Knudsen Company, Incorporated, a construction, engineering, and real estate development corporation says that "one of the biggest tasks that an organization has is to develop an understanding of what long-range planning is, and what it can do, not only for the corporation but for the individual." Specific projects for which strategic planning is actually being used may be seen in Table 2.2. As one might expect, the type of projects varies according to the company involved. As can be seen, the particular planning projects tend to be directed toward accomplishment of overall company objectives. Each phase of the strategic planning process may be seen in Figure 2.2

TABLE 2.2
Long-Range Planning Projects

Primary Products of Firm Studied	Type Planning Projects
Automotive Tires	Effects of energy crisis New Product diversification Ailing product lines
Computers	New business markets Acquisitions Venture analysis
Aircrafts	New Products
Natural Gas	Acquisitions Raw materials supply Diversification
Catalog order and retail department store	Expansion of facility Corporate financing Marketing direction
Railroad Transportation	Major construction project Capital expenditures Market Growth
Steel	Overall industry or business capital Spending policies and trends Timing of major investment
Pharmaceuticals	Plant location planning New product development Overall business strategy
Cosmetics and Toiletries	Expansion New business Resource allocation
Petroleum	Finding new energy sources New and expanded petrochemical plants Technology and manpower needs
Tobacco Products	New project development Capital planning New business entry

Service Objectives

The starting point for all strategic planning begins with the determination of the basic objectives for which the firm was established. This reason must be clearly understood. For instance, General Motors' service objective is to provide transportation. An electrical generating plant is created to provide power to the consumer. Each firm, if it is to survive in the long run, is created to provide some benefit to society.

FIGURE 2.2
Strategic Planning Sequence

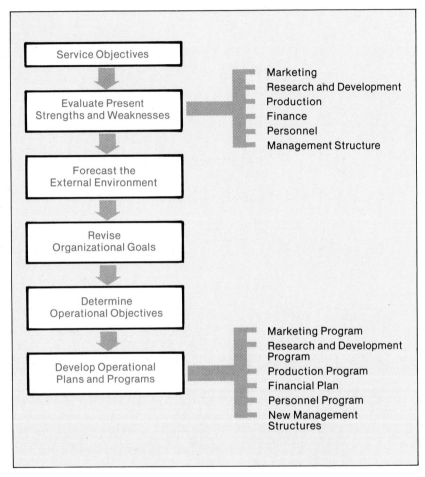

Source Adapted from Edwin B. Flippo and Gary M. Munsinger, *Management,* 4th ed. (Boston: Allyn and Bacon, Inc., 1978), p. 81.

Evaluate Present Strengths and Weaknesses

The next step in the strategic planning process is to analyze the present strengths and weaknesses of the firm. This involves an analysis of resources necessary for the accomplishment of these objectives—personnel, materials, money, physical plant, and machines. The strength/weakness evaluation should encourage the firm to be more reasonable in their expectations. If, for example, one of its strengths is strong management talent, it should be incorporated into strategic planning. For instance, E-Systems, Incorporated, has obtained numerous government contracts because it has gained a reputation of possessing strong management talent and effective planning systems. An analysis of a firm's strengths and weaknesses will permit planners to reformulate long-term goals. This competence profile may well lead to an alteration of the kind of business the firm will pursue.

Forecast the External Environment

forecasting

An attempt to project what will occur in the future is referred to as **forecasting.** It is of critical importance in the next phase of strategic planning when the long-range goals are reformulated. In this stage, an attempt to identify the external opportunities and threats to the firm is being made. Hopefully, the forecasted environment will match the strengths of the firm. At times, this is not the case and a firm's long-term goals must be modified. For instance, it would do little good to have the strengths that are needed to manufacture a high quality engineering slide rule (the hand electronic calculators have virtually made them extinct) when the forecast for demand for slide rules is on the downward trend. Specific forecasting techniques will be described in chapter 13.

Revise Organizational Goals

Once the firm is aware of the organization's strengths and weaknesses and have forecasted the environment associated with the company, the firm is then in a position to revise its long-term goals. The long-term goals of the firm are developed in view of both the strengths of the firm and the forecasted environment. If the strengths are not consistent with the changes predicted in the environment, certain capabilities of the firm may need to be developed in order for the objectives to be achieved.

Determine Operating Objectives

Once the long-term goals of the organization have been identified, the objectives of each of the functional departments such as marketing, production, finance, personnel, and research may be identified. If the goal of the organization is to be a leader in its field, marketing's goal, for instance, may be to increase sales by 20 percent. All functional goals must contribute to the accomplishment of organizational goals.

Develop Operating Plans and Programs

operating planning **Operating plans** and programs for each function are next developed. In marketing, key decisions should be made concerning such factors as product mix, sales promotion, advertising, and pricing. With respect to production, plans and programs would relate to changing technology, flexibility of present facilities, and inventory levels. Certainly, research and development programs play a key part in determining the type of products the firm will be able to offer in the years ahead. Plans concerning personnel should cover needed future skills and the skill level of current employees.

Programs developed for all of the above resources obviously require financing. Perhaps the greatest restraint is the availability of money to implement the total long-range program. Profit planning, retention of earnings, and development of short- and long-range capital resources are all important elements of this plan.

Finally, the management or administrative plan must be developed. Proposed organization structures should be designed with the emphasis on the types of decisions necessary to accomplish the tasks required by the program. In locating the appropriate decision maker, key concern is with the importance of the decision as indicated by the amount of money involved, the number of organizational units affected, the duration of the effect of the decision, and the possibility of reversing it once it is made. In addition, a control system must be designed to provide operating information so that corrections may be made when actions and environment are significantly different from the planned program.

PLANNING FOR OPERATING MANAGERS

All too often a discussion of planning is directed toward the benefits top management may derive through the use of the planning function. Sometimes we forget that all effective managers engage in planning. The planning process for both top-level and operating managers is quite similar. However, since the operating manager is lower in the organization, his or her external environment is comprised largely of company factors. A lower-level manager must develop plans that will fit within the overall company objectives and strategies, but the importance of planning remains.

As we discussed in chapter 1, time spent in the planning function at lower levels of management may not be as great at higher levels. For instance, a lower-level manager may devote a much larger percentage of his or her time to directing or controlling. However, this does not diminish the importance of planning. Also, the time frame for long-range planning for lower-level managers may be shortened. Top-level management must make decisions far into the future to be successful, but to ask a lower-level manager to think five years into the future may be unrealistic. Daily, weekly, monthly, and annual quotas must be met. It is quite possible that long-range planning for some managers may encompass a relatively short time span. However, the shorter time span does not diminish the importance of long-range planning.

STRATEGIC PLANNING VERSUS OPERATING PLANNING

The distinction made regarding planning by top management and operating managers is largely one of degree. As shown in Figures 2.3 and 2.4, a generalized planning model is given to both lower- and upper-level management. There are major differences between the two situations in the external and internal environment in which the two managers operate. External factors that top management might consider include the government, competitors, unions, suppliers, customers, creditors, stockholders, and the public. Internal factors considered by top-level management include such areas as the types of products or services provided by the firm, the structure of the organization, and the type and quality of personnel required. On the other hand, the creation of plans for lower management, while following the same general process, relates more to specific organizational concerns. External factors pertaining to lower management involve organizational objectives, policies, procedures, rules, and general company philosophy. These external considerations provide the framework for the goal-setting process. Internal factors relate to the specific task to be accomplished. The primary difference between strategic planning by top management and planning created by department or section managers is one of degree. All managers, regardless of level, establish plans.

STANDING PLANS—POLICIES, PROCEDURES, RULES, AND STANDARDS

standing plans

Once objectives and long-range strategies and plans have been established, guidelines may be needed to assist in the implementation of the plans. These are often referred to as **standing plans** because they are more detailed in nature. Policies, procedures, rules, and standards are available for this purpose. Each will be discussed separately, though, of course, some overlapping exists among the topics.

FIGURE 2.3
The Planning Process—Lower-Level Management

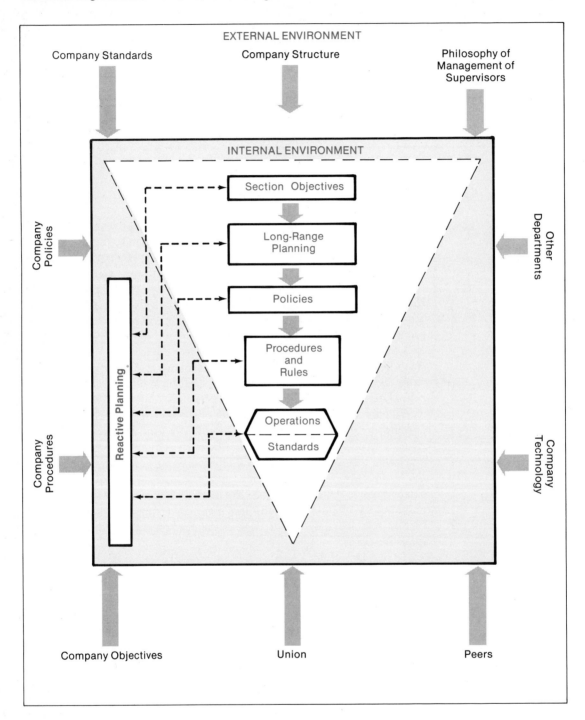

FIGURE 2.4
The Planning Process—Upper-Level Management

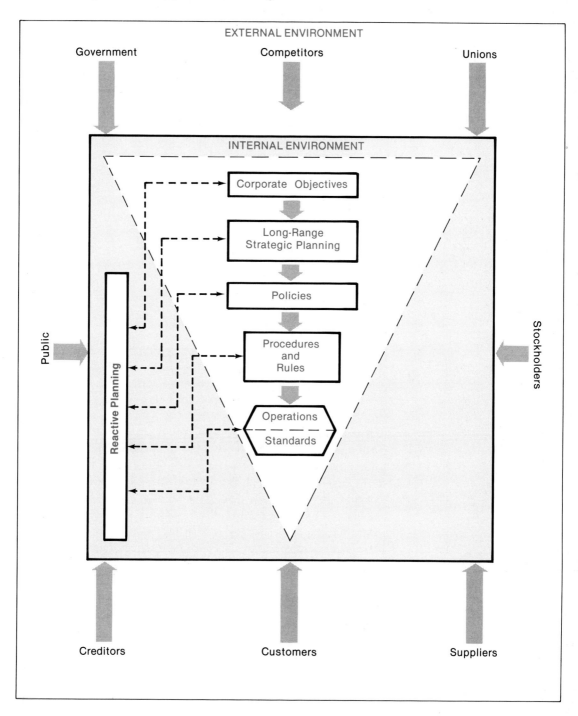

POLICIES

policy   A **policy** is defined as a predetermined, general course or guide established to provide direction in decision making. As such, it should be based
on a thorough analysis of corporate objectives. Policies cover the important areas of a firm such as personnel, marketing, research and development, production, and finance.

To formulate policies, the manager must have knowledge of, and skill
in, the area for which the policy is being created. However, there are
certain generalizations that apply to the establishment of policies. The
most important has already been stated: policies must be based on a
thorough analysis of objectives. There are several other general principles
that can help the manager create appropriate policies.

1. *Policies should be based on known principles and, as much as possible, on facts
   and truth.* For instance, it is a fact that Congress has passed the Age
   Discrimination Act. It is not a fact that a satisfied employee is a
   higher producer.

2. *Subordinate policies should be supplementary, not contradictory, to superior
   policies.* A policy for a company division should not directly conflict
   with a corporate policy.

3. *Policies of different divisions or departments should be coordinated.* They
   should be directed toward overall organization optimization instead
   of optimizing a particular department such as sales, engineering,
   purchasing, or production, to the detriment of the whole.

4. *Policies should be definite, understandable, and preferably in writing.* If a
   policy is to guide actions, persons concerned must be aware of its
   existence and this requires creating understandable directives in
   a definitive written form. These sets of guides constitute the memory
   of the organization which it uses to help cope with future events.

5. *Policies should be flexible and stable.* The requirements of policy stability
   and flexibility are not contradictory; one is a prerequisite to the
   other. Stable policy changes only in response to fundamental and
   basic changes in conditions. Government regulations can represent
   such a basic change in conditions that they can have a major impact
   on a firm's employment policies. The higher the organization level,
   the more stable the policy must be. Changing the direction of the
   enterprise is a much more complex and time-consuming task than
   changing the direction of a department or section. The higher the
   organization level, the more policy resembles principle and, con-
   versely, the lower the level, the more it resembles or becomes a rule.
   The Armco Steel Corporation provides an excellent example of a
   firm whose policies have been remarkably stable. First formulated in
   1919, these policies, outlined in Table 2.3, are still applicable today.

TABLE 2.3
Armco Policies

Ethics	To do business guided and governed by the highest standards of conduct so the end result of action taken makes a good reputation an invaluable and permanent asset.
Square Deal	To insist on a square deal always. To make sure people are listened to and treated fairly, so that men and women really do right for right's sake and not just to achieve a desired result. For everyone to go beyond narrowness, littleness, selfishness in order to get the job done.
Organization	To develop and maintain an efficient, loyal, aggressive organization, who believe in their company, to whom work is a challenge and to whom extraordinary accomplishment is a personal goal.
Working Conditions	To create and maintain good working conditions . . . to provide the best possible equipment and facilities . . . and plants and offices that are clean, orderly, and safe.
Quality and Service	To adopt ''Quality and Service'' as an everyday practice. Quality will be the highest attainable in products, organization, plant, property, and equipment. Service will be the best possible to customers, to shareholders, to city, state, and nation.
Opportunity	To employ people without regard to race, sex, religion, or national origin. To encourage employees to improve their skills by participating in available educational or training programs. To provide every possible opportunity for advancement so that each individual may reach his or her highest potential.
Compensation	To provide not only fair remuneration, but the best compensation for service rendered that it is possible to pay under the changing economic, commercial, and other competitive conditions that exist from time to time. It is Armco's ambition to develop an organization of such spirit, loyalty, and efficiency that can and will secure results which will make it possible for individual members to earn and receive better compensation than would be possible if performing a similar service in other fields of effort.
Incentive	To provide realistic and practical incentive as a means of encouraging the highest standard of individual performance and to assure increased quantity and quality of performance.
Cooperation	To recognize cooperation as the medium through which great accomplishments are attained. Success depends more on a spirit of helpful cooperation than on any other one factor.
Objectivity	To always consider what is right and best for the business as a whole, rather than what may be expedient in dealing with a single, separate situation.
Conflict of Interest	To prohibit employees from becoming financially interested in any company with which Armco does business, if such financial interest might possibly influence decisions employees must make in their areas of responsibility.

TABLE 2.3

Armco Policies (Continued)

	The above policy does not apply to ownership in publicly owned companies. This is not considered a conflict of interest but, rather, is encouraged as part of the free enterprise system.
Citizenship	To create and maintain a working partnership between industry and community in this country and throughout the world. To support constructive agencies in communities where Armco people live and work in an effort to create civic conditions that respond to the highest needs of the citizens.

Used with permission from the Armco Steel Corporation.

6. *Policies should be reasonably comprehensive in scope.* Policies conserve the executive's time by making available a previously determined decision. The manager should organize the work in such a way that subordinate personnel can handle the routine and predictable work, while he or she devotes time to the exceptional events and problems. If the body of policies is reasonably comprehensive, the cases that arise which are not covered by policy constitute exceptions.

**QUALITIES NEEDED FOR SUCCESS
AS A MANAGER IN YOUR ORGANIZATION**

- Retain a good sense of humor. If you can't have a little levity mixed with the business, forget it.
- Be demanding, but be reasonable. Set a goal of being in the top 25% of your industry in terms of financial performance.
- Don't get in "Fool's Heaven" in times of prosperity, particularly if you are in a cyclical business. Keep the team lean and hungry in both good and bad times.
- Set an example of good work habits. Don't expect anybody to work harder than you do. Never "get your dauber down" in front of your people.

GERALD L. "BUD" PEARSON, President and C.E.O., Spencer Foods, Incorporated

---

PROCEDURES AND RULES

Once broad policies have been established, more specific plans may need to be created to ensure compliance with policy. Procedures and rules might be thought of as further restrictions on the actions of lower-level personnel. They are usually established to ensure adherence to a particular policy. Although the two terms are similar, they will be defined separately.

Procedure

procedure

A **procedure** is a series of steps or functions established for the accomplishment of some specific project or endeavor. For most policies, there is an accompanying procedure to indicate how that policy should be carried out.

Rule

rule

A **rule** is a very specific and detailed guide to action which is set up to direct or restrict action in a fairly narrow manner.

An illustration of the differences between policies, procedures, and rules may be seen in Table 2.4. As may be seen from the illustration, procedures and rules may overlap as to definition. Taken out of a sequence of steps, a procedure may actually become a rule.

TABLE 2.4
Examples of Policies, Procedures, and Rules

Policy:	It is the policy of the company that every employee is entitled to a safe and healthful place in which to work and desires to prevent accidents from occurring in any phase of its operation. Toward this end the full cooperation of all employees will be required.
	Management will view neglect of safety policy or program as just cause for disciplinary action.
Procedure:	The purpose of this procedure is to prevent injury to personnel or damage to equipment by inadvertent starting, energizing or pressurizing equipment that has been shut down for maintenance, overhaul, lubrication, or setup.
	1. Each maintenance man assigned to work on a job will lock out the machine at the proper disconnect with his own safety lock and keep the key in his possession.
	2. If he does not finish the job before shift change he will remove his lock and put a seal on the disconnect. He will hang a danger tag on the control station, stating why the equipment is shut down.
	3. The maintenance man who will be coming on the following shift will place his lock on the disconnect along with seal.
	4. Upon completion of the repairs the area foreman will be notified by maintenance that work is completed.
	5. The foreman and the maintenance man will check the equipment to see that all guards and safety devices are securely in place and operable. Then the *foreman* will break the seal and remove the danger tag from the machine.

TABLE 2.4

Examples of Policies, Procedures, and Rules   (Continued)

Rules:	The following rules are intended to promote employee safety.

1. The company and each employee are required to comply with provisions of the Occupational Safety and Health Act (OSHA). You will be informed by your supervisor on specific OSHA rules not covered here which apply to your job or area.

2. Report all accidents promptly which occur on the job or on company premises—this should be done whether or not any injury or damage resulted from the incident.

3. Horseplay, practical jokes, wrestling, throwing things, running in the plant and similar actions will not be tolerated as they can cause serious accidents.

4. Observe all warning signs, such as "No Smoking", "Stop", etc. They are there for your protection.

5. Keep your mind on the work being performed.

6. Familiarize yourself with the specific safety rules and precautions that relate to your work area.

7. Approved eye protection must be worn in all factory and research lab areas during scheduled working hours or at any other time work is being performed.

8. Hearing protection is required when the noise level in an area reaches limits established by OSHA.

9. Adequate hand protection should be worn while working with solvents or other materials which might be harmful to hands.

10. Wearing rings or other jewelry which could cause injury is not allowed for persons performing work in the factory area.

11. Good housekeeping is important to accident prevention. Keep your immediate work area, machinery, and equipment clean. Keep tools and materials neatly and securely stored so they will not cause injury to you or others.

12. Aisles, fire equipment access, and other designated "clear" areas must not be blocked.

13. Learn the correct way to lift. Get help if the material to be lifted is too heavy to be lifted alone. Avoid an effort that is likely to injure you.

14. Only authorized employees are allowed to operate forklifts and company vehicles. Passengers are not allowed on lift equipment or other material handling equipment except as required in the performance of a job.

15. Learn the right way to do your job. If you are not sure you thoroughly understand a job, ask for assistance. This will often contribute to your job performance as well as your job safety.

16. Observe safe and courteous driving habits on the parking lot.

Policies, procedures, and rules are designed to direct action toward the accomplishment of objectives. If we could be assured that the persons doing the work were thoroughly in agreement with, and completely understood, basic objectives, there would be no need for policies, procedures, and rules. Moreover, it is apparent that objectives are at times unclear and even controversial. Thus, all organizations have a need for policies, procedures, and rules that can and should be more definitive and understandable than the objectives on which they are based.

STANDARDS

standard

A norm, or criteria, to which something can be compared is referred to as a **standard.** They are created to specify in detail what constitutes proper behavior and conditions. Standards permit us to determine whether or not our objectives have been achieved. As such, they provide the link between planning and controlling. Referring once again to Figure 2.1, it can be seen that standards provide a way for determining if a plan has been achieved. It would be foolish to establish plans, policies, procedures, and rules and not be able to determine whether or not they have been achieved. But, as will be described in chapter 12, standards provide the starting point for the controlling process.

performance results standards

process standards

In business, standards can be created to cover virtually every aspect of a situation. Standards can be divided into two main categories. When it is relatively simple to specify what end result is desired, they are classified as **performance results standards.** On the other hand, if we are attempting to evaluate a function for which specific standards are difficult or impossible to formulate, they are referred to as **process standards.** Examples of each type of standard may be seen in Table 2.5.

TABLE 2.5
Examples of Standards Applicable to a Production Task

Type of Standard	Example
Performance Results	
1. Quantity	20 units of Item X to be produced per hour.
2. Quality	Item X must have diameter of 2.75 inches ±0.05.
3. Time	Work order must be complete by March 2.
4. Cost	Direct costs for Work Order must not exceed $40.00.
Process	
1. Function	Standard Operating Procedure (SOP) to be followed in producing Item X.
2. Personnel	Operator must be a journeyman with minimum of six months experience on this type of job.
3. Physical Factors	Work area lighting should be evenly distributed, without glare, and with an intensity of 20 fast-candles.

Source Edwin B. Flippo and Gary M. Munsinger, *Management*, 4th ed. (Boston: Allyn and Bacon, Inc., 1978), p. 88.

Performance Results Standards

The major topics to be evaluated regarding performance results relate to

1. The quality of work
2. The quantity of work
3. The time needed to complete work
4. The cost of work

Quality standards are usually derived from the function of product or service design. For a physical product, examples would include form, dimensions, strength, color, and durability. Often, quality control inspectors are utilized to collect information from production and compare it with engineering-established requirements.

Quantity standards relate to the number of items produced during a specific time period. For instance, a time study may result in a requirement for 50 units per hour to be produced by a certain machine operator. An employment interviewer for a personnel agency may be required to place a minimum of fifteen applicants a week. In automobile assembly plants, the standard might be sixty automobiles produced each hour on the assembly line.

Standards governing *time* are often related to the quantity standards as shown in the examples above. The most common example of a time standard relates to completion of a report on a particular date. For example, a periodic accounting report will be submitted to managers by the tenth of each month.

Cost standards are established to ensure that a project is completed within set cost limits. These standards are extremely important, for it is an embarrassing situation to complete a project on time only to find that the costs are significantly higher than expected and they wipe out whatever profits might have been realized. The annual and monthly *budgets* constitute a well-known example of cost standards. Standard cost systems are also designed to enable the manager to make more effective decisions governing ongoing action.

Process Standards

Sometimes it is difficult or impossible to establish accurate standards of performance. When this occurs, process standards should be used. This type of standard relates to: personnel standards, functional standards, and physical factors standards.

Even though one may not be able to establish accurate standards of performance, one may attempt to specify and control performance through process standards. For example, a firm may try to hire a person for a particular job who possesses the highest qualifications; this would be a standard of personnel. Or, the firm may develop standards for the best content (job description) and method (standard operating procedure) for executing the job. These are standards of function. Finally, standards that attempt to provide superior physical factors in terms of equipment, lighting, ventilation, privacy, and the like may be drawn up. These are physical factors standards. The operating assumption here is that the best people, using the latest in methodology and equipment, might result in maximum efficiency without having to establish specific standards of quality, quantity, time, and cost.

REACTIVE PLANNING

reactive planning

Robert Burns' line, "The best laid plans of mice and men often go astray" is certainly applicable in today's business world. Events can occur so rapidly that plans may be useless before they can be fully implemented. Even though it is properly developed, external and internal disturbances often occur that can result in a plan being modified or even eliminated. A prudent manager recognizes that events can occur that were not planned and that he or she must attempt to anticipate these disruptions, and deal effectively with the new conditions these disruptions create. When a manager at any level prepares to adjust to unanticipated occurrences, he or she is using **reactive planning.**

Oliver R. Kirby, Vice-President for Advanced Planning for E-Systems, Incorporated, summarized the use of reactive planning when he stated, "Reactive planning fills the holes that you don't initially recognize." Clearly, it entails a recognition that unforseen events can and will occur to alter initial plans. Reactive planning therefore becomes a systematic way of modifying objectives, long-range planning, policies, procedures and rules, and standards to adapt to the real world environment. A manager who uses reactive planning is employing a true situational approach to planning.

Referring again to Figure 2.1, reactive planning encompasses all phases of the planning process. Suppose, for instance, that the competition alters their direction and thereby drastically affects the anticipated outcome of the long-range plan. Reactive planning must quickly take effect or the firm might be thrown into confusion. Changes in the plans could affect not only long-range planning but also policies, procedures and rules, and even standards. Examples which reenforce the need for reactive planning are numerous. For instance, a government policy change may have a drastic effect on a long-range business plan; it can even change corporate objectives. Also, an unanticipated stoppage of supplies of a raw material, as with the oil embargo of 1979, certainly will bring reactive planning into play.

Reactive planning does not mean that a firm has to wait for an unanticipated situation to occur before it responds. Management should attempt to anticipate these contingencies as far as possible. Naturally, not all situations can be anticipated, but the manager who tries to anticipate possible deviations will stand a much better chance of coping with the new situation brought about by the deviation.

UNINTENDED SIDE EFFECTS OF PLANS

Few things in life and organizations are absolutely pure and untainted. Every plan is likely to have certain undesired effects and the manager must not be blinded by all of the possible good results of a plan. He or she must attempt to anticipate the negative as well as the positive results of a plan. In many instances, a possible counterproductive effect of a plan can be headed off by appropriate action. For example, asking for weekly output figures in terms of poundage produced is likely to stimulate frantic juggling of orders to ensure high poundage runs on Thursday and Friday. This, in turn, is likely to lead to missing some delivery promises for smaller poundage orders. Rather than abolish the poundage reports, thereby harming the control function, the manager can ask for such reports on a semimonthly basis. This additional time should provide the flexibility for lower managers to meet both delivery dates and poundage standards. Looking at an important index too frequently can produce some undesirable side effects.

In Table 2.6 are listed a number of typical programs that many organizations adopt. Listed in the third column is a number of possible side effects that may work counter to managerial desires. All of these, and more, have been observed in many organizations. All planners—managers—must consider these possible side effects if optimum results are to be achieved.

The fact that a plan may have negative effects is not necessarily adequate justification for its abandonment. Management needs to anticipate negative consequences and make special provision for their handling. More subordinate participation can reduce some of the adverse effects, and education, patience, participation, and more effective rewards systems can remove many more of the undesired effects. Specialization cannot be abandoned, but efforts can be undertaken to ensure that the various units communicate, coordinate, and work together.

TABLE 2.6
Positive and Negative Effects of Programs

Program	Positive Effects	Negative Effects
Budgets	Allocation of resources Cost control	Resentment and antagonism Narrow focus on one's unit Unduly high concern for the present Expenditures rise to equal income
Management Information Systems	Provide proper quality of information needed at appropriate time and place	Aggressive attack on threat to security Projection of blame for errors on systems Avoidance of information provided
Contests	Increase output levels, e.g., production, sales, safety, etc.	Dishonesty in reporting Neglect of activities not under contest Aggressive behavior
Control Reports	Accurate information to enable control	Juggling of work orders to produce volume on date of report "Bleeding" the line to accelerate output by date Hurrying to spend one's budget by expiration date
Incentive wages	Increase output	Restrict output to prevent changes in output standards Reduced cooperation among personnel "I've got mine. Who cares about the next person."
Standards of performance	Control	Minimum compliance
Departmentation	Specialized units to enable better performance	Less concern for the total organization Production fights Engineering who, in turn, is at war with Sales, all of whom have little regard for Research and Development

Source Edwin B. Flippo and Gary M. Munsinger, *Management*, 4th ed. (Boston: Allyn and Bacon, Inc., 1978), p. 90.

SUMMARY

Proper establishment of objectives and plans is important for all managers regardless of level in the organizational hierarchy. Objectives identify the end results desired. Plans provide the means through which these results can be achieved. Most organizations have multiple objectives. The three most common forms of organizational objectives relate to economic, service, and personal. But, there are often problems encountered in establishing objectives. At times, there is difficulty in differentiating between the real and stated objectives of the firm. Multiple objectives as well as goal distortion create problems for the manager.

The purpose of strategic planning is to provide the means to achieve company objectives. Once the service objectives of the firm have been identified, the firm should thoroughly evaluate its present strengths and weaknesses. After the external environment has been analyzed, the organizational goals may be revised. Operational objectives and plans and programs can then be formulated based on realistic corporate objectives.

In order to facilitate the accomplishment of plans, policies, procedures, rules and standards need to be created. A policy is a predetermined, general course or guide established to provide direction in decision making. A procedure is a step-by-step means by which a policy can be accomplished. Rules provide a list of dos and don'ts that should be observed if the policy is to be achieved. Finally, standards establish a predetermined level of performance that is required if the plan is to be completed. All of these items—policies, procedures, rules, and standards—are important in the accomplishment of organizational goals.

At times, plans must be altered to conform to the needs of the situation. Reactive planning provides the means through which plans may be systematically changed to meet the needs of the situation. In addition, a person should realize that there may be an unintended side effect of plans. When plans are created, these negative effects of plans should be carefully considered.

Review Questions

1. What are the steps involved in the planning process?

2. What are the main types of objectives that can be identified for business firms in our society?

3. Distinguish between the planning process for lower-level management and upper-level management.

4. Describe and briefly discuss the strategic planning sequence discussed in the text.

5. Distinguish by definition between policies, procedures, and rules.

6. Define standards. Why is it important for a manager to develop clearly defined standards?

7. What is meant by the term reactive planning as it relates to the planning process?

8. What are some unintended side effects of plans? Discuss.

Exercises

1. It has been stated in the text that a firm can have multiple objectives. What do you feel would be the objectives of the following firms and organizations with regard to their interrelationship with society?
   A. Ford Motor Company
   B. American Airlines

C. Peat, Marwick, Mitchell & Co. (a Big-8 CPA firm)

D. New York Yankees

E. Girl Scouts of America

F. Internal Revenue Service

2. Assume that you determine your objective is to obtain a 4.0 grade point average the following semester. Develop a plan, policies, procedures, rules, and standards that could help you achieve this goal.

REFERENCES

Anderson, Carl R., and Paine, Frank T. "Managerial Perceptions and Strategic Behavior." *Academy of Management Journal* 18 (1975): 811–823.

"Future for the Corporate Planning." *Long-Range Planning,* April 1977, pp. 90–93.

Guth, William D. "Formulating Organizational Objectives and Strategy: A Systematic Approach." *Journal of Business Policy,* Autumn 1971, pp. 24–31.

Kudlu, R. J. "Elements of Effective Corporate Planning." *Long-Range Planning,* August 1976, pp. 82–93.

Leontriades, M. "Planning: A Reexamination of Fundamentals." *Journal of Economics and Business,* Spring/Summer 1976, pp. 189–194.

McCaskey, Michael B. "A Contingency Approach to Planning: Planning with Goals and Planning Without Goals." *Academy of Management Journal,* June 1974, pp. 281–291.

Powers, William J. "How Government Policies Affect Capital Investment." *Nation's Business,* November 1975, pp. 67–68.

Steiner, George A. *Top Management Planning.* New York: Macmillan, 1969.

Stephenson, E. "Assessing Operational Policies." *Omega* 6 (1976): 437–446.

Taylor, Bernard. "Strategies for Planning." *Long-Range Planning,* August 1975, pp. 27–40.

Thume, Stanley S., and House, Robert J. "Where Long-Range Planning Pays Off." *Business Horizons,* August 1970, pp. 81–87.

Townsend, Robert. *Up the Organization.* Greenwich, Conn.: Fawcett, 1971.

Vancil, Richard F., and Lorange, Peter. "Strategic Planning in Diversified Companies." *Harvard Business Review,* January/February 1975, pp. 81–90.

Case Study

OBJECTIVES AND PLANS FOR A FINANCIAL CAREER

Bill Williams has been attending State University for the past two years. Until now he has regarded school as a means of passing away four years and his grades generally reflect this attitude (his 2.2/4.0 keeps him in school but it is nothing to write home about). Bill studies when he absolutely has to and enjoys the very active social life that is available at the University. His college grades are quite different from those in high school. In high school Bill was one of the top students earning very high grades. However, since he began going to college, he has not been able to decide what he wants to concentrate on as a major. His attitude has been one of "I just haven't found the career that turns me on."

At least the above situation existed until Bill enrolled in Dr. Edens' finance class this summer. Bill had intended to spend the summer getting a good suntan and meeting as many girls as possible (a hidden goal for which many male students aspire). However, a strange thing happened; Bill was "turned on" to the field of finance. He would find himself studying many afternoons when it wasn't even raining. He even worked many of the extra finance problems though Dr. Edens did not assign them in class. Bill developed a keen respect for his professor and he often stopped by Dr. Edens' office to discuss various aspects of the course.

One day while Bill was in Dr. Edens' office he said, "I've been thinking about majoring in finance and possibly becoming a financial analyst for a major bank when I graduate."

"That's an admirable goal, Bill," replied Dr. Edens. "I hope you realize what might be involved in accomplishing that objective."

"No, not really," said Bill. "This is my first course in finance."

"What are your grades so far in college?" asked Dr. Edens.

"I have a blazing 2.2 average so far. It will improve this summer because it looks as if I will make three A's and one B. I'm really not stupid; I just have never found a reason to study that much in the past."

"I am proud of you for what you've accomplished this summer, Bill," replied Dr. Edens. "But if you're really serious about pursuing a career in finance I'll help you identify what must be accomplished before you will have the opportunity to obtain your goal. Let me list them on a sheet of paper."

1. Improve your grade point average.
2. Take all of the finance and accounting courses that are offered. At State University these courses are recognized as being quite difficult.
3. Develop good rapport with teachers in this specialty. Many of them have business contacts that could be very beneficial when you're obtaining your first job.

After Dr. Edens had developed the list, he continued his conversation with Bill by saying, "You took a management course this summer and made an A didn't you? One of the chapters in the course concerned Objectives and Plans. What I would like you to do for me is develop a plan that will help you meet your objectives. Once you have accomplished this task, we will talk some more."

Questions

1. In order to accomplish the objective Bill has established, what do you feel should be included in his short-range plans and long-range plans?
2. What are some external factors that could affect Bill's attaining his goal?

Case Study   WHO ESTABLISHES THE OBJECTIVES AND PLANS?

The organization chart for Medford Stores, a medium-sized convenience store chain located in the Southeast, is presented below. For store managers, duties are well-formulated, inasmuch as a strong attempt is made by upper management to standardize operations. Although the manager may have one or two assistants under his or her direct supervision, the "managerial" connotation is often misleading as the manager and assistants normally work different shifts.

    Upper management strives to assure uniformity of operation in all areas including ordering, stocking, customer check-out procedures, and managers' attitudes generally prevailing within a store. Because of the routine

FIGURE 2.5
Organizational Chart of Medford Stores

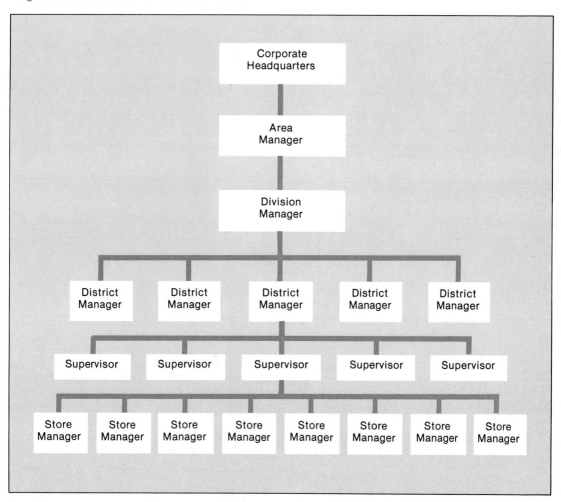

nature of work and because of a concerted effort by top management to foster conformity in store managers' duties, there tends to be little discretion on the part of managers regarding day-to-day store operations.

Furthermore, the general lack of freedom in decision making extends itself to supervisory levels of responsibility. Virtually all supervisors are promoted from the ranks of "successful managers" within Medford. As a result, those individuals who conform best to the convenience store environment are promoted. Typically a supervisor has responsibility for eight to ten stores. Normal duties include picking up the previous day's receipts, verifying daily accounting records, monitoring physical conditions of the stores, and making employment recommendations. Most matters not recognized as standard operating procedures are resolved at a higher managerial level.

The authority of the district manager is also circumscribed though to a lesser extent than the supervisor. Typically the district manager has responsibility for approximately fifty stores with five supervisors reporting directly to him. Although his district is considered a profit center, his ability to control profits is restricted to routine matters. From a practical standpoint, success or failure of a district manager depends, to a large extent, on the degree of conformity he is able to obtain from managers within his area of responsibility.

Any decisions that are not covered by standard operating procedures must be made at the division manager level. The division manager is also responsible for establishing objectives and formulating plans. All division managers are promoted from the ranks after successful accomplishment of the duties of a store manager, supervisor, and district manager.

Bob Anderson was recently promoted to division manager after having progressed from store manager to his present position in only ten years. It had been a long struggle, but Bob was pleased to finally be a division manager. Bob is now experiencing some difficulties though. The area manager called Bob in last Wednesday and questioned him about his objectives and plans for the forthcoming year. When Bob said he did not have them and was not really sure what was expected, the area manager became rather upset.

"Bob," the area manager said, "you are expected to do much more creative thinking now than in the past. You can let your subordinates put out the daily fires. Your job is much more encompassing. The very survival of Medford Stores depends on how well your objectives and plans are formulated."

Bob thanked the area manager for his comments and went to the files to find the standard operating procedures for formulating plans for Medford Stores. There were none! Bob's heart sank as he felt totally ill-equipped for this endeavor.

Questions

1. Why does the area manager feel the "very survival" of Medford Stores depends on how well objectives and plans are formulated?
2. Bob's situation is not uncommon in some firms. How could a firm ensure that people such as Bob are equipped to handle the planning function?

Chapter 3

Management by Objectives: An Approach to Planning

LEARNING OBJECTIVES

After completing this chapter you should be able to

1. State the value of a management by objectives (MBO) approach to planning.
2. Relate how the application of MBO has progressed from an emphasis on performance appraisal to planning and control and most recently to an integrated system of management.
3. Describe the essential elements of the MBO process.
4. Describe and illustrate the types and characteristics of goals established in MBO programs.
5. Explain how MBO can be used by an organization.
6. List and briefly describe the primary benefits and potential problems with MBO programs.
7. Identify important guidelines for improving the effectiveness of MBO.

A manager arrives at his office and observes two of his employees working at their desks. One employee, John James, is frantically shuffling through a mass of paperwork piled on his desk that remains to be processed. John usually arrives at the office at seven in the morning and often continues working until six or seven in the evening. He typically is behind in his work even though he is constantly busy. The other employee the manager notices is Bill Garcia. Bill comes to work at eight and usually leaves at five each day. The manager observes that Bill's desk is clean and well-organized. Bill has a reputation for completing projects on schedule and often has time to talk with other members of the firm. Does the fact that John appears "busier" to the manager than Bill mean that John is doing a better job than Bill? Of course, this may not be the case. John may be engaged in performing a number of "busy work" activities that may not contribute very much toward the accomplishment of important organizational goals.

management
by objectives An approach that concentrates on achieving results as opposed to engaging in work activities is **management by objectives** (MBO). During the past decade few developments in the theory and practice of management have received as much enthusiastic attention and application as MBO. It directs management's attention toward specific targets or end results that the organization must attain to be successful. In an MBO system, the efforts of management are goal-directed as opposed to being activity-centered. In the previous example the manager knows whether Bill or John is accomplishing the goals of the department and who merely looks busy.

In this chapter the background and development of MBO will first be discussed followed by a presentation of the MBO process. The steps to follow in developing a practical MBO system will then be presented. This discussion will be supported by an in-depth look at the types, characteristics, and the process of establishing objectives. Strengths and weaknesses of the system will also be discussed.

INSIGHTS TO SUCCESS

Set high standards for yourself and expect the same of your people.

M. LAMONT BEAN, President and C.E.O., Pay'n Save Corporation

WHAT IS MBO?

As we have discussed previously, organizations exist to achieve objectives. This is the case whether we are evaluating profit or nonprofit, private, or government organizations. Thus, all organizations are concerned about

A manager's success is determined by results not how busy he or she looks.

achieving objectives, and the attainment of objectives should be the primary concern of management. As you will recall from chapter 1, we defined management as the process of planning, organizing, directing, and controlling to accomplish organizational goals through the coordinated use of human and material resources. An MBO system causes management to focus its attention on the objectives—the end results. In essence, "MBO is simply common sense in that it is a reflection of the purpose of managing itself."[1]

Effective management practice concentrates on establishing and attaining measurable goals. *MBO provides a systematic and organized approach that allows management to attain maximum results from available resources by focusing*

1. Harold Koontz, "Making MBO Effective," *California Management Review* 20 (Fall 1977): 5.

BOONE POWELL

Chairman of the Executive Committee
Baylor University Medical Center

When the term "manager" is mentioned, a person likely thinks of presidents of major firms. But, an administrator of a major medical center has many of the same problems and responsibilities of a corporate president; the organizational environment is merely different. Boone Powell, currently Chairman of the Executive Committee of Baylor University Medical Center in Dallas, Texas, is one of those men. From the time he was named administrator and

chief executive officer in 1948, Boone Powell has had to function as a business manager. The reputation that the Medical Center has gained throughout the world supports the contention that he is a highly effective manager.

He received the Distinguished Service Award of the American Hospital Association in 1977, becoming the only Texan ever to receive this significant honor. The award proclamation read that "he has the methods of a businessman and the efficient mind of an administrator, but he also has a profound appreciation of the value of education and the application of the advantages of science."

A conversation with Powell will quickly assure a person that he is, in the truest sense of the word, a manager. He provides these comments to individuals interested in pursuing a career in management:

· *Planning* is essential to the survival of any enterprise in our society today.

· Recognize the importance of *involving people* in the planning and decision-making process—those who have a vested interest and those who have something significant to contribute. Involvement leads to commitment by those who participate to see that implementation of plans and decisions is achieved.

· Involvement also becomes an effective means of *communication*.

· Involvement at all levels—trustees, medical staff, department heads, and employees—fosters a spirit of cooperation and rapport which results in better working relationships among these groups.

· Recognize that the intricacies of a medical center operation require the understanding and support of many groups of people.

· Recognize the human element in the ultimate success of any institution.

· Be alert to the constant and rapid changes in medical science and evaluate new developments to determine those that should be incorporated into the diagnostic and therapeutic service structure of the Medical Center.

on achievable goals. Above all else, MBO represents an overall philosophy of management; it actually constitutes a way of thinking that concentrates on achieving results. As such, it forces management to predict and plan for the future as opposed to simply responding or reacting on the basis of guesses or hunches. It provides a more systematic and rational approach to management and helps prevent "management by crisis," "fire fighting," or the "seat-of-the pants" methods. MBO emphasizes measurable achievements and results and is designed to lead to improvements in both organizational and individual effectiveness.[2] The approach depends heavily on active participation at all levels of management.

BACKGROUND AND EVALUATION OF MBO

Peter Drucker was first to describe "management by objectives" in 1954 in *The Practice of Management.*[3] According to Drucker, management's primary responsibilities were to balance a number of demands and objectives in all areas where performance and results directly affect the survival, profits, and growth of the business. Drucker stated that specific objectives must be established in the following areas:

- market standing
- innovation
- productivity
- worker performance and attitude
- physical and financial resources
- profitability
- managerial performance and development
- public responsibility

Drucker argued that the first requirement of managing any enterprise was "management by objectives and self-control." As originally described by Drucker, an MBO system was designed to satisfy three managerial needs.

MBO would provide a basis for more effective planning. Drucker had in mind what might be called the systems approach to planning—that of integrating objectives and plans for every level within the organization. The basic concept of planning consists of *making it happen* as opposed to *just letting things happen.* According to Drucker, MBO was a planning system requir-

---

2. Anthony P. Raia, *Managing by Objectives* (Glenview, Ill.: Scott, Foresman and Company, 1974), pp. 10–12.
3. Peter F. Drucker, *The Practice of Management* (New York: Harper & Row, 1954.)

ing each manager to be involved in the total planning process by participating in establishing the objectives for his or her own department and for higher levels in the organization.

MBO was designed to improve communications within the firm since managers and employees frequently discuss and reach agreement on performance objectives. In the process, there is frequent review and discussion of the goals and plans of action at all levels within the firm.

Finally, Drucker thought that the implementation of an MBO system would encourage the acceptance of a behavioral or more participative approach to management. By participating in the process of setting objectives, managers and employees develop a better understanding of the broader objectives of the organization and how their goals relate to the total organization.[4]

One of the foremost advocates of MBO, George Odiorne, contends that special efforts must be undertaken to avoid the *activity trap*.[5] This trap exists when managers and employees become so enmeshed in performing assigned functions that they lose sight of the goal or reasons for their performance. As a result, they justify their existence by the energy and sweat expended, and avoid questioning whether or not they have accomplished any result deemed necessary to organizational effectiveness. For example, most students have observed professors who are so activity-centered that they never seem to accomplish the primary goals of the courses they teach. Such professors may assign a considerable amount of *busy work* not relevant to the goals of the course. The students are kept *busy*, but their efforts are not focused on the most important contents of the course. This creates a real problem when the course is a prerequisite to other courses in a student's major.

Another advocate of MBO, Douglas McGregor, stressed a slightly different emphasis. McGregor favored MBO because of its usefulness as a performance appraisal method and thought that the essence of MBO was *management by integration and self-control*. McGregor's philosophy of MBO was based upon what he termed Theory Y. Although now famous, Theory X–Theory Y will be explained in detail in chapter 8, Motivation. It is mentioned here because Theory Y provides a basis for the MBO process. The basic assumption in Theory Y is that individuals are responsible human beings capable of exercising self-direction and self-control in achieving organizational goals if they are committed to the goals.

In his approach, individual managers establish their own short-term performance objectives, and develop action plans to achieve these goals. The manager's superior (boss) would provide assistance in goal setting by creating a climate for effective participation and commitment. But, the goals are set by the subordinate, not the superior.

4. Peter F. Drucker, *Management: Tasks, Responsibilities* (New York: Harper & Row, 1974).
5. See George S. Odiorne, *Management by Objectives* (Belmont, Calif.: Pittman, 1965), and *Management Decisions by Objectives*, (Englewood Cliffs, N.J.: Prentice-Hall, 1969).

INSIGHTS TO SUCCESS

Establish goals. Realize that sheer ability without dedication is a serious deficiency. Corporations don't prosper without dedicated people.

JAMES A. SILBAUGH, Vice-President, Hormel

STAGES OF DEVELOPMENT OF MBO

In its early years, MBO programs were primarily concerned with the evaluation of the performance of managers. The programs provided a means for reducing the subjectivity in performance appraisal by developing specific objectives and performance standards for each position. An MBO performance appraisal system provided an alternative to traditional performance evaluation which was based largely on perceived personality traits of the individual being appraised. It encouraged the individual being rated to actively participate in the process of establishing specific performance goals and in appraising his or her own progress toward his or her accomplishment.

When MBO is used only as an appraisal system, the program will likely receive only mild support from top management. With MBO as an appraisal system, responsibility for implementation of the program essentially comes from the personnel department; line management's involvement is usually limited to the completion of the paperwork associated with the program. Performance reviews are conducted annually or semiannually, but they normally involve only the subordinate and his or her boss.

It is possible that less productive employees may be viewed as making greater contributions to the overall success of the firm than another person who is much more productive when MBO is used only as an appraisal system. This can occur if management fails to recognize the difference in the levels of difficulty of goal achievement and overall contributions to the firm of different employees. For example, with rigid implementation of an MBO appraisal system, Mildred Price, a highly productive employee, may have attained only 60 percent of her targeted results. However, Wayne Miller, another manager in the same department, may have achieved 90 percent of his goals, but the goals were much less demanding and ambitious than the goals of Mildred. Management should recognize the differences in the degree of difficulty in the goals of Mildred and Wayne and reward them accordingly.

MBO based on performance appraisal has been and continues to be the starting point for many companies. However, if the MBO program does not proceed beyond the performance evaluation stage, overall program effectiveness will be limited. In essence, performance appraisal is a part of the system, but perhaps the least significant. The performance appraisal aspects represent the "end results" of a properly designed MBO system.

During the late 1960s, MBO began to take on a broader perspective; it was incorporated into the organization's planning and control processes. Objectives were related to plans that provided an integrated basis for control through budgets. Results-oriented performance appraisals continued to be an integral part of the MBO program, but there was considerably more top management support than during the earlier phase. In addition, since the MBO program was closely related to the budgetary process, line management had the primary responsiblity for its success. With this approach, there was increased emphasis on the training and development of personnel throughout the organization.

Since the early 1970s, MBO has evolved into a system of management designed to integrate key management processes and functions in a logical and consistent manner. Anthony Raia, a leading advocate of MBO as a system of management, believes that MBO consists of ". . . overall organizational goals and strategic plans; problem-solving and decision-making; performance appraisal, executive compensation, manpower planning, and management training and development."[6] Phase three MBO programs are experiencing excellent success which, perhaps, in part, can be attributed to these characteristics:

- Direction and thrust come from top management, but managers at all levels are actively involved in the process.
- The increased need for teamwork involves more groups in establishing goals, action planning and reviewing performance.
- Goal setting is more flexible and covers longer time spans.
- There are more frequent performance reviews.
- There is more emphasis on individual growth and development.[7]

THE MBO PROCESS

Earlier we defined MBO as a systematic and organized approach that allows management to attain maximum results from available resources by focusing on achievable goals. This definition of MBO does not provide significant insight into the total process that must be considered in its use. It is a process that is constantly being reviewed, modified, and updated.

6. Raia, *Managing by Objectives*, pp. 14 and 15.
7. Ibid., pp. 14–18.

FIGURE 3.1
The MBO Process

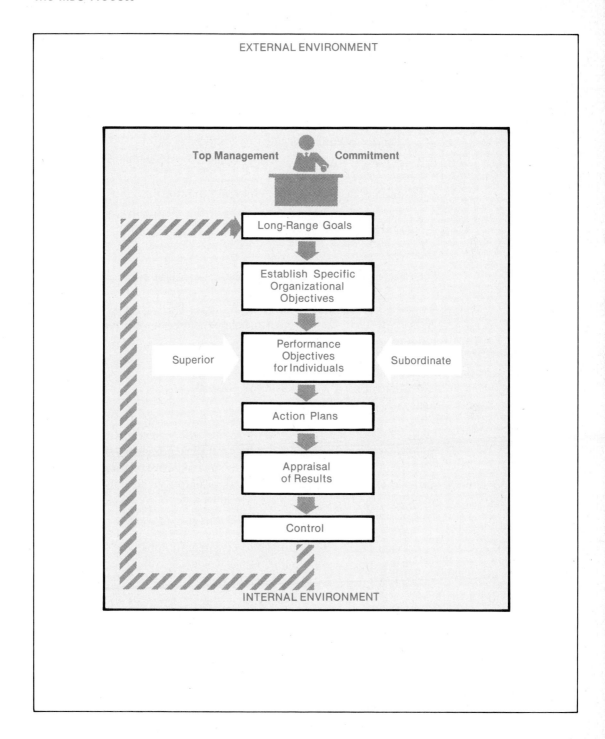

The dynamics of the system consist of the following interrelated steps as illustrated in Figure 3.1 and provided below.

- Support and commitment from top management
- Establishing of long-term goals and strategic plans (overall goals)
- Development of clear, concise objectives for the organization and each department (specific goal setting)
- Establishment of performance objectives and standards for individuals (action planning)
- Measurement of results achieved (appraisal)
- Taking corrective action to ensure the attainment of the desired results (control)

TOP MANAGEMENT SUPPORT AND COMMITMENT

Any MBO program is doomed from the start without the absolute and enthusiastic support of top management. It is because of the lack of top-level commitment that so many MBO programs fail.

ESTABLISHMENT OF LONG-TERM GOALS AND STRATEGIC PLANS

Every successful management by objectives program must begin by developing long-range goals and the strategies to accomplish these goals. Long-term plans are developed by thoughtful determination of the basic purpose or mission of the organization. Before developing long-range goals, the top management of a firm must attempt to answer such questions as these:

- What is the basic purpose of the organization?
- What business are we in and why?
- What business should we be in?

Long-range planning is essential if management is to identify areas needing improvements.

Long-term goals and strategic planning can be illustrated by a company that has an overall purpose of producing and marketing high quality color televisions. Several long-term goals and strategies consistent with the overall purpose may be developed. This company may have a goal to increase their rate of return on stockholder investment to 20 percent after taxes and to achieve a share of 15 percent of the total U.S. market for color

---

**MOST IMPORTANT REASONS FOR SUCCESS
AND EFFECTIVENESS AS A MANAGER**

1. Insistence on setting personal and corporate objectives with target dates for achieving goals.
2. Consistency in measuring progress toward goals.
3. Ability to get to the heart of a problem by understanding the subject thoroughly and asking the right questions.
4. Insistence on integrity of the Company's people and products.
5. A strong belief in listening to and evaluating thoroughly the ideas of associates and subordinates.
6. The ability to create a team effort.
7. Delegation of responsibility with adequate supervision.
8. Persistence in pursuing objectives and in problem solving.

HAROLD F. THAYER, Chairman, President, and Chief Executive Officer, Mallinckrodt, Incorporated

---

televisions within seven years. These are long-range goals because they extend beyond one year. The firm's strategic plan—the means to attain the stated goals—might include substantial quality improvements in the color television. These changes would hopefully create a greater demand and allow the firm to increase the price of the television. If the firm was able to control costs and generate greater sales volume their long-term goals should be attained.

DEVELOPMENT OF CLEAR, CONCISE OBJECTIVES FOR THE ORGANIZATION AND EACH DEPARTMENT

After long-range goals and plans are established, management must be concerned with determining specific objectives to be attained within a given time period. These objectives must be supportive of the overall purpose and key result areas. Usually they are expressed as very specific and quantifiable targets covering such areas as: productivity, market, profitability, and other areas.

In our example above of the color television manufacturer, specific organizational objectives might be represented by the following:

1. Increase sales of television model A1000 to 500,000 units—an increase of 10 percent during the current year

2. Reduce production costs per T.V. produced by 5 percent in next twelve months

3. Increase investment in new product design by 10 percent over last year

4. Increase profits by 10 percent over last year

Each of the above would be further subdivided into departmental objectives consistent with attaining the above organizational goals.

ESTABLISHMENT OF PERFORMANCE OBJECTIVES AND STANDARDS FOR INDIVIDUALS

action planning

This step in the MBO process is known as **action planning.** This phase requires that challenging, but attainable standards be developed for the purpose of improving individual or group performance. For example, specific individual standards of performance for Bob Helms, a sales representative for the Boston territory, might include the following goals:

1. Increase sales of color T.V.'s in the Boston market by 10 percent during the year

2. Reduce travel expenses by 5 percent

MEASUREMENT OF RESULTS ACHIEVED (APPRAISAL)

The next step in the MBO process is to measure and evaluate the actual performance as compared to the goals and standards established. Having specific standards of performance provides management with a basis for such a comparison. When goals are specifically stated and agreed on by both the manager and the subordinate, self-evaluation and control becomes possible. We will discuss in considerable depth the performance appraisal process in a later chapter.

TAKING CORRECTIVE ACTION TO ENSURE THE ATTAINMENT OF DESIRED RESULTS (CONTROL)

While an MBO system provides the framework for goal setting, managers in the organization must take action to correct areas where results are not being accomplished according to the plans. Such action may take the form of changes in personnel, the organization, or even in the goals themselves. Other forms of corrective action may include providing additional training and development of individual managers or employees to enable them to better achieve the desired objectives.

TYPES AND CHARACTERISTICS OF OBJECTIVES IN MBO PROGRAMS

TYPES OF GOALS

In the paragraphs below we will discuss the types and characteristics of objectives used in MBO systems. Four types of objectives can be established in MBO programs. These are:

1. routine
2. problem solving
3. innovative
4. personal development

Routine

routine objectives

Routine objectives represent recurring day-to-day activities that are expected to be performed. They represent standards of performance. As indicated in Table 3.1, a routine objective for the production manager would be to improve the percentage of due dates met on the regular production schedule from 90 to 95 percent by June 1. For the director of finance, a routine objective is to reduce bad debt losses from 5 to 3 percent of sales by January 1.

Problem Solving

problem-solving objectives

In all jobs, problems arise on a regular basis. In fact, many people believe that the basic management task is that of solving problems. A problem for the director of management information systems is often one of excessive copies of reports, many of which are tossed in the wastebasket by personnel who say they need them. A **problem-solving objective** for the director of management information systems is to reduce by 20 percent the number of copies of EDP reports prepared by June 1.

TABLE 3.1
Examples of Objectives for MBO Program

Position	Objectives
Director of Finance	Reduce bad debt losses from 5 percent to 3 percent of sales by January 1. Reduce number of accounting employees 10 percent, through transfer of operations to computer, by June 1.
Director of Management Information Systems	Add "return on assets employed" to reports for each cost center by January 1. Reduce by 20 percent the number of copies of EDP reports prepared by June 1.
Marketing Manager	Complete field testing of Product X by June 1, and add to regular line by January 1. Increase share of market of Product J from 15 percent to 20 percent in Northeast territory by January 1.
Personnel Manager	Decrease turnover of clerical employees from 20 percent to 10 percent by January 1. Complete planning and installation of supervisory training program on grievance processing by June 1.
Production Manager	Reduce welding rejects from 6 percent to 3 percent by January 1. Improve percentage of due dates met on production schedule from 90 to 95 percent by June 1.
Research and Development Manager	Complete design and development of Product X by June 1, within a cost budget of $150,000. Provide two new products for marketing field testing within next 12 months.

Source Edwin B. Flippo and Gary M. Munsinger, *Management,* 4th ed. (Boston: Allyn and Bacon Inc., 1978), p. 412.

Innovative

innovative objectives

Innovative objectives are concerned with unique or special accomplishments such as the development of new methods or procedures. Though some managers are rarely creative, MBO goal-setting sessions provide an opportunity for innovative goals to be developed and stated. Adding a return on assets employed to reports for each cost center by January 1 in the director of management information systems position could well be an innovative objective designed to improve the quality of information available. Another illustration of innovative goals might involve the credit operations of a large bank. The vice-president in charge of consumer loans might have such goals as the development of a government guaranteed loan program for low-income families or the installation of an improved credit processing system by January 1. Both of these are examples of innovative goals.

Personal Development

Personal development objectives provide the opportunity for each individual to state his or her personal goals and action plans for self-improvement and personal growth and development. Almost all MBO systems include a section on personal growth and development goals. Examples of personal development goals might include a statement such as "completing a two-week executive development program on improving leadership effectiveness by June 1." Personal development goals are important because of their potential for helping individuals improve their current skills, preparing them for increased responsibility and career advancement, and improving their current performance.

CHARACTERISTICS OF OBJECTIVES
FOR THE INDIVIDUAL

In order for MBO to achieve maximum results, objectives for each individual should be carefully prepared. They should be limited in number, highly specific, challenging, attainable, and coordinated. It has been suggested that the number of objectives for each managerial position should range from four to eight. Having more than this number leads to "spreading oneself too thin," thereby diminishing overall effectiveness. It is also suggested that each objective be assigned a priority, perhaps ranging from one to three. In this way, should time and resources prove to be more limited than anticipated, the individual has a basis for deciding which objective to pursue.

Perhaps the most emphasized characteristic of the good objectives is that they should be stated in specific terms. In most instances, this means quantification and measurability. For example, goals have far less impact when stated in such forms as "improve the effectiveness of the unit," "keep costs to a minimum," or "be alert to market changes." At the performance review, one should be able to look back and definitely answer the question, "Did I do it or not?" For instance, a goal stating that production will be increased by 1,000 units would be much clearer than one that merely encouraged increased production. Thus, in writing objectives, a special attempt should be made to phrase them in such terms as volume, costs, frequency, ratios, percentages, indexes, degrees, and phases. It is particularly important to place time limits on each objective. In 10 of 11 studies that examined the impact of such specific goals on performance, evidence was found supporting the contention that specifically stated goals will increase the level of accomplishment.[8]

Developing *challenging* and *attainable* objectives requires a delicate balance of opposing forces. Yet, both are essential in motivating the subor-

8. Ibid.

dinate. Obviously, the superior desires that objectives be set at such a level that special efforts on the part of the employee must be made. Some researchers have pointed out that if promotion and salary are related to success in attaining objectives, as they should be, the participatory approach may well be asking the subordinate to construct a "do-it-yourself hangman's kit."[9] For instance, Randal Louis might tell his parents he is going to take the maximum course load of six courses and maintain an *A* average. Randal has never made above a 2.5 average, but because he believes his parents will buy him a new car if he accomplishes this feat, he nevertheless tells them of his intentions. It is likely that Randal has just "hung" himself because these goals are unattainable.

In the initial phases of new MBO programs, one of the more common errors is the establishment of objectives that are unattainable. This is particularly the case if the time period for review is six months to a year. Anything seems possible with that much time. The superior must not allow excessively high goals to be set because this may cause a decline in future expectations and performance of the individual. Specific attention must be given to obstacles that affect accomplishment, particularly the availability of resources necessary for performance. The impact of other personnel on the subordinate's performance must be recognized and discussed.

Research indicates that challenging objectives lead to greater accomplishment only if the subordinate truly accepts the goal as reasonable, and only if goal accomplishment actually leads to organizational rewards. Challenging goals with a history of past success will lead to continued success. A series of failures creates a mental set that makes attainment increasingly more difficult. Subordinates with self-assurance do well in relation to challenging goals. It has been suggested that the subordinates' assessment of the probability of success should be that they at least have a 50–50 chance of achieving the objectives.

CHARACTERISTICS OF TEAM OBJECTIVES

team objectives

The accomplishment of most goals requires that individuals cooperate with each other. There are many factors that can affect the attainment of **team objectives.** For instance, it should be apparent that if the sales manager sets a specific objective of selling 50,000 units by March 1, it cannot be done if the production manager does not produce that number of units. One of the most recommended approaches to overall goal setting involves team meetings to establish group goals. Team goal setting is in accord with the open and supportive organizational climate that is essen-

9. Gary P. Latham and Gary A. Yukl, "A Review of Research on the Application of Goal Setting in Organizations," *Academy of Management Journal* 18, no. 4 (December 1975): 829.

tial to the success of the MBO program. In one instance, "a medium-size service company experimented with the team approach and decided to ignore individual objectives altogether, reasoning that too much inter-linking support, and cooperation are required to blame or reward any individual for the production of any single end result."[10]

If team goal-setting sessions are to be used as a prelude to the more typical individually oriented meetings, some training in group processes would be necessary. It is difficult enough for a manager to establish an open and participatory climate with an employee. But, it is far more complex and challenging to try the same thing in a group. Programs of training directed toward this end go under the title of *organization development*, a subject that will be discussed at length in chapter 10. In an MBO–team approach, French and Hollmann suggest the following se-quence: (1) team meetings of top executives to set overall organizational objectives; (2) team meetings at unit level; (3) individual person-to-person goal-setting sessions; (4) individual reviews of accomplishments; (5) team meetings at unit level to review progress and accomplishment; and (6) review at the top level to determine the degree of overall organizational success.[11] The team goal-setting process improves the chances of success of the MBO program because it improves coordination and communica-tion within the organization.

THE PROCESS OF DETERMINING OBJECTIVES

Objectives may be set (1) by the *superior,* (2) by the *subordinate,* (3) *jointly,* or (4) *jointly* with the aid of a *staff specialist.* When the superior is completely in charge of goal setting, problems often occur. Rather than involving subordinates in the process, they impose a specific, quantitative, and time-bounded goal on employees. This is not MBO; but probably should be referred to as RBO (rule by objective). The following conversation between the president of a holding company and the president of one of his subsidiaries illustrates RBO. The subsidiary president had expressed doubt as to whether he could meet the budgetary goal. The holding company president's reply was, "Do I pay you a lot of money? Do I argue with you over what you want to spend? Do I bother you? Then don't tell me what the goals should be. . . . My board and my stockholders want me to make my numbers. The way I make my numbers is for you guys to make your numbers. So, *make your numbers!*"[12] The holding company president is practicing RBO.

10. W. J. Reddin, *Effective Management by Objectives* (New York: McGraw-Hill, 1971), p. 16.

11. Richard E. Byrd and John Cowan, "MBO: A Behavioral Science Approach," *Personnel* 51, no. 2 (March–April 1974): 48.

12. Wendell L. French and Robert W. Hollmann, "Management by Objectives: The Team Approach," *California Management Review* 17, no. 3 (Spring 1975): 19.

Most MBO programs require some type of a joint determination of objectives between superiors and subordinates. The particular advantage of having an MBO staff specialist is that it assures that meetings will actually take place, with help and advice being available. The joint process can take a number of variations. Perhaps the closest to RBO would be an initial determination of goals by the superior, followed by a submission to the subordinate asking for reactions. The opposite would be an initial determination by the subordinate, followed by discussion with the superior. In other instances, both come to the meeting with a set of tentative objectives worked out as a basis for discussion.

THE APPLICATION OF MBO

The most impressive quality of MBO is that it has been successfully applied in numerous organizations. In many organizations, management by objectives represents an overall planning system in addition to providing the basis for more objective performance appraisal. Many firms have well defined MBO systems that they use in their daily activities. The following discussion illustrates the effective application of MBO in a large and diversified company.

There are two basic dimensions of the MBO system used: goal setting/planning and performance appraisal. The goal setting process used is provided in Figure 3.2. The company stresses that goals should describe results to be attained within one year. Also, these goals should motivate the individual toward the achievement of agreed on results. The purpose of each category on the goal worksheet is described below.

1. **Major direction or emphasis.** The initial step in the goal setting process is establishing priorities and determining the major work responsibilities during the coming year. This serves as an important point of reference as you establish goals and specific results expected. Each manager should ask, "What aspect of my performance has the most potential for affecting company profitability during the year?"

2. **Goals to be achieved in current year.** This section of the goal worksheet focuses on the specific results expected. Results should be consistent with long-range plans, operating plans, and the overall business environment. An example of this type of goal would be increasing sales volume by 10 percent by the end of the year through improved sales promotion techniques.

3. **Goals for next year.** The purpose of this section is to establish specific goals that are to be achieved during the following year so as to recognize important future goals and thereby avoid concentration

FIGURE 3.2
Goals Worksheet and MBO Performance Evaluation Worksheet

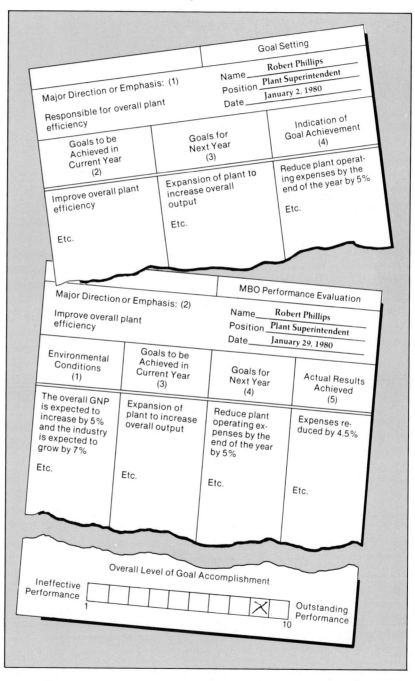

on only the current year's goals. The company emphasizes the importance of giving careful consideration to questions such as "what should be achieved this year?" and "what should be achieved next year?"

4. **Indication of goal achievement.** This section is devoted to providing an indication of what is acceptable performance with regards to the established goals. For example, a goal might be to achieve new customer sales of $2.5 million. The firm believes that it is extremely important to quantify as many of the goals as possible.

performance appraisal
system

The second phase of the MBO system with the firm involves evaluating the performance of employees. The goals of the **performance appraisal system** involves developing a clear definition of what is expected of each employee and then measuring their performance against whether or not the goals have been achieved. For the employee and his or her manager, it represents a narrowing device to get from the total job to the results and goals which are most significant.

As shown in Figure 3.2, the MBO performance evaluation system for the firm provides a system for achieving goals. The major categories included in the system are described below.

1. **Environmental Conditions.** This section is concerned with describing the environment or climate in which you will be operating in the coming year. Environmental conditions are for a one-year period and should be described as specifically as possible. For example, a statement that "the economy and the industry will experience growth" is not specific enough. A more specific statement would be that "the economy and the industry is projected to grow by 10 percent." State any assumptions that may be beyond the control or influence of the individual or his or her business unit.

2. **Major Direction or Emphasis.** Determining each manager's priorities is important because it establishes the direction of each job for the coming year. It also serves as a reference as you proceed through the goal setting and performance appraisal procedure. A question that must continually be asked is, "Do one or more of your most important results and goals relate back to your priorities and major direction?"

3. **Goals to be achieved in current year.** (Same as goals worksheet). This section focuses on the specific results expected.

4. **Goals for next year.** (Same as goals worksheet). This section is concerned with the priorities and results being sought for the following year.

5. **Actual results achieved.** This section on the MBO Performance Evaluation Worksheet is concerned with identifying the actual goals and results achieved.

6. **Overall level of goal accomplishment.** The final section on the performance evaluation worksheet is designed to evaluate an individual's overall achievement of the established goals. The scale ranges from ineffective to outstanding performance depending on goal achievement.

With both the Goal Worksheet and the MBO Performance Evaluation Worksheet, a manager is able to cross-check and ensure consistency, correctness, and proper direction. Through this process a manager can determine if the goals of the subordinates are consistent with the manager's and departmental goals. Also, it may be determined if the overall goals provide sufficient direction to achieve corporate goals.

THE BENEFITS OF MBO PROGRAMS

Many of the organizations using MBO have experienced several of the following benefits or advantages:

1. **Results in better overall management and the achievement of higher performance levels.** MBO systems provide an overall results-oriented philosophy of management that requires managers to do detailed planning. Managers also must develop action plans and consider the resources needed and control standards.

2. **Provides an effective overall planning system.** MBO helps the manager avoid management by crisis and "fire fighting."

3. **Forces managers to establish priorities and measurable targets or standards of performance.** MBO programs sharpen the planning process. Rather than just saying "do your best" or "give it your best shot," specific goals tend to force specific planning. Such planning is typically more realistic because the program calls for a scheduled review at a designated future date. The subordinate makes very sure that he or she can obtain the resources necessary for goal accomplishment and that obstacles to performance are discussed and removed. MBO forces planning of a logical sequence of activities in advance of the start of action.

4. **Clarifies the specific role, responsibilities, and authority of personnel.** Objectives must be set in key result areas and individuals responsible must be given adequate authority to accomplish them. A

production plan superintendent who has a goal of producing 10,000 units a day must be given the authority to organize and direct resources to achieve the desired level of production.

5. **Encourages the participation of individual employees and managers in establishing objectives.** If the process of MBO has been undertaken on a joint and participatory basis, the chances are that increased commitment will be obtained.

6. **MBO facilitates the process of control.** Periodic reviews of performance results are scheduled, and information collected is classified by specific objectives. Subordinates are forced to relate what was accomplished, rather than concentrate on descriptions of what they did or how hard they worked. MBO also stimulates improvement in the performance of superiors, who are forced to clarify their own thinking and to communicate this to subordinates.

7. **MBO provides a golden opportunity for career development for managers and employees.** Personal development goals are often a part of the set of objectives developed in joint sessions. MBO often demonstrates the areas where employees need additional training. Priority establishment provides realistic guides for effort, as well as enabling the concrete demonstration of goal accomplishment. This, in turn, enables a more realistic and specific annual performance review, which, of course, is the crucial event in deciding on promotions, pay increases, and other organizational rewards.

8. **Other specific strengths of an MBO system** might include:
   a. Lets individuals know what is expected of them
   b. Provides a more objective and tangible basis for performance appraisal and salary decisions
   c. Improves communications within the organization
   d. Helps identify promotable managers and employees
   e. Facilitates the enterprises's ability to change
   f. Increases motivation and commitment of employees[13]

POTENTIAL PROBLEMS WITH MBO

Although there are numerous benefits attributed to MBO, there are also certain problems that may be encountered, such as the following:

1. MBO programs often lack the support and commitment of top management.

13. See Harold Koontz, "Making MBO Effective," *California Management Review* 20, no. 1 (Fall 1977): 5-7.

2. Goals are often difficult to establish.

3. The implementation of an MBO system can create a "paper mill" if it is not closely monitored.

4. There is a tendency for goals to concentrate too much on the short run at the expense of long-range planning.

5. Some managers believe that MBO programs may be excessively time-consuming.

SITUATIONAL CONSIDERATIONS IN IMPLEMENTING AN MBO PROGRAM

In addition to the above potential problems, there are several situational factors that often affect the implementation of MBO systems.[14]

1. **Managerial approach.** If a firm's upper-level managers prefer a strongly autocratic approach with centralized decision making, extensive change in the attitudes and philosophy of top management must occur before the organization can implement an MBO program. An existing participative philosophy of management will tend to facilitate the implementation of MBO.

2. **Organization structure.** Changes in the structure of the organization including responsibility and authority relationships may be necessary as a result of the implementation of MBO. MBO may require frequent review and revision of job descriptions. Specific responsibilities of managers and employees may change significantly as the result of the MBO system and these changes may lead to confusion on the part of many of the firm's personnel.

3. **Personnel.** The successful implementation of an MBO system requires the understanding and support of the organization's personnel. In the MBO goal-setting process, it is essential that managers be skilled in the ability to deal effectively with other people. Since many managers may be lacking in this skill, extensive training in counseling, interviewing, and communications may be required.

4. **Objectives.** The establishment of challenging, yet realistic, objectives is often a source of confusion for managers in an MBO system. Goals throughout the firm must be coordinated with the overall purposes of the organization, while at the same time meeting the personal needs and objectives of individuals.

14. Bruce D. Jamieson, "Behavioral Problems with Management by Objectives," *Academy of Management Journal* 16, no. 3 (September 1973): 496–505.

5. **External environment and technology.** Changes in technology or the external environment may complicate the implementation of an MBO system. For example, a sudden economic downturn may create the need for a firm to modify its short-term goals to bring them more into alignment with the environment. Likewise, a major breakthrough in technology may cause a firm to alter its goals.

**MOST IMPORTANT REASONS FOR SUCCESS
AND EFFECTIVENESS AS A MANAGER**

- Involvement with a growth company
- Accepting a variety of responsibilities
- Making company goals my goals
- Demonstrating and insisting on thorough and objective appraisals before making decisions
- A desire to develop others

STEWART TURLEY, Chairman of the Board and President, Jack Eckerd Corporation

---

SUGGESTIONS FOR IMPROVING THE EFFECTIVENESS OF MBO

MBO programs can be made more effective if management adheres to the following guidelines:

1. Secure top management support and commitment.
2. Specify the overall objectives of the program and communicate them throughout the organization.
3. Emphasize MBO as an overall philosophy or system of management rather than just a performance appraisal technique.
4. Allocate adequate time and resources to instruct each person in the organization in the nature and philosophy of the system.
5. Recognize that all goals must be realistic and attainable and that they must contribute to the overall purposes of the organization.
6. Be willing to modify the goals as changes in the environment dictate. Continuous review is a must.
7. Be sure to clarify responsibility and authority relationships so that everyone understands what's expected in the MBO system.
8. Insist that goals be written and stated in measurable terms to be attained within a specified period of time.

9. Make the goal setting process a joint activity between superiors and subordinates.

10. Recognize that MBO will not solve all managerial problems.

SUMMARY

The attainment of organizational objectives is the primary concern of management. An approach that aids in goal achievement is management by objectives (MBO). MBO represents an overall philosophy of management—a way of thinking of an approach to planning—that concentrates on measurable goals, targets, or end results. It provides a systematic and rational approach to management and helps prevent management by crisis. To be effective, MBO depends on active participation at all levels of management.

The application of MBO in organizations has progressed through three stages—from an emphasis on performance appraisal, to one on planning and control and most recently to an integrated system of management. The MBO process consists of several important steps: attaining top management commitment and involvement; establishing long range goals and strategic plans; defining specific organization objectives; establishment of performance objectives and standards for individuals (action planning); measurement of results achieved (appraisal); and taking corrective action to ensure the attainment of the desired results (control). The types of objectives established in MBO programs include routine problem solving, innovative, and personal development. Objectives should be limited in number, stated in specific and measurable terms, and should be challenging, prioritized, and attainable.

MBO offers numerous benefits and a few potential problems for management. Some of the primary advantages of MBO are that it provides an effective planning system; forces managers to establish priorities and specific standards of performance; clarifies specific roles, responsibilities and authority of personnel; encourages participation in goal setting; aids in control; assists in career development for managers and employees; provides a more objective basis for performance appraisal as well as promotion and salary decisions; and tends to increase the motivation and commitment of personnel. The major problems that may be encountered in using MBO include lack of support and commitment of top management; difficulty in establishing goals; creation of a "paper mill"; tendency for goals to concentrate too much on the short run; and the possibility of being very time-consuming.

Review Questions

1. What is Management by Objectives (MBO)? Define and explain its value to management.

2. Compare and contrast Drucker's view of MBO with that of Douglas McGregor.

3. Briefly describe the three distinct phases of MBO programs. What is the present status with regard to MBO?

4. What are the basic steps in the MBO process? Briefly explain each.

5. What are the four types of objectives that can be established in MBO programs? Explain and provide examples of each type of objective.

6. What are the basic characteristics of objectives and how are objectives determined?

7. Briefly discuss the *benefits* and *potential problems* with MBO. Which are the most significant and why?

8. What situational factors must an organization consider when implementing MBO?

9. What suggestions for improving the effectiveness of MBO could you offer an organization?

Exercises

1. Apply the Management by Objectives concepts discussed in this chapter by developing clear-cut personal goals for yourself to cover the next year. Be sure to include specific goal statements and completion times for routine, problem-solving, innovative, and personal development. Also include specific action plans to ensure goal accomplishment.

2. Visit a firm in your area that uses MBO and ask several managers within the company their reaction to the program. This would be an excellent class project that could be part of a tour of a local business.

3. Go to the library and find three current journal articles on the application of MBO. What are the reasons for its successes and failures?

REFERENCES

Babcock, R., and Sorensen, P. F. "Long Range Approach to MBO." *Management Review* 65 (June 1976): 24–32.

Calhoun, R. E. "Results: Five Years With MBO." *Training and Development Journal* 31 (October 1977): 8–10.

Dillion, C. R. "MBO, Setting Objectives." *Supervisory Management* 21 (April 1976): 18–22.

Drucker, Peter F. *Management: Task, Responsibilities, Practices.* New York: Harper and Row, 1974, pp. 430–442.

Ford, R. C. "MBO: Seven Strategies for Success." *SAM Advanced Management Journal* 42 (Winter 1977): 4–13.

Haines, W. R. "Corporate Planning and Management by Objectives." *Long Range Planning* 10 (August 1977): 13–20.

Koontz, H. "Making MBO Effective." *California Management Review* 20 (Fall 1977): 13–15.

Migliore, R. Henry. *MBO: Blue Collar to Top Executives.* Washington: Bureau of National Affairs, 1977.

Morrisey, G. L. "How to Implement MBO in Your Organizational Unit." *Training and Development Journal* 31 (April 1977): 8–10.

Nystrom, P. C. "Save MBO by Disowning It." *Personnel Journal* 56 (August 1977): 391–393.

Odiorne, G. S. "MBO in 1980's: Will It Survive." *Management Review* 66 (July 1977): 39–42.

Odiorne, G. S. "MBO: Systematic or Mechanistic: Nine Cases with Nine Precepts." *University of Michigan Business Review* 29 (September 1977): 9–13.

Papin, J. P., and Fitch, H. G. "Participative Management by Objectives, (PMBO)." *Management International Review* 17 (1977): 69–75.

Tosi, H., and others. "How Real Are Changes Induced by Management by Objectives?" *Administrative Science Quarterly,* June 1976, pp. 276–306.

Weihrich, H. "MBO: Theory X and Theory Y." *Personnel Administrator,* February 1977, pp. 54–57.

Weihrich, H. "Management by Objectives: Does It Really Work." *University of Michigan Business Review,* July 1976, pp. 27–31.

Weihrich, H. "An Uneasy Look at the MBO Jungle: Toward a Contingency Approach to MBO." *Management International Review,* 1976, pp. 103–109.

Case Study

MBO AT THE NEW YORK CASUALTY INSURANCE COMPANY

The New York Casualty Insurance Company began a management by objectives (MBO) program two years ago. Top management of the firm was convinced that MBO would significantly improve the company's overall effectiveness in planning and would provide a system for more accurate evaluation of personnel. Prior to the implementation of MBO, the company had no formal planning system and had used a performance appraisal system that consisted primarily of evaluating such factors as quantity of work, quality of work, judgment, adaptability, etc. The performance factors were rated from 1 (very poor, unacceptable performance) to 5 (exceptional performance). All personnel including managerial employees were evaluated using this system. The considerable dissatisfaction with this rating system was a primary reason for New York Casualty implementing an MBO system. At the beginning of each year, overall company objectives as well as departmental goals are formulated and communicated to management personnel throughout the firm. The following is a description of the company's MBO program being applied in the Accounting Services Department.

Barbara Gordon, the accounting services manager, has four supervisors reporting to her. These supervisors are responsible for accounts payable, accounts receivable, payroll, and customer services. At the beginning of each year, Ms. Gordon discusses the company and departmental objectives with each of her four supervisors.

The payroll section supervisor, Dale Frazier, has been with New York Casualty for nine months. Dale had four years of experience in payroll operations at another company, and has a BBA in accounting. He is considered to be a very competent supervisor and has five clerks reporting to him. The department processes the payroll for almost 3,000 employees. Dale and Ms. Gordon had agreed on the following goals for the payroll department during Dale's first year as supervisor:

1. Establishment of a consistent account reconciliation program for the 160 payroll related accounts in the general ledger by June 1
2. Establishment of a cross-training program for the payroll clerks by June 1
3. Creation of written documentation for all of the payroll department procedures by September 1 (in accordance with the company's broader statements on policy and procedure)
4. Reduction of employee turnover to 20 percent during the year

The following is a summary of activities and events that occurred during the year:

- During the year the company experienced rapid growth, adding an average of 75 employees per month.
- Turnover of clerical personnel in the payroll department began in February.

Within the first four months, payroll lost three experienced employees. These personnel changes required considerable on-the-job training for the "new" employees.

Near the end of the year, Ms. Gordon, the accounting services manager, reviewed the progress of the payroll section with Dale. The results were as follows:

Objective 1 Not accomplished. A consistent reconciliation program has not been implemented.
Objective 2 Not accomplished. A cross-training program has not been devised. Several duties have been reassigned as new employees were hired and some jobs have been slightly redesigned.

Objective 3 Not accomplished. Written documentation has increased, but no substantial progress was made during the year toward developing an overall detailed payroll procedures manual.

Objective 4 Not accomplished.

In the conversation with Dale, Ms. Gordon made the following statement, "Dale, I'm very disappointed with the overall performance of the payroll unit. Why did your unit experience these problems?"

Dale agreed the results were not attained as planned, but believes employee turnover greatly affected the payroll unit. "Of the three people I hired," he said, "only one was as effective as those who quit."

Questions

1. If you were Barbara Gordon, how would you rate the performance of Dale Frazier, the payroll supervisor?
2. Evaluate the MBO program being used by the company. Does it meet the criteria for a successful program as discussed in the chapter?
3. Should Dale be retained?

Case Study

FEDERATION DEPARTMENT STORES' M.B.O. PROGRAM

Top management of the Federation Department Stores, Inc., a chain of 120 retail stores, had recently decided to implement a management by objectives program throughout their organization. Sam Brown, the manager of the Kansas City department store, had just completed reviewing his objectives for the company's new MBO program with his district manager, Ray Wilson. Sam was both irritated and confused as a result of his meeting with Mr. Wilson.

Three weeks before Sam had received a letter from Mr. Wilson explaining that top management had decided an MBO program would be used to assist all Federation stores improve efficiency and increase their profit contribution. The letter indicated the objectives would be used to measure performance and that salary increases and promotions would now be directly related to performance. The accompanying instructions required store managers to list the objectives they felt were appropriate for their store and then stand by for the district manager's review visit.

Sam had realized that he and the five assistant managers of the Kansas City store had a lot at stake in establishing realistic objectives for the store. After discussing the situation, Sam and the assistant managers selected objectives that they felt would be appropriate for their store. They selected performance levels which were improvements from the past year but which they felt they could exceed. Among others, they selected the following objectives:

- Increase selling efficiency as measured by the ratio of sales salaries to sales by 10 percent.

· Reduce inventory shortage to 2 percent of sales.

· Reduce register shortage to $\frac{1}{2}$ percent of sales.

· Improve customer service to the extent that there were 20 percent fewer complaint letters mailed to the home office.

The district manager had arrived late for the MBO review visit and there had not been much time for discussion. After scanning the objectives Sam submitted, the district manager explained that profit improvement was really what the home office was interested in. Rather than trying to monitor separate objectives from each store, the home office had decided that a 12 percent profit improvement would be a reasonable objective for Sam's store. This single objective would facilitate the monitoring of performance by the home office and would also reduce the amount of information the store would have to submit. The visit was cut short because the district manager had to attend a home office meeting on advertising budget to be allocated to individual stores.

Questions

1. The home office of Federation Department Stores planned to use a single MBO plan to measure the performance of each of its stores. Is this a proper way to use MBO?

2. What mistakes, if any, did the home office make in trying to establish their MBO program? Did the MBO system at Federation meet the criteria for an effective program as discussed in the chapter?

3. Will using profit as the sole measure of performance have the results the home office desires?

4. Did Sam have the right approach to setting goals?

5. What indicators of poor communications were apparent?

6. What alternatives does Sam have now in living with the single profit objective established by the home office?

Chapter 4

KEY TERMS

decision making

professional decisions

routine decisions

nonroutine decisions

intuition

scientific approach

hypothesis

professional decision maker

decision maker

state of doubt

model

physical models

schematic models

mathematical models

management information system

Managerial Decision Making

LEARNING OBJECTIVES

After completing this chapter you should be able to

1. Discuss the phases of the decision-making process.
2. State what is required for decision making to take place.
3. Describe the components of the conceptual framework of management science.
4. List and discuss the stages of the scientific method.
5. Relate the importance of model building to a manager.
6. Define and understand what is meant by a management information system.
7. Describe the steps that should be completed in developing a management information system.

Robert Halms, the president of Componic Manufacturing Corporation, a producer of electrical components, is faced with a very critical decision— should production capabilities be expanded? The firm's sales are beginning to exceed the manufacturing capabilities of the two existing plants. Presently Mr. Halms is considering three possible building sites: California, Texas, and Colorado. All sites have different strengths and weaknesses. The problem is further complicated by the fact that there is a possibility of a business turndown in which the current production facilities would be capable of meeting the demand for Componic's products.

Barbara Williams is currently the financial vice-president for Bendon Corporation. The accounting manager has just retired and his replacement must be selected. Barbara would like to promote from within but there are also several qualified applicants from outside the firm. Her alternatives are numerous and complicated. If she hires from within, the best qualified person may not be selected. On the other hand, if she hires from outside the firm, the current employees may not accept the new manager.

Billy Brown, a first-line supervisor for Kwik Corporation is disturbed because Allen Smith, one of his employees, violated a serious company policy today by failing to wear his safety glasses on a very dangerous job. The company policy states that any employee who does not follow the stated policy will receive a written reprimand on the first offense and will be terminated on the second violation. Allen has already received one reprimand but he is also one of Billy's best workers and has been with the firm for five years.

Robert, Barbara, and Billy are decision makers. The manner in which they resolve these and other problems will determine their success as managers. In fact, decision making should be viewed as if it were synonymous with managing, thereby suggesting that it accounts for a large portion of a manager's job.

Merely because an individual has a managerial title does not mean that he or she is a manager. There are many individuals with elaborate titles who are not managers in that they are not decision makers. The key to whether a person should be classified as a manager involves determining whether he or she is in a position to decide among various alternatives, and also *chooses* to make the needed decision.

On the other hand, some individuals who are in a position to make decisions cannot be considered managers. If a person has the authority to make decisions but refuses to make a decision, he or she should not be classified as a manager. Zoltan Merszei, president and chief executive officer for the Dow Chemical Company, summarized this attitude quite well when he said, "One of the most important qualities for success as a manager in our organization is to not procrastinate on decisions, hoping problems will go away if ignored." True, a decision to do nothing may, in its broadest sense, imply that a choice has been made. A constant pattern of failure to decide does not give a person the right to be called a manager.

Increasingly, managers are being measured by the results of their decisions. Companies do not want dynamic failures; they want individuals who are equipped properly to make the correct decision. This does not imply that the manager must be right 100 percent of the time; no one is that perfect. It does suggest that successful managers have a higher "batting average" than less successful managers and there is a growing tendency to evaluate managers primarily on the results of their decisions. For instance, as in the above example, it is not likely Robert, Barbara, or Billy will always be correct in their decisions. If they are to be effective, however, their ratio of success to failure in choosing the best decision must be high.

In this chapter, we will define decision making and identify some of the major factors that affect the decision-making process. Next, the steps in the decision-making process will be presented followed by an explanation of the requirements that must be fulfilled if decision making is to take place. Because models are used so extensively in the decision-making process, an explanation of the use of models will also be presented. Finally, a brief discussion of management information systems (MIS) will be provided as it relates to decision making. The intent of the chapter will be for the student to gain an appreciation of the decision-making process as it relates to managers.

DECISION MAKING DEFINED

decision making

Decision making can be described as *the process by which we evaluate alternatives and make a choice among them.* As such, decision making is a universal requirement for all of us. Basically, each individual who is involved in the decision-making process must first search for opportunities to make decisions and for alternatives to take. Next, he or she must choose one alternative; the choice of this alternative is defined as the decision. However, to place decision making in perspective, we need to distinguish between several classifications of decisions such as personal versus professional decisions and routine versus nonroutine decisions.

WILLIAM E. WINTER

President and Chief Executive Officer
The Seven-Up Company

William E. Winter, president and chief executive officer of The Seven-Up Company, has played a key role in pacing the steady expansion of the St. Louis, Missouri, firm which currently markets the third-largest-selling soft drink in the world. Winter gained his first experience in the bottling business as a part-time employee. He worked during summer vacations at the Madison, Illinois Seven-Up plant where his father was sales manager of one of the earliest Seven-Up bottling operations. Bill performed production-line assignments and case-stocking chores in the warehouse and worked as an extra hand on Seven-Up route trucks. He graduated from the University of Illinois where he received his Bachelor of Science degree in labor economics (and was elected to membership in Phi Beta Kappa).

In 1946, Winter joined the world headquarters of the Seven-Up Company in St. Louis. He began as a sales training instructor, then moved into sales counseling activities in the field. By 1950, Winter's successful promotional record rated him a transfer, and he was brought into the main offices in St. Louis as a sales promotion assistant. Within four years, a department of his own had grown up around him, and he was officially appointed sales promotion manager. Through innovation and general company growth, new responsibilities were assigned to the sales promotion department, and in 1965 Winter was made vice-president and manager over a fully integrated marketing department. In January 1969, Winter was appointed director of marketing with the responsibility for supervising departments in advertising and promotion, field sales operations, fountain syrup sales, marketing planning services, and public relations. With his appointment as executive vice-president in 1971, and president and chief operating officer in July 1974, Winter assumed additional administrative duties with overall responsibility for attainment of total corporate marketing objectives of The Seven-Up Company. Winter was appointed president and chief executive officer of The Seven-Up Company in July 1976. Domestic and international subsidiaries reporting to Winter include: Seven-Up U.S.A.; Seven-Up Canada Limited; Seven-Up International; Ventura Coastal Corporation; Warner-Jenkinson Company; and Golden Crown Citrus Corporation.

Mr. Winter believes that it takes hard work that is performed on a highly ethical and moral level to be successful today. He has always set high standards for himself and this philosophy carries over into his expectations of employees at Seven-Up. He believes nothing should be submitted to him unless it is in the best final form and accompanied by a recommendation. Concerning decision making, Mr. Winter says, "There comes a time for 'gut instinct.' At times, decision making is fun and at other times it is frightening." He realizes, however, that a president and chief executive officer doesn't get paid for easy decisions.

PERSONAL VERSUS PROFESSIONAL DECISION MAKING

Although a similar thought process exists in both personal and professional decision making, a person should be aware of the differences between the two. Here is a brief overview of personal and professional decision making.

Personal Decisions

A wide variety of decisions are considered personal. Decisions to study, go on a date, watch television, or go to bed early are examples of personal decisions made routinely by college students each day. Personal decisions can ultimately affect an organization. A personal decision to purchase a Ford rather than a Chevrolet actually helps one firm due to the sale and hurts another because of the lost sale.

A portion of a manager's time is spent discussing an employee's personal problems and what can be done about them. The supervisor should recognize that employees who are experiencing difficulties in their personal lives may bring these problems to the job. Thus, a supervisor may be involved to some degree in the personal decisions of his or her employees whether the supervisor desires to be or not.

Professional Decisions

Virtually every gainfully employed person is required to engage in decision-making activities as a part of the work he or she performs. College professors make decisions concerning the nature of what type of information they will present to their students. Physicians diagnose problems and prescribe treatments. Scientists formulate hypotheses and select experiments for testing them. Managers of baseball teams, football coaches, politicians, plumbers, and clergymen—in fact, all who are gainfully employed—are required to make decisions as part of their professional lives. Yet the administrator of a business organization is labeled a manager, whereas many of the other decision makers are not. *Managers are expected to be professional decision makers; their reason for being is to make decisions.*

Why are managers labeled professional decision makers whereas others—the physicians and scientists—are not? The answer is visibility. The manager of an organization operates in an open environment. A managerial decision affects many people (customers, stockholders, employees, the general public). The professional manager sees the results of decisions reflected in the firm's earnings report, the welfare of employees, and the economic health of the community and the country. Decisions made by professional managers may be no more or no less crucial than those of the physicians or scientists, but their decisions have impact on a greater number of people. Managers' careers cannot be made by only one good decision. Their careers must be marked by a series of decisions that are acceptable. Hence, as Levitt contends, unlike the lawyer, scientist, or physician, "the manager is judged not for what he knows about the work that is done in his field, but by how well he actually does the work."[1] To survive, the manager must be able to make **professional decisions.**

professional decisions

ROUTINE VERSUS NONROUTINE DECISION MAKING

As was the situation with Robert, Barbara, and Billy, managers are continually confronted with the need to make a variety of decisions. Professional decisions may range from such major ones as whether or not to build a new plant or to enter a new business all the way, to the rather routine decisions such as deciding which supplier to purchase the bathroom paper towels from. The two major categories of professional decision making are routine and nonroutine.

We will briefly discuss routine and nonroutine decisions and the conditions under which decisions must be made.

Routine Decisions

routine decisions

Most managers make numerous daily or routine decisions in the performance of their jobs. **Routine decisions** made by managers are governed by the policies, procedures, and rules of the organization, as well as the

1. Theodore Levitt, "The Managerial Merry-Go-Round," *Harvard Business Review* 52 (July–August 1974): 120.

personal habits of the managers. For example, decisions related to the appropriate disciplinary actions to use when an employee is habitually late to work or when an employee has violated company safety rules or how much to pay a newly hired employee may all be governed by company policies, procedures, or rules. In terms of personal decisions, deciding where to go to lunch and who to eat with are examples of routine decisions that may be determined to a great extent by habit of the individual.

Since routine decisions are relatively easy and simple for managers to make, they *free* managers for more challenging and difficult problem solving. Many organizations set forth policies, procedures, and rules that provide a framework for decision making. However, an individual manager is little more than a robot or a clerk if he or she simply adheres to the "rule book" and does not exercise personal judgment.

Nonroutine Decisions

nonroutine decisions

While routine or programmed decisions may take up a considerable portion of a manager's time, individuals *make or break it* as managers on the basis of the success of their nonroutine decision-making ability. **Nonroutine decisions** *are those that are designed to deal with unique problems or situations.* The decision to expand to foreign markets, build a new production plant or buy a more advanced computer system are all examples of nonroutine or unique decision situations. While these are examples of nonroutine decisions made by upper management, managers at all levels in the organization make nonroutine decisions. For instance, nonroutine decisions made by a first-line supervisor might include firing an employee or changing the layout or work flow procedures in his or her department.

Figure 4.1 illustrates the relationship between three levels of management and the percentage of routine and nonroutine decisions made at these different levels of management. As a manager progresses to higher levels, the number of nonroutine decisions increases. Nonroutine decisions require that managers exercise creativeness, intuition, and good judgment in resolving these types of problems.

APPROACHES TO DECISION MAKING

There are two basic approaches to decision making—intuition and research (the scientific method). Each will next be briefly discussed and broadened to include the professional decision maker.

FIGURE 4.1

Managerial Levels and the Amount of Routine versus
Nonroutine Decisions

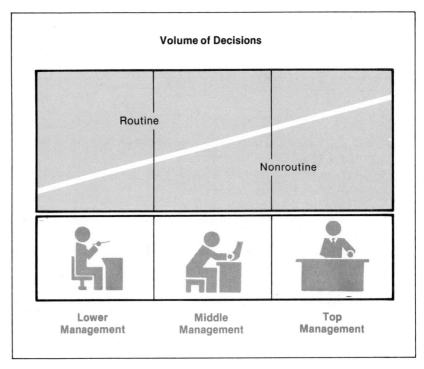

INTUITION

intuition

The individual who relies on intuition makes his or her decisions based on accumulated experience. **Intuition** is acquired through experience and accomplishments rather than through a formal decision-making process. Experience tends to be a good teacher as evidenced by the fact that many college recruiters place major emphasis on the business experience and extracurricular activities a student has accomplished while in college. They believe the learning process for a particular job may be shortened if a student has been active in other endeavors while in college. But, the decision maker who relies only on intuition, bases a judgment on his or her "feel" for the situation. Alternatives are chosen on the basis of a hunch. If the decision maker confronts a situation to which he or she has not been previously exposed, a wrong decision often results. The intuitive approach has several obvious shortcomings such as:

1. Learning from experience is usually random.
2. Although we learn experiences, there is no *guarantee* we learn from experience.
3. That which we learn from experience is necessarily circumscribed by the limits of our experience.
4. Conditions change and experiences of the past may not be good indicators of current or future conditions.[2]
5. The question may be asked, "Do you have twenty years of experience or do you have one year of experience twenty times?"

RESEARCH AND THE SCIENTIFIC METHOD

scientific approach

The research approach is based on a systematic, formal approach to decision making. It stresses that the scientific method should be used in problem solving. The **scientific approach** can be conveniently divided into four distinct but interrelated phases—observation of events, hypothesis formulation, experimentation, and verification.

Observation

The first step in the scientific method requires that a person has the desire to fully explore the relationships among the elements of a system and a curiosity to know *how* and *why* they produce a particular outcome. The process begins by observing an occurrence and then asking why it happened.

Hypothesis

hypothesis

The second step in the scientific method requires the creation of an explanation as to the hows and whys of the observed event. A **hypothesis** is a tentative statement of the nature of the relationships that exist. A hypothesis provides an explanation of the cause that brought about the observed effect.

Experimentation

The scientist subjects the hypothesis to one or a series of tests to determine whether or not the tentively stated relationship does in fact exist. Tests confirm or support the hypothesis or prove it to be unsound.

2. Items 1–4 adapted from Alvar O. Elbing, *Behavioral Decision in Organizations* (Glenview, Ill.: Scott, Foresman, 1970), p. 14.

Verification

The final step in the scientific method is verification of the findings obtained from the experiment. Sometimes this may take the form of another experiment or a series of experiments. Such is the case when a medical researcher finds that a particular drug cures a disease in a laboratory animal and then administers it to a group of human patients suffering from the same disease.

THE PROFESSIONAL DECISION MAKER

professional decision
maker

The **professional decision maker** must adopt an approach that uses the best features of both the intuitive and the research approaches, and goes one step further in that all the information that managers are able to obtain is used to assist in decision making. Intuition is an essential part of good research. This experience provides valuable insight into what may occur if a certain decision is made. The research approach, on the other hand, forces the decision maker to evaluate critically what is known and to recognize what is unknown before jumping to a decision based solely on a feel for the situation or a hunch. Professor Ralph C. Davis summarizes the need for a bond between these two approaches in this discussion of the professionally trained executive:

> A man who has nothing but background is a theorist. A man who has nothing but practical experience is a business mechanic. A professionally trained executive is one in whom there is an effective integration of these two general types of experiences, combined with adequate intelligence regarding the types of problems with which he must deal.[3]

THE DECISION-MAKING PROCESS

Decision making involves choosing among various courses of action. It is often as simple as deciding whether you will work overtime or not or as complicated as deciding on the future objectives of the firm. If an organization is to be successful, it must have people who are willing and able to make decisions that will be best for the firm. As such, decision makers are the architects of an organization. They have developed the ability to obtain solutions to problems that occur in their area of responsibility.

A complete representation of the decision-making process can be seen in Figure 4.2. As illustrated, all decisions must be made within the

3. Ralph C. Davis, *The Fundamentals of Top Management* (New York: Harper & Bros., 1951), p. 55.

You can't solve the problem until you recognize that a problem exists.

constraints of both the internal and external environment. The internal and external factors surrounding the decision maker may change, based on whether the decision is made by top-, middle-, or lower-level management, but the general process does not. For instance, the president will likely have to consider the views of the stockholders when making a decision to build a new plant. On the other hand, the production supervisor may have company policy restraints that dictate what decision can be made with regard to the reasons an employee can be terminated.

It should also be noted that the implementation of a decision does not complete the decision-making process. The arrows in the decision-making process model indicate that there is constant reevaluation and feedback to every phase of decision making. The outcome—whether good or bad—provides information through which future decisions are made. As such,

FIGURE 4.2
The Decision-Making Process

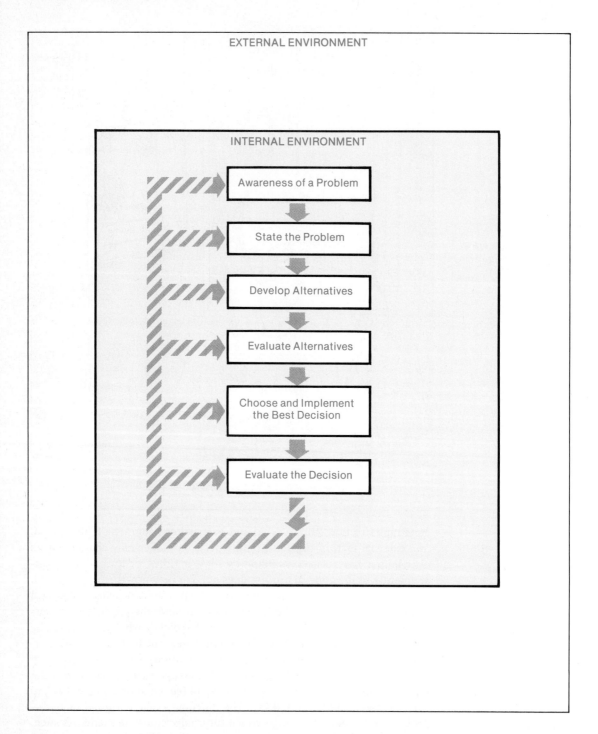

the decision making process is an on-going, dynamic course of action. For instance, if a student makes the decision to study strictly from the instructor's notes and fails the test, a different alternative would likely be chosen for studying for the next test. If an *A* is made by studying the text, a learning process has resulted. As with the student, successful managers learn from their mistakes. The less successful managers make the same mistake over and over and wonder why their decisions are consistently wrong. Elements of the decision-making process are discussed next.

AWARENESS OF A PROBLEM

When a person doesn't realize a problem exists, nothing can be done to solve the problem. We have all heard the answer to the question, "Why are you doing it this way?" The answer, "We've always done it that way," causes a person who is truly interested in problem recognition to go into a state of shock. This situation often occurs because we have stopped looking for problems that need solving. As professional managers, a fraction of our time should be spent looking for opportunities to make decisions.

Problems are recognized primarily through the planning and control functions. However, the problem itself may deal with any of the management functions of planning, organizing, directing, and controlling. The establishment of plans and the development of procedures to monitor their accomplishment makes a person aware that a problem exists.

STATE THE PROBLEM

The second step is to define the problem as clearly and concisely as possible. As Robert J. Sweeney, president of Murphy Oil Corporation, said, "A successful manager must have the ability to weed out the wheat from the chaff before deciding on a course of action." A major point for consideration is that the manager must solve the problem not the symptoms. Too often managers treat symptoms and do not identify the actual problem. Let us assume, for instance, that a large number of students are failing a particular college course (symptom). The problem may be identified as the difficulty of the textbook or the lack of ability of the students, although the real problem was that the instructor could not teach the subject matter in an understandable manner. Until the instructor can identify the real problem, the situation cannot be corrected. An example in business of an incorrect problem definition would be to define the problem of a company as not making a sufficient profit. Not making a profit may be a symptom, but not the real cause. The causes might include ineffective cost controls, excessive inventory, high turnover of personnel, or a multitude of other factors. Whatever the instance, identification of symptoms rather than causes can hurt the decision-making process and result in inappropriate decisions being made.

DEVELOP ALTERNATIVES

The manager next generates alternative courses of action that may be implemented as a solution to the problem. Naturally the number of alternatives generated is limited by the amount of time available for the decision as well as by the importance of the decision itself. Obviously, however, the best decision cannot be made if it is not considered as an alternative course of action. For instance, the company that was not making a profit might consider a number of alternatives such as cost control or incentives to workers to correct the cause of the problem. However, if the correct alternative is not considered, the problem cannot be solved.

The means for generating alternatives are numerous. Managers may get together and *brainstorm*. Through brainstorming, individuals are encouraged to identify as many possible alternatives as they can. When brainstorming is taking place, the task is to obtain a large number of potential solutions. The quality of the alternative will be judged in the evaluation stage of the decision-making process. There are also numerous quantitative techniques that have proven to be beneficial in developing alternatives. These will be described in chapters 13 and 14.

EVALUATION OF ALTERNATIVES

Each alternative that has been developed must be evaluated with respect to how it will interact with external and internal environmental conditions. In this step, answers must be provided for the question, "What will happen if this course of action is taken?" A major point for consideration is that an optimum decision at times cannot be implemented. The external environment may force a manager to make a less than optimum decision. For instance, an airline company may desire to discontinue flights to certain cities, but is not permitted to do so because of requirements from the Federal Aviation Agency to continue such service.

CHOOSE AND IMPLEMENT THE BEST DECISION

The ability to select the *best* course of action from several possible alternatives separates the successful managers from the less successful ones. The alternative offering the highest promise of attaining the objective, taking into consideration the overall situation, should be selected. This step may sound easy, but for a manager it is the toughest part of his or her job. Fear of making the wrong decision sometimes causes managers to make no decision at all. It is in this stage that weak managers sometimes fail. It is no wonder that relatively high salaries are afforded the managers who have gained a reputation for, not only having the internal strength to make decisions, but also for making the correct ones the majority of the time. It is easy to be a "Monday morning quarterback" who criticizes the coach for making the wrong decision. However, the coach had to make decisions on the field of battle and the coach hopes to make the correct decision more often than the incorrect one.

Directly or indirectly, the decision maker must implement the decision. When individuals other than the decision maker are required to implement the act, the decision maker must make certain that the appropriate steps have been taken. It is here that the decision-making process often falls short. Some managers, because they are action-oriented, believe that once the decision has been made, it will automatically be implemented. A good manager monitors the situation to ensure that his or her decisions are accomplished.

EVALUATE THE DECISION

No decision-making process is complete until the decision has been exposed to the realities of the actual business environment. Evaluation requires an objective assessment of how the decision has solved the problem. It is the process by which managers learn and develop useful experience. Without this step, the decision-making process has no value beyond providing an immediate solution to a problem. It is perhaps for this reason that some firms stress decentralized management in which lower-level managers are provided the opportunity to become more involved in the decision-making process. This process provides the younger managers with decision-making experience. Intuition and judgment increase with more exposure to decision making. Through decentralization an individual does not have to wait until he or she finally is promoted to a high level position before being given the opportunity to make decisions. It is better to make a wrong decision at a lower level, and learn from this experience, than to make a more crucial decision at a higher level and be wrong.

FACTORS AFFECTING THE DECISION-MAKING PROCESS

There are two primary factors—risk and time—that can have a major impact on the decision-making process. These factors will be discussed in this section.

RISK

The probability that an incorrect decision will have an adverse effect on the organization is referred to as *risk*. It is a factor that all managers consider (consciously or unconsciously) in decision making. For instance, Betty Harris, president of a small book publishing company, is considering paying $100,000 to a well-known author to write a book. If the book sells well the firm could make $500,000, but if it doesn't, Betty's company will lose the $100,000 plus an additional $75,000 in developmental and promotional cost. Betty decides not to take the risk because the loss of $175,000 could put the company out of business.

On the other hand, Bill Anderson, purchasing manager for General Motors, daily signs contracts for automobile parts that greatly exceed $1,000,000. The risk in these type decisions is typically low. Even the loss of $1,000,000 for General Motors would not have a disastrous affect on the firm. As the risk increases, more time and effort are often devoted to the decision-making process.

TIME

The amount of time that can be devoted to decision making is often a critical factor that must be considered. A manager would prefer to have sufficient time to thoroughly evaluate and analyze all alternatives prior to making a decision. Most business people are not afforded this luxury; they must make decisions in a time-pressure situation in which there is often not sufficient time to evaluate all alternatives. Suppose, for instance, that a customer of yours offers to purchase a large number of items for a price that is lower than you normally receive. Although the firm will make a profit on this order, the profit is not as large as normally obtained. Today there are no other orders to choose from but tomorrow there may be. However, the decision must be made today or the buyer will go to another manufacturer. The company is truly under a time-pressure situation. It is much easier to make decisions when there is enough time to thoroughly evaluate all the alternatives but managers often do not have the extra time to decide.

REQUIREMENTS FOR DECISION MAKING

As previously stated, the single most important quality that a businessperson needs is the ability to make correct decisions. This one quality often separates the successful from the less successful managers. There are, however, certain conditions that must be present before a decision

★

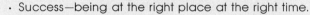

**MOST IMPORTANT REASON FOR SUCCESS
AND EFFECTIVENESS AS A MANAGER**

· Success—being at the right place at the right time.
· Effectiveness—timely decision making; rapport with people; good
operating background; development of people.

L. W. MENK, Chairman–C.E.O., Burlington Northern Incorporated

problem can exist. These conditions must be met for all types of decision
making. A decision problem must contain the following five conditions:
decision maker, problem context, courses of action, payoff relationship,
and a state of doubt.

DECISION MAKER

decision maker

While Harry Truman was President of the United States, he always kept a
plaque on his desk that stated, "The buck stops here." He was the person
responsible and he made the final decision. The **decision maker** has the
responsibility for choosing the course of action that will solve the problem
within the area for which he or she is accountable. For instance, college
students may not like a certain university housing policy that requires
freshmen and sophomores to live in dormitories. Even though the housing
regulation may adversely affect students, they do not have the authority to
make the decision to alter the housing policy. Students may only provide
input to university administrators who can make the necessary decisions
to change the policy.

The role of decision maker may be assumed by an individual or by a
group of individuals depending on how the organization is managed. This
takes into consideration the various management styles and the way in
which the organization is structured. Basically, however, if there is no
decision maker, there is no decision problem. At times, decision makers
are not easy to identify. Contrary to some thinking, everyone does not
enjoy making decisions even though they are charged with the responsibility.

PROBLEM CONTENT

The problem content includes the environment within which the problem
exists, the decision maker's knowledge of that environment, as well as the
environment that will exist after a choice is made. Because of the signifi-

cance of taking into consideration the environment in decision making, a decision that may be considered optimum in one organization may result in complete failure in another.

COURSES OF ACTION

To have a decision problem, the decision maker must have more than one alternative from which to choose. Alternatives may be many or few in number. They may merely represent the option of "doing something" or "doing nothing." A good decision maker, however, attempts to identify and evaluate as many alternatives as possible given the time and resource restrictions.

PAYOFF RELATIONSHIP

The various alternatives must be evaluated in terms of what the objective was in making the decision. The establishment of payoff relationships implies the ability to measure the costs or profits of various courses of action and the benefits that may be obtained. When the profits and costs associated with a particular alternative cannot be expressed mathematically, the decision maker suffers severely.

STATE OF DOUBT

state of doubt

The element of choice must be present to have a decision problem. Some question must exist as to which alternative is best. The **state of doubt** is the heart of a decision problem. If there was no element of choice, we would all be excellent decision makers. Choice may be required when the precise relationships among alternatives are known and the problem is simply to define what the relationships mean in terms of an objective. Choice may, on the other hand, come about because of uncertainty about the future environment or because precise relationships between alternatives are not known. Any person who has ever played five-card draw poker understands the uncertainty about the future and the imprecise relationships that can exist. The good decision maker, as with the good poker player, studies the situation thoroughly in the hope that his or her decisions will be correct more often than not. Because of the state of doubt, it is most likely a decision maker will never be 100 percent correct.

A DECISION-MAKING PROBLEM

Let us illustrate a decision-making problem through an example that some students have faced—how to choose a part-time job. Suppose you are considering two possible job positions at a local pizza restaurant that has recently opened. One of the positions is for an assistant manager and the salary is based on commission. The other alternative is as a pizza cook for which there is an hourly wage of $3.00.

Because the pizza house is relatively new, a trend has not been established as to the sales potential of the business. However, based on the experience within the school community, you estimate that there is a 20 percent chance of high sales, 50 percent chance of average sales, and a 30 percent probability of low sales. You recognize these states of nature will have a major impact on the amount of money received from the assistant manager's position. As an assistant manager, you estimate the payoff for high sales will be $6.00 an hour, for average sales it will be $4.00 an hour, and if low sales occur you will only receive $1.00 an hour. However, you will receive $3.00 an hour no matter what the sales are if you choose the job as a pizza cook. The payoff relationship between each act and state of nature is provided in Table 4.1. You are now in a position to evaluate the two alternatives.

Expected Earnings for Pizza Cook

$$= .2(3.00) + .5(3.00) + .3(3.00) = \$3.00$$

Expected Earnings for Assistant Manager

$$= .2(6) + .5(4) + .3(1) = \$3.50$$

Thus, if you are willing to accept the alternative that has the highest expected value, you will take the assistant manager position that offers commission (expected value of $3.50 versus $3.00 per hour). However, as with other managers, there may be other factors that must be considered before an actual decision is made. Your financial situation may prevent you from taking the chance of only receiving one dollar per hour if sales

TABLE 4.1
The Pizza House Job Matrix

Alternatives	High Sales	Average Sales	Low Sales
Probabilities	.20	.50	.30
Hourly Wage	$3.00	$3.00	$3.00
Commission	$6.00	$4.00	$1.00

are poor. Other alternatives also might have been evaluated. For instance, there may have been other jobs available to consider. However, although there are numerous considerations, the example does provide the student of management with a brief appreciation of the thought process that should go into managerial decision making.

MODEL BUILDING

model

A procedure quite beneficial to a manager in all phases of the decision-making process is model building. A **model** is defined as an abstraction of a real world situation. It is an attempt to portray reality through various means *without having to work directly with the real world.* For instance, suppose a manager must make a major decision involving many millions of dollars as to where to build a new factory. Once funds have been spent on the plant, the decision is irreversible. Model building permits the decision maker to develop alternatives that can be evaluated prior to making the *real* decision which commits funds. As such, model building is an extremely useful tool for managers in the decision-making process.

In business, models can be expressed in many ways and can have many meanings. This is true because managers must constantly deal with highly complex business systems that must be simplified to be understood. Model building provides the means for simplifying a difficult situation. For instance, the plant manager might develop a three-dimensional model of the plant planned for construction. Then, as if shifting furniture in a doll house, he or she can move the equipment around to see what effect the shift of the equipment might have on plant operations. If the plant was built and then the movement of the equipment was attempted, the results could prove to be quite costly.

The model builder must first determine the purpose of the model as it relates to depicting a real world situation. The purpose of the model should be consistent with the overall objectives of the firm. Next, it must be decided which parts should be included. This factor alone is a major advantage of model building. If there are certain components that would be included in the real world, but have no effect on the problem under consideration, they can be omitted. As in the above plant equipment example, the electrical hookup may be omitted because most likely its placement can be decided on after the equipment has been installed. Finally, the model builder must define the interrelationships that exist among the parts. Does one piece of equipment produce a part that will be used by another machine? The understanding of these interrelationships is vital in model building.

In a true sense, the model is a tool for extending the manager's understanding of the organization. Models are more widely employed than commonly realized. Many times a manager may not even realize a model is being used. If a manager envisions what would occur if a particular decision is made, model building is actually taking place. The manager has a picture (model) of the relationships that will result if a particular decision is made. Whether they recognize it or not, managers are constantly using models to support their decision-making activities.

One means by which we can examine models is through the language the modeler employs. By language, we mean *the technique chosen to communicate understanding.* Models may use physical, schematic, or mathematical "languages." Our primary concentration later in the book will be on mathematical models.

PHYSICAL MODELS

physical models

Physical models were among the first to be used in management and are the most familiar. Systems represented by physical models can include people, ships, airplanes, automobiles, houses, dams, shopping centers, factories, retail stores, and so on. **Physical models** generally *look like* the system they represent. Physical models can, however, be more abstract representations. A photograph captures the physical appearance of a person as does a portrait, but in painting the portrait, the artist can de-emphasize or exaggerate features to make the subject appear more handsome.

SCHEMATIC MODELS

schematic models

Line drawings, flow charts, graphs, maps, organization charts, and similar items that represent the major features of a particular system are **schematic models.** Schematic models may or may not be related in *scale* to the

GENERAL PHILOSOPHY ABOUT MANAGING YOUR ORGANIZATION

Our corporate philosophy is to maintain open door communications from "bottom to top." We try to attract the most capable associates in the retailing industry and then let them perform. Through close communication, we are able to make immediate decisions which are in the best interest of our Company and its associates. We share operational and financial information with our people in order that they will be in a position to make the best possible day-to-day decisions concerning their particular area of responsibility. Ours is a team effort, with every job to be done to the best of our individual and collective abilities.

SAM M. WALTON, Chairman and C.E.O., Wal-Mart Stores, Incorporated

object being abstracted. Elements of a highway system are represented by road maps, which are two-dimensional scale models. On the other hand, schematics depicting electrical circuitry found on the back of a radio or television set usually are not drawn to scale.

Schematic models have been widely used in management to define components of the organization and to analyze problems. Schematics are used to describe processes and procedures as well as physical components. For example, a computer programmer uses schematic models—the flow-chart—to illustrate the steps that must be accomplished in writing a program. Although schematic models are useful to managers in each major business function, production management (now called production and operations management) has, perhaps, utilized them more than any of the others. Production and operations management models will be discussed in chapters 13 and 14.

MATHEMATICAL MODELS

mathematical models

An equation or set of equations that defines and represents the relationship among elements of a system is a **mathematical model.** Mathematical models portray in quantitative terms the essential elements and interrelationships among elements of the systems they describe. The language used, mathematics, is a powerful one, because it is not so subject to misinterpretation. For mathematical models to represent reality, we must know a good deal about reality and in many instances this by itself is a problem. The primary limitation to the application of mathematical models in assisting management is the constraint imposed by our inability to measure the relationships among elements of the environment.

A SITUATIONAL APPROACH TO DECISION MAKING

The six situational factors identified in chapter 1 must again be considered when the decision-making process is discussed. Failure to effectively evaluate these factors can severely affect decision making. In order to illustrate how the situational factors might impact the decision-making process, two successful but diverse organizations will be discussed. The first firm is a leader in the manufacture of electronic calculators while the other firm is a major producer of paper bags that are used in packing groceries.

Assume that the electronic calculator manufacturer has an objective of growth and survival in this rapidly changing, complex, dynamic, and highly competitive industry. The situational factors will likely have a major impact on effective managerial decision making. The external environment exerts significant pressure on decision making in the electronics industry. For instance, competitors are constantly developing new products that could severely affect the survival of the firm. Stockholders want a higher return on investment because of the high risk involved in the electronics industry. Customers desire the latest in electronics wizardry.

The technology in this organization is typically quite high and constantly changing. Adaptability to change is the norm rather than the exception. The organizational structure that may prove to be optimum for a decision maker under these conditions is one that embraces decentralization. With decentralization, decisions are made at lower levels in the organization by individuals who are closest to the problems. Rapid decision making tends to be facilitated within this type of structure. In order to survive in this organizational environment, the managerial approach tends to be one of adaptability and acceptance of lower-level personnel participating in the decision-making process.

In the high technology, rapidly changing electronics industry, merely recognizing that a problem exists often proves difficult. The number of alternatives may be numerous and the ability for a manager to evaluate, choose, and implement the optimum decision is typically complex and difficult. In order to be a successful decision maker in this environment, the manager must adapt to the situational factors that affect the decision-making process.

Recognition of the situational factors for a firm whose objectives are to produce paper bags in a stable industry is also critical, but a manager who is successful as a decision maker for an electronics manufacturer may find the environment in the paper product industry less appealing. Technology in this industry is much less dynamic than in the electronics industry. Changes occur, but they occur slowly. The external environment changes less rapidly, but must still be considered.

Because of the environment in which the firm operates, a more centralized organizational structure may need to be developed in which a majority of the decisions are made by top-level management. If a decision is to be made, it is thoroughly coordinated through the chain of command, often resulting in decisions being made more slowly. But, because speed may not be essential in this environment, a more deliberate approach to decision making may be superior.

The managerial approach needed to cope with this type of environment may be less participative and adaptive. Because decisions are centralized, the amount of participation involved is limited. Also, the personnel who will be able to work within this type of environment will likely differ from those in the electronics industry. Decision making then takes a more structured, methodical approach. The problems are often easier to identify. Alternatives may be fewer and the ability to choose, evaluate, and implement a decision may exert less pressure on the decision maker.

Decision makers who are highly successful in one environment may be a dismal failure in another and vice versa. There are certain managers who enjoy making high-risk decisions and others who would prefer not to be placed in this situation. In addition, some individuals are quite comfortable making decisions under a time pressure situation while other equally successful managers require more time to thoroughly evaluate the situation. The above comments should not be taken to mean that a manager who prefers high risk and time restrictions is more successful than a person who prefers the alternate situation. The decision maker for a firm needs to be chosen on the basis of who will function best within a particular environment. This involves matching the "right" person to the situation. Once the situational factors are evaluated, the stage is set for the decision-making process to function properly.

MANAGEMENT INFORMATION SYSTEMS

management
information system

Since the advent of high speed computers, management has been fascinated with the amount and speed with which data could be prepared. Correct and timely information is extremely valuable to a manager in the decision-making process. A means that facilitates managers in obtaining timely and accurate information is a **management information system** (MIS). While the computer has made management aware of the importance of a properly designed MIS, the use of a MIS should not depend on a computer; a firm without a computer can also have a very effective management information system.

Basically, MIS will be defined as a technique for providing management with *timely, accurate,* and *useful* information with which to make decisions. Historically, a major problem management has confronted is to be capable of obtaining information that meets these three requirements. Management has encountered numerous instances in which the information is timely and accurate, but was not useful in making decisions. The type of information received might not be relevant to the type of problems facing management. For example, timely and accurate information of how many parking spaces are being used will be of little value to the production manager who is concerned with today's problems.

As previously stated, the development of a management information system does not necessarily require the use of a computer; the computer has merely made it possible to obtain the data with the speed that would make the information useful. Thus, a MIS should be designed without considering what computer should be selected. A computer system can be chosen once the management information system has been designed.

The procedure that is used in the design of a MIS is relatively simple. The details are what cause the problem. Described below are the general steps that should facilitate the development of a useful MIS.

STUDY THE PRESENT SYSTEM

A person cannot tell where they want to go until they know where they have been. Possible questions to ask are: (1) What is the present flow of information? (2) How is the information used? and (3) How valuable is this information in terms of decision making? At one stage in his career one of the authors was a team member in charge of developing one of the first state highway information systems. One of the agencies that had to be integrated into the system was the state highway patrol. In conversations with local troop members, it was discovered that one weekly report that caused considerable difficulty in preparation was being sent to headquarters. For each troop (there were thirteen) it took one officer four hours to prepare the report. Once the author went to headquarters to determine how the data was used in the decision-making process, an interesting situation was discovered. Each weekly report was neatly filed by a secretary and the data was never used. However, if the report was not submitted, a letter of reprimand was sent to the unit commander.

DEVELOP A PRIORITY OF INFORMATION MANAGERS NEED

Once the current system is thoroughly understood, the next step involves prioritizing the information a manager needs. There is certain information a manager must have if proper decisions are to be made; there are also data that are merely *nice* to have, but not critical for the manager to perform his or her job. The management information system that is designed must concentrate on providing the high priority information. Reports lower in the priority list will be generated on an "if possible" basis.

Once individual managers have developed his or her priority list, the separate lists will be integrated into a priority list for the entire organization. Certain departments may discover that the report that they identified as top priority will be far down the list. The needs of the entire organization must be taken into consideration with this list.

DEVELOP THE INFORMATION SYSTEM

A system will now be developed that satisfies the needs of the organization. Reports are prepared that will provide this information. As items lower on the priority list are considered, their benefit to the organization diminishes. At a certain point on the list the costs do not justify the information and these items will not be included.

FIGURE 4.3
Highway Safety Information System

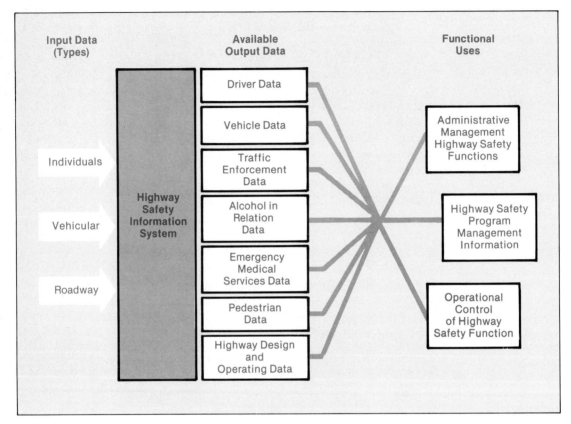

The management information system that was prepared for one state government is presented in Figure 4.3. As can be seen, there are many types of input data necessary to satisfy the needs of the system. The highway safety information system provides various types of information that is available for both administration and operations. All areas are tied together into a complete information system. Data that comes in from one department of the state can provide the information used in another department. If a person has a car wreck and is given a ticket, this information not only is used by law enforcement agencies but also forms a data base to identify high accident locations. When properly designed, the important information an organization needs in the decision-making process is available.

Another factor to consider in designing an MIS relates to whether the information that does arrive is timely and/or accurate. If the manager receives it a day after the decision was required to be made, it is useless.

INSTALL A COMPUTER

The mistake many firms make is that they purchase a computer and then attempt to design the information system around the computer. If a computer is needed to provide accurate and timely information—often this is not the case—the computer is chosen that will provide the best capability of processing the data that is needed by management.

It is expected that the future will see an expansion of management information systems in business. As it becomes necessary for business decisions to be made faster and with more accuracy, they will become increasingly important. As such, MIS becomes a valuable facilitator to the decision-making process.

SUMMARY

A person who has the authority to make decisions, but refuses, should not be classified as a manager. Decision making is the most important responsibility of a manager. The actual decision-making process is simple to state but is often difficult to implement. Once an individual is aware a problem exists, the problem should be clearly stated and then alternatives to the solution of the problem can be developed. Next, each alternative is evaluated and the best alternative is chosen to be implemented. The decision making process continues as the decision is evaluated to determine if the proper decision was made.

Before a decision can be made, certain basic requirements must be achieved. Naturally, a decision must be made by a decision maker. Problem content, courses of action, and the payoff relationships must be identified. A most important consideration is identifying the state of doubt of selecting a particular decision. It is because of this state of doubt that even the best managers will occasionally make incorrect decisions. However, good managers make correct and effective decisions more often than not.

Model building allows alternatives to be identified, developed, and evaluated. A model is an abstraction of a real world situation. Some of the most common models available for use by managers include physical, schematic, and mathematical models. These models let the manager portray the real world through various means indirectly.

Management information systems (MIS) provide another way to assist the manager in the decision-making process. MIS is a technique that provides management with timely, accurate, and useful information to assist in the decision-making process. The benefits of MIS have been significantly enhanced since the development of high speed computers.

Review Questions

1. Define and discuss the process of decision making. How important do you feel it is to a manager?

2. Distinguish between personal decisions and professional decisions. Why are managers expected to be professional decision makers?

3. What effect does risk and time have on decision making?

4. Discuss the strengths and weaknesses of the person who makes decisions based on intuition and the person who makes decisions based on research.

5. What are the basic requirements that must be present in decision making?

6. Distinguish between physical models, schematic models, and mathematical models. Give an example of each.

7. Define management information system. What steps should be followed in developing a MIS?

Exercises

1. We are all decision makers. In a one-hour period during the day list the top five decisions you made. Were they based primarily on intuition, the scientific approach, or the professional approach? Why?

2. Visit a successful business person. Discuss the importance of professional decision making with him or her.

3. Make a list of the different types of models you observe during a twenty-four hour period.

4. Develop a small decision-making problem in which there are three alternatives and three states of nature. Remember that the probabilities must total one.

REFERENCES

Brown, Rex V. "Do Managers Find Decision Theory Useful?" *Harvard Business Review*, May/June 1970, pp. 78–89.

Grayson, C. Jackson, Jr. "Management Science and Business Practice." *Harvard Business Review*, July/August 1973, pp. 41–48.

Gremion, Catherine. "Toward a New Theory of Decision Making." *International Studies of Management and Organization*, Summer 1972, pp. 125–141.

MacCrimmon, Kenneth. "Managerial Decision Making." In Joseph McGuire, ed., *Contemporary Management*. Englewood Cliffs, N.J.: Prentice-Hall, 1974.

McKenney, J. L. and Keen, P. G. W. "How Managers' Minds Work." *Harvard Business Review*, May/June 1974, pp. 79–90.

Simon, Herbert A. *The New Science of Management Decision.* rev. ed. Englewood Cliffs, N.J.: Prentice-Hall, 1977.

Thierauf, Robert S., and Grosse, Richard A. *Decision Making Through Operations Research.* New York: Wiley, 1977.

Turban, Efraim. "A Sample Survey of Operations Research at the Corporate Level." *Operations Research,* May/June 1972, pp. 708–721.

Vroom, Victor H. "A New Look at Managerial Decision Making." *Organizational Dynamics,* Spring 1973, pp. 66–80.

Wright, Peter. "The Harassed Decision Maker." *Journal of Applied Psychology* 59 (1974): 555–561.

Case Study

A CASE OF THE REQUEST FOR SPECIAL FAVORS

Bill Thompson is the manager of the payroll department of the Wellingham Manufacturing Company. Bill reports to the company comptroller. A major function of the department is processing the company biweekly payroll for the more than 2,000 employees of the company. The workload in payroll is very task and deadline oriented. The workload is even more demanding during holiday periods—such as during Thanksgiving, Christmas, or New Years.

At the beginning of December, Betty Jones, a twenty-year-old clerk, informs Bill Thompson she needs to take a week of vacation between Christmas and New Year's Day in order to "visit her family during the holidays." Since the payroll is processed every other week, it has been customary for the payroll department manager and clerical personnel to schedule vacations during the weeks that the payroll is not processed. Betty, an efficient worker, has been employed since March and became eligible for one week of vacation in October. (An employee is eligible for one week of vacation after six months or two weeks upon the completion of one year.) At the time Betty was employed, specific vacation arrangements were not discussed, only the minimum time for eligibility.

Betty's request for a one week vacation during the holiday period would make it difficult for the payroll department to meet its deadlines. The department would lose two days during the period because Christmas Eve and Christmas Day are holidays. Thus, Bill was very concerned about getting the payroll processed that week, especially with Betty on vacation.

Bill and Betty discussed workload requirements during the week in question. He told her the department needs her effort that week, particularly since it is a short week. Betty responded by saying, "My husband has made plans for us to go and he says we're going." Bill feels that while Betty is a satisfactory performer, she apparently lacks commitment to the job and company. He is also concerned about the effects on other members of the work group if he approves Betty's vacation request.

Questions

1. What decision should Bill make regarding Betty Jones' request for vacation? In order to assist Bill, use the decision-making process developed in the chapter.

2. In making the decision, what additional situational factors should be considered other than the fact that she intends to take the vacation against the wishes of the supervisor?

Case Study

A DECISION TO MOVE A BANK TELLER

Commerce is a small midwestern town in a rural area. Two new farm-related industries recently opened factories in the area and created an increase in the general business activity for Commerce. Due to the increased business, First National Bank of Commerce, the largest of the three banks in town, experienced long waiting lines for the paying and receiving tellers. On the basis of a questionnaire sent out to its customers, the bank's executives decided to open a new drive-through facility. The bank purchased a vacant lot across the street and built one drive-through window facility. Room for expansion was possible if the new service proved to be as popular as expected.

Eight tellers were employed by the bank. All were considered good workers and had good relations with the customers. Mrs. Williams, age 48, a widow, was chosen by a bank vice-president to be the teller in the new drive-through facility. She had been with the bank for nine years. The reasons given for her selection were as follows: (1) she can service customers rapidly; (2) she has a responsible attitude toward the work to be accomplished (she helps others when her work is finished and the other tellers seek her advice when they have a problem), and (3) she works well without supervision. An additional teller was employed inside the bank to take Mrs. Williams' place.

The opening day for the new window was hectic, but thanks to Mrs. Williams' organization and work habits the opening was considered to be a success by the customers and by bank officials. Mrs. Williams complained of a headache, but she attributed it to "opening day jitters." As the following week progressed, Mrs. Williams' headaches increased and she was becoming despondent. The next week Mrs. Williams was late twice and made some errors on her accounts. The bank president then told the vice-president to reevaluate his choice of Mrs. Williams as the teller for the new drive-through facility.

Questions

1. What other factors should the vice-president have considered prior to moving Mrs. Williams to the new drive-in facility?
2. What do you believe are the real causes of the difficulties that Mrs. Williams experienced?
3. At what point did the decision-making process break down?

THE ORGANIZING FUNCTION

Part 3 stresses how important the organizing function is to a manager. First, the organizing function is described and then the ways a firm can be organized are presented. Next, staffing the organization is discussed. We close this part of the book with a presentation on the effect an informal organization can have on a firm. Finally, status, power, and politics are discussed in relation to how a knowledge of these topics can help a manager effectively carry out his or her job.

Chapter 5

The Organizing Function: Process and Structure

LEARNING OBJECTIVES

After completing this chapter you should be able to

1. Identify and describe the basic components of the organizing process.
2. List and describe the primary means of departmentation.
3. Identify approaches used in dividing responsibility.
4. Distinguish between responsibility, authority, and accountability.
5. Describe and demonstrate an understanding of the basic principles of authority, responsibility, and accountability.
6. Identify the basic types of organization structures and the advantages and disadvantages of each.
7. Explain the situational approach to organization.

Most likely you have belonged to various student organizations such as clubs, sororities, or fraternities. At the first meeting of the semester, things may have been very hectic, with little sense of direction until someone shouted, "Hey, let's get organized!" Members then began to plan and ask volunteers to do certain tasks that had to be performed if the organization was to be a success.

The process of getting organized is essentially the same for all types of organizations. Once objectives and plans have been formulated, management must develop an orderly way for bringing together the resources—human and material—that are essential to accomplish what's intended. This task is referred to as the organizing function of management. But, what exactly is an organization? The word organization is heard on television and radio and read in newspapers and magazines virtually every day. We hear of organized crime and have a picture of evil. To some of us the word *organization* causes us to think only of large firms such as General Motors, U. S. Steel, or the Bell Telephone Company. We rarely think of the local grocery store, service station, cleaners, or nursery school as an organization.

ORGANIZATION DEFINED

Organizations, large or small, have at least these three common characteristics:

- They are composed of *people.*
- They exist to achieve *goals.*
- Each has some degree of *structure* that results in a definition and limitation of the behavior of its members.

organization

Thus, an **organization** can be defined as *two or more people working together in a coordinated manner to achieve group results.* Since most of us spend a considerable part of our lives working in organizations, it is important for us to fully understand how organizations function and how to manage them. To be effective, a manager must be capable of organizing **human resources, physical factors,** and **functions**—production, marketing, finance, personnel—in a manner to ensure the achievement of the goals of the firm. This process is crucial to the success of a business, church, government agency, university, or any other organization where people work together as a group.

human resources
physical factors
functions

THE PROCESS OF ORGANIZING

The managerial function of organizing is illustrated in Figure 5.1. Consistent with the concepts and ideas presented in earlier chapters, the

FIGURE 5.1
The Organizing Process

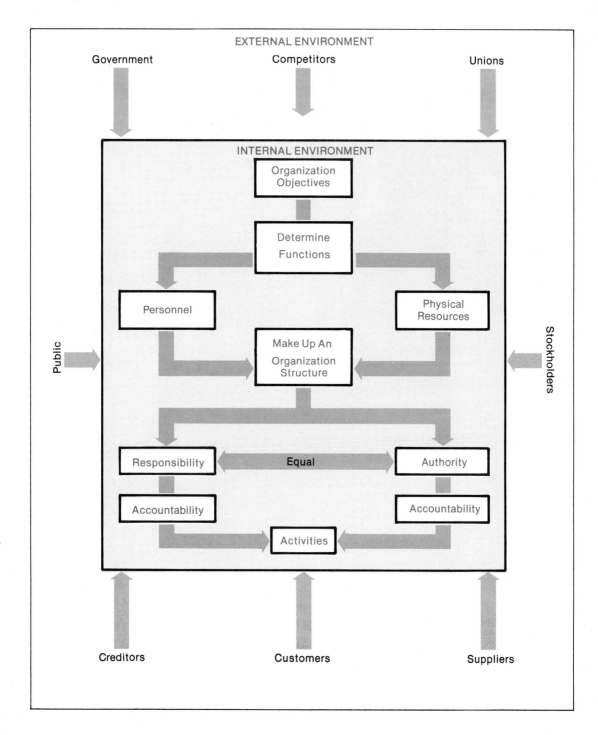

DOROTHY H. MOORE

*Vice-President, Corporate Secretary,
and Director of Stockholder Relations
Michigan General Corporation*

MICHIGAN GENERAL "A young woman today should begin early to obtain the necessary training and education to be successful," says Dorothy H. Moore. "I want my daughter, who just completed high school, to look past tomorrow and think about a career twenty years from now. She needs to realize that she can be a doctor, lawyer, or choose from any number of careers if she is willing to work with a long-range goal in mind."

Ms. Moore graduated from high school when she was 15. This presented a problem because she was more restricted at home than were older classmates. "To escape my mother's rules, I married too young and consequently didn't go on to college," Ms.

Moore recalls. After the marriage did not work out, she was faced with the necessity of finding a job to support her four children.

From the beginning of her working days, Dorothy was determined to succeed. At one of the first places she was employed, she handled the secretarial work for two attorneys. When she asked for a raise, she was offered only $15. "At that point, I found another job. I was and still am willing to do any work necessary but I want to be paid for it."

She worked for a period with a Dallas attorney for whom she felt great respect. When he moved to New York City, she later obtained a secretarial job with Ira G. Corn, Jr., a financial consultant, and Joseph P. Driscoll, an independent oilman. Corn and Driscoll cooperated on several investments and eventually co-founded two large companies, including Michigan General. As her work expanded, Ms. Moore became Mr. Corn's personal secretary and within three years, was being introduced formally as his assistant. "In those early days with the two men," she remembers, "no one ever told me what to do. I looked to see what needed to be done, got things organized, and did it. I took over as acting office manager and if the floor needed mopping I would do that. My advice to anyone is do a good job, look for things to do. Don't wait to be told." She attributes much of her success to her ability to organize personnel and other resources.

When Michigan General was organized in 1968, Ms. Moore helped with the details of putting the various mergers together. In 1973, Ms. Moore became the second woman to be named to Michigan General Corporation's board of directors. In 1978, she was elected a vice-president of the company. Although she has a number of college hours, Dorothy regrets that she never obtained a degree. "A formal education is extremely important because it prepares one for life and it teaches a student to finish what he starts. It opens doors all through life," she points out.

Her tips for success also include a recommendation that an employee be 100 percent loyal to the company. "Make your boss's job easier. Make yourself hard to replace. If you can't be loyal or feel that success and advancement is not possible, the thing to do is look for another job. But always be determined to work hard to attain that long-term goal."

external environment exerts its influence on the organizing process. Organizing consists of establishing *relationships* (responsibility and authority) among the organizational *components* (personnel, functions, and physical factors) for the purpose of *structuring* (line, line and staff, functionalized, project), and directing them toward some common *objective.* Thus, the essential elements of the organizing process are

- establishing objectives
- determining the functions that need to be accomplished
- assessing personnel requirements
- determining the physical resources necessary to achieve the objectives (inputs)
- grouping the functions, physical resources, and the personnel into a coordinated organization structure
- assigning responsibility and authority
- determining the levels of accountability of personnel within established structure
- determining the work activities

Our discussion in this chapter will focus on the organizing process and the design of the appropriate organization structure. We will discuss functions, departmentation, responsibility and authority relationships, principles of organizing, types of organization structures, and a situational approach to organizing.

FUNCTIONS

Once objectives have been established, it is then necessary to determine the type of functions or work that must be performed within the organization. A *function* is work that can be identified and distinguished from other work.

On the typical baseball team, several distinct functions or work activities must be performed effectively if the team is to win ball games. Players on the team must perform the basic functions of fielding, throwing, and hitting, the baseball. A good team must develop specialists capable of performing each of these activities. For instance, a team would have a pitching staff consisting of starters, long-term relievers, and short-term relievers. The team also has infielders who specialize in playing either third base, short-stop, second base, or first base.

As in the baseball example, the basic functions or work activities can be defined in any business, government, or educational organization. For instance, the major functions of a manufacturer would be *production, marketing,* and *finance.* For a retailing company, the basic functions would be *buying* and *selling* of merchandise and *extending credit.* The major functions in a bank would include *depositing* or receiving a customer's money and making loans to borrowers. In a university, *teaching, research,* and *service* are the primary functions that must be performed.

Functions performed by individuals within the organization must be identified, defined, and separated from the work performed by other people. Each function can be further divided into smaller work activities, which is often referred to as **specialization of labor.** Specialization or division of labor has been a major element of the traditional approach to the organizing process. It has been absolutely essential for the achievement of efficiency in mass-production industries. In fact, most work activities performed in nearly all organizations are of a specialized nature.

In many of today's organizations, specialization of labor is referred to as **work simplification.** The work simplification approach to job design organizes jobs into small, highly specialized components. Organizations have several options as to the degree of specialization associated with each job. For instance, if a company produces small transistor radios, several different approaches might be available, such as:

specialization of labor

work simplification

1. Each employee assembles the entire radio.
2. Each employee assembles several major components of the radio (the plastic casing and primary transistor circuit board).
3. Each employee assembles one component of the radio (the case).
4. Each employee performs a few routine operations (such as putting the knobs on for tuner and volume control).

Specialization or work simplification offers the following advantages:

· Allows workers to concentrate skills on a narrow range of work, thus increasing output
· Facilitates the selection and training of workers to perform identifiable activities
· Leads to more efficient utilization of a worker because he or she can practice and develop specialized skills
· Contributes to better consistency of quality in products or services

Despite the advantages of specialization of labor, its application may not always be desirable. In some organizations, certain jobs have become oversimplified. Too much specialization in the design of jobs may create boredom and fatigue among the employees. For example, some people would find it very difficult to perform a job on an assembly line that required the tightening of a certain $1\frac{1}{2}''$ diameter bolt 10,000 times a day. The height of specialization is found in assembly-line work and has often caused employee turnover, absenteeism, and a deteriorating quality of output resulting in increasing operational costs. The problem of too much specialization in work activities will be discussed in chapter 8, Motivation.

DEPARTMENTATION

departmentation

Specialization of labor is normally accomplished by the process of departmentation. **Departmentation** involves the grouping of related functions or major work activities into manageable units to achieve more effective and efficient overall coordination of organization resources. The primary means for departmentation are by *function, product, customer, geographic territory,* and *project.* In most large organizations several of these bases for departmentation are used.

Departmentation by Function

Departmentation by function is perhaps the most common means of grouping related functions (see Figure 5.2). Departmental lines are drawn on the basis of specialized functions such as production, marketing, engineering, finance, and personnel, and assist management in making efficient utilization of the resources of the organization. However, departmentation by function may create problems for management in the sense that personnel in these specialized functions may become more concerned with their own department than with the overall company.

FIGURE 5.2
Departmentation by Function

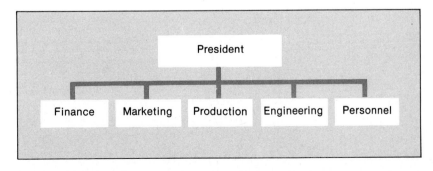

FIGURE 5.3
Departmentation by Product

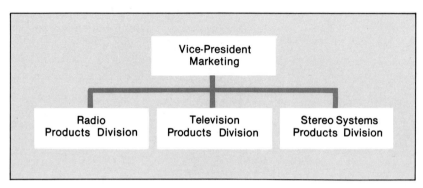

FIGURE 5.4
Departmentation by Customer

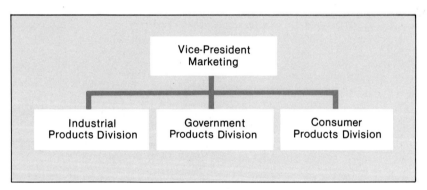

FIGURE 5.5
Departmentation by Geographic Territory

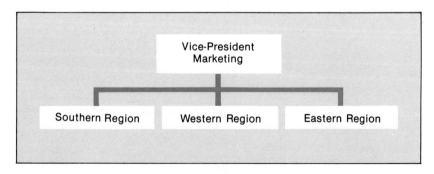

Departmentation by Product

This means of departmentation is concerned with organizing according to the type of product being produced and/or sold by the firm. This means of departmentation enhances the use of specialized knowledge of particular products or services and is often used by rather large, diversified companies. As shown in Figure 5.3, a large electronics firm is organized into three product divisions.

Departmentation by Customer

Departmentation by types of customers is used by organizations that have a special need to provide better service to different types of customers. As illustrated in Figure 5.4, a diversified manufacturing company has an industrial, government, and consumer products division. Large retailers and banks use departmentation along customer lines to provide better service to different customer groups.

Departmentation by Geographic Territory

Grouping activities according to geographic territory is used by organizations that have physically dispersed and/or independent operations or markets to serve. The marketing function of the company shown in Figure 5.5 is organized into the Southern, Western, and Eastern regional divisions. Geographic departmentation offers the advantages of better service with local or regional personnel, often at less cost.

Departmentation by Project

Departmentation by project is a method of bringing together personnel with various work backgrounds to form a team. Figure 5.6 provides an illustration of departmentation for the special project of developing an aircraft plan. Engineer "B" and Financial Planner "C" are to accomplish this special project. The team has been assigned a specific task or objective to be accomplished within a given time period. On completion of the project, Engineer "B" and Financial Planner "C" will return to their regular work assignments. Departmentation by project has received considerable usage in recent years by the construction and aerospace industries.

FIGURE 5.6
Departmentation by Project

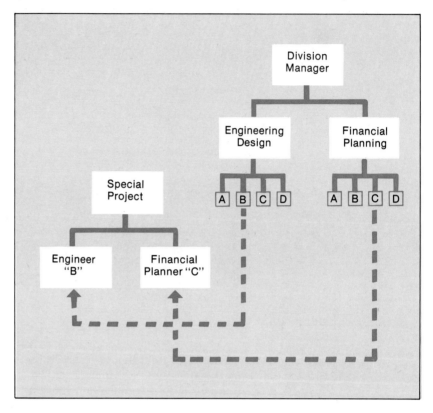

Departmentation: A Combination Approach

As illustrated in Figure 5.7 most organizations make use of several different bases for departmentation. In this case, the manufacturing company is departmentalized by type of functions performed; i.e., Production, Engineering, Marketing, etc.; type of products—industrial and consumer; and by geographic territory.

RESPONSIBILITY

As was shown in Figure 5.1, the organizing process begins with the establishment of objectives and the determination of the functions that need to be accomplished in the organization. Once functions have been

FIGURE 5.7
Organization Chart Illustrating Departmentation

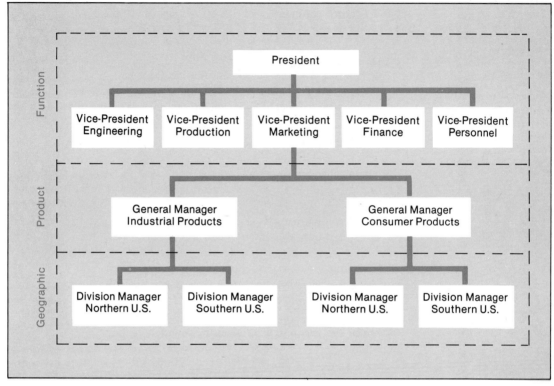

identified, it is then necessary to determine the personnel and physical resources needed to achieve the objectives of the organization.

The *functions, personnel,* and *physical resources* are then grouped together by some means of departmentation into a coordinated organization structure. At this point, it is necessary to assign appropriate levels of responsibility and authority to the personnel.

responsibility   **Responsibility** is an obligation to perform certain work activities. For example, if we say that James Lewis, a manager, is responsible for the data processing center, we mean that he has an obligation to plan, organize, direct, control, and coordinate the work of computer operators and analysts. But, that's not all! He also has the obligation for the maintenance of the computer equipment and programs, plus numerous other activities that are essential to the success of the data processing department.

A key consideration every manager must keep in mind is that responsibilities or obligations to perform certain functions must be clearly defined. Nothing is more frustrating to a manager or a worker than not to know the nature, scope, and details of his or her specific job responsibilities. For instance, suppose that Susan James, a first-line supervisor for a large insurance company, had the following conversation with her boss, Phil Williams.

> *Susan:* Is my unit responsible for processing the new commercial fire insurance policies or should Joe Davis' unit handle them?
>
> *Phil:* I don't think it really matters too much which unit handles these new commercial fire policies so long as it's done correctly and thoroughly.
>
> *Susan:* But, what am I expected to do?
>
> *Phil:* I'll get back to you later on this—I'm busy at the moment.

Obviously, the above comments by Phil would prove to be ambiguous and frustrating to Susan. Susan doesn't know what her specific responsibilities are with regard to the new commercial fire insurance policies and gets no help toward clarifying her role from Phil. Accomplishing the objectives of processing the commercial fire insurance policies may be quite difficult to attain. In order to perform any job adequately, an individual must understand the objectives, functions, and specific responsibilities. As illustrated in Figure 5.1, objectives, functions, and specific responsibilities must be closely integrated if there is to be effective organization.

Personnel in the organization are delegated responsibilities or work assignments by their superiors. When a superior delegates a responsibility to a subordinate, a relationship based on an obligation exists between the two. By delegating, *one cannot relieve oneself of any portion of the original responsibility; delegation allows only for someone else to do the work.* Responsibility is, thus, a series of obligations established between two levels in an organization.

delegation

This concept of **delegation** creates a risk for the manager, for he or she is ultimately responsible for either the success or the failure of an operation. As a result, some managers have attempted to reduce the risk by avoiding delegation and doing tasks themselves. Delegation may sometimes be considered an admission of managerial failure. Delegation of responsibility and authority is absolutely essential if the manager is to provide opportunities for the development of people.

Division of Responsibility

Objectives determine the work to be performed. The total work load must be divided among the available personnel. Individual jobs, or units of responsibility, are created by selecting and grouping functions into individual assignments. The basic guide that governs this process is that of

★

GENERAL PHILOSOPHY ABOUT MANAGING YOUR ORGANIZATION

· Remember and apply "The Golden Rule!"

· Have *honest,* intelligent, energetic, highly motivated people in responsible positions.

· Decentralize as far down as possible into *profit centers* with quality general managers responsible for *results* measured over the *long* term. Beware of managing to achieve *short*-term goals!

JOHN R. HILL, JR., Chairman and C.E.O., Gifford-Hill & Company, Incorporated

---

functional similarity

functional similarity. In Figure 5.8, functions J, L, and Q are shown to be sufficiently similar in objectives and content to comprise the work assignments for Job 1, a press operator. Therefore, a person with the skills and abilities necessary to execute this job must be found. Job 2, the quality

**FIGURE 5.8
Job Design**

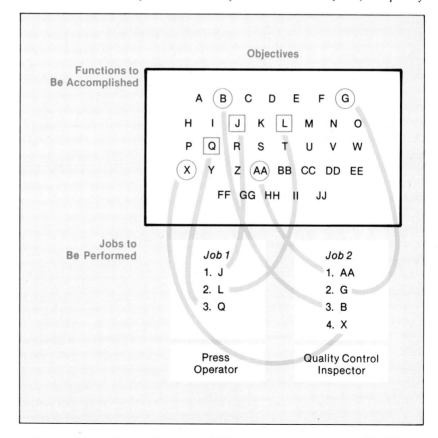

Source Adapted from Edwin B. Flippo and Gary M. Munsinger, *Management,* 4th ed. (Boston: Allyn and Bacon, Inc., 1978), p. 192.

control inspector, consists of functions AA, G, B, and X. The same principles also guide us in the creation of sections, departments, and divisions. Jobs with similar objectives and requirements are grouped to form a section. A person with the background necessary to supervise these functions effectively should be assigned as the manager.

Although functional similarity is desired, the extent to which it can be applied depends on several factors.

Sufficient Volume of Work There must be a sufficient volume of work to enable some specialization. In the small firm, personnel will have to cope with a wide assortment of jobs. But, with increases in volume, the concept can be applied more rigorously. For example, let's compare the operations of a small grocery store versus a large supermarket. In the small store, one person might perform such functions as stocking shelves, working in the produce section, checking, and sacking groceries. In the large supermarket, personnel will tend to specialize in one or only a few of the basic functions. It's common to have individual managers of the produce section, stocking, checking, and sacking functions.

Personnel Qualifications A second factor that may work against the concept of functional similarity is the qualifications of the personnel who are presently employed. It may be that certain employees have seniority or other restrictive qualifications and cannot be assigned certain tasks. However, the manager attempts to develop a unit of responsibility based on the capabilities of the "typical" person.

Functions Similar to Others in the Organization A third complicating factor is that the particular function in question is often similar to other functions. For example, the function of inventory control would appear to fit logically with the purchasing function. The purchasing department buys the material and thus has need for records of inventory levels. However, production uses these materials and, in scheduling, must work with these same inventory records. Inventory control could then be placed in either section.

Separation of Functions for Control or Motivation A fourth complication is the occasional necessity for separating similar functions for purposes of control or motivation. For instance, inspection is a function that is intimately involved in production; inspectors frequently work side by side with production employees. However, the inspector should not be unduly influenced by the production manager's interest in quantity and cost. Thus, inspection, although similar to production, should be separate from production to protect its own independence.

Combining Dissimilar Functions Finally, there are occasions when two dissimilar functions must be combined for purposes of effective action and control. Though purchasing is clearly differentiated from selling in a factory organization, buying and selling are so interdependent in department stores that one person is often made responsible for both. The theory is that "a well-bought dress or hat is half sold."

Other Guides in Dividing Responsibility

In addition to the principle of functional similarity, there are other guides in dividing and delegating responsibility; among these are (1) avoiding overlaps, (2) avoiding gaps, and (3) avoiding delegation of responsibility for work that does not contribute to the objective.

An *overlap* in responsibility occurs when two or more persons are made responsible for the same function. This often happens when responsibility is unclear or when work is unknowingly duplicated in different parts of the organization. A *gap* in responsibility results from a failure to foresee all requirements for effective accomplishment of goals. A function should be performed but has been assigned to no one. As a result, it may not be accomplished, and the organization suffers. Or, the organization politician, who searches for power, may jump in and volunteer to take on the job even though it bears no similarity to his or her main task. *Avoiding delegation of responsibility for work that does not contribute to the objective* would appear so obvious as to be implicit. However, there are many examples of activities that in no way contribute to organization objectives.

AUTHORITY

authority

Once responsibility has been assigned, it is then necessary to delegate the authority necessary to accomplish the job. Just as responsibility is a concept based on and derived from functions, authority is derived from responsibility. Viewed in terms of management, **authority** is the right to decide, to direct others to take action, or to perform certain duties in achieving organizational goals.

The concept of authority is often difficult to understand. As defined above, there are at least three key characteristics of authority.

1. Authority is a *right.*
2. Exercising authority involves making *decisions* and taking actions or the performance of duties.
3. Authority is used to achieve organizational *goals.*

Whatever the source—formal or informal—authority is absolutely essential if the manager is to organize and direct the use of resources to attain the goals of the organization.

Division of Authority

Because authority is derived from responsibility, its division should be along the same lines. This is made evident in a widely accepted basic principle of management that states *responsibility should equal authority.* This principle indicates that a delegation of responsibility should carry with it an equal amount of authority. In other words, a manager who is given a job to do (responsibility) should have adequate authority (or rights) to get the job done.

The concept as stated sounds good in theory. Yet one of the most common complaints of first-level supervisors is that they have more responsibility than authority. Authority deals with rights, and these must be made specific in terms of the responsibility delegated. For example, if a supervisor is made responsible for staffing a department, he or she can be delegated any one of the following levels of authority:

1. rights of recruitment, screening, and hiring of all personnel
2. rights of recruitment, screening, and hiring subject to prior approval from above
3. no rights of recruitment and screening, which have been allocated to a staff personnel department, but rights of accepting or rejecting candidates
4. no rights of hiring since one must take whomever the personnel department sends.

In the last instance, the supervisor is responsible for getting a job done but lacks the authority to adequately perform the job by hiring personnel he or she considers best qualified.

Amount of Authority:
Centralization vs. Decentralization

It is important that management determines the appropriate levels of responsibility and authority to be delegated. If a limited amount of authority is delegated, the organization is usually characterized as being **centralized.** On the other hand, if a significant amount of authority is delegated to lower levels, the enterprise is described as being **decentralized.**

centralization

decentralization

Some managers act like kings and feel they should make all the decisions.

Centralization and decentralization are the opposites with many different degrees in between them. The real question is not whether a company should decentralize, but rather how much. In determining the actual amount of decentralization existing in an organization, the nature and location of decision making must be assessed. In a highly centralized structure, individual managers and workers at lower levels in the organization have a rather narrow range of decisions or actions they can initiate. By contrast, the scope of authority to make decisions and take actions is rather broad for lower-level managers and employees in decentralized organizations. For example, in a highly centralized organization structure, upper management makes all decisions regarding the hiring or firing of personnel, approval of purchasing of equipment supplies, or other such activities. In a decentralized structure lower-level management may make these decisions.

Although the trend today seems to favor decentralization, all forms of decentralization cannot be classified as effective and not all centralization classified as ineffective. Decentralization is advocated by many who believe that a greater share in management decision making should be given to lower organizational levels. If virtually all decisions and orders come from one central source, organization members tend to act as robots and unthinking executors of someone else's commands. Decentralization tends to create a climate for more rapid growth and development of personnel, and as has been discussed in earlier chapters, a primary responsibility of managers, on any level, is the development of people.

In addition to the human relations implications of decentralization and centralization, there are other factors that will affect a manager's decision in this regard. Centralization—

1. produces uniformity of policy and action;
2. results in few risks of errors by subordinates who lack either information or skill;
3. utilizes the skills of central and specialized experts;
4. enables closer control of operations.

On the other hand, decentralization—

1. tends to make for speedier decisions and actions on the spot without consulting higher levels;
2. results in decisions that are more likely to be adapted to local conditions;
3. results in greater interest and enthusiasm on the part of the subordinate to whom the authority has been entrusted; (These expanded jobs provide excellent training experiences for possible promotion to higher levels.)
4. allows top management to utilize their time for more study and consideration of the basic goals, plans, and policies of the enterprise.

Additional factors to be taken into account concerning the degree of centralization are discussed below.

Size and Complexity of the Organization The larger the enterprise, the more authority the central manager is forced to delegate. If the firm is engaged in many separate businesses, the limitations of expertise will usually lead to decentralization of authority to the heads of these units.

Each major product group is likely to have different production problems, varying kinds of customers, and varied marketing channels. If speed and adaptability to change are necessary to success, decentralization is a must.

Dispersion of the Organization When the difficulties of size are compounded by geographic dispersion, it is very evident that a greater degree of decentralization must occur. General Motors Corporation is a prime example of decentralization because of size and geographic dispersion. However, not every decision or every function must be decentralized. Control of operations may have to be pushed down to lower levels in the organization, while control of financing may still be centralized. Because of the increasing complexity of federal and state legislation affecting employment practices and unionization, centralization of labor relations is often established for purposes of uniformity throughout the company.

Competency of Personnel Available A major limiting factor in many organizations is the adequacy or inadequacy of present personnel. If the enterprise has grown up under centralized decision making and control, past experience has often equipped subordinate personnel poorly to start making major decisions. They were hired and trained to be followers, not leaders and decision makers. In some convenience store chains this has developed into a major problem. Store managers are promoted to supervisors because they are able to perform basic store functions, not on their decision-making ability. Supervisors are promoted to general managers not because of their decision-making ability but because they can ensure that lower managers follow standard operating procedures. In such a situation, a person who eventually makes it to the top is not equipped to cope with the large number of decisions to be made that are not based on established practices and procedures, and those who were inclined toward more independent thought and action may well have been driven away from the centralized firm.

Adequacy of Communications System The size, complexity, and geographic dispersion lead to the delegation of larger amounts of authority for decision making to lower levels in the organization. The manager can seek to avoid decentralization through the development of a communication system that provides for speed, accuracy, and capacity of information needed for top management to exercise centralized control. In effect, although size and geography may preclude being on the spot, one can attempt to control subordinates by detailing standards of performance and process, and by ensuring that information flows quickly and accurately to the central authoritative position.

ACCOUNTABILITY

accountability

Once a sufficient amount of authority has been delegated to enable the individual to complete the task for which he or she is responsible, the individual can then be held accountable for results. **Accountability** is an important concept for managers to understand. Managers are not only accountable for their own actions and decisions, but they are also accountable for the actions of their subordinates. Before we can hold an individual accountable for results, we should make sure of the following:

- The responsibilities are thoroughly understood.
- The person is capable of fulfilling the obligation.
- Sufficient authority has been delegated.

PRINCIPLES RELATED TO AUTHORITY, RESPONSIBILITY, AND ACCOUNTABILITY

There are several important principles that relate to the concepts of authority, responsibility, and accountability. These principles will be briefly discussed below and are summarized in Table 5.1.

Single Accountability

single accountability

Perhaps the most widely known principle of management governing the relationship of accountability is that of **single accountability.** Each person should answer to only one immediate superior—one boss to each employee. Single accountability enables better coordination and understanding of what is required, and improves discipline. If an employee has two or more bosses, it is possible to receive contradictory orders.

Though this concept of single accountability is sound, it does have certain limitations. In many organizations, it is no doubt an unreality. In actuality, in many instances a person is accountable to more than one boss as the size of the organization increases.

Equal Authority and Responsibility

As previously discussed, an important principle of management is that authority should equal responsibility. Following this principle ensures that work will be performed more efficiently and with a minimum amount of frustration on the part of personnel. By not delegating an adequate amount of authority, energies and resources are wasted and employee dissatisfaction often results.

TABLE 5.1
Principles of Authority, Responsibility, and Accountability

Principle	Definition of	Reason for	Possible Causes of Violation	Possible Results of Violation
Single Accountability	A person should report to only one boss. ("one boss")	Clarity and understanding, to ensure unity of effort and direction, and to avoid conflicts	Unclear definition of authority	Dissatisfaction or frustration of employees and perhaps lower efficiency
Authority Should Equal Responsibility	The amount of authority and responsibility should be equal. (Responsibility = Authority)	Allows work to be accomplished more efficiently, develops people, and reduces frustration	Fear on the part of some managers that subordinates might "take over"	Waste of energies and dissatisfaction of employees thereby reducing effectiveness
Scalar Chain of Authority (Chain of Command)	There should be a clear definition of authority in the organization. ("to go through channels")	Clarity of relationship avoids confusion and improves decision making and performance	Uncertainty on the part of the employee or a direct effort by the employee to avoid chain of command	Poor performance, confusion and/or dissatisfaction
Span of Control	There is a limit to the number of employees a manager can effectively supervise.	Increased effectiveness in direction and control of a manager	Overloading a manager due to growth in number of personnel	Lack of efficiency and control resulting in poor performance

Scalar Chain of Authority (Chain of Command)

chain of command

The principle of the scalar chain of authority suggests that there should be a clear definition of authority in the organization. This concept is often referred to as the **chain of command.** Following this principle is very important to management because its application clarifies relationships, avoids confusion, and tends to improve decision making, thus, leading to more effective performance. When the scalar chain is in effect, a person communicates in the organization by *going through channels.*

Span of Control

span of control

The number of employees a manager can effectively supervise is referred to as the **span of control.** Adherence to this principle enables the manager to achieve maximum effectiveness in directing and controlling personnel. While there is a limit to the number of employees a manager can effectively supervise, the precise span of control varies according to the situation.

The "correct" or optimum span of control for a manager in one situation may be to supervise eight people; for another manager, in a different situation and/or time, the span of control would be different. Joan Woodward, a British researcher who conducted studies in 100 English manufacturing firms, discovered that the type of technology had a significant impact on spans of control actually used in business organizations. Classifying production technology on the basis of (1) unit or small-batch processing (for example, made-to-order goods such as custom-tailored clothing), (2) mass production (assembly line operations), and (3) process production with continuous flow (producing materials or products such as oil, chemicals, or pharmaceuticals), she discovered that spans were largest in mass production. The jobs in a mass production situation tend to be more routine and similar to one another, thus leading to a longer effective span of control.[1]

ORGANIZATION STRUCTURES

As described previously, organizing is the process of bringing together functions, personnel, and physical resources for the purpose of achieving objectives. The primary formal relationships which we discussed in this process were responsibility, authority, and accountability. Now let's

1. Joan Woodward, *Management and Technology* (London: Her Majesty's Stationery Office, 1958), pp. 8–30.

> ★
>
> **GENERAL PHILOSOPHY ABOUT MANAGING YOUR ORGANIZATION**
> - Keep a lean and mean staff.
> - Delegate responsibility and authority to operations personnel.
> - Manage on a low key basis.
> - Establish good relationship with all employees and keep communication channels open.
> - Inform top people on major decisions.
>
> R. P. TIMMERMAN, President, Graniteville Company

organization structure

consider the means of providing a pattern for organizing these formal relationships. This framework is known as an **organization structure.** The development of an appropriate organization structure provides the overall *guidelines* essential for effective employee performance. While we usually think of the large company when we discuss organization structures, every firm, large or small, has a structure. The organization structure provides the guidelines for clarifying and communicating the lines of responsibility, authority, and accountability within the firm. Although there are many variations of organization structure used in industry today, we will discuss only four basic types. These are line, line and staff, functional, and the project structure.

LINE ORGANIZATION

line organization

A **line organization** structure shows the direct, vertical relationships between different levels within the firm. A "pure" line organization would consist of personnel performing or managing functions essential to the successful existence of the firm. In a line organization structure, authority would follow the scalar or vertical chain of command. Figure 5.9 is an illustration of a simple three-level line organization structure for the modern manufacturing company.

Several advantages are quite often associated with the pure line organization structure.

1. A line structure tends to *simplify* and *clarify* responsibility, *authority,* and *accountability* relationships within the organization. The levels of responsibility and authority of personnel operating within a line organization are likely to be precise and understandable.
2. A line structure *promotes fast decision making and allows the organization to more rapidly change directions since there are few people to consult when problems arise.*

FIGURE 5.9
A Line Organization Structure

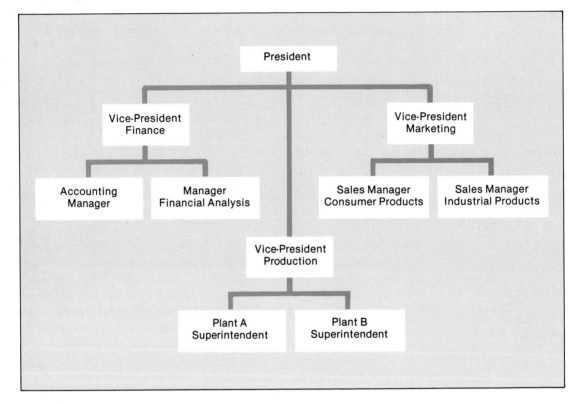

3. Since pure line organizations are small, there are the advantages of *greater feeling* of *closeness* of management to the employees and all personnel usually have an opportunity to know what's going on within the firm.

Despite the above advantages, there are also certain disadvantages of the line structure. The major disadvantage of a line organization structure is its increasing lack of effectiveness as the firm grows larger. At some point, speed and flexibility do not offset the lack of specialized knowledge and skills. In other words, a line structure may force managers to "wear too many hats" and thereby possibly reduce their effectiveness. In a line organization structure, the firm may have a tendency to become overly dependent on one or a few key people who can perform numerous jobs. If the organization is to remain purely line, one solution is for management to seek help by creating additional levels of organization to share the managerial load. This, however, will result in a lengthening of the chain of command and a consequent loss of some of the values of speed, flexibility, and central control.

LINE AND STAFF ORGANIZATION

line and staff organization

At some point in the growth of a firm, there will be a need for specialists. When a provision is made for these specialists, one has altered the structure from being a line organization to **line and staff organization.** The staff function provides advice and support to the organization. Types of staff personnel may be either *general* or *specialized.* A general staff position is usually an assistant with a background very similar to the boss. Specialized staffs are the type most frequently encountered. They provide expertise developed by means of concentration on a narrow portion of the firm's activities. As shown in the line and staff organization chart in Figure 5.10, staff functions include personnel, research and development, and public relations.

Three separate types of specialized staffs can be identified: (1) advisory, (2) service, and (3) control. It is possible for one unit to perform all three functions. For example, the personnel manager may advise line managers on the appropriateness of recognizing a particular labor union. The department simultaneously provides a service by procuring and training needed production and sales personnel. A control orientation enters when the personnel manager audits salaries actually paid to ensure conformity to line-approved pay ranges. Some staffs are predominantly one or the other in character; for example, a staff economist advises the establishment of long-range plans, a maintenance staff unit repairs plant and equipment, and a quality control staff unit enforces authorized product standards. It is apparent that the potential for conflicts in coordination between line and staff tends to grow as one moves from advice to service to control. One can possibly ignore advice, but service is needed, and control is often unavoidable.

There are both advantages and disadvantages of a line and staff organization structure. The primary advantage is that it uses the expertise of specialists. The actions of a manager can become more scientific, by means of concentrated and skillful analysis of business problems. In addition, the manager's effective span of control can be lengthened—that is, he or she can supervise more people. Some staff personnel operate as an extension of the manager, and assist in coordination and control.

Despite the fact that a line and staff structure allows for increased flexibility and specialization, it may create conflicts. When we introduce various specialists into the organization, line managers may feel that they have "lost authority" over certain specialized functions. These managers

FIGURE 5.10
Line and Staff Structure of Typical Manufacturing Company

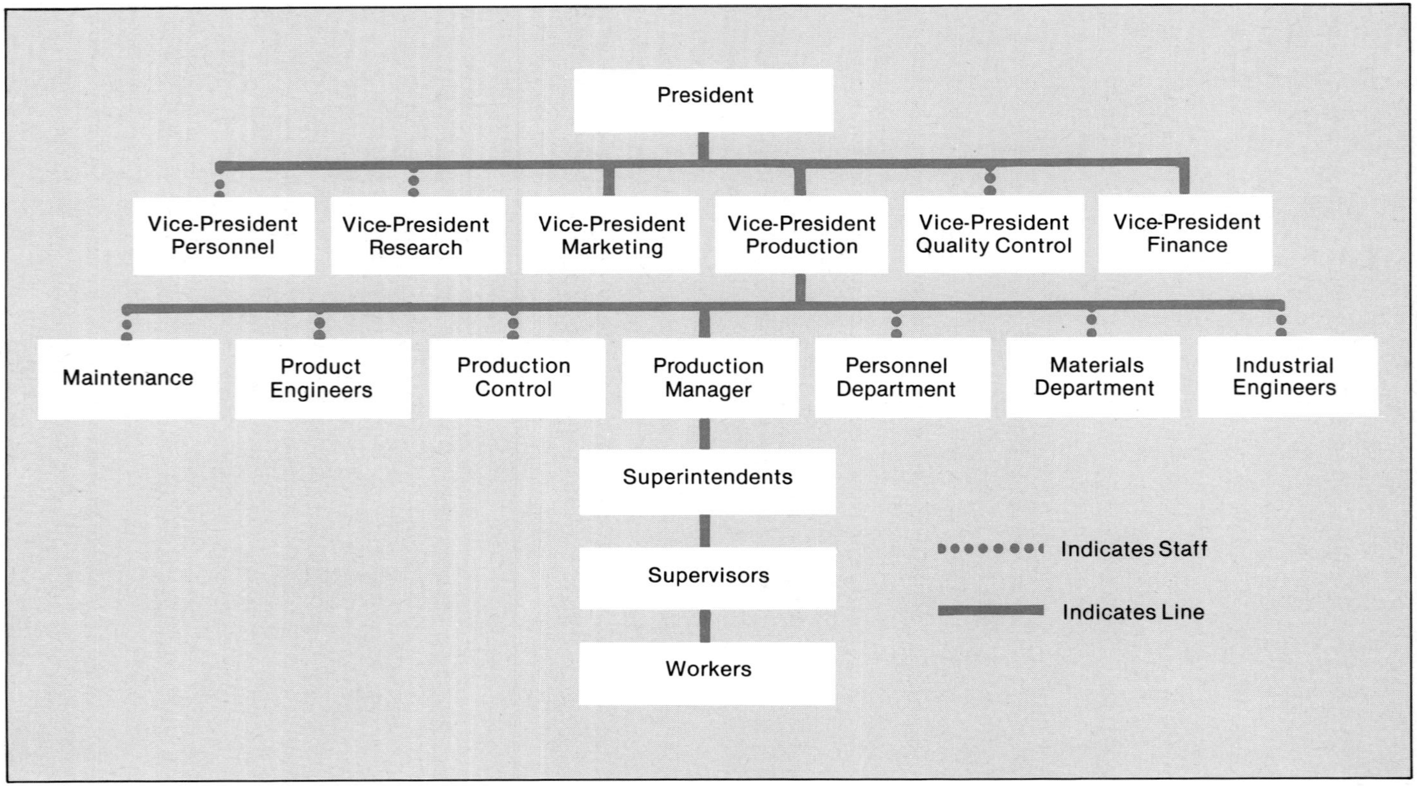

do not want staff specialists telling them "what to do or how to do it" even though they recognize the specialists' knowledge and expertise. It is important to use staff personnel without destroying the unity of command. The *right* of the line manager still remains, though the *ability* to exercise this right may have been considerably weakened. The problem is not so much the type of structure, but the individual personnel within the organization. Some staff personnel have a difficult time adjusting to the role of being an advisor especially if line managers are reluctant to accept his or her advice. Staff personnel may resent not having authority and this may cause a line and staff conflict.

There is a tendency for the specialist to seek to enlarge personal influence by assuming line authority in her or his specialty. This is compounded by a realization that the fundamental purpose of all staff is to produce greater economy and effectiveness of operation. This means that staff must attempt to introduce changes that result in more efficiency. These changes will not always be welcomed with open arms by line personnel. Thus, the introduction of specialized, noncommand personnel into what was once a fairly simple organization structure complicates relationships.

FUNCTIONAL ORGANIZATION

If a staff specialist is given command or line authority over other personnel in regard to his or her specialty, a functional authority relationship has been created. **Functional authority** is direct line authority over specialized functions or activities. These relationships give rise to what has become known as a **functional organization** structure. In a pure line organization there is limited use of specialists by management. In the line and staff organization, specialization of particular functions characterizes the structure, but the specialists have only advisory authority. However, in the functional structure, specialists are given authority to issue orders in their own name in designated areas of the work. The chain of command of line authority and the notion of single accountability (or having one boss) is broken creating multiple accountability.

Even though few, if any, organizations are established on a completely functionalized basis, it is quite common to functionalize the relationship between one or two specialists and the remainder of the organization. If a function is considered to be of crucial importance, it may then be necessary for the specialist to exercise direct rather than advisory authority. The violation of single accountability is undertaken deliberately. The possible losses resulting from confusion and conflicting orders from multiple sources may be more than offset by increased effectiveness in the performance of the specialty.

functional authority

functional organization

FIGURE 5.11
Functional Organization Structure

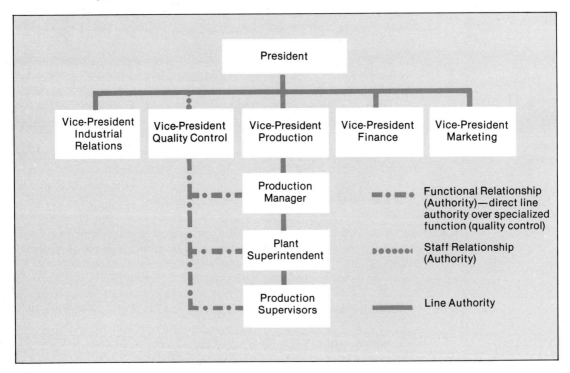

Good examples of specialties that have been given functional authority in many organizations include quality control, safety, and labor relations (see Figure 5.11). Quality control is a very important function in most manufacturing organizations, and its level of authority and stature within the organization has increased over the years. A staff quality control department would merely advise; if, however, that unit is given the authority or right to issue orders (e.g., to correct defects) in its own name, it can no longer be called staff.

Likewise, safety and labor relations specialists may also exercise functional authority over personnel in other areas throughout the organization, but only in relation to their specific specialties. A safety manager may issue compliance guidelines and give direct interpretations of the Occupational Safety and Health Act (OSHA) throughout the organization. The labor relations specialist often will have complete authority in contract negotiations with the union. In each of the above illustrations—quality control, safety, and labor relations—the traditional chain of command has been split. As long as this splitting process is restricted, coordination and unity of action are not in excessive danger. Many organizations that utilize functional relationships attempt to confine its impact to managerial rather than operative levels. Thus, a department supervisor may have to account to more than one boss, but the employees are protected from this possible confusion.

Despite the advantages of a functional organization, the major disadvantages of such structures are: (1) the potential conflicts resulting from the violation of the principle of single accountability; and (2) the tendency to keep authority centralized at higher levels in the organization. If the functionalized structure is used extensively, there may be a tendency for the line department supervisor to become little more than a figurehead. The structure can become very complicated when there are corresponding functional specialists on various levels in the organization.

PROJECT ORGANIZATION

The line, line and staff, and functional organization structures have been the traditional approaches to organization. The primary concern of these forms of organizations has been the establishment and distribution of authority to coordinate and control the firm by emphasizing vertical, rather than horizontal, relationships. However, work processes may flow horizontally, diagonally, up or down, depending on the problem and distribution of talents. Work requirements often result in the need for an organization based on the specific nature of work projects. The organizations that have emerged to cope with this challenge have been referred to as project structures or matrix organizations.

project organization

A **project organization** provides a highly effective means by which all of the necessary human talent and physical resources can be focused for a time on a specific project or goal. They are temporary organization structures designed to achieve specific results by using a team of specialists from different functional areas within the organization. The *team* focuses all of its energies and skills on the assigned project. Once the specific project has been completed, the project team is broken up and personnel are reassigned to their regular positions in the organization. Many business organizations and government agencies make use of project teams or task forces to concentrate their efforts on a specific project assignment like the development of a new product or new technology, or on the construction of a new plant.

Perhaps the most famous example of the successful use of the project form of organization has been by the National Aeronautic and Space Administration (NASA). The significant space achievements of the United States have been due in part to the project organization structures used by NASA. For each major space goal, a project team was assigned. The terms used to describe our objectives in space exploration, such as the *Gemini Project* and *Apollo Moon Project*, are very familiar project organizations to millions of us.

Project organization structures are probably most valuable when the work is—

1. definable in terms of a specific goal and target date for completion that have been established;
2. somewhat unique and unfamiliar to the existing organization;
3. complex with respect to interdependence of activities and specialized skills necessary to accomplishment;
4. critical in terms of possible gain or loss;
5. temporary with respect to duration of need.

Figure 5.12 illustrates a highly simplified project organization that is attached to an existing organization. Personnel are assigned to the project from the existing permanent organization and are under the direction and control of the project manager. In simple terms, the project manager will specify what effort is needed and when it will be performed, while the concerned department managers may decide who in their unit is to do the work and how it is to be accomplished. Home base for most personnel is the existing department—engineering, production, purchasing, personnel, or research and development.

The authority over the four project members is shared by both the project manager and the functional managers in the permanent organization. The specialists are temporarily on loan to spend a portion of their time on the project assignment. However, it is apparent that authority is one of the crucial questions of the project structure. A deliberate conflict has been established between the project manager and managers within the permanent organization. The authority relationships are overlapping, presumably in the interest of assuring that all problems will be covered.

Project managers and department heads are often forced into using means other than formal authority to accomplish results. Informal relationships become more important than formal prescriptions of authority. In the event of conflict and dispute, discussion and consensus are required rather than the forcing of compliance by threat or punishment. Full and free communication, regardless of formal rank, is required among those working on the project. More attention is allocated to roles and competencies in relation to the project than to formal levels of authority.

The effectiveness of the project management concept demonstrates that people can work for two or more managers and that managers can effectively influence those over whom they have no clear authority. There is the possibility of conflict and frustration, but the opportunity for prompt, efficient accomplishment is great.

FIGURE 5.12
Project Structure

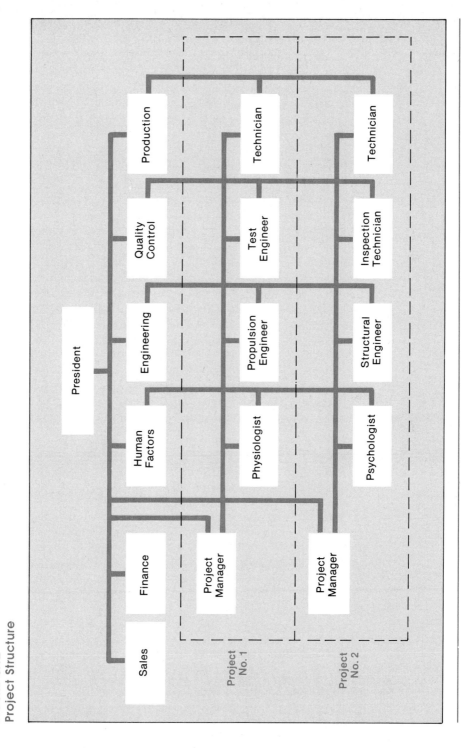

Source Edwin B. Flippo and Gary M. Munsinger, *Management*, 4th ed. (Boston: Allyn and Bacon, Inc., 1978). p. 220.

THE SITUATIONAL APPROACH TO ORGANIZATION

There is no one best way to organize that meets the requirements of all situations. The most appropriate structure requires that the situational factors discussed in chapter 1 be considered. Management must analyze and diagnose the relevant factors and develop a structure that meets the needs of the situation.

If the external environment in which the firm operates is stable, there are few changes in requirements made on the firm by customers, government, unions, and the public. For instance, the firm may produce one or only a few products and all employees belong to one union. Under these rather stable or predictable conditions, a more uniform organization structure is appropriate. In this type of structure, objectives can be specifically defined, decisions made mostly at the top of the organization, tasks preprogrammed and specialized, and a large number of detailed standards established to cover all activities. Employees are closely monitored by narrow spans of control, resulting in the formation of a *tall* (many levels) organization structure. Their prime contacts are with superiors, who in turn are the primary means of coordinating all activity in conformance with plans.

In an environment characterized by dynamic and uncertain conditions (such as the aerospace industry) a more flexible organization structure is appropriate. In such an organization, the emphasis must be on flexibility in reaction to changes in the environment, technology, objectives, personnel needs, or managerial approaches. Because there can be no *all knowing* top management that is simultaneously everywhere, decision making must be decentralized within the organization. Consequently, we cannot specialize all tasks, specify all roles in advance, or set numerous detailed performance standards. We are more heavily dependent on organizational members to interact on the basis of unique problems and integrate themselves in response to the demands of the situation.

In an industry that has rather stable or predictable technology in terms of skills, knowledge, methods, and equipment, a uniform or stable organization structure is usually appropriate. In other words, if the methods of accomplishing the work are well developed, a stable structure is necessary. However, if the technology is complex, uncertain or rapidly changing (e.g., as evidenced by the technology required in producing electronic pocket calculators) the firm is more dependent on individual initiative and skill for effective performance.

For example, the Woodward studies which were previously discussed revealed technology has an important effect on the type of organization structure that is most effective. When the firms in the Woodward studies were grouped on the basis of different types of production technology being used, regardless of the product or size of the company, certain organizational patterns were apparent.

Classifying the firms into three categories (1) unit production, (2) mass production, and (3) process production, Woodward concluded there were several important relationships between the types of production technology a firm used and its organization structure and managerial practices. In general, complex production technologies (mass and process production) require a greater number of organizational levels and more managers to do the job effectively.

Having more managers and levels within an organization necessitates more effective supervision and coordination. Spans of control of lower-level managers are greater in mass production than in unit and process production. Narrow spans of control are usually found in unit and process type organizations where employees perform highly skilled work in small groups. In mass production firms, workers usually perform relatively unskilled work often in large groups, thereby permitting managers to supervise a larger number of employees than in the other types of organizations. Finally, the most successful firm in each of the three categories tended to have an organization structure that was most appropriate for the type of technology they used. In essence, Woodward's findings support the notion that there is *no one* best approach to designing an organization structure that meets the needs of all situations.[2]

Managerial approaches are also an important situational component to be considered in designing or modifying an organization structure. The traditional approach tends to lead to more formalized roles and job descriptions for employees, and centralized decision making. This creates a more stable or predictable organization structure. On the other hand, the participative approach emphasizes more employee involvement in decision making and less rigid adherence to narrow job descriptions. This creates the need for more flexible organization structures.

The nature and aspirations of the firm's personnel also has an effect on the organization structure. Personnel differ with respect to goals, backgrounds, experiences, and personalities and these factors affect the type of organization structure utilized. Research and development personnel may not be as productive when placed in a rigid organizational structure. On the other hand, some individuals even desire a more formalized structure. For instance, people who make a career of the military have to be able to work well in a highly structured environment to be successful.

Management may feel its objective must change in order for the firm to survive. Such would be the case where a company was following the objective of stability and gradual growth. If the objectives were changed to encompass rapid growth and diversification with an aggressive marketing plan, most likely the structure would have to be altered. To cope with an environment requiring fast decision making, the structure might be changed from centralized to decentralized.

2. Ibid.

There is considerable evidence to suggest the organization structure must be adapted to major situational factors. In research conducted by Lawrence and Lorsch, it was found that firms in the container industry, characterized by stable environments, tended to develop more rigid or stable structures.[3] Those operating in the more volatile and rapidly changing environment of the plastics industry tended to develop flexible organization structures. In environments characterized by intermediate degrees of uncertainty and change, tailor-made structures designed to produce values of both spontaneity and repetitiveness were created. Even within the single organization, varying types of structures will be used. For the research and development unit, with its imperfect technology and high degree of uncertainty, a flexible structure is typically utilized.[4] In the production division, however, the buffered environment of the inner technological core enables a more uniform or stable structure to be established.

Thus, the situational or contingency approach stresses that there is no one best way to design an organization structure. The situational factors of the external environment, objectives, technology, managerial approaches, and personnel must be integrated and balanced in order for an optimum structure to be developed.

SUMMARY

An organization exists any time two or more people work together to achieve a group result. However, in order to be effective, organizations must be managed. The second function of management—organizing—consists of establishing appropriate levels of responsibility and authority among the personnel, determining the functions and physical factors within the organization for the purpose of structuring, and directing them toward common objectives.

The specific steps of the organizing process are as follows: establishing objectives; determining the functions that need to be accomplished;

3. P. R. Lawrence and J. W. Lorsch, *Organization and Environment: Managing Differentiation and Integration* (Boston: Division of Research, Harvard Graduate School of Business Administration, 1967).

4. In a study of research and development units of firms in the United Kingdom, it was found that such units vary their structures in response to market environments. The more effective units had better coalignment. See L. Burns and G. M. Stalker, *The Management of Innovation* (London: Tavistock, 1964).

assessing personnel requirements; determining the physical resources necessary to achieve the objectives; grouping the functions, physical resources, and personnel into a coordinated organization structure; assigning responsibility and authority; and determining the work activities.

Determining the functions to be performed raises the issue of how much specialization of labor is desirable. Specialization of labor is usually accomplished by the process of departmentation. Departmentation involves grouping related functions or major work activities into manageable units to achieve more effective and efficient overall coordination of the resources of the firm. The primary means for departmentation are by function, product, customer, geographic territory, and project. In most organizations, a combination of these means of departmentations is used.

Delegation of the appropriate levels of responsibility and authority is essential to sound organization. Derived from functions, responsibility is an obligation to perform certain work activities. It is crucial to the success of a firm that responsibilities be clearly defined. Once responsibilities have been assigned to personnel, it is then necessary to delegate enough authority to get the job done. Authority is the right to decide, to direct others to take action or to perform certain duties in achieving organizational goals. A basic principle of management is that authority should equal responsibility.

Depending on the extent of the delegation of authority, an organization is said to be either centralized or decentralized. In a centralized organization, decisions are made primarily by upper management, whereas in a decentralized structure, lower levels in the organization play a more active role in decision making. Once responsibility and authority have been delegated, the individual can be held accountable for results. There are four important principles of authority, responsibility, and accountability. The principles include: *single accountability*—a person should have only one boss; *authority should equal responsibility; scalar chain of authority*—clear definition of authority (through channels); and *span of control*—a limit to the number of people a manager can effectively supervise.

The means for organizing the functions, resources, and the formal relationships is the organization structure. Four basic types of organizations are the line, line and staff, functional, and the project structure. A line structure is the simplest and most basic form of organization. The line and staff structure allows for increased flexibility and specialization with the introduction of staff specialists who serve as advisors. However, it creates more conflicts over authority. In the functional organization, the staff specialists are given authority to issue orders in designated areas of work. Finally, project or matrix organization structures provide a highly effective means by which all of the necessary human talent and physical resources are allocated for a time to a specific project.

**Review
Questions**

1. What is an organization? What are the common characteristics of all organizations?

2. Discuss (and illustrate) the essential elements of the organizing process. What external factors affect the process?

3. What is meant by specialization or work simplification? What are the advantages of work simplification?

4. What does the term departmentation mean? What are the primary means for departmentation?

5. Define and illustrate the following:
   a. Responsibility
   b. Authority
   c. Accountability

6. What factors should be considered when assigning responsibilities within an organization?

7. What is meant by centralization and decentralization?

8. What are the advantages and disadvantages of centralization and decentralization of authority?

9. Briefly discuss the primary factors to be considered in determining the degree of centralization that is appropriate for an organization.

10. Briefly summarize four important principles of management governing authority, responsibility, and accountability relationships. In your answer, define the principle, the possible causes for violation, and possible results of the violation of the principle.

11. What are the four basic types of organization structures? Draw a simple chart to illustrate each.

12. Briefly discuss the appropriateness of each type of organization structure.

13. What is meant by the situational approach to organization?

Exercises

1. Analyze the organization charts of a local retail store (e.g. Sears), a bank, a manufacturing company, and your college or university. How are these firms organized and what are the basic means of departmentation used? What changes, if any, would you suggest for the managers of these organizations? Draw new charts if necessary.

2. Go to the library and review two current journal articles describing corporate reorganizations. At the next class meeting report to the class *one* example of a company that has been reorganized. In your three minute presentation briefly describe the company as well as the reasons for and advantages of the reorganization.

REFERENCES

Allen, B. A., and LaFollette, W. R. "Perceived Organizational Structure and Alienation Among Management Trainees." *Academy of Management Journal,* June 1977, pp. 334–341.

Bowers, David G. *Systems of Organizations: Management of Human Resource.* Ann Arbor: University of Michigan Press, 1976.

Clutterbuck, D. "The Science of Organization." *International Management,* June 1975, pp. 53–54.

Cummings, L. L. and Berger, C. J. "Organization Structure: How Does It Influence Attitudes and Performances." *Organizational Dynamics,* August 1976, pp. 34–49.

Dressler, Gary S. *Organization and Management: A Contingency Approach.* Englewood Cliffs, N.J.: Prentice-Hall, 1976.

Franklin, J. E. "Down the Organization: Influence Process, Across Levels of Hierarchy." *Administration Science Quarterly,* June 1975, pp. 154–163.

Gibson, James L.; Ivancevich, John M.; and Dennelly, James H., Jr. *Organizations: Behavior, Structure, and Processes.* Dallas: Business Publications, Inc., 1976.

Limerick, D. C. "Authority Relationships In Different Organizational Systems." *Academy of Management Review,* October 1976, pp. 56–68.

Ouchi, W. G. "Relationship Between Organizational Structure and Organizational Control." *Administrative Science Quarterly,* March 1977, pp. 206–216.

Schleh, E. C. "Using Central Staff to Boost Line Initiative." *Management Review,* May 1976, pp. 17–23.

Schmidt, S. M. and Kochan, T. A. "Interorganizational Relationships: Patterns and Motivations." *Administrative Science Quarterly,* June 1977, pp. 220–234.

Steers, R. M. "When Is An Organization Effective? A Process Approach." *Organizational Dynamics,* August 1976, pp. 50–63.

Wieland, George F., and Ullrich, Robert A. *Organizations: Behavior, Design, and Change.* Homewood, Ill.: R. D. Irwin, 1976.

Case Study   THE ORGANIZATION OF QUALITY CONTROL

Robert Belham was production manager for Memorand, Inc., a small component parts manufacturer. He had been with the firm for fifteen years and had progressed from foreman to his current position. Robert—Bob as his employees call him—is completely dedicated to the company and its future. He has had numerous opportunities to obtain a higher paying and more prestigious position with competing firms but has chosen to remain with Memorand because he liked his job and the employees.

Kathy Wells is in charge of the quality control section with Memorand and reports directly to Bob. She has been with the company for ten years, having started as a departmental secretary for Mr. Belham. Bob has been highly supportive of her getting a college degree and has allowed her to take time off to attend classes at the University. After several years of attending the University, she recently obtained a degree in industrial management with a specialty in quality control. Because of the patience and support that Mr. Belham gave her, Kathy has a strong loyalty to Bob and to Memorand.

A very difficult situation occurred yesterday that has now caused a severe strain to be placed on the relationship between Bob and Kathy. The firm was awarded a very lucrative contract by CBU with the provision that Memorand would produce the parts within one week. If Memorand completes the order on time, they have the potential for obtaining additional contracts from CBU which would increase overall company sales by at least 10 percent a year. The order comes at the right time because business has been relatively bad for Memorand and there was a good chance that the firm would have to reduce its work force.

As Kathy met with Bob yesterday morning the following conversation took place:

Kathy: "Bob, the quality of the parts we're making for CBU is not as good as those we normally make. I believe we should slow down and inspect all the parts to ensure that we don't send out an inferior product."

Bob: "Are the parts below standard?"

Kathy: "No, but there are a lot of marginal parts being produced. I believe that if we are to improve our chances of obtaining additional orders we must slow down the production line."

Bob: "If we slow down the production line, we won't make the deadline we promised CBU. If we don't make the deadline most likely Memorand will not even have a chance to receive follow-up contracts. I expect you to see to it the production schedule is met."

After receiving such firm demand, Kathy left the office. She felt she was right but didn't know what to do.

Questions

1. How would you reorganize the relationship of the production department and the quality control section to ensure that the conflict experienced by Kathy and Bob would not occur in the future?

2. If you agree with Kathy, what do you think she should do? Discuss.

3. Do you believe Bob was correct in his assessment of the situation? Discuss.

Case Study

MATERIALS ORGANIZATION AT NEWCO MANUFACTURING

Tom Johnson, the newly employed materials manager for the Newco Manufacturing Company, was concerned about the lack of organization in his department. Newco was a small company of 250 employees that manufactured small electrical motors. Mr. Johnson reported to the vice-president of manufacturing, Charles McDowell, and had fifteen people in his department performing such functions as stocking, receiving, inventory control, purchasing, and outside sales.

Because the workflow was not very predictable, the previous materials manager told the department's personnel to do whatever they thought necessary. This would involve working the parts issue windows while mechanics were ordering parts, stocking the parts bins when time permitted, receiving parts when deliveries were made, and shipping orders to customers. Employees answered the phone and handled outside sales as required. Employee complaints had been frequent regarding such matters as inadequate pay, unclear work assignments, and lack of competent leadership.

Tom had received a rather detailed account about the materials operation from his boss, Mr. McDowell. McDowell described the materials department as performing very poorly and attributed this to a lack of overall direction, ineffective organization, and incompetent personnel. McDowell described several of the department's personnel as "dope heads" or "long hairs" who did as little work as possible. The turnover rate had been in excess of 200 percent per year for the past three years. McDowell suggested that Johnson "clean house" by firing most of the employees in the department and start with a fresh crew.

Johnson was obviously shaken by the comments made by Mr. McDowell and the complaints of the personnel in the department and considered finding a new position. However, he chose not to leave the company until he had given the assignment his best efforts for at least a few months.

Questions

1. Using concepts and principles discussed in this chapter, what actions would you recommend that Mr. Johnson take to improve the materials department?
2. What type organization chart would you recommend Mr. Johnson develop?
3. Should Mr. Johnson "clean house" as suggested by Mr. McDowell?

Chapter
6

Staffing the Organization

LEARNING OBJECTIVES

After completing this chapter you should be able to

1. Describe the importance of the staffing function of management.
2. Identify the components of a human resources system.
3. Explain the process of determining the personnel needs of the organization and be able to define the various aspects of the staffing process.
4. State the legal requirements that must be met in staffing an organization and be able to identify the major provisions of federal laws affecting the selection process.
5. Explain each phase of the recruitment and selection process.
6. Describe the special concerns in selecting managerial personnel.

Graham Johnston, the personnel manager for National Insurance Company, was faced with a difficult problem of trying to recruit programmers and systems analysts. The data processing center employed a total of forty-five people, including ten programmers and four systems analysts. During the past six months, seven programmers and three systems analysts have quit for better positions. The people who have departed National were experienced and competent in their positions. A major reason given for leaving the company was a better salary and greater advancement opportunity. Because of the shortage of experienced programmers and analysts, the replacements hired by the company possess little prior experience. This situation has caused the data processing center to continuously run behind schedule.

Lynn Marlow had recently been promoted to division personnel manager with the Northwest Tire Manufacturing Company. One of her first assignments was to recruit several recent college graduates for the company's manager training program. Lynn had recently received a memo from her boss, Bill Furgason, the vice-president of personnel, advising her to be certain to comply with all federal and state laws—especially the affirmative action guidelines—when recruiting and hiring new personnel. Since she had graduated with a degree in Personnel Administration from the University of Washington five years ago, she felt confused about possible recent changes in the laws governing the selection of personnel. When she asked for guidance from Bill, she received the reply, "Compliance is complicated because there are so many laws and guidelines issued from different sources which may be inconsistent or difficult to put into practice. Lynn, you probably need to attend the five-day course on the 'Legal Aspects of Personnel Administration' at the university."

Harry Miller, vice-president of finance at Sure Oil Corporation, had to make a difficult decision about who would be the new accounting manager. Harry was faced with a dilemma—should he promote Dale Barks to the position or should he hire someone from outside the firm? Dale, 29, joined Sure six years ago after completing a B.B.A. in accounting. His initial position was as a junior accountant and he was promoted to a supervisory position two years ago. He's a competent accountant and has performed well as a supervisor. However, Harry is concerned that Dale may not be experienced or mature enough to handle such a responsible position as accounting manager. Harry thinks to himself, "The accounting manager has seven supervisors reporting to him, and after all, there is a lot of difference in supervising accountants and clerical personnel as opposed to a group of managers." Harry also believes that Sure may need some "new blood" in their managerial ranks so he is considering hiring a person from outside the firm to fill the position.

In the above situations, Graham, Lynn, and Harry are each concerned with various phases of the staffing function. The situations illustrate some of the types of challenges that confront managers responsible for making staffing decisions.

The success of a firm depends, to a great extent, on its effectiveness in selecting quality personnel. It does little good to have high market potential for a product or service if capable personnel are not present to direct the effort to achieve the market potential. The need for sound selection and development practices is crucial for all types of organizations—banks, retail stores, manufacturing plants, hospitals, universities, or professional football teams. For example, the success of a professional football organization like the Dallas Cowboys can largely be attributed to the capability of top management of the club as well as the quality of the players drafted into the Cowboy organization. The Cowboy's basic approach to building a winning team has been to select high quality talent via the yearly National Football League Player's Draft, and then training and developing the players selected. The Cowboy's method of building a sound organization and a winning team is in direct contrast to several other teams that recruit older, more experienced personnel. The Cowboy's approach to staffing has been studied by several successful business firms. For instance, Bud McMahon (see the career profile at the beginning of the chapter) has personally visited several of the more successful sports organizations—including the Cowboys—to study their approach to recruitment of professional athletes. Whether an organization is a professional sports team, a business firm, a nonprofit institution, or a government agency, effective recruitment and development of human resources are essential to their success and effectiveness.

A HUMAN RESOURCES SYSTEM

human resources
systems

In recent years, many organizations have developed comprehensive **human resource systems** such as the Kemper Insurance Company approach illustrated in Figure 6.1. At Kemper, the goal is "to have fully effective personnel at all levels of the organization to meet present and future needs." Kemper's Human Resource System includes six major elements and a total of twenty-six components. All twenty-six of the

FIGURE 6.1
Kemper Human Resource System

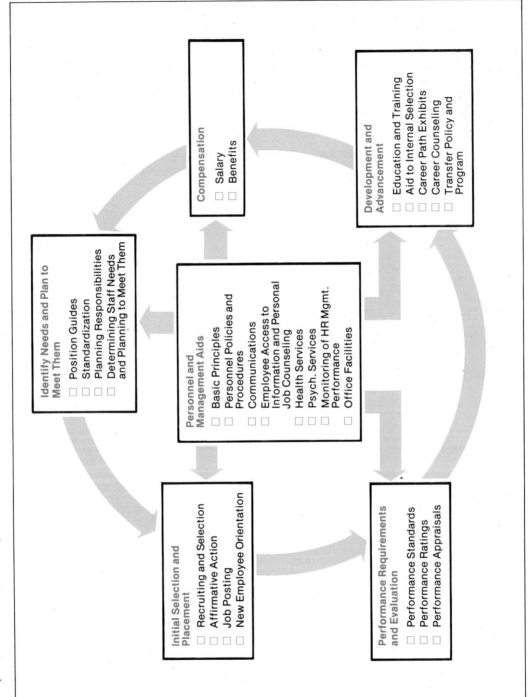

Identify Needs and Plan to Meet Them

☐ Position Guides
☐ Standardization
☐ Planning Responsibilities
☐ Determining Staff Needs and Planning to Meet Them

Compensation

☐ Salary
☐ Benefits

Development and Advancement

☐ Education and Training
☐ Aid to Internal Selection
☐ Career Path Exhibits
☐ Career Counseling
☐ Transfer Policy and Program

Personnel and Management Aids

☐ Basic Principles
☐ Personnel Policies and Procedures
☐ Communications
☐ Employee Access to Information and Personal
☐ Job Counseling
☐ Health Services
☐ Psych. Services
☐ Monitoring of HR Mgmt. Performance
☐ Office Facilities

Initial Selection and Placement

☐ Recruiting and Selection
☐ Affirmative Action
☐ Job Posting
☐ New Employee Orientation

Performance Requirements and Evaluation

☐ Performance Standards
☐ Performance Ratings
☐ Performance Appraisals

Used with the permission of Kemper Insurance Companies.

components are integrated into a coordinated management system consisting of the following key areas:

1. Identification of needs and plans to meet them
2. Recruitment, selection, and placement of personnel
3. Performance, requirements, and evaluation
4. Training, development, and advancement
5. Compensation
6. Personnel and management aids

A detailed study of each component in the Kemper Human Resource System is beyond the purpose of this chapter. However, it is important to recognize the scope of a total personnel system in today's complex business organization. The remainder of this chapter is concerned with the first two components of a human resource system—the assessment of personnel needs and recruitment of personnel.

INSIGHTS TO SUCCESS

I do not believe there is, nor do I believe there should be, a clearly delineated track for promotion. When there is, it seems that the person who gets himself on that track and heads upward gets the feeling he has it made. This is followed by a noticeable reduction in productivity and personal growth.

M. W. TAYLOR, Vice-President—Maintenance, Continental Airlines

---

THE STAFFING PROCESS: ASSESSING REQUIREMENTS

In the final analysis, personnel selection involves choosing people who meet the requirements of a job. The selection process is not an easy task as there are many factors that must be considered. For example, a manager must forecast current and future personnel needs as well as determine the appropriate methods or process to recruit and select new employees. Also, the organization must comply with numerous federal, state, and local legal requirements that govern the selection process. In addition, the performance of each individual employed by the organization should make contributions toward the achievement of the objectives of the firm. This is exemplified by the comments of Mr. C. Richard Blundell, Vice-President of General Foods, Inc.

MR. W. L. (BUD) McMAHON

Vice-President of Salaried Personnel
Corning Glass Works

CORNING As vice-president of salaried personnel for Corning Glass Works, Mr. W. L. (Bud) McMahon is responsible for approximately 9,000 salaried employees located throughout the world. Twenty years in various personnel assignments provided the experience to progress to this position of responsibility within Corning Glass Works.

Bud received his B.S. from St. Bonaventure University and his M.S. from the University of Pittsburgh. After a few years as the company's industrial hygienist, he was assigned to help initiate the Management Development Department. From there he was appointed to the Research and Engineering Division as a personnel manager and later promoted to manager of manpower development of the corporate staff. He was appointed a vice-president in 1971.

In response to a question on critical decisions he has made, he quickly identified the time in 1975 when Corning was confronted with the need to follow a retrenchment strategy. Because of the general economic conditions, management found it necessary to terminate a high percentage of the firm's managerial, technical, and professional employees. These decisions were especially difficult because Corning is a "close" company in small communities and involved in the reduction. Bud says, "This was an extremely traumatic experience, but Corning provided very generous assistance in placing the employees that were separated. The company received national recognition and praise for its innovative out placement program for employees who were terminated. I hope I never have to experience this type of thing again."

Mr. McMahon feels that "a successful corporation devotes as much—or more—time to managing its people as it does its money and technology." Bud believes,

Providing that the basic incentives are competitive, clarity of corporate and individual business objectives becomes essential in order to establish authority and responsibility in the decision-making process. Achieving this end in a multi-business, worldwide corporation is a difficult, but essential, task if the goal is to delegate more complete responsibility to all levels of management.

Bud believes that the key to success is the ability to make the informal system work for you.

It is vital that the personnel selection process in today's complex business environment have clearly established goals and objectives which have been agreed to and supported by top management of the enterprise. The personnel function must conduct its role in both a leadership and an anticipatory mold if it is to be effective as a resource in the achievement of the overall objectives of the enterprise.

Figure 6.2 illustrates the basic elements of the staffing process. It is important to note the staffing process begins with a careful review of the organization's objectives prior to the specific analysis of the work requirements and forecast of specific personnel needs.

MANPOWER PLANNING

manpower planning

The staffing process starts with a careful forecast of manpower required to accomplish organizational objectives. **Manpower planning** is "necessary to assure that the organization will have the right numbers and kinds of people available when and where they are needed to perform useful work."[1] Manpower planning, when performed properly can do the following:

1. Enable management to anticipate shortages and surpluses of labor allowing the development of plans for avoiding or correcting problems before they become serious.
2. Permit forecasts of recruitment needs in terms of both the numbers and types of skills sought.
3. Help in the analysis of sources of supply of labor in order to focus recruitment efforts on the most likely supply sources.
4. Provide for identification of replacements or "back-up" for present key managers from either inside or outside the organization.
5. Integrate manpower plans with financial plans and forecasts.[2]

JOB ANALYSIS

job analysis

Once manpower plans have been developed, the next phase in the staffing process is to determine the human qualifications required to perform the jobs. The process to accomplish this is **job analysis.** It involves determining the responsibilities and operations of a job leading to the development

---

1. Lewis E. Albright, "Staffing Policies and Strategies," *ASPA Handbook of Personnel and Industrial Relations,* edited by Dale Yoder and Herbert G. Heneman, Vol. 1. (Washington, D.C.: Bureau of National Affairs, 1974), pp. 4–21.
2. Ibid.

FIGURE 6.2
The Staffing Process

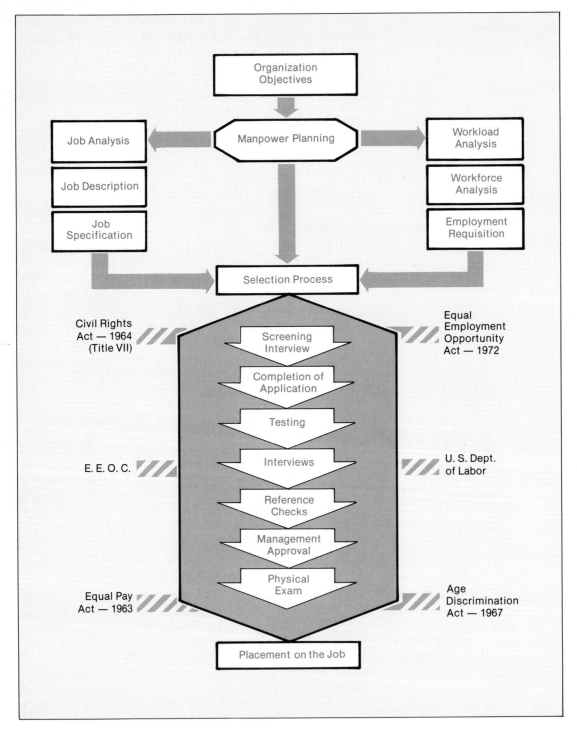

of a job description. There are several methods that may be used in conducting job analysis including the following:

1. Observations of and interviews with present employees performing the jobs
2. Questionnaires completed by present employees or supervisors of the work
3. Analysis by experts
4. A diary of activities performed by present employees

JOB DESCRIPTION

job description

The **job description** is a product of the job analysis process. As shown in Figure 6.3, a job description summarizes the purpose, principal duties, and responsibilities of a job. A job description includes statements on the following items:

1. duties to be performed
2. supervision given and received
3. relationships with other jobs
4. equipment and materials needed
5. physical working conditions

Job descriptions facilitate the recruitment process by clarifying the specific nature of objectives and responsibilities of jobs. Job descriptions are also a helpful tool in the orientation and training of new employees. While job descriptions exist in many large firms, managers sometimes do not understand or use them properly. For instance, some managers believe that having job descriptions restricts management's flexibility and creativity in staffing the organization. However, to be useful to the manager, job descriptions must be translated into a statement of human requirements.

JOB SPECIFICATION

job specification

The statement of the minimum acceptable human qualities necessary to perform the job is the **job specification.** The job specification pinpoints such characteristics required for the job as

1. education
2. experience
3. personality
4. physical abilities

FIGURE 6.3
Job Description: Manager, Fleet Equipment Fabrication

JOB TITLE: Manager, Fleet Equipment Fabrication

BASIC FUNCTION:

This position is accountable for the effective management of the Fleet Equipment Fabrication Department. This department produces the service equipment required by the company's field activities.

DIMENSIONS:

Sales: The mill door cost of the equipment produced per year is $4.5 MM

Personnel: Two exempt and one-hundred non-exempt

Payroll: $0.8 MM

NATURE AND SCOPE:

This position, along with the Plant Manager, Manager of Quality Control, Manager of Production Control, Manager of Manufacturing Engineering, Manager of Materials and Building Engineer reports to the Vice-President of Manufacturing.

The Fleet Equipment Fabrication Department is responsible for the manufacture of all of the service equipment used by the company in support of its field operations and for the manufacture of similar equipment sold to customers. This department procures all of its own operating supplies including raw material, paint, welding supplies, nuts, bolts, etc., and maintains its own inventory of finished goods.

The incumbent is responsible for insuring that orders placed upon his department are met in accordance with acceptable delivery and quality. Because the work centers are involved in fabrication and the products utilized for this operation are purchased parts, the incumbent's job is complicated by uncontrollable facets such as delivery, quality and diversity of these required items. He must continually attempt to achieve a work center job schedule to insure sufficient work for all areas and small backlogs.

The incumbent's job is further challenged by the evolution and substitution of equipment fabricated. This constitutes a low volume, highly diversified conglomerate of components to be ordered, stocked and assembled— where work load is determined by component availability rather than a firm schedule.

The position of Manager, Fleet Equipment Fabrication acts with relatively complete freedom within the broad policy structure as established by the Vice-President of Manufacturing and has the following people reporting directly to him:

Project Coordinator (1):

Assists the Manager and acts for him in his absence. General functions include insuring continuity of work flow through the various production processes.

Coordinating all projects. Working out material substitutions with vendors, to insure that the new product fits application. Assists the shop foreman where required.

Materials Supervisor (1):

Insure through stock monitoring and updating, that sufficient stockage is maintained. Is also accountable for issuing and accounting for usage.

Shop Foreman (1):

Directs all personnel activities within the fabrication area. These duties are: Monitoring and distributing CCU work loads that will satisfy delivery needs (date and quantity), rescheduling project requirements that vary from program, in process and final inspection and counseling.

Recommends new fabrication tools and directs maintenance for specific field problems.

Fleet Secretary (1):

This position provides administrative and secretarial assistance to all positions shown above.

Contacts made by the Manager, Fleet Equipment Fabrication will include all of the various departments within the company, many of the component suppliers who supply Fleet inventory as well as machinery and equipment suppliers and others.

Those internal contacts are: **Engineering** to clarify designs and/or offer suggestions regarding same. **Data Processing** to update, alter or initiate programs. **Sales** to receive assistance on priority, order clarification and substitutions. **Payroll** to resolve any problems involved. **Purchasing** to expedite, change specifications and quantity problems. **Production Control** coordinating plant furnished equipment. **O.C.G.** scheduling.

Skills required in this position will include proficiency in mechanical engineering with strong background in administration preferred and with some knowledge of company field activities.

PRINCIPAL ACCOUNTABILITIES:

1. Selects and staffs his department.
2. Devises operational organization and staffs same.
3. Originates policy and procedures for his department within corporate guidelines.
4. Appraises performance and makes salary adjustments.
5. Supervises the technical personnel development program.
6. Develops budgetary requirements of personnel and facility needs for one to five years.
7. Monitors operating statement for expense guidance.
8. Personally guides jobs requiring special handling because of technical and/or time requirements.
9. Forecasts future need of departments including facilities, personnel and equipment.

It should be noted that the Civil Rights Act of 1964 prohibits specific requirements in terms of race, color, national origin, religion, or sex if the organization cannot prove that the characteristic is necessary for job success. The job specification is the standard to which the applicant is compared in each step of the recruitment procedure.

WORKLOAD ANALYSIS

Not only must we know the type of person required for a job but also the number of people necessary to meet organizational needs. Determining the number of personnel needed by an organization requires a prediction of future workloads.

workload analysis

Workload analysis involves estimating the type and volume of work that needs to be performed if the organization is to achieve its objective. Workload analysis requires that forecasts of work to be accomplished be prepared. These forecasts are then translated into person-hour requirements. Work programs are often stated in terms of units produced, products assembled, boxes packed, customer calls, vouchers processed, and so forth. These are then converted into the number of person-hours by means of time study of the units, or by utilizing average past work experience. For example, we may conclude that a specified number of products to be produced will require 1,000 person-hours of work during a forty-hour work week. Thus, by dividing the 1,000 person-hours required by the forty hours in the work week would indicate a need for twenty-five workers.

WORKFORCE ANALYSIS

After determining the number of workers required, a workforce analysis is needed. **Workforce analysis** consists of identifying the skills of current personnel to determine if workloads can be accomplished by these employees. In some organizations a computerized personnel data bank (Manpower Information System) assists in providing this information. The following is typical of the information included:

workforce analysis

1. Personal History—age, sex, marital status, etc.
2. Skills—education, job experience, training, etc.
3. Special Qualifications—memberships in professional organizations, special achievements
4. Salary and Job History—present salary, past salary, dates of raises, and various positions held

5. Company Data—benefit plan, retirement information, and seniority
6. Capacity of Individual—test scores, health
7. Special Preferences of the Individual—geographic location, work assignments

EMPLOYMENT REQUISITION

In most large organizations, an employment requisition is issued whenever a job becomes available. The requisition is the product of an analysis of a company's personnel requirements and must be closely coordinated with the job specification. In firms where job specifications are detailed, employment requisitions are usually brief, typically including such information as the job title, starting date, pay scale, and a brief summary of principal duties.

LEGAL ASPECTS OF STAFFING

Before discussing the process of selecting personnel, a summary of major federal legislation and its impact on the staffing process will be presented. Table 6.1 provides a brief summary of several of the more significant federal laws affecting the recruitment and selection practices of organiza-

TABLE 6.1
Major Federal Legislation Affecting The Staffing Process*

Law	Date	Major Provisions	Enforcement Agency
Equal Pay Act	1963	Prohibits wage discrimination on the basis of sex (Act was an amendment to the FLSA)	Wage and Hour Division of the U. S. Department of Labor
Civil Rights Act	1964	Prohibits discrimination in employment on basis of race, color, religion, sex, or national origin	Equal Employment Opportunity Commission (EEOC)
Age Discrimination Act Amended	1967 1978	Prohibits discrimination on basis of age—provides specific protection for people 40–70 years of age	Wage and Hour Division of U. S. Department of Labor
Equal Employment Opportunity Act	1972	Increased enforcement power of the EEOC	Equal Employment Opportunity Commission (EEOC)

* For a more indepth appreciation of major federal legislation affecting the staffing process see James M. Higgins, "A Manager's Guide To The Equal Employment Opportunity Laws," *Personnel Journal*, August 1976, pp. 406–412.

tions. Every manager involved in selecting new employees must comply with federal, state, and local laws in staffing the organization. The impact of recent federal laws is illustrated by the following comments of W. L. McMahon, Vice-President of Corning Glass:

> Recruitment of personnel in today's organization requires careful consideration of federal laws. This has greatly increased the complexity of selecting qualified personnel at all levels in the company. We must comply with several equal employment opportunity laws often without a clear understanding of how to comply. Compliance is further complicated by the fact that guidelines may have been issued from different sources. The guidelines are often presented in different formats and may provide information that is inconsistent or difficult to implement.

EQUAL PAY ACT OF 1963

The Equal Pay Act prohibits wage discrimination on the basis of sex. The legislation was designed to prevent organizations from paying a female employee less than a male for equivalent work on jobs requiring equal skills and effort, and jobs that are performed under similar working conditions. The Act is enforced by the Wage and Hour Division of the U. S. Department of Labor.

Initially the law applied only to nonsupervisory employees covered by overtime provisions of the Fair Labor Standards Act of 1938. However, in 1972, the Act was extended to include executive, administrative, and professional employees.

In recent years, the number of complaints filed with the Wage and Hour Division has increased dramatically primarily as a result of the Women's Rights Movement. During a recent year, some 17,000 women were awarded a total of $4.6 million in back wages because of violations in the 1963 Equal Pay Act.[3]

CIVIL RIGHTS ACT OF 1964

The Civil Rights Act has had a very significant impact on personnel selection. Title VII of the Act prohibits discrimination on the basis of race, color, religion, sex, or national origin in selection, promotion, and other areas of employment.

The Equal Employment Opportunity Commission (EEOC) was established by the Civil Rights Act to seek compliance with the law and to

---

3. The Conference Board, *The Personnel Function: Changing Objectives and Organization* (New York: The National Industrial Conference Board, 1977), p. 5.

investigate alleged discrimination in employment. Employment procedures include recruitment, interviewing, advertising, application forms, tests, pay, training, and other areas. The EEOC issues compliance guidelines and sometimes requires employers to develop and implement affirmative action programs designed to increase the number of minority and female employees.

The federal courts have had the primary responsibility for interpreting and enforcing the Act. Court decisions have significantly affected the personnel selection policies and practices. Several court decisions have clarified and strengthened a strict interpretation of the Civil Rights Act.

In *Phillips* vs. *Martin Marietta*, the court ruled that the company had discriminated against a women who was denied a job because she had young children. In the *Myart* vs. *Motorola* case, a black man was denied a job because of a low score on an intelligence test. The court told Motorola that they could use the test only if the test was a predictor of job success.

In a highly significant case, *Griggs, et.al.* vs. *Duke Power Company*, the U. S. Supreme Court ruled that pre-employment requirements including tests must be job related.[4]

THE AGE DISCRIMINATION IN EMPLOYMENT ACT OF 1967 AS AMENDED IN 1978

This law protects individuals between the ages of forty and seventy years of age from discrimination in employment—selection, retention, promotion, compensation, and other conditions of employment. Like the Equal Pay Act, the Age Discrimination Act is enforced by the Wage and Hour Division of the U. S. Labor Department.

EQUAL EMPLOYMENT OPPORTUNITY ACT OF 1972

This law significantly increased the enforcement power of the EEOC by authorizing EEOC to initiate suits against employers for noncompliance with the law. The 1972 EEO Act also extended coverage to state and municipal employees and to employees in educational institutions, and reduced the number of employees necessary to bring a company under its jurisdiction from twenty-five to fifteen.[5]

The above legislation, in addition to several Presidential Executive Orders, prohibits discrimination in all employment practices on the basis

4. William F. Glueck, *Personnel: A Diagnostic Approach* (Dallas: Business Publications, Inc., 1974), pp. 189–191.

5. *ASPA Handbook of Personnel and Industrial Relations*, Volume 1, p. 4–109.

of race, color, religion, sex, national origin, or age. If an employer is sued for discrimination in employment, the employer must prove that discrimination was not present. Organizations cannot use selection procedures—tests, interviews, special requirements—unless they are related to the performance of the specific position. Many practices, which in the past were routine, are now illegal or vigorously challenged by the federal

MOST IMPORTANT REASON FOR YOUR FIRM'S SUCCESS

Good key people (employees)

HUGH O'NEILL, Chairman, Leaseway Transportation Corporation

government. The following are guidelines for Equal Employment Personnel Selection Practices:

1. Employment advertising must conform to the requirements for nondiscrimination. Advertisements cannot indicate any preference as to sex, race, age, etc. unless these are bona fide occupational qualifications.
2. Application blanks, tests, and interviews must be related to job requirements.
3. Requirements such as photographs, birth certificates, arrest records, and names of other family members on employment applications are no longer permitted.
4. Marital status and family situation are no longer deemed acceptable recruiting standards.
5. Employers must maintain a variety of records as to the sex and race of on-job applicants as well as employees. For certain job classifications, organizations must supply data to the EEOC on rejection ratios showing minority status and sex of applicants. Data identifying race, national origin or religion of applicants must be kept separate from data used in making selection decisions.

RECRUITMENT AND SELECTION OF PERSONNEL

recruitment

Few activities are more important to an organization than the recruitment and selection of quality personnel. **Recruitment** is the process of searching for prospective employees and stimulating them to apply for available jobs. Personnel recruitment can range from locating individuals within the firm who are qualified to a very sophisticated and extensive executive search. Final selection of employees comes only after careful evaluation of applicants during the various phases of the selection process. Figure 6.4 illustrates the personnel selection process.

Personnel can be recruited using internal and/or external sources of qualified applicants. There are advantages and disadvantages of both internal and external sources of applicants. Internal recruitment or promotion from within is an important source of personnel for positions above the entry level. Promotion from within has several *advantages;* it

1. increases morale of employees;
2. improves the quality of selection since an organization usually has a more complete evaluation of the strengths and weaknesses of internal applicants as opposed to those from outside the firm;

FIGURE 6.4
The Personnel Selection Process

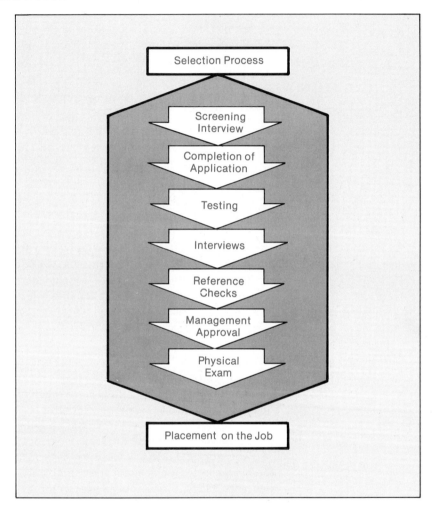

3. motivates present employees to prepare for more responsible positions;

4. attracts better quality of external applicants if chances for promotion from within are good;

5. assists the organization to more fully utilize personnel.

According to William F. Comiskey, a partner with Arthur Young and Company, a large public accounting firm,

A policy of promotion from within is essential if the firm is to attract and retain competent and progressive personnel. Most people want an opportunity for promotion to more responsible jobs; and if this opportunity is not present, they will look elsewhere.

Despite the advantages of internal recruiting, there are several *disadvantages* to be considered. Two of these are the following:

1. There may be an inadequate supply of qualified applicants.
2. Internal sources may lead to inbreeding of ideas—current employees may lack new ideas on how to do a job more effectively.

Richard C. Farr, Vice-President, Corporate Management, Heublein, Inc.; says,

As a general rule, our policy is to fill middle- and upper-level positions internally. However, there may arise a need to hire someone from the outside if the organization needs a person with special experience, knowledge, or skills not available within our company.

External sources of applicants permit an organization to overcome many of the disadvantages of recruiting internally. There are several external means a firm can use in recruiting personnel. Some of these include:

1. Advertisements in newspapers, journals, or on radio or T.V.
2. Public and private employment agencies and executive search firms
3. Recommendations of present employees
4. Recruitment at schools and colleges
5. Unsolicited applicants
6. Labor unions
7. A combination of two or more of the above.

These sources allow the firm to attract a pool of applicants for available positions. At this point, it is necessary to screen these applicants against the hiring requirements.

The ultimate objective of recruitment is to select individuals who are most capable to meet the requirements of the job. This is primarily a matter of comparing applicants' skills, knowledge, and education, to the duties and responsibilities of the job as specified on the **job specification.** This process involves the following phases:

1. preliminary screening interview
2. completion of employment application blank

3. testing
4. interviewing
5. background and reference checks
6. physical exam
7. final selection and induction

A summary of a selection procedure that can be used by a firm is presented in Figure 6.5.

PRELIMINARY SCREENING INTERVIEW

preliminary screening
interview

Preliminary screening interviews are typically used to eliminate the obviously unqualified applicants for reasons such as excessive salary requirements, inadequate education, inability to speak coherently, lack of job related experience or other reasons. An applicant who appears to qualify for a position is asked to complete the employment application.

EMPLOYMENT APPLICATION

employment
application

Almost all organizations use an **employment application** form in selecting new employees. The application collects more objective biographical information about an applicant such as education, work experience, special skills, general background, marital status, and references (see Figure 6.6 for an example of an employment application). Information obtained from the employment application significantly assists managers in selecting quality personnel. Some organizations design and use a weighted application blank by determining relationships between biographical facts and job success. For example, one bank discovered that newly hired secretaries are least likely to quit the job if they are over thirty-five years of age, married, not a college graduate, and have more than three years of experience.[6] Biographical analyses can also be used to predict the quality of job performance. It is important to remember that information requested on an employment application should not lead to discrimination against applicants. Questions referring to an applicant's age, sex, race, religion, national origin, or family status may violate Title VII of the Civil Rights Act of 1964.

6. Stanley R. Novack, "Developing An Effective Application Blank," *Personnel Journal* 49 (May 1970): 421.

FIGURE 6.5
Summary of a Selection Procedure

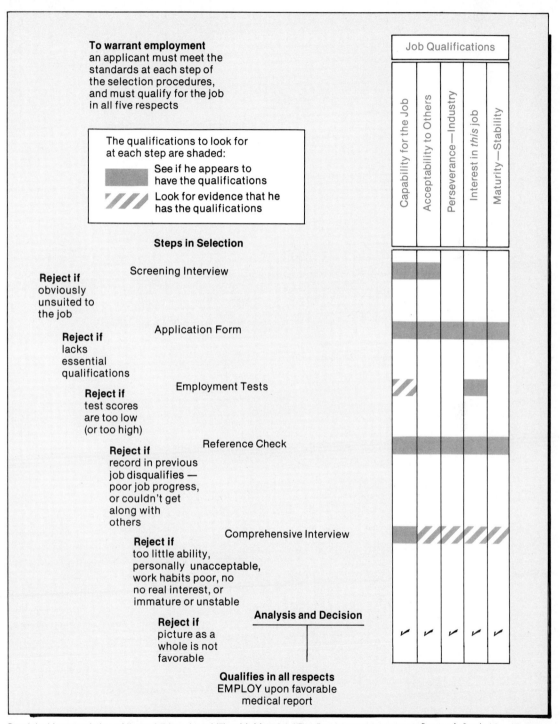

FIGURE 6.6
Employment Application—Otis Engineering Corporation

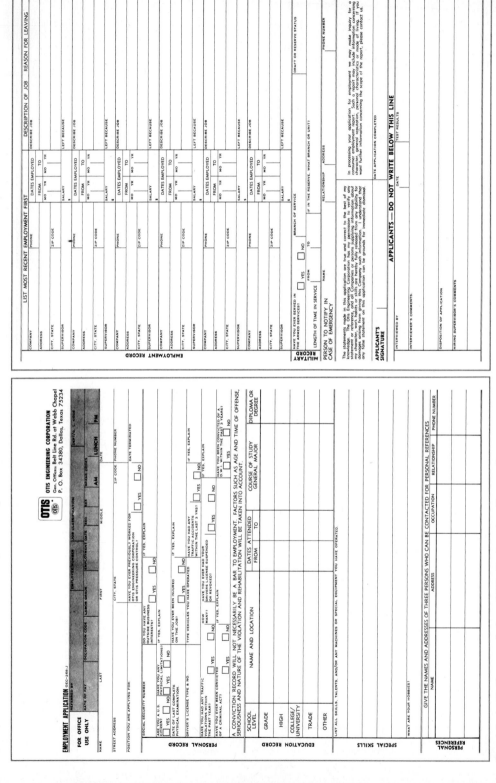

Reprinted with the permission of Otis Engineering Corporation.

TESTING

testing
Traditionally, **testing** has been an integral component in the selection process. Tests have been used to screen applicants in terms of skills, abilities, aptitudes, interest, personality, and attitudes that cannot be objectively judged in other ways. Tests to determine specific skills such as typing or shorthand are in wide use. However, in recent years many organizations have significantly curtailed or eliminated their psychological and intelligence pre-employment testing programs. This has occurred because some tests have been found to be instruments of discrimination against minorities.

Testing is used in screening recruits in some organizations in which one would normally not expect tests to be administered. For example, the Dallas Cowboys and several other National Football League clubs give prospective players an intelligence test prior to the NFL Players Draft. The Cowboys have found the test they use to be a predicator of a player's ability to learn the Cowboys' system and to be successful in the League.

However, if all organizations, large and small, are considered, it is apparent that most are *not* using intelligence and psychological testing. In order to meet legal requirements, tests must possess validity and reliability.

validity
Test **validity** is concerned with the relationship between the score on the test and performance on the job. A test is *valid* if the score on the test is a predicator of job success. Does the test measure what we want to measure? Validity is highly specific in nature. A test may be valid for one objective and invalid for another. For instance, the Otis Test of Mental Ability may be highly valid for measuring abstract intelligence. It certainly will be far less valid in predicting the success of a supervisor.

reliability
Reliability is concerned with the degree of consistency of test results. If a test possesses high reliability, a person tested a second or third time with the same test, under the same conditions will obtain approximately the same score.

An organization choosing to use testing in the employment process should be careful to avoid potential discriminatory aspects of tests and use tests only as an "aid" in the process, not as the determining factor.

INTERVIEWING

interview
The **interview** is the most widely used and probably the most important method of assessing the qualifications of job applicants. In general there

are several objectives to be achieved in interviewing job applicants such as these:

1. assessing potential for advancement
2. determining the ability to get along with others
3. assessing personality
4. determining if the person will fit into the organization.

There are two basic types of interviews: direct (patterned) and unstructured (nondirected). In recent years, there has been increased interest in the use of a directed or patterned interview. In **patterned interviews,** the interviewer follows a predetermined series of questions in interviewing applicants. The interviewer asks questions and records the applicant's responses. The use of a patterned or structured interview usually yields more complete, consistent, and reliable information about an applicant. Also, its use permits the comparison of several applicants and tends to minimize interviewer bias and prejudices.

patterned interview

Unstructured or nondirected interviews have no predetermined interviewing strategy or list of questions. Broad, rather open-ended types of questions such as "Tell me about yourself" are part of the unstructured interview. The unstructured interview may be useful in assessing characteristics of an individual such as ability to communicate, personal values, personality, and other factors.

Other types of interviewing techniques have also been used for special purposes. One of these techniques, the group interview, has been frequently used in the selection of managerial trainees. Group interviews are used where a small group of five or six applicants is observed and evaluated in small group discussions by two or more company managers or interviewers. The panel interview is a situation in which an applicant is interviewed by several people at the same time.

stress interview

The **stress interview** is another approach that is sometimes used in the selection of managers and potential managers. The stress interview attempts to make the applicant defensive by putting pressure on the person in order to observe his or her reactions to stress and tension.

One of the authors, in an early stage of his career, was exposed to a stress interview when he applied for a sales position. The initial interview for the job had gone well, so a second interview was scheduled with the firm's sales manager. On meeting the sales manager, the author was bluntly told he was not qualified for the position. At that point, the author had no idea a stress interview was in progress. The author was put on the defensive, but being a rather confident person, maintained he was the best qualified person for the job. At the end of the two-hour stress interview, the author was offered the job. Not until several months later was it discovered that a stress interview had been conducted and that the job would not have been offered to the author if he had not responded to the *stress* with confidence.

Regardless of the type of method used, the interview is the most important element in the selection of new personnel. Since most managers must rely on interviewing when selecting new employees, and evaluating candidates for promotion, following sound practices is essential. The following guidelines have been found to be helpful in conducting effective interviews:

1. **Plan for the interview**—review job specification and description as well as the applications of candidates.
2. **Create a good climate for interview**—try to establish a friendly, open rapport with the applicant.
3. **Allow sufficient time for an uninterrupted interview.**
4. **Conduct a goal-oriented interview**—seek the information needed to assist in the employment decision.
5. **Avoid certain types of questions**—try not to ask "leading" questions or questions that may imply discrimination.
6. **Seek answers to all questions and check for inconsistencies.**
7. **Record the results of the interview immediately upon completion.**[7]

Over the years, the interview, much like testing, has received considerable criticism concerning its ability to predict success on the job. In interviewing an applicant for employment, many factors influence the decision of the interviewer. For example, the interviewer may allow a first impression of an applicant to unduly influence the outcome of the interview. In a large insurance company, the personnel manager was a great believer in the importance of initial impressions in evaluating applicants for jobs. He placed considerable emphasis on his initial reactions to an applicant's handshake, speed of walking, and eye contact. For male applicants, the personnel manager was careful to observe whether the applicant could pass the "firm handshake," "fast walk," and "eye contact" tests. The manager strongly believed that if the applicant had a "firm handshake" and maintained good eye contact when meeting others as well as the ability to keep up with the personnel manager's walking pace, the applicant was both confident and aggressive. Many managers rely on similar, but sometimes questionable practices in selecting personnel.

Interviews can be instruments of discrimination, and for this reason, they have received close scrutiny by the EEOC in recent years. Charges of possible discrimination have led to an increase in the use of the patterned

---

7. *ASPA Handbook of Personnel and Industrial Relations,* Volume 1, pp. 152–154.

interview as was mentioned above. The patterned or structured interview has significantly higher reliability and validity than other methods of interviewing.

An effective means of assessing the success of an organization's interviewing process is to compare performance of employees with the evaluation of these same employees when they were interviewed for the job. In other words, how effective or valid is the interview in predicting job success?

BACKGROUND AND REFERENCE CHECKS

Once an applicant successfully clears the interviewing "hurdles," the practice of many organizations is to conduct background and reference checks. The purpose of checking a person's background and references is to verify the information provided by the applicant in the interview and on the employment application.

In recent years, thorough and reliable reference checks have often been difficult to obtain because of the Privacy Act of 1974. It is quite likely the reference check will "become a process of verifying that the prospective employee was at a certain place doing a certain job for a specified period of time at a verified compensation level."[8] Under the law, the former employer may be required to obtain a release from the ex-employee to provide information to prospective employers about his or her quality of performance.

MANAGEMENT APPROVAL

In most large organizations, many of the above functions are performed by a personnel department. However, the personnel department does not usually make the final decision as to which person is selected for a particular position. Under most circumstances, the manager or supervisor who will be the immediate superior of the new employee will make the final hiring decision. The selection decision is usually made after interviewing the applicants and reviewing the recommendations of the personnel department. The immediate supervisor knows the needs of his or her unit or department and is in the best position to evaluate the qualifications and characteristics of prospective employees. The supervisor or manager should be able to identify factors in the applicant's background or work experience that would be helpful to the new employee in fitting into the work unit.

8. Lawrence A. Wanger, "Employee Reference Request Revisited," *The Personnel Administrator* 20 (November 1975): 62.

INSIGHTS TO SUCCESS

Regarding the matter of financial reward, I have never, except one time in my career, asked for a pay increase. And that was when I was very young and very new in the company; I had been with the company a couple of years. There were eight or ten of us who had been employed at the same time as engineers. We felt that we had gone a bit long without an increase in salary and recognition. A couple of us were chosen to go in and speak to the boss about a raise. I have never since then asked for a pay raise. I would have to be hurting pretty hard to do it. One might think that, given my salary today, that is an easy thing to say. But my salary wasn't always what it is today.

JAMES E. LEE, President, Gulf Oil Corporation

PHYSICAL EXAMS

After a prospective employee has successfully completed the other phases in the selection process, most organizations require a physical exam. The physical exam has at least these three basic goals:

1. To determine if the applicant can meet the physical demands of the job
2. To provide a record to protect the organization against claims for previously incurred injuries
3. To prevent communicable diseases from entering the firm

PLACEMENT ON THE JOB: ORIENTATION

Once an individual has been selected for a particular position, he or she must receive an orientation to the organization. Orientation is the process of introducing the new employee to the organization. Every new employee goes through an orientation period regardless of whether the firm has a formal orientation program. The new recruit must "learn the ropes" or "rules of the game" if he is to succeed. Much of the new employee orientation takes place on an informal basis—during coffee breaks, at lunch, or during work—by interactions with employees often referred to as "old timers." However, most organizations have formal orientation programs designed to acquaint new personnel with the areas as shown in Figure 6.7.

FIGURE 6.7
Orientation Outline

1. History and nature of the business

2. Goals of the company

3. Basic products/services provided by the firm

4. Organization structure

5. Policies, procedures, and rules covering such areas as:
   a. Work schedules
   b. Salaries and payment periods
   c. Physical facilities
   d. Attendance and absenteeism
   e. Working conditions and safety standards
   f. Lunch and coffee breaks
   g. Discipline and grievance
   h. Parking

6. Company benefits
   a. Insurance programs
   b. Pension and/or profit sharing plans
   c. Recreational programs—bowling, tennis, golf, etc.
   d. Vacations and holidays

7. Opportunities
   a. Advancement, promotion
   b. Suggestion systems

8. Specific departmental responsibilities
   a. Department functions
   b. Job duties/responsibilities/authority
   c. Introduction to other employees in work group

SPECIAL CONSIDERATIONS
IN SELECTING MANAGERIAL PERSONNEL

In recruiting and selecting nonmanagerial personnel it is usually possible to use more objective factors in identifying potentially successful employees. However, more subjective judgment is often involved in selecting managerial personnel. In selecting managers, concern is typically focused on an evaluation of skills, abilities, attitudes, and characteristics many of which are intangible. Some of these include:

1. Planning skills
2. Communication ability

3. Decision-making skills
4. Organizing ability
5. Motivation and leadership skills
6. Conceptual skills—an overall understanding of the organization
7. Adaptability to change
8. Qualities such as self-confidence, aggressiveness, and empathy

The recruitment and development of quality managerial personnel is essential to the continuing success of every organization. Because of this, organizations must be concerned with determining needs for managerial personnel and identifying persons with managerial potential.

DETERMINING EXECUTIVE NEEDS

Decisions concerning the number of executives required by an organization involve a comparison of (1) predicted future needs and (2) present inventory of talent. Determining needs for managerial personnel requires an "inventory" of personnel presently available within the organization. Inventory is a term often used in relation to the counting of tangible objects such as raw materials, goods in process, and finished products. In the inventory of managerial and executive talent, however, the items are generally intangible. The inventory is not simply a counting of heads; it includes a cataloging of present and potential abilities and attitudes. It is an assessment not only of skills, experience, and abilities, but also personal motivation. It sometimes happens that a person who appears to be properly prepared for a promotion indicates a desire to transfer, to change occupational area, or to remain on the present job.

In making up the inventory, a decision must be made as to the personnel to be included. Certainly, present lower- and middle-management personnel will be included. In some companies all salaried personnel compensated on a monthly or semimonthly basis are included. Each first-level supervisor may be asked to submit recommendations of those deemed to have the potential for advancement. For each individual included, detailed information must be gathered to supplement and update existing data, such as education, experience, performance ratings, health, psychological test results, recreational interests, hobbies, and civic groups. Such data can be computerized in order that (1) assessments as to current adequacy of talent reservoirs can be made, and (2) searches can be made to fill particular vacancies arising. Figure 6.8 illustrates the Xerox Corporation's approach to such an inventory. The Xerox system provides management with personal history and performance data on present personnel who may be qualified to fill anticipated vacancies resulting from retirements, resignations, termination, promotions, or expansion.

FIGURE 6.8
Manpower Information System

Top form (right portion):

NAME	HIRE DATE	DATE PREPARED
Mary R. Wells	9/1/66	6/1/76

Career Objectives

Manager Branch Operations in two years.

Vice President and Region General Manager in five years.

Check one ☐ Not interested in promotional move at this time but would like to develop within current job   ☒ Would like additional responsibility   ☐ Would like to change career path

Education

Washington University 9/53–9/57 St. Louis, Mo.	Business Admin Economics	B.A.
St. Louis University 6/57–12/59 St. Louis, Mo.	Masters Business Admin	MBA

Xerox Courses: Field Management Action Workshop, FED

Other Data

Graduated with honors from Washington University

Speak German fluently

Pre-Xerox Experience

| 12/59 – 2/63 | Sales Rep., Brunswick Corp. St. Louis, Mo. Directed sales of Hospital equipment to dealers. |
| 2/63 – 9/66 | Sales Manager, Brunswich Corp. St. Louis, Mo. Directed Medical sales team. |

Xerox Experience

9/66 – 3/69	Territory Rep. Xerox St. Louis, Mo.
3/69 – 3/70	Financial Planning Analyst Xerox Rochester Provide support to sales planning through close liaison with finance on sales force size and impact. Create data base for sales analysis system.
3/70 – 3/72	Market Manager Xerox Rochester Direct responsibility for development of marketing plans and approach to the automotive industry. Potential market 4 million dollars. Increase 10% realized in first six months of program.
5/72 – 9/74	Branch Manager II Xerox Denver, Co.
9/74 – Pres.	Branch Manager I Xerox San Fran., Cal.

● IF ADDITIONAL SPACE IS REQUIRED, USE EXTRA SHEET AND CHECK HERE ☐

● WOULD YOU RELOCATE? ☒ YES ☐ NO

NOTE: Your Manager will provide you with a complete copy of your HRP after it has been validated.
Form 56598 (3/76) Printed in U.S.A.

Bottom form:

NAME	EEO INFORMATION PLEASE CIRCLE	EMPLOYEE NO.	Previous Reviews		
Mary R. Wells	1 2 3 4 5 M (F)	3514	YR	RATING	
			5/74	4	

TITLE Branch Manager I   MONTHLY MIDPOINT 4186   12/74 RATING 3

ORGANIZATION LOCATION San Francisco, Western Region   MOS. IN POSITION 20   6/75 RATING 4

PERFORMANCE APPRAISAL

1 Unsatisfactory Performance	2 Meets Minimum Performance	3 Normal, Reasonable Expected Level of Performance	4 Consistently Exceeds Expected Level of Performance (X)	5 Exceptional Performance

Provide Summary Comments

Mary always meets or exceeds job targets. She is an aggressive, highly results-oriented manager who works well under heavy job demands. She motivates her people well and promotes strong team spirit; however, she must allow her people greater participation in the decision-making process. In this way, they will be provided with an optimum of development related experience. Mary does not try to solve problems with a status quo approach. Her approaches to problems are creative. She assimilates new concepts readily and acts decisively. She is flexible and cooperative and requires little direct supervision to accomplish even the most complex tasks.

APPRAISAL OF PROMOTABILITY – CHECK ONE

A Immediately Eligible for Promotion (X)	B Eligible in 12 Months after Further Development	C Eligible in 24 Months after Further Development	D Recommend Transfer for Further Development	E Not Eligible in 24 Months, Should Continue to Develop in Present Job	F Recommend Less Responsibility	G Too Soon to Appraise

Suggested Positions
Use exact Titles and Organization

	Title	When Ready		
		Now / Current 1 year / 2 years	Now / Previous HRP 1 year / 2 years	
1	Manager, Branch Operations, Region	X	X	
2	Regional Sales Manager, Region	X	X	
3				

My signature indicates I have held a Career Guidance Session and discussed Career Objectives with my subordinate.

DATE PREPARED 6/1/76   PREPARED BY _Charles G. White_   REVIEWED BY _John M. Columbus_   DATE _6/30/76_

I have reviewed my HRP and discussed the contents with my manager. My signature means that I have been advised of my performance and appraisal of promotability, it does not necessarily imply that I agree with the HRP's contents.

EMPLOYEE SIGNATURE _Mary R. Wells_

EMPLOYEE NAME Mary R. Wells

DATA FOR KEYPUNCHING

						DEVELOPMENTAL OR PROMOTIONAL POSITIONS & WHEN READY								
EMPLOYEE NUMBER 4	AOP 5	JOB CODE 1 6	YRS 13	PREV HRP 14	JOB CODE 2 15	YRS 21	PREV HRP 22	JOB CODE 3 24	YRS 30	YRS 31	PREV HRP 32
3 5 1 4	B	H 0 0 2 5 1 5	0	1	H 0 0 4 0 2 4	2					

Used with the permission of Xerox, Inc.

Many companies maintain *back-up* organizational charts to show listings of available talent for each key managerial position in the organization. For example, Associated Dry Goods, Inc., a large retailing firm with over 51,000 employees and sales of $1.5 billion, utilizes such a *back-up* chart. This company has an organizational chart that includes the names of at least two individuals as replacements for each key position. The chart also includes an assessment of eligibility for promotion and targeted for certain key positions.

TECHNIQUES FOR IDENTIFYING MANAGERIAL TALENT

Identifying individuals with potential executive talent has become an increasingly important activity in large organizations. In general, the activity has taken these two directions:

1. Determining the significant personal characteristics or behaviors that seem to predict managerial success
2. Establishing managerial talent assessment centers

Personal Characteristics

Over the years, there has been considerable interest in determining the personal characteristics related to managerial success. Major companies such as AT&T, Sears, General Electric, Standard Oil, and many others have engaged in research within their firms to identify a series of traits or characteristics that were necessary for success. The studies related measures of job performance such as productivity, salary level, and quality of work of successful managers with personal characteristics and attitudes of these managers. Some of the characteristics of managers included in these studies were: grades in college, level of self-confidence, organized orderly thought, personal values of a practical and economic nature, intelligence, nonverbal reasoning, and general attitudes. Research at AT&T found a significant relationship between grades in college and salary level achieved. In a study of 10,000 managers in the Bell System, it was found that 51 percent of those in the top 10 percent of their college class were located in the top third of the salary levels in the company. For the most part, studies of personal characteristics of managers have not yielded accurate predictions of managerial success.

Assessment Center

assessment center

In an effort to improve managerial selection, a second technique for identifying talent has become popular in recent years. This approach is the **assessment center** designed to provide for the systematic evaluation of the potential of individuals for future management positions. In the typical assessment center, a series of activities is designed to test the potential manager's skills, abilities, attitudes, and judgment. Figure 6.9 illustrates a three-day assessment center that uses a number of different bases on which to evaluate executive candidates. The assessment center approach was introduced to American business in the mid-1950s by the American

FIGURE 6.9
Typical Assessment Center Schedule

Day 1	Orientation of dozen candidates
	Break-up into groups of four to play a *Management Game* (observe and assess organizing ability, financial acumen, quickness of thinking efficiency under stress, adaptability, leadership)
	Psychological Testing (measure and assess verbal and numerical abilities, reasoning, interests, and attitudes) and/or **Depth Interviews** (assess motivation)
	Leaderless Group Discussion (observe and assess aggressiveness, persuasiveness, expository skill, energy, flexibility, self-confidence)
Day 2	**In-Basket Exercise** (observe and assess decision making under stress, organizing ability, memory and ability to interrelate events, preparation for decision making, ability to delegate, concern for others)
	Role-playing of Employment or Performance Appraisal Interview (observe and assess sensitivity to others, ability to probe for information, insight, empathy)
	Group Roles in preparation of a budget (observe and assess collaboration abilities, financial knowledge, expository skill, leadership, drive)
Day 3	**Individual Case Analyses** (observe expository skill, awareness of problems, background information possessed for problems, typically involving marketing, personnel, accounting, operations, and financial elements)
	Obtainment of **Peer Ratings** from all candidates
	Staff assessors/meet to discuss and rate all candidates
Weeks later	Manager, with assessor experience, meets with each candidate to discuss assessment with counseling concerning career guides and areas to develop

Source Edwin B. Flippo and Gary M. Munsinger, *Management,* 4th ed. (Boston: Allyn and Bacon, Inc., 1978), p. 237.

Telephone and Telegraph Company and has grown in popularity since. More than 200 large companies now utilize assessment centers.

A survey of thirty-three companies reveals that the three most widely used assessment techniques are in-basket exercises (thirty-one firms), business games (thirty firms), and leaderless group discussion (thirty-one firms).[9] An in-basket consists of a set of notes, messages, telephone calls, letters, and reports the candidate is expected to handle within a period of one or two hours. The candidate's decisions can be rated by assessors with respect to such abilities as willingness to take action and organizing of interrelated events.

A business game is a competitive simulation where teams are required to make decisions concerning production, marketing, purchasing, and finance in competition with each other. The leaderless group discussion assesses participant activities in taking the lead in discussion, influencing others, mediating arguments, speaking effectively, and summarizing and classifying issues. In addition, various other exercises are often designed to fit the firm's particular situation. For example, J. C. Penney utilizes the "Irate Customer Phone Call," made by an assessor, in order to rate the candidate's ability to control emotions, demonstrate tact, and satisfy the complaint.[10] Psychological tests and depth interviewing are frequently used techniques but generally show lower levels of accuracy in predicting future success. Personality tests, in particular, appear to be the weakest predicator.

In determining the predictive accuracy of the assessment center approach, the initial study at AT&T was most impressive. Assessor ratings were not communicated to company management for a period of eight years in order not to contaminate the results. In a sample of fifty-five candidates who achieved the middle-management ranks during that period, the center correctly predicted 78 percent of them.[11] Of seventy-three persons who did not progress beyond the first level of management, 95 percent were correctly predicted by the assessment staff. As a result, this company has maintained its centers, processing an average of 10,000 candidates a year. Reviewing ratings and actual progress of 5,943 personnel over a ten-year period demonstrated a high validity of assessment center predictions.[12]

9. Joseph M. Bender, "What is 'Typical' of Assessment Centers?" *Personnel* 50 (July–August 1973): 51.

10. William C. Byham, "Assessment Centers for Spotting Future Managers," *Harvard Business Review* 48 (July–August 1970): 158.

11. Douglas W. Bray and Donald L. Grant, "The Assessment Center in the Measurement of Potential for Business Management," *Psychological Monographs,* whole no. 625, vol. 80, no. 17, (1966), p. 24.

12. James R. Huck, "Assessment Centers: A Review of the External and Internal Validities," *Personnel Psychology* 26 (Summer 1973): 198.

SUMMARY

People are the most important asset of any organization. Most firms today realize that acquiring and developing quality human resources is absolutely essential if the organization is to survive and grow. This statement provides an excellent short summary of the significance of staffing to every organization. In most large firms, a human resources or personnel department is responsible for administering the organization's recruitment, selection, training, and compensation functions. However, every manager, regardless of function, must understand and participate in the staffing process.

Personnel selection involves choosing people to meet the requirements of a job. Staffing begins with a careful forecast of manpower required to accomplish the objectives of the organization. Once manpower plans have been developed, job analysis allows the organization to determine the specific qualifications required to perform the job. Job analysis leads to the development of a job description that is a summary of the specific purposes, duties, and responsibilities of the job. Another product of job analysis is a job specification that states the minimum qualifications persons need to do the job. Next, management must predict future workload requirements and complete an analysis of the work force available.

Prior to discussing the specific phases of the recruitment process, the legal aspects of staffing were discussed. Every manager involved in selecting new employees must comply with federal, state, and local laws. Four of the most significant federal laws affecting the staffing process include the Equal Pay Act of 1963, the 1964 Civil Rights Act, the Age Discrimination Act of 1967, and the 1972 Equal Employment Opportunity Act. These laws are concerned primarily with prohibiting discrimination in employment, pay, and promotions on the basis of race, color, religion, sex, national origin, or age.

After the preliminary steps in the staffing process have been completed, the actual recruitment process begins. Personnel can be recruited using internal or external sources. If a firm is seeking applicants from outside the organization, recruitment usually consists of several important steps. First, preliminary screening interviews are often used to eliminate obviously unqualified applicants. If an applicant appears qualified, he or she is then requested to complete an employment application. Next, some form of test may be given the applicant, although in recent years, the use of certain types of tests has declined.

The next step in the process is the interview which is probably the most widely used and perhaps the most important method of assessing the qualifications of job applicants. If an applicant is judged acceptable in the interviews, many organizations conduct background and/or referred checks prior to seeking final management approval to employ the individual. The final step in the process is that the prospective employee is given a physical exam prior to placement on the job.

<table>
<tr><td>Review
Questions</td><td>

1. Describe and discuss the different phases in the staffing process.

2. Distinguish between a job description and job specification.

3. What are the major federal laws that have the potential to impact the staffing process?

4. Describe the advantages and disadvantages of promotion from within.

5. What are the general objectives that need to be achieved in interviewing job applicants?

6. What are the steps that are involved in the personnel selection process?

7. What is the purpose of an assessment center? Discuss.

</td></tr>
<tr><td>Exercises</td><td>

1. Assume you are a personnel director for the following type of firms and have a vacancy that requires the skills identified below. What phase(s) of the personnel selection process do you believe would require special attention?
    a. Faculty member for a major university that stresses research
    b. A general laborer for a construction firm
    c. A skilled welder for work on an assembly line
    d. A senior secretary who is required to take dictation and type 70 words per minute
    e. A first-level production supervisor

2. Consult the personnel wanted section of a major Sunday newspaper. Evaluate the positions that are available for the following career fields. Can you detect a general pattern of job requirements that are needed for an applicant?
    a. Personnel and human resource manager
    b. Computer specialist
    c. Car salesperson
    d. Production supervisor

</td></tr>
</table>

REFERENCES

Bray, Douglas W., and Grant, Donald L. "The Assessment Center In The Measurement Of Potential For Business Management." *Psychological Monographs*, whole no. 625, vol. 80, no. 17 (1966), p. 24.

Bender, Joseph M. "What Is 'Typical' Of Assessment Centers?" *Personnel*, July–August, 1973, p. 51.

Bucalo, J. "Personnel Directors: What You Should Know Before Recommending MBO." *Personnel Journal*, April 1977, pp. 176–8.

Byham, William C. "Assessment Centers For Spotting Future Managers." *Harvard Business Review*, July–August 1970, p. 158.

Conference Board. *The Personnel Functions: Changing Objectives And Organization*, 1977, p. 5.

Davies, G. S. "Consistent Recruitment In A Graded Manpower System." *Management Science*, July 1976, pp. 1215–20.

Gery, G. J. "Equal Opportunity—Planning and Managing The Process of Change." *Personnel Journal*, April 1977, pp. 184–5.

Gillespie, J. F., et al. "Human Resources Planning and Valuation Model." *Academy of Management Journal*, December 1976, pp. 650–6.

Glueck, William F. *Personnel: A Diagnostic Approach*. Business Publications, Inc., 1974, pp. 189–191.

Hakala, D. R. and Huggins, K. M. "ERISA: Impact On Business Financial Management." *University of Michigan Business Review*, November 1976, pp. 19–23.

Henderson, J. A. "What The Chief Executive Expects Of The Personnel Function." *Personnel Administration*, May 1977, pp. 40–45.

Higgins, James M. "A Manager's Guide To The Equal Employment Opportunity Laws." *Personnel Journal*, August 1976, pp. 406–412.

Hoffman, W. H., and Wyatt, L. L. "Human Resources Planning," *Personnel Administration*, January 1977, pp. 19–23.

Hollingsworth, A. T., and Preston, P. "Corporate Planning: A Challenge For Personnel Executives." *Personnel Journal*, August 1976, pp. 386–9.

Huck, James R. "Assessment Centers: A Review of the External And Internal Validities." *Personnel Psychology*, Summer 1973, p. 198.

Mandel, Milton M. "The Employment Interview." Research Study No. 47. New York: American Management Association.

"Manpower Research: A Key To The Future." *Personnel Management*, February 1977, pp. 16–18.

Novack, Stanley R. "Developing An Effective Application Blank." *Personnel Journal*, May 1970, p. 421.

Phillips, S. M., and Fletcher, L. P. "Cost of Funding Benefits Under the ERISA: A Statistical Survey." *Journal of Risk and Insurance*, December 1976, pp. 569–85.

Rogers, R. G. P. "Personnel Moves Center Stage." *Personnel Management*, October 1976, p. 3.

Shaw, M. E. "Behavioral Sciences: A New Image." *Training and Development Journal,* February 1977, pp. 26–31.

Sprin, S. and Soloman, L. "Key Element in EDP Personnel Management's Functional Job Analysis." *Personnel Journal,* November 1976, pp. 552–6.

Wanger, Lawrence A. "Employee Reference Request Revisited." *The Personnel Administrator,* November 1975, p. 62.

Case Study

A CASE OF ALLEGED DISCRIMINATION

John Williams, a black clerical employee, has been with the Della Corporation for over fifteen years. During his tenure he has held various positions, all within the same department. He has advanced to the position of Senior Clerk, a semisupervisory position concerned with work direction, but not hiring, firing, or promoting authority. He has attained this position not as much through outstanding work as through longevity in the department. Over the years he has developed a very abrasive personality. This normally is demonstrated by such things as never greeting the other employees in the morning, never doing any of the "dirty work," and acting like answering questions imposes a real imposition on him.

This insensitive type of personality has had an adverse effect on the working effectiveness of the section as evidenced by an above average turnover rate of the clerical staff and reduced accuracy and efficiency of the work performed in the department. When terminated employees are questioned on their exit interviews, statements such as "Don't like John" or "Can't stand to work in that department" are common. On several occasions John's supervisor has discussed these comments with him. John tends to pass these off as merely racially discriminatory remarks.

John's supervisor does not know how to react in this situation because it is based on such intangible evidence. None of his actions by themselves warrant termination. The personnel director has cautioned the supervisor that she must be careful of disciplinary action because of the discrimination implications. John has no room for advancement into another position in the department because of educational requirements and cannot change departments easily because his entire work experience has been in one area.

Questions

1. What should John's supervisor do?
2. How much consideration should be given to John's longevity and minority status?
3. How difficult would it be to terminate John in view of the laws discussed in this chapter?

Case Study

ABSENTEEISM OF A LONG-SERVICE EMPLOYEE

Quality Business Forms, Inc. has a policy stating that employee absenteeism should not exceed four days during a ninety-day work period without medical verification. If an employee does not have medical reasons for excessive absences, he or she may be subject to disciplinary action.

Ed Thompson has been employed by Quality for over twenty-one years. In the past three years he has had an abnormal amount of absences which his supervisor chose to ignore due to Ed's long tenure with the company. When Ed's supervisor was transferred and another individual in the department, Alice Randall, assumed the supervisory position, she immediately advised Ed that his absenteeism was excessive and that it would have to cease or disciplinary action would be taken. Ed claimed to have been injured five years previously on his job and that his absences were a result of that injury. A review of Ed's health records was undertaken and no such injury had ever been reported.

Ed's attendance improved during the first six months under Ms. Randall's supervision, but began to deteriorate during the latter part of the year. Ed, warned again about the absenteeism, came back with his previous excuse. At this point, Ms. Randall contacted the personnel manager for assistance in dealing with Ed. She was told that further disciplinary steps should be taken along with a complete physical evaluation by the corporate medical doctor. The physical exam was given immediately and no physical abnormalities were found.

This information was given to Ed verbally by the doctor, but Ed did not accept the findings. He was then counseled by the personnel manager, his supervisor, and his department manager. Ed listened very intently to what was being said and took notes. Ed was told that the next step in the disciplinary procedure would be dismissal if his absenteeism continued. He said he understood and that he would work when he felt good and would not work when he did not feel good.

Thirty days later Ed and his supervisor were called in to the personnel office at 7:00 in the morning and Ed was terminated. It was a shock to Ed that he had actually been fired, since it was necessary for the president of the company to approve the termination of employees with a long service record. A discrimination charge was filed but was dropped after no grounds could be established. A Workmen's Compensation claim came in, but could not be substantiated. The last item was an unemployment claim that was to be levied against the corporation, but on an appeal it too was found in favor of the corporation.

Questions

1. Do you agree with the standards developed by the firm with regard to absenteeism?

2. What responsibilities rest with an employer in regards to when a long-term employee should be terminated?

3. How much documentation is really needed to be fair?

Chapter 7

KEY TERMS

activities

interactions

sentiments

informal relationships

role

informal work groups

group

synergistic effect

cohesiveness

norm

contact chart

status

status symbol

power

politics

The Informal Organization

LEARNING OBJECTIVES

After completing this chapter you should be able to

1. Describe the importance of the informal group in the organization.
2. Distinguish between the formal and the informal organization.
3. Identify the basic characteristics of the informal group.
4. List the values and losses associated with the informal organization.
5. Explain the importance of status, power, and politics in an organization.

Jim Brown, the general manager of Ampex Manufacturers, is frustrated. One of his supervisors, Bob Evans, is constantly being asked to supply advice to many people in the organization. On numerous occasions he has seen Bob with the vice-president of production and the vice-president of finance. Not only do people from upper management seek Bob's attention, but also many lower-level employees from several different departments apparently desire Bob's advice and opinion. Jim thinks to himself, "What ever happened to the chain of command."

Alice Garcia, the production supervisor for United Wholesaling Company has just been told by Barbara Adams, one of her new employees, that she will quit on Friday. The reason Alice gave for leaving was, "I just don't fit in around here. The other workers don't seem to like me and I cannot find anyone to talk to."

Tommy John, a supervisor for Grey Productions, told Bill Stephens, the new machine operator, that extra money above his hourly wage could be earned if he worked faster. Because Bill really wanted to buy a new car, he began his job by *busting quota* every day. At first Bill was taking home 30 percent more money each week than the average employee. After only one month, however, Bill's production had dropped to the average level in the department. Whereas, at first, Bill did not seem interested in socializing with the other employees, Bill is now seen going to coffee and lunch with the other workers and laughing and joking with them. The supervisor thinks to himself, "The old informal group pressure got to a good worker again."

Jim, Alice, and Tommy have learned from experience that the informal organization can have a significant impact on the work environment. Inserting the human element into an organization reduces the clear, logically designed official structure desired so much by some managers. These managers are proud of the formal organization structure that has been developed. As may be seen in Figure 7.1, it is very logical and orderly. Everyone knows exactly who they report to and the tasks they are expected to do. Some managers believe they can sit back in their executive suites and the company will "run itself" because of the beautiful structure that has been developed.

When the human factor is inserted, this most beautiful creation is often altered. In fact, the manner in which a company is organized and the way the employees interact to accomplish the task may be completely different. In jest, but a somewhat realistic illustration, the manner in which the

FIGURE 7.1
The Formal Organization

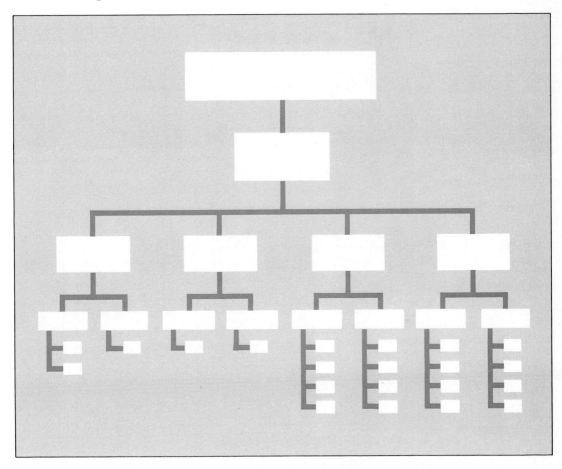

informal group operates within the formal organization might be as shown in Figure 7.2. As may be seen, the president of the firm is *out to lunch* although he has the official *right* of command. Apparently most of the actual decisions in the firm are made by one person and everyone is attempting to get a share of his consideration. There are also two *rising stars* who are receiving attention from several devoted organizational members. Some of the employees are in a maze and don't know where they are going while others are covered with cobwebs and are doing nothing. A fight appears to have broken out between two employees while other members are more attracted to a member of the opposite sex than they are with their jobs. As may be seen, organizational members often do

FIGURE 7.2
The Informal Organization

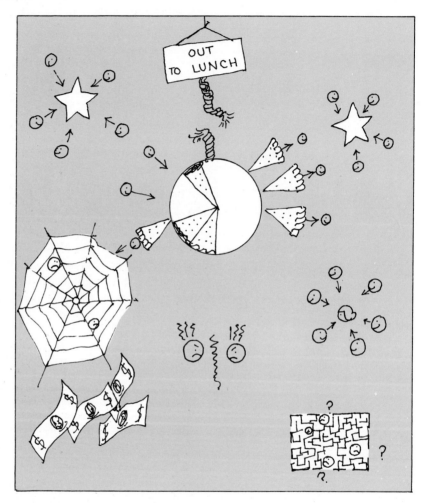

not conform to the formal structure that has been officially prescribed. Rather, they develop friendships and relationships with individuals in other departments. They also choose their own informal leaders that may or may not be the same as those selected by the formal organization.

In this chapter we will examine the nature of the informal organization and attempt to gain an appreciation of the influence—both positive and negative—it can have on the formal organization. Included within the discussion will be a presentation of the characteristics associated with the informal work group. The ultimate objective of the chapter will be to gain an appreciation of the factors a manager should consider when dealing with the informal group. Status, power, and politics will also be discussed as topics that relate to the informal organization.

THE FORMAL VERSUS THE INFORMAL ORGANIZATION

It would be foolish for managers to assume that they could identify and control every relationship among all persons within the organization. There are, however, managers who sincerely believe they can. However, the uncooperative nature of the informal work group frustrates these attempts. For this reason, the manager must appreciate both the formal and informal relationships in the organization. They may be studied separately, but ultimately they must be integrated into a total organizational package. As suggested by George Homans, a more complete view of organizational behavior—both formal and informal—would include three elements: activities, interactions, and sentiments.[1] **Activities** are concerned with what a person actually does. **Interactions** are the interpersonal contacts and relations that one has with others. **Sentiments** deal with the emotional reactions that we have to other people, the organization, and the physical factors. Sentiments would also encompass the person's sense of self-worth, level of aspiration, and identification with selected values.

activities
interactions
sentiments

INSIGHTS TO SUCCESS

Work hard in your chosen profession, have a good attitude toward your organization or get out. Become an excellent front line employee because this is the source of most managers. After getting a job, seniors should prepare a self-development plan which is designed to prepare himself/herself for a first line manager job.

J. H. BANDY, Chief, Audit Division, Internal Revenue Service

As may be seen in Figure 7.3, the manager of the formal organization establishes the activities and interactions for his or her employees. The official document describing what must be accomplished is the job description. Although they are not specifically stated, the person is also expected to possess certain sentiments about the work, the organization, and his or her manager. *Traditional* managers tend to emphasize the values of organizational and personal loyalty. Such managers often can tolerate incompetence more readily than disloyalty. The official organization

1. George C. Homans, *The Human Group* (New York: Harcourt, Brace, 1950).

J. ALVIN WAKEFIELD

Vice President—*Personnel*
Avon Products, Inc,

AVON J. Alvin Wakefield believes that the management of people is one of the most exciting career endeavors that a person can choose in today's rapidly changing busi-

ness environment. His enjoyment of personnel management is one of the major reasons for his rapid advancement to his present position as vice-president—personnel for Avon Products, Inc. Mr. Wakefield joined Avon in 1973 as manager—employee relations. In 1974 he assumed the position of director—home office operations and in 1976 Mr. Wakefield was appointed general manager—home office. In 1977 he became group director—personnel, with worldwide personnel responsibilities. Later that same year, he was elected vice-president—personnel.

Mr. Wakefield attended C. A. Johnson High School in Columbia, South Carolina. He received a B.A. in English Literature in 1960 from New York University, and completed his M.B.A. at Pace University Graduate School. Mr. Wakefield is a former chairperson of the Council of Concerned Black Executives and present Board member as well as a member of: Advisory Board of The Black Theatre Alliance, The Black Executive Exchange Program, 100 Black Men, and Black Retail Action Group.

Mr. Wakefield believes that a major portion of his job consists of making things happen through people. He says, "The key for success in any business is the proper utilization of a company's human resources. At Avon we have a strong people orientation and a corporate personnel philosophy which makes the job of the Personnel Department easier." As a black who is involved in the field of personnel management, Mr. Wakefield feels that he is making a major contribution to the management of the corporation's most important asset—its people.

FIGURE 7.3
The Formal and Informal Organization

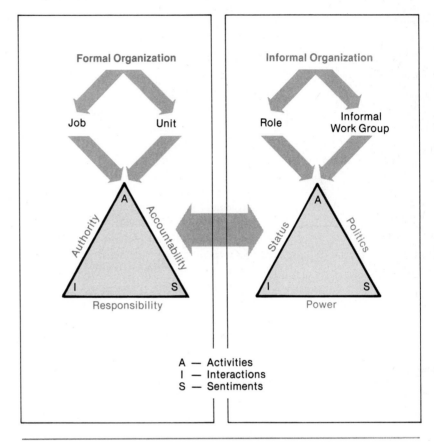

A — Activities
I — Interactions
S — Sentiments

Source Adapted from Edwin B. Flippo and Gary M. Munsinger, *Management,* 4th ed. (Boston: Allyn and Bacon, Inc., 1978), p. 248.

attempts to specify the actions, interactions, and sentiments that various sections, departments, and divisions of the firm should undertake. As has been discussed in a previous chapter, the basic relationships involved in this process are responsibility, authority, and accountability.

The official structure is only a portion of the story. There emerges another structure consisting of **informal relationships.** These are created, not by officially designated managers, but by any and all organizational members. Though not identical to responsibility, authority, and accountability, the major informal relationships are status, power, and politics. It should be noted that each of these three predominantly informal relationships has significant inputs from the formal organization and they can also affect the

informal relationships

formal organization. At this point, our attention will turn to the role and characteristics of the informal organization. Status, power, and politics will be discussed later in the chapter.

ROLE

role

The concept of role is broader than that of its counterpart in the formal organization—the job. A **role** consists of the total pattern of expected behavior, interactions, and sentiments of an individual. As may be seen in Figure 7.3, these three patterns exist in both the formal and informal organization. In the formal organization it includes, but goes beyond, the official content of the job description. If a person is officially designated a supervisor, pressure may be exerted to dress, talk, and act similar to other managers in the organization. If managers in a particular firm typically dress formally, the manager who fails to wear the proper "uniform" is not fulfilling the expected role.

Individuals who are members of an informal group also are presented with an expected role they act out. Whether the informal group is supportive or nonsupportive of management has a major impact on the roles of the group members. If the group decides they should not support a decision made by top management, the pattern of their behavior (role) may reflect indifference or slowing down on the job. Failure to conform to the expected role may result in a member being outcast from the informal group.

A person may have many roles that they must constantly play. For instance, when working toward a doctorate, one of the authors was a student, a teacher, a consultant, and a military officer in the reserves. For each of these acivities there was a different role and failure to immediately change roles at the proper time often resulted in difficulties. Being a military officer on the weekend with considerable authority followed on Monday morning by playing the humble role of a doctoral student was sometimes no easy task. Students who go back to school part-time while working as a supervisor in a firm often encounter the same difficulties.

INFORMAL WORK GROUPS

informal work groups

Referring again to Figure 7.3, it can be noted that just as the formal organization establishes certain official units by creating different levels of authority, the informal organization will develop **informal work groups.** Because of the impact the groups may have on an organization, firms are training their managers in ever increasing numbers to be able to cope with the informal group. Gerritt Starke, Director of Corporate Personnel for Kemper Insurance Company, says, "We teach our managers/supervisors to be alert to the formation of 'informal work groups' and that such groups can be either a positive or a negative influence on a department or company objective." Corning Glass Works also has an extensive management development program devoted to both understanding how the informal group functions and designing ways to have the informal group work in a positive manner. At Sherwin-Williams, effort is directed towards making the formal and informal work group one and the same. This means that each work group is managed by a team leader who is both technically and interpersonally competent. Supervisors and employees are trained in effective team skills and use these skills in day-to-day problem solving.

Various disciplines have been involved in research regarding the informal work groups in such fields as psychology, sociology, anthropology, social psychology, and psychiatry. As a result, certain basic elements of the group have been identified. Among these characteristics are group goals, cohesiveness, norms, structure, leadership, participants, and size. These will be discussed next.

Group Goals

group

synergistic effect

A **group** is defined as two or more people who join together to accomplish a desired goal. A strange situation occurs though when people join groups. A **synergistic effect** takes place and the sum of the parts becomes greater than the whole. That is, one plus one becomes greater than two. Through the synergistic effect, the informal work group achieves a much more powerful meaning. People in groups have much more influence than each individual has alone.

Although managers often do not like to recognize the existence of informal work groups, it is important that they do. When the goals of the work group are similar to those of management, no major problems exist. However, the goals of the work group can sometimes mean the difference between the success or failure of the organizational goals. If the goals of the informal work group are in agreement with the organization, productivity may improve. On the other hand, if they are contrary to each other, the firm may confront barriers to success. The goals of the informal work group will affect the type of members the group will attract, the type of work that is accomplished within the group, and the standards (norms) that are acceptable to the group members.

Cohesiveness

cohesiveness

The degree of attraction that the group has for each of its members is referred to as **cohesiveness.** It is identified by such attitudes as loyalty to the group, a feeling of responsibility for group efforts, defending against outside attack, friendliness, and congeniality. Cohesive work groups are powerful instruments that can work for or against the formal organization. For instance, a highly cohesive group whose goals are in agreement with organizational objectives can use this strength to assist the firm in increasing productivity. On the other hand, a highly cohesive group that is not in agreement with organizational objectives can have an extremely negative effect on the accomplishment of the firm's goals. Because of this potential power, some managers attempt to reduce cohesion in order to maintain control.

Norms

norm

The formal organization has its performance standards, and the informal work group has its norms. A **norm** is a standard of behavior that is expected from group members. Those who violate the group norms are helped to see the errors of their ways. Informal pressures to conform to group norms are often more powerful than the official sanctions used by managers to enforce conformance to organizational standards. A worker who is a high producer (very acceptable to the formal organization) may be sanctioned by the informal organization until his or her production falls back in line with the informal group's norms. In the example at the beginning of the chapter, Bill Stephens was influenced to conform to the group norm of expected output. Group norms are unwritten rules that new members, if they are to remain members, gradually learn. Norms are frequently established concerning how hard one should work, whether one should be friendly, the degree to which one should cooperate with management, and whether or not one should be innovative.

INSIGHTS TO SUCCESS

Trite—but true: "You earn your salary during working time—you earn promotions on your own time."

H. DORMAN, Vice-President—Administration, Equifax, Incorporated

Leadership

An entirely different procedure is at work in selecting a leader for the informal work group. In the formal organization the leader (manager) is placed in his or her position of authority by top management. By filling a particular supervisory position, the individual is designated the leader. This is not the case with the informal group. The informal group leader *emerges* from the group. There is no formal election; the process of identifying a leader merely occurs. Typically, the person who adheres closest to the norms of the group is the leader. There is no formal title attached to this individual. He or she is the one who is looked to for guidance in achieving the group's goal. Should the leader begin to deviate from group norms, another leader who is closer to the group norm will emerge to take his or her place.

Structure

Although not capable of being placed into a formal organizational chart, the informal group has its own organizational structure. As with the formal structure, informal groups may also have different levels in the chain of command. It may even be charted by management, as will be discussed later, but the members themselves have not drawn up a formal structure. Gerritt Starke, Director of Corporate Personnel for Kemper Insurance Company, states, "We should recognize that 'informal work groups' exist at all levels of the organization. A formal organization chart can be very misleading in terms of who has 'real' authority/influence."

The dynamic nature of the informal structure constantly changes. As different members enter into and exit out of the group, the structure is modified. The structure is heavily based on the communication patterns that develop among group members. If many people attempt to gain the advice of one individual, this individual is often the informal leader and the structure develops around this individual. Just as formal organizations have vice-presidents, the informal group may have an equivalent counterpart. The structure evolves, rather than being formally laid out, but often it is more effective than the formal organizational structure.

contact chart

One means by which the organizational structure of the informal work group may be studied is through the use of a **contact chart.** These charts are developed to identify the connections that an individual has with other members of the organization. As may be seen from the contact chart in Figure 7.4, all contacts do not follow the formal organization chart. In various instances, certain levels of management are bypassed; others show cross-contact from one chain of command to another. Individual #17 appears to be very popular based on the number of workers contacting the employee. The difficulty with a contact chart is that the reasons for these relationships are not shown. It is possible that these contacts could work either for or against the organization. Individual #17 could be assisting other employees accomplish their tasks. On the other hand, this individual could be *talking down* the organization and promoting disharmony among company employees. In any event, once a manager has identified the major contact points, he or she is in a position to either encourage or discourage the individual within the work group.

FIGURE 7.4
A Contact Chart

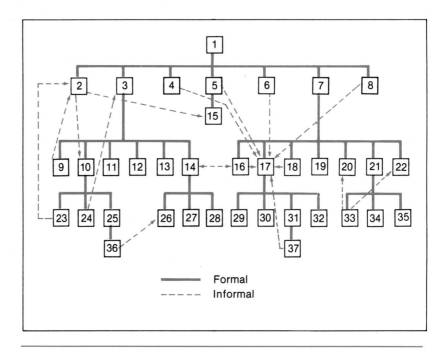

Source Edwin B. Flippo and Gary M. Munsinger, *Management*, 4th ed. (Boston: Allyn and Bacon, Inc., 1978), p. 262.

Size

The size of the informal group is a major factor affecting group effectiveness. Because interpersonal relationships are the essence of informal organizations, the informal group tends to be small so that its members may interact frequently. But when groups get too small, difficulties arise. The dyad, or two person group, is a perfect example. When a decision is required and there isn't a consensus, one of the other group members must lose.

There has been considerable research devoted to determining the most effective group size. This research leads to the following conclusions:

- When quality of a complex group decision is important, the use of seven to twelve members under a formal leader is most appropriate.
- When consensus in a conflict situation is important, the use of three to five members with no formal leader will ensure that each member's view will be discussed.

· When both quality and consensus are important, five to seven members seem most appropriate.[2]

There tends to be greater group conflict in even-sized groups, and there is more conflict in groups of two and four members than there is in those of six members. In seating arrangements, members who sit across from each other tend to engage in more frequent and often argumentative communication. If consensus is the goal, members with high conflict potential should be seated alongside each other.

Thus, when dealing with the subject of effective informal organization, we are primarily concerned with smaller groups. Obviously, many organizations consist of thousands of members. The initial approach to organization must therefore be formal in nature, resulting in the design of official units, jobs, and formal relationships of authority, responsibility, and accountability. Within this formal organization, a limitless number of small informal work groups will be spontaneously established, and hopefully will be aligned with overall organization objectives.

BENEFITS AND COSTS OF THE INFORMAL ORGANIZATION

Management often has mixed emotions about the informal work group. On the one hand, the work group is capable of contributing to greater organizational effectiveness. On the other, the informal organization is not without its drawbacks and there are certain costs involved. However, if management is properly trained to understand and work with the informal groups, the benefits should exceed the costs. As may be seen in Figure 7.5, the benefits outweigh the costs. However, as with the seesaw, if management is not careful, the losses may exceed the benefits. Both the benefits and costs resulting from the informal work group will be discussed next.

BENEFITS OF THE INFORMAL ORGANIZATION

It is fortunate that management cannot destroy the informal organization because it is capable of providing significant benefits to an organization's effectiveness. These potential values of the informal work group are discussed below.

2. L. L. Cummings, George P. Huber, and Eugene Arendt, "Effects of Size and Spatial Arrangements in Group Decision Making," *Academy of Management Journal* 17 (September 1974): 473.

FIGURE 7.5
Benefits and Costs of the Informal Work Group

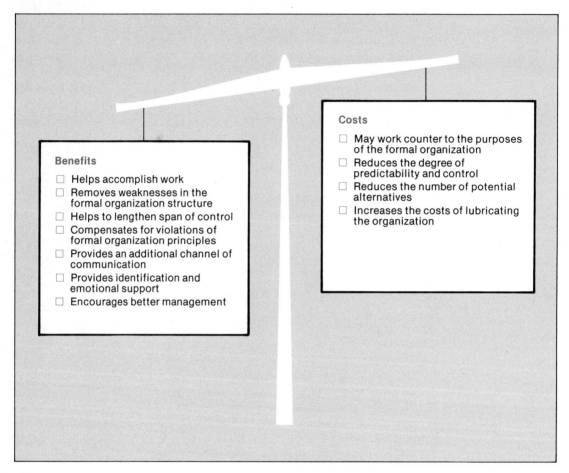

Benefits

☐ Helps accomplish work
☐ Removes weaknesses in the formal organization structure
☐ Helps to lengthen span of control
☐ Compensates for violations of formal organization principles
☐ Provides an additional channel of communication
☐ Provides identification and emotional support
☐ Encourages better management

Costs

☐ May work counter to the purposes of the formal organization
☐ Reduces the degree of predictability and control
☐ Reduces the number of potential alternatives
☐ Increases the costs of lubricating the organization

Assists in Accomplishing Work

For a manager to be effective, his or her subordinates must be permitted a certain degree of flexibility in accomplishing the assigned tasks. Advance approval of every move is detrimental to achieving success. If people in any organization acted only when they were told to act, followed standard instructions to the letter at all times, and contacted others only when duly authorized, a business would have to cease operations. However, the traditionalist tends to rely more heavily on formal decisions based on a scientific study of business problems.

There are also occasions when the formal command is wrong or inadequate for the situation. If the atmosphere is heavily traditional, subordinates may exhibit *malicious obedience* by executing the command faithfully despite personal knowledge that their action will ultimately result in failure. Many a young manager has discovered that a subordinate can "Yes, sir" him all day, follow every directive to the letter, and watch him fail miserably. If more faith is placed in informal relationships, subordinates may voluntarily adapt the formal order to the requirements of the actual situation. When loosely structured, groups are often able to achieve organization objectives more effectively in an informal manner.

Helps to Remove Weaknesses in the Formal Structure

The formal organization often has a number of gaps that the informal group can fill. For example, let us consider a person who is promoted to a position that exceeds his or her current capabilities. This is not an unusual occurrence in the armed services, for instance, where a young officer is appointed unit commander. Without the advice and assistance of an experienced sergeant, young officers might not survive their first assignment. In fact, most likely there are many officers who have been unsuccessful in the military because they have failed to recognize the power of the informal organization. The formal orders and regulations say that he or she is the commander, with certain responsibilities and authorities. By admitting one's temporary weaknesses, help may be obtained from other officers and enlisted personnel. In effect, deficiencies in the formal structure have been removed by sharing decision making with others. In time, the informal group may resemble the formal organization more closely.

Lengthens the Effective Span of Control

As we indicated in chapter 6, the number of people a supervisor can effectively manage is referred to as the span of control. As individuals and small groups learn to interact more effectively and are permitted to do so by their supervisors, the manager should be able to devote less time to each individual member. This could well contribute to a lengthening of one's effective span of control.

Compensates for Violations of Formal Organization Principles

The development of informal relationships also influences the effectiveness of certain traditional principles of formal organizations. For example, it has been pointed out that even though authority should equal responsibility, the principle is often violated. As a result, the employee tries to develop informal contacts with personnel over whom one has no formal authority. Favors are traded and friendships formed. One quickly learns that the formal prescription of authority often is not a sufficient base for operation. Yet, this still does not negate the desirability of having responsibility equal authority.

**QUALITIES NEEDED FOR SUCCESS
AS A MANAGER IN YOUR ORGANIZATION**

- The willingness to fight hard for what is right.
- A continuous search for better understanding of a business.
- An ability to forecast, but a willingness to accept change and cope with it when forecasting is in error.
- Flexibility
- The ability to identify competent people in the organization and to help plan their careers.
- The ability to motivate.
- Not willing to procrastinate on decisions, hoping problems will go away if ignored.
- Early job rotation of the star performers so that their careers are broadened rather than narrowed.

ZOLTAN MERSZEI, President and C.E.O., The Dow Chemical Company

---

Provides an Additional Channel of Communication

The informal organization provides an additional channel of communication for the enterprise. To some traditional managers, the "grapevine" constitutes an obstacle to be destroyed. They seek to channel and control most, if not all, communications through the official chain of command. However, the grapevine can add to organization effectiveness if the manager will use it. The grapevine is fast and usually accurate in the information it transmits.

The use of the grapevine does not decrease the importance of the official channel of communication and command. The grapevine can spread much information in a short period, but it cannot provide the authority that is necessary for much of the action that will take place.

Provides Emotional Support for Employees

Over one-half of all voluntary resignations in many organizations occur within the first six months of employment. This is often due to poor induction procedures when little help is provided the new employee in joining and being accepted within the group. Friendships, or at least speaking acquaintances, are highly essential to a satisfactory working environment for most people. In one hospital where the termination rate among janitorial personnel was high, the formation of cleanup teams reduced turnover considerably. Such personnel felt isolated and uncomfortable when working alone among physicians, nurses, and patients.

Encourages Better Management

Awareness of the nature and impact of the informal organization often leads to better management decisions. The acceptance of the fact that formal relationships will not enable full accomplishment of organization tasks stimulates management to seek other means of motivation. If most of the work is done informally, the manager will seek to improve his or her knowledge of the nature of the people in general and his or her subordinates in particular. Managers should realize that organization performance can be affected by the workers who grant or withhold cooperation and enthusiasm. Means other than formal authority must be sought to develop attitudes that support effective performance.

COSTS OF THE INFORMAL ORGANIZATION

The informal organization is not without its drawbacks. Here are the possible costs of informal work groups.

May Work Counter to the Purposes of the Formal Organization

It is apparent to most managers that individuals and groups can and sometimes do work contrary to the formal goals of an enterprise. If the goals of the informal group could always be the same as those of the organization, few would object to the encouragement of its formation. However, there are results such as work restriction, pressuring other workers to exhibit disinterest in company requirements, disloyalty, insubordination, and unauthorized actions that work at cross-purposes with other functions in the organization.

Reduces the Degree of Predictability and Control

One of the basic purposes of an organization is to ensure predictability and control of individual behavior so that the individual will work effectively toward organizational goals. This depends, however, on people interpreting and executing the formal guidelines. If we recognize and accept the greater possibility of good from permitted flexibility, we also must accept the risks that accompany this lesser degree of control. The human element can and does add much to an organization's effectiveness; it also can and does add much to the degree of uncertainty.

Reduces the Number of Practical Alternatives

In *The American Soldier*, a four-volume study of the United States Army during World War II, it was concluded that the natural unit of personal commitment was the informal group, not the total formal organization.[3] The soldiers reported that one of the major reasons for moving forward in combat was to avoid letting the other fellow down. The solidarity developed in the informal group greatly strengthened the motivation of individual members.

The significance of this finding creates problems in the interchangeability of personnel. If natural groups are broken up by moving individual members in and out of them, the degree of motivation and cooperation is reduced. This may well mean that management should think in terms of moving groups around, rather than individuals. If management wishes to capitalize on the considerable values issuing from the development of primary work groups, it must lose some flexibility in decision making.

Increases the Time Required to Complete Activities

If the cooperative efforts of the informal work groups can be aligned with the objectives of the firm, management has the best of both worlds. The collective power generated can be quite phenomenal. Informal work group activities such as gossiping, betting pools, long coffee breaks, and general horseplay are time consuming and may be detrimental to efficient opera-

---

3. Samual A. Stouffer et al., *The American Soldier*, vol II (Princeton: Princeton University Press, 1949), p. 1974.

tions. These are acts that will tax the patience of the rigid, rational manager. Yet, if an effective work group is to be established, some of these activities will have to be permitted and should even be encouraged. The manager must realize that, despite concern for goal accomplishment, he or she must allow the group time and opportunity to maintain itself in good working order. People can usually sustain action for a longer period of time under an informal atmosphere than they can when the situation is highly rigid, controlled, and formal.

STATUS, POWER, AND POLITICS

Status, power, and politics are involved in both the formal and informal organization. However, the informal relationships associated with status, power, and politics go well beyond the formal prescription in an organization. The forthcoming discussion of these concepts will concentrate on the manner in which status, power, and politics primarily affect factors associated with the informal work group.

STATUS

status   A person's rank or position in a group is called **status.** It is an important relationship that has considerable effect on the morale and efficiency of any organization. Status is an inevitable component of human relationships in all aspects of life, business and nonbusiness. In this section, we wish to examine the sources of status in business organizations, the symbols that denote status levels, and the functions of a status system.

Status Sources

The sources of status, or social rank, can be of both an informal and a formal nature. Examples of these sources are as follows:

Formal Organizational Sources
1. Occupation or Job
2. Organization Level

Personal Sources
1. Education
2. Age
3. Seniority
4. Race
5. Religion
6. Parentage
7. Sex
8. Competence
9. Associates

It is apparent that certain occupations are accorded more prestige than others. For example, white-collar jobs are usually more highly esteemed than blue-collar jobs. Within particular companies, management has discovered, often with great surprise, the following status differentials: long-distance telephone operators had higher social rank than operators handling local calls; cooks who worked on white meat had higher status than those who worked on dark; and cafeteria personnel who handled fish dishes had less prestige than those who served beef. As can be seen, the status of one's occupation depends on the rank accorded it by one's peers, and not by management alone. The job assigned to a person and the level of organization in which it is placed are significant sources of status; in general, the higher the organization level, the higher the level of prestige.

A particular individual can possess high status even though that person works in a low-status job. If one does a low-status job extremely well, this skill is often generally recognized and respected. For instance, a junior accountant recently employed as an auditor may develop a better reputation than a senior staff accountant. The senior staff accountant may have the lower status although filling a higher position. If the president of the firm bumbles and muddles through the job, the status level is also substantially reduced.

Finally, there is status that comes from one's associates. This is social rank that comes from friendship, kinship, or social organizations. Membership in a certain fraternity or club and graduation from certain schools are examples of status being assigned to a person on the basis of the status accorded the larger group. Membership in these groups is often based on possession of some of the other personal sources of status.

INSIGHTS TO SUCCESS

I would suggest that college seniors in the last year should concentrate as much of their study and activity as possible on people-oriented courses, and focus especially on interpersonal relationships.

ROY A. WESTRAN, President, Citizens Insurance Company of America

Status Symbols

status symbol

A visible, external sign of one's social position is referred to as a **status symbol.** A stranger can enter an organization and if aware of status hierarchies, is able to quickly obtain a social fix by reading the various symbols. However, one must recognize that status symbols often vary from firm to firm. For example, one would usually expect that higher status positions are accompanied by more elaborate office furnishings. In one organization, however, the high-status positions were given antique roll-top desks, whereas the lower jobs were equipped with new, shiny, modern furniture. Symbols sometimes change with the times. Some typical status symbols in business are the following:

- Job titles
- Pay
- Bonus/stock plans
- Size and location of desk or office
- Location of parking space or reserved parking
- Type of company car assigned
- Secretaries
- Privacy
- Use of executive clubs
- Cocktail party invitations
- Furnishings, including rugs, pictures, tables and similar items
- Privileges, including freedom to move about, not punching the time clock, and freedom to set own working hours and to regulate coffee break
- Ceremonies of induction
- Number of windows in office

Within the company, however, many of the symbols are within the control of management, and constitute the basis for many conflicts. Executives have gotten down on their hands and knees to measure and compare the sizes of offices. Windows are counted, steps from the president's office are paced off, secretaries who can take fast dictation are sought (even though the supervisor may never give dictation), parking space is fought for, and company cars are wangled. A humorous, fictional example of status symbols by organization level is presented in Table 7.1. Some reflection on this table leads one to believe that there is more truth than fiction here.

Some managements have sought to abolish the whole problem of awarding status symbols by attempting to equalize all privileges, offices, and furnishings. For instance, NCR has eliminated the executive dining rooms and uses open-landscaped offices. In some universities the department head position is rotated among the department members, thereby reducing the status attached to the position. Windowless buildings have been constructed, office sizes are completely standardized, and only one type of company car is available. However, as long as there are differences in status, some type of symbol will be worked out by the group.

TABLE 7.1
Status Symbols

Visible Appurtenances	Top Dogs	V.I.P.'s	Brass	No. 2s	Eager Beavers	Hoi Polloi
Brief cases	None—they ask the questions	Use backs of envelopes	Someone goes along to carry theirs	Carry their own—empty	Daily—carry their own—filled with work	Too poor to own one
Desks, office	Custom made (to order)	Executive style (to order)	Type A, "Director"	Type B, "Manager"	Cast-offs from No. 2s	Yellow Oak—or cast-off from Eager Beavers
Tables, office	Coffee tables	End tables or decorative wall tables	Matching tables, type A	Matching tables, type B	Plain work table	None—lucky to have own desk
Carpeting	Nylon—1-inch pile	Nylon—1-inch pile	Wool-twist (with pad)	Wool-twist (without pad)	Used wool pieces—sewed	Asphalt tile
Plant stands	Several—kept filled with strange exotic plants	Several—kept filled with strange exotic plants	Two-repotted whenever they take a trip	One medium-sized—repotted annually during vacation	Small—repotted when plant dies	May have one in the department or bring their own from home
Vacuum water bottles	Silver	Silver	Chromium	Plain painted	Coke machine	Water fountains
Library	Private collection	Autographed or complimentary books and reports	Selected references	Impressive titles on covers	Books everywhere	Dictionary
Shoe shine sevice	Every morning at 10:00	Every morning at 10:15	Every day at 9:00 or 11:00	Every other day	Once a week	Shine their own
Parking space	Private—in front of office	In plant garage	In company garage—if enough seniority	In company properties—somewhere	On the parking lot	Anywhere they can find a space—if they can afford a car

Reprinted by permission of the publisher, from Morris S. Viteles, "What Raises a Man's Morale," Personnel, (January 1954), p. 305. © 1954 by American Management Association, Inc. All rights reserved.

Status Functions

Status produces several desirable values such as the following:

- **Assisting in Meeting the Needs of the Individual.** Most people wish to be accorded some degree of respect by others. They want to have their abilities and accomplishments recognized, and status symbols constitute tangible evidence of this respect.
- **Facilitating the Process of Communication.** We receive many messages daily from people we do not know personally. The status title of the person or position helps us to evaluate the worth of the message. For example, if a medical doctor tells you something about your backache, it will likely have more meaning than if the service station attendant diagnosed the problem.
- **Serving as a Motivational Device for Management.** Management has discovered that employees will strive for prestige and prestige symbols, as well as for money. Therefore, nonfinancial incentives can be worked into a more comprehensive incentive system. A job title change is often as satisfying as more money. A change to a job of lesser pay but more prestige is often a change a particular person will find satisfying, providing that the pay is still sufficient. Thus, status as a motivating tool has its greatest use in situations where monetary requirements have been met to a reasonable degree. If management is aware of status systems and the symbols it can control, more comprehensive and coordinated incentives can be developed.

POWER

power

The ability of one person to influence the behavior of another person is referred to as **power.** Like status, power is neither completely informal nor formal in nature. The concept of power goes well beyond the capacities provided by the formal organization. Therefore, it is included in this section of the text.

Power is an emotionally laden term, particularly in cultures that emphasize individuality and equality. To label a manager as a *power seeker* is to cast doubt on that manager's motives and actions. Some of these negative views issue from older analyses that have suggested that power is evil, that it corrupts people, that it is largely comprised of naked force, and that the amount is limited in supply. Certainly, the modern business corporation constitutes a major concentration of economic power that has materially improved the standard of living of millions of people. When such concentrations lead to abuse, control rather than its elimination, would appear to be the more desirable course of action. Power can be a highly effective instrument for the good of people.

Sources of Power

The sources of power are many and varied, and are not restricted to the legitimate ones provided by management. These sources are presented in the following paragraphs.

Formal Authority as a Result of Position   Significant power results from a person being placed in a formal position of authority. It results from a person occupying a certain position in the organizational structure and being granted legitimate authority.

Informal Authority   Some managers assume that power and authority are identical concepts. Undeniably, formal authority arising from one's position is a very important source of power, but it is not the only source. Power is the broader concept.

In many situations, informal authority is an important source of influence or power in the organization. This concept serves to emphasize the influence that subordinates have with their superiors. An order is received from a superior and the subordinate can choose among several alternative actions:

- Refuse to obey, thus not delegating informal authority over himself.
- Reluctantly accept the order and execute it on a minimal basis.
- Accept and execute the order with a neutral or indifferent attitude.
- Accept and execute the order with enthusiasm, intelligence, and ingenuity.

The amount of informal authority granted an individual is materially greater in the last alternative. In the Vietnam War, the power of the informal group became significant as entire units refused as a group to follow the formal orders given by officers. Thus, a manager must realize that subordinates can give or withhold their cooperation, which, in effect, means giving or withholding power.

Rewards and Punishments   Rewards and punishments as sources of power are also partly determined by the authority structure of the organization. However, the informal group can also either reward a person through acceptance and liking of a co-worker or punish by rejection and the "silent treatment."

Expertise or Knowledge   Even though an individual has limited formal authority, expertise in a particular area will also give that person considerable influence or power. Expertise power is often a difficult problem for management to confront. For instance, if a computer programmer becomes so familiar with a system that even his or her supervisor could not adequately supervise the person, problems can result. The supervisor may feel that he or she cannot even reprimand the programmer for fear of losing the expertise the worker possesses.

Another major problem is involved in line and staff relationships—the line has the power that issues from authority, whereas the staff has the power that issues from knowledge. The formal right to manage a firm remains, but the capacity to manage it has been diluted and spread among a number of experts. The person possessing knowledge and expertise has power regardless of the formal authority relationships within the organization.

Identification with Individuals Who Are Respected The particular personality and characteristics of an individual will also affect the degree to which other persons wish to identify and be associated with that person. If one is liked and respected, we are more likely to be influenced by that person. If he or she is associated with persons occupying high and visible power positions, we are more inclined to pay greater attention. If a person has access to many sources of power, the concept of *exaggerated response* is often encountered. One president of a large enterprise inquired about the hiring procedures currently in effect. After a three-week delay, he received a comprehensive and detailed report covering all facets of hiring, with an emphasis on the current status of minority group members. At this point, it was discovered that a friend of his had a son who wanted a summer job, but because the young man had already found a position elsewhere, the president was no longer interested.

Significance of Power to the Manager

Research has shown that a good manager must have a concern for acquiring and using power. In a number of studies, it was found that over 70 percent of managers have a higher need for power than does the general population.[4] And the better managers have a stronger need for power than a need to be liked by others. This need for power is not a desire to be dictatorial, nor is it a drive for personal enhancement. Rather, it is a concern for influencing others on the behalf of the organization. It is a need for socialized power rather than for personal power. When managers feel a greater need to be liked than a need to influence others, they tend to be less effective in many organizations.

The control of situational factors, both in and out of the organization, is of significant concern to the modern manager. It has been noted that when

4. David C. McClelland and David H. Burnham, "Power is the Great Motivator," *Harvard Business Review* 54 (March–April 1976): 102.

organizations grow so large and complex that no one individual has the capacity to manage all of the interdependencies, a dominant managing group will develop. This coalition is sometimes formalized into a presidential or executive office. It will exist, however, whether or not it is actually recorded on a chart. If the president of the firm heavily depends on the vice-president of finance to develop the crucial programs, that vice-president is likely to be a member of the dominant coalition and have actual power in excess of that suggested by the official chart. Within the organization, smaller and sometimes more temporary coalitions are formed so that a task involving significant interdependencies can be executed. The formation, use, and dissolution of such coalitions are sometimes called *politics.*

POLITICS

In everyday conversations with the general public, the politician would most likely receive low marks of approval. Political scandals have regularly hit the front page of the daily newspaper since before the days of Watergate. Even though the politician's image is low, politics and politicians are with us in all forms of organized society, and not just the politicians who are in government. Political action can and does provide positive values in promoting cooperation among individuals and groups with differing interests and objectives.

politics **Politics** can be described as a "network of interaction by which power is acquired, transferred, and exercised upon others."[5] Let's think about this definition in order to gain a thorough appreciation of what it means. The politician is working with and through many people. As such, politics transcend the traditional organizational structure boundaries. In the process of these interactions the medium of exchange is power. Just as the dollar is used as the medium of exchange in our economic system, power provides virtually the same function in politics. The shrewd politician acquires power and transfers it to another person when it can *purchase* something of value. Politicians use this medium of exchange in the network that they establish to exert pressure on others in order to gain their desired end result. Just like the accountant, the politician has a balance sheet. When power is transferred, something is received in return. To the politician, a favor given now is power to be extracted in the future. Thus, we are all politicians to a certain extent; some are better at it than others.

5. John M. Pfiffner and Frank P. Sherwood, *Administrative Organization* (Englewood Cliffs, N.J.: Prentice-Hall, 1960), p. 311.

Role of Politics in Business Organizations

If all actions could be foreseen and prescribed for with accuracy, perhaps there would be little need for politics. This would also assume that all conflicts could be resolved in some rational manner acceptable to all. Inasmuch as neither of these two circumstances is likely, the individual will be asked to adjust and accommodate to varying conditions and pressures. Perhaps *adjustments* and *accommodations* are more understandable terms for this political process. Though going exclusively by the rule book could under certain circumstances be construed as one form of politicking, accommodation usually requires additional interactions to be forthcoming. It sometimes involves a bending of the rules, an exchange of favors, and offers of reward for the cooperation that management textbooks often indicate will be forthcoming automatically. It often comes as a shock to some students of management who discover that merely doing the job as expected will not extract the expected rewards.

To make the implications of politics more concrete, let us assume the following example. An engineer heading up an industrial engineering department has developed a new procedure for processing work in a particular line executive's production department. According to the formal rules of the game, he or she would elect to follow the first suggestion listed below:

1. The engineer submits the recommendation for approval by the line executive. The supporting data are provided and persuasive arguments are presented. This failing, the engineer appeals to a common line superior, who will decide the case and issue an order accordingly.

2. The engineer attempts to get to know the line executive on a personal basis. This involves casual conversation, inquiries about respective backgrounds, and the like.

3. The engineer attempts to simulate a friendship that is not felt.

4. The engineer arranges to lunch with the line executive in the company dining room to promote her or his views on a casual basis.

5. The engineer invites the line executive to lunch away from the company premises at the former's own expense.

6. The engineer offers to exchange favors that are possible within the regular operating rules and policies; for example, he or she agrees to do an immediate restudy of a particular job rate that has been resulting in serious difficulties between the line executive and the union.

7. The engineer agrees to favors involving a slight bending of the procedures and policies; for example, agreeing to delay introduction of a new method and rate, even though fully developed and ready to go, at the request of the line executive.

8. The engineer agrees to a favor involving a more serious bending of the procedures and policies; for example, "discovering" that the particular job rate mentioned in item 6 above is too tight, when it is not, and loosening it up for the benefit of the line executive.

9. The engineer agrees to cover for the line executive; for example, the line executive wishes to use the industrial engineering department as an excuse for failing to meet schedules because of presumed work interferences.

10. The engineer, with the assistance of understanding accountants, agrees to a transfer of industrial engineering budget funds to the line executive's department.[6]

The others listed are not formally required and can be construed as various forms of adjustment and accommodation. There are doubtless other possible actions that might be undertaken to persuade the line executive to cooperate. The available alternatives depend on the extent of power possessed by the two parties.

In instances where one has control over items or services that can be adapted to personal as well as organizational use, the power is even greater. There have been cases where personal furniture has been constructed on company time with company materials, as well as instances where personal cars have been repaired in company motor pools.

The degree of politicking is limited not only by the formal organization restrictions, but also by one's personal code of ethics and conscience. The fact that at times politics may be unethical should not preclude a discussion of the subject. That such actions as the above do exist in various business organizations is undeniable. Few businesses are run completely and rigidly by the book, and such politicking cannot be condemned per se. Some accommodations are constructive, whereas others are perhaps destructive of both organized activity and individual morals.

Values of Political Action

It is apparent some degree of politics is a fact of organized life, regardless of the caliber of people involved or the degree of formalization of organization rules and regulations. No doubt some political maneuvering can

6. Edwin B. Flippo and Gary M. Munsinger, *Management*, 4th ed. (Boston: Allyn and Bacon, Inc., 1978), p. 282.

make a net contribution toward organization effectiveness. Where there is head-on conflict and where interdependencies make some degree of cooperation essential, concessions worked out between the parties often involve some bending or reinterpretation of the rules. On many occasions, the various conflicting interests are all highly legitimate and rest on solid ground. Some type of informal accommodation, compromise, or exchange is essential for a degree of reconciliation that permits the basic work of the organization to continue. One is usually safe, personally, if one sticks to the rule book and the letter of the law. Unfortunately, one also becomes known as a pathological bureaucrat who is more interested in being right, according to the rules, than in accomplishing the objective as revealed by the situation. On the other hand, organizations could evolve into complete chaos if everyone acted as a power politician above the law, and the formal organization. It is clear that neither extreme is the answer.

SUMMARY

The official organizational structure portrays only a portion of the story of the interactions that exist within a firm. There emerges another structure consisting of informal relationships. Managers need to recognize the existence of the informal work groups in organizations if they are to effectively accomplish their tasks. This is necessary because of the synergistic effect that occurs when individuals join groups. Employees have much more influence in a group than they have alone. Although some managers attempt to reduce the influence of informal work groups, they continue to exist and bring with them both benefits and costs to the organization.

Status, power, and politics are concepts that all managers constantly observe. A person's rank or position in a group is referred to as status. Status symbols are visible signs of a person's social position and have several important values of status. It assists in meeting the needs of an individual, aids in the communication process, and serves as a motivational device for management.

Power, on the other hand, refers to the ability of one person to influence the behavior of another person. As with status, it is neither completely formal nor informal. The primary sources of power are: formal authority; informal authority; the ability to provide rewards and punishment; expertise; and identification with individuals who are respected. Power is important to managers because it permits them to benefit others on the behalf of the organization.

Politics in an organization provides positive values in promoting cooperation among individuals and groups with differing interests and objectives. Politics is a means by which power can be acquired, transferred, and exerted on others. Through politics, adjustments and accommodations are made to varying conditions and pressures. Some degree of political actions will occur in any organization regardless of the caliber of people involved or the degree of formalization or organization rules and regulations.

Review Questions

1. Why should a manager be aware of informal work groups?
2. What are the characteristics of the informal work group?
3. In your own words, describe the values and losses that may be attributed to the informal work group.
4. What is the purpose of a contact chart?
5. Define: Status; Power; Politics.
6. What are the three functions of status?
7. In your own words describe the various sources of power. What is the significance of the understanding of power to a manager?
8. What is the role of politics in today's business organization?

Exercises

1. Develop a contact chart and a sociogram for an organization of which you are a member. Interpret the results.
2. Visit three businesses. Attempt to identify the various status symbols associated with the organization.
3. Collect five articles from your daily newspaper that relate to the use of power. Describe how power was used to obtain results or why it failed to achieve results.

REFERENCES

Aldag, R. J., and Brief, A. P. "Relationships Between Leader Behavior Variability Indices and Subordinate Responses." *Personnel Psychology*, October 1977, pp. 586–601.

Burke, R. J., and Weir, T. "Team Building for More Effective Work Groups." *Canadian Banker and TCB Review*, November 1976, pp. 40–45.

Franklin, J. E. "Down the Organization: Influence Processes Across Levels of Hierarchy." *Administrative Science Quarterly*, June 1975, pp. 154–163.

Hall, R. H., et al. "Patterns of Interorganizational Relationships." *Administrative Science Quarterly*, September 1977, pp. 457–474.

Herker, D., and Aldrich, H. "Boundary Spanning Roles and Organization Structure," *Academy of Management Review*, April 1977, pp. 217–230.

Kelly, J. "Manager and Behavioral Technology." *Canadian Business Magazine*, April 1977, pp. 73–74.

McKenna, R. F. "Blending the Formal with the Informal System." *Journal of System Management*, June 1975, pp. 38–41.

Mayes, B. T., and Allen, R. W. "Toward a Definition of Organizational Politics." *Academy of Management Review*, October 1977, pp. 672–678.

Miles, R. H., and Perreault, W. D. "Organizational Role Conflict: Its Antecedents and Consequences." *Organizational Behavior and Human Performances*, October 1976, pp. 19–44.

Miller, J. "Isolation in Organizations: Alienation From Authority, Control, and Expressive Relations." *Administrative Science Quarterly*, June 1975, pp. 260–271.

Moschis, G. P. "Social Comparison and Informal Group Influence." *Journal of Marketing Research*, August 1976, pp. 237–244.

Phifer, S. H. "Performance Standards and the Circle of Influence." *Supervision*, October 1976, pp. 2–3.

Pilnick, S. "Getting to Grips with the Group Sub-culture." *Personnel Management*, July 1975, pp. 34–37.

Quinn, R. E. "Coping with Cupid: The Formation, Impact, and Management of Romantic Relationships in Organizations." *Administrative Science Quarterly*, March 1977, pp. 30–45.

Schmidt, S. M., and Kochan, T. A. "Interorganizational Relationships: Patterns and Motivations." *Administrative Science Quarterly*, June 1977, pp. 220–234.

Villarreal, J. J. "Sub-Optimal Activities within an Organization." *Managerial Planning*, November 1976, pp. 30–33.

Case Study

THE YOUNG ACCOUNTANT BECOMES AN INFORMAL LEADER

Upon graduation, Dave Maddala went to work as an accountant for Bradford, Inc., a manufacturer specializing in producing oil field parts. Dave brought with him an excellent record from his four years in college. Not only was Dave an excellent student, he was also extremely involved in all forms of campus activities. As both a junior and a senior, he was president of his class. People felt comfortable around Dave and his opinions were well-respected by the students and faculty.

Donald Dean, the department head took great pride in having hired Dave. He bragged to his superiors about how he was able to attract Dave to Bradford. As expected, when Dave began with Bradford, he started with the same intensity that earned him the respect in college. Dave learned the job quickly and within a very short period of time was identifying and initiating changes that could improve operations. Dave followed the chain of command and cleared each modification with Mr. Dean. This pleased Mr. Dean for he was able to take the credit for the changes with his superiors.

In the department there were ten other accountants who reported to Mr. Dean. However, as the employees came to recognize Dave's expertise, they began to go to him with their particular problems. Dave's personality was the type that made it easy for others to talk to him. Even though Dave was junior in age, the members regarded him as a true professional. As time went on, employees would even go to Dave with their personal problems.

A strange situation ultimately developed. Although not in the formal structure, another layer in the organization had developed. If an employee had a problem he or she would first go to Dave. If Dave could not solve it, he would go to Mr. Dean. Upward communication tended to go entirely through Dave.

Although Mr. Dean did not have the reputation of being extremely "swift" it did not take him long to see what had evolved. Although the department had gained in efficiency since Dave had joined the firm, Mr. Dean did not like the loss of power that he envisioned was occurring. He even felt that his career was in jeopardy. Dean reasoned that the only way to eliminate this "bad" situation was to ensure that Dave was either transferred or terminated.

Dean immediately began his harassment campaign. He would reprimand Dave in front of his peers. Anything that Dave recommended would be immediately disapproved. It did not take long for the other employees to recognize that if they associated with Dave they were in trouble. Various instances of harassment were noticed for those that even spoke to Dave. Ultimately, Donald's strategy worked; Dave quit. But an unanticipated situation also occurred. Six of his best accountants also resigned and the department was thrown into complete confusion.

Questions

1. Why had Dave Maddala become the informal leader?
2. To what extent was Dave a "threat" to his supervisor, Donald Dean? How important are the issues of status, power, and politics?
3. How can a strong informal group affect the operations of a department such as accounting?

Case Study

THE POWER OF THE INFORMAL GROUP

Don Prier had recently been hired as production planning manager for Surefire Airlines. Immediately after reporting to his new job, Don recognized that there were difficulties with the time control section. This section consisted of sixteen clerks and a supervisor who reported to him.

The basic function of the time control section was to maintain records on all rotatable parts used on a fleet of eighty-five passenger aircrafts.

Records reflected the date a part was installed or removed and total aircraft flying time. To maintain identification, serial numbers were recorded for each controlled part. The FAA required strict control of life-limited parts. Parts that had operated beyond their approved limit had to be removed and overhauled.

The problem that Don noticed was that there were numerous instances of inaccurate records. The records were in violation of FAA regulations and poor record-keeping resulted in excessive overhaul costs. When Don studied the situation he observed that the employees had formed an extremely strong informal work group. The members would accept or reject new employees into the work group based on factors completely unrelated to the job. Some outsiders observed that if a new employee's bowling score was not above 175 that he or she had little chance for success within the group. The group members bowled three times a week and had a great time together. Those who did not like to bowl and socialize frequently were ignored and made to feel uncomfortable to the point that they would quit. This resulted in an annual turnover rate of approximately 400 percent. Don realized that this problem had to be solved immediately or major problems could result for Surefire Airlines.

Questions

1. How did the informal work group affect the operations of the production planning department?
2. What action(s) should Don Prier take in coping with the informal group?

THE
DIRECTING
FUNCTION

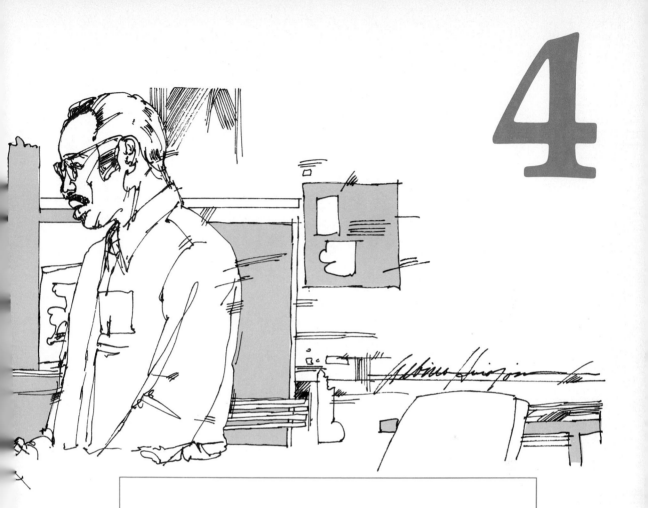

4

In Part 4 the various aspects of the directing function are presented. First, the basic theories of motivation are discussed in relation to management practices. This is followed by a look at the factors a manager must consider in developing effective leadership. Next, the effects of organizational climate, change, and development are described as they apply to the directing function. Part 4 is concluded with a discussion of the communication process, the barriers that affect communication, and the facilitators that may be used to improve a manager's communication ability.

Chapter 8

KEY TERMS

motivation

motives

behavior

Theory X

Theory Y

hierarchy of needs

hygiene factors

motivators

satisfiers

dissatisfiers

job enrichment

need for achievement

need for power

need for affiliation

expectancy

valence

behavior modification

organizational behavior modification

reinforcers

equity

job enlargement

self-fulfilling prophecies

Motivation

LEARNING OBJECTIVES

After completing this chapter you should be able to

1. Describe the process of motivation.
2. Identify the basic philosophies of human nature as contained in Theory X and Theory Y.
3. Describe the basic needs of man as presented in Maslow's hierarchy of needs theory and be able to explain how organizations attempt to satisfy these needs.
4. Identify Argyris' maturation theory and how it relates to motivation.
5. Describe the hygiene and motivation factors contained in Herzberg's motivation theory.
6. Explain how such motives as the needs for achievement, power, and affiliation affect the behavior of individuals.
7. Describe how expectancy theory can be useful to managers in motivating employees.
8. Explain organizational behavior modification and how the technique can be applied in organizations.
9. Describe the role of money as a motivator, programs of job enrichment, and the application of the self-fulfilling prophecy.
10. Explain the situational approach to motivation.

"You either do it my way or you're fired!" This type of motivation may have worked at the turn of the century, but today many employees would tell their supervisor to "take this job and shove it." Today's "new breed" of employees does not respond to "traditional" values that might have motivated them twenty or thirty years ago. Employees in today's organizations are better educated, more highly skilled, and work with more advanced technology. They have significantly higher expectations which creates difficult challenges for managers.

In general, our society has achieved a higher standard of living and people expect the improvements resulting from this higher living standard will continue. In addition to this, there have been rather significant changes in the make up of the labor force. In 1978, 41 percent of the labor

force was female compared to 30 percent in 1960. Along with the increased size and complexity of today's organizations, the proportion of manual workers relative to the number of professional and technical workers in the total labor force has declined. These changes provide a significant challenge to managers to provide a climate in which employees will contribute toward the accomplishments of organizational goals.

In view of these major developments, the manager must ask, "How do I motivate my employees to perform more effectively and efficiently?" This question reflects one of the most challenging aspects of a manager's job and it is frequently asked by managers in all types of organizations. The topic of motivation is one of the most important and frequently discussed subjects in management. In this chapter, we will discuss various philosophies of human behavior. The objective of our discussion is to provide managerial insight into the following concepts:

- The process of motivation
- Philosophies of human nature
- Theories of motivation
- Approaches and techniques available to enhance motivation
- The impact of the situational factors on the motivation process

MOTIVATION DEFINED

motivation

Motivating a worker today is considerably more complex than the simple application of the "carrot and the stick" approach used by many managers of yesterday. **Motivation** is the process of influencing or stimulating a person to take action that will accomplish a desired goal. In an organization, personnel are said to be *motivated* if they perform their jobs efficiently and effectively.

motives

In Figure 8.1, a basic, but simple, model of motivation is illustrated. Everyone has certain needs. A person cannot be motivated until a need is activated (this need activation is referred to as a motive). **Motives** explain *why* people engage in certain behavior, and are the drives or impulses within an individual that cause the behavior.

An aroused need (motive) will cause some type of behavior to take place. Such behavior is directed toward a particular goal or want that the person has learned will satisfy the need. For example, if a person feels hunger, he or she has a need for food. This results in action designed ultimately to obtain food. In our complex society, this typically entails searching for and obtaining a job so that money can be secured. The successful accomplishment of this goal or want results in food being obtained and, thus, the satisfaction of the need. Or, a person may feel a

FIGURE 8.1
The Motivation Process

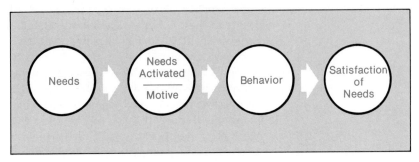

need to associate with other people. This leads to actions of searching out other individuals and associating and interacting with them in the hope of obtaining the goal of friendship.

This simple explanation of motivation does not represent the true complexity of the process. Any single act by a particular person may well be reflecting a number of different needs. Striving for a promotion may be caused by a need for material possessions or a need for recognition. The same act by another person may be due to different needs. One person may seek friendships to satisfy his or her need for association with other people, whereas another individual may wish to use friendships for advancing a career. One person seeks recognition through hard work; another seeks it by being the fastest driver on the highway. The same need can be expressed in a number of different ways.

Management has traditionally relied on the use of rewards such as increased pay, job security, and good working conditions, or punishments such as dismissal, demotions, or withholding rewards to motivate employees to achieve high performance. However, management in today's environment cannot rely on the *manipulation* of pay, benefits, or working

INSIGHTS TO SUCCESS

Once you have demonstrated your technical or professional ability in an organization, and are being considered for supervisory responsibilities, one of the most important things becomes how you relate to other persons, how you get along with others, how you motivate them. Technical and professional skills and performance are still important. But other abilities begin to take on increasing significance. Your job begins to move from doing an operation to managing an operation.

JAMES E. LEE, President, Gulf Oil Corporation

conditions to motivate personnel to perform effectively. Motivation is a much more complicated process.

The modern manager must be sufficiently aware of basic human needs to understand much of the behavior that he or she observes. A manager cannot assume that all people are alike, or that other people are like him or her. The one major commonality is that there is a reason for all **behavior.** The manager would do well not to condemn any act as being idiotic, pointless, or senseless. In the eyes of the individual, the behavior makes sense. The manager must seek to understand the forces that energize the behavior. It is the responsibility of the manager to develop programs that will make use of the enormous energy that is within every person.

behavior

PHILOSOPHIES OF HUMAN NATURE

Human behavior has puzzled managers throughout history. People appear to have a capacity for tenderness, sympathy, and love while at the same time possessing tendencies toward cruelty, callousness, hate, and destruction. If individuals are basically tender, loving, and sympathetic, they may need little external regulation. On the other hand, if individuals are cruel or callous they may need to be closely controlled and regimented for the good of society.

McGregor's Theory X and Theory Y

Douglas McGregor stressed the importance of understanding the relationships between motivation and behavior.[1] In observing the practices and approaches of traditional managers, McGregor believed that managers usually attempted to motivate employees by one of two basic approaches. He referred to these approaches as **Theory X** and **Theory Y. Theory X,** or the traditional view of management, suggests that managers are required to coerce, control, or threaten employees in order to motivate employees. In contrast to this, McGregor proposed an alternative philosophy of human nature which he referred to as **Theory Y.** Following Theory Y, a manager basically believes people are capable of being responsible and mature. Thus, they do not require coercion or excessive control by the manager in order to perform effectively. McGregor's basic belief was that Theory Y was a more realistic assessment of people.

Theory X, Theory Y

Table 8.1 illustrates the different assumptions of these two philosophies of human nature. The Theory Y assumptions represent the manager's

1. Douglas McGregor, *The Human Side of Enterprise* (New York: McGraw-Hill, 1960).

JERRY O. WILLIAMS

Vice-President, Planning and Administration
Maremont Corporation

MaReMONT

Although Jerry O. Williams has a B.S. in Electrical Engineering and an M.S.E. in Operations Research, he decided to get out of "pure" engineering functions because of the lack of enough interaction with people. Jerry said, "I found out I enjoyed the functions of organizing, motivating, and planning more than I did working with devices and apparatus." Jerry gives the following reasons for selecting a career in management. He—

- Wanted to be involved in the decision-making process
- Wanted to have some impact on the process that was charting the company's and his own future
- Enjoyed working with people and got tremendous satisfaction in motivating and directing a diverse group of people to accomplish a common goal
- Desired to develop and guide people for larger roles in the corporation

After being with a large company like General Electric and then going to a smaller company (Stanford Research Institute), Jerry felt he would like to be in a medium-sized company where he could have a greater impact on decisions. In order to do this, he went back to General Electric to establish his credentials in strategic planning. Next, he accepted a position with Maremont Corporation to initiate their planning process. Maremont manufactures automobile parts and has approximately 8,000 employees.

Because Jerry has been associated with both engineering- and managerial-related jobs, he can make the following point with regard to earning potential, "A career in management is better than other fields like engineering which starts with a high salary but levels off much sooner than management." With regard to the importance of education to a manager, Jerry states, "With the proliferation of M.B.A.'s, a person needs to have a graduate degree just to participate. This does not guarantee success. However, it does make it possible for a person to participate." When it comes to company loyalty, he also has some interesting observations. He says, "A person should be loyal as long as he is working for a company. However, when it comes to career, do what is best for your career. 'Look out for number one.' Others look out for you only as it affects their careers."

Finally, when Jerry was asked what he believes are the most important qualities for success, he described the following:

- Perseverance in achieving goals.
- Enjoy what you are doing and the money will come.
- Develop interpersonal relationships.
- Anticipate the needs of the organization and be able to fill those needs.
- Be dependable—Get the job done on time and correctly.
- Be creative.
- Be a little impatient. Not always satisfied with the status quo. Look for other ways to do things and do them faster.
- Flexibility. Be able to adjust to new techniques, procedures, and policies without getting frustrated.
- Understand the political environment and be able to work within the system.

It's obvious Jerry has followed his own advice as he is now a very successful executive who has much more potential for advancement.

TABLE 8.1
A Comparison of McGregor's Theory X and Theory Y
Assumptions about Human Nature

Theory X	Theory Y
The average person inherently dislikes work and will avoid it if possible.	The expenditure of physical and mental effort in work is as natural as play or rest.
Because of the dislike of work, most people must be coerced, controlled, directed, and threatened with punishment to get them to perform effectively.	People will exercise self-direction and self-control in the service of objectives to which they are committed.
The average person lacks ambition, avoids responsibility, and seeks security and economic rewards above all else.	Commitment to objectives is a function of the rewards associated with achievement.
Most people lack creative ability and are resistant to change.	The average person learns, under proper conditions, not only to accept but to seek responsibility.
Since most people are self-centered, they are not concerned with the goals of the organizaion.	The capacity to exercise a relatively high degree of imagination, ingenuity, and creativity in the solution of organizational problems is widely, not narrowly, distributed in the population.

Source Based on Douglas McGregor, *The Human Side of Enterprise* (New York: McGraw-Hill Book Co.), 1960.

boundless faith in the capacity and potential of people. If one accepts the Theory Y philosophy of human nature, managerial practices such as the following will be seriously considered: (1) abandonment of time clocks, (2) flexible working hours on an individual basis, (3) job enrichment, (4) management by objectives, and (5) participative decision making. All are based on the beliefs that abilities are widespread in the population and each person is trusted to behave in a responsible manner. Thus, management should structure the organizational environment in a manner that will release this tremendous human potential. However, one should not conclude that McGregor advocated Theory Y as the panacea for all managerial problems. The Theory Y philosophy is not utopia, but McGregor argued that it did provide a basis for improved management and organizational performance.

ARGYRIS'S MATURITY THEORY

The research of Chris Argyris has also aided managers in developing a more complete understanding of human behavior. Argyris emphasizes the importance of the process of maturity. He suggests that there is a basic difference between the demands of the mature personality and the demands of the typical business organization. Argyris concludes that if plans, policies, procedures, and rules are prescribed in detail, an employee will need to be submissive and passive, which suggests a *Theory X* type organization. The demand is for the subordinate to concentrate on the orders as given and not question or attempt to understand these orders in a broader perspective. In brief, such a detailed prescription may ask individuals to work in an environment where

1. They are provided minimal control over their work-a-day world.
2. They are expected to be passive, dependent, and subordinate.
3. They are expected to have a short time perspective.
4. They are induced to perfect and value the frequent use of a few shallow abilities.
5. They are expected to produce under conditions leading to psychological failure.[2]

When the mature employee encounters the conditions described above, three reactions are possible:

1. **Escape.** An employee may escape by quitting the job, being absent from work, or attempting to climb to higher levels in the firm where the structure is less rigid.
2. **Fight.** A person can "fight the system" by exerting pressure on the organization by means of informal groups or through formally organized labor unions.
3. **Adapt.** The most typical reaction by employees is one of adaptation by developing an attitude of apathy or indifference. The employee "plays the game" and pay becomes the compensation for the penalty of working.

Of the three reactions above, Argyris considers adaptation to be the least representative of good mental health.

However, managers cannot assume that all employees are mature as defined by Argyris or Theory Y types as defined by McGregor. These assumptions may be very valid when managers are dealing with highly educated professional, technical, and managerial employees. Security may mean more to the industrial worker than to the highly educated professional. The industrial worker may value the freedom of thought permitted by the highly structured and repetitive tasks which may be boring to others.

It could be argued that a highly structured environment requires employees to act in an immature manner. In fact, managers have conditioned employees to prefer that type of behavior. Many people can and have adjusted to tightly regimented work situations which Argyris contends would demand immature behavior. One need only observe workers on an assembly line to recognize this conclusion. The resulting condition

2. Chris Argyris, *Personality and Organization* (New York: Harper & Row, Inc., 1957).

or adaptation is one of indifference and apathy which may be a successful acceptable adaptation. However, only a fraction of the jobs in American business are of the highly structured, totally controlled type. To the degree that an open job market operates effectively, there will be some matching of varying human needs and organizational demands. One writer points out that 85 percent of American workers indicated that they were satisfied with their jobs, that fewer than 2 percent actually work on an assembly line, and that the typical employee does not even work for a manufacturing organization.[3]

The philosophical theories of human nature discussed above provide the basis for a manager's approach to motivation and leadership. As such, the theories of both McGregor and Argyris should be kept in mind as we present the various concepts of human motivation in this chapter and as we discuss leadership styles in chapter 9.

INSIGHTS TO SUCCESS

Give each assignment 100 percent effort and learn what you can from each assignment. Be particularly conscious of people and what motivates them—it's people you will be managing.

R. H. SCHWARZ, Vice-President, Kaiser Aluminum & Chemical Corporation

---

THEORIES RELATING TO MOTIVATION

There are nearly as many theories of motivation as there are psychologists who develop them. Because of the vast amount of difference associated with the theories, the acceptance of one may actually mean that another theory will be rejected. None of the theories provides a universally accepted approach that explains *all* human behavior. Human beings are far too complex. However, a basic understanding of these theories can be useful to managers as they attempt to motivate people in their organizations. Our purpose in presenting these different theories of human motivation is not to identify one as being superior. Rather, our purpose is to develop a thought process that will ultimately lead a manager to develop his or her own concept of motivation.

MASLOW'S HIERARCHY OF NEEDS

Though there obviously are individual differences, many psychologists believe that there are certain patterns or configurations of human needs. A

3. Irving Kristol, "Is the American Worker Alienated?" *The Wall Street Journal*, January 18, 1973.

FIGURE 8.2
Maslow's Need Hierarchy and How Needs Are Satisfied by the Organization

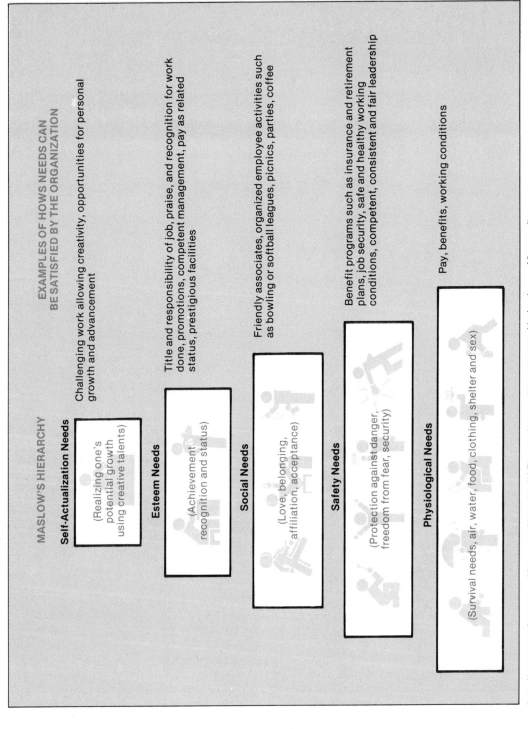

MASLOW'S HIERARCHY

Self-Actualization Needs

(Realizing one's potential growth using creative talents)

Esteem Needs

(Achievement recognition and status)

Social Needs

(Love, belonging, affiliation, acceptance)

Safety Needs

(Protection against danger, freedom from fear, security)

Physiological Needs

(Survival needs, air, water, food, clothing, shelter and sex)

EXAMPLES OF HOWS NEEDS CAN BE SATISFIED BY THE ORGANIZATION

Challenging work allowing creativity, opportunities for personal growth and advancement

Title and responsibility of job, praise, and recognition for work done, promotions, competent management, pay as related status, prestigious facilities

Friendly associates, organized employee activities such as bowling or softball leagues, picnics, parties, coffee

Benefit programs such as insurance and retirement plans, job security, safe and healthy working conditions, competent, consistent and fair leadership

Pay, benefits, working conditions

Data (for diagram) based on Hierarchy of Needs in "A Theory of Human Motivation" in *Motivation and Personality*, 2nd Edition, by Abraham H. Maslow. Copyright © 1970 by Abraham H. Maslow. By permission of Harper & Row, Publishers. Inc.

common approach to establishing this need pattern is that of developing a universal need hierarchy. Abraham Maslow has proposed one widely accepted pattern which is illustrated in Figure 8.2. Examples of how an organization might help to satisfy these basic needs are also presented. Maslow states that individuals are motivated to satisfy certain unsatisfied needs. His theory of human motivation is based on the following assumptions:

- Individuals have certain needs that influence their behavior. Needs that are not satisfied motivate or influence behavior. Thus, satisfied needs do not motivate behavior.
- Needs are arranged according to a hierarchy of importance from the basic physiological to the complex self-actualization needs.
- An individual's needs at any level on the hierarchy emerge only when the lower-level needs are reasonably well satisfied. A need does not have to be totally satisfied for it to no longer motivate behavior.[4]

hierarchy of needs

According to Maslow's **hierarchy of needs** theory, an individual's needs are arranged in a hierarchy from the lower-level physiological needs to the higher-level needs for self-actualization. The physiological needs are the highest priority because until they are reasonably satisfied other higher level needs will not emerge to motivate behavior. Next, we will discuss the five basic needs presented in Maslow's hierarchy and ways in which these needs can be at least partially satisfied by an organization.

Physiological Needs

It is generally agreed that the basic needs such as food, clothing, and shelter are our first concern. The organization helps individuals satisfy their basic needs by providing good salaries, benefits, and working conditions. Once these basic needs are satisfied to a reasonable degree, the individual then becomes aware of higher-level needs.

Safety Needs

Once the physiological needs are reasonably well satisfied, the next higher level of needs becomes important as motivator. According to Maslow, these are the needs for safety or security. These needs cause the individual

---

4. Abraham Maslow, *Motivation and Personality* (New York: Harper & Bros., 1954).

to become concerned about security, protection from danger, and freedom from fear. In an organization, these needs may be satisfied by job security, benefit programs including insurance and retirement plans, and safe and healthy working conditions.

Social Needs

These needs reflect an individual's desire for love, affiliation, and acceptance in relationship with other people. In a work environment, social needs are concerned with relating to friendly associates, identification with a *good* company, and through participation in organized activities such as bowling or softball leagues, picnics, or parties.

Esteem Needs

These needs represent the individual's concern for feeling important and respected by others. The esteem or ego needs relate to the need for achievement, recognition, and status. Individuals seek approval and recognition from others. Job title and responsibilities, praise, and competent management are all important factors in satisfying the esteem needs.

Self-Actualization

Once esteem needs are reasonably well satisfied, the highest level of need, self-actualization, becomes important. Self-actualization or self-fulfillment is the need to realize one's capacities and potentialities by achieving specific goals. A person attempting to satisfy this need seeks challenging work assignments that allow for creativity and opportunities for personal growth and advancement.

A person is never completely satisfied on any need level, but a sufficient amount of gratification of lower priority needs must be met if the individual is to seek to satisfy upper-level needs. Maslow suggests a hypothetical example for an average citizen who is 85 percent satisfied in physiological needs, 70 percent in safety needs, 50 percent in love needs, 40 percent in the self-esteem category, and 10 percent in self-actualization needs.

The use of the universal need hierarchy by a manager in motivating employees is based on the concept that *reasonably well satisfied needs do not motivate.* Therefore, if an individual's lower-level needs are fairly satisfied, management cannot use these needs to motivate behavior.

HERZBERG'S MOTIVATION-HYGIENE THEORY

One of the most stimulating and controversial theories of human nature proposed in recent years is that of Frederick Herzberg.[5] Herzberg's Motivation-Hygiene Theory grew out of research directed toward determining what factors lead to satisfaction on the job. The usual approach is one of examining a number of factors such as the work itself, pay, working conditions, supervision, status, security, and the like.

The Herzberg theory proposes that there are in reality *two* significantly different classes of factors and thus two different continuums. One class,
hygiene factors referred to as **hygiene factors,** makes up a continuum ranging from dissatisfaction to no dissatisfaction. As illustrated in Figure 8.3, hygiene factors relate to the environment and are external to the job. Herzberg indicates that these factors do not serve to promote job satisfaction; rather, their absence or deficiency can create dissatisfaction. Hygiene factors "maintain" an employee; they do not make a person healthy, but rather prevent unhealthiness. An organization that meets the hygiene need of its employees will eliminate dissatisfaction, but will not create job satisfaction.

motivators The second class of factors or needs referred to as **motivators,** makes up a continuum leading from no job satisfaction to satisfaction. As illustrated in the exhibit, the work itself, recognition, achievement, possibility of

FIGURE 8.3
Motivation and Hygiene Factors

Dissatisfaction	No Dissatisfaction	No Job Satisfaction	Job Satisfaction
Hygiene Factors (Needs)		Motivation Factors (Needs)	
Environment		The Job	

- ☐ Pay
- ☐ Status
- ☐ Security
- ☐ Working conditions
- ☐ Fringe benefits
- ☐ Policies and administrative practices
- ☐ Interpersonal relations

- ☐ Meaningful and challenging work
- ☐ Recognition for accomplishment
- ☐ Feeling of achievement
- ☐ Increased responsibility
- ☐ Opportunities for growth and advancement
- ☐ The job itself

5. Frederick Herzberg, *Work and the Nature of Man* (Cleveland: World, 1966).

growth, and advancement are motivation needs. These are concerned with the work itself, rather than its surrounding physical, administrative, or social environment. They are internal to the job itself and if the worker is to be truly motivated, the job itself is the major source of that motivation.

satisfiers, dissatisfiers Herzberg's theory seems to suggest a clear delineation between **satisfiers** (motivators) and **dissatisfiers** (hygiene) in terms of absolute categories—i.e., pay is categorized as a hygiene factor for each individual. Pay may be a dissatisfier to some individuals and a satisfier to others. Thus, it can be argued that hygiene and motivation factors should not be considered as absolute categories.

Specific criticisms of Herzberg's theory include the following:

1. The research methodology using the critical incident technique of asking people to reflect back on experiences may cause people to recall only the most recent experiences. Also, analysis of the responses derived from this approach is highly subjective.

2. The theory is most applicable to knowledge workers—managers, engineers, accountants, and other professional level personnel. Thus, it is not possible to say that the findings apply equally to other occupational groups. Most studies have shown that when the employees were professional or managerial level employees, the theory is applicable. However, studies of lower level or manual workers are less supportive of the theory.

3. The theory focusses too much attention on "satisfaction" or "dissatisfaction" rather than on the performance level of the individual. Satisfaction may or may not be directly related to job performance.

Despite these criticisms, Herzberg's two-factor theory has made a significant contribution toward improving a manager's basic understanding of human behavior. As a result, managers must be aware of the potentially successful application of the theory as our work force becomes increasingly better educated and develops higher expectations of management, and as organizational life becomes more complex.

There is a fairly close relationship between Maslow's hierarchy of needs theory and Herzberg's motivation hygiene theory (see Figure 8.4). As may be seen, Herzberg's *motivators* are most closely related to the esteem and self-actualization needs on Maslow's hierarchy. The hygiene factors closely correspond to the physiological, safety, and social needs. Herzberg's basic contention is that most organizations give inadequate attention to the *motivation factors* in the work environment. Most of the efforts of managers are concentrated on meeting the lower-level needs which are satisfied by the *hygiene factors.* But, just because the hygiene or maintenance needs are satisfied—by good pay, benefits, or working conditions—this

FIGURE 8.4
Maslow and Herzberg Related

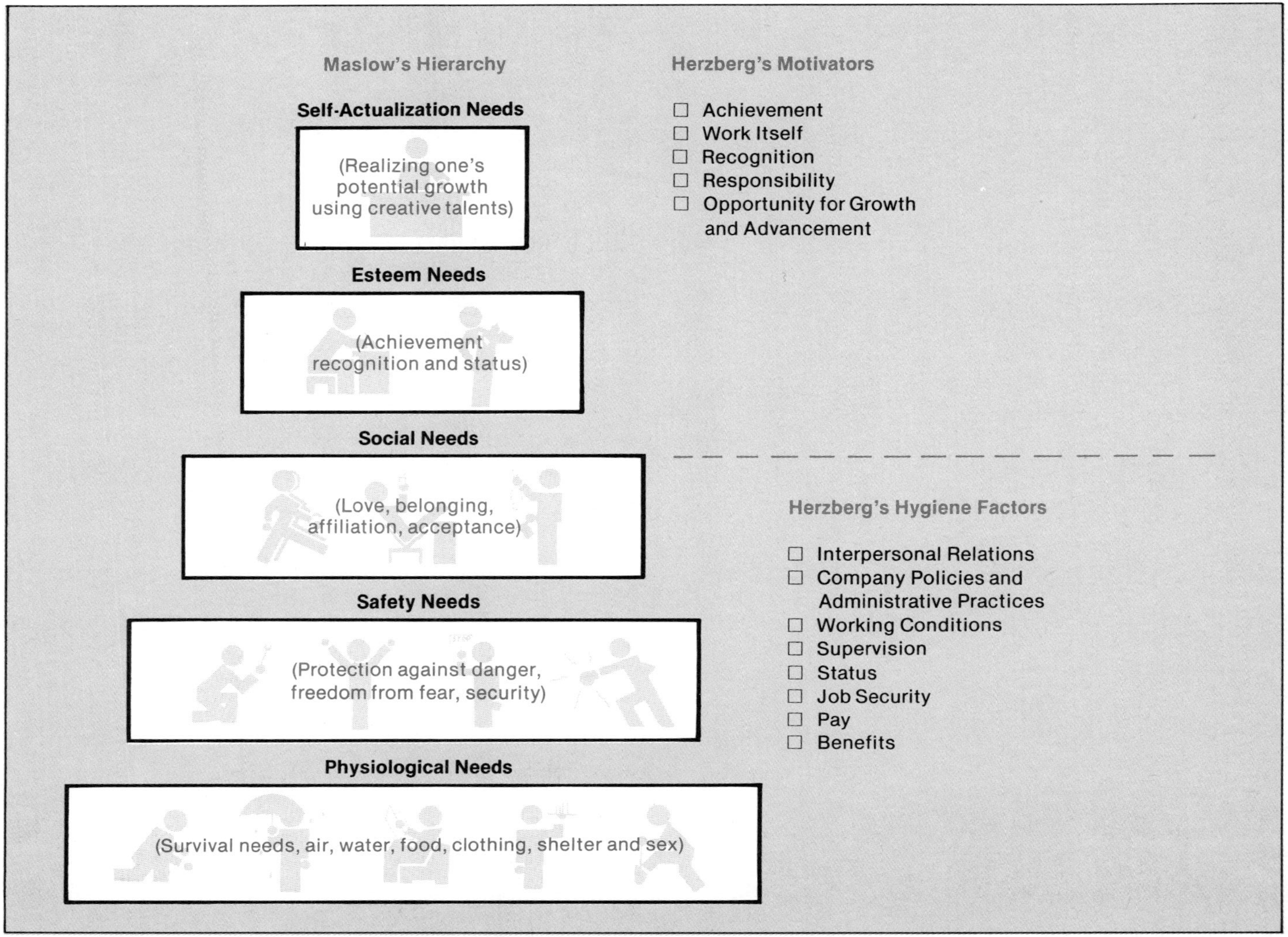

Maslow's Hierarchy

Self-Actualization Needs

(Realizing one's
potential growth
using creative talents)

Esteem Needs

(Achievement
recognition and status)

Social Needs

(Love, belonging,
affiliation, acceptance)

Safety Needs

(Protection against danger,
freedom from fear, security)

Physiological Needs

(Survival needs, air, water, food, clothing, shelter and sex)

Herzberg's Motivators

☐ Achievement
☐ Work Itself
☐ Recognition
☐ Responsibility
☐ Opportunity for Growth
   and Advancement

Herzberg's Hygiene Factors

☐ Interpersonal Relations
☐ Company Policies and
   Administrative Practices
☐ Working Conditions
☐ Supervision
☐ Status
☐ Job Security
☐ Pay
☐ Benefits

does not mean that the individual's performance will be positively influenced. To achieve effectiveness, the organization must satisfy both the hygiene and motivation needs of its employees. Most organizations have given considerable attention to the hygiene needs, but inadequate attention to the motivation needs of its personnel. This is understandable; hygiene needs can be met in a more tangible or specific manner than can the motivational needs. It may be easier to provide employees with improved pay, fringe benefits, or working conditions than a job that is more responsible or challenging.

job enrichment

Advocates of Herzberg's two-factor theory of motivation suggest that management can assist employees in meeting their motivational needs by providing employees with more challenging and responsible jobs. According to Herzberg, increasing the level of autonomy, skill variety, task significance, and feedback will lead to better job performance and more satisfied employees. This is known as **job enrichment** which will be discussed later in the chapter.

McCLELLAND'S THEORY OF HUMAN MOTIVES

need for achievement
need for power
need for affiliation

Whereas Maslow's theory stresses a universal hierarchy of needs, the research of David McClelland stresses that there are certain needs that are learned and socially acquired as the individual interacts with the environment. McClelland's theory concerns three motives—the **need for achievement (*n Ach*)**, the **need for power (*n Pow*)**, and the **need for affiliation (*n Aff*)**. A *motive* is a reason that explains behavior. McClelland had conducted numerous studies attempting to define and measure these basic motives. To varying degrees, each of us possesses these motives. However, one of the needs will tend to be more characteristic of the individual than the other two.[6]

Need for Achievement

A person with a high need for achievement tends to be characterized as an individual that—

1. wants to take personal responsibility for finding solutions to problems;
2. is goal-oriented;
3. seeks a challenge—and establishes moderate, realistic and attainable goals that involve risk but that are not impossible to attain;
4. desires concrete feedback on his or her performance.

6. David R. Hampton, Charles E. Summer, and Ross A. Webber, *Organizational Behavior and the Practice of Management* (Glenview, Ill.: Scott, Foresman, 1978), pp. 11–15.

People exhibiting a high *n Ach* have found the above pattern of behavior personally rewarding. McClelland's research has shown that a high *n Ach* is probably a strong or dominant need in only 10 percent of the U.S. population. Persons high in the need for achievement tend to gravitate toward entrepreneurial and sales positions. In these occupations an individual is better able to "manage" himself or herself and satisfy the basic drive for achievement.

Need for Power

A high need for power means that individuals seek to influence or control others. Such individuals tend to be characterized by the following types of behavior:

1. Is concerned with acquiring, exercising, or retaining power or influence over others
2. Likes to compete with others in situations that allow him or her to be dominant
3. Enjoys confrontations with others

McClelland says that there are two basic aspects of power—positive and negative. Positive use of power is absolutely essential if a manager is to effectively accomplish results through the efforts of others. The negative "face" of power is when an individual seeks power for his or her own personal benefit, which may prove detrimental to the organization.[7]

Need for Affiliation

The need for affiliation is related to the desire for affection and establishing friendly relationships. A person with a high need for affiliation tends to be characterized as one who—

1. seeks to establish and maintain friendships and close emotional relationships with others;
2. wants to be liked by others;
3. enjoys parties, social activities, and "bull" sessions;
4. seeks a sense of belonging by joining groups or organizations.

The most effective mixture of these three motives depends on the situation. In studies of over 500 managers, it was concluded that the most

7. D. C. McClelland and David H. Burnham, "Power Is the Great Motivator," *Harvard Business Review* 54 (March–April 1976): 103.

effective top managers have a high need for power, a low need for affiliation, and are high in the need to use this power in a participative manner for the good of the organization. Managers also have a strong need for achievement, but it is not strong enough to interfere with the management process. After all, management is getting things done through the efforts of others, and not shoving them aside so that you can do the task yourself.

Outstanding sales personnel tend to be high in the need for achievement and moderately high in the need for affiliation. Entrepreneurs who develop ideas and promote specific enterprises tend to be high in achievement motivation. They delight in personally solving problems and getting immediate feedback on the degree of success. Entrepreneurs sometimes are unable to make the transition to top-level management positions. Their need for personal achievement gets in the way of the requirements for effectively influencing the organization's employees.

VROOM'S EXPECTANCY THEORY OF MOTIVATION

It is essential for managers to develop an understanding of human needs and the variety of organizational means available to satisfy the needs of employees. However, the *needs* approach to motivation as developed by Maslow and Herzberg does not adequately account for differences in individual employees or explain why people behave in certain ways in accomplishing goals. Victor Vroom developed an approach to motivation known as the expectancy theory which attempts to explain behavior in terms of an individual's goals, choices, and the expectations of achieving these goals.[8] It assumes people can determine which outcomes they prefer and make realistic estimates of the chances of obtaining them.

The key concepts of the expectancy theory are that motivation depends on

expectancy

- An individual's **expectancy** (his or her perception of the chances or probability) that a particular outcome will occur as a result of certain behavior.

valence

- How much value an individual places on a specific outcome (this is known as **valence**).

These factors—expectancy and valence—determine motivation. Both must be present before a high level of motivation can occur. In other words, a high expectancy or a high valence alone will not ensure motivation . For example, if an employee had a low expectancy (perceived little chance) of

8. Victor Vroom, *Work and Motivation* (New York: John Wiley and Sons, 1964).

receiving a pay increase even though he or she placed a high value on money, the employee would not be highly motivated to work hard to attain the increase.

All employees in an organization do not share the same goals or values regarding pay, job security, promotions, benefits, or working conditions. For instance, Sam Johnson, a supervisor in the systems and programming division, places a high value on receiving a promotion to a more challenging and responsible position. Sam perceives that excellent performance in his current supervisory position is essential to achieving his desired promotion. Thus, Sam will seek to perform in a superior manner in order to achieve the promotion. Another employee, Bill Thomas, an office supervisor, values stability and job security and is not interested in promotion because he does not want more responsibility. Thus, Bill will not be motivated by an opportunity for a promotion.

A key factor in the expectancy model is how the employee perceives the goals or values, not what the manager believes the employee should seek or value. Thus, employees are motivated by what they perceive or expect in terms of rewards as a result of a given behavior. A manager's ability to motivate employees depends on a thorough knowledge of each individual employee as to their background, goals, experiences, etc. The manager needs to identify what sparks motivation in the employee.

A major contribution of the expectancy theory is that it explains how the goals of employees influence their behavior on the job. The employees' behavior depends on their assessment of the probability that the behavior will actually lead to the attainment of the goal.

In summary, the manager who wishes to use the expectancy model of motivation should devote attention to the following activities:

1. Ensuring that employees have sufficient training to do the task assigned.
2. Removing organizational obstacles to proper performance.
3. Instilling employees' confidence concerning capacity to perform.
4. Selecting organizational rewards that will meet specific employee needs.
5. Communicating clearly the relationship between rewards and performance.
6. Administering the reward system in a consistent and equitable fashion so that employees will perceive a relationship between performance and the rewards they receive.

SKINNER'S BEHAVIOR MODIFICATION

Although most managers over the years have used informal versions of the expectancy model, the concept is carried to its fullest with reinforce-

behavior modification

ment theories or under programs labeled organizational **behavior modification.** Reinforcement theory is based primarily on the research of B. F. Skinner and has been increasingly applied in business situations.

Reinforcement theory is concerned with the ways in which behavior is learned as the result of either positive or negative consequences. People tend to repeat behaviors that they have learned will produce pleasant outcomes. Behavior that is reinforced will be repeated and behavior that is not reinforced will not be repeated. If you have found out that an "A" can be obtained by studying, you continue to study. On the other hand, if you discover you can obtain an "A" by "playing politics" with the teacher, then you will likely continue this practice.

Skinner contends that people's behavior can be controlled and shaped by rewarding (reinforcing) desired behavior while ignoring undesirable actions. Over time, the reinforced behavior will tend to be repeated, whereas the unrewarded behavior will tend to be extinguished and disappear. Punishment of undesired behavior is to be avoided since it may contribute to feelings of restraint and actions of rebellion. Thus, over a period of years, the conditioner can control human behavior without the person becoming aware of being controlled. In his book, *Beyond Freedom and Dignity,* Skinner says that people can be controlled and shaped while at the same time feeling free.[9]

Skinner's theory of shaping behavior is useful to managers but one should not assume that human behavior is simple to understand and/or modify. Some Skinner-oriented conditioning techniques are compatible with the participative management recommendations of Argyris and McGregor and the job enrichment programs suggested by Herzberg. Obtaining immediate feedback of results on an enriched job is a form of instant reward related to behavior on the job. The primary technique suggested by Skinner is organization behavior modification.

**MOST IMPORTANT REASON FOR SUCCESS
AND EFFECTIVENESS AS A MANAGER**

Managers succeed if they understand and can motivate people. Managers who understand leadership will be successful. Add the characteristics of loyalty and willingness to give the job all the time it requires. Very few clock watchers ever make it to the top.

CHARLES W. MERRITT, President, Commercial Metals Company

---

organizational
behavior modification

Organizational behavior modification (OBM) rests on two fundamental concepts: (1) people act in ways they find most personally rewarding, and

9. B. F. Skinner, *Beyond Freedom and Dignity* (New York: Alfred A. Knopf, 1971).

reinforcers

(2) by controlling the rewards, people's behavior can be shaped and determined. In OBM, rewards are termed **reinforcers** because the goal is to stimulate continuation of the rewarded behavior. What reinforcers actually work in managing people is determined by a manager's trial and error and experience. What is successful with one employee may not work with another because their needs and wants differ. Praise is used most frequently because it is most readily available. But, it becomes less effective whenever it becomes predictable or is continuously applied. Money is also used, as are public or private letters of commendation, time off, increased status, and the like.

In OBM, punishment is rejected as a reinforcer because it suppresses the undesired behavior while at the same time stimulating anger, hostility, aggression, and rebellion. And, at times, it is difficult to identify the punishment. In one instance, placing prisoners in solitary confinement on bread and water turned out to be a high status symbol and led to repetition of offenses. When the bread and water was changed to baby food, the status symbol disappeared, leading to a significant reduction in the number of undesirable acts. When undesired behavior is not rewarded, it tends to disappear over time.

In reinforcing desired behavior in a positive fashion, it is important to allocate the rewards soon after the behavior occurs so that the person perceives a clear and immediate linkage. Fast and accurate feedback of information to the performer in itself constitutes a reinforcer.

Organization behavior modification has been used successfully in a number of organizations to improve performance. In one firm, positive reinforcement was used to reduce absenteeism.[10] Each day an employee came to work on time, he or she received a playing card. At the end of the week, the highest poker hand received $20.00. Over a three-month period, the absenteeism rate of the experimental group decreased 18 percent, whereas that of a control group actually increased. In their use of OBM, Michigan Bell Telephone identified specific desired behaviors such as the following:(1) service promptness in answering calls, (2) shortness of time taken to give information, (3) use of proper references in handling the call, and (4) attendance.[11] Praise and recognition were the dominant reinforcers. The results were an improvement in attendance by 50 percent and above standard productivity and efficiency levels.

The Emery Air Freight OBM program is one of the biggest success stories to date.[12] It used the simple reinforcers of information feedback

10. Ed Pedalino and Victor U. Gamboa, "Behavior Modification and Absenteeism," *Journal of Applied Psychology* 59 (December 1974): 694–698.

11. W. Clay Hamner and Ellen P. Hamner, "Behavior Modification on the Bottom Line," *Organizational Dynamics* 4 (Spring 1976): 12.

12. "At Emery Air Freight: Positive Reinforcement Boosts Performance," *Organizational Dynamics* 1 (Autumn 1973): 41–50.

and praise to condition employee behavior. In responding to customer questions about service and schedules within a standard 90-minute period, performance moved from 30 percent of the standard to 90 percent within a few days. Employees were provided with feedback charts through which they could monitor their own performance. Employees who did not achieve the desired results were reminded of the goal and then praised for their honesty. This 90 percent achievement remained stable for over three years. As a result of the application of OBM, estimated savings to Emery Air Freight were placed at $650,000 per year.

If the manager desires to use OBM, the following actions are necessary:

- Identifying the desired performance in specific terms, for example, improving attendance rate or answering questions within one hour
- Identifying the rewards that will reinforce the desired behavior, for example, praise, money, time off
- Making the reward a direct consequence of the behavior
- Selecting the optimum reinforcement schedule

Despite the successes achieved by behavior modification, it has been criticized as being a manipulative and autocratic approach to the management of people. People are conditioned to change their behavior in the direction required by management and the organization. Some critics argue that OBM is not consistent with the theories of such behavioral scientists as Maslow, Argyris, or McGregor. The assumption underlying these theories is that people are motivated by their own internal needs and are capable of a degree of self-control. On the other hand, OBM assumes that the causes of human behavior are in the environment and therefore external to the individual.

APPROACHES AND TECHNIQUES AVAILABLE TO ENHANCE MOTIVATION

In addition to the above theories of motivation, there are several approaches and techniques that the practicing manager should consider.

THE ROLE OF MONEY AS A MOTIVATOR

One of the oldest and longest standing rewards or reinforcers of behavior is money. Frederick Taylor was among the first to introduce individual incentive wage plans into American industry during the rise of scientific management. Managers are hopeful that money can be utilized for two basic purposes: (1) to attract and retain qualified personnel in the organization, and (2) to motivate these personnel to higher levels of performance. In the hierarchy of human needs presented earlier in this chapter, money can serve to satisfy the basic physiological and security needs. Money also can become a status symbol, thus contributing to egotistic needs. Without contending that it is the only or most important reward, we can state that money plays a significant role in most motivational programs.

If you will recall, Herzberg's motivation-hygiene theory tends to place money in the hygiene category. Herzberg's research indicates that salary has more potency as a job dissatisfier than as a job satisfier. This view argues that monetary systems can only produce peace and harmony at best (satisfy the employee's hygiene needs), but have little potential for motivating higher levels of performance. The conclusions of Herzberg's theory have been challenged on the basis that many organizations have not established clear reward systems that directly link pay and perform-ance. It can be argued that if an organization establishes a direct relation-ship between pay and performance then money may actually serve as a motivator.

If money is to motivate behavior, employees must both desire it and believe that it will be forthcoming if they behave in the manner pre-scribed. Determining the degree of importance of money to employees requires knowledge of each individual's current need level. If employees have a need for higher pay and expect to receive it if they perform more effectively, then pay can motivate performance.

EMPLOYEE PERFORMANCE AND EQUITY

equity A major concern of managers is the issue of **equity** in relation to the distribution of pay and other rewards. Managers must deal with employ-ees who continually compare the pay and rewards they are receiving with the rewards being received by other employees. The degree of perceived equity is important to each employee. Equity involves an individual comparing his or her performance and the rewards received with the performance and rewards others receive for doing similar work.

Even though the employee values money, for example, and expects that it will be paid if he or she performs, comparisons will be made to the rewards received by others. Thus, if the employee likes money and believes that an $800 raise will be forthcoming when performing well, motivational force decreases if he or she perceives that other employees are receiving $1,000 for the same performance level. When an employee receives compensation from the organization, perceptions of equity are affected by two factors: (1) comparison of the compensation received to such factors as one's input of effort, education, training, and endurance of adverse working conditions, and (2) the comparison of the perceived equity of pay and rewards received to those received by other people. Equity usually exists when individuals perceive that they are receiving equitable pay and rewards based on their own performance (internal comparison) and in relation to the rewards received by others (external comparison).

JOB ENRICHMENT VERSUS JOB ENLARGEMENT

In the past two decades there has been considerable interest in and application of job enrichment in a wide variety of organizations. Strongly advocated by Frederick Herzberg, *job enrichment* refers to basic changes in the content and level of responsibility of a job so as to provide for the satisfaction of the *motivation* needs of personnel. The individual is provided with an opportunity to derive a feeling of greater achievement, recognition, responsibility, and personal growth in performing the job. Although job enrichment programs have not always achieved positive results, such programs have demonstrated improvements in job performance and in the level of satisfaction of personnel in many organizations.

Such companies as AT&T, Polaroid, Texas Instruments, Monsanto, Weyerhauser, General Motors, Corning Glass and many other firms have achieved excellent results after implementing job enrichment programs. In most instances productivity and job satisfaction increased accompanied by reduction in employee turnover and absenteeism.[13]

According to Herzberg, there are a number of principles for implementing job enrichment.

1. **Increasing job demands.** Changing the job in such a way as to increase the level of difficulty and responsibility of the job.

2. **Increasing a worker's accountability.** Allowing more individual control and authority over the work, while retaining accountability of the manager.

3. **Providing work scheduling freedom.** Within limits, allowing individual workers to schedule their own work.

4. **Providing feedback.** Making timely periodic reports on performance to employees (directly to the worker rather than to the supervisor).

5. **Providing new learning experiences.** Work situations should encourage opportunities for new experiences and personal growth of the individual.[14]

13. See "Case Studies in the Humanization of Work," in *Work In America*. Report of a Special Task Force to the Secretary of Health, Education and Welfare. (Cambridge, Mass.: M.I.T. Press, 1973), Appendix pp. 188–200.

14. Frederick Herzberg, "One More Time: How Do You Motivate Employees?" *Harvard Business Review* 46 (January–February 1968): 53–62.

FIGURE 8.5
Job Enrichment versus Job Enlargement

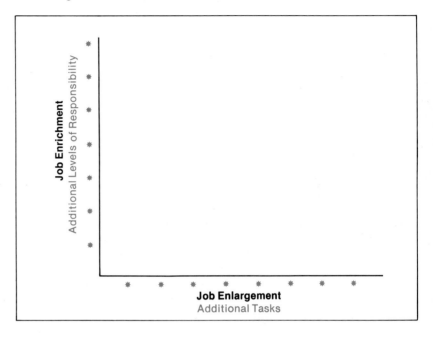

Many people have attempted to differentiate between **job enrichment** and **job enlargement** by using the diagram presented in Figure 8.5. Job enlargement is said to provide a horizontal expansion of duties. For example, instead of knowing how to operate only one machine, a person is taught to operate two, or even three. But, no additional responsibility is provided. On the other hand, job enrichment entails providing a person with additional responsibilities. There may be other tasks to perform, but responsibility is given with the tasks. For instance, the worker may be given the responsibility of scheduling the three machines. Increased responsibility means providing the worker with increased freedom to do the job—make decisions and exercise more self-control over the work.

job enrichment
job enlargement

SELF-FULFILLING PROPHECY

A manager's expectations have a significant influence on employee motivation and performance. According to J. Sterling Livingston,

- A manager's expectations of employees and the way he or she treats them largely determine their performance and career progress.
- A unique characteristic of superior managers is their ability to create high performance expectations that subordinates fulfill.

- Less effective managers fail to develop similar expectations, and, as a consequence, the productivity of their subordinates suffers.
- Subordinates, more often than not, appear to do what they believe they are expected to do.[15]

self-fulfilling
prophecies

High performance expectations tend to be **self-fulfilling prophecies.** A manager communicates expectations through both verbal and nonverbal means.

There have been numerous studies that support the notion of the self-fulfilling prophecy. In one such study, eighteen elementary school teachers were informed that about 20 percent of their students were "intellectual bloomers." The teachers were told that these youngsters would achieve remarkable progress during the school year. In actuality, the 20 percent sample of students was chosen at random and did not differ in intelligence or abilities from the remainder of the students in the classes. The only variable was the teacher's expectations of the group of "intellectual bloomers." The students did actually achieve significantly greater progress during the school year. Thus, the teacher's expectations of the students became a self-fulfilling prophecy.

Similar results have been achieved by managers. More often than not, if managers have high expectations of their employees, the employees' performance will meet those expectations. For example, the high expectations of the manager of a large computer center at a major university substantially changed the life and work of a janitor. The manager believed that George Johnson, a janitor with limited formal education, had the potential to become a computer operator. The computer center manager had high expectations and believed that George could learn the new job. After several months of training, George Johnson did become a successful computer operator, and ultimately progressed to the point of providing training to others. This illustrates how the expectations of one person (in this case the manager of the computer center) can have a significant impact on the actions of another.

ADDITIONAL MOTIVATIONAL CONSIDERATIONS

Management should recognize there are many factors that affect job performance. These factors include: (1) skills and abilities of personnel, (2) levels of education and training of employees, (3) existing technology, (4) available equipment and tools to perform the job. A manager may not be able to "motivate" an employee to better job performance if the

15. J. Sterling Livingston, "Pygmalion In Management," *Harvard Business Review*, July–August 1969.

employee does not possess the education, skills, training, and equipment to perform the job effectively. If any one of these factors is inadequate, performance may be adversely affected. An employee may possess the necessary skills and be highly motivated to perform a certain job efficiently, but his or her overall performance level may be quite low because he or she may not know how to do the job. This is a problem that is sometimes overlooked by managers who believe that an employee is simply *not motivated* when in fact the employee does not understand what it is he or she is required to do or lacks the proper training or equipment to perform efficiently and effectively. It does little good, and may cause considerable harm, if managers persist in *driving* employees in an effort to motivate them when motivation is not the problem.

MOTIVATION: IMPLICATIONS FOR MANAGEMENT PRACTICE

From our discussion of the above theories of motivation, several implications for managers can be derived.

- Managers should recognize and try to develop a better understanding of human behavior if they are to create a climate that encourages greater employee performance and satisfaction.
- Human needs that are reasonably well satisfied do not motivate behavior. The lower-level needs on Maslow's hierarchy (physiological, safety, and social) are fairly well satisfied for many U.S. employees and therefore have little significant influence in motivating behavior. Thus, management should devote more of its attention toward providing a climate for the satisfaction of the upper-level needs of esteem and self-actualization.
- Personnel have been underutilized and *overmanaged*. Organizations should try to provide more responsible and challenging jobs that allow a greater degree of self-control by the individual.
- Many managers have adopted the Theory X assumptions regarding the expected behavior of their subordinates. These managers have created a climate of distrust and one that encourages immature actions on the part of the employees. These conditions do not lead to more effective performance or a higher level of employee satisfaction.

A SITUATIONAL APPROACH TO MOTIVATION

We have discussed several theories and concepts of human motivation that may be useful to managers. From our analysis, it should be clear that there is *no one* best approach (or theory) to motivation that will be effective

FIGURE 8.6
A Situational Approach to Motivation

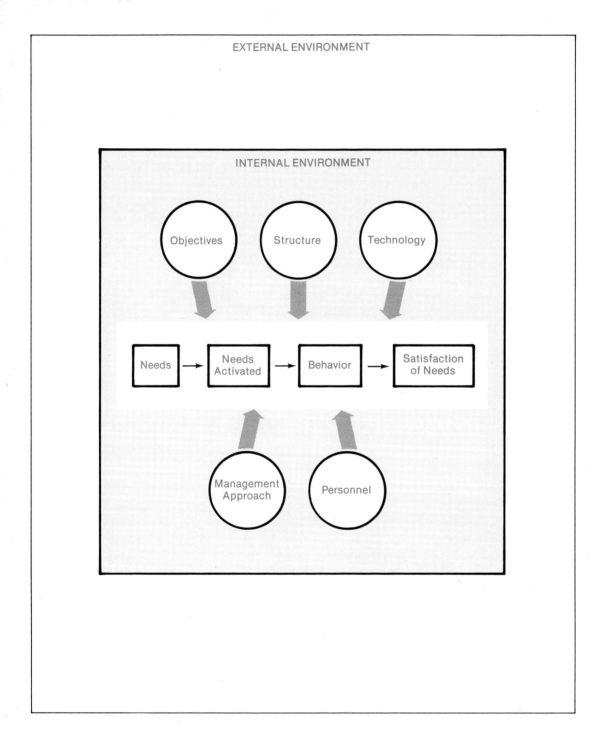

or appropriate for all employees in an organization or work unit. The theories presented in this chapter provide approaches a manager can use in motivating employees. However, the manager must adapt his or her motivational style to meet the needs of the situation. As can be seen in Figure 8.6, a number of situational factors must be considered before a manager is able to optimize his or her ability to motivate.

Because all employees have different needs and aspirations, the motivational factors for one individual most likely will be different from another. Thus, a manager must evaluate each person in order to determine what will stimulate that person to exert effort above and beyond what is normally expected. If possible, an environment should be created so that each employee can be motivated to his or her fullest potential. Thus, the manager must be capable of adapting his or her motivational approach to meet the needs of personnel in a changing environment.

The fact that there are a number of factors that affect the level of performance does not in any way diminish the significance of the element of motivation. In the last few decades, significant accomplishments in the areas of technology and education have positively affected performance. While there has been increased knowledge of human behavior and motivation in the working environment, this area still has great potential for improving performance. It has been estimated that most individuals perform only up to 20 or 30 percent of their capability. Through a better understanding of human behavior and the modern theories of motivation, management may be able to create a climate within their organization that inspires individuals to perform at a level greater than 30 percent of their potential.

SUMMARY

Motivation is one of the most important and frequently discussed subjects in management. Today's employees are better educated, more highly skilled, and often do not respond to traditional values that may have motivated them 20 or 30 years ago. Motivation is the process of influencing or stimulating employees to take action that will accomplish a desired goal. In an organization, personnel are said to be motivated if they perform their jobs effectively and efficiently. Management has traditionally relied on the use of rewards such as increased pay, job security, good working conditions, or punishment such as dismissal, demotions, or withholding rewards to "motivate" employees. But today, management cannot rely on the manipulation of pay, benefits, or working conditions to motivate personnel to perform effectively. Motivation is a much more complicated process.

Managers must attempt to understand human nature and a person's basic needs if they are to create a climate for motivation. McGregor's Theory X and Theory Y and Argyris's maturity theory have aided managers in developing a better understanding of human behavior. The theories of Maslow, Herzberg, McClelland, Vroom, and Skinner are very helpful to managers as they attempt to gain a more complete appreciation of man's basic needs and the reasons for human behavior.

Maslow's hierarchy of needs is a widely accepted theory which supports the idea that man is motivated by unsatisfied needs. According to Maslow, a person's needs are arranged in priority from the basic physiological to the complex self-actualization needs. The key point for managers to accept is that needs that are fairly well satisfied do not motivate behavior. Herzberg's motivation-hygiene theory classifies man's needs into two categories—hygiene factors and motivators. The hygiene factors correspond to the lower-level needs on Maslow's hierarchy, while the motivators represent the upper-level needs of man. Herzberg contends that despite the fact that most managers and organizations concentrate on satisfying the hygiene needs, this action does not motivate employees. He feels firms should direct more attention to the motivators and to enriched or more challenging jobs, but at the same time firms should not forget to be concerned about the hygiene needs. McClelland's theory stresses that there are certain needs that are learned. He argues that each person's need for achievement, power, and affiliation affects his or her behavior in the work environment.

The needs approach to motivation as developed by Maslow and Herzberg does not adequately explain individual differences in the way people behave in accomplishing goals. Victor Vroom's expectancy theory of motivation attempts to explain behavior in terms of an individual's goals, choices, and the expectations of achieving the goals. Employees are motivated by what they expect in terms of rewards as a result of their behavior. B. F. Skinner contends that behavior can be controlled and shaped by reinforcing desired behavior. The primary approach suggested by Skinner is organization behavior modification (OBM) which has been successfully applied in a number of organizations. Under this approach, people act in the way they find most rewarding and by controlling rewards, people's behavior can be directed and/or modified.

In addition to the major theories of motivation, managers should also develop an understanding of the role of money as a motivator and the importance of equity between an individual's performance and the pay he or she receives. Managers should also be aware that their expectations have a significant influence on employee motivation and performance. Finally, managers should realize that there is no one best approach to or theory of motivation that will be effective or appropriate for all employees in an organization. The truly effective manager is one who can adapt his or her motivational approach to meet the needs of the situation.

Review Questions

1. How would you define motivation?

2. What is the "carrot and the stick" approach to motivation?

3. Compare and contrast McGregor's Theory X and Theory Y. What are some examples of managerial practices that are consistent with a Theory Y philosophy of human nature?

4. What is Argyris' maturation theory? How does it apply to motivation?

5. Relate Herzberg's theory of motivation to the theory developed by Maslow.

6. Describe McClelland's theory of human motives. How does it relate to motivation and what are the basic characteristics of individuals described by the theory?

7. What is expectancy theory and how can managers use it in the motivation process? Provide examples.

8. Briefly describe organization behavior modification. How can it be used in motivating people? Give illustrations.

9. What is the role of money as a motivator? How important is the issue of equity of pay in terms of motivation? Explain.

10. What is meant by job enrichment and how does it differ from job enlargement? How would you apply job enrichment? Give an example.

11. What is the notion of the "self-fulfilling prophecy?" How is it related to management and motivation?

12. "There is *no one* best approach (or theory) to motivation that is appropriate for all employees in an organization." Comment.

Exercises

1. Interview three managers—for example, a bank president, a college dean, and a local retailer. Ask these managers to describe their approach to creating a climate for motivating personnel within their organization. Compare their comments with the concepts on motivation presented in this chapter.

2. Using Maslow's hierarchy of needs as a guide, describe how *your* various needs have been satisfied on any job(s) you have held. Were any of your needs not met? Why or why not? How could they have been satisfied?

3. Go to the library and prepare critiques of recent journal articles relating to "new" approaches to the motivation of managers and/or employees utilized by business organizations.

REFERENCES

Armstrong, J. "How to Motivate." *Management Today*, February 1977, pp. 60–63.

Bennis, Warren G. "The Coming Death of Bureaucracy." In Patrick E. Connor, ed., *Dimensions of Modern Management*. Boston: Houghton Mifflin, 1974, pp. 496–505.

Gallagher, W. E., Jr., and Einhorn, H. J. "Motivation Theory and Job Design." *Journal of Business*, July 1976, pp. 358–373.

Giblin E. J. "Motivating Employees: A Closer Look." *Personnel Journal*, April 1976, pp. 68–71+.

Hackman, J. R. "Is Job Enrichment Just A Fad?" *Harvard Business Review*, September 1975, pp. 129–138.

Kovach, K. A. "Improving Employee Motivation In Today's Business Environment." *Michigan State University Business Topics*, Autumn 1976, pp. 5–12.

McClelland, D. C., and Burnham, D. H. "Power Is the Great Motivator." *Harvard Business Review*, March 1976, pp. 100–110.

Mack, H. "Some Lessons in Motivation." *Supervisory Management*, August 1976, pp. 2–7.

Morse, John J., and Lorsch, Jay W. "Beyond Theory Y." *Harvard Business Review*, May–June 1970, pp. 61–68.

Pinder, C. C. "Concerning the Application of Human Motivation Theories in Organizational Settings." *Academy of Management Review*, July 1977, pp. 384–397.

Prenting, T. O. "Job Enrichment: How Important Is the Work Itself." *University of Michigan Business Review*, January 1976, pp. 26–30.

Rosenthal, Robert. "The Pygmalion Effect Lives." *Psychology Today*, September 1973, pp. 56–60ff.

Speigel, D. "How Not to Motivate." *Supervisory Management*, November 1977, pp. 41–45.

Whitehall, A. M. "Maintenance Factors: The Neglected Side of Worker Motivation." *Personnel Journal*, October 1976, pp. 516–519+.

Zedeck, S. "Information Processing Model and Approach to Study Motivation." *Organizational Behavior and Human Performance*, February 1977, pp. 47–77.

Case Study

A PHILOSOPHY OF MOTIVATION

Trent Pratter is the advertising manager for a major tire manufacturer. There are eight advertising specialists who report directly to Trent. Within Trent's department there is a wide diversity of talent and experience. It is obvious to most outsiders that some of the specialists are far superior in their advertising talents than others.

Wayne Sanders is one of the specialists who is recognized for his superior talents. He is able to develop and implement a campaign from start to finish. His creativity is second to none. Billy Miller, on the other hand, does a minimum amount of work—just enough to get by. He does what is required but virtually nothing extra. If he is assigned a project, he typically complains that he is working too hard. He always appears to be busy, but rarely gets much accomplished.

Trent openly recognizes that Billy does not produce as much as the other employees, but believes that he can make Billy more productive. Therefore, rather than reward people like Wayne, he concentrates his attention and special privileges on individuals like Billy. If there is a seminar for professional development, Billy is typically chosen to attend. Billy is afforded time off whenever he wants it. Wayne works a minimum of 60 hours a week but never receives any recognition for his work. In fact, it would appear to an outsider that Trent rewards inefficiency and condemns effectiveness. All his efforts are directed toward helping the "underdog."

Over a period of years there has been a tendency for the best qualified advertising specialists to leave the company and the less capable to remain. This trend was continued the other day as Wayne turned in his resignation. Trent is confused and requests your assistance in resolving the problem.

Questions

1. What caused Wayne Sanders to terminate his employment?
2. How would the situation approach to motivation be helpful to Trent in analyzing the problem?
3. What advice would you give to Trent regarding his approach to motivation?

Case Study

MOTIVATING A DISSATISFIED MANAGER

Alice Ross had been a district sales manager with Finn Productions for ten years. She was recognized by her peers and supervisors as a person who ran a good department. However, everyone realized that Alice was extremely ambitious and was seeking a higher-level management position. When one of her sales representatives did a good job in a particular quarter, Alice would attempt to take the credit. However, if a problem arose, it was not Alice's fault.

When the marketing manager retired, Alice applied for the position. The company decided to do a thorough search because of the responsibility and importance associated with the position. When the search was concluded, the decision was made to go "outside" for a person to fill the position. The consensus of top management was that Alice, although a good district sales manager, might have difficulties in working with her new peer group. They felt that she might alienate the other managers if she tried to take credit for their work.

Alice was heart-broken. She had wanted that particular job for a long time and had dedicated all of her energies toward obtaining it. She became very despondent and her work deteriorated. The department functioned in spite of her, not because of her. Decisions were made slowly if at all and she began to be late with her sales reports. Although her sales staff continued to be productive, Alice could not take the credit.

When the new marketing manager took over one of the first major problems that he confronted was how to motivate Alice to her former level of performance. He recognized that Alice had been with the company for a long time but something had to be done. Alice was receiving an excellent salary for doing virtually nothing.

Questions

1. As the new marketing manager, what approach would you use to motivate Alice?
2. Do you believe that Alice can be motivated to once again become a productive member of the organization? Why or why not? Discuss.

Chapter 9

KEY TERMS

leadership

formal power

reward power

coercive power

expert power

referent power

trait approach

behavioral theories of leadership

Likert's systems of management

managerial grid

Ohio State leadership studies

initiating structure

consideration

leadership continuum

situational theories of leadership

Fiedler's contingency leadership model

leader-member relations

task structure

position power of the leader

Reddin's leadership theory

Hersey and Blanchard's situational leadership theory

task behavior

relationship behavior

task–relevant maturity

Effective Leadership

LEARNING OBJECTIVES

After completing this chapter you should be able to

1. Define the process of leadership.
2. Explain that there is *no one* most effective leadership style.
3. Define the types of power a leader may possess.
4. Describe the trait, behavioral, and situational theories of leadership.
5. State the behavioral leadership theories developed by Likert, Blake and Mouton, Tannenbaum and Schmidt, and researchers at Ohio State University.
6. Identify the two basic dimensions of leadership behavior.
7. Describe the situational leadership theories developed by Fiedler, Reddin, and Hersey and Blanchard.
8. State the importance of an approach to leadership that gives adequate consideration to the situational dimensions.

The sales manager has just learned that his sales representatives had exceeded their territorial quotas by 25 percent making this the most successful year in the last five.

A production supervisor has received the monthly production reports indicating that her employees had exceeded the production quantity standard by 20 percent, while at the same time maintaining quality standards.

A group of scientists in a research department has just made a critical breakthrough on a project that they had been working on night and day for the past eighteen months.

A leader is involved in each of the situations above but an entirely different relationship exists between the leader and the followers. There is more to the study of leadership than merely understanding the qualities associated with an individual manager or leader.

The questions then must be asked, "What does it take to be an effective manager?" and "What is the most effective leadership style?" These questions have perplexed and challenged managers (and students of management) for generations. Literally thousands of research studies concerning leadership have been conducted to provide greater insight into these questions. However, these studies of leaders and the leadership process have not yielded any set of traits or qualities that are consistently related to effective leadership. The basic conclusion that can be drawn from these studies is that there is *no one* most effective leadership style. What we do know is that effective leadership is absolutely essential to the survival and overall growth of every organization.

As we noted at the beginning of chapter 1, 50 percent of all new businesses fail within the first two years. Despite high salaries and excellent opportunities in large corporations, there continues to be a shortage of competent managers who are effective leaders. The lack of capable leadership is not just confined to business organizations, but has also been felt in government, churches, education, and all other types of organizations. The problem is not created because of a lack of people who want to be leaders or managers, but rather a scarcity of skilled people who are capable of performing effectively in leadership positions. The primary challenge of leadership or management is to guide an organization toward the accomplishment of its objectives. The leader achieves this by influencing and encouraging employees of the organization to attain the highest level of performance possible within the limitation of available resources, skills, and technology.

Many large businesses and even countries have made successful turn-arounds as a result of a change in leadership. Even though we don't have all the answers, a more complete knowledge of the skills, attitudes, and values that are related to effective leadership would greatly improve our ability to select, train, and develop more effective managers. This is precisely the purpose of this chapter. We will first define leadership and then discuss the more significant theories of leadership. Finally, an integrative approach to leadership will be presented which should prove beneficial to individuals as they develop their leadership styles.

LEADERSHIP DEFINED

leadership

Leadership is the process of motivating and directing others toward the accomplishment of goals. Leadership involves any attempt at influencing the behavior of others for goals or purposes that may or may not coincide with the goals of the organization. In this chapter our discussion will be primarily concerned with managers as leaders. By definition a good manager is a good leader, but a good leader may not necessarily be an effective manager.

As the result of a consulting assignment with a mobile home manufacturer, one of the authors observed a production manager exerting effective leadership, but ineffective management. A team of consultants had prepared a feasibility study for the president of a newly formed mobile home manufacturer. The study recommended that the new plant produce a relatively low-priced mobile home because the firm was in a low-income geographic area. However, the company hired a production manager with an excellent reputation as a competent leader who had several years of experience with a manufacturer of higher priced, higher quality mobile homes. Against the advice of the consultants, and without the knowledge of the board of directors, the production manager decided to direct his production supervisors and workers to produce a higher priced mobile home. The results proved to be disastrous for the newly established company.

The sales staff was not able to sell this high-priced unit causing the firm to invest over $350,000 of their working capital in inventory of mobile homes that could not be sold. This was a major factor contributing to the firm's

---

INSIGHTS TO SUCCESS

★

A leader must *lead*, not drive. People are unpredictable, different from one another, often irascible, frequently petty, sometimes vain, but always magnificent if they are properly motivated.

ZOLTAN MERSZEI, President, The Dow Chemical Company

MR. ROBERT C. WILSON

President and Chairman
Memorex Corporation

MEMOREX Robert C. Wilson, President and Chairman of Memorex Corporation, is the only person who has twice won the annual Gallagher's President's Report Award for his successful leadership with two different companies.

Mr. Wilson received his degree in mechanical engineering from the University of California at Berkeley in 1941. He joined General Electric as a test engineer and, except for three years service with the U. S. Navy in World War II, devoted the next twenty-eight years to a career at G.E. As the General Manager of the consumer radio receiver business, he is credited with establishing the basis for being fully competitive with the Japanese. He was named a Corporate Vice-President of G.E. in 1966. In 1969, he joined Rockwell International as Corporate Vice-President, and President of its Commercial Products Group as well as a member of the Board of Directors. Subsequently, he became an Executive Vice-President of Rockwell. Late in 1971, Mr. Wilson became President and Chief Executive Officer of Collins Radio Company, which was then in serious financial difficulty. The recovery of Collins was rapid and dramatic. More importantly, during the turn-around the basis was established for long-term profitable growth. Collins was subsequently acquired by Rockwell International and has become the "brightest jewel in the Rockwell crown."

In 1974, Mr. Wilson became President and Chairman of Memorex Corporation, a manufacturer of information storage and communications products, whose financial difficulties had led it to a loss of $90 million in 1973. Under Mr. Wilson's leadership, Memorex became profitable in 1975 and has established a continuing record for profitable growth.

Mr. Wilson's approach to management is to achieve quality and integrity in every company activity. Wilson believes that excellence, both in a company and an individual, is the only real measure of worth. For a company it brings customer confidence; in an individual it brings recognition and advancement. The essential ingredient in achieving excellence in a company is the attitude of those related to the company—customers, suppliers, investors, and especially, employees.

Mr. Wilson has demonstrated his professional managerial capabilities in a long series of responsibilities with General Electric, Rockwell, Collins Radio, and Memorex. These assignments covered products ranging from steel mill drives to yachts and geographies from Ireland to Japan.

bankruptcy within nine months of their starting date. In this illustration the production manager exercised effective leadership because he significantly influenced the behavior of his workers. However, he was an ineffective manager in this instance because he had his workers pursuing goals that were not in the best interest of the company.

Thus, a company can actually go bankrupt even though leadership has been effective in influencing the behavior of others to accomplish goals—if these goals are wrong for the company. Also, it should be noted that a person can have the title of *manager* but have very little influence over the behavior and actions of others. On the other hand, an individual might not carry the title of *manager* but be an important informal leader exercising considerable influence over the behavior of others in the work group.

A leader is able to influence others because he or she possesses power. We have discussed the various types of power in chapter 7. However, we will briefly review these below. Power can be in one or any combination of the following forms:

formal power
- **Formal power**—derived from authority or legitimate position in the firm.

reward power
- **Reward power**—based on the leader's ability to administer and control rewards (such as pay, promotions, and praise) to others for complying with the leader's directives.

coercive power
- **Coercive power**—based on the leader's ability to administer and control punishments (such as the power to fire, demote or reprimand) to others for not following the leader's requests.

expert power
- **Expert power**—based on the special knowledge, expertise, skill, or experience possessed by the leader. For example, employees may view Frank Wilson, an engineer, as a "real pro" in the engineering department. While Frank is not the manager of the department, other engineers and managers may go to him for technical assistance with structural design problems.

referent power
- **Referent power**—based on the leader's possession of personal characteristics that make him or her "attractive" to other people. Some individuals are said to possess "charisma" which is one form of referent power. Another form of referent power can be derived from one's association with another powerful leader. For instance, Bob Haldeman and John Ehrlichman possessed this form of referent power because many people believed they were acting with the approval of President Nixon. Another illustration might be the Assistant Vice-President for Academic Affairs at a university. This individual may possess referent power because the deans and department heads believe he or she represents the views of the Vice-President for Academic Affairs.

THE TRAIT APPROACH TO LEADERSHIP

The leader has always occupied a strong and central role in traditional management theory. Most of the early research on leadership attempted to: (1) compare the traits of people who become leaders with those who remain as followers; (2) identify characteristics and traits possessed by effective leaders. Research studies comparing the traits of leaders and nonleaders have found that leaders tend to be somewhat taller, more outgoing, more self-confident, and more intelligent than nonleaders. But, a specific combination of traits has not been found that would differentiate the leader or potential leader from the follower. As portrayed in the illustration on the next page, it is difficult to identify the leader from an initial impression.

There has been considerable research to compare the traits of effective and ineffective leaders. Traits such as aggressiveness, ambition, decisiveness, dominance, initiative, intelligence, physical characteristics (looks, height, and weight), self-assurance, and other personality factors were studied to determine if they were related to effective leadership. The major question was, Could such traits differentiate effective from ineffective leaders? Perhaps the underlying assumption to the trait research has been that *leaders are born, not made.* Although research has demonstrated that while this is not the case, many people still believe there are certain *inborn* traits that make a person a good leader. Research has not shown that certain traits can distinguish effective from ineffective leaders.

trait approach

However, the **trait approach** to the study of leadership is not dead. Edwin Ghiselli[1] has continued to conduct research in an effort to identify personality and motivational traits related to effective leadership. Ghiselli's research has centered on these factors:

Abilities
- supervisory ability
- intelligence
- initiative

Personality Traits
- decisiveness
- self-assurance
- supervisory ability—ability to direct others
- maturity
- masculinity–femininity
- working-class affinity

1. Edwin Ghiselli, *Explorations in Managerial Talent* (Pacific Palisades: Goodyear Publishing Company, Inc., 1971).

Who is the leader?

Motivational Traits
- need for occupational achievement
- need for self-actualization
- need for power over others
- need for financial reward
- need for security

Ghiselli's studies, which are well respected because of their scientific quality, have revealed that certain traits are important to effective leadership. The traits identified by Ghiselli as most significant for effective leadership are (in order of importance):

1. **Supervisory ability**—the performance of the basic functions of management including planning, organizing, directing and controlling the work of others.
2. **Need for occupational achievement**—the seeking of responsibility and the desire for success.
3. **Intelligence**—creative and verbal ability—including judgment, reasoning, and thinking capacity.
4. **Decisiveness**—ability to make decisions and solve problems capably and competently.
5. **Self-assurance**—the extent to which the individual views himself as capable of coping with problems.
6. **Initiative**—ability to act independently and develop courses of action not readily apparent to other people. Self-starter—able to find new or innovative ways of doing things.

In spite of the contributions of Ghiselli, the trait approach to the study of leadership has left unanswered many questions concerning what is required for effective leadership. Perhaps one of the major problems with the trait approach is defining who is effective. Does the mere fact that a person has a powerful position make the individual a leader? Former President Nixon had the position power, but many questioned whether or not he was an effective leader after news of the Watergate scandal became widely known to the public. Failure to adequately answer this question has caused the trait approach to lose its influence as a means of studying leadership.

BEHAVIORAL THEORIES OF LEADERSHIP

Dissatisfaction with the results of the trait approach to the study of leadership has caused a rather significant change in the emphasis of leadership research. This shift in emphasis began to focus attention on the actual behavior and actions of leaders as opposed to the traits or characteristics of leaders.

behavioral theories
of leadership

Several major theories were developed during the 1950s and 1960s that approached leadership from the standpoint of identifying the types of behavior or styles that are available to leaders. Four **behavioral theories of leadership** will be presented below. Two of these—Likert's Systems of Management and Blake and Mouton's Managerial Grid®—advocated a universal style that was best for all leaders. Two other theories of leadership behavior—Ohio State, and Tannenbaum and Schmidt—suggested that a variety of factors determine the appropriate leadership behavior of managers. Each of these will be discussed below.

LIKERT'S SYSTEMS OF MANAGEMENT

Likert's systems of management

Rensis Likert, Director of the Institute for Social Research at the University of Michigan developed a universal theory of leadership. Likert's theory consists of a continuum of styles ranging from autocratic to participative. Four basic styles or **Likert's systems of management** were identified as follows: *System I*, Exploitative Autocratic; *System II*, Benevolent Autocratic; *System III*, Consultative; and *System IV*, Participative Team. Only the last style or System IV was deemed best in the long run for all situations.[2]

System I—Exploitative Autocratic

Managers make all decisions. They decide what is to be done, who will do it, and how and when it is to be accomplished. Failure to complete work as assigned results in threats or punishment. Under this system, management exhibits little confidence or trust in employees. A typical managerial response with this system is, "You do it my way or you're fired." According to Likert there is a low level of trust and confidence between management and employees when System I is used.

System II—Benevolent Autocratic

Managers still make the decisions, but employees have some degree of freedom and flexibility in performing their jobs so long as they conform to the specified procedures. Under this system, managers take a very paternalistic attitude—"I'll take care of you if you perform well." With System II, there is a fairly low level of trust between management and the employees which causes employees to use caution when dealing with management.

System III—Consultative

Managers consult with employees prior to establishing the goals and making decisions about the work. Employees have a considerable degree of freedom in making their own decisions as to how to accomplish the work. A manager using System III might say to an employee, "Charlie, I'd

2. Rensis Likert, *The Human Organization* (New York: McGraw-Hill, 1967).

like your opinion on this before I make the decision." Management tends to rely on rewards as opposed to punishments to motivate employees. Also, the level of trust between the employees and management is fairly high creating a climate in which employees feel relatively free to openly discuss work-related matters with management.

System IV—Participative Team

This is Likert's recommended system or style of management. The emphasis of System IV is on a group participative role with full involvement of the employees in the process of establishing goals and making job-related decisions. Employees feel free to discuss matters with their manager who displays supportive rather than condescending or threatening behavior. It is contended that the entire organization should be designed along System IV lines, with work being performed by a series of overlapping groups. The leader provides a link between the group and other units at higher levels in the organization. Decision making is widespread throughout the enterprise, with the power of knowledge usually taking precedence over the power of authority.

Measurement of the type of style in the Likert framework is usually accomplished by having organization members assess their management on a series of scales (Likert scales) for such items as the character of motivational forces, communication processes, confidence and trust, decision-making processes, interaction-influence process, and goal-setting and control processes. A profile showing the management system existing within the organization is developed through this subordinate survey of opinion (see Figure 9.1). For example, when the question, "Extent to which superiors willingly share information with subordinates?" is asked, the employee can answer on the continuum from "provide minimum information" all the way to "seeks to give subordinates all relevant information and all information they want;" (see question 3C2 in Figure 9.2). It has been found that the positions on these scales can be significantly altered through managerial training programs.

Blake and Mouton's Managerial Grid®

Managerial Grid

Perhaps the most widely known of all leadership theories is the **Managerial Grid** developed by Robert R. Blake and Jane S. Mouton.[3] The Managerial Grid is illustrated in Figure 9.3. The two dimensions of the 9 × 9

3. Used with permission of Blake, Robert R. and Mouton, Jane S. *The New Managerial Grid* (Houston: Gulf Publishing Company, 1978), p. 11.

FIGURE 9.1
Likert Chart—Management Systems*

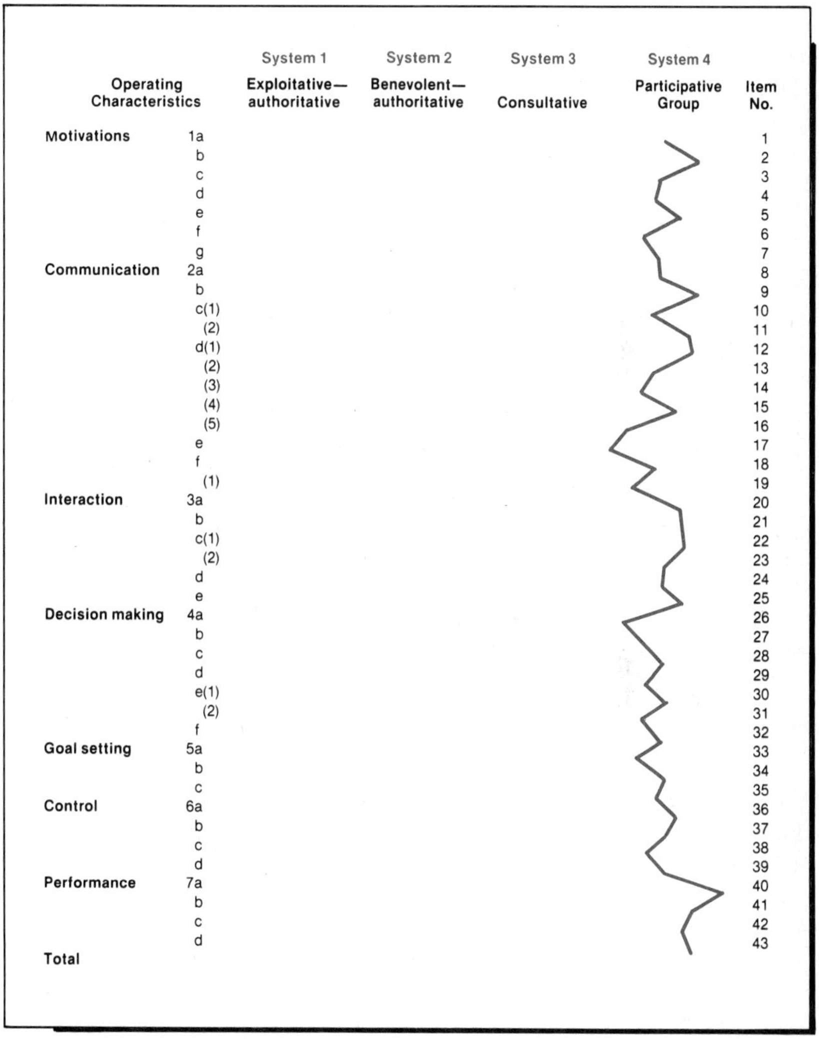

Operating Characteristics		System 1 Exploitative— authoritative	System 2 Benevolent— authoritative	System 3 Consultative	System 4 Participative Group	Item No.
Motivations	1a					1
	b					2
	c					3
	d					4
	e					5
	f					6
	g					7
Communication	2a					8
	b					9
	c(1)					10
	(2)					11
	d(1)					12
	(2)					13
	(3)					14
	(4)					15
	(5)					16
	e					17
	f					18
	(1)					19
Interaction	3a					20
	b					21
	c(1)					22
	(2)					23
	d					24
	e					25
Decision making	4a					26
	b					27
	c					28
	d					29
	e(1)					30
	(2)					31
	f					32
Goal setting	5a					33
	b					34
	c					35
Control	6a					36
	b					37
	c					38
	d					39
Performance	7a					40
	b					41
	c					42
	d					43
Total						

*Management system used by the most productive plant (Plant L) of a well-managed company, as seen by middle- and upper-level managers.
From Rensis Likert, *The Human Organization* (New York: McGraw-Hill, 1967). Used with permission.

Grid are labeled "concern for people" and "concern for production." A score of 1 indicates low concern and a score of 9 shows a high degree of concern. The Grid depicts five major leadership styles representing the degree of concern for "people" and "production."

FIGURE 9.2
Sample of Questions on Likert Scale Relating to Communications Within the Organization

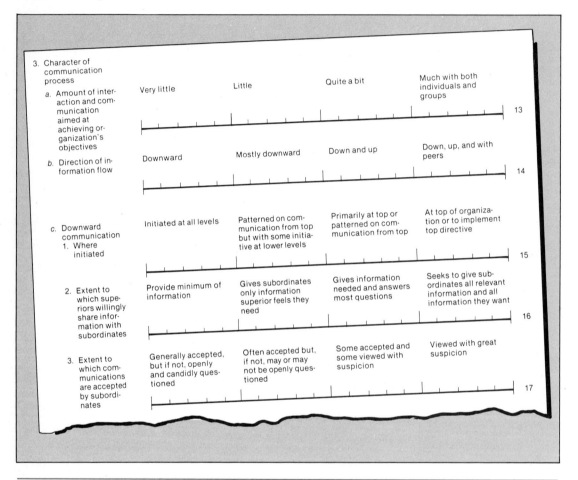

From Rensis Likert, *The Human Organization* (New York: McGraw-Hill, 1967). Used with permission.

1,1 Impoverished Management—The manager has little concern for either people or production.

9,1 Authority-Obedience—The manager stresses operating efficiently through controls in situations where human elements cannot interfere.

FIGURE 9.3
Blake and Mouton's Managerial Grid®

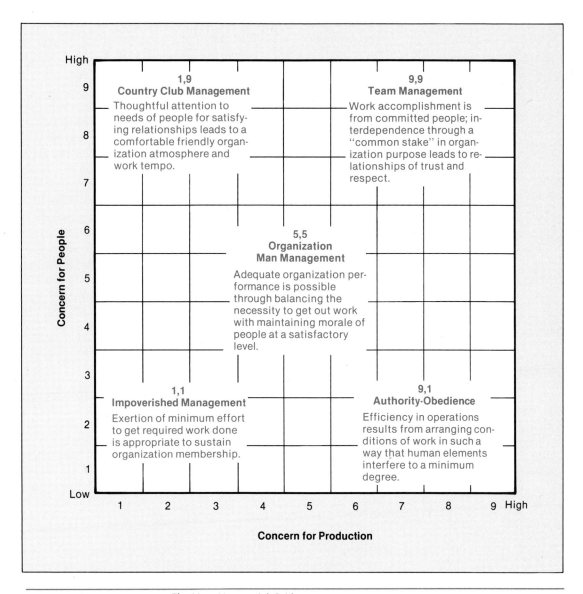

1,9 **Country Club Management**—The manager is thoughtful, comfortable, and friendly, and has little concern for output.

5,5 **Organization Man Management**—The manager attempts to balance and trade off concern for work in exchange for a satisfactory level of morale—a compromiser.

9,9 **Team Management**—The manager seeks high output through committed people, achieved through mutual trust, respect, and a realization of interdependence.[4]

According to Blake and Mouton, the first four styles listed do not represent the most effective leadership style. They strongly suggest that only the 9,9 position of maximum concern for both output and people is the most effective style of leadership. Blake and Mouton argue that using the 9,9 team approach will result in improved performance, lower employee turnover and absenteeism and greater employee satisfaction. The use of job enrichment and subordinate participation in managerial decision making contributes to this 9,9 situation where both the organization and its human members are accorded maximum and equal concern. The Managerial Grid concept has been introduced to many managers throughout the world since its development in the early 1960s and has influenced the management philosophies and practices of many of them. Blake and Mouton have conducted Grid training seminars around the world.

OHIO STATE LEADERSHIP STUDIES

Ohio State leadership studies

Beginning in 1945, researchers in the Bureau of Business Research at Ohio State University made a series of in-depth studies of the behavior of leaders in a wide variety of organizations. The key concern of the **Ohio State leadership studies** was the leader's behavior in directing the efforts of others toward group goals. After a considerable number of studies had been completed, two important dimensions of leader behavior were identified:

initiating structure

1. **Initiating Structure**—the extent to which the leader establishes goals and defines and structures their roles and the roles of subordinates toward the attainment of the goals.

consideration

2. **Consideration**—the extent to which leaders have relationships with subordinates characterized by mutual trust, respect, and consideration of employees' ideas and feelings.

4. Ibid.

FIGURE 9.4
Ohio State Leadership Model

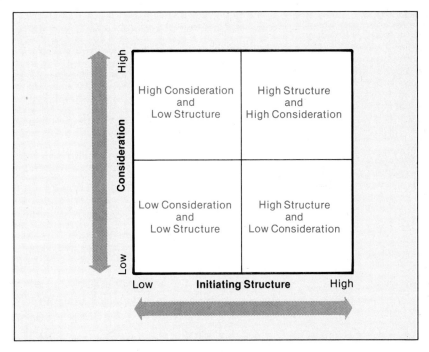

Initiating structure and consideration were identified as separate and distinct dimensions of leadership behavior. As illustrated in Figure 9.4, there are four basic leadership styles representing different combinations of leadership behavior. A manager can be high in both consideration and initiating structure, low in both, or high in one and low in the other. Though there are two important elements of leadership behavior, the *one* most effective combination that meets the needs of all situations was not suggested by the Ohio State model. Rather, the combination or appropriate level of initiating structure and consideration was determined by the demands of the situation.

INSIGHTS TO SUCCESS

A person should be patient and recognize that there is no substitute for experience and demonstrated performance; that a job well done is the best credential for the next more responsible job; that management entails the ability to motivate, persuade, and otherwise lead people to achieve goals, more so than any other factor.

JOHN A. HILL, Manager—Manpower Planning, Jones and Laughlin Steel Corporation

Among the many situational variables that must be related to leadership behavior are the following:

- expectations of the led
- degree of task structuring imposed by technology
- pressures of schedules and time
- degrees of interpersonal contact possible between leader and the led
- degree of influence of the leader outside of the group
- congruency of style with that of one's superior

The following observations can be made with regard to the type of leadership styles proposed in the Ohio State model:

- If a group expects and wants authoritarian leadership behavior, it is more likely to be satisfied with that type of leadership.
- If group members have less authoritarian expectations, a leader who strongly emphasizes initiating structure will be resented.
- If the work situation is highly structured by technology and the pressures of time, the supervisor who is high in consideration is more likely to meet with success as measured by absenteeism, turnover, and grievances.
- If task structuring precludes individual and group self-actualization, it will be useless to look for motivation from this source.
- When subordinates have little contact with their supervisor, they tend to prefer a more autocratic style.
- If employees must work and interact continuously, they usually want the superior to be high in consideration.

TANNENBAUM AND SCHMIDT'S LEADERSHIP CONTINUUM

Robert Tannenbaum and Warren H. Schmidt described a series of factors that they thought influenced a manager's selection of the most appropriate leadership style. Their approach advocated a continuum of leadership behavior supporting the notion that choosing an effective leadership style depended on the demands of the situation. As illustrated in Figure 9.5, leadership behavior ranges from "Boss-Centered" to "Subordinate-Centered," which is similar in concept to the other dimensions of leadership behavior discussed above. Tannenbaum and Schmidt emphasized that a manager should give careful consideration to the following factors before selecting a leadership style:

FIGURE 9.5
Continuum of Leadership Behavior

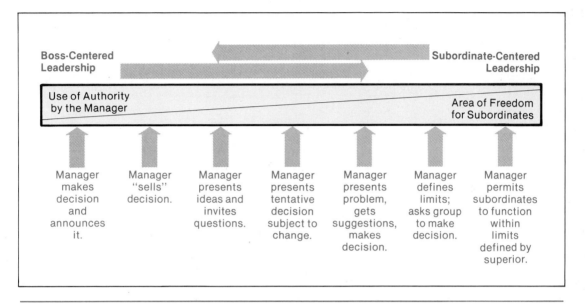

- **Characteristics of the manager**—background, education, experience, values, knowledge, goals, and expectations.
- **Characteristics of the employees**—background, education, experience, knowledge, goals, values, and expectations.
- **Requirements of the situation**—size, complexity, goals, structure, and climate of the organization, as well as the impact of technology, time pressure, and nature of the work.

leadership continuum

According to the Tannenbaum and Schmidt **leadership continuum** a manager may engage in a more participative leadership style when subordinates

- Seek independence and freedom of action.
- Understand and are committed to the goals of the organization.
- Are well educated and experienced in performing the jobs.
- Seek responsibility for decision making.
- Expect a participative style of leadership.

If the above conditions do not exist, managers may need to adopt a more autocratic or "boss-centered" leadership style. Thus, in essence, managers must be able to diagnose the situations confronting them and then attempt to choose a leadership style that will improve their chances for effectiveness. The most effective leaders are neither "task centered" nor "people-centered," but rather they are flexible enough to select a leadership style that fits their needs as well as the needs of their subordinates and the situation.

SITUATIONAL LEADERSHIP STYLES

situational theories of leadership

The current trend in the study of leadership has been toward a situational approach. In the next section, we will discuss several approaches to the study of leadership that can be classified as situational. Increased knowledge and understanding of these theories can be of significant benefit to managers and those who aspire to managerial positions. We will present these three **situational theories of leadership:**

1. Fred Fiedler's Contingency Leadership Model
2. William J. Reddin's 3-D Theory of Leadership
3. Hersey and Blanchard's Situational Leadership Model

Fiedler's Contingency Leadership Model

Fiedler's contingency leadership model

The contingency theory developed by Fred E. Fiedler has received considerable recognition as a situational approach to leadership.[5] **Fiedler's contingency leadership model** suggests that there is no one most effective style that is appropriate to every situation. He says that there are a number of styles that may be effective depending on the situation. The framework is made up of eight significantly different situations and two basic types of leadership orientations. Three major elements seem to determine whether a given situation is favorable to a leader. These are:

leader-member relations

- **leader-member-relations**—the degree to which the leader feels accepted by subordinates. The atmosphere may be friendly or unfriendly, relaxed or tense, and threatening or supportive.

task structure

- **task structure**—clearly defined goals, decisions, and solutions to problems.

position power of the leader

- **position power of the leader**—the degree of influence over rewards and punishments, as well as by his or her official authority.

5. Fred E. Fiedler, *A Theory of Leadership Effectiveness* (New York: McGraw-Hill, 1967).

TABLE 9.1
Framework of Fiedler's Contingency Leadership Model

Situation	Degree of Favorableness of Situation to Leader	Leader-Member Relations	Task Structure	Position Power of Leader
1	Favorable	Good	Structured	High
2	Favorable	Good	Structured	Low
3	Favorable	Good	Unstructured	High
4	Moderately Favorable	Good	Unstructured	Low
5	Moderately Favorable	Poor	Structured	High
6	Moderately Favorable	Poor	Structured	Low
7	Moderately Favorable	Poor	Unstructured	High
8	Unfavorable	Poor	Unstructured	Low

Source Edwin B. Flippo and Gary M. Munsinger, *Management*, 4th ed. (Boston: Allyn and Bacon, Inc., 1978), p. 381.

The concept of leader-member relations is similar to the consideration or relationship behavior concepts, while task structure and position power are closely related to initiating structure or task behavior as discussed previously. By mixing these three elements, eight situations can be identified in Table 9.1.

These eight situations vary in accordance with the degree of favorableness of a situation to a leader—which is the leader's influence and control over the group. A leader has maximum influence in situation one and very little in situation eight. Research evidence indicates that a task-oriented, controlling leader will be most effective when the situations are either very favorable or easy (1, 2, and 3) or very difficult.[6] The more permissive, considerate leader performs more effectively in the intermediate situations which are moderately favorable to the leader (4, 5, 6 and 7). Another way to illustrate Fiedler's framework is seen in Figure 9.6. The task-oriented style of leader is more effective in situations 1, 2, 3, and 8 while the relationship-oriented style is more effective in situations 4, 5, 6, and 7. As demonstrated by Fiedler's theory, the most effective leadership style is contingent on many situational factors.

REDDIN'S THEORY OF LEADERSHIP

Reddin's leadership theory

Another situational leadership theory has been developed by William J. Reddin. **Reddin's leadership theory** proposes that four basic types of

6. William J. Reddin, *Managerial Effectiveness* (New York: McGraw-Hill, 1970).

FIGURE 9.6
Appropriateness of Leadership Styles to Situation

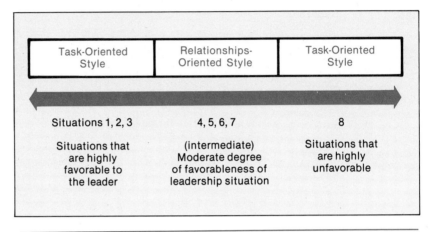

Source Adapted from Edwin B. Flippo and Gary M. Munsinger, *Management*, 4th ed. (Boston: Allyn and Bacon, Inc., 1978), p. 381.

situational styles can be identified, as depicted in Figure 9.7. Dividing the total area into the four cells results in situations where the manager can be—

1. separated from both task and human considerations,
2. highly related to people with limited emphasis on tasks,
3. highly concerned with the task with limited attention being allocated to interpersonal relationships, or
4. highly concerned with both task and relationships.

Within each of these four cells, two types of styles are identified—one that is more effective in dealing with a situation and another that is less effective. In Figure 9.7, these are indicated by the letters *a* and *b*, though their specific location in the illustration is suggested by the authors and not by Reddin.

In the Reddin framework, there are eight basic styles—four more effective and four less effective. In cell 1, the 1a position is the less effective style of "deserter" and the 1b position is the more effective one of "bureaucrat." Bureaucrats who are dedicated to enforcing the policies and rules of an organization can make an effective contribution if the policies and rules are correct. In cell 2, "Less effective" style 2a is extremely high on relationships and very low on task. This is referred to as a "missionary" style which tends to be found among members of voluntary agencies and in personnel departments. A more effective style for this cell would be 2b,

FIGURE 9.7
Reddin's 3-D Theory of Leadership

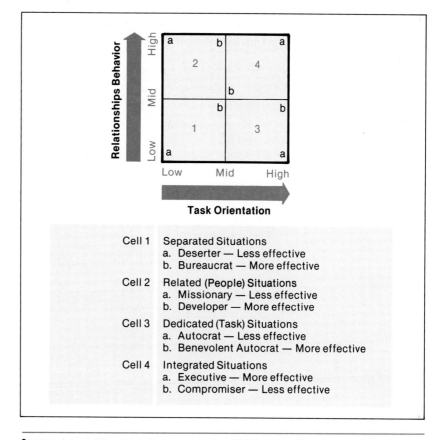

Cell 1	Separated Situations a. Deserter — Less effective b. Bureaucrat — More effective
Cell 2	Related (People) Situations a. Missionary — Less effective b. Developer — More effective
Cell 3	Dedicated (Task) Situations a. Autocrat — Less effective b. Benevolent Autocrat — More effective
Cell 4	Integrated Situations a. Executive — More effective b. Compromiser — Less effective

Source Adapted from Edwin B. Flippo and Gary M. Munsinger, *Management*, 4th ed. (Boston: Allyn and Bacon, Inc., 1978), p. 300.

"developer," where the orientation is more toward helping people to develop their skills and abilities, which will ultimately pay off in organization task accomplishment. However, leaders high on relationships and low on task can make a desired contribution in certain organizations or in certain portions of an organization. In cell 3, the 3a position is the less effective style of "autocrat," whereas the 3b location depicts the "benevolent autocrat." Only in cell 4 is the more effective style in the "a" position. This depicts the "executive," who develops balanced teamwork, coordination, and participation as an avenue toward higher performance. The less effective position, 4b, is termed "compromiser," the leader who develops teamwork through a trade-off or negotiation tactic. Thus, there is no one generally effective style applicable to all situations.

Though research continues, it has been found that styles tend to be associated with general situational constraints. Benevolent autocrats are more often found on the production floor, developers in the personnel department, bureaucrats in middle positions in large organizations, and executives among top management.

HERSEY AND BLANCHARD'S SITUATIONAL LEADERSHIP THEORY

Hersey and Blanchard's situational leadership theory

Paul Hersey and Kenneth Blanchard have developed a situational leadership theory that has attracted considerable attention on the part of managers.[7] **Hersey and Blanchard's situational leadership theory** is based on the notion that the most effective leadership style varies according to the level of maturity of the followers and demands of the situation. Their model uses two dimensions of leadership behavior—task and relationship—that are similar to the classifications used in the leadership models developed by Ohio State, W. J. Reddin, and the Managerial Grid. Hersey and Blanchard argue that an effective leader is one who can diagnose the demands of the situation and the level of maturity of the followers and use a leadership style that is appropriate. Their theory is based on a relationship between these factors:

task behavior

1. The amount of **task behavior** the leader exhibits—(providing direction and emphasis on getting the job done)

relationship behavior

2. The amount of **relationship behavior** the leader provides (consideration of people, level of socio-emotional support)

task–relevant maturity

3. The level of **task-relevant maturity** followers exhibit toward the specific goal, task or function that the leader wants accomplished

The key concept of their leadership theory is the level of task-relevant maturity of the followers. Maturity is not defined as age or psychological stability. The maturity level of the followers is defined as:

- *A desire for achievement*—(level of achievement motivation) based on the need to set high but attainable goals
- *The willingness and ability to accept responsibility*
- *Education and/or experience and skills* relevant to the particular task

---

7. Paul Hersey and Kenneth Blanchard, *Management of Organizational Behavior: Utilizing Human Resources*, 3rd ed. (Englewood Cliffs: Prentice-Hall, Inc., 1977), pp. 94–95.

A leader should consider the level of maturity of his or her followers only in relation to the work or job to be performed. Certainly, employees are "mature" on some tasks as they have the experience and skills as well as the desire to achieve and are capable of assuming responsibility. For example, an accountant may be very "mature" in the manner in which he or she prepares accurate quarterly IRS tax reports, but may not exhibit the same level of maturity when preparing written audits of the company's operations. The accountant needs very little direction or task-related behavior from his or her manager in preparing the tax reports, but may require considerably closer supervision and direction over the preparation and writing of audits.

**QUALITIES NEEDED FOR SUCCESS
AS A MANAGER IN YOUR ORGANIZATION**

· Finding the fine line between a workaholic and an 8:00 to 5:00'er that lets you make sure you keep your perspective with regard to other responsibilities, i.e., family, community, church, self. Time should be an ally, not an enemy.

· Putting people where they can perform profitably for the Company and themselves.

· A "can do" attitude.

· Understanding the difference between leadership and dictatorship.

BERL M. SPRINGER, President, Southwestern Public Service Company

Hersey and Blanchard argue that leadership style and effectiveness can be measured and they have designed an instrument for this purpose—The Leader Effectiveness & Adaptability Description (LEAD). The LEAD provides feedback on leadership style and the effectiveness of the individual completing the instrument.[8]

As illustrated in Figure 9.8, the appropriate leadership style used by a manager varies according to the maturity level (represented by M1 through M4) of the followers. There are four distinct leadership styles that

8. See Paul Hersey and Kenneth Blanchard, "So You Want to Know Your Leadership Style?" *Training and Development Journal,* February 1974, pp. 22–32. This article contains the Leader Adaptability and Style Inventory (LASI) an instrument that can be used to examine your leadership behavior, style adaptability, and effectiveness. Since this article, the LASI has become the Leader Effectiveness and Adaptability Description (LEAD). Information, LEAD inventories and training materials may be obtained from the Center for Leadership Studies, 17253 Caminito Canasto, Rancho Bernardo, San Diego, CA 92127.

FIGURE 9.8
Situational Leadership

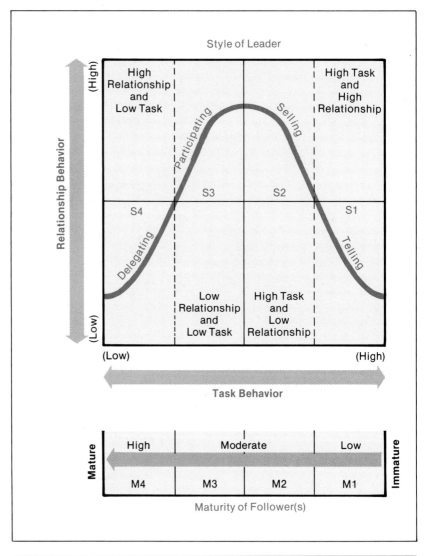

Style of Leader

Relationship Behavior

(High)

High Relationship and Low Task

High Task and High Relationship

Participating

Selling

S3

S2

S4

S1

Delegating

Telling

(Low)

Low Relationship and Low Task

High Task and Low Relationship

(Low)   (High)

Task Behavior

Mature	High	Moderate	Low	Immature
	M4	M3	M2	M1	

Maturity of Follower(s)

Source Paul Hersey and Kenneth Blanchard, Center for Leadership Studies, California American University, 1977.

are appropriate given different levels of maturity. As the task-relevant maturity level of followers increases, the manager should reduce task behavior and increase relationship behavior. These are illustrated by the classifications of the styles as:

S1—Telling	High Task
	Low Relationship
S2—Selling	High Task
	High Relationship
S3—Participating	High Relationship
	Low Task
S4—Delegating	Low Relationship
	Low Task

With the *S1 (Telling) high task, low relationship* leadership style, the leader uses one-way communication, defines the goals and roles of employees and tells them what, how, when, and where to do the various work. This style is very appropriate when dealing with subordinates who lack task-relevant maturity. For example, in supervising a group of relatively new, inexperienced employees, a high level of task directed behavior and low relationship behavior would be an appropriate approach to effective leadership. Inexperienced employees need to be told what needs to be done and how to accomplish their jobs.

As employees learn their jobs, the manager begins to use an *S2 leadership style.* There still is a need for a high level of task behavior since the employees do not have the experience or skills to assume responsibility, but the manager provides a higher level of socio-emotional support—high relationship behavior. The manager encourages the employees and demonstrates greater trust and confidence in them.

As we move toward *S3 leadership style,* the employee begins to exhibit an increase in task-relevant maturity. As employees become more experienced and skilled, as well as more achievement motivated and more willing to assume responsibility, the leader should reduce the amount of task behavior, but continue the high level of socio-emotional support and consideration. A continuation of a high level of relationship behavior is the manager's way of reinforcing the employees' responsible performance. Thus, S3 becomes the appropriate leadership style—high relationship and low task behavior.

The *S4 leadership style* represents the highest level of follower maturity. In this stage, the employees possess a very high level of task maturity. They are very skilled and experienced and possess high achievement motivation and are capable of exercising self-control. Thus, the leadership style that is most appropriate for this situation is S4—Low Relationship and Low Task. At this point the employees no longer need or expect a high level of supportive behavior from their leader.

We should not conclude from the above discussion that the process of deciding the appropriate leadership style is simple to determine. The ability to diagnose the maturity level of the followers as well as the specific needs of the situation is indeed complex. The leader must have indepth insight into the abilities, needs, demands and expectations of followers and be aware that these can and do change over time. Also, managers must recognize that they must adapt or change their style of leadership whenever there is a change in the level of maturity of followers for whatever reason—change in jobs, personal or family problems, or change in complexity of present job due perhaps to new technology. For example, Bill Woodall, the sales manager has been using an S4 leadership style in supervising John Chriswell, a normally highly productive sales representative. But, suppose that John's pending divorce has recently been adversely affecting his performance. In this situation, Bill might increase both the level of task and relationship behavior in order to provide John with the direction, support and confidence he may need to cope with his problems and improve his performance.

In summary, Hersey and Blanchard's theory provides a useful and understandable framework for situational leadership. In essence, their model suggests that there is *no one* best leadership style that meets the needs of all situations. Rather, a manager's leadership style must be adaptable and flexible enough to meet the changing needs of employees and situations. The effective manager is one who can change styles as employees develop and change or as required by the situation.

AN INTEGRATED APPROACH TO LEADERSHIP

The notion that there is one "best" leadership style has been criticized as being unrealistic and overly simplistic. Is it logical to assume that the *same* leadership style would be equally effective in managing such diverse groups as auto assemblers, research scientists, clerk-typists, college professors, lawyers, or construction workers? We think not! From our previous discussion of the several situational leadership theories, it should be apparent that there is no one best style of leadership that is equally effective for all circumstances. The most effective leadership style is one that meets the needs of the particular situation at hand. This requires a careful consideration of forces in the leader, the followers, and the specific situation.

The development of an integrated approach to effective leadership requires that we consider several important situational factors. As shown in Figure 9.9, forces in the leader, the followers, and the situation all interrelate to determine the most effective leadership style. Although the situational factors are presented in a different format, the importance of giving careful consideration to these factors remains. The *management approach* is associated with the leader. The followers represent the *personnel.* The situation includes the *structure,* the *technology, objectives* and the *external* environment. Each of these elements will be discussed as it is a determinant of effective leadership style.

FIGURE 9.9
An Integrated Approach to Leadership

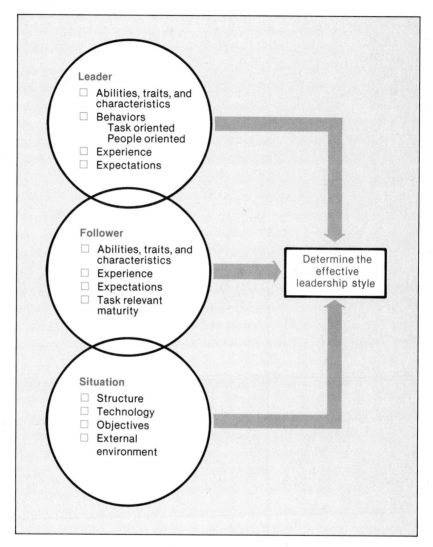

LEADER

All of us have different combinations of abilities, personalities, experiences, and expectations. Because of these factors each of us develops different patterns of accomplishing tasks. If it has been discovered that a certain behavioral pattern has worked successfully in the past, this approach will likely continue in the future. A person who has found that being an autocratic manager will get the job done will likely continue this pattern unless events occur that show this style is no longer appropriate. The same situation may evolve for a person who has developed participative patterns. A participative style may also continue to be used unless it is proven that it is no longer a realistic approach.

With the integrated approach to leadership, managers must recognize the leadership style they are presently using. Then, an evaluation is made as to what managerial approach will be most effective based on a careful consideration of the nature of the followers and the situation. The leader adapts his or her style to meet the needs of the followers and the situation. This does not mean that an individual's basic beliefs change. However, it does mean that for the time he or she is in a particular leadership role his or her leadership style must be adapted to the followers and the situation.

FOLLOWERS

As with the leader, followers have different abilities, personalities, experiences and expectations. With the integrated approach to leadership it is recognized that the followers do not necessarily obey an order that is given by the leader. If the followers feel that it is in their best interest to abide by the wishes of the leader, the task will be accomplished.

Thus, followers are a major factor for consideration in the integrated approach to leadership. If the followers are inexperienced, lack the education or skills, and do not seek more individual responsibility for their job, the most effective leadership style will tend to be more directive or autocratic, emphasizing task accomplishment. On the other hand, if personnel are highly educated, experienced, and seek responsibility for decision making, a more participative style of leadership is most appropriate. At times a manager may need to strongly emphasize task accomplishment and a statement like "Let's get the job done" may be necessary to accomplish the job. At other times a much more participative style suggested by a comment such as "I need your help and advice if this job is going to be done" will provide the most effective leadership. A manager must take into consideration the needs, goals, capabilities, and experiences of the followers if his or her effectiveness is to be achieved.

SITUATION

The remaining four factors of structure, technology, objectives, and the external environment comprise the situation (see Figure 9.1). Each must be considered if a leader is to determine his or her most effective style.

Structure

Managers in a very highly structured, centralized environment may tend to adopt a more autocratic style of leadership. It is quite difficult to apply a more participative leadership if rules and regulations describe all tasks that must be performed. On the other hand, in a decentralized and/or less structured organization where tasks are not clear and precise, a more participative style of leadership may produce the best results.

Leadership style is also affected by the manager's level within the organization. A first-line supervisor may be prevented by rules and regulations from developing a more permissive style whereas a vice-president may find that a more democratic style produces superior results.

Technology

At times the state of the art is a major determining factor of the most effective leadership style. On an assembly line it is likely that a supervisor may lean toward an autocratic style. When teams of highly skilled workers are used instead of a traditional assembly line, the manager may use a more participative style of leadership.

Objectives

As the objectives of the firm change, a change in leadership style may be necessary. For example, if a firm determines that it should be an innovative organization, personnel changes may require a modification of leadership styles. The personnel who are hired to make the transition to an innovative firm may not accept the autocratic style of its predecessor. As the level of professional and technical capabilities increases, the style of leadership may lean toward a more relationship-oriented leadership style. On the other hand, if the firm's goal is survival, the leadership style may again move toward a greater emphasis on task accomplishment.

External Environment

The external environment has considerable influence on determining the most effective leadership style. Obviously, economic, political, social, and cultural forces must be considered. For example, during periods of economic crunches or slowdowns which cause a decline in sales for a company, some managers tend to become more direct, cost-conscious, and place greater emphasis on the efficiency of task accomplishment.

During the past two decades, there has been a significant increase in the educational level of the people entering the work force. There have also been changes in social and cultural values which, in effect are demanding that leaders must be able to adapt to the situation. These trends support the conclusion that there is no one best style of leadership that will meet the needs of all followers or the demands of every situation.

SUMMARY

Effective leadership is absolutely essential to the survival and growth of every organization. Leadership is the process of motivating and directing others toward the accomplishment of goals. But, what is required to be an effective manager and what is the most effective leadership style? These questions have been of concern to managers for generations and have been the subject of thousands of research studies. Despite volumes of leadership research, no simple list of traits or characteristics have been identified that are consistently related to effective leadership. In fact, the basic conclusion of these studies is that there is no one most effective leadership style.

Three basic theories of leadership were discussed in this chapter—trait, behavioral, and situational. The early studies of leadership attempted to identify the traits and characteristics of effective leaders. Traits relating to physical characteristics, personality, or intelligence were studied to determine if they were related to effective leadership. For the most part, research has not shown that traits alone can distinguish effective from ineffective leaders. Despite these findings, the trait approach to the study of leadership has continued. Edwin Ghiselli has identified six traits/ characteristics that his extensive research indicates are related to effective leadership. These include supervisory ability, need for occupational achievement, intelligence, decisiveness, self-assurance, and initiative.

Dissatisfaction with the trait approach to the study of leadership caused the research emphasis to concentrate on the behavior and actions of leaders. The behavioral theories identified two basic dimensions of leadership behavior. Although these two behaviors have been referred to by several different names, they are the leader's behavior and concern for (1) the accomplishment of tasks (task behavior), and (2) the relationship with people (relationship behavior). One of the most widely known leadership theories is the Managerial Grid. The two dimensions of leadership behavior identified in the 9 × 9 Managerial Grid was "concern for people" and "concern for production." Five basic styles of leadership on the Grid were do nothing (1,1), task centered (9,1), country club (1,9), organization man (5,5), and team builder (9,9). Blake and Mouton, the developers of the Grid theory, suggest that the 9,9 style of leadership is the most effective and achieves the best results in terms of performance.

In recent years, considerable attention has been given to the situational approach to the study of leadership. The basic conclusion of this approach is that the most effective leaders are neither task centered nor people centered. But rather, effective leaders must be flexible enough to adopt a leadership style that fits their needs as well as the needs of their subordinates and the situation.

The theories of Fred Fiedler, William J. Reddin, and Paul Hersey and Kenneth Blanchard suggest there is no one most effective style of leadership that is appropriate to every situation. In Fiedler's theory, the degree of favorableness or unfavorableness of the leader–member relations, task structure, and position power of the leader determine the style of leadership that is most effective. In Reddin's model there are eight styles of leadership—four more effective and four less effective. Finally, Hersey and Blanchard's theory is based on the notion that the most effective leadership style varies according to the level of maturity of the followers and the demands of the situation. Their theory offers four basic styles or combinations of task and relationship behavior of the leader. If the leader is dealing with highly "mature followers" the appropriate leadership style might be low emphasis on both relationships and task behavior.

Perhaps the most realistic approach to leadership is an integrated one that carefully considers the forces in the leader, the followers, and the situation. To be truly effective in achieving goals, the leader must recognize that no one approach will be equally effective for all circumstances.

Review Questions

1. What is meant by the term leadership? Why is it an important subject?

2. What is the distinction between management and leadership? Is it possible to be a good leader but an ineffective manager?

3. In the chapter, what caused the bankruptcy of the mobile home company?

4. Briefly describe and contrast the types of power a leader may possess to influence the behavior of others.

5. What is the trait approach to the study of leadership? To what extent are certain traits related to effective leadership?

6. List several significant traits identified by the research of Edwin Ghiselli as being important for effective leadership.

7. What are the four basic styles or systems of management identified by Rensis Likert? Explain each.

8. Describe the five leadership styles presented in the Managerial Grid. Which style is recommended as most effective by Blake and Mouton?

9. What were the Ohio State leadership studies? What basic dimensions of leadership behavior were identified? What were some of the factors that determined the most effective style of leadership?

10. What basic conclusion can be derived from the Tannenbaum and Schmidt leadership continuum? What factors should be considered before choosing a given style of leadership?

11. What is the basic contention of Fiedler's theory of leadership? In what situations are *task-centered* leaders most effective? People-centered leaders?

12. Explain Figure 9.7, a model illustrating W. J. Reddin's leadership theory. What basic styles are presented?

13. Briefly explain Hersey and Blanchard's situational leadership theory. What is the key concept of their theory?

14. Explain Figure 9.8.

15. What basic conclusions can be drawn from the various situational leadership theories?

Exercises

1. Assume you have just been promoted to the position of office manager in charge of 12 clerical personnel—8 typists and 4 general clerks. The previous manager was removed from the position because the office staff was not able to complete their work on schedule. In addition, the office experienced excessive turnover of employees and several of the employees had expressed concern about poor quality of work and attitudes of the clerical staff. Under the previous manager, the employees showed little interest in their jobs and generally viewed the office manager as a ''soft touch.''

   a. What style of leadership would you utilize as you assume the position of office manager? Why?

   b. Explain, in terms of situational leadership theory presented in this chapter, how your leadership style would change should output improve and employee turnover decrease.

2. Go to the library and make a copy of the article ''So You Want To Know Your Leadership Style?'' by Paul Hersey and Kenneth Blanchard, *Training and Development Journal*, February 1974, pp. 22–32. Complete the Leader Adaptability and Style (LASI) instrument contained in the article. Then read the article. What is your leadership style as per the LASI? Discuss in class.

REFERENCES

Barrow, J. C. "Variables of Leadership: A Review and Conceptual Framework." *Academy of Management Review*, April 1977, pp. 231–251.

Bennis, W. "Leadership: A Beleaguered Species?" *Organization Dynamics*, Summer 1976, pp. 2–16.

Chapman, J.B. "Comparison of Male and Female Leadership Styles." *Academy of Management Journal*, September 1975, pp. 645–650.

Fiedler, F. E. "Job Engineering For Effective Leadership: A New Approach." *Management Review*, September 1977, pp. 29–31.

Fox, W. M. "Limits to the Use of Consultative-Participative Management." *California Management Review*, Winter 1977, pp. 17–22.

Green, S. G., and Nebeker, D. M. "Effects of Situational Factors and Leadership Style on Leader Behavior." *Organizational Behavior and Human Performance*, August 1977, pp. 368–377.

Helmich, D. L., and Erzen, P. E. "Leadership Style and Leader Needs." *Academy of Management Journal*, June 1975, pp. 397–402.

Jago, A. G., and Vroom, V. H. "Hierarchical Level and Leadership Style." *Organizational Behavior and Human Performance*, February 1977, pp. 117–123.

Katz, R. "Influence of Group Conflict on Leadership Effectiveness." *Organizational Behavior and Human Performance*, December 1977, pp. 265–286.

Leister, A., and Others. "Validation of Contingency Model Leadership Training: Leader Match." *Academy of Management Journal*, September 1977, pp. 464–470.

Likert, R. "Management Styles and the Human Component." *Management Review*, October 1977, pp. 23–28.

Putnam, L. and Heinen, J. S. Women in Management: The Fallacy of the Trait Approach." *Michigan State University Business Topics*, Summer 1976, pp. 47–53.

Smith, D. F. "Developing Effective Leadership in Front-Line Supervision." *Personnel Journal*, June 1975, pp. 453–460.

Zaleznik, A. "Managers and Leaders: Are They Different?" *Harvard Business Review*, May 1977, pp. 67–68+.

Case Study   CHOOSING AN APPROPRIATE LEADERSHIP STYLE

Allen Russell was chosen six months ago to be manager of the research and development department for Western Engineering. The senior vice-president who made the decision reasoned that the R&D Department could use the expertise of a person who was experienced in production problems. Allen had been a line foreman and had an excellent reputation for getting the job done. He was well organized and was credited with being able to solve problems prior to their reaching upper-level management. The primary emphasis of the research and development department was to conduct practical research for the purpose of developing marketable products. Thus, top management believed Allen would do well in this assignment because of his knowledge of production operations.

When Allen arrived at his new job he could not believe how "unorganized" the researchers were. They might come to work at 10:00 and leave at 3:00 (Allen did not realize that many of them worked late at night). The employees were all dedicated researchers and considered themselves professionals. They did not feel that a task had to be lined out in detail for the job to be done.

Allen believed that these conditions were not conducive to maximum productivity. He had been taught on the production line that efficiency is a direct result of the organization and structure of tasks. If it works in one situation, it should work in another.

The first decision that Allen made was to install a time clock. He reasoned that if the department members were to be productive they must be at their desks during certain hours of the day. The researchers in Allen's department expressed disbelief of this decision. Before Allen became supervisor most of the researchers were working an average of twelve hours a day. Although they might not be at the office between eight and five, they were recognized as being very productive. Many of the researchers actually liked to work Saturday morning because the activity level of the plant was lower and they could concentrate better. Without realizing it, Allen was actually telling the departmental members to reduce their work time by one-third.

When Allen arrived at work at 8:00 on Monday he was pleased to see that all of the researchers clocked in at the proper time. They remained at their desk the entire day and left promptly at 5:00. He reasoned that everything was going to be great. The employees had accepted him as their superior. This euphoria did not last for long. People throughout the company began calling him to ask why their particular project was not finished. When he checked with the person who was responsible for the project, he found out that they had been working on it, but had not had time to complete it. In virtually every instance this was the case.

Allen came to the conclusion that the researchers were "goofing off" and he issued numerous letters of reprimand. Meanwhile, several key employees resigned to take other positions. The situation continued to deteriorate until there was virtually no useful work being conducted in the department. When the vice-president finally asked Allen what was causing this inefficiency, he responded, "They were all a bunch of super-egos but he could get them in shape." The vice-president is not so sure that this was the problem and asks for your advice.

Questions

1. What assumptions did management make with regard to making Allen Russell the research and development department manager?

2. How would you describe the leadership style of Allen? How appropriate was this style to the management of the research and development department?

3. What style of leadership would likely be most effective in managing a group of researchers?

4. Assume that you are the vice-president of Western (Allen's boss). What action would you take to improve the situation?

Case Study   FAILURE TO TAKE A PROMOTION

Nancy Rodgers had been employed with Stockton, Inc. as an accountant since she had graduated from college five years ago. She enjoyed her work and the close association she had made with the other accountants and staff within the office. During this time Nancy gained a reputation for being highly efficient and for being able to react quickly to a crisis. When she was evaluated by her supervisor each year, Nancy consistently received the highest rating in the department. She had no idea that these excellent evaluations might ultimately return to haunt her.

When the departmental supervisor was promoted to the position of controller, Nancy was a prime contender for the supervisory position. Everyone liked Nancy and her superiority on the job was recognized by all. It did not take long for management to make the decision that Nancy was the one to become the new department head. The promotion would mean a substantial increase in salary and respectability within the firm.

The only problem was that Nancy did not want the promotion. She enjoyed the work she was doing and had absolutely no aspiration to obtain a managerial position. The new controller was shocked to find out that Nancy rejected the offer. He felt that it was a "slap in his face" and took a personal offense that the person he recommended would refuse the offer. When a new supervisor was selected from outside the firm, the bad feelings that the controller had regarding Nancy were communicated to the new supervisor. The controller's attitude was not directed toward Nancy's work (her efficiency was a well-known fact). The tone of his comments related to "company loyalty," "dedication," and "faithfulness." This attitude ultimately filtered down to the employees in Nancy's department. Many of her "friends" were not as close to Nancy as they once were. The few friends that remained were not accepted by the other members of the work group. When the time for her annual evaluation arrived, it was not nearly as good as it had been in the past.

Nancy became extremely depressed by the loss of respect and friendships within the department. This was reflected in her work as she began making numerous errors. Also, ideas that she presented to her peers and the departmental manager were frequently rejected. Her drop in efficiency caused her to receive several reprimands by the manager. After the third reprimand Nancy was told that she was terminated. She was given two weeks pay but was asked to leave the company immediately.

Questions   1. What caused this situation to develop?

2. In view of the circumstances, do you feel it would have been in Nancy's best interest to accept the promotion?

3. What mistake(s) did the new controller make regarding Nancy? Discuss.

4. What approach to leadership would have been appropriate in this situation? In other words, how should the company and especially the controller have reacted to Nancy not wanting to become the department supervisor?

Chapter 10

organizational climate

participative climate

change sequence

management development programs

sensitivity training

organization development

team development

Organizational Climate, Change, and Development

LEARNING OBJECTIVES

After completing this chapter you should be able to

1. Describe the importance of surveying the organizational environment prior to making changes.
2. Explain the reason for the trend toward a more participative climate.
3. Identify the situational factors that should be considered in bringing about change.
4. List the sequence of events that must take place for change to occur.
5. Identify sources of resistance to change and the approaches that can be used in reducing resistance to change.
6. Describe the techniques that are available to implement change.

As you try to settle down to study most likely you will have observed that there are certain places where you can concentrate better than others. Studying in front of the television may result in a limited attention span whereas in your bedroom may result in greater concentration (provided you don't decide to rest your eyes too much). Each potential place to study provides a different climate. It is much the same in a business firm; certain organizational climates are more conducive to maintaining higher levels of productivity than others. But, just as most students have a particular location (thereby a particular climate) that provides them with the best opportunity to learn, companies are also different in that there is an optimum climate to achieve maximum productivity.

When a person—perhaps your parents, girlfriend, or boyfriend—suggests that you should change your study habits, there may be a tendency to resist. You like studying in front of the television; who has a right to tell you how to do things? But, there are times when a change or modification of a particular behavior might be beneficial to long-run effectiveness. Your parents or teachers may have suggested that grades will improve if study habits are altered. You have been studying in front of the television all of your life and have maintained a C average. Perhaps if you studied away from the television, a B average could be attained. Nevertheless, even if a person realizes that the change may be for the best, there still may be a certain amount of resistance.

MOST IMPORTANT REASONS FOR SUCCESS AND EFFECTIVENESS AS A MANAGER

No executive can be more effective than the team of people working for him; and nowhere is this more apparent than in a people-oriented business like broadcasting. Much of the success and effectiveness I've achieved can be traced to finding talented managers, encouraging them to function as a team, and creating an organizational climate in which they can operate smoothly, creatively, and happily.

ELTON H. RULE, President, American Broadcasting Companies, Incorporated

---

Companies confront much the same type situation on a day-to-day basis, but on a much more complicated level. Just as the student mentioned above may not want to change his study habits, employees also may be reluctant to change even though the organization's very survival may be in jeopardy. As mentioned in an earlier chapter, we live and work in a highly dynamic, ever-changing environment. In order to be competitive, a business and its employees must constantly adapt to external and internal pressures. It has been said that nothing is certain except "death" and "taxes." Realistically, for a firm this need not be so. Corporations can manipulate their resources so that taxes will not have to be paid. Salaries and bonuses may be increased to eliminate profits; individual executives may pay taxes but the corporation may not. A firm can also perpetuate its existence through incorporation; presidents may pass on but the corporation remains. The only thing certain is that *change* will occur.

This chapter first concentrates on the importance of selecting the proper organizational climate for a firm. Next, a discussion of the importance of understanding change in a business environment is presented. Finally, the various approaches that have been used in business to implement change will be discussed. The intent of the chapter is to prepare a person to recognize the importance of the organizational climate to a firm and how he or she may change the firm to the best possible environment to achieve maximum results.

ORGANIZATIONAL CLIMATE

There are times when an organization must alter its entire personality or climate in order to survive. But what are the types of organizational climates that a firm may wish to emulate and why should one particular climate prove superior to another? A knowledge of organizational climate is important before specific types of change methods should be considered. In the situational approach to management, one must first determine the types of climate that should achieve a desired output before any change should take place. Once this information is obtained, attention may then be devoted to specific types of change techniques which are needed.

CLIMATE DEFINED

organizational climate

The psychological environment of the firm is described as the **organizational climate.** Just as individuals have different personalities, an organization also has its own distinct climate or personality. Two firms, manufacturing similar type products, may have completely different climates.

Organizational climate is similar in concept to meteorological climate. Just as the latter is comprised of such variables as temperature, humidity, and precipitation, organizational climate is composed of such factors as friendliness, supportiveness, risk-taking, and the like. Just as the weather of the Southwestern United States may be described as warm and pleasant, the employee may characterize his or her organization as being open and supportive. This perception is gradually formed over a period of time

D O R I S   C.   E T E L S O N

Vice-President—Service Standards
Howard Johnson's

Doris C. Etelson has been in the restaurant business since she started working at her family's restaurant as a girl—"from pot-sink up." Her success as a manager is even more significant when one considers that Doris wears two hats—a family person and a successful business executive. The Etelsons were married in 1950, and for the first years of their marriage, Mrs. Etelson owned and operated a cafeteria in an industrial plant. She stopped working between 1958 and 1961 to care for her two young daughters.

In 1961, she joined Howard Johnson as a food supervisor for seven restaurants. Doris became head supervisor for twenty-five restaurants in 1965 and in 1968 became area manager. She was named staff assistant to a divisional manager in 1970 and advanced to director of administration in 1972. While working upward in Howard Johnson's, Doris was also obtaining her college degree in economics from the State University of New York in 1974 and is currently working toward her M.B.A. In 1977, she was named to her present position as vice-president—service standards. Her current job entails finding ways of upgrading the quality of customer service at Howard Johnson's and the development of new concepts. The job carries with it a profit and loss responsibility.

Progression into top management has not been an easy one, but from the beginning, Doris has had a clear-cut goal of going "as far as I could in management and to take it step by step." Her husband owns a successful air-freight company in Newark, New Jersey, and she works in Boston. In order to maintain two successful careers, every weekend Mrs. Etelson drives or hops on a plane to visit Mr. Etelson. Twice a week, her husband takes a plane to Boston. Two days a week, they are apart. They have been able to keep this schedule because their children are in their twenties and are no longer at home and because Mr. Etelson has encouraged his wife's career. Her husband, she says, is a "totally emancipated man. He's my best supporter in pursuing career goals."

For Mrs. Etelson, the most important aspect of any job is the "ability and willingness to make a tremendous effort. I'm constantly preparing for the next job, willing to do more than necessary. I have a policy of total involvement in whatever I'm doing. I definitely aspire to move to the very top of my potential." Doris Etelson is a person of tomorrow. "Looking ahead means making changes. Change is never easy, but the only alternative is standing still." The career pattern of the Etelsons is one that may increase significantly in the future as more and more women aspire to fulfill their full potential.

as the person performs an assigned activity under the general guidance of a superior and a set of organizational guides. The climate existing within a firm has an impact on the person's degree of satisfaction with the job, as well as on the level and quality of his or her performance. The assessment of how good or bad the organization's climate is, is in the eyes of the employee. One person may perceive the same environment as *bad* and another perceive the environment as *good*. An employee may actually leave an organization in hopes of finding a better climate.

FACTORS THAT DETERMINE ORGANIZATION CLIMATE

As may be seen in Figure 10.1, typical factors that affect organizational climate are provided under the headings of work group, organization characteristics, supervisor, and administrative processes.[1] Certainly, the nature of the immediate work group will affect one's conception of the quality of climate. The factor *commitment* refers to whether or not this group is just going through the motions associated with a job. If such a state does exist, it would be very difficult for a particular individual to derive high levels of output and satisfaction. The factor of *hindrance* is concerned with the degree to which a great deal of *busywork* of doubtful value is given to the group. *Morale* and *friendliness* within the group are factors with which most readers are familiar.

There is much evidence that suggests the leadership style of the immediate supervisor will have a considerable effect on the climate of the group and vice versa. If the manager is *aloof* and distant in dealing with subordinates, this will have an impact. If he or she is always pushing for output, this alters the environment. *Thrust* refers to supervisory behavior characterized by personally working hard and setting an example. *Consideration* is a leadership characteristic that was discussed at length in chapter 9.

Moving from the immediate group, there are a number of variables that affect the type of organizational climate. Organizations vary on such attributes as size and complexity. Large organizations tend toward higher degrees of specialization and greater impersonalization. Labor unions often find that large firms are easier to organize than the smaller ones because the smaller firms tend to be closer and have more informal relationships between employees and management. Complex organizations tend to employ a greater number of professionals and specialists

1. Many of the factors were taken from the Organizational Climate Description Questionnaire generated by Halpin and Croft as described in Andrew W. Halpin, *Theory and Research in Administration* (New York: Macmillan, 1966), chap. 4. Another widely used measure is that of Litwin and Stringer found in G. Litwin and R. Stringer, *Motivation and Organizational Climate* (Cambridge, Mass.: Harvard University Press, 1968).

FIGURE 10.1
Factors That Determine Organizational Climate

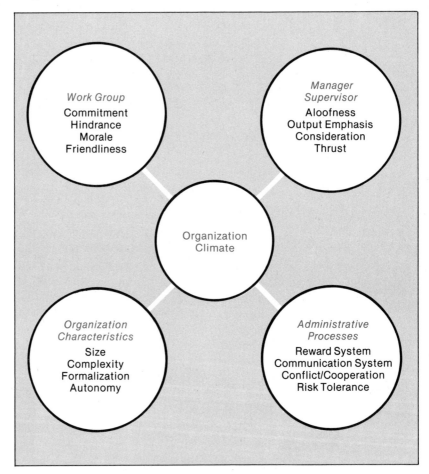

which alters the general approach to solving problems. Organizations also vary in the degree to which they write things down and attempt to program behavior through rules, procedures, and regulations. They can also be distinguished on the basis of the degree of decentralization of decision-making authority, which affects the degrees of autonomy and freedom of personnel within the organization.

Organization climate can be affected by administrative processes. Firms that can develop a direct link between performance and rewards tend to create climates conducive to achievement. Communication systems that are open and free-flowing tend to promote participation and creative atmospheres. The general attitudes that exist toward the handling of risk and the tolerance of conflict will, in turn, have considerable impact on the type of teamwork effected. They also affect the amount of organizational innovation and creativity.

As shown in Figure 10.1, there are sixteen factors that affect organization climates. From these factors organization members will develop a subjective impression of "what kind of place this is to work for." This general impression will have some impact on performance, satisfaction, creativity, and commitment to the organization.

TYPES OF CLIMATES

participative climate

There are a number of possible types of organizational climates. The one advocated by most behavioralists, such as Rensis Likert and Robert Blake, is the open and/or **participative climate.** This climate would be characterized by such attributes as these:

· trust in subordinates
· openness in communication
· considerate and supportive leadership
· group problem solving
· worker autonomy
· information sharing
· establishment of high output goals

Some behaviorialists contend this is the *only* viable climate for *all* situations.

The opposite of the open and supportive climate would be a *closed and threatening* one. It, too, would be characterized by high output goals. But such goals are more likely to be declared and imposed on the organization by autocratic and threatening leaders. There is greater functional rigidity in this climate, which results from strict adherence to the formal chain of command, shorter spans of control, and stricter individual accountability. The emphasis is on the individual rather than teamwork. Employee reactions are often characterized by *going through the motions* and doing as one is told. Despite criticism by behavioralists, such climates may not adversely affect performance output in a highly structured situation. Such a closed and threatening climate will almost surely contribute to a decrease in employee satisfaction, with possible subsequent increases in absenteeism and turnover.

THE PARTICIPATIVE CLIMATE

As has been indicated previously in this text, the prevailing managerial approach in most organizations has been one characterized as being highly structured. Consequently, most of the attempts to alter organizational climates have been directed toward creating a more open and participative climate. The theme of participation developed by individuals such as McGregor, Herzberg, and Maslow relates primarily to self-actualization, motivator factors, consultative and democratic leadership, job enrichment, organization development, and management by objectives.

Values of Participation

The possible values of involving more people in the decision making process within a firm relate primarily to productivity and morale. Increased productivity can result from the stimulation of ideas and from the encouragement of greater effort and cooperation. If employees are psychologically involved, they will often respond to shared problems with innovative suggestions and unusual efforts. In one company, management was faced with the problem of stocking a reserve supply of coal in anticipation of a possible coal strike. The thirty-seven men involved were told the reason for the extra effort. They were also informed that management did not know what extra effort could be expected from the men. However, it was believed that a period of only three months was available to them for the establishment of a reserve supply. The group discussed the problem and directed several questions to management, one of which concerned the effect that this *crash* effort would have on their vacations. Management replied they hoped that vacations could be eliminated during these three months, but any reasonable request would be respected. After further discussion, the group finally decided that they could stock sixty carloads of coal on each shift. This was even more than had been hoped for by management, which had considered a figure of fifty-five cars more likely. During these three months, the men worked seven days a week and exceeded the figure they had set. The supervisors noted the morale during this period was higher than it had been previously. Team spirit and improved attitudes were readily apparent.

In another instance, the expansion of the work planning responsibilities of a group of ten female assemblers at Texas Instruments led to a reduction in assembly time for one product from 138 hours to 41 hours over a period of nine months.[2] These employees had previously participated in a

---

2. M. Scott Myers and Earl D. Week, Jr., "Behavioral Change Agents: A Case Study," *Management of Personnel Quarterly* 6 (Fall 1967), p. 16.

twenty-four-hour training program in work simplification and cost reduction. Texas Instruments was systematically attempting to manage in a consultative and participative manner. It also has a program of employee profit sharing through which monetary benefits of increased productivity can be shared.

However, not all attempts at participative management have been successful. In 1965, Non-Linear Systems of Del Mar, California, attributed a 30 percent increase in productivity to a participative philosophy of management. They also reported elimination of specialized inspectors, thereby trusting the employee, with a consequent decrease in customer complaints of about 70 percent. When sales dropped because of the aerospace slump of 1970, from $6 million in 1965 to $3.5 million in 1971, the participative experiment was abandoned. The president stated, "I may have lost sight of the purpose of business, which is not to develop new theories of management."[3] Behavioral consultants maintain that the motivational programming was working, but top management failed in its development of strategic planning and forecasting. Tighter financial and inventory controls were introduced and a *turnaround* was effected. A portion of the credit for this was attributed to enlarged work skills developed during the participative experiment.

Open and participative climates are more often successful in improving the levels of morale and satisfaction. Specific values in this area would include:

1. Increased acceptability of management's ideas
2. Increased cooperation with members of management and staff
3. Reduced turnover
4. Reduced absenteeism
5. Reduced complaints and grievances
6. Greater acceptance of changes
7. Improved attitudes toward the job and the organization

In general, the development of greater employee participation appears to have a direct and immediate effect on employee morale. Employees take a greater interest in the job and the organization. They tend to accept, and sometimes initiate, changes not only because of their understanding of the necessity for change but also because their fear of insecurity has been reduced by knowing more about the change. Thus, even though a credibility gap may exist for practicing managers in the area of productivity, most experience and research indicate a positive relationship between

3. "Where Being Nice to Workers Didn't Work," *Business Week* (January 20, 1973), pp. 90–100.

> **QUALITIES NEEDED FOR SUCCESS**
> **AS A MANAGER IN YOUR ORGANIZATION**
> · A willingness to accept change
> · A skill in motivation of people
> · Technical ability
> · An attitude that pushes one to go that extra mile
> · Being in the right place at the *right time*
>
> H. C. GOODRICH, Chairman & C.E.O., Inland Container Corporation

employee participation and measures of morale, turnover, and absenteeism. However, there has been little evidence presented that would suggest a positive relationship exists between job satisfaction and productivity. If productivity is not harmed by participation, it would appear that these supplementary values would make a program worthwhile. If productivity is actually decreased, then serious decisions will have to be made concerning management's philosophy of organizational and human values.

Limitations of Participation

Despite the values of a participative approach to management, there are some limitations. There are certain prerequisites to and limitations on greater employee participation in decision making. The requirements for greater participation in decision making are: (1) sufficient time; (2) adequate ability and interest on the part of the participants; and (3) restrictions generated by the present structure and system.

If immediate decisions are required, time cannot be spared for group participation. The manager decides what to do and issues the order accordingly. Should management decide to switch from a practice of autocracy to one of increased participation, some time for adjustment on the part of both parties will be required. Participation calls for some measure of ability to govern oneself instead of leaning on others. In addition, it requires time for the subordinate to learn to handle this new-found freedom and time for the supervisor to learn to trust the subordinate.

Whether or not greater involvement in decision making can be developed largely depends on the ability and interest of the participants, both subordinates and managers. This is not an easy concept to implement. Obviously, if the subordinate has neither knowledge of nor interest in a subject, there is little need to consult. As organizations and technology become increasingly complex, and as management becomes more

FIGURE 10.2
Limits to Participative Freedom

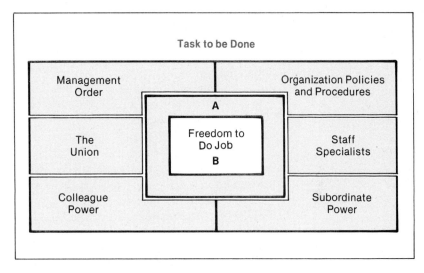

Task to be Done

Management Order		Organization Policies and Procedures
The Union	**A** Freedom to Do Job **B**	Staff Specialists
Colleague Power		Subordinate Power

Source Adapted from Edwin B. Flippo and Gary M. Munsinger, *Management*, 4th ed. (Boston: Allyn and Bacon, Inc., 1978), p. 405.

professionalized, it is likely that employee participation will become more characterized by cooperation seeking or information gathering. It should also be noted that not all personnel are equally desirous of participation. Managers must face the fact that some employees, hopefully just a few, do not seek more responsibility and greater involvement in their job.

Finally, as indicated in Figure 10.2, the area of job freedom left to the individual may be quite restricted, but can be expanded. His or her task is pregoverned by management directives, organization policies and procedures, the union contract, relations with the union steward, staff specialists, and the degree to which one can obtain the cooperation of subordinates. The greater the area in the *Freedom To Do Job* section, the greater the degree of participative freedom that is available. In the illustration, *A* would have more freedom to accomplish the job than *B*.

TO CHANGE OR NOT TO CHANGE: SITUATIONAL FACTORS TO BE CONSIDERED

Perhaps the most important question to ask regarding the subject of change is, "Is this change necessary?" There are some who unwisely believe that changes should be made merely for the sake of change. A manager who makes a change merely to satisfy a personal desire may create a disruptive effect on his or her section. When one of the authors was working as a consultant for a manufacturing firm, he inadvertently noticed a note on the desk of a new vice-president who had been brought in from the outside to attempt to improve the performance of a division that was doing poorly. The note said, "Do not make any major changes for three months." The new executive obviously wanted to be aware of the total situation before changes were made. If he began to make changes immediately, inappropriate changes could be made and an entire division could be further damaged.

Organizations and people desire some degree of stability in order to accomplish their assigned tasks. But there are times when changes are necessary and failure to deal effectively with them can have a disastrous effect. The six situational factors should be considered as factors that affect change. This section will concentrate on understanding how each of the factors affect the change process (see Figure 10.3). The external environment is discussed first because it is the overriding factor that creates the need for change in an organization. The other situational factors provide the internal means by which change may be realized.

EXTERNAL ENVIRONMENT

Most change is necessary because the external environment has been altered. If the external environment was relatively stable and consistent, there would be little need for change to occur. However, because business today operates in a dynamic, rapidly moving environment, management must constantly be alert to factors in the external environment that make change necessary.

For example, an economic recession will often cause a firm to make rather drastic changes. A company may temporarily reduce production output, lay off employees, and curtail capital investments.

OBJECTIVES

A change in objectives of the organization can have a major effect on every aspect of the firm. If the direction of the firm is altered to conform to the external environment every phase of the firm will likely be affected. For instance, if the firm decided that for survival it must alter its objectives from a conservative, moderate growth organization to an innovative rapid growth firm, many changes would need to take place. Personnel may have to be retrained to cope with these new goals. A more participative mana-

FIGURE 10.3
Factors Affecting the Change Process

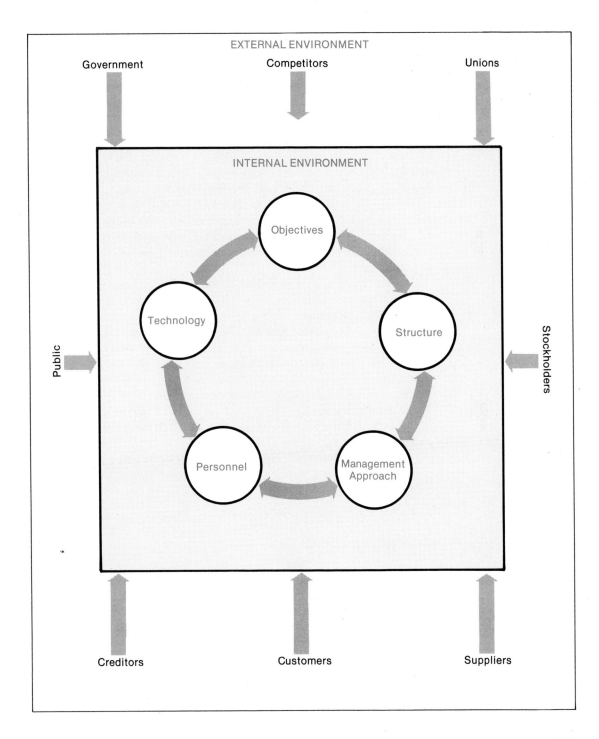

gerial approach is likely to be needed. The organizational structure may need to be decentralized to permit faster decision making and new technology may be needed.

PERSONNEL

Because of an alteration in the external environment, the type personnel that the firm needs in order to succeed may require evaluation. If in-house personnel cannot be developed, the firm may be forced to recruit their work force from outside sources. It may be that the current work force may have to go through a retraining phase—encompassing management development programs, sensitivity training, and organizational development—in order to implement the necessary changes to accomplish the objectives of the firm.

There is developing an increasing concern for individual job satisfaction and for increased awareness for social well being. For instance, a change may be made to enrich a job by giving the worker more responsibility. There may be no evidence that this change will actually increase profits or serve the customer better, but the change may be made in order to increase an individual's job satisfaction. Volvo has begun to use teams to manufacture their cars. Worker satisfaction has increased although there is little tangible evidence as to increased profits.

The demand for greater concern for social well being may also encourage change. For instance, a change may be made in the organizational philosophy to encourage the hiring of unskilled workers. This change may not result in immediate, if any, profits; it was accomplished because the company had altered their company philosophy to include social well being.

MANAGERIAL APPROACH

The managerial approach used by the firm may also need to be altered to adapt to the external environment. As discussed in chapter 9, an adaptive or situational approach to leadership is recommended. A method that some firms use in changing a managerial approach is to bring in a new president with full decision-making authority. The style of the new chief executive rapidly permeates the entire organization. There will likely be quite a few terminations as managers who cannot conform to the new style leave the firm. Bringing in a new chief executive with a completely different managerial approach is a drastic one; often it is necessary to ensure survival of the firm.

> **QUALITIES NEEDED FOR SUCCESS**
> **AS A MANAGER IN YOUR ORGANIZATION**
>
> · Dedication, interest, cooperative attitude, concern for people, and pride in team accomplishments.
> · Energy, enthusiasm, loyalty, willingness to try new methods, and alertness to opportunities.
>
> M. G. MITCHELL, Chairman & President, Chicago Bridge & Iron Company

Some managers have achieved considerable success in reviving *sick* companies. One such executive is Robert C. Wilson, who has successfully revitalized Collins Radio and Memorex companies. He turned Collins Radio around from a $64 million dollar loss in 1972 to a $13.3 million profit in only twelve months. Wilson became President of Memorex, a firm that was nearly bankrupt, in 1974. The company had experienced a loss of $90 million in 1973 and had debts totaling $300 million. By the end of 1975, Memorex had made a profit of $8.2 million and profits for 1977 were $56 million. Mr. Wilson took a very direct managerial approach that met the needs demanded by the situation.[4]

Less drastic means by which managerial approaches have been changed are through sensitivity training, management development programs, and organizational development.

STRUCTURE

Changes in the structure call for rather fundamental changes in the *guts* of an organization. A small scale change may mean that the content of a job is altered or a new procedure designed for collecting control information is developed. A large scale change might entail progressing from a centralized structure to a decentralized organization or vice versa. If the firm is now decentralized, personnel at lower levels will be provided additional decision-making responsibility. Because a change in structure has been made, additional training may be needed to provide the employees with the particular abilities they will need to adapt to the new environment. In the centralized environment all decisions were made by top management. The decision-making process may have to be developed in people who have grown accustomed to merely acting on directives they receive.

---

4. "Corporate 'Architect' Helps Troubled Companies Build Stable, Profitable Organizations," *The AMBA Executive* 7 (February 1978), p. 3.

TECHNOLOGY

A wide range of possibilities exists when a change in technology is discussed. A small change results when a new machine is purchased that accomplishes a similar task in a faster, more efficient manner. Even this small change may evoke resistance. A major technological change involves much more consideration. Implementing this type of change may not be possible with the present work force. This might be the situation that management confronts when a new computer is purchased where the work was previously accomplished manually. Some of the current personnel can be retrained to go into other jobs throughout the firm, but it is likely that new computer personnel will enter the firm. A modification of current management style may be necessary to entice the type personnel that will be needed to facilitate effective use of the new technology.

THE CHANGE SEQUENCE

change sequence

Identifying the factors that may create a need for change does not explain the sequence of events that are needed to bring about change in an organization. The **change sequence** is illustrated in FIGURE 10.4. As may be seen, management must first recognize that there is a need for change. Then the specific change method(s) must be chosen. The actual change process cannot begin until these stages are completed.

RECOGNITION OF THE NEED FOR CHANGE

Conditions existing in the external environment may be quite different than what management perceives them to be. Managers must train themselves to constantly seek improvement activities (areas for change). This is not always easy because of the tendency to lapse into a condition of euphoria; if it was successful in the past it will continue to be successful in the future. People who have been successful under an old system often resist; the old way was the vehicle that was used to bring them to power. If the system is modified, some may feel that their power will be reduced. There are three basic conditions—curiosity and discontent, open-mindedness, and respect for oneself[5]—a manager must develop in order to recognize that change is needed and have the courage to implement the change.

5. Addison C. Bennet, "The Manager's Responsibility for Work Improvement," *Improving the Effectiveness of Hospital Management* (New York: Preston Publishing Company, 1972), pp. 161–162.

FIGURE 10.4
The Change Sequence

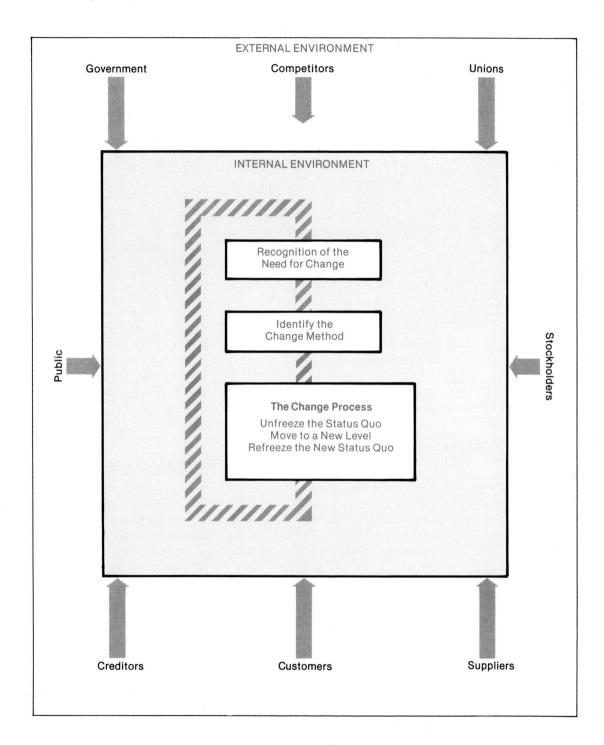

Curiosity and Discontent

The two terms provide perhaps a strange combination with regards to establishing a condition to recognize that a change is desired. A person should have sufficient curiosity to ask searching questions regarding why a task is being performed in a certain manner. "Curiosity may kill the cat" but it is vital in recognizing where change is needed. Discontent, on the other hand, has the implication that a person should not constantly be satisfied with the current situation. Discontent does not mean that an individual should fight the system. He or she is not satisfied to merely let things go along in their old and established pattern and concede that the old way is the best way. Through curiosity and discontent managers place themselves in a position to recognize when a change may be needed.

Open-Mindedness

Managers who believe that their way is always the best will only recognize that a change is needed if they personally make the discovery. Subordinates' opinions are not considered. A manager who is open-minded recognizes and permits subordinates to make suggestions. He or she believes that there are many times when "two heads are better than one" and that useful ideas can evolve from lower-level personnel if they are provided the opportunity.

Respect for Oneself

It is often easier to "travel in the well-worn ruts of the past" rather than make a decision to change a procedure that will likely produce some resistance. Managers who have respect for themselves do not fear to attempt a modification that will likely draw initial resistance but will eventually result in a better operation. These individuals believe in their ability.

IDENTIFYING THE CHANGE METHOD

Management has at its disposal numerous methods or techniques. Specific techniques include management development programs, sensitivity training, and organization development. The technique chosen should meet the needs of the organization in reacting to the external environment and the identification of the type of climate that will provide for the greatest productivity in the organization. Specific techniques will be discussed later in the chapter.

THE PROCESS OF CHANGE

The steps involved in the change process are easier to describe than they are to implement. Simply stated, the change process as outlined by Levin involves three fundamental stages: (1) unfreeze the status quo, (2) move to the new level, and (3) refreeze at the new level which becomes the new status quo.[6] Each stage of the change process will next be briefly discussed.

Unfreezing the Status Quo

If individuals are to change their present attitudes, current beliefs must be altered or unfrozen. Resistance to change must be eliminated or reduced if a change is to be effective. Once the factors that caused resistance to change are lowered, the manager is in a position to implement the desired change. Sources of resistance to change and approaches to reduce resistance to change will be discussed later in the chapter.

Unfreezing in the change process generates self-doubt and provides a means of remedying the situation. Employees must be made to feel that ineffectiveness is undesirable, but it can be remedied. If organization members are to be receptive to change, they must feel that they can change.

Moving to a New Level (Changing)

The initiation of a change can come from an order, a recommendation, or a self-directed impetus. A manager with authority can command that a change be made and enforce its implementation by threats, punishments, and close supervision. If this path of implementing change is taken, the manager will likely find that the change must be constantly monitored. Change is more permanent and substantial if a person truly wants and feels a need to change.

The most effective approach to initiate change is for a two-way relationship to exist between the change agent (the person who is attempting to implement the change) and the changee (the person who will be changed). Rather than a one-way flow of commands or recommendations, the change agent should observe the rule of reciprocity. The change agent makes suggestions on a tentative basis, and the changees should be encouraged to contribute and participate. Change agents should be responsive to suggestion, either by reformulating the change or by providing

---

6. Kurt Levin, "Frontiers in Group Dynamics," *Human Relations* 1 (1947): 34.

explanations as to why the suggestions cannot be incorporated. Specific techniques for initiating change will be discussed at a later stage of the chapter.

Refreezing the New Status Quo

If a student changes to a new set of rigid study habits for a week and then reverts to former practices, the change has not been effective. Too often changes are introduced that do not stick. If the change is to be permanent, changees must be convinced that it is in their own and the organization's best interest. One of the best ways to accomplish this purpose is to systematically collect objective evidence of the success of the change. A student who sees his grades go from a C to a B average because of a change in study habits has obtained excellent evidence of the success of the change. People should have feelings of competence and pleasure in using the new behavior.

But, the change will be completely accepted only if the reward system of the organization is geared to the new form of behavior. If a university states that all their faculty must begin to publish articles and there is no reward attached to publishing, it is likely that few faculty members could be motivated to make this change. An employee's job may be substantially enriched in terms of content and self-supervision, but if the change is not accomplished by properly enriched pay and status symbols, dissatisfaction is likely to result. People tend to repeat behavior that they find rewarding.

SOURCES OF RESISTANCE TO CHANGE

A change involves some loss to the person who is affected by the change. Attachments to old and familiar habits, places, and people must be given up. In major and unexpected changes, there is often daze, shock, recoil, and turmoil.[7] Some of the many sources of resistance to change are looked at next.

INSECURITY

Once a person has operated in a particular environment for a long time, he or she begins to feel comfortable. A change of environment often brings

7. Ralph G. Huschowitz, "The Human Aspects of Managing Transition," *Personnel* 51 (May–June 1974): 13.

about uncertainty; one does not know exactly what to expect. The feeling of insecurity surrounded virtually all of us as the transition was made from high school to college. The same sense of insecurity continues as the move is made from undergraduate to graduate work or when individuals move from one job to another or to a new city. And, it is perhaps because of this feeling of insecurity that some people seemingly become perpetual students.

POSSIBLE SOCIAL LOSS

A change has the potential to bring about social losses. As was discussed in chapter 7, the informal work group may be extremely powerful. If change causes individuals in the group to be transferred, the power of the group is likely diminished. A change may cause established status symbols to be destroyed or an individual of lower status may even be awarded a high status symbol.

The impact that a change can have on the social environment was vividly illustrated when one of the authors was doing a consulting job for a regional medical center. The hospital had been a small local 100-bed hospital but because industry was moving rapidly into the area the board of directors had decided to expand the hospital to 300 beds. In one department all personnel reported directly to the department head and a close rapport had developed among the members. On a rotating shift, staff members would have to work the evening and night shift but they still maintained close contact with the other department members.

Because of the great increase in workload the work force was expanded and a decision was made to have three shifts with a shift supervisor for each shift. The department head now had only three people reporting directly to him and it was believed that the work could be performed much more efficiently. But the social loss was drastic. Subordinates no longer had a close relationship with the department head; some, because they were on a different shift, rarely saw the department head. This created a tremendous social loss to several long-term employees and resulted in termination of over 50 percent of the personnel in six months.

ECONOMIC LOSSES

Technology may be introduced that can produce the same amount of output with fewer personnel. While most companies make an honest attempt to transfer or retrain employees who have been affected by the change, the fear remains. When the computer was first introduced, the number of clerical personnel needed was often drastically reduced. The

Regardless of the benefit of a change, employees often resist even minor ones.

computer firms attempted to lessen this fear by claiming that the number of jobs had actually increased through the use of the computer. This did not help the employee who was capable of only accomplishing the clerical work. To him it was a major economic loss.

INCONVENIENCE

Even if there were no social or economic loss associated with a change, the change does represent a new way of doing things. As such, new procedures and techniques may have to be learned. This means that physical and mental energy must be expended (for some people this is not an enjoyable task). When a new phone system was installed at a university, there initially were many complaints. The new phone system meant that time and effort had to be expended. It took approximately one year for the system to be accepted by a majority of the university personnel.

RESENTMENT OF CONTROL

Taken as a whole the American people are very independent. When employees are told that a change must take place, they are made to realize that they do not have control over their destiny. Even though the change may be for the better, a certain amount of resentment takes place.

UNANTICIPATED REPERCUSSIONS

Because the organization is a system, a change in one part is likely to have unforeseen repercussions in another portion. For example, a newly enriched job is likely to demand a change in supervisory behavior. The supervisor may resist this change in his behavior even though he initially supported the concept of job enrichment.

UNION OPPOSITION

Labor union representatives are at times inclined to oppose on principle any change suggested by management. Employees are often more comfortable with a fighting union than they are with one inclined to cooperate with management on changes designed to promote organizational interest.

APPROACHES IN REDUCING RESISTANCE TO CHANGE

One of the authors while working as a personnel administrator for a large insurance company observed that an anticipated change in computers brought about considerable employee resistance. Management of the company had announced that a new computer system with greatly increased capacity would be installed in about six months. The new computer would cause substantial changes in many of the clerical jobs being performed by office personnel. Uncertain as to what to expect from the change in computer systems, numerous employees began expressing fear and concern about the impact of the change.

Before management took any action, the level and intensity of the discussion by the employees caused a rather severe slowdown in work flow in the office. Customer and agent complaints rose substantially during the six-week period after the announced change. Management took action to correct the situation by holding a series of small group meetings to explain the new computer system and how it would affect each job and each work group. While there would be several major changes in job functions affecting some individuals and work groups, management made a commitment to all employees that no one would be dismissed as a result of the installation of the new computer. The company would provide retraining programs to increase the affected employees' skills thereby improving their adaptability to the new system. The situation that occurred at the insurance company might have been avoided through following the approaches described below.

MAKE ONLY NECESSARY CHANGES

Changes should be made only when the situation demands, not because of a whim on the part of a manager. A manager who gains a reputation for making change for the sake of making change most likely will rapidly discover that the support for any change, whether beneficial or not, will receive only minimum acceptance. This tactic relates well to the shepherd who constantly cried "wolf" and when there actually was a wolf, no one believed him.

ATTEMPT TO MAINTAIN USEFUL CUSTOMS AND INFORMAL RELATIONSHIPS

As was mentioned in chapter 7, the informal work group has real value from the standpoint of interpersonal understanding and cooperation. When possible, changes should be made to coincide with the culture of the personnel within the organization. When safety shoes were first introduced, few would wear them willingly because of their appearance. When they were redesigned to resemble dress shoes, resistance faded. The granting of fictional rank to civilian consultants who are to work with military personnel makes their integration into ongoing operations more understandable and acceptable. A staff expert who wants a change introduced may find it advisable to have the announcement made by a line executive with some sharing of the credit. Changes that go against established customs and informal norms will likely experience resistance and a minimum chance of acceptance.

BUILD TRUST

If a manager has obtained a reputation for providing reliable and timely information to his employees in the past, the explanation as to why a change is to be made will likely be more believable. The change may still be resisted but if the manager is trusted by the employees it should be minimized. On the other hand, managers who have gained a reputation for providing incomplete or inaccurate information will often find it difficult for employees to believe that the change is "good" for them.

PROVIDE INFORMATION IN ADVANCE

Whenever possible the manager should provide the reasons for the change, its nature, planned timing, and the possible impact upon the organization and its personnel. Withholding information that could seriously affect the lives and futures of particular individuals, such as keeping secret the planned closure of a plant in order to preserve the workforce level until the last possible moment should be avoided if possible. The firm that gains a reputation for these type actions will have a difficult time in making future changes. Although there are occasions when competitive survival requires that information be closely held until shortly before introduction, they should be accomplished on an *as required* basis.

ENCOURAGE PARTICIPATION

When possible subordinate participation should be encouraged in establishing the change. A person who is involved in implementing change procedures will likely be more supportive of the change. It will be recalled from chapter 8 that Theory Y contends that abilities are widespread in the population. Many valuable ideas may be gained by permitting employees a degree of participation in implementing the change.

GUARANTEE AGAINST LOSS AND SHARE GAINS

To promote acceptance of technological changes, some organizations guarantee no layoffs as a result of such changes. In cases of a change in methods and output standard, employees are often guaranteed retention of their present level of earnings during the learning period.

PROVIDE COUNSELING

At times some form of nonthreatening discussion and counseling may not only prevent rebellion, but have some chance of stimulating voluntary adaptation. Nondirective counseling has been used effectively in many change situations. The approach rests on a fundamental belief that a person has the ability to solve his or her problems with the aid of a sympathetic listener. The role of a counselor is one of understanding rather than passing judgment. This requires a somewhat permissive, friendly atmosphere, with actions and statements that exhibit continuing interest but not judgment. In most instances, managers with authority are unable to establish this type of atmosphere. Successful nondirective counseling must usually be undertaken by staff psychologists. What the manager can do is to permit some subordinate ventilation of feelings, particularly those of frustration and anger. Just talking about the "good old days" will assist in the transition process. Discovering that others have similar feelings and doubts will often make the transition less painful; "misery loves company."

ALLOW FOR NEGOTIATION

Resistance to change can be reduced by the process of negotiation. Negotiation is the primary method used by labor unions to effect modification of proposed managerial changes. For example, in return for accepting many changes in work rules, a west-coast employer at one time provided a $29 million benefit fund to aid longshoremen through early retirement and a type of annual wage guarantee.

TECHNIQUES FOR IMPLEMENTING CHANGE

One Monday morning, employees of a midwestern railroad company arrived at their office at the usual time. They tried the door and were surprised to find it locked. Soon they discovered a notice attached to the corridor wall, which read essentially that effective immediately this office of the company had been eliminated. The rooms were empty and all equipment had been moved to a more central office about 600 miles away. No one was laid off, but if an employee wished to retain employment, he or she would have to be on the train the next afternoon headed for the consolidated central office. Should an employee wish to resign, personal effects on his or her desk would be mailed back. Over the preceding weekend, moving vans had cleared the local office of all equipment and had transported it to the new office.

This, of course, is one way to introduce a change. The change may be technically justified, assuming that the railroad is in serious financial difficulties. The manner of introducing the change is, however, subject to criticism. The Chamber of Commerce of the city attempted to expel the railroad from membership. The company's general approach was to make the change an accomplished fact, utilizing the power of the "new" status quo. Rapidity of execution was, they felt, the only answer to resistance that could never be overcome anyway. Other less dramatic techniques which management has found useful in bringing about change will next be discussed.

MANAGEMENT DEVELOPMENT PROGRAMS

management
development programs

Many firms use **management development programs** (MDP) to assure their managers are capable of learning more effective approaches to management. As such it is considered by some to be a technique for change. With MDP, specific areas that have been identified as possible weaknesses are included in a development program. The training programs may be administrated by either *in-house* or external personnel. An illustration of a management development program which was developed for a major independent telephone company is provided in Figure 10.5. The intent of a program is not only to learn new methods and techniques but to develop an inquisitive thought process. Too often personnel within a firm become so accustomed to performing the same task day after day that they forget how to think. A properly designed management development program places a person in a frame of mind to analyze problems and is often used to provide the foundation for a change to occur.

SENSITIVITY TRAINING

sensitivity training

In 1946, Leland Bradford, Kenneth Benne, and Ronald Lippitt inadvertently developed the technique of **sensitivity training** as they were studying leaderless discussion groups. While trying to change behavior through reducing the restraining forces of buried fears, the feedback provided the group by outside observers was so revealing that an observer-moderator was placed in the group itself. Alternative titles frequently used are T-group training and laboratory training.

As the title indicates, the general goal of sensitivity training is to develop awareness of and sensitivity to oneself and others. More specifically, the goals of sensitivity training include the following:

FIGURE 10.5
Course Content for a Management Development Program

I. Management Development Program Title:
"Improving Group Effectiveness and Team Building"

II. Objectives:
(1) To identify the reasons for group formation
(2) To understand the types of groups and their attributes
(3) To discover the implications of research on group dynamics
(4) To acquire an understanding as to forces in intro- and inter-group processes
(5) To learn the characteristics of teamwork and ways to achieve it
(6) To provide experience in analyzing and diagnosing work group dimensions
(7) To acquire an appreciation for various team building techniques

III. Description and Evaluation:
The course is designed to provide greater understanding of, and ability to work with and through, groups. Special emphasis is given to understanding the various need levels of groups and what can be done to more effectively appeal to those levels. Actual practice in team building techniques is given, as well as experience in analyzing work groups. Evaluation is made of the major contingencies affecting groups. Observing group behavior through various media is a portion of the course content.

IV. Size of Class:
The class should have a maximum enrollment of 20 participants so as to allow the group process to be seen in action in the group itself, yet small enough to allow for active participation.

V. Assignment of Instructor:
The instructor allocates an equal amount of time to lecture and active class discussion with approximately one-third of the time devoted to various media presentations and group involvement. The course is designed for a two- or three-day session.

VI. Enrollment Requirements:
Middle- and upper-level managerial experience desired

- Increased openness with others
- Greater concern for needs of others
- Increased tolerance for individual differences
- Less ethnic prejudice
- Awareness and understanding of group processes
- Enhanced listening skills
- Greater appreciation of the complexities of behaving competently
- Establishment of more realistic personal standards of behavior

Sensitivity training has not received unanimous approval by industry leaders. It has been labeled "psychotherapy" rather than proper business training. Moderators have been criticized as having an insufficient background in psychology and psychiatric methods. It has been suggested that individual defense mechanisms that have been built up to preserve the personality over a period of years may be destroyed, with little help being provided in replacing them with more satisfactory behavioral patterns. It is contended that one cannot exist without a few defenses.

Also, in business organizations, managers frequently must make unpleasant decisions that work to the detriment of particular individuals and groups. Excessive empathy and sympathy will not necessarily lead to a reversal of the decision, and may exact an excessively high emotional cost for the decision maker. Many business organizations have internal environments characterized by competition and autocracy. The power structure may not be compatible with openness and trust. In some instances, an effective manager must practice diplomacy by retaining a portion of the truth, or perhaps even telling different stories to two different persons or groups. Truth is not always most conducive to effective interpersonal and group relations. Sensitivity training would also tend to ignore organizational values that are derived from aggressiveness, initiative, and the charismatic appeals of a particular leader.

ORGANIZATION DEVELOPMENT

organization development

The **organization development** (OD) movement has been strongly advocated by behaviorists such as Chris Argyris and Warren Bennis. OD is a planned and calculated attempt to move the organization as a unit from one state to another, typically to a more behavioral environment. Its education and training strategies are designed to develop a more open, real, and compatible environment regardless of existing differences in personalities, cultures, or technologies. More specific goals of the educational strategy are provided in the following list:

- Decision making on the basis of competence rather than authority
- Creatively resolving conflict through confrontation designed to replace win-lose situations with win-win types
- Reducing nonbeneficial competition and maximizing collaboration
- Increasing commitment and a sense of "ownership" of the organization objectives throughout the workforce
- Increasing the degree of interpersonal trust and support
- Creating a climate in which human growth, development, and renewal are a natural part of the enterprise's daily operation
- Developing a communication system characterized by mutual openness and candor on solving organizational problems

A major criticism of organization development is that efforts in changing values have been directed toward white-collar managers, professionals, and technicians. Certainly, value changes among blue-collar rank and file would be much more difficult to effect. Neither have there been significant organization development attempts in the areas of labor union-management bargaining, relationships among nations, or improving the interface between students and police. Organization development seems most adaptable to organizations with a single formal power structure.

Team Development

team development

One of the major techniques in the arsenal of the organization development consultant is **team development.** This technique was found to be the one most widely used in a recent survey of firms.[8] Instead of sending isolated individuals off to a sensitivity training session attended by strangers, a type of sensitivity session is conducted for the members of an operating unit, away from the job site. To overcome the natural reluctance of subordinates to exhibit candor with colleagues and superiors, the services of outside third-party consultants are deemed essential.

In effect, the consultants serve three functions: (1) they first contact all members separately to determine what they feel are the major obstructions to effective functioning of the unit; (2) they feed this gathered information to the convened group in a manner that preserves the confidence of information contributors; and (3) they serve as a catalyst in the ensuing discussion, which is designed to encourage honest feedback, leveling, and candor. Obviously, the entire process is ego-threatening to the superior, and he or she must first be willing to engage in such an examining process.

With the support of the consultant, the supervisor learns to demonstrate openness to constructive comment and suggestions concerning how the unit's collaborative processes are functioning. In one such unit, all the members of the group, with the encouragement of the consultant, testified that they felt their supervisor to be a cold, unfeeling, *illegitimate person.* In this case, the OD model did not work. The supervisor stated that he felt that the group had him pegged correctly but that he had no intention of changing. But he did explain that his reasons for behaving in this manner issued from wartime experiences where he had lost most of his friends in combat. He had no intention of making another friend. The group atmosphere did improve after these reasons were revealed, and everyone now knew that the supervisor did not discriminate among his subordi-

8. W. J. Heisler, "Patterns of OD in Practice," *Business Horizons* 18 (February 1975): 82.

nates. It is reported that his behavior did change in ensuing months in response to their changed attitudes.

In a second organization, an executive was disturbed with failures of subordinates to follow instructions communicated to them by memo. In this instance, it was suggested that several copies of his past memos be distributed and that each member write out an interpretation. After each was read, it was evident that the problem was more one of communication than of deliberate disobedience. One of the changes introduced into the unit's functioning in the future was far fewer memos being written by the manager. Face-to-face oral direction with opportunities for immediate feedback and questioning became the new norm.

The above illustration provides insight into the flavor of a team development session. Specific attention is not devoted to the unit's technical task, but rather to its coordination, cooperation, and collaborative processes in executing that task. The outside party can gather information concerning these processes, and act as a catalyst in permitting this and other information to surface.

In a reported study of OD effectiveness in a large automotive division, it was discovered that the program did produce favorable interpersonal relations. Subordinates perceived their bosses to be more open to suggestions, more trusting and supportive, and more adept in using the problem-solving technique of conflict resolution. There was no impact on the rate of production. There was, however, a significant improvement in quality of output which, in turn, had a favorable impact on the division's profit position.

Survey Feedback

Another major method in the organization development repertoire is the systematic collection and measurement of subordinate attitudes by anonymous questionnaires. If we are to obtain truthful information concerning attitudes, the employee must feel comfortable, secure, and confident in giving answers to the questions posed. Usually this is most likely to occur if anonymity is preserved. Here again the services of a third party, the outside consultant, are useful.

Two basic types of questionnaires can be used: (1) the attitude survey, and (2) the opinion survey. The attitude survey is usually of the objective type, using either multiple-choice answers or Likert-type scales of agreement to disagreement for each subject. Various subjects are covered, such as communications, the reward system, degree of collaboration, leadership style, and processes of decision making. An example of multiple choice question on the reward system is provided below:

How do you feel about the opportunity to advance in this organization?

———a. If I work hard and do a good job, I will get ahead in this company.

———b. The only way to get ahead in this company is know someone with "pull."

———c. Hard work and loyalty to the company are not rewarded in this operation.

———d. If you stick around long enough, you'll get ahead.

———e. There is not opportunity to advance in this company.

———f. Usually the best person wins out, but occasionally "pull" is more important.[9]

Attitude surveys require a scaling of these answers according to some set of values established by the organization. A questionnaire survey would only report the percentage of replies—that is, 45 percent marked choice a, 30 percent choice b, etc.

To assess these results objectively, it is significant to note that they are evaluated primarily in relative terms. We can compare in terms of the following criteria:

1. Scores for the entire organization now and in the past
2. Scores for other organizations if a standard instrument has been used
3. Scores for each department now and in the past
4. Scores by organization level
5. Scores by sex
6. Scores by seniority
7. Relative scores on each question
8. Scores for each question for each category of personnel cited above

In using these questionnaires in an OD program, the results must be communicated back to employees on a group-by-group basis. When the group is convened, the specific distributions of ratings on each item are presented. Members are questioned concerning whether they feel the rating is truly reflective of the thinking of the group. Ordinarily, the response is noncommittal for the first several items, but the superficiality of the process usually irritates one of the earlier items. He or she usually selects an item that everyone knows is a real stickler in the group's processes.

When the superior demonstrates openness to the initial tactfully stated criticisms, other members of the group tend to own up to their own

9. Edwin B. Flippo and Gary M. Munsinger, *Management,* 4th ed. (Boston: Allyn and Bacon, Inc., 1978), p. 542.

responses on the questionnaire. For example, in one group the manager was rated rather low on communicative ability. After the unfreezing process had taken place with the catalytic help of the consultant, one member revealed why he had rated his leader so low. He stated that every time he came in with a problem, inside of two minutes the manager would switch the subject to something that was bothering him, with the effect that the subordinate's problem was never discussed. When a few others chimed in with agreement, the manager indicated that he had not been aware of this particular behavioral pattern. He said that he would attempt to correct it, and hereby authorized each person to stop and point it out should it happen again. In another instance, a departmental secretary said that she became quite irritated when the supervisor would lean over and read miscellaneous letters on her desk. The supervisor authorized her to remind him of this should he revert to this bad habit.

The objective and analyzed data of the survey provide the basis and the excuse for convening the group to discuss processes of coordination and collaboration. Pet peeves are aired, and if the possessor finds that he or she is alone, they tend to disappear. The superior also finds that extreme opinions seldom spread among all subordinates. The information revealed is directly and immediately relevant to organizational functioning. In using these questionnaires in an OD program, it is important that the results be communicated to employees on a group-by-group basis.

SUMMARY

The psychological environment of a firm is referred to as the organizational climate. As such, the organizational climate is quite similar to an individual's personality. There are times when a particular climate is not conducive to the long-run success of the firm. Many advocate the open and participative climate as the best climate for all situations because it is often successful in improving the morale and satisfaction of all employees. Despite the values associated with the participative climate, there are limitations which at times restrict its use.

When an organization is contemplating a change, the most important question to ask is: "Is this change necessary?" Each of the situational factors will likely be affected if a change is undertaken. However, if a change is to be made, there is a specified change sequence that should be followed. First, management must recognize that there is a need for change and then choose a specific change method. Within the change process the status quo is unfrozen, moved to a new level, and then refrozen. Unfortunately, even though a change may be best for the organization, resistance is still likely to exist. Insecurity, possible social or economic losses, inconvenience, and resentment of control are all contributing factors to resistance to change. There are, however, numerous approaches that have been used successfully in reducing resistance to change. Management development programs are used to assure that managers are capable of learning more effective approaches to dealing with resistance to change. The goal of sensitivity training is to develop awareness of and sensitivity to oneself and others. Organization development is a planned and calculated attempt to move the organization as a unit from one state to another. Specific organization development techniques include team development, surveys, and customized methods.

Exercises

1. Identify the major changes that have occurred in your life during the past year. How did you react to these changes?

2. Visit three businesses. Attempt to assess the type of climate that exists in each of the firms.

3. Assume that you are the president of a college or a university and you would like to make the following changes:
   A. Students must be professionally attired at all times.
   B. Faculty members must be at their office by 8:00.
   C. All single students must live in the dormitory.

   Assuming that all of the above mentioned changes are made for a logical reason, what type resistance to these changes could you expect? How could you possibly overcome some of the resistance to these changes?

Review Questions

1. Define organizational climate. What are the factors that interact to determine the type of organization climate that exists in a firm?

2. Identify the values and limitations of a participative climate.

3. What is the primary reason for making a change in business? Relate the situational factors to making a decision to change.

4. List and describe the change sequence discussed in the text.

5. What are the sources of resistance to change as described in the text?

6. Describe the approaches that may be used in reducing resistance to change.

7. Define each of the following terms:
   A. Management Development Program
   B. Sensitivity Training
   C. Organization Development

REFERENCES

Allen, R. F. "Changing Community and Organizational Cultures." *Training and Development Journal,* July 1977, pp. 28–34.

Bensahel, J. G. "How to Overcome the Resistance to Change." *International Management,* September 1977, pp. 66–67.

Biggart, N. W. "Creative-Destructive Process of Organizational Change: The Case of the Post Office." *Administrative Science Quarterly,* September 1977, pp. 410–426.

Butterfield, D. A., and Powell, G. N. "Case for Subsystem Climates in Organizations." *Academy of Management Review,* January 1978, pp. 151–157.

Carlson, H. C. "Organizational Research and Organizational Change." *Personnel,* July 1977, pp. 11–22.

Drucker, Peter F. "Management's New Role." *Harvard Business Review,* November–December 1962.

Gordon, G. G., and Goldberg, B. E. "Is There a Climate For Success?" *Management Review,* May 1977, pp. 37–44.

Greiner, Larry E. "Evolution and Revolution as Organizations Grow." *Harvard Business Review,* July–August 1972, pp. 37–46.

Hellriegel, Don, and Slocum, John W., Jr. "Organizational Climate." *Academy of Management Journal,* June 1974, pp. 255–280.

Howe, R. J., and Others. "Introducing Innovation Through Organizational Development." *Management Review,* February 1978, pp. 52–56.

"Is Organization Development Catching On? A Personnel Symposium." *Personnel,* November 1977, pp. 10–22.

Kuzmits, F. E. "Considering An Organizational Development Program?" *Personnel Administration,* October 1977, pp. 29–32.

Land, G. T. "Managing Change—Key to Tomorrow." *Internal Auditor,* June 1977, pp. 15–18.

Mealiea, L. W. "T. A. Approach to Employee Development," *Supervisory Management,* August 1977, pp. 11–19.

Miller, E. C. "Organization Development: A Dynamic New Force? *Personnel,* November 1977, pp. 32–41.

Morano, R. A. "How to Manage Change to Reduce Stress," *Management Review,* November 1977, pp. 21–25.

Pheysey, D. C. "Managers' Occupational Histories, Organizational Environments and Climates for Management Development." *The Journal of Management Studies,* February 1977, pp. 58–78.

Severiens, J. T. "Product Innovation, Organizational Change and Risk: A New Perspective." *SAM Advanced Management Journal,* Fall 1977, pp. 24–31.

Stein, R. T. and Lija, E. "Impact Models As a Method for Planning Change." *Management Review,* Spring 1977, pp. 47–61.

Taylor, D. "Coping With Change," *Management Today,* October 1977, pp. 81–83.

Case Study

A CHANGE IN ENVIRONMENT

Until one year ago Wayne, Don, and Robert had been supervisors with a small chain of thirty-nine grocery stores. Each supervisor had responsibility for thirteen stores and reported directly to the company president. All three supervisors worked well together and there was a constant exchange of information which was quite useful in coordinating the activities of the stores. Each supervisor had specific strengths that were useful in helping the others. Wayne coordinated the deployment of the part-time help at all thirty-nine stores. Don monitored the inventories and Robert interviewed prospective new employees prior to sending them to Wayne and Don for review. It was a complete team effort directed toward getting the job done.

One year later a completely different environment existed at the chain. The president, wishing to relieve himself of many daily details, decided to promote Robert to vice-president. Another supervisor, Phillip, was hired for Robert's position. Robert had a completely different idea of how the activities of the supervisors should be conducted. Under Robert's leadership each supervisor was now responsible for the activities at only his stores. If a problem occurred the supervisor was to discuss it with Robert and he would provide the solution. When either Wayne, Don, or Phillip attempted to solve problems on their own, they were reprimanded by Robert. After a few "chewing outs" Wayne, Don, and Phillip decided not to fight the system and did as Robert wanted; they rarely saw each other any more. If Don had a problem at his stores that caused him to work all night, that was not any concern of Wayne or Phillip.

The only problem with the new system was that efficiency dropped drastically. For instance, Wayne was a good coordinator of part-time help. He had the type of personality that could talk a person into coming to work at 5:00 on Saturday when the individual had a date at 6:00. Wayne's stores remained well staffed with part-time help but the others suffered. Many times the part-time help did not show up and either Don or Phillip had to act as the replacement if the store manager could not be convinced to work overtime. On the other hand, Wayne's inventory control suffered because Don was the best qualified in this area.

Robert accused the three supervisors of working against him and threatened them with dismissal if operations did not get better. Wayne, Don, and Phillip felt that they could not be productive in this environment and found other positions. When the president discovered what had occurred, Robert was fired. It took the president six months to get the operations back to the level of efficiency that it had achieved previously.

Questions

1. What different organizational environment was created as a result of promoting Robert to vice-president?
2. How do you feel that this situation could have been avoided? Discuss the possibility of the use of the participative approach in this instance.

Case Study

RUMORS AT DUNCAN ELECTRIC

David Garcia is a supervisor for Duncan Electric Corporation, a manufacturer of high quality electrical parts. David had been with the firm for five years and had a reputation for having one of the best teams in the plant. David had picked the majority of these employees and was proud of the reputation they had achieved. But, a problem was now brewing that had the potential of destroying his department.

For weeks now, rumors of a substantial reduction in manpower at Duncan Electric have been circulating. Dave has not received any confirmation from the corporate office regarding the reduction. The rumors, all claiming to be from reliable sources, range from minor reductions to large scale reduction in manpower. Every day someone claims to have the inside story and every day the story changes. Dave, who has a reputation for leveling with his people, successfully discounted the rumors for a while. But, as the doubts began to grow, work output began to suffer. His employees were now spending time trying to verify the latest rumor. Speculation increased to the point that the best qualified employees were starting to shop around.

The action by these employees did not make sense, unless there was to be a very large-scale layoff. On the other hand, he recognizes that most employees are smart enough to get out while comparable jobs are available. They realize that the job market will be saturated after the layoff. Dave was convinced that a minor layoff was the worst that could possibly happen and he was demoralized to see things falling apart for no good reason.

On Friday, Bob Phillips and Henry Barham, two of the most skilled employees in the department, told David that they had taken a job with a competitor. This situation was what David feared most; the most qualified workers will leave and the least qualified workers will remain. Instead of having one of the best departments at Duncan Electric, he may now have the worst.

Questions

1. What extent has the rumors of the anticipated change in the work force done to the morale of the employees?
2. What should management do to reduce the fear of the anticipated change?
3. What should David do in a situation like this?

Chapter 11

KEY TERMS

communication	filtering
sender	perception sets
signal	empathy
receiver	listening
downward channels	body language
upward channels	transactional analysis
barriers to communication	parent
timing	child
communication overload	adult
short-circuiting	conflict management
cultural differences	arbitration
semantic	mediator

Organizational Communication

LEARNING OBJECTIVES

After completion of this chapter you should be able to

1. Identify the basic components of the communication process.
2. Describe the techniques involved in both downward and upward communication.
3. List the barriers that can cause breakdowns in communication.
4. Explain techniques that are available to facilitate communication.
5. Describe how conflict management is important as a facilitator in the communication process.

"But Professor Sundy, what I meant to say on the test was what you described as the answer. You knocked off ten points. I don't think you should have taken off so many points."

Professor Sundy replied with a disappointing statement, "Bobby, you may have meant to write the correct answer but what you put down on the test was totally incorrect. You did not communicate to me that you had any understanding of the subject. I even considered taking off more points."

Pat Steen, the production foreman for Abbot Electronics, had just been told by his supervisor that production output had to be increased if the company was to meet the deadline on a large contract. He called his workers together and said, "We are under a big push to get the contract completed. I will make it worth your while if output increases."

Outwardly the workers told Pat that they would try to meet his request. Inwardly, the majority were thinking, "Pat has made these promises before and has never come through. I just don't trust him anymore. I am not going to work harder just to make him look good and receive no reward. His word is just no good."

Alice Stevens, the office manager for Apex Supply was experiencing problems. Her car wouldn't start this morning, she had been reprimanded by her boss for sending an incorrect report forward, and she couldn't sleep well the night before. Just at that moment Phyllis Rule came to Alice to discuss a problem with regard to how to fill out the new report. After describing the problem in detail to Alice, Phyllis asked, "What do you think I should do?"

"Perhaps all my car needs is a new battery," was Alice's reply as she started off into the room. At that point, Phyllis left the office. Alice just wasn't listening to her problem.

The situations of Bobby, Pat, and Alice provide illustrations of breakdowns in communication. Breakdowns in communication occur frequently in all organizations where people work together to accomplish results. Unless these barriers are removed, the work cannot be accomplished effectively.

Perhaps the worst criticism that managers can receive from their peers, superiors, and subordinates is that they cannot communicate effectively. This was further stressed by Marvin F. Glade, Executive Vice-President for Kimberly-Clark Corporation, when he said, "Unless an individual is capable of clear and timely communication with deputies, peers and principals he or she is near totally ineffective." In a previous chapter management was defined as the accomplishment of objectives through the efforts of other people. In order for an employee to achieve the goals of the manager he or she must know what the supervisor desires to be accomplished. When the goals of the manager do not match what has actually been completed, a breakdown in communication is often found to be the source of the difficulty. A statement by a frustrated manager such as "You did what you thought I meant very effectively. Unfortunately, that was not what I wanted you to do," reveals that communication did not take place.

communication **Communication** will be defined as the achievement of meaning and understanding between people through verbal and nonverbal means in order to affect behavior and achieve desired end results. In an organization, communication has two primary purposes. First, it provides the means by which the objectives of the firm may be accomplished. The manner in which plans are to be implemented and actions coordinated to achieve a particular goal must be communicated to the individuals who must accomplish the task. Second, communication provides the means by which members of the firm may be stimulated to accomplish organizational plans willingly and enthusiastically.

The inability to communicate effectively can severely hamper a manager in the accomplishment of his or her duties. In fact, a person can actually cease to be effective as a manager unless communication skills can be improved. At times we see a manager performing tasks that a subordinate should be doing. The supervisor may say that he or she is doing the job because the worker is not capable of completing the assigned job. Often this is not the case; the manager may feel incapable of communicating his or her desires effectively. Rather than stand a chance of this occurring, the manager decides to do the work of the subordinate. In these instances, the failure to communicate has caused the efficiency of the unit to deteriorate because both the subordinates and the manager are not accomplishing the work for which they were hired.

The one redeeming feature of communication is that it is a learned quality. A person who truly desires to improve his or her ability to communicate can improve if proper attention is given to the task. The basic purpose of this chapter entails understanding the communication process. Concentration will first be placed on items that can cause a breakdown in communication. Next, factors that can assist or facilitate the communication process will be presented. Finally, means by which conflict can be managed will be discussed.

THE COMMUNICATION PROCESS

Certain basic processes are involved if effective communication is to occur. Ideas must be translated into a set of symbols and then transmitted to another person. This person receives the symbols and attempts to interpret them. If the person who receives the symbols interprets them in the manner that the sender intended, communication takes place. The first person can learn of this success only by receiving feedback from the second person. Communication must always take place between two or more people. Shouting for help on a desert island is not communication; similarly, if the professor lectures and no one listens or understands, there is no communication.

The basic elements of the communication process are illustrated in Figure 11.1. As a minimum the process includes the *sender*, the *signal*, and the *receiver*. As may be seen from the directional lines, feedback from the receiver to the sender is needed. Each basic component of the communication process will next be discussed.

SENDER

The individual(s) who attempts to transmit a message to a receiver is referred to as the sender. Each of us have different backgrounds, experiences, and goals. When communication is attempted, messages are transmitted through speaking, writing, acting, and drawing. The messages are highly dependent on our backgrounds and experiences. Because of these differences, the vocabulary and perception sets of the **sender** may be different from the receiver. The sender must be aware of these differences if effective communication is to be achieved.

sender

SIGNAL

The medium of communication through which the signal may be transmitted may be either words, actions, pictures, or numbers. The senses of sight, sound, touch, smell, and taste assist in communication. Communication can often take place without a word being spoken. Because there are so many ways that communication can be affected, breakdowns often occur because the **signal** has been improperly interpreted. These breakdowns will be discussed at a later stage in the chapter.

signal

RECEIVER

The individual for whom the message is transmitted is referred to as the receiver. He or she also has diverse backgrounds, experiences, and aspirations that may be significantly different from those of the sender. The **receiver** interprets the signals from the sender through listening, observing, and reading. The signals may be interpreted quite differently from what was intended by the sender.

receiver

FIGURE 11.1
The Communication Process

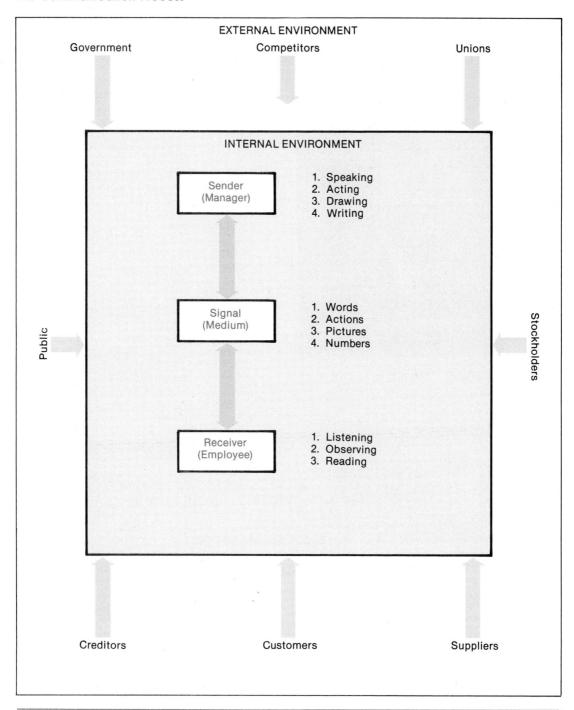

Source Adapted from Edwin B. Flippo and Gary M. Munsinger, *Management,* 4th ed. (Boston: Allyn and Bacon, Inc., 1978), p. 436.

MR. RAYMOND M. ALDEN

President
United Telecommunications, Inc.

United Telecom ▦ Raymond M. Alden is currently president and chief operating officer of United Telecommunications, Inc., the second largest independent telephone system in the United States. Alden holds an electrical engineering degree from Stanford University and was a member of the National Academy of Engineering's Committee on Telecommunications from 1973 to 1976. He began his telephone career with Hawaiian Telephone Company and served with them in various capacities including chief engineer, vice president—operations, and as director. Mr. Alden joined United Telecom in 1964 as executive vice president—operations and was elected a direc-

tor of the corporation in 1968. He became president of United in 1973.

He describes certain precepts that have contributed to, and as he states, "even accounted for" the success he has experienced. Although he qualifies this statement by saying that, "Their truth is an issue I leave for the consideration of philosophers," they have produced satisfactory results for him.

- Clear thinking leads to effective action. The best evidence of clear thinking is the ability to produce clear and concise statements about the subject under consideration. Expository writing is therefore an essential skill for managers, and it is preferable that this ability be developed in conjunction with scientific or philosophic disciplines.

- All rational people try to do what they believe to be right. Conflict and disagreement are, therefore, essentially communication problems.

- If time is taken into account, as it should be, in the setting of goals and the identification of guiding principles, then there is no conflict among the interests of owners, workers, managers, and customers of an enterprise. Management is not, as it has sometimes been characterized, the art of balancing conflicting interests. Rather, it is the art—or skill—of identifying, defining, and quantifying common interests.

- Above the level of survival, all factors that effectively motivate people can be reduced to a single essence: the development of self-esteem.

Mr. Alden is a senior member of the Institute of Electrical and Electronic Engineers, a member of the National Society of Professional Engineers, and was a trustee of the Engineers Foundation of Kansas from 1969 to 1975. Alden is a vice-president and director of the Greater Kansas City Chamber of Commerce. He also serves on the boards of the C. J. Patterson Company, the United Missouri Bank of Kansas City, and Farinon Corporation.

WHAT SHOULD BE COMMUNICATED?

In the past, the manager has tended to communicate not much more than the orders necessary to effect plans. Today, communication takes on a much larger scope. As W. D. Johnson, Vice-President of Personnel for Baxter-Travenol Labs, Inc., stated, "Communications with employees should be a part in getting managers to share more information, not only with subordinates, but with the general public as well." One of the factors is derived from the research of the behavioral scientists, who have demonstrated the motivational qualities of information. Human relations research has also underscored the need for subordinates to be heard and understood by their supervisors, thus introducing a high degree of subjectivity into the organization's communication framework.

The depression of the 1930s also was a major factor in enlarging the scope of business communications, for the confidence of the American public in its private business system was severely shaken. Managements became more interested in informing both the public and employees alike in order to demonstrate that the grant of power to run the economy was being well handled.

A third factor was the suddenly increased power of labor unions in the 1930s and 1940s. The union can often force a sharing of information through both economic and political pressures. The National Labor Relations Board, for example, has often ordered a company's management to open its records to the union in order that collective bargaining "in good faith" may be effected. Many managements have realized that union members are also their employees and have moved to effect an understanding with them to offset the increased power of labor union representatives.

Determining what specific topics are to be communicated is often a very difficult problem. The manager who believes that everything is suitable for transmission will not only clog the channels with insignificant trivia, but may harm operations by releasing information that should be retained. The National Association of Manufacturers has suggested that the following should be communicated:

1. information about the company—its operations, products, and prospects
2. information about company policies and practices related to personnel and their jobs, such as vacations, seniority, and pay systems
3. information about specific situations that arise in the company, such as a change in management or a change in plant layout
4. information about the general economic system in which a company and its employees operate

Within these broad areas, many specific details must be considered. For example, management should inform its employees of the company's products, believing that their understanding will inspire interest, loyalty, and cooperation. But, on the other hand, disclosure of future product plans may jeopardize the company's future in a highly competitive industry. In matters more closely related to the employee's interests, such as seniority and pay, the tendency is toward providing all information that could possibly be desired.

The two best guides for determining what information to provide relate to answering the following questions:

1. What must personnel know in order to relate effectively to others and to the organization as a whole?
2. What do employees want to know before cooperation will be given willingly and with enthusiasm?

The typical employee wants to know such things as—

1. his or her standing in relation to the official, formal authority structure;
2. his or her standing in relation to the informal organization with respect to individual status, power, acceptance, and so forth;
3. events that have bearing upon future economic security;
4. operational information that will enable him or her to develop pride in the job.

ORGANIZATIONAL CHANNELS OF COMMUNICATION

An important component of communication processes is the channel through which the signals flow between sender and receiver. If only superiors and subordinates are considered, these channels are of two types, downward and upward.

DOWNWARD CHANNELS

downward channels

The traditionalist manager is likely to emphasize the importance of the **downward channels** of communication. He or she is aware of the necessity for conveying management's orders and viewpoints to subordinates. It is believed that the logic of these orders will stimulate desired action. Some of the various channels available to carry the information downward are provided in Table 11.1.

TABLE 11.1
Downward Channels of Communication

The Chain of Command	Orders and information can be given face-to-face or in written fashion and transmitted from one level to another. This is the most frequently used channel and is appropriate on either an individual or a group basis.
Posters and Bulletin Boards	Many employees refuse to read such boards, and thus this channel is useful only as a supplementary device.
Company Periodicals	A great deal of information about the company, its products, and policies can be disseminated in this manner. To attract readership, a certain percentage of space must be devoted to personal items about employees, and thus the periodical plays a part in developing the social life of the organization.
Letters and Pay Inserts	This is a form of direct mail contact and is ordinarily used when the president of the organization wishes to present something of special interest. Letters are usually directed to the employee's home address. The use of pay inserts ensures exposure to every employee
Employee Handbooks and Pamphlets	Handbooks are frequently used during the hiring and orientation process as an introduction to the organization. Too often, however, they are unread even when the firm demands a signed statement that the employee is acquainted with their contents. When special systems are being introduced, such as a pension plan or a job evaluation system, concise, highly illustrated pamphlets are often prepared to facilitate understanding and stimulate acceptance.
Information Racks	In a relatively small number of organizations, racks containing free paperback literature of all types are provided. Mixed in with books on hobbies and sports are pamphlets on the profit system, the company, management techniques, and the like.
Loudspeaker System	The loudspeaker system is used not only for paging purposes, but also to make announcements while they are "hot." Such systems can also be misused, as in the case where the president of a company sent his greetings from his cool vacation place in the mountains to the hot, sweaty workers on the production floor.
Grapevine	Though the grapevine is an informal means of communication, it has been suggested that management should "feed, water, and cultivate" its growth by providing factual information to combat rumors.
Annual Reports	A review of typical annual reports would indicate that they are increasingly being written for the benefit of the employee and the union as well as for the stockholder. It is a channel that appears to be designed for one group, the owners, to which others "tap in," hoping to obtain information not intended for them.
The Labor Union	The union can be very helpful in communicating certain philosophies to company employees. The union voice, added to the management voice, can be highly persuasive.

INSIGHTS TO SUCCESS

1. Be mentally prepared to work on "off shifts" (4 P.M. to 12 midnight or midnight to 8 A.M.) in early part of career.
2. Realize that those in management usually work longer hours than those in service departments.
3. The ability to communicate both orally and in writing is essential.

JOHN F. LIVINGSTON, Vice-President—Manufacturing, Graniteville Company

---

There are doubtless many other channels that are used every day by management in attempting to communicate with subordinates. Middle- and low-level managers are usually contacted personally and by such written devices as memoranda, policy manuals, and authorized schedules. External means, such as radio, television, and the press, can be used to contact employees as well as the general public.

UPWARD CHANNELS

upward channels

The behaviorists have emphasized the establishment of **upward channels** of communication from subordinate to supervisor. This is necessary not only to determine if subordinates have understood the information that was sent downward, but also to meet the needs of the human ego. An upward flow of information is also necessary if management is to coordinate the various activities of the organization. As may be seen in Table 11.2, there are many channels from which to choose for the upward flow of information.

BARRIERS TO COMMUNICATION

Effective communication means that the receiver correctly interprets the message of the sender. Often this is not the case because of various breakdowns that can occur in communication. If a manager tells an employee to "produce a few more parts" and the employee makes two, but the manager wanted two hundred, a breakdown in communication certainly took place. If a manager is to develop his or her communication ability, the manners in which communication breakdowns can occur must be fully understood.

TABLE 11.2
Upward Channels of Communication

The Chain of Command	Theoretically, the flow of communication is two-way between superior and subordinate. The superior should have an open-door attitude as well as some of the skills of a counselor. If one has more courage, group meetings can be held in which expression of gripes and attitudes is encouraged.
The Grievance Procedure	A systematic grievance procedure is one of the most fundamental devices for upward communication. The subordinate knows that there is a mechanism for appeal beyond the authority of the immediate supervisor. If this grievance procedure is backed up by the presence of a labor union, one is even more encouraged to voice true feelings.
The Complaint System	In addition to grievance procedures, some firms encourage all types of upward communication by establishing means of preserving the identity of the complainant. "Gripe boxes" may be established, into which an employee can place a written complaint or rumor, which management will investigate. In one firm, a blackboard was divided into halves, one side being for employee complaints or rumors, the other for management's replies. An answer of some sort was guaranteed within a twenty-four hour period.
Counseling	Though all supervisors have a counseling obligation, the authority barrier makes true communication difficult. For this reason, special staff counselors may be provided to allow employees to discuss matters with them in privacy and confidence.
Morale Questionnaires	This channel also preserves the identity of the employee when answering specific questions about the firm and its management.
An Open-Door Policy	An open-door attitude on the part of each supervisor toward immediate subordinates is to be highly commended. With regard to higher management it is seldom used, because the employee is usually reluctant to bypass his or her immediate supervisor.
Exit Interview	If the employee leaves the organization, there is one last chance in the exit interview to discover feelings and views about the firm in general and reasons for quitting in particular. Follow-up questionnaires are also used at times, because employees are reluctant to give full and truthful information at the time of departure.
Grapevine	Though management may be reluctant to feed and cultivate the grapevine, it should always listen to it. The grapevine is a spontaneous and natural phenomenon that serves as a means of emotional release and provides management with significant clues concerning the attitudes and feelings of organization members. If the grapevine should ever become silent, that is the time to worry.

TABLE 11.2
Upward Channels of Communication (Continued)

Labor Union	A prime purpose of the labor union is to convey to management the feelings and demands of employees. Collective bargaining sessions constitute a legal channel of communication for any aspect of employer-employee relations.
The Informer	The communication barrier of formal hierarchy can be removed through the use of management informers among the rank and file. Their formal use has been in the field of labor relations; it is to be hoped that this use has diminished with the introduction of federal legislation. The use of this channel goes a questionable step beyond merely listening to the grapevine.
Special Meetings	Special employee meetings to discuss particular company policies or procedures are sometimes scheduled by management to obtain employee feedback. The keystone of teamwork in the Pitney Bowes Company is monthly meetings in all departments involving all employees. In addition, a central employee council of 13 employee representatives meets with top executives on a monthly basis. Employees on this main council are elected for two-year terms and devote full time to investigating company problems and improving communication processes.
The Ombudsman	Though little used in this country, it has been suggested that corporate justice in nonunionized firms requires a special person to act as the president's eyes and ears. In essence, the ombudsman acts as a complaint officer to which employees may go when they feel they have exhausted the typical avenues of receiving an acceptable hearing. An ombudsman has only the rights of acceptance or rejection of complaints, investigation, and recommendation of action to the top organizational official. Most complaints center around salary, performance appraisal, layoff, and fringe benefits. In many instances, low-level managers make voluntary adjustments precluding specific recommendations from the ombudsman. Though the position has existed for about 150 years, only recently have some American business firms adopted the concept. Xerox Corporation inaugurated the position in 1972 and reports that 40 percent of the final decisions clearly favored the employee, 30 percent were against the employee, and 30 percent represented some type of compromise.*

*"Where Ombudsmen Work Out," *Business Week*, May 3, 1976, pp. 114-116.

barriers to communication

As seen in Figure 11.2, successful management decisions must pass through the *bottleneck* or **barriers to communication** if organizational goals are to be achieved. If the barriers are excessive, communication may be reduced to the point that the firm's objectives cannot be achieved. Barriers

FIGURE 11.2
Successful Management Decisions Must Pass Through the "Bottleneck"
or Barriers to Communications Prior to Achieving Desired Results

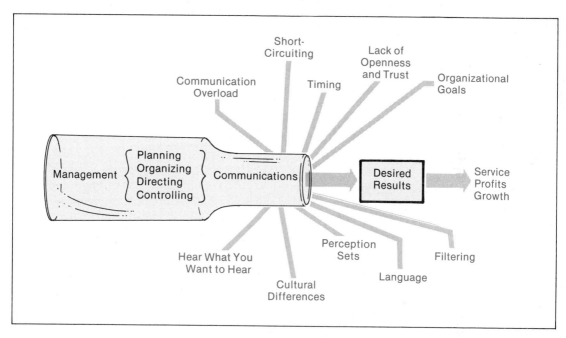

may be classified as either technical, semantic, or psychological. With this information, managers are in a position to improve their communication ability.

MOST IMPORTANT REASON FOR SUCCESS
AND EFFECTIVENESS AS A MANAGER

The ability to develop business plans and strategies and then communication of them to the people who can share in and build on these concepts.

L. W. LEHR, President, U. S. Operations, 3M Company

TECHNICAL

Environmental barriers to communication are referred to as technical breakdowns. Some of these include timing, communication overload, cultural differences, and short-circuiting.

Timing

timing

Timing of when communication should be transmitted to superiors, subordinates or peers is extremely important to a manager. Just as timing is quite critical to when a boy asks a girl for a date—if you ask too late she may already have a date and if you ask too early she may not know if she has to go home to visit her parents for the weekend—a manager must determine the best time to transmit a message. A presentation that would be acceptable at one time might be unacceptable at another.

Communication Overload

communication overload

With the many channels and media available as well as the changed philosophy toward a greater sharing of information, it is little wonder that communication overload often occurs. **Communication overload** occurs when the sender attempts to present too much information to the receiver at one time. There are only so many facts and figures that a person can absorb at a particular time. When excessive information is provided, a major breakdown in communication can occur. As a professor, one of the authors experienced communication overload in a classroom. While teaching a statistics class that met one day a week for four hours, excessive overload was encountered. For the first hour students were eager to take notes. Progressing toward the fourth hour students began to have blank stares. By the end of the fourth hour few students could tell another person what had been said by the instructor. Communication overload had definitely occurred. Some students have discovered that their grades suffer when they attempt to take all of their classes in the morning on Monday, Wednesday, and Friday. By the end of the last class many of the students have no idea what the teacher has said and their grades often suffer.

Short-Circuiting

short-circuiting

It is perhaps a difficult lesson for a young manager to learn but everyone, especially peers and subordinates, may not be as pleased to see you perform successfully. Successful completion of a task may actually be viewed as a threat to their security. As such, attempts may be made, either consciously or unconsciously, at **short-circuiting** the communication of your excellent results to another person, typically a supervisor. If the person who is attempting the short-circuiting is able to gain the attention of the supervisor there is a possibility that when you attempt to communicate a "less receptive ear" may be present. Because the message has been short-circuited, the effectiveness of the communication may be reduced.

Cultural Differences

cultural differences

Cultural differences can also cause a breakdown in communication. In the United States, time is a highly valuable commodity and a deadline suggests urgency. In the Middle East, the giving of a deadline to another conveys meanings of rudeness, and is likely to be ignored. If a client is kept waiting in the outer office for thirty minutes in the United States, it means that a person may have low status. In Latin America, a thirty-minute wait means nothing. If a contract offer has not been acted on in this country over a period of several months or a year, the conclusion is that the party has lost interest. In Japan, long delays mean no slackening of interest, and delay is often a highly effective negotiation tactic when used on impatient Americans.

Americans conduct most business at an interpersonal interval of from five to eight feet, and a distance of one to three feet suggests more personal or intimate undertakings. The normal business distance in Latin America is closer to the personal distance of the United States. Thus, we observe the highly interesting communication difficulties of a back-pedaling American as his or her Latin American counterpart presses ever closer. Regarding status symbols, an American manager's office that is spacious, well furnished, and located on the top floor conveys meanings of high prestige. In the Middle East, size and decor of office mean little or nothing, and in France, the manager is likely to be located in the midst of subordinates in order to control them.

SEMANTIC

semantic

Barriers to communication can be caused because of **semantic** problems resulting from language barriers and different meanings being applied to the same words.

Language

A manager must have fully in mind the type of audience addressed, whether it is a staff engineer, a skilled mechanic, or a ditch digger. Each may have a different vocabulary set. Words that the staff engineer might fully understand have little meaning to the ditch digger or vice versa. Breakdowns in communication often occur when the sender does not tailor the signal to match the knowledge base of the receiver.

All of us have a common level of vocabulary (see Figure 11.3 for an illustration). If we speak with level 4 type words both the statistician and the ditch digger will understand. As we progress above this base level

FIGURE 11.3
Common Vocabulary Base

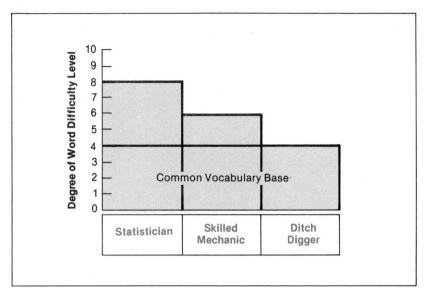

more and more people will not be able to comprehend the message. If the statistician uses words above the scale of 6, communication with the skilled mechanic is lost. It will cease at level 5 with the ditch digger. Naturally, there will be times when higher level words must be used to communicate a technical concept but if a manager can concentrate their messages in the common vocabulary base, he or she should experience a much better chance of being understood.

Two systems for judging the reading difficulty of written material are the Flesch system and the *fog index* suggested by Robert Gunning.[1] The Flesch system analyzes factors such as sentence length and the number of human interest words used in the written presentation. Standards of readability are established for each of these factors, with seventeen words, for example, constituting the standard sentence length.

Using either of these systems, most best-selling novels test at seventh- or eighth-grade level. In an analysis of United States Air Force documents, Air Force Regulations were placed at sixteenth-grade level and Numbered Letters at eighteenth grade. In an early use of the Flesch scale, Davis analyzed the readability of seventy-one employee handbooks and discovered that 92 percent were too difficult for their intended readers.[2] In a

1. Robert Gunning, "How to Improve Your Writing," *Factory Management and Maintenance* 110 (June 1952): 134.

2. Keith Davis, "Readability Changes in Employee Handbooks of Identical Companies During a Fifteen-Year Period," *Personnel Psychology* 21 (Winter 1968): 413–420.

follow-up study of twenty-nine handbooks fifteen years later, little or no improvement was noted. Eighteen of the twenty-nine were lacking in understandability and appeal for employees who were not college graduates. It is apparent that the subject matter of a handbook is not as appealing as a novel or popular magazine. This, combined with readability levels beyond employee capabilities, will assure that only publication, rather than communication, is accomplished.

The objective of both of these systems is to reduce the amount of pompous jargon and inflated prose. Of course, there is more to communication than can be revealed by these mechanistic counts of syllables and sentence lengths. The sender of symbols must have a clear and coherent grasp of the idea one hopes to transmit. The Flesch and Gunning indexes merely aid the writer in keeping the audience in mind.

The Meaning of Words

When the sender uses words that the receiver either does not understand or the receiver applies a different meaning to, a communication breakdown can certainly occur. A major difficulty with the American language is that multiple meanings may be attached to a word. For instance, the word *charge* has several different meanings. A manager may place an employee *in charge* of a section. The company *charges* for their services. When two individuals attach different meanings to a word, a breakdown in communication can occur.

The use of jargon can also create a barrier to communication. Virtually every industry develops certain jargon that is used in everyday business. The statistician, computer programmer, typist, or ditch digger likely develops expressions peculiar to his or her specific profession. When speaking to an individual not associated with the trade jargon, a breakdown in communication may occur. It is likely for this reason that many firms provide new personnel with a list and definition of terms associated with the particular industry.

PSYCHOLOGICAL

Although technical factors and semantic differences are credited with causing breakdowns in communication, psychological barriers tend to be the major reasons for miscommunication and communication breakdowns. These include various forms of distortion and problems involving interpersonal relationships.

Knowledge of What You Want to Say

The old expression, "The mouth was in gear before the mind was operating" provides one form of breakdown in communication. Directives, orders, and even comments that are not well thought out can develop an image that the sender does not know what they actually want. A manager who asks for one thing and expects another has had a breakdown in communication.

Filtering

filtering

Managers often discover that information that has been provided them by subordinates has been **filtered.** As subordinates contribute information to superiors, they know that it will be used for at least two purposes: (1) to aid management in controlling and directing the firm (and therefore the worker) and (2) to evaluate the worth of their performance. Because of this, employees are often tempted to filter, alter, and color information to present a more favorable image to the manager. Managers at all levels are tempted to filter information as it progresses up the chain of command. Even the president may filter information before it goes to the board of directors.

Because the data has been filtered, an incorrect impression of the true situation may occur. There have been many managerial attempts to reduce both the number and thickness of the authority filters that clog organization communication channels. It should be apparent that decentralization reduces the number of levels of authority within the organization. One organization reduced the number of managerial levels from eight to four, with a consequent speeding up of the communication process. Such reorganizations are drastic and require considerable efforts in the area of retraining and establishing realistic control standards.

The consultant can also serve as a means of reducing communication filters. In one company, there was a steady decrease in productivity for no reason that could be identified by management. The consultant systematically interviewed all employees over a six-month period. The results of these many interviews indicated strong feelings on the part of many employees that work standards were too high, that older employees resented the high wage scales of the new, and that temporary transfers to new jobs to avoid layoff were widely resented. In each case, management had felt that it had communicated effectively its intent to the employees.

Lack of Trust and Openness

It was stressed in chapter 10 that a basic requirement for change entailed openness and trust on the part of the manager by his or her subordinates.

When employees feel that the manager does not possess these qualities a barrier to communication has occurred. A manager may say to an employee, "If you complete this project on time, I am certain you will get a raise." If similar statements have been made in the past and no raise has been forthcoming, the manager has lost the trust of the worker.

In the communication process illustration (see Figure 11.1) it should be noted that the directional lines go both ways. The sender needs feedback to know whether or not communication has occurred. If employees perceive the manager as being open and receptive to their ideas, communication is encouraged. On the other hand, should the manager give the impression that feedback is not desired, and that his or her statements should never be questioned, communication is stifled.

Perhaps the most important approach toward the problem is the development of *leadership skills* among all supervisors. If supervisors can acquire the skills of openness and receptiveness, lack of trust and openness can be reduced. The fact that communication problems exist in many business organizations is made evident by various surveys conducted by Opinion Research Corporation among 2,147 supervisors, engineers, and white- and blue-collar employees in eight companies.[3] Among the various findings were (1) over half of all employees believed that telling one's supervisor everything felt about the company would probably get her or him into a "lot of trouble"; (2) almost three-quarters of all employees felt that management was not interested in employee problems; (3) most employees rated their supervisors as "good" on job knowledge and operating problems, but only one-third said that he or she was "good" on handling complaints and encouraging suggestions; (4) less than one-quarter felt that management usually took prompt action in connection with employee complaints; and (5) almost three-quarters of the supervisors felt that they needed more training in communication practices, particularly in how to listen. That such training is worth the effort is suggested by a study in six offices of a large public utility.[4]

In relating the perceived degree of openness between supervisor and subordinate with employee satisfaction, a clear-cut effect was discovered. The greater the openness of either superior or subordinate, or both, the greater the degree of employee satisfaction with the company, the job, and the supervisor. Equal degrees of openness on the part of both tended to result in greater satisfaction, as contrasted with situations where only one or the other was more open. Though not proved, it was suggested that an open attitude on the part of the subordinate was a direct result of such an attitude on the part of the supervisor.

3. Alfred Vogel, "Why Don't Employees Speak Up?" *Personnel Administration* 30 (May–June 1967): 20–22.
4. Ronald J. Burke and Douglas S. Wilcox, "Effects of Different Patterns and Degrees of Openness in Superior-Subordinate Communication on Subordinate Job Satisfaction," *Academy of Management Journal*, 12 (3) (September 1969): p. 326.

We Hear What We Expect to Hear

We are often conditioned in the communication process to hear what we expect to hear, not what is actually said. Because of past experiences we have developed a concept of what will be said. At times we hear what we want to hear. An employee who has been reprimanded quite a few times by a certain supervisor may even interpret a compliment by the manager as a negative statement.

Perception Sets

perception sets

Languages are very complex mechanisms, and the same word will not have the exact same meaning for everyone because of differences in **perception sets.** Even if both parties are in agreement as to which formal meaning is involved, there are the differences in individual backgrounds that give varying connotations to words. The word *management,* for example, may be defined by both parties as the planning, organizing, directing, and controlling of the activities of others. If the first party's parents have been managers and the second's parents have been labor union organizers, it is apparent that the word *management* will evoke drastically different meanings. It is difficult enough if words are representative of tangible objects such as chair, pencil, or hat. But one can imagine the difficulties in using such terms as *liberal, conservative, philosophy, group dynamics,* and *communication.*

FACILITATORS TO COMMUNICATION

Once a person recognizes that breakdowns in communication can occur, a manager is then in a position to work toward improving their communication ability. As previously mentioned, the major factor that should be remembered is that communication is a learned art. If a person truly desires to improve his or her communication ability there are means available to assist in this undertaking.

EMPATHY

empathy

An expression that has come out of the college community during the past few years is, "I see where you are coming from." Although likely not realizing this fact, empathy is being expressed. **Empathy** is the ability to identify with the various feelings and thoughts of another person. It does not mean that you necessarily agree with the other person but while you are with the individual you can appreciate why they speak and act as they

Barriers to communication can be reduced if individuals desire to improve their communication ability.

do. If a person is bitter, you are able to relate to this bitterness; if scared, you understand this fear.

Taken in its broadest meaning, an empathetic person is communicating. It is for this reason that a manager should take the time to understand as much as possible about the people with whom he or she must work daily. With this information, the manager is in a much better position to understand why people act as they do. The manager may not agree with the individual, but if the time is taken to understand the reason for certain action, problems may more easily be resolved. Research has indicated that women tend to be much more concerned with money than men.[5] Until

5. Pryor, Mildred Golden and R. Wayne Mondy, "How Men and Women View Their Jobs—and What This Means to the Supervisor," *Supervisory Management* 23 (November 1978): 17–25.

recently, women have received lower pay for the same work as men. A male manager must be able to understand this difference in attitude. If a manager has empathy and understands these differences the ability to communicate has a greater likelihood of being enhanced.

LISTENING

listening

One of the most effective tools a manager has at his or her disposal to facilitate communication is the ability to listen. A person who is constantly talking is not learning. **Listening** assists a manager in discovering problems and determining solutions to problems.

Communication cannot take place unless messages are received and understood by the other party. It has been observed that the average speaking speed is 120 words per minute. One is able to listen more than four times as rapidly. The question therefore arises, what does the listener do with the free time that results from this difference in speeds?

At least three types of listening have been identified: marginal, evaluative, and projective. The speed of listening provides the opportunity for marginal listening, a dangerous type that can lead to misunderstanding of and even insult to the speaker. For instance, most of us have experienced a situation where we have been speaking to a person but we know that their mind is a million miles away. The individual may occasionally hear some words, but the majority of the message was not understood.

Evaluative listening requires the second party to allocate full attention to the speaker. The excess time is devoted to evaluating and judging the nature of the remarks heard. Often, we are forming rebuttal remarks while the sender is still speaking, thus moving into a type of marginal listening. As soon as the sender says something that is not accepted, communication ceases and the receiver begins to develop a response in his or her own mind. Thoughts such as, "This person does not know what he is talking about. I was in Vietnam and I know the way it was" can significantly reduce, or even eliminate, the communication process. Instead of one idea being transmitted and held by two people, we often end up with two ideas neither of which is really communicated to the other. If the listener allocates too much time to disapproving or approving of what is heard, it is doubtful whether he or she has the time to understand fully. This is particularly true when the remarks are loaded with emotion or concern over the security and status of the receiver.

The third type of listening holds the greatest potential for effective communication. Listeners fully utilize their time by attempting to project themselves into the position of the speaker and understand what is being said from the speaker's viewpoint. We should first listen without evaluation. After feeling that we understand what has been said, we can then evaluate what has been said. Rogers suggested a rule to be followed to ensure some degree of projective listening: "Each person can speak for himself only *after* he has related the ideas and feelings of the previous speaker accurately and to that speaker's satisfaction."[6] There is no need to agree with the statements, but there is a need to understand them as the speaker intended. Only in this way is it possible to frame a reply that will actually respond to the speaker's remarks. Effective listening is empathic listening. It requires an ability to listen for feeling as well as for words. The person attempts to place himself or herself in the "shoes of the other person."

IMPROVE READING SKILLS

Reading skills have received great attention in our society. The amount of written material a manager must plow through seems to increase yearly, and some attempt should first be made to consolidate and reduce it. However, the ability to read rapidly and with understanding is an essential communication skill, particularly in larger organizations. It has been found that reading speeds can be doubled and tripled with little or no loss in comprehension.

OBSERVATION

As in the case of listening, there are too few attempts to increase skill in observation outside of training for law enforcement. Most of us have heard reports where there were many witnesses to a traffic accident. When the police arrived and questioned the witnesses there were many different versions to what actually occurred. "The blue car went through the stop light," said one witness. "No, that is not correct," said another, "the light was green." Most people miss a great deal by not carefully observing important elements in the environment. It was mentioned earlier that some managers are very adept at assessing the general atmosphere of an organization by merely strolling through its work places. Observation of furnishings, housekeeping, dress of personnel, and activities can convey much information. Using our powers of observation to supplement listening and reading will add immeasurably to our understanding of what is actually transpiring.

6. Carl R. Rogers and F. J. Roethlisberger, "Barriers and Gateways to Communication," *Harvard Business Review* 30 (July–August 1952): 48.

WORD CHOICE

It has been mentioned previously that there is a certain threshhold of words that virtually everyone can understand. If a manager desires to communicate effectively he or she must make certain that the choice of the words transmitted by the sender is in the vocabulary set of the receiver. Generally simple or common words provide the best means through which communication is accomplished.

BODY LANGUAGE

Most students have already been introduced to the concept of body language as it assists in the communication process. A guy seldom has to be told by a young lady, "I want a date with you." It is likely that this inclination is communicated by a pleasant smile, where there was not one previously. It is something that an observant student soon recognizes, but often words are not said.

body language   Appreciation of the importance of understanding of **body language** in the communication process is also quite important for a manager. All people—managers, superiors, and subordinates—give off unintentional signals which can provide significant insight into the exact meaning that a person is attempting to communicate. The manager particularly must be constantly aware of the signals that he or she is presenting. Employees grasp at these small symbols to determine what the "boss" means. A frown, even though the words were positive in nature, may be taken wrong. A sarcastic smile when "you did a good job" was mentioned will not likely be interpreted to mean that the worker actually did a good job. A blank stare may mean to the employee that the manager is not interested.

A manager must also be aware of the signals that a subordinate may be giving off. Sweaty hands or nail biting in the presence of the supervisor may mean that the worker feels quite ill at ease. Managers need to recognize these signs and be prepared to adjust their action.

ACTIONS

The manager must also recognize that one communicates by what one does or does not do. If a person comes to work one day and finds her or his desk moved from a location in a private office to one in an open area, communication of a sort has taken place. If no verbal explanation accompanies the action, people will interpret it their own way; the missing symbol or signal will be supplied by the observer. And despite any verbal statement to the contrary, such a move will likely be interpreted as a demotion for the person.

In one company, management had introduced a change in procedure for a small crew of employees. The new method was timed and piece rates were established. None of the personnel produced more than half of the standard amount and were therefore on a time-wage basis rather than piece rates. They all filed grievances protesting the unfairness of the standard. Management tried everything it could think of to correct the problem, from all-day time studies to providing each employee with a private instructor in the new method. A check on similar jobs in other companies revealed that the standard was in line. Thus, management concluded that a concerted work restriction was involved.

The next move was one of communication by *action.* An engineer was sent to the production department, and he proceeded to measure various angles and spaces on the floor. He volunteered no information to the group. Finally, one man's curiosity got the best of him and he asked the engineer what he was doing. The engineer indicated that management wanted to see if there was sufficient room to locate certain machinery that could do the work of this crew. He continued about his business of measuring. The next day, all work crew members were producing amounts well above the established standard.

TRANSACTIONAL ANALYSIS

transactional analysis

If we can understand both ourselves and the people with whom we must work daily, communication should be significantly enhanced. A method which has proven useful in accomplishing this task is **Transactional Analysis,** referred to as TA. Because a manager is constantly working with a variety of people, any approach that has the potential of increasing understanding should be explored as a potential facilitator to communication. Various aspects of TA that have proven useful in facilitating the communication process will be briefly introduced.[7]

With TA there are three ego states that are constantly present and at work within each individual—the *Parent,* the *Adult,* and the *Child.* The states interrelate and the ego state that dominates can have a tremendous effect on communication potential.

7. For an expanded coverage of transactional analysis see Thomas A. Harris, *I'm O.K.—You're O.K.,* Harper & Row Publishers, Inc., 1969.

Parent

parent   The **Parent** may take on the characteristic of either the *Nurturing* or the *Negative Parent.* When the Nurturing Parent dominates, the person gives praise and recognition, comfort in time of distress and reassurance in time of need. Statements such as "You have done a good job" or "I am certain the problem will work out all right" might be associated with the Nurturing Parent. On the other hand, the Negative Parent is overcontrolling, suffocating, critical, and oppressive. Comments such as "Women should be seen and not heard" or "Be careful, you can hurt yourself with the knife" might be associated with the Negative Parent. When the Negative Parent dominates the person tends to lecture, believes that his or her moral standard is best for everyone, and often will not accept other ideas.

Child

child   The **Child** may take on the characteristics of either the *Natural Child,* the *Little Professor,* or the *Adaptive Child.* The Natural Child is spontaneous, impulsive, untrained, expressive, self-centered, affectionate and curious. The Little Professor tends to be intuitive, manipulative, and creative. The Adaptive "Child" tends to react in a way determined by parental figures.

Adult

         A person who tends to evaluate the situation and attempts to make
adult   decisions based on information and facts is the **Adult.** No emotions are involved and the individual tends to function like a computer with all decisions based on logic.

   Knowledge of which ego state a person is in can often assist in the communication process. The manager must recognize that a person will not always be in the Adult state and make decisions based entirely on logic. In fact, the greatest amount of creativity is associated with the Child. Also, the manager will be able to recognize when communication is impossible. For instance, the manager who is in the Adult state may attempt to speak to the Adult of the employee. The Child state of the employee returns the conversation to the Parent of the manager. The following conversation is given to illustrate such a communication problem.

   Manager: This task needs to be completed today.

   Employee: Why are you always pushing me to work harder?

In the above illustration, communication has broken down because the employee is not addressing the problem that the manager was attempting to communicate.

The manager should also be aware of the ego state in which he or she resides. If properly interpreted, it permits the manager to recognize and possibly change his or her actions. Should you recognize that you are in one state and an employee is in a state that precludes effective communication, it may be best to postpone communication. For instance, if the manager is in the Child state and the employee is in the Adult state, communication may be postponed to another time. The employee who is in the Adult state is serious about his work at this time and joking remarks may be misinterpreted.

MANAGEMENT OF CONFLICT

An organization is comprised of individuals who have been brought together to accomplish certain specified objectives. Unless it is a very unusual company, these employees have different backgrounds, experiences, aspirations, and personalities. These differences alone can create a situation of potential conflict and a breakdown in communication. Even the most happily married couple who are perfectly matched may have occasional disagreements.

A firm brings together even more diversity of ideas and sets the stage for potentially greater conflict. When these individuals are brought together in a highly structured environment, a potential for major disagreements exists. It may be nothing more than a difference in opinion of how to accomplish the same goal or as critical as a disagreement as to what the goals actually are. At times, conflict occurs because of unclear authority in that a person does not have a clearly defined role within the firm. Also, roles may overlap which has the potential to create considerable conflict among employees. Unless a person believes in a utopian world, conflict will occur in any organization.

In its broadest interpretation conflict management is a facilitator to communication because it has the ability to resolve disagreements between individuals within the organization that could have an adverse effect on attaining organizational goals. When this definition is applied, a person should rapidly see that all conflict is not bad. In fact, a certain amount of conflict is healthy. There may be an optimum level of conflict that should be developed and maintained for the good of the organization. Too little conflict may lead to mediocrity, apathy, and at times, destruction. The Penn Central Railroad went quietly into bankruptcy when its board of directors offered no challenging questions to management. If former President Nixon had not surrounded himself with "yes men" the events of Watergate might not have occurred. Certainly, the conflict surrounding the civil rights movement led to societal decisions more in keeping with the long-run interests of the United States.

Although conflict can be beneficial to an organization, it can also be detrimental to the overall effectiveness of a firm. The situational approach is of value to us in deciding how much conflict in an organization is desirable. There are times when cooperation should take precedence over conflict. But there are also occasions when the suppression of opposing viewpoints can be highly detrimental to long-run organizational effectiveness. The modern manager must consciously attempt to overcome his or her strong tendency to prefer unquestioning acceptance of the status quo. This attitude might result in the firm peacefully slipping into stagnation or bankruptcy.

INTERPERSONAL CONFLICT MANAGEMENT

conflict management

The techniques of dealing with conflict between two or more individuals are numerous. They range from the use of force by a superior over a subordinate to the problem solving approach. Possible ways of dealing with interpersonal **conflict management** are discussed below.

Force

When force is used in the resolution of conflict, official authority may compel one party to accept a solution. The old expression, "He may not be right but he is still the boss," applies in this instance. The party for which the decision was directed may not agree with the results but if he or she is to stay within the organization, the directive must be accepted.

Withdrawal

A solution that some individuals use in resolving conflict is to withdraw or avoid the person with whom the conflict exists. Conflict is reduced, but the reason that originated the conflict remains. It would be the same thing as seeing a person you do not want to speak to approaching you on the street and you walk around the block to keep from having to speak to the individual.

Smoothing

When smoothing is used, a manager attempts to provide a semblance of peaceful cooperation by presenting an image that "we're one big happy family." With this approach, problems are rarely permitted to come to the surface but the potential for conflict remains.

Compromise

Neither party gets all it wants when compromise is used. This is the most typical way of dealing with labor management conflict. For example, management may offer to increase wages by 8 percent, while the union may be seeking a 12 percent pay hike. A compromise figure of a 10 percent pay increase may result in a reasonable settlement of the conflict.

Mediation and Arbitration

arbitration

mediator

Both arbitration and mediation call for outside neutral parties to enter the situation to assist in resolving the conflict. **Arbitration** is used considerably in union/management grievance conflicts. The arbitrator is given the authority to act as a judge in making a decision. The decision rendered is usually final in that both union and management agreed in advance to this condition. A **mediator,** on the other hand, can only suggest, recommend, and attempt to keep the two parties talking in the hope of reaching a solution. The United States could be considered a mediator in the Arab/Israeli conflict.

Superordinate Goals

At times, a goal may be encountered that supersedes the conflict of two opposing factions. If the firm is in danger of going out of business both union and management have been known to put aside minor conflict and work toward the common goal of survival. There have been instances where union members have taken a decrease in pay and benefits in order to assist in the survival of the firm.

Problem Solving

The preferred behavioral approach to conflict management is problem solving. As usually practiced, problem solving is characterized by an open and trusting exchange of views and facts. A person realizes that conflict is caused by relationships among people and is not within the person. With the problem solving approach, an individual can disagree with your ideas and still remain your friend. It is a healthy approach in which rarely is one person completely right and the other person completely wrong. Granting a concession is not a sign of weakness and a person does not feel that they have to win every battle to maintain his or her self-respect.

When the problem solving approach is in effect, a person recognizes that a certain amount of conflict is healthy. For instance, if a difference of opinion exists between two individuals and they openly discuss their difficulties a superior solution often results. With problem solving a person is actually encouraged to bring difficulties into the open without fear of reprisal. When this occurs, a situation that initially appeared to be a major problem may evolve into only a minor instance which is easily resolved.

STRUCTURAL CONFLICT MANAGEMENT

Conflict can also be managed by changing structures and processes that can have an effect on behavior. These methods for resolving conflict are discussed next.

Procedural Changes

There are times when conflict can occur because a procedure is illogically sequenced. When a credit manager and a sales manager were both about to be fired because of an irreconcilable personality conflict, it was discovered that the processing of credit applications too late in the procedure was the cause of the difficulty. The credit manager was forced to cancel too many deals already made. When the credit check was placed earlier in the procedure, most of the conflict disappeared. In another instance, the personnel director and the production manager were in continuous disagreement. At times the conflict actually came to blows. Then it was discovered that the production manager was not being permitted to review the applicants at an early stage of the hiring sequence and provide input as to his feelings regarding an applicant. When the procedure was changed, many of the difficulties were resolved.

Organizational Changes

The organization can be changed to either promote or reduce conflict. There are times when a department becomes too complacent, and although there is little conflict, very little is accomplished. To reduce undesired conflict within an organization, transfers of incompatible personnel can be made. Often this procedure is quite acceptable but a manager must be careful that the workers are transferred for the proper reason. To transfer a worker that is incompetent merely because you as a manager are afraid to deal with the individual does an injustice to the overall goals of the organization. Some managers begin to suspect why an employee who is to be transferred to their department arrives there with "too glowing" recommendations. The question is asked, "If he is that good, why don't you keep him?" But, if transfers are handled on a professional basis both the company and the employee benefit.

When the conflict is between two units of the organization, special liaison personnel can be assigned. A traditional problem exists between production and marketing. Production personnel have been taught to cut costs and the technique to accomplish this goal is to produce as few variations of a product as possible. Marketing personnel want products consisting of different colors, styles, and shapes. A person who understands and appreciates the problems of both departments can greatly assist in resolving conflict.

Physical Layout Changes

Changes in the design of the physical work places have been used effectively to reduce or eliminate conflict. Office space can be designed to either force interaction or to make it difficult. Personnel can use desks as barriers and buffers. Some offices have dividers which separate each worker. However, if a manager desires to stimulate a problem-solving atmosphere, a more open office arrangement may be permitted. When known antagonists are seated in conference directly across from each other, the amount of conflict increases. When they are seated side by side, the conflict tends to decrease.

Expand Resources

The incompatibility of goals that stimulated much conflict can be reduced if resources can be expanded until all have more. Thus, in a growing organization everything looks rosy. When hard times come, the contest begins for one's share of the smaller pie. As enrollment goes down in some colleges and universities, the battle begins to emerge. Should everyone get a graduate assistant, should the senior faculty members get one, or should the most productive but perhaps junior member get the assistant? The same question must be asked when summer teaching assignments are made. Under these conditions, skills in conflict management of the highest order are demanded. Whatever the situation, the effective use of conflict management will have a major impact upon organizational effectiveness.

SUMMARY

Effective communication refers to the achievement of meaning and understanding between people through verbal and nonverbal means. The basic components of the communication process consist of the sender, the signal, and the receiver. A weakness in any of these components reduces effective communication.

There are numerous channels of communication through which a manager transmits information. Downward channels provide means through which management's orders and viewpoints are transmitted to subordinates. Upward channels provide means through which subordinates can communicate with their superiors.

Effective communication is often not achieved because of various breakdowns that can affect the communication process. Barriers may cause communication to be reduced to the point that the firm's objectives cannot be achieved. Barriers may be classified as either technical, semantic, or psychological. Technical barriers include improper timing, communication overload, short-circuiting, and cultural differences. Semantic barriers result from different meanings being applied to the same word. Psychological barriers include various forms of distortion and problems involving interpersonal relationships.

Although there are many barriers to communication, there are means available to eliminate or reduce these breakdowns. The use of empathy and the development of good listening skills can facilitate the communication process. In addition, reading and observation skills as well as making better choices of words can aid the manager in better communication with employees. The study of transactional analysis and developing the ability to read body language has been used to improve a manager's ability to communicate.

Management of conflict is important within an organization because there are so many different backgrounds, experiences, aspirations, and personalities among employees. In its broadest interpretation, conflict management can be used to overcome communication problems by resolving disagreements between individuals within the organization. Conflict management may be classified as interpersonal or structural. Interpersonal conflict management deals with conflict between two or more individuals. Structural conflict management is concerned with changing the structures and processes that can have an effect on behavior.

**Review
Questions**

1. Define communication. Describe the basic communication process.

2. Distinguish by definition between downward and upward communication. What are examples of both type channels of communication?

3. What is meant by the phrase "barriers to communication?" Distinguish between technical, semantic, and psychological barriers.

4. List the topics that have been identified as facilitators to communication. Briefly define each.

5. Explain how empathy may be used to assist a person become a better listener.

6. Describe how conflict management can be used as a facilitator to communication.

Exercises

1. In a twenty-four hour period, identify factors and situations which created barriers to communication. Attempt to secure at least one example of each of the barriers to communication identified in the text. What facilitators of communication could have been used to reduce these barriers to effective communication?

2. Visit a business of your choice. Attempt to identify the various means of both downward and upward communication.

3. This is an exercise regarding observation skills. With one of your classmates go to the window and observe what is occurring on the outside for ten seconds. Each of you will now write down what you saw. After completing the list compare your list with your partner's list. Compare the differences.

REFERENCES

Allen, T. H. "Communication Networks: The Hidden Organization Chart." *Personnel Administrator*, September 1976, pp. 31–35.

Davis, Keith. "Cut Those Rumors Down to Size." *Supervisory Management*, June 1975, pp. 2–6.

Deutsch, A. R. "Does Your Company Practice Affirmative Action In Its Communication?" *Harvard Business Review*, November 1976, pp. 16 +.

Farinelli, J. L. "Fine Tuning Employee Communications." *Public Relations Journal*, January 1977, pp. 22–23.

Genfun, H. "Managerial Communication." *Personnel Journal*, November 1976, pp. 568–569 +.

Hargreaves, J. "Six Keys to Good Communications." *International Management*, December 1976, pp. 54–56.

Hill, J. W. "Look It Up—Or Can You?" *Business Horizons*, April 1977, pp. 61–68.

Huseman, R. C. "Managing Change Through Communication." *Personnel Journal*, January 1978, pp. 20–25.

Leavitt, Harold J. *Managerial Psychology*, 2nd ed. Chicago: University of Chicago Press, 1964.

Muchinsky, P. M. "Organizational Communication: Relationships to Organizational Climate and Job Satisfaction." *Academy of Management Journal*, December 1977, pp. 592–607.

Rice, J. A., and Colby, J. B. "Communication Barriers: Individual Quirks and Corporate Personalities." *Supervisory Management*, April 1976, pp. 2–10.

Roberts, Karlene H., and O'Reilly, Charles A., III. "Failures in Upward Communication: Three Possible Culprits." *Academy of Management Journal*, June 1974, pp. 205–215.

Rogers, Carl R., and Roethlisberger, J. J. "Barriers and Gateways to Communication." *Harvard Business Review*, July/August 1952.

Rosenberg, Marshall B. "Words Can Be Windows or Walls." In Walter R. Nord, ed. *Concepts and Controversy in Organizational Behavior*, 2nd ed. Pacific Palisades, Calif.: Goodyear Publishing, 1976, pp. 485–490.

Sullivan, B. "Tearing Down the Barriers." *Industry Week*, March 1, 1976, pp. 38–40.

Sussman, L. "Communications: What Are Your Assumptions?" *Supervisory Management*, January 1976, pp. 35–37.

Thompson, D. B. "Ultimate Word: The Grapevine." *Industry Week*, May 10, 1976, pp. 29–33 +.

Wilkinson, R. "And While on the Subject of Communication." *Industrial Management*, November 1976, p. 21.

Wood, M. M. "The Give-and-Take of Communication." *Supervisory Management*, June 1976, pp. 24–28.

Case Study

THE PROMISE

Philip Jackson was a graduate from a large midwestern university that had an excellent reputation for preparing business graduates to take responsible jobs in industry. Philip was in the top 10 percent of his graduating class and was extremely active in social activities on campus. On graduating, Philip had many job opportunities. He took the time to study the firms and the type of positions that were available. He ultimately decided to take a position with Bedford International, a large conglomerate.

Philip and twenty other recent college graduates were hired as management trainees. All of the management trainees were to start as first-line supervisors. There were no formalized training sessions, just on-the-job training. But, after one year, the individual trainees were all promised advancement to higher-level positions.

Philip was considered to possess excellent management potential. During the quarterly progress reviews, he was told that his performance was exceptional in all areas. His employees showed less turnover, lower absenteeism, and higher performance than other similar groups.

Due to the large number of trainees hired, and the low turnover rate of managers at Bedford, few openings for the next managerial positions were available. Philip felt that recognition was nearly impossible. At the end of one year, no new positions were available, yet many promises had been made regarding his advancement opportunities. At the end of eighteen months, there were still no new positions available.

A few weeks later, Philip was approached by a professional recruiter and after several interviews, he received an offer from another company. The offer Philip received included a 20 percent increase in salary and an increase in managerial responsibilities. Philip felt obligated to talk to his supervisor prior to accepting any offers. In his conversation with the supervisor Philip reminded his supervisor of the promises that had been made but not fulfilled.

Questions

1. What do you believe Philip should do with regard to the job offer?
2. How do you believe Philip's supervisor should answer the questions that Philip asked?
3. What problems in communication are evident from this case?

Case Study

GARY JONES, MANAGEMENT TRAINEE

Gary Jones, a recent graduate of Michigan State University, had just joined Bellingham Electric Company as a management trainee. Bellingham was one of the largest manufacturers of electric light bulbs, transformers, and generators in the United States with headquarters in Detroit. Gary had first made contact with the company through the placement office at Michigan State. Bellingham had achieved excellent results over a period of many years in recruiting management trainees through college placement offices. In a typical year, the company would hire 200 management trainees from their college recruiting efforts.

The company had a well-established management training program, lasting one year, during which time the trainee was assigned to a branch location to learn various phases of company operations. The program designed to prepare individuals for branch management includes training in the following areas: shipping and receiving, inventory control, purchasing, personnel, production, order service, and outside sales. In addition to this on-the-job experience, the trainee is returned to Detroit four times during the year for one week of classroom type instruction and to "compare notes" and review individual progress with members of upper management.

Gary was assigned to a branch operation in Indianapolis, Indiana, and was under the direct supervision of Mr. Clayton Thomas, the branch manager. Mr. Thomas, 55, had been with Bellingham for thirty-two years, having joined the company at the end of World War II. He had not attended college, but had worked his way "up the ranks" and believed that this way of making it into management provided better training for a management position than the company's one year rotation program. Gary was assigned to perform various jobs in the branch but not according to the planned program. Gary was asked to "fill-in" as needed and he became very concerned about not receiving the type of training required to prepare him for his first management position.

During his second trip to headquarters for a one-week training session, Gary discussed his problem with the Coordinator of Management Training and Development, John Wilson. Mr. Wilson assured Gary that he would look into the matter.

On his return to the branch, Gary was severely reprimanded by Mr. Thomas for discussing his problem with Mr. Wilson. The conversation proceeded as follows:

Mr. Thomas: "Gary, why did you discuss your problems with John Wilson? You work for me, at least as long as you are at this branch."

Gary: "I don't know—I guess I was just frustrated with the training I have received."

Mr. Thomas: "You are just like a lot of young college graduates. You think your degree should entitle you to special treatment. Well, I'm sorry, but in my book it doesn't mean a thing."

Gary: "What should I do now?"

Mr. Thomas: "Go back to work and don't cause any more trouble."

Questions

1. What action do you think Gary Jones should take?
2. To what extent should Mr. Wilson have discussed Gary's problem with the local branch manager, Mr. Thomas?
3. What evidence is there of a breakdown in communication between the branch office and the intentions of headquarters? Discuss.

THE
CONTROLLING
FUNCTION

5

The fourth management function is presented in Part 5. You will appreciate how important the controlling function is and learn how it closely interrelates to the planning function.

Chapter 12

KEY TERMS

control

control process

standards

quantity control

quality standard

time standards

budgetary standards

initial controls

overseeing controls

comparison controls

strategic control points

inappropriate controls

budget

financial budget

operating budget

cash budget

capital budget

planning-programming budgeting system

zero base budgeting

Management and Control

LEARNING OBJECTIVES

After completing this chapter, you should be able to

1. Describe the factors involved in the basic control process.
2. Explain why the planning and controlling functions are so closely related.
3. State the procedure for setting strategic control points.
4. List and briefly describe the ways actual performance may be compared to standards.
5. Explain the importance of a properly developed budget for a manager.
6. Describe how the process of control varies for different levels of management.
7. List the techniques which are beneficial in administering disciplinary action.

The fact that you know exactly where you desire to go and have created a beautiful plan to get there does not mean your objectives will automatically be achieved. The final function of management is concerned with ensuring that results are achieved according to plan. This is known as the control process. Stated another way, controls provide the manager with the means of finding out if the tasks are performed properly. One might think that if the functions of planning, organizing, and directing are completed satisfactorily, there would be little need for the control function. This could not be further from the truth! Events often occur which have not been considered in managerial planning. Controls provide management with the capability of recognizing a deviation from a plan. Then, a manager is in a position to make the necessary corrections that will bring the situation back into agreement with the objectives for which the plan was initially developed.

> Joan Lynwood, the keypunch supervisor for Multifact Productions, has recently observed that the number of keypunch errors in her department has exceeded the 3 percent standard during the past week.

> Robert Seay, a department head for State University, has just been advised that he has exceeded his annual travel budget by $500.

> Alyson Sanders, a nursing supervisor for McGovern Regional Medical Center, has noticed that her employees have exceeded the number of overtime hours allocated to the department by fifty hours.

In the above situations, standards had been established that enabled managers to recognize that potential problems existed and to exercise the control function when necessary to correct the deviation. Joan may have discovered that one of the keypunch operators was experiencing personal problems which resulted in the operator making excessive errors. Robert can explain his difficulty because he has had to do extensive recruiting to fill two new faculty positions. Alyson realizes that she must cut back on the number of overtime hours because they are not actually needed. A properly designed control system alerts managers of the existence of potential problems and permits them to take corrective actions when necessary. The control function, therefore, is a valuable part of the management process.

This chapter will first concentrate on the basic control process. Next, the various types of controls that are available to the manager will be discussed. Procedures for establishing strategic control points will then be provided, followed by a discussion of the importance of budgets to a manager. Finally, an appreciation of the effects of disciplinary action on

> **INSIGHTS TO SUCCESS**
>
> After people in an organization reach a certain level of productivity, I feel that extraordinary incentives must be used to move them up one more notch, such as good "down and up" communication, perhaps part ownership in the company, achievement recognition, etc.
>
> JOHN W. DIXON, President and Chairman, E-Systems, Incorporated

members of an organization will be discussed. The overall objective of the chapter is to provide the student of management with a clear understanding of the need for adequate controls within the firm.

THE NATURE OF CONTROL

control

Control is the process of comparing actual performance with established standards for the purpose of taking action to correct deviations. For instance, Joan Lynwood, the keypunch supervisor, knew that if the number of defects was above the 3 percent standard, a potential control problem existed. Thus, effective control requires comparing actual performance with preestablished goals. If results differ from established standards, corrective action may need to be taken.

Effective control depends on sound planning by management. As we discussed in chapter 2, objectives and plans provide the basis for the control process. The ultimate goal of the control function is to ensure that the objectives of the organization are achieved. As such, the planning and control functions are highly dependent on each other. Plans must be properly prepared and in agreement with the objectives of the firm. Controls ensure that actions undertaken to implement the plans are correct.

Referring again to the planning model discussed in chapter 2 (see Figure 12.1), it can be seen that standards are the end result of the planning process. Before standards can be established, objectives or goals must first be developed. These objectives serve as the desired end results. Next, long-range plans are created to specify the manner in which objectives are to be accomplished. Appropriate policies, procedures, and rules must be created to state, in greater detail, the manner in which the goals will be achieved. Finally, standards must be developed to determine if the various aspects of the plan have been achieved. But, whereas standards are the end result of planning, they provide the starting point for the control process. Thus, *standards serve as the link between planning and control* (see Figure 12.2).

FIGURE 12.1
The Planning Process

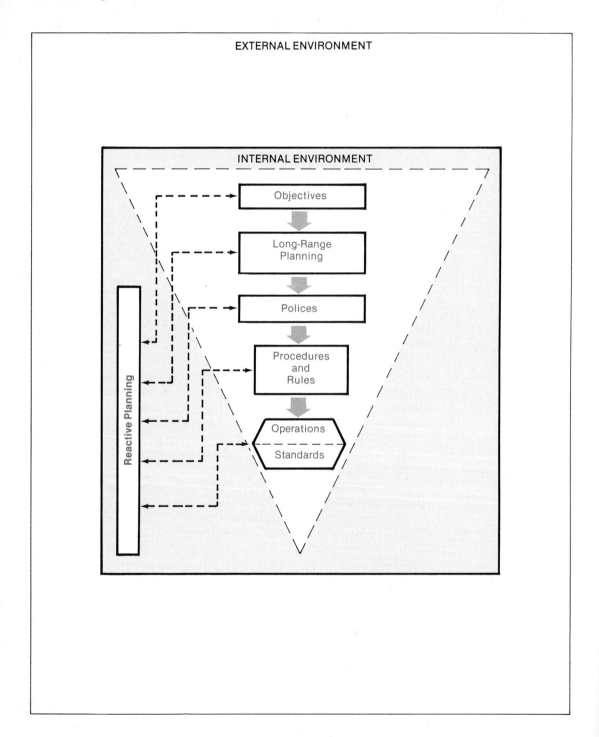

FIGURE 12.2
The Planning and Control Process

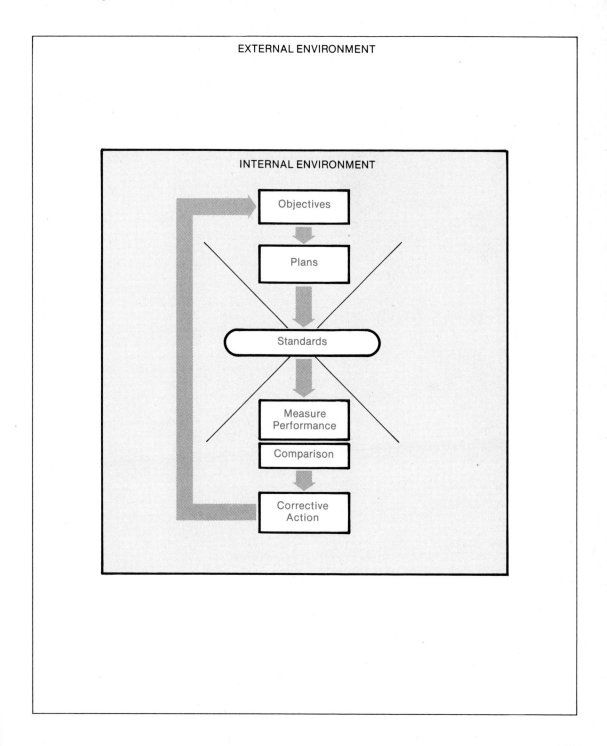

JOAN D. MANLEY

Group Vice-President, Books, Time Inc.
Chairman of the Board, Time-Life Books Inc.

TIME The woman behind the books at Time Inc. is Joan Manley, currently a group vice-president where she is responsible for all book publishing activities in the company. Mrs. Manley is the chief executive officer of Time-Life Books Inc., one of the ten largest nongovernment book publishers in the world. This is quite a rapid progression for a person who graduated from the University of California in 1954 with an A.B. in English and history. Joan then entered the business world as a secretary, the experience of which she says has been invaluable. "Being a secretary to the right person is an extremely good position," she said. "I have always felt it is a good place to spend some years, for either sex."

Joan joined Time-Life Books as an assistant to the publisher when it was first established as a separate division of Time Inc. in 1960. In 1963, she was named circulation manager and in 1966 circulation director. Her reputation as a skilled professional grew rapidly and in 1970, Joan became publisher of Time-Life Books and in 1971, was chosen as the first woman vice-president of Time Inc. In 1975, she became the first woman to hold a group vice-presidency.

Joan says the two most important parts of her job are long-term planning and the selection and training of key personnel. "A chief executive's problem is always in the future, not in the present. If I am paying attention to today's problems, it means I didn't do something properly a few years ago. Of course, part of planning is correcting and adjusting. You can't glue yourself to a plan. You must always reassess and readjust the emphasis."

"On people—guessing right and then maximizing their individual assets is the key." Joan says, "One of the keys to being a good boss is not to get in the hair of the people who are actually doing the work." She admits she sometimes finds it difficult to step aside so others won't "find me in their path."

Conventional wisdom has it that committees are the types of organizations that put together camels when various members want horses, cows, elephants, or sheep. Joan Manley disagrees. She believes that the use of committees can improve communication and decision making. Time-Life Books spends two to four million dollars on a series of books before the first copy is shipped. All the various departments have to be convinced that the chances for success are good before such an investment can be justified. "Wherever an enterprise requires a variety of talents, it's best to have them in agreement. An adversary role can at times be productive, but most of the time it's not. Decision making by committee is not a cop-out. Its value is in specialization and pooling of talents."

She attributes her success to three factors: her skill in bringing out the best in other people, her good luck in working for talented and bright bosses, and the women's movement. "The women's movement has become shrill, but its timing has benefited me personally." Joan is childless by choice. She says she is certain many women could have children and at the same time exercise the type of responsibility she does. "But, I can answer only for myself. I personally would find it extremely difficult to raise children and have this kind of job. I don't think I could do both."

THE PROCESS OF CONTROL

control process   The **control process** involves three critical areas: establishment of standards, comparison of performance to standard, and taking corrective action. A discussion of each phase follows.

ESTABLISHMENT OF STANDARDS

standards   There can be no control process without standards. **Standards** specify the type of performance results that are desired. As such, they must be tied closely to organizational objectives. For instance, a clothing manufacturer may have a goal of achieving 10 percent of the market share for men's suits. If the forecasted sales for the industry is $500 million, then the objective of the company is to achieve sales of $50 million. This $50 million then becomes a standard by which to measure performance, but if it is not broken down into controllable units, this goal may be difficult to achieve.

Specific standards for the different sales managers might be allocated as follows: Northern District, $15 million; Southern District, $10 million; Eastern District, $12 million; and Western District, $13 million. Progressing still further in establishing standards, each district manager will likely assign a sales quota to their sales representatives. For instance, Joe Drake, a sales representative for the State of Missouri, might be given a sales quota (standard) of $500,000. Through this process of progressive controls the company will be in a position to realize where difficulties may exist in accomplishing their objectives.

You may also establish standards to assist you in maintaining a high grade point average. Your objective may be to obtain a 3.0 average. This objective then becomes a standard by which actual performance may be measured. You have numerous combinations by which to obtain the 3.0 average. All the grades may be a *B* or they may be half *A*'s and half *C*'s. By establishing standards, you are then in a position to allocate your time in the proper manner to achieve the objective. For instance, you may find it best to make all *B*'s rather than spend the extra time on some courses to make an *A* and perhaps make a *D* in another course because insufficient time was available.

ACTUAL PERFORMANCE COMPARED TO STANDARDS

It does little good to have standards unless actual performance is compared to these standards. In an organization, the most important means by

quantity control

quality standard
time standards
budgetary standards

which performance can be compared to standards relate to: (1) quantity, (2) quality, (3) time, and (4) budget (cost.). With **quantity control,** the standard has been established in terms of volume or numbers. The **quality standard** for a product relates to degrees of conformity to such factors as form, dimension, composition, and color. **Time standards** entail monitoring the time that is required to complete a project. **Budgetary standards** are concerned with the comparison of actual to planned expenditures. While the importance of each one is likely to depend on the goals of the firm, all types are typically being used to varying degrees in business. It is likely that a combination of these four types will be in use at any one time within the firm.

CORRECTIVE ACTION

If no significant deviations are discovered, the manager only needs to continue to monitor the activity. Corrective action is needed to either correct deviations from planned performance or alter the plan to allow for obstacles that cannot be removed. The goal is to restore effective, coordinated action.

There are two general types of corrective action—immediate and basic. The type most frequently recognized is the immediate; something must be done now to correct the situation and get back on track. For example, a particular project is a week behind schedule and, if not corrected, will seriously affect other projects. The first problem is not to worry about who caused the difficulty, but rather to get the project back on schedule. Depending on the authority of the official concerned, the following corrective actions may be ordered: (1) overtime hours may be authorized for project personnel; (2) additional personnel and equipment may be allocated; (3) a full-time director may be assigned to personally push the project through; (4) an extra effort may be asked from all personnel, perhaps through the use of participation approaches; or, (5) if all these fail, the schedule may have to be readjusted, thereby requiring changes all along the line.

After the degree of stress has lessened through any of the above measures, attention can then be devoted to the second type of corrective action. Just how and why did events stray from their planned course? What can be done to prevent a recurrence of this type of difficulty? Many managers fail at this phase. Too often they find themselves "putting out daily fires" and they never discover the actual cause of the problem. For instance, managers may find themselves having to constantly interview and hire new people to replace those that are leaving the firm. A manager may be working twelve hours a day attempting to locate new employees. But, the high turnover problem is not solved merely by employing new personnel. The manager must take some type of corrective action after he or she has determined what has actually caused the high turnover. A supervisor may be extremely difficult to work with or the pay scale may not be competitive for the area. Whatever the problem, it must be identified and corrected or the high turnover problem is likely to continue. The dull work of basic corrective action must be done for the sake of future economical and effective operations.

As illustrated by the project that was not on schedule, the manager may discover various fundamental causes for the difficulty. The schedule may not have been met because of a continuing difficulty in one department. Or, it may be discovered that not only was this particular project in trouble, but most of the projects in this company are behind schedule. In the first event, investigation may reveal that poor equipment in the one department or poor control on the part of the department supervisor is the major source of trouble. Thus, basic corrective actions would involve new or improved equipment or new or improved management. The project that initially revealed the difficulty will not likely be helped by this action; however, future projects should be improved.

If most of the projects in a firm are usually behind schedule, an even more serious type of basic corrective action may be demanded. There may be a drastic overhaul of general control procedures or a reexamination and reconstitution of sales policies and relationships between sales and production control. There might even be a reorganization of the entire company.

SPECIFIC TYPES OF CONTROL

The control function can be divided into three basic types—initial, overseeing, and comparison controls. *Initial controls* take place as resources enter the organization. *Overseeing controls* are used during the process when the products and services are being produced. *Comparison controls* are used after the final product or service has been produced. Each type of control will next be briefly discussed along with specific means available to accomplish the control process.

Initial Controls

initial controls

The manager uses **initial controls** primarily as a preventative measure. With initial controls, an attempt is made to monitor the resources— material, human, and capital—that come into the organization for the purpose of ensuring that they can be used effectively to achieve organizational objectives. An effort is made to control the resources that enter the organization. Specific types of initial controls will be described next.

Material Controls The material resources an organization requires must meet specified quality standards and be available when needed by the firm. If Ethan Allen purchased lower quality wood with which to manufacture furniture, their image for producing high quality furniture could not be maintained. In order to assist in ensuring material control, statistical sampling is often used (to be discussed in greater detail in chapter 14). With statistical sampling, a portion of the items received into the firm are studied in an attempt to estimate the quality of the entire lot. For instance, a certain percentage of lumber (say 5 percent) would be studied to estimate the quality of all lumber received. The quality and reliability of material can be determined with acceptable accuracy without having to expend the time and resources to inspect each item.

Personnel Selection Controls If a firm is to maintain its present level of operations, there must continue to be an infusion of new personnel into the company. This constant search for new employees is caused by such factors as deaths, retirements, loss of employees to other organizations, and any growth that the firm is experiencing. In order to obtain new people who are capable of sustaining the organization, certain controls must be established regarding the selection of individuals employed by the firm. Skill requirements of each job must be determined and new employees should meet or exceed these skills before being employed. It would likely do little good to hire an accountant to fill an electrical engineering position or vice versa. Controls are needed to ensure that the skill level and job requirement are matched.

Capital Controls The firm must have sufficient capital available to achieve its objectives. Equipment must be obtained and financed. However, when funds are expended on capital goods, we are exchanging today's dollars in the anticipation of future profits. A firm wants to purchase capital equipment that will produce the greatest cost savings or profit for the company. This is no easy matter when we are looking into the future. However, there are numerous techniques available to assess capital expenditure alternatives. One of the most useful approaches takes into consideration the time value of money (a dollar received today is more valuable than a dollar received ten years into the future). The procedure for using net present value and the benefits of the technique will be described in chapter 13.

Overseeing Controls

overseeing controls

Overseeing controls are used to monitor the actual creation of products or services. This type of control is accomplished largely by observation and

*The greatest
opportunity for the
discovery and
correction of undesired
deviations takes place
while the work is being
performed.*

by conference between supervisor and subordinate. Overseeing controls occur as the actual work activities are being performed. A large portion of the operating manager's time is devoted to this function.

The greatest opportunity for the discovery and correction of undesired deviations takes place while the work is being performed. If an entire lot of fifty units is completed by a worker, and inspection reveals that all fifty are too small, there is little that can be done about it. If, during the operation, someone has personally checked the work, much material and labor would have been saved. The amount of overseeing necessary depends on such factors as skill and attitude of the worker, the skill of the manager, and the discipline of the workplace.

Comparison Controls

comparison controls

Comparison is the function of determining the degree of agreement between performance results and performance standards and can take place on or away from the point of operation. It can be applied to the cumulative performance results of departments or of the entire organization. The objective of **comparison controls** is to determine whether deviations from plans have taken place, and, if necessary, to bring them to the attention of the responsible managers.

There are several differences between the overseeing and comparison phases of control. Both involve relating what is going on to what should be going on. Overseeing occurs while the work is in progress. Comparison comes later and relies on information received after a step in the project is completed or on the results of the entire project.

A second difference between the two functions occurs as a result of the contrast in timing. Overseeing has to be accomplished by the immediate supervisor. Comparison, however, can be done not only by the supervisor but also by higher line managers or various staff officials. Because it relies on reporting, it can be separated physically from the point of operation.

Finally, overseeing requires face-to-face contacts and personal observation as the method of obtaining information. The manager must evaluate work in both qualitative and quantitative terms and must be adept in human relation skills. Comparison, however, is usually concerned with only a quantitative and statistical evaluation of actions that have reached some state of completion. A monthly production report comparison of the quality of all parts for three shifts is provided in Figure 12.3. As can be seen, Shifts I and II are above the 90 percent standard, while Shift III is slightly below standard. Though observation can be used to gain such information, it more frequently involves written reports, charts, graphs, and similar forms of communication. Specific types of comparison controls will be described next.

Evaluation of Employee Performance Given a particular task to be accomplished, we would all likely perform at different levels of efficiency. Just as one student may be quite proficient in English and another in math, we all have different abilities. But, if we are to improve, we must know our deficiencies and determine what can be done to overcome these obstacles. An effective employee performance system is a means of control whereby an individual learns of his or her strengths and weaknesses and is told what should be done to overcome deficiencies. Employee performance evaluation systems that give each worker the same ratings do not benefit the individual who is a superior performer nor does it assist the substandard worker who desires to improve.

FIGURE 12.3
Monthly Quality Comparison Report by Shifts

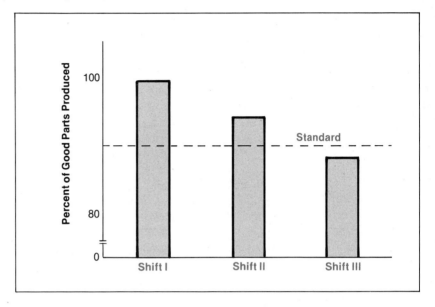

Quotas Much of comparison control relates to quotas that have been established for individuals, units, departments, or divisions. Sales quotas specify the amount of sales an individual, district or region is expected to sell. Production quotas specify the amount of an item that needs to be produced. Control of quotas at every level is important if the organization is to achieve its objectives.

Statistical Quality Control The purpose of quality control is to ensure that a certain level of excellence is attained. Statistics are one of the primary tools at the disposal of a manager to identify deviations in quality. As greater levels of quality are built into a product, costs increase significantly. It is, therefore, quite important to identify in the planning stage what quality level is desired to meet company objectives.

For example, there are significant differences in the quality of watches, and of course, the higher the quality the greater the cost. An individual who purchases a high quality watch may desire a time piece that may deviate only a few seconds during an entire year. On the other hand, a student may purchase a watch of lesser quality because he or she does not see the importance of being a few minutes early or late for class, feeling perhaps that the instructor will tell the same joke again at the first of the class.

Network Controls A means by which the progress of a particular project may be monitored is referred to as network controls. With network controls critical areas of a project can be identified and carefully monitored to assure a successful completion time. Two of the best known means of network controls are PERT and CPM which will be described in chapter 14.

Controls Through Financial Analysis The financial statement provides valuable information with regard to whether a company, department, or unit is effectively utilizing its financial resources. Intelligent interpretation of financial data provides an excellent means through which management can control its financial welfare. In order to analyze the financial position a firm would likely begin with ratio analysis. Financial ratio analysis provides management with a basis for comparing current to past performance. In addition, financial ratios can be compared not only to past trends within the company, but also to other divisions within the company and to other firms in the industry. If the ratios are not in line with what is considered acceptable, the manager is in a position to make corrections. There are four basic types of ratios:

- *Liquidity ratios* measure a firm's ability to meet its current obligations.
- *Leverage ratios* measure whether a firm has effectively used outside financing.
- *Activity ratios* measure how efficiently the firm is utilizing its resources.
- *Profitability ratios* measure the overall operating efficiency and profitability of the firm.[1]

ESTABLISHING STRATEGIC CONTROL POINTS

Management is concerned with directing and monitoring a system comprised of resources, processes, activities, and outputs. The problem that management often encounters is the determination of the phases of the system that should be monitored. However, this is not always that easy. Theoretically, every resource, processing activity, and output should be measured, reported, and compared to some predetermined standard. This can be extremely costly and time consuming as all activities are not

---

1. For an excellent discussion of financial ratios see J. Fred Weston and Eugene F. Brigham, *Managerial Finance*, 6th ed. (Hinsdale, Ill.: The Dryden Press, 1978), pp. 23–62.

strategic control points

equally important. A manager must determine what to measure and when to measure an activity. These critical areas will be referred to as **strategic control points.** It is an area that must be monitored if accomplishment of the organization's major objectives is to be achieved.

These control points have a number of basic characteristics. First, it is a point established to regulate key operations or events. If a difficulty occurs at these strategic control points, the entire operation may grind to a halt. For instance, if the personnel manager does not control the quantity and quality of employees that are to be employed by the company, an inferior product may result even though the material inputs are of a superior quality.

**QUALITIES NEEDED FOR SUCCESS
AS A MANAGER IN YOUR ORGANIZATION**

· Willingness to make a decision
· Ability to weed out the wheat from the chaff before deciding on a course of action
· Desire to apply the above talents to the job

ROBERT J. SWEENEY, President, Murphy Oil Corporation

A second major characteristic of a strategic control point is that it must be capable of identifying problems prior to serious damage occurring. If the control point is properly located, action can be taken to stop or alter a defective process before major harm is done. It does little good to discover after the fact that a million defective parts have been produced. The control point should be located so deviations can be quickly identified and corrections made.

In the early days of one of the authors' careers, he had the opportunity of observing how the improper selection of strategic control points virtually caused a major tire manufacturer to be forced to cease operation. In the manufacture of a tire, four basic phases were required (see Figure 12.4). The mixing department must obtain the proper blend of rubber for the type of tire that is being produced. The tread is then shaped with specific attention being given to length, width, and thickness. The next phase, building, entails placing the various components such as the tread, steel belting and white walls together. In the molding department, the tires are heated and shaped into final form.

A major problem occurred which forced the tire company to reevaluate their entire control procedure. The old system of control consisted only of

FIGURE 12.4
Example of Placement of Strategic Control Points

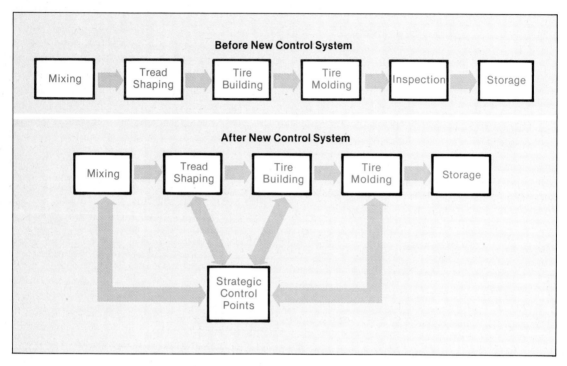

inspecting tires after they had been molded. Because there was already a large investment in a tire at this stage, a tire would have to have a major defect before it would be rejected. Recognition of the deficiency in the control process occurred when the tire manufacturing firm received an order for several million dollars from a company that purchased tires and sold them at retail outlets under a different brand name. The retail chain, after careful inspection of the tires, rejected the order and demanded that the entire batch be redone. The tire manufacturing firm nearly went out of business because of this decision. Due to the large investment that was tied up in rejected inventory, the firm had to go heavily into debt to reaccomplish the order.

It was after this experience that major changes were made in the control process. A separate quality control department, reporting directly to the president, was established. Quality control inspectors were hired and given authority to stop operations, even over the advice of the production superintendent, if they felt it was needed to maintain high quality. Strategic control points were located in the four major departments (see Figure 12.4). If a problem occurred in the mixing department, it would be discovered before the tire progressed through the other stages. Because of this intensive effort to improve quality the firm was able to survive and prosper.

A third consideration concerning the choice of strategic control points suggests that they should indicate the level of performance for a broad spectrum of key events. At times, this comprehensiveness conflicts with the need for proper timing. Net profit, for example, is a comprehensive strategic control point, indicating the progress of the entire enterprise. Yet, if one waits until the regular accounting period to obtain this figure, one loses control of the immediate future. It does little good to recognize that you are now bankrupt; you need to have accounting figures ahead of time so that corrective action may be taken.

Economy is the fourth consideration in the choice of proper control points. With computer and management information systems available, there is a strong temptation to demand every conceivable bit of organizational information. But there is only a limited amount of information that an executive can effectively use. If every bit of information is available to the executive, it is quite possible that critical information will be lost in the masses of data. Simply stated, "You can't see the forest for the trees."

Finally, the selection of various strategic control points should be balanced. If only credit losses are watched and controlled, for example, sales may suffer because of an overly stringent policy in accepting credit risks. If sales are emphasized out of proportion, then credit losses will mount. There is a tendency to place tight control over tangible functions, such as production and sales, while maintaining limited control over the intangible functions such as personnel development and other staff services. This often leads to a state of imbalance where production line executives are held to exact standards, and staff executives are seemingly given "blank checks."

CONTROL AND LEVELS OF MANAGEMENT

A manager, unless he or she is the president or chief executive officer, links two levels of organization. As may be seen in Figure 12.5, each management level plans for, organizes, and directs the lower level. Lower levels of management of course require more specific planning, organizing, and directing. The higher level manager issues orders to a lower level supervisor to accomplish tasks generally planned by top management. As tasks are accomplished, results are provided both the immediate supervisor and the other levels of management. This enables the immediate supervisor to control within the limits of his or her specific plan. The immediate supervisor must then provide the information to higher management to ensure that higher level plans are being fulfilled. This infor-

FIGURE 12.5
Organization Levels and Linking Management Functions

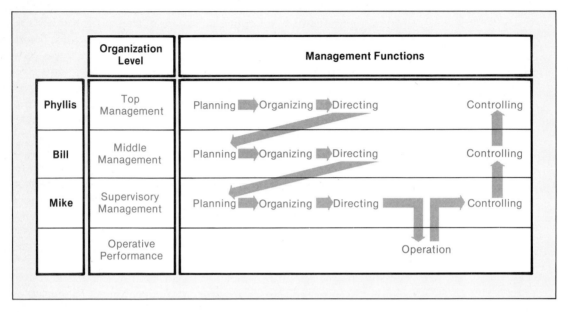

Source Edwin B. Flippo and Gary M. Munsinger, *Management,* 4th ed. (Boston: Allyn and Bacon, Inc., 1978), p. 461.

mation enables each level of management to determine if the actions of the lower levels are conforming to general plans and objectives and if corrective measures need to be taken.

Let us now progress through an illustration of the types of controls a person confronts as he or she moves from a supervisory management position to a top management position. Mike Miller is a shift foreman for a firm that manufactures aluminum window and door frames. Each Monday, Mike is provided a weekly schedule of items that must be produced each day for that week. With this schedule, Mike plans, organizes, and directs the activities that must be accomplished this week. He knows the standards that have been established for each piece of equipment and monitors each of his employees to ensure that the correct number of frames are being manufactured. If an employee is deficient in any task, Mike must take immediate corrective action to ensure that the daily and weekly schedules are achieved. Each day, Mike sends a report of activities to the general manager, Bill Alexander.

Bill Alexander supervises the activities of ten shift foremen within a division. He must plan, organize, and direct the efforts of the shift foremen. As such, he works in a much longer time frame and views his task as coordinating the work of the foreman. He studies the reports of each of the foremen and determines if they need help to solve particular problems. If a foreman is consistently below standard, Bill will analyze the situation to determine what action must be taken. Rarely will any decision be made entirely on one day's performance of one of the shifts, but the general overall trend is studied. Bill submits a weekly performance report of his sections to Phyllis Towne, the vice-president of operations.

Phyllis also accomplishes the various functions of management, but from a different perspective. She has five divisions reporting directly to her. She views control as that of ensuring that the overall objectives of the firm are achieved. She attempts to ensure that a consistent level of quality is maintained, but she must also consider the cost of reaching the quality standard. Her plans tend to be longer in nature and she views controls as assisting her in solving problems that the divisions may be unable to handle. For instance, if quality is declining because of an aging piece of equipment, she has the authority to purchase new machinery. She is only slightly concerned with the day-to-day operations of the plants.

REASONS FOR NEGATIVE REACTIONS TO CONTROLS

Although strategic control points and the various types of control that we have discussed are important in effective management, controls are often viewed in a negative way by employees being "controlled." When the term "controls" is mentioned, it makes some of us realize that other people have the power to regulate our activities. There is a natural resistance toward controls because a certain amount of individual freedom has been taken away. But in business, some controls are necessary if the organization is to accomplish its objectives in the most effective manner. Employees may not like to be controlled, but they will likely accept the fact that some controls are necessary if the organization is to function successfully. It is when controls are established which are inappropriate, unattainable, unpredictable, uncontrolled, or contradictory that major negative resistance is encountered.[2]

INAPPROPRIATE CONTROLS

inappropriate controls

Controls that do not conform to the needs of the situation are referred to as **inappropriate controls.** In many instances, workers recognize before management where controls need to be placed if efficiency is to be

2. Robert N. Anthony and Regina E. Herzlinger, *Management Control in Non-Profit Organizations* (Homewood, Illinois: Irwin, 1975), pp. 222–226.

increased. Inappropriate controls can inhibit the accomplishment of the goals of a department or unit within the organization. For instance, in one firm because of an immediate need for more highly trained machine operators, the control system was changed from a measurement of skill level to one that measured numbers of machine operators that were "trained." Many more workers completed the training program, but there was considerable grumbling among the production foremen because the skill level of the machine operators had actually declined. True, more people were available to run the machines, but performance had dropped to the point that the quality level could not be attained. The controls that had been established were inappropriate to meet the needs of the situation.

UNATTAINABLE STANDARDS

Employees realize when a standard is unrealistic. When unattainable controls are established, it may actually cause some employees to work below their capabilities. Realizing that a standard cannot be achieved, workers may view unrealistic controls as a means of lowering their productivity. Resentment is created because the standards were unattainable.

UNPREDICTABLE STANDARDS

When the control system is unpredictable and constantly changed, much frustration and resentment to the control process can result. For instance, if a production manager is told that he should strive to achieve maximum output and once this high output level has been achieved, told that quality is more important, resentment to the control process can result. The production manager could not predict what standard he was to be evaluated on.

NO CONTROL OVER THE SITUATION

A most frustrating encounter that can occur to anyone is to be reprimanded for something that he or she cannot control. Suppose, for instance, that a manager is told that he will be evaluated regarding the profit and loss of his department, but he does not have the authority to change budget items. Frustration becomes extremely high in instances such as these and can work to the detriment of the entire control system.

CONTRADICTORY STANDARDS

At times, various controls may be established that do not complement each other. It may appear to the manager that if one standard is achieved that it would be impossible to accomplish the other. For instance it might appear to some managers that high quality and maximum output are contradictory in nature. To a marketing manager, a control system that stresses both increased sales and reducing the uncollectable debts rate may appear contradictory.

OVERCOMING NEGATIVE REACTIONS TO CONTROLS

Although there are numerous reasons that may cause people to resist controls, there are also means which a manager can use to assist in reducing negative reactions to controls. While some of the reasons discussed below may appear obvious, the lack of effectiveness of some control systems makes it clear that they are not observed at times. Some of the basic means through which negative reactions to controls may be overcome are discussed next.

JUSTIFIABLE

If employees believe that there is a need for a particular control system, compliance is much easier to obtain. For instance, the firm may have to increase the quality of their product in order to obtain future contracts. These contracts will not only mean profit for the firm but job stability for the employees. A control system will have higher acceptability if the reason for the control appears justifiable to those who must comply.

UNDERSTANDABLE

Employees who know exactly what is expected of them with regard to a control system tend to exhibit less resistance. For instance, a statement by a manager that quality should increase does not clearly convey what is expected. A requirement that the number of defects should decrease by 10 percent is precise and understandable. It is when workers do not understand what is expected of them that frustration and resentment can occur.

REALISTIC

A realistic control system is one that permits the organization to achieve its goals and is also obtainable by the employees who work within the control system. For example, at times it may appear that controls are established merely to harass the worker. Excessive standards that are higher than needed to accomplish the purpose of the organization are not only expensive, but often resisted by company employees.

TIMELY

For a control system to be effective, information regarding deviations needs to be communicated to employees as quickly as practical. It does little good to tell a person that his or her performance was below standard three weeks ago. If a problem is to be corrected, it must receive immediate attention.

ACCURATE

Nothing could be worse than to have a control system that provides inaccurate information. If information feedback from the control system has proven incorrect in the past, it may be difficult to convince a person that his or her efforts are below standards. If students consistently find grading errors of a professor, belief in his grading system may be questioned. A student who receives a D may have reason to suspect the grade is inaccurate even if it is not.

DISCIPLINARY ACTION: GUIDELINES FOR MANAGEMENT

John Phillip, a machine operator for Terry Manufacturing, was not wearing his safety glasses when his supervisor came to his work area. The glasses are required by a company directive to be worn by all personnel when working in that particular location of the plant.

Jodi Haun, an accounts receivable specialist for Southeast Utilities, has arrived one hour late for work four times this week and it is only Thursday. She has never called in to explain the reason for being late.

Betty Garcia, an airline hostess for Tree Top Airline, has been advised that the public relations office has received a large number of passenger complaints regarding her attitude and performance on the plane.

In the above three instances, a potential for disciplinary action exists. However, because the details of each circumstance are not known, a person cannot readily determine if disciplinary action is actually required. But, if a control system did not exist to identify problems when they occurred, potential problems would go unrecognized. The purpose of establishing controls is to determine if deviations have taken place regarding a particular standard. It follows that a natural by-product of controls is disciplinary action.

We all have different visions of what is meant by disciplinary action. Perhaps as a child you did not do what your parents wanted and received a severe scolding or spanking. In business, the purpose of disciplinary action takes on a similar, but perhaps broader connotation. But disciplinary action continues to have negative connotations for most people. In a business sense, it is a penalty that is applied to assure conformity in future actions. However, disciplinary action should be used as a type of education to influence favorable behavior in the future and not as a form of punishment. Many of the problems a manager faces relate to disciplinary actions. Approximately half of all grievance cases appealed to an impartial arbitrator by labor unions involve disciplinary action. Management's decisions are overturned in approximately half of these cases. It is evident from the above statistics that managers are not applying disciplinary action in a manner that is generally acceptable.

Because of the difficulties that often arise, managers have identified guides to assist in handling disciplinary cases. Some of these are listed here:

- The manager should exhibit the attitude of assuming that all employees desire to conform to reasonable organization requirements. One should not appear to invite trouble.
- The act, rather than the person, should be condemned.
- Although the act may be the basis for penalty, a model of future desired behavior should be communicated.
- Reasonable promptness is important so that the employee can connect the penalty to the violation.
- A managerial listening role is highly essential to (a) effect greater understanding of the reasons for the act, and (b) prevent hasty decisions that may lead to unjustified penalties.
- Negative disciplinary action should be administered in private so that the employee can save face among colleagues.
- Definite, but tactful, follow-up should occur to determine the degree of success of the conditioning effort.
- Consistency and flexibility, though apparently contradictory, are both desirable elements of a superior's style of disciplining.

INSIGHTS TO SUCCESS

1. Develop a strong personal commitment to excellence.
2. Generate a drive and desire that will create a willingness to make personal sacrifices and do more than expected.
3. Dedicate yourself to be the "best the company has ever had" in whatever position you may be in. We move from successes.
4. Never stop studying and learning—continue to "grow."

WALTER S. BRAGER, Group Vice-President, Regional Management & Operations, Oscar Mayer & Company

The last guide deserves further discussion as it relates to the situational approach to management. A manager has at his or her disposal numerous styles which are available to handle disciplinary action. These styles range from a strictly legalistic one in which rules are made to be enforced, to a purely humanitarian approach which is based on the concept that rules are for educational, guidance, and developmental purposes. For instance, John Phillip's supervisor might say, "If I find you without your safety glasses again, the company regulations state that I am supposed to fire you." On the other extreme, the supervisor could see the situation as a learning experience and say, "John, when this machinery is running, small pieces of metal are thrown into the air. Before the company required safety glasses, there were five machinists who had eye damage as a result of particles of metal being thrown into the air. I think it is a good rule and believe you would want to wear your safety glasses from now on." However, on a general basis, it is likely that an effective supervisor should be neither completely legalistic nor completely humanitarian.

CONTROLLING AND THE BUDGETING PROCESS

Though there are many devices that managers can use in controlling costs or expenditures, perhaps the most widely known and used is the budget. Most of us have a general impression of what is referred to as the budgeting process. Perhaps you earn $75 a week working part time at a local grocery store while attending college. Since you buy most of your own clothes and lead a very active social life, you must allocate or budget your income to achieve the goal of maximum satisfaction. If you go over budget in one area, for example by buying four new shirts, you may find that you cannot afford those exciting dates on Friday and Saturday nights.

budget   A **budget** is merely a formal statement of financial resources—planned expenditures of money for personnel, time, space, or equipment. Budgetary control is concerned with the comparison of actual to planned expenditures. Most areas of operations in a business enterprise—sales, production, materials, labor, manufacturing expense, capital expenditures, and cash—can be reduced to expenditures in the budget.

TYPES OF BUDGETS

financial budget
operating budget

In many organizations, budgets are the primary document used by managers in planning and controlling operations. There are basically two broad categories of budgets: **financial budget** and **operating budget.** An overview of the components of these two types of budgets is provided in Figure 12.6.

FIGURE 12.6
Types of Budgets

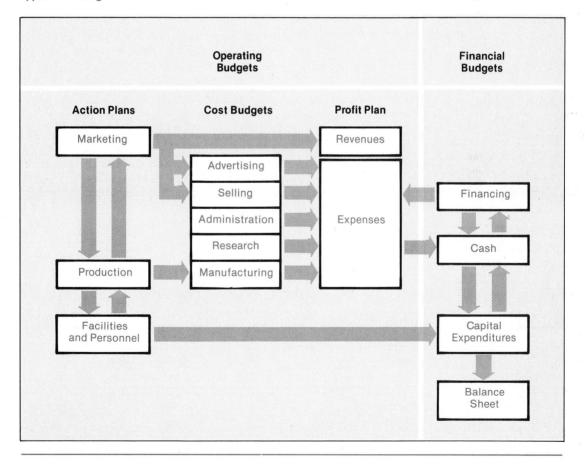

From Gordon Shillinglaw, *Managerial Cost Accounting*, 4th ed. (Homewood, Ill.: Richard D. Irwin, 1977), p. 137. Copyright © 1977 by Richard D. Irwin, Inc.

- *Operating budgets* indicate the revenues and expenses the business expects from producing goods and services during a given year. As illustrated in Figure 12.6, these budgets consist of action plans, cost budgets, and a profit plan.

- *Financial budgets* indicate the amount of capital the organization will need and where it will obtain the capital. Two financial budgets are usually developed. These are the **cash budget** and the **capital budget.** The cash budget summarizes planned cash receipts and disbursements while capital budget indicates planned capital acquisition usually for the purpose of purchasing additional facilities or equipment.

AN ILLUSTRATION OF BUDGETARY CONTROL

The use of a budget as a control device is relatively simple. Figure 12.7 shows the monthly budget for a keypunch department. The major expense items include direct labor (wages for the unit's keypunch operators), indirect labor (the department manager's salary), operating supplies (keypunch cards), maintenance expenses (repair of machines), and miscellaneous expense. As shown in Figure 12.7, actual expenditures are compared with budgeted or planned expenditures. In this department, actual exceeded budgeted expenditures for direct labor and operating supplies by $800 and $250 respectively. Actual spending for maintenance and miscellaneous was under the budgeted amount by $440. Budgetary control enables the manager to identify significant deviations in actual

FIGURE 12.7
Departmental Operating Budget

BUDGET KEYPUNCH DEPARTMENT
January 1-31

Item	Budget	Actual	Over	Under
Direct Labor	$10,000	$10,800	$800	
Indirect Labor	1,800	1,800		
Operating Supplies	1,250	1,500	$250	
Maintenance	1,800	1,400		$400
Misc. Expense (telephone)	190	150		40
Total	$15,040	$15,650	Over $610	

versus budgeted or planned expenses and to take corrective action when necessary. For example, the $800 over budgeted expenses for the wages of keypunch operators may have been caused by the necessity to pay overtime wages. This may have resulted from ineffective work scheduling or the sudden appearance of a "rush job." This situation, if it occurred in several successive periods, may cause the manager to take actions such as requesting additional personnel or improving the scheduling of work to correct the problem. In any event, budgeting control is a very useful tool of managers at virtually every level of an organization.

BENEFITS OF THE BUDGETING PROCESS

The fact that virtually every type of organization—profit or nonprofit—operates within the framework of budgets attests to their benefits. Budgeting is very significant as a part of both the planning and controlling process. Budgets are widely used by managers to plan, monitor and control various activities and operations at every level of an organization. There are several important advantages for preparing and using budgets. Some of the benefits of the budgeting process are listed here:

1. Provides standards against which actual performance can be measured. Budgets are a quantified plan which allows management to more objectively measure and control performance. If, for instance, a department knows that the budgeted expenditure for supplies is $1,000 per month, the manager is then in a position to monitor and control the expenses for supplies.

2. Provides managers with additional insight into actual organizational goals. Monetary allocation of funds as opposed to merely *lip service* more often than not is the true test of a firm's dedication to a particular goal. For instance, suppose that two firms of relatively equal size had a stated policy of hiring minority personnel. Firm A allocates $100,000 and Firm B provides $10,000. A manager from Firm A likely realizes that a much stronger commitment to minority hiring is expressed by Firm A as opposed to Firm B.

3. Tends to be a positive influence on the motivation of personnel. People typically like to know what is expected of them and budgets clarify specific performance standards.

4. Causes managers to divert some of their attention from current to future operations. To some extent, a budget forces managers to anticipate and forecast changes in the external environment. For example, an increase in transportation costs created by higher priced petroleum might force the firm to seek an alternative transportation or distribution system.

5. Improves top management's ability to coordinate the overall operation of the organization. Budgets are "blueprints" of the company's plans for the coming year and greatly aid top management in coordinating the operations/activities of each division or department.

6. Enables management to recognize and/or anticipate problems in time to take the necessary corrective action. For example, if production costs are substantially ahead of the budgeted amount, management will be alerted to make changes that may realign actual costs with the budget.

7. Facilitates communications throughout the organization. The budget significantly improves management's ability to communicate the objectives, plans, and standards of performance, which is important to the organization. Budgets are especially helpful to lower-level managers by letting them know how their operations relate to other units or departments within the organization. Also, budgets tend to pinpoint an individual manager's responsibility and improve his or her understanding of the goals of the organization. This process usually results in increased morale and commitment on the part of managers.

8. Helps managers recognize when change is needed. The budgeting process requires managers to carefully and critically review the company's operations to determine if the firm's resources are being allocated to the *right* activities and programs. The budgeting process causes management to focus on such questions as: What products appear to have the greatest demand? What markets appear to offer the best potential? What business are we in? Which business(es) should we be in?[3]

LIMITATIONS OF THE BUDGETING PROCESS

Although there are numerous benefits that can be attributed to the use of budgets, potential problems may also arise. If the budgetary process is to achieve its maximum effectiveness, these difficulties must be recognized and an attempt made to reduce the potential damaging side-effects associated with the use of budgets. Some of the major problems are the following:

1. The attitude by some that all funds allocated in a budget must be spent may actually work against the intent of the budgetary process. Some managers have learned from experience that if they do not

3. Irwin, "Budgeting."

spend the funds that have been budgeted, their budget will be reduced the following year. Managers have found that they can actually hurt their department because of their conscientious cost effectiveness approach. A manager who operates in this type of environment may make an extraordinary effort to spend extra funds for reasons that may be marginal at best.

2. A budget may be so restrictive that supervisors are permitted little discretion in managing their resources. The actual amount that can be spent for each item may be specified and funds cannot be transferred from one account to another. This has sometimes resulted in some unusual situations. There may be funds for typewriter paper but no money available for typewriter ribbons.

3. Budgets may be used to evaluate the performance of a manager as opposed to evaluating the actual results that the individual has accomplished. If this philosophy is prevalent within the firm, a poor manager may be recognized as superior because he or she met the budget, but a good manager may be reprimanded for failure to follow the exact budgetary guidelines. With this corporate philosophy, the amount of risk a manager will be willing to take may be severely reduced. Managers may spend a majority of their time ensuring that they are in compliance with the budget when their time might be best spent in developing new or innovative ideas.

SPECIFIC BUDGETING SYSTEMS: PPBS AND ZBB

planning-programming budgeting system
zero base budgeting

In recent years, two specific budgeting systems have received considerable attention. These two approaches are the **planning-programming budgeting system** (PPBS) and **zero base budgeting** (ZBB). Although PPBS and ZBB have been used infrequently in business organizations, the techniques have been applied by numerous federal, state, and local governments.[4]

Planning-Programming Budgeting System

PPBS was designed to aid management in identifying and eliminating costly programs that were duplicates of other programs and to provide a means for the careful analysis of the benefits and costs of each program or activity. The essential elements of PPBS include the following:

---

4. Anthony and Herzlinger, *Management Control in Non-Profit Organizations.*

1. Careful analysis and specification of basic objectives in each major program area. A vital starting point for PPBS is to answer such questions as "What is our basic purpose or mission" and "What, specifically, are we trying to accomplish?"
2. Analyze the output of each program in terms of the specific objectives. In other words, how effectively are we achieving our goals?
3. Measure and analyze the total costs of the program over several years. For example, in budgeting for additional schools, you would need to consider not only the initial costs of construction, but also costs of operating and maintaining the facilities in future years.
4. Determine which alternatives are the most effective in achieving the basic objectives at the least cost.
5. Implement PPBS in an organized and systematic manner so that over time most budgetary decisions are subject to rigorous analysis.[5]

PPBS was first applied by the Defense Department in the preparation of their 1962 budget, but was used by all other federal government agencies beginning in 1966. However by 1971, the system was abandoned by the federal government although it has continued to be used by the Defense Department and some public and private institutions of higher education. PPBS was not accepted by most departments and agencies of the government nor did it have the support of the U. S. Congress. The system was implemented under Presidential edict with an inadequate amount of time to explain the advantages of PPBS, much less the techniques involved in using it.

Zero-Base Budgeting

ZBB, originally developed by Texas Instruments, received widespread recognition when Jimmy Carter implemented the system when he was Governor of Georgia. In 1977, President Carter required that ZBB be used in preparing budgets in the Executive branch of the federal government. ZBB requires management to take a fresh look at all programs and activities each year rather than merely building on last year's budget. In other words, last year's budget allocations are not considered as a basis for this year's budget. Each program, or "decision packages" as they are called, must be justified on the basis of a cost-benefit analysis. There are three main features of zero base budgeting:

5. See Anthony and Herzlinger, *op cit.*, p. 223 and 224 and James A. F. Stoner, *Management*, (Englewood Cliffs, New Jersey: Prentice-Hall, Inc., 1978), pp. 600–677.

1. The activities of individual departments are divided into *decision packages.* Each decision package provides information so that management can compare costs and benefits of the program or activity.

2. Each decision package is evaluated and ranked in the order of decreasing importance to the organization. Priorities are established for all programs and activities. Each of these is evaluated by top management to arrive at a final ranking.

3. Resources are allocated according to the final rankings of the programs by top management. As a rule, decisions to allocate resources for high priority items will be made rather quickly, whereas greater analysis or scrutiny will be given lower priority programs or activities.[6]

ZBB is not a panacea for solving all problems associated with the budgeting process. Organizations may experience problems in implementing ZBB. Most managers are reluctant to admit that all of their activities are not of the highest priority or to submit their programs to close scrutiny. However, it does establish a system whereby an organization's resources are allocated to the higher priority programs. Under this system, programs of lower priority are reduced or eliminated. Thus, the benefits of zero-base budgeting appear to outweigh the costs.[7]

A SITUATIONAL APPROACH TO CONTROL

The amount of control supervisors, middle management, or top management imposes on their subordinates is dictated by the six situational factors that have provided the central theme throughout the text. The degree of control that is helpful or harmful to the organization often varies from department to department and from firm to firm. Appreciation of the situational factors assists the manager in determining the proper balance between organizational needs and an individual's personal freedom. For instance, let us take the illustration of two similar products being produced: a high quality watch and, although quite marketable, a watch of much lower quality.

Because the objective of one of the firms is to manufacture and sell a high quality watch, the other situational factors may have to be aligned if the optimum level of control is to be achieved. Precision instruments

6. See James A. F. Stoner, *Management* (Englewood Cliffs, N.J.: Prentice-Hall, 1978), pp. 608–609.

7. Gordon Shillinglaw, *Managerial Cost Accounting: Analysis and Control,* 4th ed. (Homewood, Ill.: Richard D. Irwin, 1977), pp. 142–143.

(technology) and skilled personnel will likely be required. Very rigid quality levels must be obtained if the objectives are to be achieved. It is likely that skilled craftspeople will be required to monitor the quality of the watch. Because these craftspeople consider themselves professionals, they readily accept the responsibility of assuring the highest quality level for their product. The organizational structure may have to be modified to attract craftspeople who are dedicated to their profession. In order to employ these individuals, a more permissive atmosphere may need to be developed. Thus, the managerial approach used by supervisors may need to be altered. All of the situational factors need to be considered and aligned if the proper level of control is to be achieved as needed to meet the organizational objective of manufacturing high quality watches. The amount of personal freedom exerted by the control system is likely to be quite high.

On the other hand, if the objective of another firm is to produce a lower quality mass produced watch, the alignment of the situational factors to obtain the proper level of control may be quite different. Since the quality of the product will be lower and the firm will be mass producing the watches, the technology of the equipment and skill requirements of the workers may not be as demanding. An organization may need to be developed that is conducive to mass production. In this environment of specialization, workers may not see themselves as craftspeople, and their dedication to manufacturing a quality product may not be as high. Thus, a control system may have to be developed that takes much of the inspection process away from the employee and places it with a separate quality control division. Because the watch is being mass produced, the managerial approach in accomplishing the control process may lean toward a more authoritative approach. In this environment, the control process may actually reduce the amount of personal freedom in order to achieve the organizational objectives of mass producing a lower quality watch.

SUMMARY

Control is the process of comparing actual performances with established standards for the purpose of taking corrective action. However, before standards can be established, objectives and plans must be developed. Thus, standards serve as the link between planning and control.

The control process involves three critical areas: establishment of standards, comparison of performance to standards, and taking corrective action. In an organization, the most important means by which performance can be compared to standards relate to quantity, quality, time, and budget (costs). Corrective action is needed to either remove deviations from planned performance or alter the plan to allow for obstacles that cannot be removed.

The control function can be divided into three basic types—initial, overseeing, and comparison controls. Initial controls take place as resources enter the organization. Overseeing controls are used during the process when the products and services are being produced. Comparison controls are used after the final product or service has been produced. However, at all times a manager must determine what to measure and when to measure an activity. These critical areas are referred to as strategic control points.

Managers must constantly be alert to the realization that there will be a certain amount of negative reactions to controls. Some of these negative reactions are caused as a result of inappropriate controls, unattainable standards, unpredictable standards, and contradictory standards. However, there are means by which negative reactions to controls may be overcome. If controls are justifiable, understandable, realistic, timely, and accurate, they will likely receive the least resistance.

A natural by-product of controls is disciplinary action. In business, disciplinary action is used to assure conformity in the operations of the business. Although there are difficulties that often arise through the use of disciplinary actions, there are guides that assist in handling disciplinary cases.

Perhaps the most widely known and applied device that managers use in controlling cost and expenditures is the budget. A budget is merely a formal statement of financial resources; it is a planned expenditure of money for personnel, time, space, or equipment. Although there are numerous benefits that may be associated with the budgeting process, it also has limitations. A budget will not solve all of a manager's monetary problems.

In recent years, two specific budgeting systems have received considerable attention. The Planning-Programming Budgeting System (PPBS) was designed to aid management in identifying and eliminating costly programs that were duplicates of other programs and to provide a means for the careful analysis of the benefits and costs of each program or activity. Zero Base Budgeting (ZBB) requires management to take a fresh look at all programs and activities each year rather than merely building on last year's budget.

The amount of control that a manager imposes on a subordinate is determined by the situation. The degree of control that is helpful or harmful to the organization often varies from department to department and from firm to firm. Understanding the situational factors assists the manager in determining the proper balance between organizational needs and an individual's personal freedom.

Review Questions

1. Define control as a process for assisting a manager to accomplish his or her objectives.

2. Explain in your own words why the functions of planning and controlling are so closely related.

3. What are the steps that are involved in the control process?

4. What are the four means by which actual performance may be compared to standards? Briefly discuss each.

5. Why are budgets so important to a manager? Discuss.

6. Distinguish between initial controls, overseeing controls, and comparison controls. When would each type be used?

7. What factors should a manager consider in establishing strategic control points?

8. What effect does the level of management have on the process of control?

9. What are some guidelines that a manager should follow when disciplinary action must be used?

Exercises

1. Develop objective(s), plans, and standards for obtaining an "A" in this course. What type control measures must be developed for you to accomplish this goal?

2. Think of the following type businesses and managers. What type controls do you believe they must have to ensure that they accomplish their objectives:
   1. A small convenience store
   2. A college or university
   3. A firm that manufactures a high quality hand calculator
   4. An insurance agency
   5. An automobile repair shop

REFERENCES

Austin, D. L. "Conflict: A Professional Approach." *Personnel Administrator*, July 1976, pp. 28–32.

Brooker, W. M. A. "Eliminating Intergroup Conflicts Through Interdepartmental Problem Solving." *S. A. M. Advanced Management Journal*, Spring 1975, pp. 16–25.

Buffa, Elwood S. *Basic Production Management.* 2nd ed. New York: John Wiley and Sons, Inc., 1975.

Buffa, Elwood S. *Modern Production Management.* 4th ed. New York: John Wiley and Sons, Inc., 1973.

Burns, J. H. "Managing the Profit of Conflict." *Management Accounting,* December 1975, pp. 21–24.

Cuthill, R. "How to Cope with Inter-Personal Conflicts." *Canadian Business Magazine,* September 1976, pp. 89–90.

DeWelt, R. L. "Control: Key to Making Financial Strategy Work." *Management Review,* March 1977, pp. 18–25.

Elliot, C., and Haynes, J. "Resolving a Growing Conflict: Management and Computer Specialist." *University of Michigan Business Review,* March 1977, pp. 9–13.

"Harnessing Conflict for Management Improvement." *The C.P.A. Journal,* July 1975, pp. 62–63.

Hayburst, G. "Proposal for a Corporate Control System." *Management International Review,* 1976, pp. 93–103.

Hopeman, Richard J. *Production: Concepts, Analysis, Control,* 3rd ed. Columbus, Ohio: Charles E. Merrill Publishing Co., 1976.

King, John Russel. *Production Planning and Control: An Introduction to Quantitative Methods.* New York: Pergamon Press, 1975.

Morano, R. A. "Managing Conflict for Problem Solving." *Personnel Journal,* August 1976, pp. 393–394.

Moreau, D. "When War Breaks Out in the Company." *The Director,* March 1977, pp. 35–36.

Nelson, E. G., and Machin, J. L. J. "Management Control: Systems Thinking Applied to Development of a Framework for Empirical Studies." *The Journal of Management Studies,* October 1976, pp. 274–287.

Ouchi, W. G. "Relationship Between Organizational Structure and Organizational Control." *Administrative Science Quarterly,* March 1977, pp. 95–113.

Plossl, G. W. *Manufacturing Control: The Last Frontier for Profits.* Reston, Va.: Reston Publishing Co., 1973.

Stewarts, Robert. "Patterns of Work and the Dictates of Time." *Personnel Management,* June 1976, pp. 507.

Szilagyi, A. P. and others. "Role Dynamics, Locus of Control, and Employee Attitudes and Behavior." *Academy of Management Journal,* June 1976, pp. 259–276.

Thamhain, H. J., and Wilemom, D. L. "Conflict Management in Project Life Cycles." *Sloan Management Review,* Spring 1975, pp. 31–50.

Thomas, K. W., and Schmidt, W. H. "Survey of Managerial Interest with Respect to Conflict." *Academy of Management Journal,* June 1976, pp. 315–318.

Thompson, A. "How to Share Control." *Management Today,* September 1976, pp. 70–73.

Whitehead, R. "Controlling Your Quality Cost." *Industry Week,* June 7, 1976, pp. 34–39.

Case Study   A PROBLEM OF INVENTORY CONTROL

As supervisor of ten stores in a convenience store chain, Mike Pressley is responsible for their general operation. Each of these small stores has a day manager and two assistant managers who work the evening and midnight shifts. These "managers" are not really managers because they have no subordinates reporting directly to them. The day manager is typically the senior person and has chosen the day shift. (A person might want to visit a convenience store to gain a better appreciation of the work environment.)

Mark McCall is the day manager of one of the stores that Mike supervises. Mark has been at the store for three months and sales have been increasing steadily. Mark maintains his store in good order and the first two monthly inventory checks have been satisfactory. But, as Mike reads the inventory report for this month he becomes quite disturbed. Inventory is $1,000 short for the previous month (anything over $200 is considered out of the ordinary).

Mike realizes that this report is extremely serious. Other managers have been terminated for inventory shortages of this amount. He likes Mark but something must be done to keep this situation from occurring in the future. Mike sits down and reviews the situation regarding the store. The following points come to mind:

- The store is located close to a school. When Mark took control of the store, school was not in session. There might be some shoplifting occurring.
- One of the assistant managers has been with the store for only one month. There is a possibility that there could be internal theft.
- The other assistant manager broke up with his girlfriend last month. There is a possibility that he has not been paying close attention to his job.

Questions   1. What type of controls, if any, should Mike instigate?
                    2. If the inventory is short next month, what do you think Mike should do?

Case Study   DIFFERING PHILOSOPHIES

Collins and Bradford (C&B) is a manufacturing company with sales of approximately $250 million. C&B employs twelve college trained accountants at its headquarters. These positions are divided between financial accounting, cost accounting, accounts payable, and auditing. Tom Brown came to work at C&B in the financial accounting department. He had a B.B.A. from a major university and two years of previous work experience in accounting. He caught on quickly, did a good job, and was well liked by his supervisor and fellow employees. After eleven months, a position became available in the cost accounting department that offered Tom a higher salary and an opportunity to develop professionally in another area.

After three months in the cost accounting department it became apparent to Tom that he and his supervisor, Ed Blake, simply could not work together. Tom disagreed with Ed's training techniques and Ed's philosophy on how certain problems should be handled. It also became evident that they had a severe personality conflict. After a full month of deliberation on what to do, Tom decided to go to John Collins, Ed's supervisor, and ask for a transfer. He explained that he wanted to remain at C&B but that neither he nor the cost department were benefiting from his being in his present position.

Ed and John had been friends and working associates for years and John's initial reaction was to blame Tom for the bad situation. He surveyed the other accounting positions and did not see any openings coming up in the near future. John felt that he had three alternatives—to create an additional accounting position in another department and transfer Tom, to work with Ed and Tom to reconcile the problems, or to terminate Tom.

Questions   1. What might have caused the conflict between Tom and Ed? How can this type of conflict be controlled so as not to adversely affect a firm's operations?

2. What action should John take? Is he limited to the three alternatives mentioned at the end of the case?

3. If you were Tom Brown, what would you do?

SITUATIONAL
APPLICATIONS

6

Part 6 is devoted to understanding specific topics of interest to managers. In chapters 13 and 14 we'll look at the various production and operations management tools and techniques that are available to a manager. Following this is a discussion of the variety of factors that must be considered when managing a small business. In the last chapter of this section the various conditions that affect managing the multinational corporation will be discussed.

Chapter 13

KEY TERMS

process layout

product layout

flow process chart

operations chart

worker machine charts

stopwatch method

work sampling

break-even analysis

fixed costs

variable costs

discounted cash flow

make/buy planning decision

purchase/lease decision

linear programming

demand forecasting

trend

cyclical

seasonal

random

moving averages

exponential smoothing

regression analysis

time series analysis

Production and Operations Management I

LEARNING OBJECTIVES

After studying this chapter you should be able to

1. Identify some of the traditional production management techniques.
2. List the basic production and operations management techniques.
3. Explain how many of the quantitative techniques are used in business today.
4. Describe how financial models may be used by managers in decision making.
5. Identify the basic requirements needed to work a linear programming problem.
6. Explain the forecasting techniques of moving averages, exponential smoothing, regression, and times series analysis.

Brian Jones, vice-president of production for Marlboro Corporation, is faced with a critical decision. He must make a choice between two machines that will be used to increase production efficiency at Marlboro. One piece of equipment costs $200,000 and is capable of providing a savings of $40,000 a year over the next ten years. The other machine costs $150,000 but will generate a savings of $40,000 over the next seven years. Brian thinks to himself—"Gee, I wish I knew more about evaluating financial alternatives."

Barry Williams, the director of production for Ampex Corporation, has been asked by the President of Ampex to evaluate the feasibility of closing one of the factories in Chicago. Ampex has factories and warehouses across the nation and Barry must determine how the decision to close the factory will affect the total cost for the firm. Barry has been told by a person in another department that linear programming might provide assistance in making this decision.

Lisa Thompson, the director of planning for Finn Manufacturing, has been asked to develop a five-year forecast of demand for Finn's product. Based on this forecast, Finn Manufacturing will make the decision whether or not to expend five million dollars to build a new plant. Lisa is glad she has concentrated on learning how to use the various forecasting techniques while in school.

David Channel, a production foreman for Edens Manufacturing, has been instructed by his manager, the plant superintendent, to analyze the methods used by the workers in assembling the products made in Dave's department to determine if more efficient methods/procedures can be developed. David has heard of techniques that could be beneficial for the assigned job but does not know how to use them. He wishes that he had not skipped his production and operations management class so much while in college.

Brian, Barry, Lisa, and David could all benefit from the use of production and operations management techniques. They provide managers with a wide variety of principles and procedures related to production economies, quality control, inventory control, work measurement, scheduling, cost control, and others. Procedures that assist in more effectively accomplishing the purpose for which the firm was created are included. In this and the following chapter, specific approaches useful to a manager will be developed. They will be described from the standpoint of how they are being used in business today. A major portion of the explanation is

> **INSIGHTS TO SUCCESS**
>
> The initial years of a career are important in building a strong understanding of company operations. We encourage individuals to take advantage of the many types of training positions available in the company and to treat each job as equally important to advancement. A generalized initial career, including staff, factory, branch, and overseas accounting, rather than an initial specialized career will provide individuals greater opportunity for advancement.
>
> J. W. ENGLAND, Vice-President and Comptroller, Deere & Company

devoted to gaining an appreciation of what techniques are available, what the manager needs to know in order to use them, and how they have been used to solve actual business problems.

Only a few years ago, production and operations management was taught exclusively as it related to the factory environment. Production management was then assumed to be completely factory oriented. The techniques assisted in the production process for plants or factories. For instance, production management techniques might be utilized to optimize the procedures for manufacturing automobiles. Today, production and operations management takes on a much broader application in that any organization including hospitals, schools, and government agencies may conceivably benefit through the use of the techniques. Most of the quantitative techniques now apply to both factory and service industries and the term has also been expanded to include production and operations management.

BASIC CONCEPTS OF TRADITIONAL PRODUCTION MANAGEMENT

There are several concepts that at one time were used primarily in the manufacturing environment. Although today they have been used in other than factory settings, the following tools and concepts have been identified as traditionally production and will be discussed separately.

SITE SELECTION

Every firm has different reasons for choosing a particular site for locating a new facility. There are many factors to consider, however, if a firm is to achieve long-run benefits from proper site selection. Factors such as the

D O R O T H Y   T I V I S   P O L L A C K

Vice-President
Formfit Rogers, A Division of Genesco Incorporated

FORMFIT ROGERS It has been a long road from Fargo, North Dakota to New York City for Dorothy Pollack. Dorothy describes herself as a "depression child" who quit school to go to work to help support her family. Her first job was with the daily newspaper in Fargo. She worked for Gifford Herron, the city editor, a famous newsman, whom she says had a great influence on her professional life.

Dorothy left Fargo for the bright lights of New York and began her career as a free-lance writer turning out soap operas and love stories for McFadden and Fawcett publications. After a brief stint with the Foreign Department of the UPI during World War II, she became a fashion model. She was a successful fashion model for ten years and had some interesting observations about modeling.

> The idea that this is a glamourous profession is crazy, you work like a truck horse. Finally, I got tired of it and set about finding a job where I could use some of the fashion know-how I'd absorbed standing in front of the cameras. That's when I discovered the sad truth that models are generally considered to be idiots—decorative, but dumb.

After her ten years as a model, she landed a job with *Vanity Fair* as assistant advertising manager.

> It was my good fortune to work for a very smart lady (this is the most important job benefit—to work for somebody who's brighter than you are) and to be in on the beginning of great and exciting changes in this industry.

Dorothy later joined Formfit Rogers as vice-president responsible for advertising, promotion, and fashion merchandising. In this capacity she is on the Executive Committee which makes all management and operating designs decisions for the company. She feels that her varied background and twenty years experience in the industry have proven invaluable. In response to the question as to why she chose management, Dorothy responded with this comment:

> I really like to make decisions, have the opportunity to grow, learn and rely on my judgment. It's my basic nature to work hard, to try to inspire my staff to turn every problem into a chance to do something wonderful. I prefer not to be the one who is bossed.

Although Ms. Pollack does not have a great deal of formal education, she says that "nothing is more important in today's market." This is especially true for women—"those who want to get into management do need that MBA; it's their foot in the door, it's the fast way to get started. This is the era of the professional who comes prepared." She believes that the most important quality for success as a manager is the *desire* to succeed. "You have to really want to get up that ladder, to give up certain things, to keep climbing and to enjoy the upper rungs when you get there." She strongly believes, "If a woman has the talent to turn the Profit and Loss sheet around, she will be as eligible as a man. Believe it or not, realism will win—maybe sooner than we think."

supply of skilled labor, union activities, living conditions, and, of course, actual costs are some items that warrant consideration. For many reasons, a site that may be completely satisfactory for one company may be totally unacceptable for another.

In order to objectively evaluate different site opportunities, a firm must identify factors they feel are important in choosing a particular location and those items they feel would possibly be detrimental to long-run success. For instance, it may be extremely important for the area surrounding the site to have skilled workers and an ample supply of natural resources. Next, these factors are ranked according to their relative importance. Each site that is considered is then compared to these factors and scored. The site with the highest score is likely to be the best in terms of the company objectives.

PLANT LAYOUT

The type of plant layout that will prove to be optimum for the manufacture of a particular product deserves special consideration. Generally, layouts may be identified as being process or product. The selection of one over another depends on the type of product to be manufactured, the type of equipment to be used in the process, and the amount of the particular product to be produced.

product layout
When we think of **product layouts** a person is generally referring to assembly lines. A large amount of a single product can be produced at a relatively low cost per unit when product layouts are used. Equipment is sequenced to permit a product to go from start to finish through the use of automated equipment and assembly lines. The manufacture of automobiles in the United States provides an excellent example of a product layout.

process layout
On the other hand, when **process layouts** are used, pieces of equipment that perform virtually the same function are grouped together. For instance, all drills would be placed in one area and presses placed in another area. It is likely that additional manpower and handling time will be required for a process layout. When smaller quantities of a product are to be manufactured (normally referred to as batch processing), most likely the process layout will prove to be superior.

The selection of one layout over another involves analyzing the cost effectiveness of moving the product from an unfinished to a finished stage. The layout that maximizes employee effectiveness and minimizes handling cost is likely to be advantageous.

WORK METHODS

There are certain tasks that an individual can do better than a machine and others that machines can handle better. For instance, people do a better job in areas that require exercising judgment and developing concepts. On the other hand, machines have proven to be superior in areas where repetitive and routine tasks are to be performed. It becomes the manager's job to provide a balance between the two.

Numerous techniques are used to maximize the efficiency associated with a particular process. The flow process chart, operations chart, and worker-machine chart have proven to be beneficial for this purpose.

Flow Process Charts

flow process chart

The symbols that are used in a **flow process chart** to depict the flow of a job are:

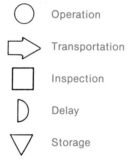

Operation

Transportation

Inspection

Delay

Storage

Each task to be accomplished is identified along with the time it will take. A manager then is able to study the sequence of tasks to determine if there is a better way to accomplish the job. A simple flow process chart is presented in Figure 13.1.

Operations Charts

operations chart

In a production operation, the movement of the right and left hand are analyzed through the use of an **operations chart.** Its use is essentially appropriate when the time from start to finish of an operation (cycle time) is fairly short. A major benefit of an operations chart is that it permits a manager to view a task to see if it is being completed in an optimum manner.

FIGURE 13.1
Flow Process Chart

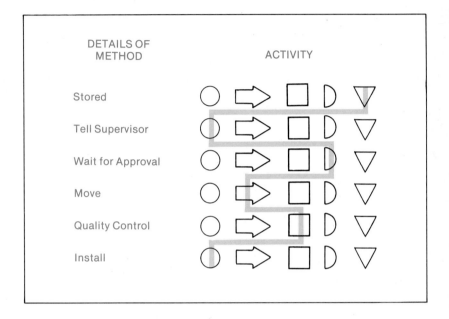

Worker Machine Charts

worker machine charts

These charts are beneficial when both a worker and a machine are used to perform a particular task. Through studying the **worker machine charts** a manager is able to determine if there is excessive idle time associated with either the worker or the machine. If the worker is idle, he may be assigned an additional machine to control. On the other hand, if the machine is expensive and needs to be kept operating a majority of the time, it may be worth the cost of an additional worker to help operate the machine even though the idle time of the worker goes up.

Principles of Motion Economy

The principles of motion economy presented in Table 13.1 are useful in improving efficiency and reducing fatigue. They relate to principles concerning the use of the human body, arrangement of the work place, and design of tools and equipment. Although there is nothing sophisticated or mysterious about the principles, they have been extremely beneficial in job design.

TABLE 13.1
Principles of Motion Economy

Use of the Human Body	Arrangement of the Work Place	Design of Tools and Equipment
1. The two hands should begin as well as complete their motions at the same time.	9. There should be a definite and fixed place for all tools and materials.	17. The hands should be relieved of all work that can be done more advantageously by a jig, a fixture, or a foot-operated device.
2. The two hands should not be idle at the same time except during rest periods.	10. Tools, materials, and controls should be located close in and directly in front of the operator.	18. Two or more tools should be combined whenever possible.
3. Motions of the arms should be made in opposite and symmetrical directions and should be made simultaneously.	11. Gravity feedbins and containers should be used to deliver materials close to the point of use.	19. Tools and materials should be prepositioned whenever possible.
4. Hand motions should be confined to the lowest classification with which it is possible to perform the work satisfactorily.	12. Drop deliveries should be used wherever possible.	20. Where each finger performs some specific movement, such as in typewriting, the load should be distributed in accordance with the inherent capacities of the fingers.
5. Momentum should be employed to assist the worker wherever possible, and it should be reduced to a minimum if it must be overcome by muscular effort.	13. Materials and tools should be located to permit the best sequence of motions.	21. Handles, such as those used on cranks and large screwdrivers, should be designed to permit as much of the surface of the hand to come in contact with the handle as possible. This is particularly true when considerable force is exerted in using the handle. For light assembly work the screwdriver handle should be so shaped that it is smaller at the bottom than at the top.
6. Smooth continuous motions of the hands are preferable to zigzag motions or straight-line motions involving sudden and sharp changes in direction.	14. Provisions should be made for adequate conditions for seeing. Good illumination is the first requirement for satisfactory visual perception.	
7. Ballistic movements are faster, easier, and more accurate than restricted (fixation) or "controlled" movements.	15. The height of the workplace and the chair should preferably be arranged so that alternate sitting and standing at work are easily possible.	
8. Rhythm is essential to the smooth and automatic performance of an operation, and the work should be arranged to permit easy and natural rhythm wherever possible.	16. A chair of the type and height to permit good posture should be provided for every worker.	22. Levers, crossbars, and handwheels should be located in such positions that the operator can manipulate them with the least change in body position and with the greatest mechanical advantage.

Source R. M. Barnes, *Motion and Time Study: Design and Measurement of Work*, 6th ed. New York: John Wiley, 1968.

LABOR MEASUREMENT

There are two basic techniques for determining labor standards: stopwatch and work sampling. Both are used extensively in the factory to determine the time it should take a worker to accomplish a particular task.

Stopwatch Method

With this approach a stopwatch is used to estimate the time it will take to complete a task. After timing a particular task an appropriate number of

stopwatch method

times, the times are averaged to arrive at a standard time. A weakness that has been associated with the **stopwatch method** is that workers often either speed up or slow down when they know that they are being timed.

Work Sampling

work sampling

An approach that has been used effectively in overcoming the deficiencies involved in the stopwatch method is **work sampling.** Workers are observed at random times to determine the proportion of their time that is being spent on different tasks. Statistical sampling techniques are used to determine the number of observations that are needed to obtain the degree of reliability desired.

QUANTITATIVE TOOLS FOR PRODUCTION AND OPERATIONS MANAGEMENT

Our intent in discussing the quantitative tools should not be taken to mean that a manager is always expected to know the detailed mathematics of each approach. James F. Olson, Manager, corporate strategic planning for General Mills, Inc., reinforced the authors' philosophy with regard to quantitative tools when he stated, "I would urge students to become as familiar as possible with all techniques but to remain enough detached from them to allow clear thinking to take place." A manager should at least have an appreciation of the following:

- the tools available
- the situation for which the tools are designed
- how the tools are used in business

This approach will be taken because of an apparent misconception that has evolved regarding the use of quantitative techniques by students of management. The myth is that these tools cannot be used without a total and complete theoretical and mathematical appreciation of the quantitative techniques. *This need not be the case!* A prudent manager wants to utilize his or her resources to their maximum. Thus, a manager must be capable of recognizing what tools are available and when they should be used. Once the manager has made this determination, the mathematician, statistician, or computer specialist may be called on to perform the actual calculation. These individuals are trained to implement a quantitative technique once you, as the manager, have made the decision as to which tool is appropriate and identified the factors that should be considered in the problem.

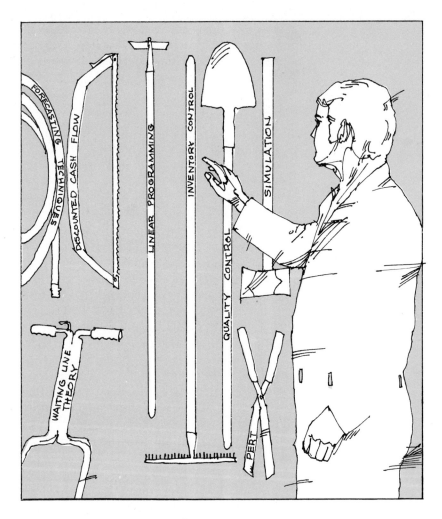

Another major point that should be made regarding the use of any quantitative tool is that the manager must still use his or her personal judgment once an answer has been obtained. As D. E. Eckdahl, senior vice-president, engineering and manufacturing of NCR, stated:

> Since no mathematical model can satisfactorily emulate all aspects of most decision problems, it is essential that sound judgment is exercised in evaluating mathematical models rather than unquestioning reliance on simple quantitative results.

Until all factors that may affect a decision are considered, a manager must still exercise sound judgment in deciding whether or not to use the solutions that have been derived from the use of quantitative techniques.

As these techniques are discussed, the comments of P. J. Durosko, director of manufacturing for the Armstrong Rubber Company, should be remembered. He said;

> The importance of a specific production and operations management technique varies with time, project attention, business cycles, and performance achievement in various aspects of the business. The needs of the time dictate the techniques as well as the capabilities and understanding of the concepts by the project manager and his team.

**MOST IMPORTANT REASONS FOR SUCCESS
AND EFFECTIVENESS AS A MANAGER**

Being able to accurately predict changes in the consumer's demands and consequently reacting faster than others to these changes. Of course, it is absolutely essential that you keep equipment modern and up to date so as to be cost efficient.

R. P. TIMMERMAN, President, Graniteville Company

MANAGERIAL USES OF QUANTITATIVE TECHNIQUES

A major point for a student of management to realize is that many companies are making extensive use of various quantitative tools. The need may be different for each firm, but the fact remains they are being used. This was vividly illustrated when the authors surveyed a sample of major firms in the United States as to which primary quantitative tools they used (see Table 13.2). Each firm had a minimum of $250 million in sales annually. As you can see, their use of the quantitative tools apparently depended on the nature of the business and the specific desires of management, but they were being used.

The rest of this chapter and the next chapter concentrate on providing an overview of some of the production and operations management quantitative tools that have transcended the boundaries of traditional production. The discussion in this chapter is devoted primarily to the quantitative tools that have been found useful in the planning function. A person should remember, however, that although the tools have been beneficial in the planning stage, their use is not confined strictly to the planning function.

TABLE 13.2
Use of Quantitative Techniques

Primary Product of Firm	Primary Quantitative Techniques Used
Vehicle components and assemblies	Inventory control models Economic modeling
Railroad transportation	Discounted cash flow techniques PERT, CPM Simulation
Pharmaceuticals, proprietary remedies, confections, cosmetics and toiletries	Simulation
Petroleum	Simulation Mathematical programming Discounted cash flow techniques Probability theory (Bayesian statistics, payoff and risk analysis)
Construction, engineering, and real estate development	Simulation Mathematical programming PERT, CPM
Tires and tubes	Inventory control models Discounted cash flow techniques
Automobile accessories	Simulation Probability theory (Bayesian statistics, payoff and risk analysis) Inventory control models
Industrial and agriculture products	Inventory control models
Petroleum products	PERT, CPM Discounted cash flow techniques
Building products	Simulation Probability theory (Bayesian statistics, payoff and risk analysis) Inventory control models Discounted cash flow techniques
Steel	Inventory control models Mathematical programming Discounted cash flow techniques
Building products	Inventory control models PERT, CPM
Electrical equipment	Inventory control models PERT, CPM
Paper products	Discounted cash flow techniques Simulation Mathematical programming
Computers	PERT, CPM Simulation
Natural gas	Discounted cash flow techniques
Toiletries and grooming aids	Inventory control models Discounted cash flow techniques Simulation
Aircraft	Discounted cash flow techniques PERT, CPM

TABLE 13.2
Use of Quantitative Techniques (Continued)

Primary Product of Firm	Primary Quantitative Techniques Used
Computers	Discounted cash flow techniques Simulation
Tires	Inventory control models Discounted cash flow techniques
Heating and refrigeration equipment	Inventory control models Discounted cash flow techniques
Construction and engineering	PERT, CPM
Engines and trucks	Inventory control models Discounted cash flow techniques Mathematical programming
Petroleum	Discounted cash flow techniques
Catalog order and retail department store	Inventory control models Simulation
Beverages and food concentrates	Discounted cash flow techniques

PLANNING TECHNIQUES

In this section, several techniques will be presented that have been used effectively for business planning. As previously mentioned, their placement in the planning section should not be taken to mean that the technique is reserved solely for the planning function. The quantitative techniques may be appropriate for use in solving other management problems.

FINANCIAL MODELS

One of the most valuable tools for a business planner is financial modeling. Since factors relating to profit and loss are so vitally important to the growth and even survival of a firm, it is advantageous for any planner to understand the techniques that are available. In this section, several basic financial approaches will be discussed.

Break-even Analysis

break-even analysis

One approach to use to determine the amount of a particular product that must be sold if the firm is to generate enough revenue to cover costs is **break-even analysis.** In order to progress in a break-even study the student of management must be capable of identifying the following items:

1. Fixed cost
2. Variable costs
3. Price of the item

fixed costs

Fixed costs are costs that do not change with the level of output. Items that normally are considered fixed are the salaries of top management, rent, property taxes, and other similar expenses. On the other hand, variable costs **variable costs** are those costs that are directly related to changes in output. Items that might be included as variable costs are direct materials and labor expenses that are used in manufacturing a particular product. However, these definitions are not always as clear-cut in reality as we would like them to be. There is often a gray area in which some costs can at times be considered either fixed or variable, but this should not deter the student of management from understanding and appreciating the concept.

The typical approach to show how to use break-even analysis is through graphical illustration. As seen in Figure 13.2, the vertical axis is designated as the total revenue produced while the horizontal axis shows the units of

FIGURE 13.2
Break-even Analysis

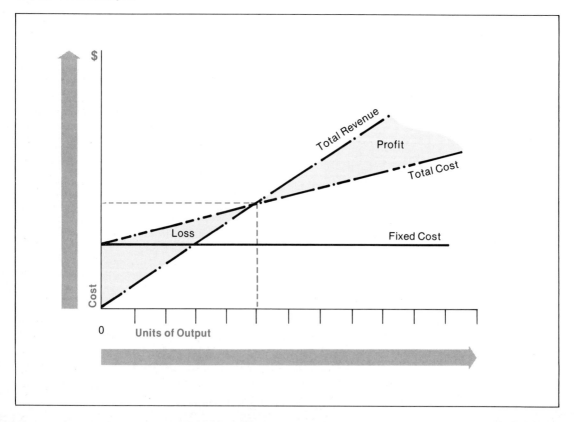

output. Our task is to determine the units of output at which we will break-even. If we sell units beyond the break-even point the firm will make a profit; sales lower than the break-even point result in a loss.

Since it is assumed fixed costs do not change, they are placed on the graph as a straight horizontal line. Variable costs, on the other hand, change with the level of production and the cost line slopes upward. The variable cost line is drawn starting at the point where fixed costs intercept production costs. The resulting line is total costs. Next, our total revenue line is drawn showing the total amount of revenue (price times number of units sold) at all possible combinations of production. When the total revenue line intersects the total cost line the break-even point has been identified.

But how reliable is this one point in space? Would you bet your firm's survival on its accuracy? Likely not, but its benefits are substantial if used with full appreciation of the weaknesses of the technique. If you drew a beam on the break-even point with a shotgun and fired, the pattern of the shots would spread out around the break-even point. This is about as accurate as you might expect because of the nature of correctly identifying fixed and variable costs. But, the break-even analysis has been used effectively because it forces a manager to plan. An individual who plans is in a position to make better decisions than a nonplanner.

Discounted Cash Flow

A dollar earned today does not have the same value as a dollar that will be earned one year from today. This is because if you invest this dollar today, a year later it will be worth the dollar plus interest. Thus, the time value of money becomes quite important in business planning. Take for example the signing of a superstar professional athlete for over a million dollars. We are often awed by these large amounts and wonder how a team can afford to stay in business by paying these salaries. But, the managers of these clubs are usually business people and understand the time value of money. This was vividly illustrated in the signing of Tony Dorsett by the Dallas Cowboys, described in the article in Figure 13.3. As you can see, even though the contract was in excess of one million dollars, this amount was paid back in one year when the time value of money was considered. The signing of a superstar or placing an order for new equipment have the same implications—the decision should take into consideration the time value of money.

discounted cash flow   In business planning the **discounted cash flow** technique is used extensively. As may be seen in Table 13.3, a wide diversity of firms are deeply involved in the use of discounted cash flow techniques for solving business problems, but most involve capital investment decisions. Taking into consideration the time value of money can mean the difference between a firm achieving a profit or loss.

FIGURE 13.3

Touchdown Tony: What Price Glory?

Dorsett: *Sound Investment.*

There's really no need to feel sorry for the Tony Dorsetts of this world, but things aren't quite as rich as they seem. Headlines suggest that Dorsett's five-year Cowboy contract calls for $1.1-$1.2 million. A million dollars or so over five years is worth more than $200,000 a year? Right? Not really.

We checked with a well known local sports executive, who prefers to remain anonymous. Aided by his accountant, our executive gave us this "hypothetical" example of a Dorsett-like, million-dollar, superstar contract.

A five-year contract calls for a salary beginning the first year at $40,000, and increases by $20,000 each year until it reaches $120,000 in year five. Total salary over five years: $400,000.

Next, the contract adds $600,000 in deferred payments. The first payment begins 10 years after the contract is signed and payments continue at $20,000 a year for the next 30 years.

The trick here is a financial principle money wizards call "net present value." Ordinary folks call it common sense. Because the salary payments are spread over five years the superstar forfeits the right to earn interest from the beginning on the entire $400,000. He thus loses the interest he needs to cover the declining value of his dollar (the inflation pinch). In effect, that delay makes the $400,000 he eventually will receive in salary worth only $312,120 in today's money. Applying the same logic to the deferred payments, one finds the $600,000 spread out over 30 years worth only $104,291 in today's money. Total value of the million dollar contract: $414,411 in today's dollars.

Now, let's assume that a player such as Dorsett could draw 7,900 fans for each 1977 home game, not too far-fetched if you note the season ticket boom tony has triggered. The Cowboys' take from 7,900 extra tickets at 11 home games would be about $414,000. Invest that money at eight percent for 40 years and it will grow to nine million dollars. In today's dollars that would be $414,411, fully repaying the Cowboys for the "million dollar" contract. Meaning that Touchdown Tony would pay for himself — in just one season. Hypothetical, of course.

"Touchdown Tony: What Price Glory," *D Magazine*, August 16, 1977. Copyright © 1977, Dallas Southwest Media Corporation. Reprinted with permission.

INSIGHTS TO SUCCESS

The basic function of the plant is to convert resources (raw materials, labor, energy) into a marketable product, with maximum efficiency.

JAMES A. MARK, General Manager, Chemical Division, Sherwin-Williams Company

---

Let us take a simple illustration to provide us with an appreciation of the discounted cash technique. Suppose that two machines are being considered for purchase, Machine A and Machine B. Both cost the same amount, $10,000, and the revenue that will be generated is the same, $21,000. The only difference is that the revenue is generated over a different time frame. As may be seen in Table 13.4, Machine A generates $1,000 in revenue in year 6 while Machine B generates $6,000. If we assume an interest rate of 10 percent, let us see what happens when the decision maker views the final results as depicted in the table. Because

TABLE 13.3
Uses of Discounted Cash Flow Techniques

Company	Uses
AMF Inc.	Evaluation of strategic alternatives
Bendix Corporation	Plant expansion Machinery purchase
Carrier Corporation	Plant expansion Major capital expenditures
Crown Zellerbach	Make or buy decisions Lease or buy decisions Plant expansion decisions Alternative courses of action
Glidden Division, SCM Corporation	Capital expenditure request model— Corporate-wide Capital investment analysis system New product planning
Inland Steel Company	Capital investment decisions Lease or buy Repair or replace
Kellogg Company	Project justification and decision making Justification of new technologies All capital expenditures
Kimberly-Clark	Maintenance analysis Project evaluation Lease/buy decisions
Lear Siegler	Capital equipment purchases Plant expansion Make or buy
Oscar Mayer & Co.	All major economic analyses Effect of anticipated inflation on Investment analysis Investment risk analysis
Proctor & Gamble Company	New product decisions Evaluation of capital appropriations Evaluation of engineering alternatives
The Signal Companies, Inc.	All major capital investment decisions (new plants, equipment) Lease vs. purchase Acquisitions
Southern Railroads	Investment decisions RR rate and pricing decisions Merger and acquisition analysis
The Southland Corp.	Building decisions
3M Company	Investment analysis Decisions for capital expenditures Make or buy and lease and buy

Machine A produces a large portion of the revenue during the first few years, management is able to reinvest this revenue at 10 percent. Although Machine B will ultimately produce as much revenue as Machine A, it does not produce high revenue until the end of the life of the equipment and

TABLE 13.4
Discounted Cash Flow Example

Cost of Equipment	Machine A $10,000	Machine B $10,000	Present Value of $1.00	Total Present Value Machine A	Machine B
Year	Revenue per year				
1	6,000	1,000	.909	5454	909
2	5,000	2,000	.826	4130	1652
3	4,000	3,000	.751	3004	2253
4	3,000	4,000	.683	2049	2732
5	2,000	5,000	.621	1242	3105
6	1,000	6,000	.564	564	3384
				16,443	14,035
		Less Cost of Equipment		10,000	10,000
		Net Discounted Cash Flow		$6,443	$4,035
		Difference in Cash Flow		└─$2408─┘	

the revenue cannot be reinvested early. This provides a difference in cash flow of $2,408, quite a significant difference when the decision maker evaluates the alternative. It is likely that Machine A will be purchased if there are no other external factors to be considered.

Make/Buy Decisions

make/buy planning decision

When a **make/buy planning decision** is considered by a manager, he or she is concerned with evaluating the benefits of making the product *in-house* or going *outside* to another manufacturer. A prime factor that a manager should consider relates to whether the manufacturing costs in-house are lower than the cost to go outside. But this is not the only factor to consider. The manager must also ask whether the space that will be used to manufacture the product in-house could be used more advantageously. If the space could be used more effectively (make more money), through manufacturing other products, the decision might be made to produce the product outside the firm.

Purchase/Lease Decisions

purchase/lease decision

Another financial alternative that many business people are considering is whether to purchase or lease equipment. Such a decision is called a **purchase/lease decision.** Realistically, at times it is better to purchase and at other times it becomes more advantageous to lease. The answer may again be derived through evaluating the time value of money. If a manager were to purchase the equipment, such things as interest expense, depre-

TABLE 13.5
Uses of Linear Programming

Company	Uses
Bendix Corporation	Minimizing transportation costs for the truck fleet Production scheduling
Glidden Division, SCM Corporation	Product formulation Analysis of competitors products Capacity planning (long range)
Inland Steel Company	Evaluating energy impact of facility and policy decisions Allocating products to certain production facilities
Kaiser Steel Corporation	Proportioning of raw materials to satisfy quantitative constraints
Kellogg Company	Analyzing production capacity for budgets Long-range production planning Minimizing transportation costs for finished products
Kimberly-Clark	Distribution planning between multiple production locations New plant location-distribution cost comparison
Lear Siegler Inc.	Work Flow Transportation Analysis
Oscar Mayer & Co.	Product formulation Identifying new plant locations Design of distribution transportation systems
Proctor & Gamble Company	Allocations of material suppliers to manufacturing plants Warehouse and plant site selection Production planning
3M Company	Selection of manufacturing facility for new product

ciation, and salvage value must be evaluated to come up with a net discounted cash flow value. However, if a firm were to lease the equipment, only the lease payment could be used with regard to tax savings in computing a net discounted cash flow value. Under the leasing arrangement, there is no salvage value and although leasing may be attractive at times, the decision should certainly be evaluated as to which decision would be best for the firm.

LINEAR PROGRAMMING

linear programming

With **linear programming,** we are attempting to allocate limited resources among competing demands in an optimum way. As may be seen in

Table 13.5, linear programming is used for a variety of reasons in industry, but its use depends on the nature of the needs of the firm. Summarizing the uses presented in Table 13.5, and other uses, linear programming has been used effectively in industry to solve these and other type problems:

- Locations and closures of plants, warehouses, and retail stores
- Production scheduling
- Distribution planning between factory and warehouse
- Product mix problems
- Optimizing use of transportation facilities
- Strategic and tactical planning
- Blending problems

Linear programming does have many uses in the business world. But what must a student of management know prior to being capable of using linear programming? There are two basic areas that the manager must be able to define—the *objective* and *constraint* functions. Once this has been accomplished, the manager is in a position to turn the problem over to the quantitative specialist. The objective function is what the decision maker is attempting to maximize or minimize. It is a statement of how each component part relates to either cost or profit. For instance, if we are attempting to determine the optimum number of tables and chairs to manufacture in order to maximize profits, we would first have to determine the contribution to profit of both items. If chairs contributed $5 (selling price of $11 minus cost of $6) and tables contributed $7 (selling price of $17 minus cost of $10) the objective function would be stated as:

$$\text{Maximize} = \$5 \text{ (chair)} + \$7 \text{ (table)}$$

Once the objective function has been identified, the manager must next determine what restrictions or constraints he or she confronts in the problem. If the resources of personnel, material, and equipment were unlimited, there would be no need for linear programming. But since this is unlikely, managers must know what restrictions are placed on their ability to make decisions. For instance, there may be only fifty hours available in the machine shop to work on either table or chairs (definitely a restriction). Also, there may be only seventy hours available in the paint shop. If it takes one hour to machine a chair and two hours to machine a table and four hours to paint a chair and two hours to paint a table, we come up with the following constraint equation:

$$1 \text{ (chair)} + 2 \text{ (table)} \leq 50 \text{ (machine shop constraint)}$$
$$4 \text{ (chair)} + 2 \text{ (table)} \leq 70 \text{ (paint shop constraint)}$$

One should notice the inequality signs ($\leq$) in both equations. We are merely stating that the maximum amount of time in either the machine or paint shop does not have to be used. The inequality could also go the other direction ($\geq$) which means that a minimum amount of time must be used. Once the objective and constraint functions have been identified, the manager may turn the problem over to the analyst.

With all the benefits that can be derived through the use of linear programming, one might ask why it is not used in other types of projects. There are certain assumptions that must be met before linear programming should be used.

1. The variables (in our examples, tables and chairs) must be assumed to be divisible. We must, for example, be able to assume that we can make a fraction of a table.
2. Both the objective and constraint functions must be assumed to be linear. If it costs $5 to paint one table, it costs $10 to paint two tables. We do not get faster as we perform the task again and again.
3. We know precisely the costs or profits associated with the constraints and objective functions. There is no margin of error in these figures.[1]

In using linear programming, the manager's job is to develop the constraint and objective functions. The manager is the individual who is closest to the problem and best capable of providing this information. The actual mechanics of linear programming are often performed with the assistance of a computer.

FORECASTING

An effective business planner must be capable of estimating with a certain degree of accuracy what will occur in the future. Naturally, we can never be completely correct in projecting the future, but a high *batting average* in accomplishing this task often separates the successful from the less successful manager. In this section, we will concentrate on some of the forecasting techniques that have proven beneficial to business planners.

Terminology

A general overview of terminology used in forecasting will first be presented and is illustrated in Figure 13.4. The four basic components that demand forecasting should be appreciated in **demand forecasting** are the following:

---

1. Richard B. Chase and Nicholas J. Aquilano, *Production and Operations Management* (Homewood, Ill.: Richard D. Irwin, Inc., 1977), p. 50.

**FIGURE 13.4
Forecasting**

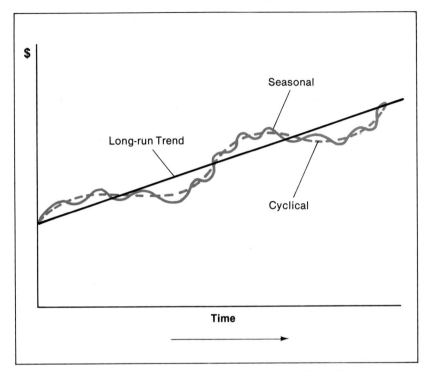

* Random patterns are not shown because we do not know when they will occur.

- long-term trend
- cyclical
- seasonal
- random demand

trend   As you can see in Figure 13.4, the **trend** line projects the long-run estimate of the demand for the product being evaluated. Long-run projections are typically said to be five years or more into the future. In this instance, it shows that the long-run demand for this product is increasing.

cyclical   But a business planner needs more than just a long-run trend. **Cyclical** variation occurs around the trend line. A business recession may cause sales to go down or, on the other hand, demand may be above the trend line in a recovery period. A common view of cyclical variations is greater than one year but less than five with the typical cyclical span being three years. Cyclical consideration is important because of the severe peaks and valleys associated with the demand for some products. Even though there is a trend for increased demand for the product, a firm may presently be in a valley in the business cycle which may affect production, inventory, and labor requirements.

seasonal

A business person often needs to evaluate demand patterns in a shorter time frame than cyclical. This is known as **seasonal** demand and the forecasted period is typically thought to be twelve months or less. During a twelve month period the demand for many products fluctuates drastically. Electric shaver sales are concentrated heavily in the holiday seasons; swim suits are sold in the spring. Knowledge of these seasonal demand patterns is quite important to the business planner because of production, inventory, and labor requirements.

random

Finally, **random** demand patterns are the ones that accelerate the early retirement of many business planners. With random demand there is no pattern. By definition it occurs for reasons that the business manager cannot anticipate, even with the most sophisticated forecasting techniques.

With this brief discussion of business forecasting completed, it is now time to consider some specific tools available to the business forecaster. It should be remembered that forecasting tools are especially needed in the factory environment. For instance, it is important to forecast sales adequately because production forecasts, labor forecasts, material forecasts, and cash forecasts depend on the projection of sales. The following discussion should not be considered all encompassing but is presented to give the student of management an appreciation of some of the tools that are available.

Moving Averages

moving averages

A simple technique for smoothing the effects of random variation is through the use of **moving averages.** Since we do not want to make a business decision based on a random occurrence that may never again happen, business people have attempted to remove this one-time occurrence through moving averages. As may be seen in Table 13.6, the

TABLE 13.6

Moving Average Example

Quarter	Actual Demand	Three Quarter Moving Average	Five Quarter Moving Average
Q 1	3000	—	—
Q 2	2350	2767	—
Q 3	2950	2758	3075
Q 4	2975	3342	3025
Q 1	4100	3275	3065
Q 2	2750	3133	3548
Q 3	2550	2533	2980
Q 4	2300	2683	2915
Q 1	3200	3092	3035
Q 2	3775	3442	—
Q 3	3350	—	—

different time periods are averaged to get both a three month moving average and a five month moving average. The greater the number of months that are averaged, the less effect the random variations will have on the demand estimation. To compute a three month moving average, periods one, two, and three are averaged. This provides the first figure for the three month moving average. To get the next month's estimate, the first month is dropped and the fourth month is added and again averaged. Through the use of moving averages the effects of random variation are reduced and the demand estimate is smoothed.

Exponential Smoothing

exponential smoothing

One of the major difficulties associated with moving averages is that a large amount of historical data must be used. When the **exponential smoothing** technique is applied the manager needs only three types of data:

- the forecast from the previous period
- the actual demand that resulted from this forecasted period
- a smoothing constant

While the first two pieces of data are relatively easy to obtain, determining the smoothing constant requires that the manager personally identify what he or she feels is a good response rate. This smoothing constant depends to a large extent on the past demand for the product. If it has been relatively stable, the smoothing constant will likely be small. However, if the product is experiencing rapid growth, the manager may wish to have a large smoothing constant to ensure that the firm is keeping up with actual demand.

Let us envision how exponential smoothing might be helpful through considering two entirely different products; one has a stable demand and the other has experienced a rapidly increasing demand. The manager has chosen a low smoothing constant (.05) for the stable product and a high smoothing constant (.50) for the rapid growth product. In both instances the previous forecast was 1,000 units and actual demand was 2,000 units. Two entirely different projections for future demand result, as may be seen below:

New Forecast = Past Forecast
     + Smoothing Constant (Actual Demand − Past Forecast)

New Forecast (Stable Product) = 1000 + .05 (2,000 − 1,000)
        = <u>1,050</u> units of forecasted demand

New Forecast (Rapid Growth Product) = 1000 + .5 (2,000 − 1,000)
         = <u>1,500</u> units of forecasted
          demand

The manager is attempting to maintain a balance in planning activities through the use of exponential smoothing. If the product has been relatively stable in demand there is no reason to believe that a rapid surge in sales will occur through other than perhaps random fluctuation. However, when a high smoothing constant is chosen, the manager realizes that demand shifts rapidly and requires swift action in order to be competitive. The identification of the proper smoothing constant represents the major difficulty in working exponential smoothing problems.

Regression Analysis

With the increased use of high speed computers and sophisticated statistical packages, the manager has at his or her disposal a more useful tool for forecasting—regression analysis. Its use has obtained respectability in accomplishing many forecasting functions ranging from estimating product demand to development of profiles of successful versus less successful employees within a particular firm.[2]

regression analysis

Regression analysis is used to predict one item (known as the dependent variable) through knowledge of other item(s) (known affectionately as the independent variables). The task of the manager involves first determining what you would like to predict and then identifying the independent variables to determine if they actually are capable of predicting a particular outcome. Suppose, for instance, the manager would like to determine the relationship that advertising and size of the sales force has upon company sales. The basic equation that would develop is as follows:

Y (Company Sales) = Advertising (X_1) + Sales Force Size (X_2)
(dependent variable)   (independent variable(s))

If there does exist a relationship the equation that might result is given below:

$$Y = 2 (X_1) + 4 (X_2)$$

Interpreted, the manager would determine that for each added dollar spent on adding to the sales force, total sales would increase by four dollars. However, for every dollar spent on advertising total sales would increase by only two dollars. The manager might use this model to assist in developing a marketing plan to achieve the greatest company sales. Naturally, the manager must determine the reliability of the model but we do not wish to take away from the enjoyment of a statistics class to learn the detailed mechanics associated with regression analysis.

---

2. R. Wayne Mondy and Frank N. Edens, "An Empirical Test of the Decision to Participate Model," *The Journal of Management* 2 (1977), pp. 11-16.

Time Series Analysis

time series analysis

Another approach to the use of regression is **time series analysis.** Here the same mathematical approach is used except that the independent variable is expressed in units of time. For instance, we might like to project the number of car sales in a particular district for the coming year. In order to accomplish this projection, we would need the car sales for previous years as shown in Table 13.7. Given this data, the prudent manager turns the work over to the brilliant analyst and the following equation is given to the manager:

$$Y \text{ (auto sales)} = -21{,}230 + 361 \text{ (Year)}$$

Substituting 1973 into the equation we have:

$$Y = -21{,}230 + 361 \text{ (73)} = 4{,}762$$

Thus, the estimated number of cars that will be sold in this district for the coming year is 4,762. The $-21{,}230$ represents a constant that results from the calculation of the regression equation. As with the previous illustration, the manager must study the accompanying statistics to determine the reliability of the model. But, it provides the manager with a valuable tool for planning and decision making.

TABLE 13.7
Auto Sales

Cars Sold	Year
400	1960
600	1961
1550	1962
1500	1963
1500	1964
2400	1965
3100	1966
2600	1967
2900	1968
3800	1969
4500	1970
4000	1971
4900	1972

SUMMARY

Only a few years ago, production and operations management concentrated primarily on the factory environment. Today, production and operations management takes on a much broader application in that any organization may conceivably benefit through the use of the techniques. Most of the quantitative techniques now apply to both factory and service industries. There are, however, several concepts that at one time were used primarily in the manufacturing environment. Site selection, plant layout, work methods, operations charts, worker machine charts, principles of motion economy, and labor measurement are some examples of traditional techniques.

A major point for the student of management to realize is that many companies are making extensive use of the various quantitative tools. One of the most valuable tools for a business planner is financial modeling. Two of the most commonly used financial models are break-even analysis and discounted cash flow analysis. Break-even analysis helps determine the amount of a particular product that must be sold if the firm is to generate enough revenue to cover costs. With discounted cash flow analysis, the time value of money becomes important. A dollar earned today does not have the same value as a dollar that will be earned in the future. Linear programming is used as a planning tool to assist management in allocating limited resources among competing demands in an optimum way.

An effective business planner must be capable of estimating with a certain degree of accuracy what will occur in the future. The basic components that should be understood in demand forecasting are long-term trend, cyclical demand, seasonal demand, and random demand. Some of the quantitative tools that are available to forecast demand include moving averages, exponential smoothing, regression analysis, and time series analysis. These forecasting tools will not provide the manager with all the answers concerning the future, but they do assist the manager in planning and decision making.

Review Questions

1. Why do we currently refer to production and operations management as opposed to merely production? What changes in attitudes have brought this about?

2. What are the traditional production management concepts and techniques?

3. Distinguish by definition and an example between moving averages, exponential smoothing, time series analysis, and regression analysis. What is the purpose of each?

4. According to the text, what should a manager know when considering using each of the various quantitative techniques?

5. Why is the time value of money so important to a manager?

6. Define:
   a. Break-even analysis
   b. Fixed costs
   c. Variable cost
   d. Discounted cash flow

Exercises

1. How might the discounted cash flow technique be used in the following instances?
   a. Purchase of a major league ball player
   b. Purchase of a fleet of trucks
   c. Decision by you to purchase or lease your business automobile
   d. A decision as to whether to go to college or go to work after completing high school

2. Think of five different type businesses. How could the following quantitative planning techniques be useful in their operations?
   a. Moving averages
   b. Exponential smoothing
   c. Time series analysis
   d. Regression analysis

REFERENCES

Adam, N., and Surkis, J. "Comparison of Capacity Planning Techniques in a Job Shop Control System." *Management Science*, May 1977, pp. 1011-1015.

Araten, M., and Dukman, B. "Linear Programming and Financial Cost Models for Industrial Enterprise." *Omega*, 1976, pp. 279–288.

Booler, J. M. P. "A Method for Solving Crew Scheduling Problems." *Operational Research Quarterly*, 1976, pp. 55-62.

Buffa, Elwood S. *Modern Production Management*, 4th ed. New York: John Wiley and Sons, 1973.

Chase, Richard B., and Aquilano, Nicholas J. *Production and Operations Management*, 2nd ed. Homewood, Ill.: Richard D. Irwin, Inc., 1977.

Clay, M. J. "Evaluating the Production Function." *Accountancy*, May 1977, pp. 82+.

Cummings, L. L. "Needed Research in Production/Operations Management: A Behavioral Perspective." *Academy of Management Review*, July 1977, pp. 500-504.

Daellenbauh, Hans G., and George, John A. *Introduction to Operations Research Techniques*. Boston: Allyn and Bacon, Inc., 1978.

Green, T. B. "Why Are Organizations Reluctant to Use Management Science/ Operations Research? An Empirical Approach." *Interfaces*, August 1976, pp. 59-62.

Harwood, G. B., and Hermanson, R. H. "Lease or Buy Decisions." *Journal of Accountancy*, September 1976, pp. 83-87.

Jenkins, J. O., et. al. "Computer-Based Scheduling of Technical Resources." *Omega*, 1977, pp. 317-332.

Knotts, Ulysses S., Jr., and Swift, Ernest W. *Management Science for Management Decisions*. Boston: Allyn and Bacon, Inc., 1978.

Lebell, D., and Krasner, O. J. "Selecting Environmental Forecasting Techniques from Business Planning Requirements." *Academy of Management Journal*, July 1977, pp. 373–383.

Lindsey, B. A. "Forecasting for Control." *Management Accounting*, September 1976, pp. 41-43.

McNamara, J. R. "Linear Programming Model for Long Range Capacity Planning in an Electric Utility." *Journal of Economics and Business*, Spring/Summer 1976, pp. 227-235.

Morey, R. "Operations Management in Selected Non-manufacturing Organizations." *Academy of Management Journal*, March 1976, pp. 120-124.

Petry, Glenn H. "Effective Use of Capital Budgeting Tools." *Business Horizons*, October 1975, pp. 57-65.

"Production Comes Back with a Bang." *Director*, August 1975, p. 120.

Rippe, R. D. "Integration of Corporate Forecasting and Planning." *Columbia Journal of World Business*, Winter 1976, pp. 54–61.

Robinson, S. M. "Characterization of Stability in Linear Programming." *Operations Research*, May 1977, pp. 435-447.

Sprague, L. G., and Sprague, C. R. "Management Science?" *Interfaces*, November 1976, pp. 57-62.

Soyster, A. L., et. al. "Conservation Linear Programming with Mixed Multiple Objectives." *Omega*, 1977, pp. 193-205.

Case Study

EXPONENTIAL SMOOTHING

Barry Smiler is the production manager for a firm that manufacturers high quality watches. His job is to maintain a smooth flow of production of these watches. In order to determine what levels of output to produce, Barry relies heavily on sales forecasts. If he produces too many watches, inventory will increase and this can be extremely costly to a company in the quality watch business. Should inventory become excessive, workers may have to be laid off or terminated. On the other hand, if too few watches are produced, the sales force gets extremely unhappy since orders cannot be filled. Barry is aware of exponential smoothing and decides to use it to assist him in estimating next month's demand. He realizes that last month's sales forecast was for 10,000 watches, but actual demand for watches during the month was 12,000. Barry also realizes that demand changes rapidly so he decides to use a .5 smoothing constant.

Questions

1. What is the forecasted demand for next month?
2. If demand were relatively constant, what size smoothing constant would you recommend that Barry use?

Case Study

BREAK-EVEN ANALYSIS

Phyllis Stevens, a junior management major at Midwestern State University, has been elected promotional manager for the Society for the Advancement of Management (S.A.M.), a professional organization of which she is a member. She is thinking of recommending that S.A.M. sell miniature flags of the university to the student body. Students can take these flags to football games and wave them to cheer their team on to victory! (The team is expected to have a winning season.)

Phyllis is aware of break-even analysis so she develops some cost figures for producing the flags. She estimates that the fixed cost for the project will be $200. The flags will be made by members and she estimates that the variable cost to make each flag is fifty cents. They will sell them for $1.

Questions

1. How many flags must the organization sell in order to break even?
2. How many flags must the group sell to make a profit of $100?
3. If Phyllis thinks that the maximum number of flags that the group can sell is 500, do you feel that S.A.M. should take on the project? Discuss.

Chapter 14

KEY TERMS

simulation

waiting line theory

queuing theory

quality control

statistical quality control

variable sampling

attribute sampling

control chart

inventory control

ordering costs

carrying costs

ABC method

network

Program Evaluation and
Review Technique

Critical Path Method

event

activity

optimistic time

most likely time

pessimistic time

expected time

critical path

Production and Operations Management II

LEARNING OBJECTIVES

After completing this chapter you should be able to

1. Describe how simulation and waiting line theory may be used to solve business problems.
2. Explain the basic quantitative techniques available for use in the control function.
3. Describe how PERT may be used to assist in both planning and controlling.

In chapter 13, our discussion was directed toward gaining an appreciation of some of the quantitative tools that are especially beneficial in planning. But, as was previously mentioned, the fact that these tools are discussed as being useful in the planning function should not be thought to mean that they are beneficial only in that area. The same general theme will be followed in this chapter. Concepts will be presented that have been successful in helping managers solve problems. Simulation and waiting line theory will first be discussed. These will be followed by a brief presentation of the techniques that have been applied successfully to the control function of management. Included in these topics are inventory control, quality control, and network models (PERT and CPM). Again, their presentation will follow the format of presenting the techniques from the standpoint of how managers can use them in their jobs.

SIMULATION

In front of a radar scope in the western United States sits a young officer with his eyes fixed to the scope. He is controlling an Air Force fighter jet whose target is a Russian bomber flying toward San Francisco. The conversation is progressing in the following manner:

> *The young controller:* "Tango Papa O1, this is Ringdove. You have a Russian bomber in your 12 o'clock position closing fast. Looks as if its target is San Francisco."
>
> *The fighter pilot:* "Roger, Ringdove. I have a visual and am going in for the kill. Ringdove, Ringdove, my engine just flamed out. I am bailing out!"

Will San Francisco be destroyed? Will the fighter pilot be saved? These and other type problems occurred daily to one of the authors when he was a United States Air Force aircraft controller. The Russian bomber was on the radar screen, but a real bomber was not attacking San Francisco. The pilot who *bailed* out was merely in another room "simulating" the problem. The purpose of this exercise was to train the young controller for possible real-life situations. A fighter pilot would hate to have to bail out and lose his plane in order for the controller to be trained. It was much better to simulate the occurrence, representing the real-life situation as much as possible. Businesses, as well as the military, have found **simulation** to be a valuable tool to assist in the planning and decision-making processes.

simulation

With the advent of the high speed electronic computers, simulation has come of age. Its value has been recognized for many years but its use had previously been restricted because manual simulation takes so much time and tended to make the technique impractical. In chapter 4 a model was

Simulation permits the manager to ask many "what if" questions before having to make the decision in the real world.

defined as an abstraction of the real world. Thus, a simulation model is an attempt to represent a real world situation through mathematical logic in an attempt to predict what will occur in an actual situation. Its uses are many and widespread.

As may be observed in Table 14.1, firms are using simulation for a variety of reasons ranging from "economic analysis of alternate hog cutting methods" by Oscar Mayer & Company to the calculation of locomotive fuel requirements by Southern Railway. In all instances simulation assists the manager by permitting him or her to ask many *what if* questions without having to make the decision in the real world.

A major factor that should be realized is that simulation transcends the boundaries of many of the other quantitative techniques that have been

MR. GENE BARHAM

General Manager
Fisher Controls Company

A college degree in chemical engineering but a desire to pursue a career in management has produced an interesting career progression path for Gene Barham, currently a general manager for Fisher Controls Company. When Gene graduated from college in 1959, he had already made up his mind that he wanted ultimately to be in management. "I've always wanted to run my own show," says Gene, "and as a general manager with Fisher Controls this is the closest thing there is to running your own business within a major corporation. There is relative independence, as long as you do well!"

Gene began his career in the technical end of the chemical business in the agriculture product plant in Luling, Louisiana, with Monsanto Company. His managerial skills were soon recognized and in 1967 he was promoted to manufacturing superintendent and transferred to Muscatine, Iowa. Next, he was plant manager at Bridgeview in Chicago for two years, and he then served for three years as a plant manager at Ligonier, Indiana. Gene saw another portion of the business world in 1975 as he was made marketing manager of blownware products for the Monsanto Commercial Products Company. This experience in marketing provided the necessary ingredient to progress to general manager, Fisher Controls Company, a division of Monsanto Company, in 1977.

Gene believes that the ability to communicate and get people to work toward common objectives is the real key to getting results. A major responsibility of a manager is to provide a clear set of directions for everyone to work toward. Gene is very committed to developing people and depends heavily on others in the organization. He says, "People who work with me have a lot of freedom to accomplish results, as well as opportunities for cross training. It is good for them and for the company."

TABLE 14.1
Uses of Simulation Techniques

Company	Primary Uses
Bendix Corporation	Inventory control Production scheduling
Carrier Corporation	Energy modeling
Crown Zellerbach	Inventory control Production planning
Glidden Division, SCM Corporation	Price–profit analysis Production scheduling C&R capacity analysis system
Inland Container Company	Determine the impact of the number of pugh ladles on hot metal distribution Evaluate productivity effect of additional pollution control equipment
Kaiser Steel Corporation	Hot strip mill production rates under different conditions
Kimberly-Clark	Plant layout Inventory control Process system design
Lear Siegler, Inc.	Projecting results based on assumptions tied to math models to project economic impact on sales volumes, profits and cash flow
Oscar Mayer & Company	Product layout within an order filling cooler Economic analysis of alternate hog cutting methods Plant design problems
Proctor & Gamble Company	Design of manufacturing facilities Design of communication facilities Understanding of chemical processes
The Southland Corporation	Analysis of operations EDP teleprocessing system Distribution center layout Vehicle delivery programs
3M Company	Distribution system Inventory control

and will be discussed. As such, it is not a separate quantitative tool; rather it is a procedure that has been used effectively in conjunction with other mathematical tools, such as inventory control, quality control, waiting line theory, and mathematical modeling. When a manager operates in an uncertain environment, simulation may be considered.

Simulation is a quantitative technique that many students of management often shy away from because they believe it is too sophisticated for them to use. They apparently reason that they must know computer

INSIGHTS TO SUCCESS

Don't expect true managerial responsibilities until earned on the job.

FRED DeCHANT, Personnel Director, Georgia-Pacific Corporation

programming and how to operate the computer to use simulation. This certainly need not be the case for most firms have their own in-house programmers capable of interpreting the needs of the user and developing the necessary computer programs.

On the other hand, this does not mean that the manager has nothing to do. He or she must be capable of clearly defining the problem that needs solving and identifying the factors that may be associated with the problem. The general steps associated with developing a simulation model are presented in Figure 14.1. Once the problem has been identified a simulation model is developed and run. The results are analyzed and then if the manager again desires to ask other *what if* questions regarding the problem, they can be asked. The manager is in a position to ask many questions regarding the other factors that could affect the problem.

Assume for a moment that you are employed by Oscar Mayer and you are attempting to determine the optimum manner to cut up a hog to maximize profits. The problem has not been defined, but what are some of the possible factors that could affect obtaining optimum results? Perhaps the manager desires to determine whether to automate a production line or hire additional workers. What happens as the size of the hogs vary? The hog cutting methods may have to be changed. Through simulation a person is once again able to see that there is more than one way to skin a hog!

FIGURE 14.1
Steps in Simulation

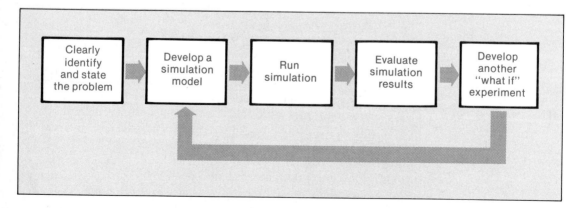

Southern railroads also have found simulation quite beneficial. Have you ever wondered why more trains don't arrive at the same time on a single track? Trains are different lengths and weights; they travel at different speeds, and typically must share a common track to get from one place to another. At times there are two or more tracks that the cars could travel, but the majority of the time there is only one. Simulation provides the manager with the ability to recognize the many variables that are involved and ask questions regarding solutions to the problem.

Even Procter and Gamble Company utilizes simulation to assist in solving some unusual problems. Gary O. Walla, management science manager for Procter and Gamble Company, provides the following example of how they use simulation.

Pulp forms the basic raw ingredient for manufacturing paper and can be made in a variety of grades that are dependent on the chemical processing and the blend of wood species. Procter and Gamble refines pulp from trees and they use simulation to aid in the design of a woodyard, assuring maximum operating efficiency with a minimum of capital investment.

A woodyard serves as a surge area for wood arriving from various sources by unscheduled rail cars and trucks. The wood is in the form of short and long logs and must be stored until used in the pulp mill. Naturally, rail cars require different unloading equipment than trucks and the simulation helps determine the optimum number of unloading stations for both. Additionally, different equipment is needed to handle long logs than short logs for both rail cars and trucks. After long logs are unloaded, they are cut into short logs before they can be stored, an operation which requires other special equipment. Finally, the operation of the pulp mill needs a constant feed of a well controlled blend of wood species to be efficient. Wood must be stockpiled sufficiently to assure a constant feed regardless of the weather which can bring the tree cutting operations to a standstill for a couple of weeks, or equipment failures in the woodyard which require repair. In net, the simulation of the flow of materials through the woodyard helps size equipment and stockpiles of logs to assure constant availability of the proper wood species for input to the pulp mill.

Examples of how simulation has been used effectively in business are extensive. Its use is expected to receive additional attention by managers in the future. As the risk of making a particular decision increases, managers will need to evaluate many options prior to making a commitment to allocate resources. Simulation provides an excellent tool for evaluating alternatives and finding solutions to problems.

WAITING LINE/QUEUING THEORY

Friday is payday and you want to get to the bank to cash your check in time to do some shopping before the stores close. You know the main

waiting line theory
queuing theory

bank is closed, but the one-window, drive-in bank is still open. As you pull into the drive-in bank lane, your heart sinks; there are ten cars ahead of you and the line does not appear to be moving very fast. You may not realize it but you have now confronted a **waiting line theory** or **queuing theory** problem.

A waiting line problem occurs when arrivals at a service facility (the bank's drive-in window) want service (all the drivers of the cars want banking service). The problem that exists is that all customers do not require the same type of service (some may want to merely cash a check and others want to deposit an entire week's receipts) and customers do not arrive at regular intervals (it has at times appeared that everyone arrives at once and you are a second too late). A waiting line problem involves a tradeoff or balance of costs. If the line is constantly too long, some customers may get angry and change banks; this results in lower deposits and lost revenue for the bank. But, there is another cost that must be considered. It also costs to add an additional drive-in window and pay the salary of another teller. From a managerial standpoint, waiting line problems assist the manager in determining if it is worth the additional investment to add the new drive-in window.

**MOST IMPORTANT REASONS FOR SUCCESS
AND EFFECTIVENESS AS A MANAGER**

- Ability to make decisions
- Able to delegate responsibility to subordinates.
- Capable of creating and maintaining a sense of direction
- 100% sold on the free enterprise system
- Able to be a good listener when necessary
- A good judge of people
- Approach each project enthusiastically

WARREN E. McCAIN, Chairman of the Board, Albertson's, Incorporated

---

Another illustration of a waiting line problem that virtually everyone has seen relates to the number of checkout counters at a grocery store. Just how many should be kept open at a given time? Customers may get quite angry if they have to wait an excessive amount of time to be checked out. But it also costs the store if checkers are behind the cash registers with nothing to do. Again, a balance must be achieved. When the store was built, a waiting line problem should also have been considered. The store developer must consider how many checkout counters to initially install. For every checkout counter it costs because store space is valuable. However, if insufficient counters are included, lost revenue may result.

TABLE 14.2
Uses of Waiting Line/Queuing Theory

Company	Uses
Bendix Corporation	Maintenance Skilled trades study
Kimberly-Clark	Process systems layout Process design capacities of component units
Southern Railroads	Shop assembly line procedures Scheduling locomotive maintenance
Oscar Mayer & Company	Production line balancing Plant design problems Production scheduling
The Southland Corporation	EDP system
Glidden Division, SCM Corporation	Queuing theory developing Industrial Engineering standards Line balancing developing Industrial Engineering standards
Proctor & Gamble Company	Design of communication facilities Design of manufacturing facilities
Crown Zellerbach	Maintenance evaluation
Kaiser Steel Corporation	Hot Metal Delivery System Study

Businesses have found that waiting line or queuing theory can assist in the solution of a variety of problems. As may be seen in Table 14.2, the uses are quite widespread but differ depending on the specific needs of the firm. A major petroleum firm uses queuing theory to determine if they need to construct additional docking facilities. If a ship is delayed in unloading, it costs the firm a certain amount per day. The ship cannot make money for the firm if it is not transporting petroleum. But, if additional docks are constructed, this also is expensive. Again, a balance must be achieved.

The mathematics of waiting line problems is often quite complicated. But, as with the other quantitative tools, this should not keep the manager from using the approach. He or she must first recognize that queuing theory is appropriate to solve the problem and be able to identify the costs that are involved in the balancing process. At this point the brilliant quantitative expert may again be brought in to accomplish the mathematical manipulation.

CONTROL TOPICS

As was mentioned in chapter 12, there are numerous control techniques available for use by a manager. Three approaches will next be presented: quality control, inventory control, and network models. Again, it should be emphasized that the techniques can be used in other managerial functions.

QUALITY CONTROL

quality control   Of all the quantitative techniques discussed, **quality control** is the one that is likely to be in the vocabulary of the majority of Americans. When a person states that they got a "lemon" the immediate impression is that the product they purchased was of inferior quality. As was mentioned in chapter 12, quality of a product is the combination of several factors such as form, dimension, composition, and color. For a particular product, all of these factors may have to be considered with regard to quality.

But, what exactly is meant when the term quality is mentioned? Quality is the degree of conformity to a certain predetermined standard. As was mentioned in chapter 2, standards result ultimately from the establishment of objectives. If the company has an objective of gaining a reputation for manufacturing a high quality product, standards will have to be high. In order to meet these high standards, there would likely have to be a very rigid quality control program. On the other hand, other firms may not have as their objective to be recognized as producing the highest quality product in the industry. Increased quality generally results in higher prices. Therefore, some firms may target their appeal to a market that desires lower prices and will accept lower quality. Certain standards remain, but they are not as rigid as with the high quality product.

There are numerous ways to maintain quality of a product. A company could make the decision to have a 100 percent inspection of all items manufactured. But, even with a total inspection program, some defects will not be discovered. When you insert the human element into a quality control environment, mistakes will occasionally be made. Some items that are good may be rejected and other items that are bad will be accepted.

In many instances it is impossible to have a 100 percent inspection. For instance, if the standard for the life of a light bulb were 200 hours, you would have to burn the light for the assigned number of hours to determine if it met standards. Naturally, you would have no product to sell in this situation. Tire manufacturing companies set standards for their tires in order that they will be capable of being driven a certain number of miles. If each tire were placed on a machine and run the assigned number of miles to determine if they can meet standards, there would be no product to market. In still other instances, the cost to inspect each item to determine if they conform to standard is prohibitive. If each nail in a keg were inspected separately, the cost to inspect might be higher than the price of the nails.

statistical quality control   The technique that is available to overcome the above deficiencies is known as **statistical quality control.** In statistical quality control, a portion of the total number of items is inspected. For instance, five out of one hundred items may be selected, and an estimate be made as to the characteristics of the other ninety-five. Naturally, some degree of error exists. For instance, if out of one hundred items only five are defective (this amount of error may be perfectly acceptable), it is conceivable that all five defectives might be selected and the entire lot would be rejected. On the other hand, there might be only five good parts out of the one hundred parts manufactured. These five good parts might be the ones drawn and the batch would be accepted. With sampling there is risk, but the benefits of sampling are far superior to other procedures in many instances.

There are two basic types of sampling plans—sampling by attributes and sampling by variables. Both are appropriate for use but under different circumstances.

Sampling by Variables

variable sampling

A plan developed for **variable sampling** consists of determining how closely an item conforms to an established standard. In essence, degrees of goodness and degrees of badness are permitted. For instance, a stereo speaker is designed to project a certain tone quality. All speakers will not project precisely the same tone quality. Some speakers will have quality that is above the established standard and some will have tone quality that is below standard. This does not necessarily mean that the speaker will be rejected. Only when the quality is outside a certain established limit will it be rejected.

Sampling by Attributes

attribute sampling

With sampling by variables, degrees of conformity are considered; with **attribute sampling,** the item is either acceptable or unacceptable. The product is either good or bad; there are no degrees of conformity to consider. For instance, if a key punch operator makes only one off-punch in a general purpose computer card, that card is rejected. It is not 99 percent correct.

Control Charts

control chart

A procedure that measures the process during actual operations is referred to as a **control chart.** They are used with both variable and attribute sampling although the statistical procedure for developing the charts is different. First the standard is determined (see Figure 14.2). A variable sampling plan in the manufacture of tire treads might have standards which test thickness, weight, length, and width. The company creates a desired level of acceptability through the standards. In the example of the

FIGURE 14.2
Example of Control Chart

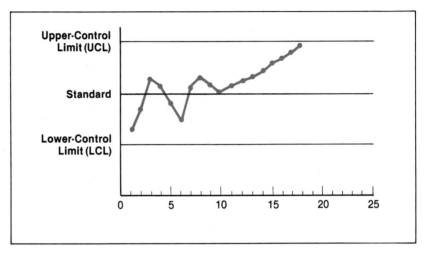

key punch operator, a certain percent of defects would constitute the standard.

Once the standard has been established the manager must determine the amount of deviation that will be acceptable. The amount of deviation that will be acceptable above the standard is referred to as the *upper control limit* (UCL) and the amount of deviation below the standard is referred to as the *lower control limit* (LCL). If a product that is being evaluated falls within the two extremes between the UCL and LCL, it will be accepted. If it falls outside the limit, it will be rejected. Although the statistics involved in the development of control charts are beyond the scope of this text, the concept is nevertheless sound.

Another benefit that accrues through the use of control charts is that potential problems may be recognized prior to their actual occurrence. As may be seen in Figure 14.2, from day 10 until day 17 the quality of a product is progressively getting worse. Although still within the limits of acceptability, if the problem is not corrected, the process will very shortly likely go above the upper control limit. When a manager sees this pattern developing he or she is in a position to take corrective action.

What a Manager Should Know

Through an understanding of the objectives of the firm, a manager establishes standards and levels of quality that are in line with these goals. He or she realizes that as quality increases, costs go up. Quality represents a cost! There is an optimum level of quality for each company consistent with maximizing profits. The manager, working in conjunction with statistical and accounting personnel, will be able to develop a plan that is consistent with attaining these goals. The primary task of a manager at upper levels is determining the quality level that is appropriate. A lower-level supervisor monitors the quality on a day-to-day basis to ensure that the stated level of quality is being maintained.

INVENTORY CONTROL

inventory control

Our exposure to inventory and **inventory control** occurs almost daily. You hear that a car dealership has excessive inventory and will offer you a special deal to reduce his inventory. A furniture dealer provides you with a similar offer. While there may be a bit of sales promotion in these instances, inventory does represent a cost that must be controlled. A product in inventory constitutes an idle, but valuable resource. Suppose that the car dealership mentioned above keeps a million dollars in extra inventory for one year. At a 10 percent interest rate, $100,000 would be lost because items in inventory do not draw interest. Much of the resources of some major companies are in inventory; failure to control inventories can mean the difference between a profit or a loss to a firm.

INSIGHTS TO SUCCESS

Seek involvement in areas outside your specialty field in order to obtain breadth of experience. Try to secure a more responsible and challenging assignment every 2–4 years.

G. ROBERT BAER, Group Vice-President, Ball Corporation

Purposes of Inventory

One of the major purposes of inventory is that it permits independence of operations between two activities. For instance, if Machine A makes a product that will be used in a later stage by Machine B and Machine A breaks down, Machine B will have to cease operation unless inventory has been previously built up.

Inventories also provide for continuous operations when demand for the product is not consistent. Electric razors are sold primarily during the Christmas holiday season. But, a manufacturer of electric razors typically keeps production going through the entire year. Inventory is built up during the year and sold during the holiday seasons. Stability is assured in that a skilled work force can be maintained and equipment usage can be kept at an optimal level.

Another purpose of inventory is to be capable of filling orders when they are received, thereby maintaining customer satisfaction. If orders arrived on a constant basis there would be no need to maintain inventory. But if five orders come in this month and a hundred are processed the next month, a company might be hard pressed to fill the hundred requests unless an inventory had been maintained.

Costs Involved

As with several of the quantitative techniques, inventory control involves a balancing of two general types of costs—ordering costs and carrying costs. **Ordering costs** relate to the clerical expenses associated with preparing the order. **Carrying costs** include all of the expenses that would be associated with maintaining the product before it is sold or used. Taxes, insurance, interest on capital invested, storage, electricity, and spoilage would be some of the items associated with carrying costs. The purchase cost is the price of the product multiplied by the number of items ordered.

ordering costs
carrying costs

Thus, the total cost associated with a particular order follows the following general formula:

Total Cost = Ordering Cost + Carrying Cost + Purchase Cost

It is the task of the manager to purchase in amounts that will minimize total cost (Economic Order Quantity, EOQ). You realize that if you order less frequently, ordering costs will go down, but carrying costs go up. On the other hand, if you submit frequent orders, ordering costs go up but carrying costs are reduced. This balancing process is graphically presented in Figure 14.3. The optimum number of items to order at any one time is at the lowest point on the total cost curve. This lowest point would be where carrying costs and ordering costs intersect.

In order to determine the Economic Order Quantity, calculus is used in the development of the mathematical model. Again, the manager does not have to be a quantitative wizard to determine EOQ. A manager, however, must be capable of identifying two primary costs: carrying (C) and ordering (O). Through the power of calculus, an EOQ formula is then determined from the total cost equation. The basic equation for EOQ is presented below.

$$\text{Economic Order Quantity} = \sqrt{\frac{2\left(\substack{\text{Ordering}\\\text{Cost}}\right)\left(\substack{\text{Annual}\\\text{Demand}}\right)}{\text{Carrying Costs}}} = \sqrt{\frac{2\,(O) \times (D)}{C}}$$

FIGURE 14.3

Economic Order Quantity Illustration

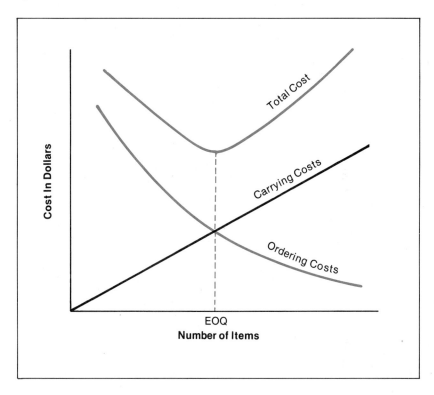

If we assume that annual demand is 10,000 units, carrying cost is $20 per unit, and ordering cost is $40, we will determine that the optimum number to order is 2,000. We cannot choose another order quantity that would lower the total cost (see Figure 14.3).

It should be remembered that the model described above is one of the simplest to develop. The sophistication level of the model depends on the actual needs of the company and the demands of the environment. The manager must be capable of realizing when inventory control procedures may be useful and must identify what costs may be associated with the problem. Then specialists such as accountants and mathematicians are called upon to assist in the development of the model. The manager provides the guidelines and ensures that necessary output is received.

The ABC Method of Inventory Control

There are times when it is impractical to monitor every item that is in inventory with the same degree of intensity. A procedure that permits the manager to determine which items should be under close scrutiny relates

ABC method

to the ABC method. With the **ABC method,** inventories are classified into three groups according to cost.

- A Category—Small number of items but large dollar value
- B Category—Moderate number of items and cost
- C Category—Large number of items but low dollar value

Through the ABC classification, a manager is able to develop a sophisticated system to monitor the Category A items. Items in the category might include automobiles, machinery and tractors. Category B items would have a less sophisticated inventory control system. Category C items might not even be controlled as the cost associated with monitoring the items would be prohibitive, such as pencils and paper. Through the ABC method, a manager is capable of utilizing resources allocated to inventory in an optimum manner.

NETWORK MODELS

network

The number of separate tasks that must be accomplished to build a skyscraper or a dam across a river are almost impossible to conceive for the average person. We are often fascinated at how the construction manager in charge of a project of this magnitude is able to coordinate all the tasks and arrive at a finished product. When the project is nonrecurrent, large, complex, and involves multiple organizations, the manager needs a tool that will assist in coordinating this complicated **network** of interdependencies. He or she needs to be able to think through the project in its entirety and see where resources can be shifted or rescheduled to ensure that the project is completed within the time and cost constraints.

Program Evaluation and Review Technique

Critical Path Method

The primary techniques available to accomplish the above mentioned tasks are **Program Evaluation and Review Technique** (PERT) and **Critical Path Method** (CPM). PERT was developed to assist in the rapid development of the Polaris submarine program. During approximately the same time period (1957–58), researchers for E. I. DuPont de Nemours and Company and computer specialists from what was the Remington Rand's Univac division combined their talents to develop a method to schedule and control all activities involved in constructing chemical plants. The result of their effort was a network model termed *critical path method.*

Both PERT and CPM have received widespread acceptance since their beginning in 1957–59. The manner in which some firms have used the techniques may be seen in Table 14.3. As may be seen, their use primarily involved construction projects, but some firms such as 3M Company even use the technique to assist in the development of new products. Firms that do major construction work for the government are required by contract to use PERT.

TABLE 14.3
Uses of PERT or CPM

Company	Uses
Bendix Corporation	Plant construction Project work
Carrier Corporation	Plant construction Government projects
Kimberly-Clark	Control of major projects Systems design
The Signal Companies, Inc.	Petroleum process unit construction Industrial building construction
Southern Railway	Major plant construction project Installation of new MIS system at major RR yards Time schedule for preparing five-year plan
3M Company	Construction projects Introduction of new products Marketing plans
Oscar Mayer & Company	Plant construction New product development and production startup Allocation of craft personnel
The Southland Corporation	Facility construction Establishment of a new operation
Glidden Division, SCM Corporation	Plant construction
Lear Siegler	New product development Major program control (particularly government contracts)
Procter & Gamble Company	Facilities construction New product introduction
Kellogg Company	New product development Construction project control Forecasting New plant construction
Crown Zellerbach	Construction Most capital projects Planning inputs
J. Ray McDermott & Co., Inc.	Plant construction
Kaiser Steel Corporation	Construction of new facilities

PERT

Network analysis is common to both PERT and CPM. Because of their similarity only PERT will be discussed in its entirety. Two definitions are first needed—an event and an activity.

event   An **event** is a meaningful specified accomplishment (physical or intellectual) in the program plan, recognizable at a particular instance of time. It does not consume time or resources. A circle or node provides the representation of an event.

activity   An **activity** is the time consuming element of the program. It is represented by an arrow.

In order to assist in the understanding of PERT, a project will be developed. The project entails obtaining a production contract award for an aircraft. The principal steps to be taken by a project manager in this problem are described below.

1. Define the objective of the project and specify the factors (time, cost) that must be considered as the variables to be controlled. For instance, how quick must the project be completed or how much money is allocated for completion of the project.
2. List all of the significant activities that must be performed for the project objectives to be achieved. As one might expect, a manager who is unfamiliar with the project would find it difficult to accomplish this task. The activities for this project are as follows:

Preparing specifications
Establishing quantity requirements
Negotiating contract
Administrative delay
Preparing test facilities
Developing airframe
Developing engine
Assembling airframe
Installing engine
Preparing test
Testing
Obtaining headquarters approval
Evaluating by contractor
Negotiating contract

3. Develop a statement of the relationship among project activities. The order in which each task is to be accomplished is also specified. A PERT network is then developed through this information. (See Figure 14.4.) As may be seen, the prototype airframe and the prototype engine must be completed before the test model is completed.

4. Determine the expected times that will be required to complete each activity. PERT requires that three time estimates be provided.

optimistic time

Optimistic time—If everything goes right and nothing goes wrong, the project can be completed in this amount of time.

most likely time

Most likely time—The most realistic completion time for the activity.

pessimistic time

Pessimistic time—If everything goes wrong and nothing goes right, the project will be completed in this amount of time.

The expected time for the completion of each activity may be seen in Figure 14.5. For instance, the optimistic time for the activity "developing airframe" is 36 weeks, the pessimistic time is 56 weeks, and the most likely time is 40 weeks. Inserting these figures into the expected time formula, we determine that 42 weeks is the expected time to complete the activity.

expected time

Expected time is then computed by applying the three time estimates to the following formula:

Expected Time =

$$\frac{\text{Optimistic Time} + 4\ (\text{Most Likely Time}) + \text{Pessimistic Time}}{6}$$

critical path

5. Determine the **critical path,** that is, the longest path from start to finish of the project. There are numerous computer programs that are available to perform the mechanics of this task. The actual work of the manager terminates once the three time estimates have been obtained. The critical path for this project is represented by the broken line seen in Figure 14.6. If any activity along the critical path is a week late, the entire project will be delayed an additional week.

6. Determine the probability of completing the entire project or a particular activity on time. This in itself is a major feature of PERT. Because of the three estimates, the manager is able to obtain an estimate of whether the project will be completed on schedule. The optimistic and pessimistic times have been determined to assist in this operation. If there were but one time estimate, the most likely

FIGURE 14.4
PERT Network with Activities and Events Included

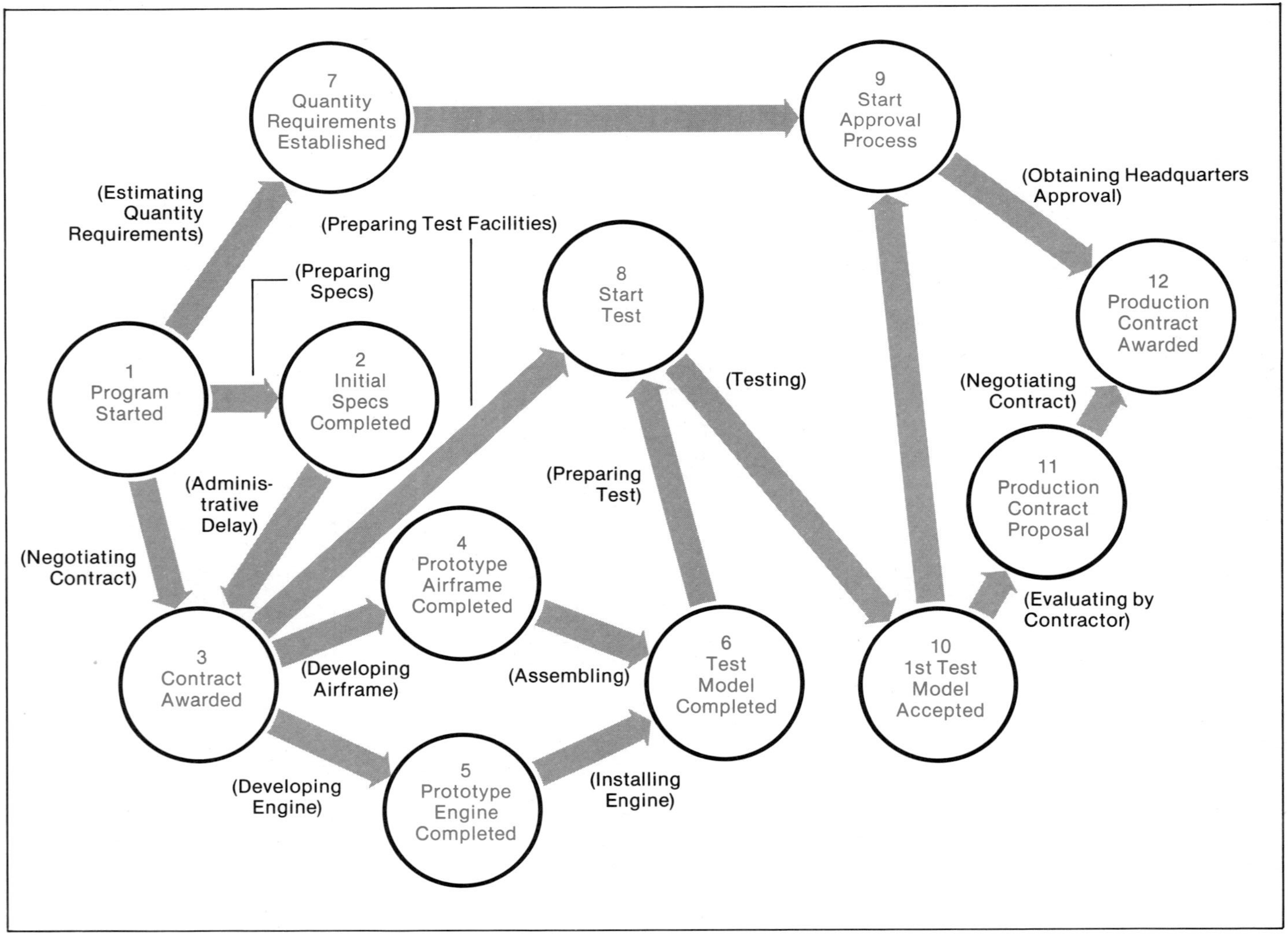

FIGURE 14.5
Expected Times to Complete Each Activity

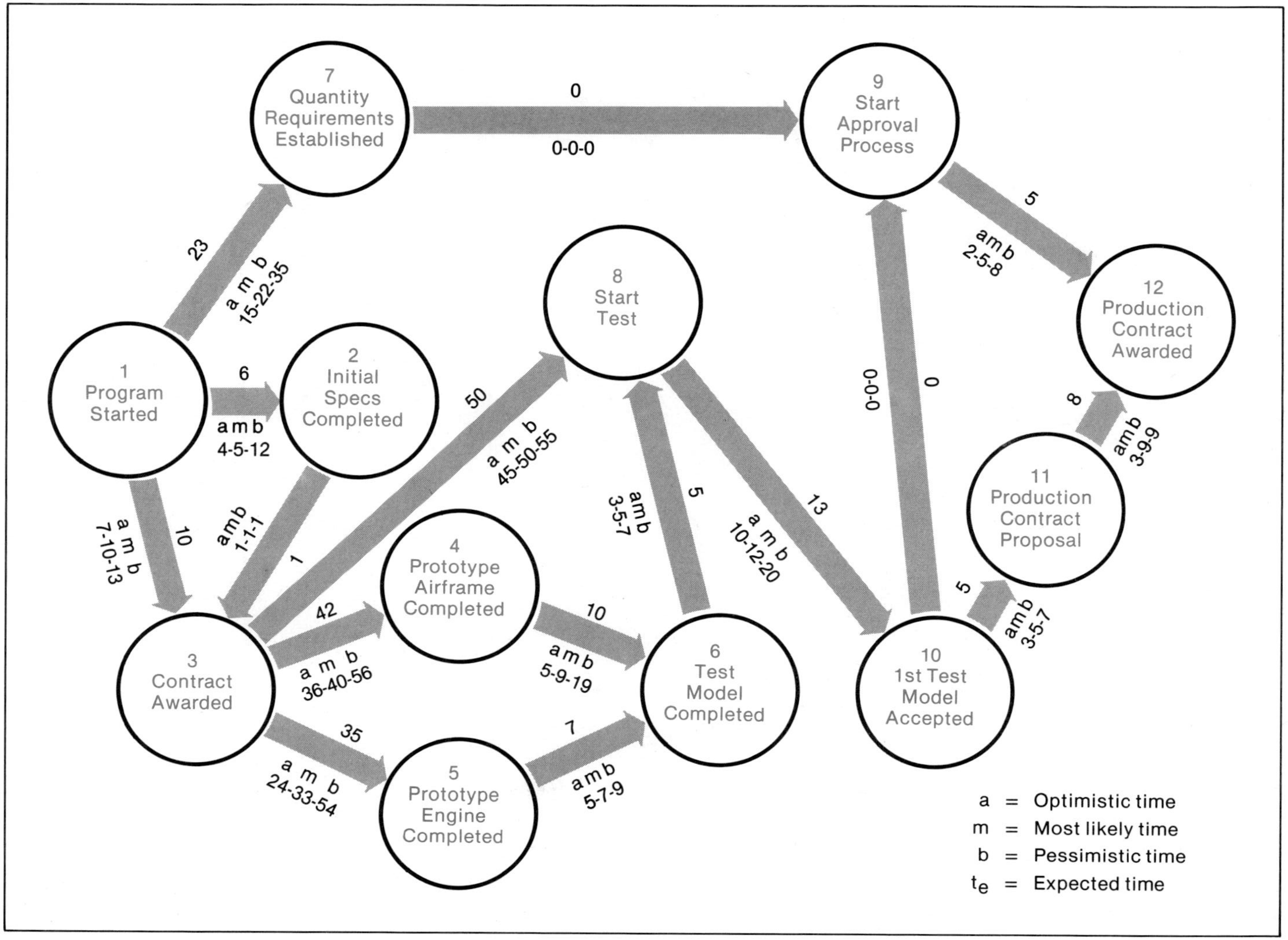

a = Optimistic time
m = Most likely time
b = Pessimistic time
t_e = Expected time

FIGURE 14.6
Critical Path for Project

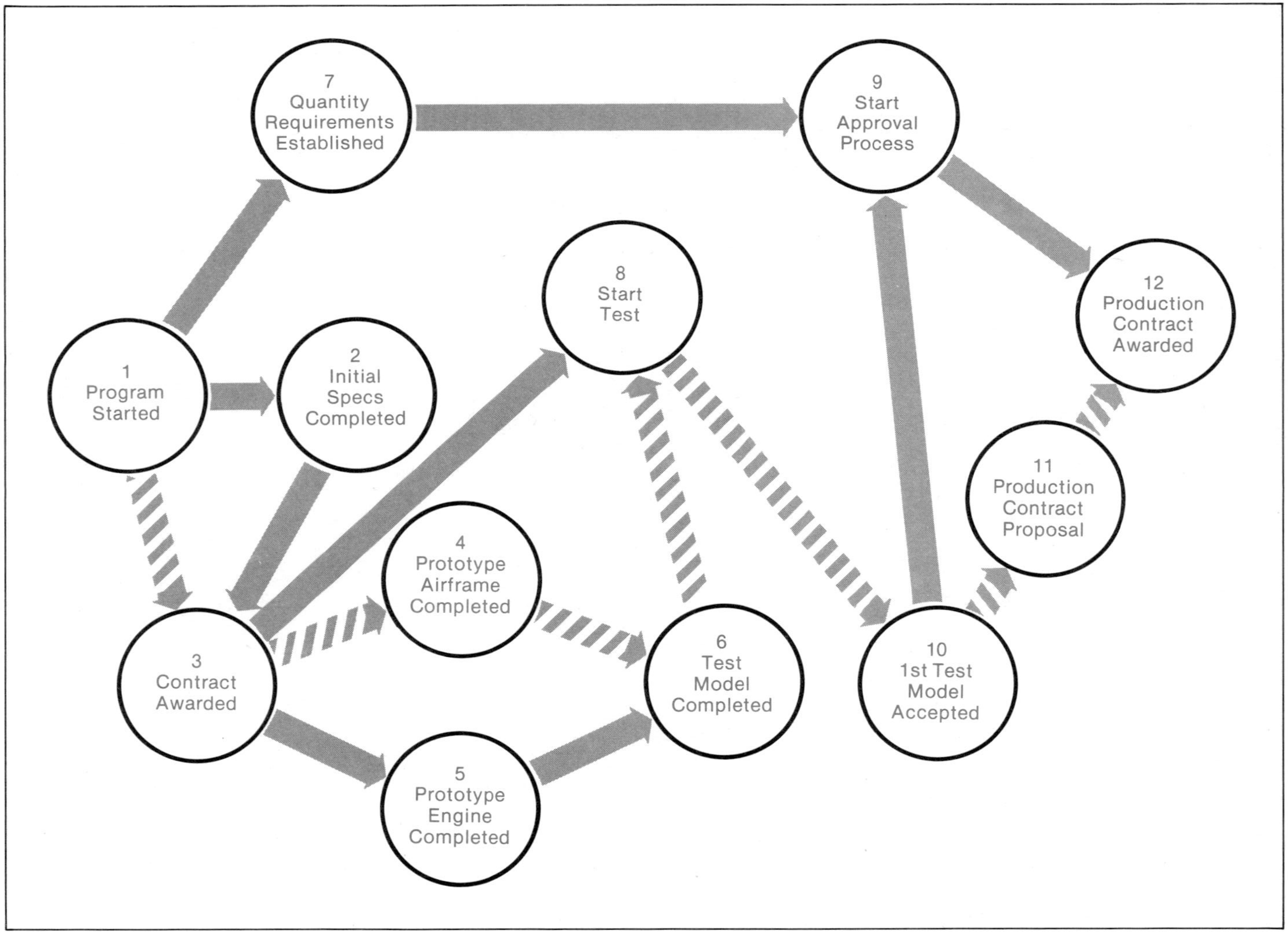

time, probabilities could not be computed. A manager usually finds it beneficial to relate the optimistic and pessimistic times to the most likely time.

For instance, the activity "developing engine" would likely cause greater concern to the manager than the activity "developing airframe." The difference between the optimistic time and pessimistic time for "developing engine" is 30 weeks (54-24) while the difference for the activity "developing airframe" is but 20 weeks (56-36). A manager will likely monitor the activities that have the greatest difference between optimistic and pessimistic time because they provide the greatest potential for not meeting the completion date.

Once the critical path has been identified, the manager is able to quickly determine what activities must be carefully monitored. If an activity along the critical path slips one day, the entire project will be delayed one day. Activities that are not on the critical path may not have to be monitored as carefully as those on the critical path. The manager is also in a position to determine which activities are not likely to be completed on time and carefully monitor them.

PERT may serve both as a planning and a control function. It *forces* a manager to thoroughly think through a project and identify the tasks that must be accomplished and how they interrelate in the completion of the project. It serves as a control function in that a critical path (the longest path from start to finish of the project) is identified. Thus, a manager is able to work with extremely complex projects and still maintain control over the project.

Critical Path Method

The developers of CPM were dealing with projects for which the time and cost of tasks (activities) required to complete the project were known. In CPM the points or nodes of the CPM network represent activities rather than events. Also, there is but one time estimate in CPM because it was designed to accommodate situations in which sets of standardized activities were required for the completion of a complex project. Time for completion of a task was relatively easy to determine accurately. Because there was but one time estimate, probabilities of completing the project on time were not available. With these minor exceptions, PERT and CPM provide for accomplishment of similar functions.

PRODUCTION AND OPERATIONS MANAGEMENT: A WRAP-UP

The quantitative planning techniques discussed in this and the previous chapter were provided to stimulate the student to gain further insight into what tools are available. A person should not be misled into believing that these techniques are the only ones that a manager has at his or her disposal. A course in statistics should dispel this notion. But, a manager should always remember that they are but tools to be used, just as a calculator or a piece of machinery. You need not know the inner workings of either; the primary concern is the end result. Thus, a manager needs to be able to select the correct tool which will solve the problem at hand and not become overly concerned with the details of each technique. When this has been achieved, the production and operations tools become a valuable part of a manager's repertoire of knowledge.

SUMMARY

Additional quantitative concepts and techniques that have proven successful in assisting managers solve problems are simulation and queuing theory. Simulation is a technique which permits managers to ask many "what if" questions without having to make the decision in the real world. With the advent of high speed electronic computers, simulation has come of age. A simulation model is used to represent a real world situation through mathematical logic in an attempt to predict what will occur in an actual situation. Queuing or waiting line theory is used by management to determine how much service to provide at the time of greatest need. Although the mathematics of a waiting line problem is often quite complicated, businesses have found that the technique can assist in the solution of a variety of problems.

There are numerous control techniques available for use by managers. Four approaches are quality control, inventory control, Program Evaluation and Review Technique (PERT) and the Critical Path Method (CPM). When a manager uses quality control, a product is evaluated regarding the degree of conformity to a certain predetermined standard. If a firm has an objective of gaining a reputation for manufacturing a high quality product, standards will have to be high. There are two basic types of sampling plans—sampling by attributes and sampling by variables. A plan developed for variable sampling consists of determining how closely an item conforms to an established standard. With sampling by attributes, the item is either acceptable or unacceptable. A procedure that measures the quality control process is referred to as a control chart.

Inventory control is a vital technique that can mean the difference between a profit or a loss to a firm. Inventory control involves the balancing of two general types of costs—ordering costs and carrying costs. It is the job of the manager to use inventory control as a means to minimize total cost. A procedure which permits the manager to determine which items warrant careful control is referred to as the ABC method of inventory control.

When a project is nonrecurrent, large, complex, and involves multiple organizations, the manager needs a tool that will assist in coordinating this complicated network. The primary techniques available to accomplish this task are PERT and CPM. Both serve as planning and control devices.

Review Questions

1. Define simulation. Why does the technique have so much potential to a business person of today?

2. Give the sequence that should be followed in developing a simulation problem.

3. Why is a waiting line or queuing theory problem called a process of balancing? When would this technique be used?

4. What are the costs that are involved in developing an inventory control problem? Define each.

5. Why do we often use sampling techniques in quality control?

6. In terms of quality control define the following:
   a. Standard
   b. Upper confidence limit
   c. Lower confidence limit

7. Distinguish between sampling by attributes and sampling by variables. Give an example of each.

8. Distinguish between PERT and CPM.

9. Define the following:
   a. Optimistic time
   b. Most likely time
   c. Pessimistic time
   d. Expected time

Exercises

1. Think of five instances where it would be impossible or impracticable to inspect every item.

2. Develop a small PERT network for a task that you are very familiar with. Make sure that you are accomplishing this project with another individual.

3. Visit a local automobile dealership. Estimate the number of cars on the lot and the value of these cars. Assume that the dealer has 20 percent more cars than he currently needs. If the interest rate is 10 percent, how much money is the dealership losing each year?

REFERENCES

Brennan, J. M. "Up Your Inventory Control." *Journal of Systems Management,* (January 1977), pp. 39–45.

Buffa, Elwood S. *Modern Production Management,* 4th ed. New York: John Wiley and Sons, 1973.

Bures, Jaroslav P. "Time Framing a PERT Chart." *Management Accounting,* (October 1974), pp. 24–26.

Chase, Richard B., and Aquilano, Nicholas J. *Production and Operations Management,* 2nd ed. Homewood, Ill.: Richard D. Irwin, Inc., 1977.

Clayden, A. D. "Decision Simulation Model for Health Services Management." *Operational Research Quarterly* (1977), pp. 505–515.

Daellenbauh, Hans G., and George, John A. *Introduction to Operations Research Techniques.* Boston: Allyn and Bacon, Inc., 1978.

Davis, Edward W. "C.P.M. Use in Top 400 Construction Firms." *Journal of the Construction Division,* March 1974, pp. 39–49.

DeWelt, R. L. "Make Inventory a Working Asset." *Journal of Purchasing and Materials Management,* Spring 1977, pp. 14–22.

Elam, Rick. "General Purpose Simulation System: A Management Tool." *Managerial Planning,* May/June 1977, pp. 29–34.

Henderson, R. I. "Creating a Quality, Quality Control Program at Southern Protective Products." *Supervisory Management,* March 1977, pp. 25–30.

Hostage, G. M. "Quality Control in a Service Business." *Harvard Business Review,* July/August 1975, pp. 98–106.

Knotts, Ulysses S., Jr., and Swift, Ernest W. *Management Science for Management Decisions.* Boston: Allyn and Bacon, Inc., 1978.

Mittelstaedt, Arthur H., and Berger, Henry A. "The Critical Path Method: A Management Tool for Recreation." *Parks and Recreation,* July 1972, pp. 14–16.

"More Companies Adopt Control Circles." *Industry Week,* August 29, 1974, pp. 67–68.

"Nuclear Simulator Streamlines Operator Training." *Electrical World,* July 15, 1976, pp. 48–50.

Parsons, J. A. "Inventory Policy Checking Via Control Charts." *Journal of Systems Management,* October 1976, pp. 20–21.

"Production Control Through E.D.P." *Textile Industry,* September 1976, p. 199.

Reuter, Vincent G. "ABC Method of Inventory Control." *Journal of Systems Management*, November 1976, pp. 26–33.

Robertson, J. C., and Davis, F. G. "How to Evaluate Internal Control by Using Statistical Sampling: A Simplified Step-By-Step Approach." *Practical Accountant*, November/December 1976, pp. 34–48.

Shoemaker, R., and Staelin, R. "Effects of Sampling Variation on Sales Forecasts for New Consumer Products." *Journal of Marketing Research*, May 1976, pp. 138–143.

Smith, Martin R. "A 10-point Guide to Making Quality Control Management Effective." *Management Review*, April 1975, pp. 52–54.

Wiley, J. M. "Just Enough Queuing Theory." *Datamation*, February 1977, pp. 87+.

Case Study

PRODUCTION APPLICATIONS

Robert Channell is vice-president of operations for a firm that manufactures minicomputers. Robert works in an industry that is quite dynamic and constantly changing. A product that is in the forefront today may be out-of-date tomorrow because of the rapid technological changes that take place in the minicomputer industry. The firm that Robert works for is known for quality equipment and delivery that is on time. The environment in which the company operates is constantly changing. This makes it very difficult to forecast market demand and schedule production. Robert believes in using the quantitative tools that are at his disposal. Although he does not have a math background, he has experts that can be called upon when needed.

Assume for a moment that you are Robert Channell, vice-president of operations. Answer the following questions.

Questions

1. Comment on the usefulness of the quantitative technique(s) discussed in chapters 13 and 14. Which of these tools do you feel would be the most beneficial for you? Explain.

2. What information should you provide your experts in order to use these techniques?

Chapter 15

Managing Small Businesses

LEARNING OBJECTIVES

After completing this chapter you should be able to

1. Define the types of small businesses according to the classification standards established by the Small Business Administration.
2. Identify the primary reasons for the high failure rates of small businesses.
3. Describe how situational forces affect the management of small businesses.
4. List the major personality characteristics of the typical entrepreneur.
5. State the pitfalls an individual may encounter in starting a new business.
6. Describe the types of financial, procurement, and management assistance available to small businesses from the U. S. Small Business Administration (SBA).

One of the great freedoms we have in this country is the freedom to start and manage our own business—"to be our own boss." Today, this right continues to be a prime motivator for many people. There are approximately 14,000,000 businesses in the United States, including nearly 3,000,000 corporations; almost 97 percent of these are classified as small businesses. As shown in Figure 15.1, approximately 77 percent of all business establishments in the United States have nine or less employees. Small businesses provide income to millions of families in the United States.

FIGURE 15.1
Percent Distribution of Employment and Establishments by Employment-Size Class

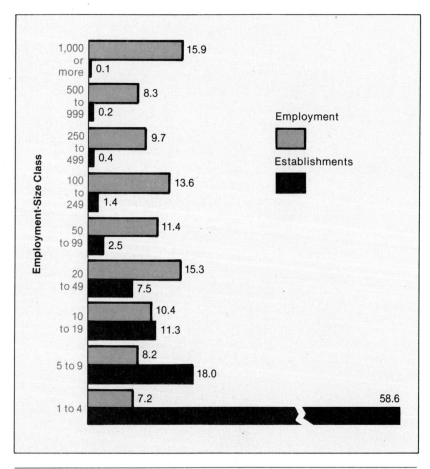

Source U. S. Department of Commerce, Bureau of the Census.

Believing that the development of the small business is vital to the success of our economic system, Congress passed the Small Business Act in 1953. The intent of the Small Business Act is summarized by the following:

> It is the declared policy of the Congress that the Government should aid, counsel, assist and protect, insofar as is possible, the interests of small business concerns in order to preserve free competitive enterprise . . . to maintain and strengthen the overall economy of the nation.[1]

Even with the assistance provided by the government of the United States, the failure rate of small businesses continues at an extremely high rate. Statistics reveal that 50 percent of all new businesses fail within the first two years of operation and 70 percent fail within five years. However, in spite of the obstacles that are confronted in starting a small business, there continues to be a vast influx of people each year that decide to challenge the odds. Of the over 70,000 new businesses started each year, 95 percent are classified as small businesses.

At times in the chapter one might sense the authors are being unduly pessimistic with regard to recommending that a person start his or her own small business. This is certainly not the case. But a person should be fully aware of the difficulties that he or she may confront if a decision is made to start a small business. Thus, the successful start and continued operation of a small business requires that careful consideration be given to the major situational factors that have been discussed throughout the text. After a discussion of the importance of the small business in our economic system, these situational factors will be presented from the standpoint of how they can affect the operation of a small business.

THE SMALL BUSINESS

Almost every large corporation began as a small business. Thousands of small businesses are so successful that they become a big business. After six years in the computer industry, Sam Wyly decided that he was tired of working for the "other guy." So, in 1963, he purchased a used computer and started his own business, University Computing Company. From this meager beginning, UCC evolved in a period of just ten years into a multinational organization with operations in fifty U. S. cities and twenty-one foreign countries. Wyly's success story proves once again that the American dream of developing a successful small business can be realized.

1. U. S. Congress, *Reconstruction Finance Corporation Liquidation Act; Small Business Act of 1953*, Public Law 163, 84th Congress, 1st Session, 1953.

MR. SAM WYLY

Chairman and Chief Executive Officer
Wyly Corporation

Sam Wyly can be characterized as a true entrepreneur. Sam grew up in the small town of Delhi, Louisiana, where his father was publisher of the town's weekly newspaper. Working around the paper was young Wyly's first job. After graduating from Louisiana Tech University with a degree in engineering, Sam earned his master's degree in business administration from the University of Michigan, specializing in the then new field of computer science.

Sam spent his first half-dozen years in the computer industry as a salesman for IBM's Service Bureau Corporation in Dallas, and then as a sales manager for Honeywell Computer Systems. With this valuable experience and a desire to develop a company on his own, Wyly founded University Computing Company (UCC) on Dallas' Southern Methodist University campus in 1963. From that meager beginning, UCC evolved into a multinational organization with operations in fifty cities and in twenty-one countries. UCC at different times has been the parent of companies in the leasing and insurance business (Computer Leasing Company and Gulf Insurance Group). UCC was also the parent of DATRAN, the pioneer data communications specialized common carrier.

In 1973, Wyly Corporation was formed to succeed UCC as the parent company of University Computing with Sam Wyly becoming chairman. He is also director and controlling stockholder of two companies outside Wyly Corporation—Bonanza International, Inc., the nationwide restaurant chain, and Earth Resources Company, an oil refining and metals exploration company. Sam Wyly has proven once again that the "American Dream" is still possible.

★

> **MOST IMPORTANT REASON FOR SUCCESS**
> **AND EFFECTIVENESS AS A MANAGER**
>
> · Dedication to the task at hand and pursuit of excellence in discharging that responsibility.
> · Willingness to undertake any task I was asked to do, even if it was outside my normal functional responsibility.
> · An entrepreneurial spirit, coupled with drive and energy.
>
> PHILLIP HARTLEY SMITH, Chairman and President, Copperweld Corporation

small business

Small Business
Administration (SBA)

Despite the fact that there are millions of small businesses, there is no commonly agreed-on definition of what constitutes a **small business.** The United States Congress, in the Small Business Act of 1953, specified the following two requirements: (1) it must be independently owned and operated, and (2) it must not be dominant in its field.[2] The Act created the **Small Business Administration (SBA),** an agency empowered to set more specific criteria in conjunction with the number of employees and the dollar volume of business. For the purpose of determining who may receive special financial assistance under the act, the SBA has established the guidelines as presented in Table 15.1.

The flexibility of the Small Business Administration in classifying small businesses is demonstrated by the fact that in 1966 the nation's sixty-third largest company was identified as a small business for the purpose of providing assistance to the company in obtaining government contracts. The firm was American Motors, and the key characteristic was its marginal standing in the automobile industry. Though this company had approximately 28,000 employees, its sales comprised less than 4 percent of total industry output.

TABLE 15.1
SBA Classification of Small Businesses

Types of Business	Classification Standards
Manufacturing	1. Up to 1,500 employees (varying industrial standards may be applied)
Retailing	2. Up to $7.5 million in annual sales
Wholesaling	3. Up to $22.5 million in annual sales
Services	4. Annual receipts up to $8 million
Construction	5. Annual receipts up to $9.5 million
Agriculture	6. Annual receipts not exceeding $275,000

Source U.S. Small Business Administration

2. Ibid.

The Committee for Economic Development (CED) has also developed a definition of a small business. To qualify as a small business, the CED stated that a firm must meet at least two of the following:

1. Management of the firm is independent. Most often the managers are also the owners.
2. Capital is supplied and ownership is held by an individual or small group.
3. The firm's primary area of operations is local. Markets need not be local, but the owners and workers are in one home community.
4. The business is small compared to the largest firms in its field. This would vary according to the industry. A large firm in one industry might seem small in another.[3]

As noted in the above CED definition, the small enterprise is one in which the owner-operator knows personally the "key" personnel. In most small businesses, this key group would ordinarily not exceed twelve to fifteen people. Regardless of the specific definition of a small business, it is a certainty that this category makes up the overwhelming majority of business establishments in this country.

SITUATIONAL FACTORS AFFECTING THE MANAGEMENT OF SMALL BUSINESS

The small business enterprise offers unique challenges and opportunities—and considerable difficulties—that differ from those encountered by large businesses. In fact, the six situational factors may have a greater impact on small businesses than on large companies. A large firm usually has the resources to "weather" adverse conditions. Believing that the small business person must be able to recognize and deal with the various situational factors, they will be presented next.

EXTERNAL ENVIRONMENT

There are a number of external environmental conditions that affect a small business. In the discussion following, we will cover three types of environments that all small businesses confront—economic, political and legal, and social.

3. H. N. Broom and Justin G. Longenecker, *Small Business Management,* 4th ed. (Dallas: Southwestern Publishing Company, 1975), p. 3.

Economic Environment

Unlike the large corporation, the small business can concentrate on a restricted economic market in one locale or in one segment of an industry. But, this condition is a two-edged sword. If economic conditions become depressed in one portion of the industry the small business may suffer severely whereas the large, diversified firm may be capable of relying on other segments of the firm to offset the adverse conditions. However, in some situations the small business may be able to choose a more favorable economic environment in which to operate.

In numerous instances a small business may find itself in competition with a large enterprise. They often will seek to protect themselves by serving a particular market segment. Computer manufacturers, which are competing against IBM, often decide not to go "head-to-head" against the "giant's" strength. Rather, they direct their effort at their weakness. The same situation exists for a small grocery store that is competing for sales against the major chains such as Safeway and A&P. Because of the volume sales of the giants, the small stores cannot compete against prices. Factors such as staying open late and offering shorter service lines frequently provide the means for the small business to survive.

The flexibility of being small is somewhat offset by weaker power because of limited resources. On occasions, a major customer can take advantage of the small company by insisting on excessively favorable terms in price, quality, or delivery. It is difficult to push around a supplier larger than the small firm itself. Small businesses often find it more difficult to secure adequate financing from institutional lenders because of their size. Lenders are aware of the fact that the small business has less depth in management. They are also aware of the statistics with respect to small business failure—one of the major reasons for the establishment of special loans under the Small Business Act of 1953. However, many small businesses are able to secure a loan simply on the basis of the personal reputation of the owner.

Unlike many large enterprises, the small business is typically unable to exert a major influence on the economic environment. Whereas some suggest that large enterprises are engaged in *closed enterprise,* there is usually little doubt that the small firm is involved in a highly competitive *free enterprise system.* In this environment the small business that is able to maintain lower operational costs will be the most profitable and have the greatest chances of remaining in business.

Political and Legal Environment—Government Regulation

It would seem that the political and legal environment for small businesses would be no different from that of large enterprises. One could also contend that this aspect of the environment would be considerably simpler for the small business since it is unlikely to be subject to prosecution under such laws as Sherman Antitrust Act or the Employees Retirement Income Security Act. Since over 75 percent of the small businesses employ fewer than ten people, many federal laws do not apply to them.

There are, however, many laws that apply equally to small and large enterprises and that require considerable expertise and resources. Though burdensome, the large enterprise can utilize its staff of specialists and larger capital resources to meet legal and/or administrative requirements. The small business, on the other hand, often has few if any staff experts and may experience difficulty in complying with government regulations. For example, a firm with fifty or sixty employees must fill out about seventy-five to eighty government report forms a year.[4] One wholesaler estimates thirty-six person-days per year to comply with government reporting.

As a tangible example of this problem, the Occupational Safety and Health Act applies to all firms with one or more employees (in addition to the owner). Basically, the approach in this revolutionary law is one of setting comprehensive and specific standards, governmental policing of company practices and workplaces, and enforcement by citations and fines. Standards governing physical conditions and work practices are published in a voluminous *Federal Register.* Some have stated (as illustrated on the next page) that if small businesses are required to adhere rigorously to these detailed specifications, many would be forced into bankruptcy. However, considering the millions of business establishments as compared with the hundreds of OSHA inspectors, the odds of receiving a surprise inspection are quite low.

Another major factor that must be considered is that of ecology. In a survey of the presidents of fifty small companies, over 80 percent ranked the costs of coping with ecological requirements as one of the top three problems facing the business.[5] Many small firms have been charged with excessively polluting sewer systems, waterways, and the air. Prevailing winds can carry animal and waste odors generated from hog and cattle feedlots as far as two miles. Small laundries that bleach blue jeans have added blue water and sludge to municipal sewer systems. Most small businesses operate on "thin" margins and have reduced their operating costs by pouring wastes into available streams, air, land, and sewers. This, combined with the lack of expert staff and alternative production facilities, makes coping with new ecological demands a very critical problem.

---

4. "Reporting to Government—How Paper Work Swamps Business," *U. S. News and World Report,* May 29, 1972, p. 96.

5. Dale D. McConkey, "Will Ecology Kill Small Business?" *Business Horizons* 15 (April 1972): 62.

In a few instances, the owner-manager of small businesses has found means to cope with environmental problems and to do so at a profit. For example, animal waste solids from feedlots have been collected, sterilized, and sold as organic fertilizer, or converted to gas to be used to heat a home. Some laundry managers who were forced to buy a special tank truck to remove excessive sludge have expanded into the septic tank drainage business. The pressing necessity for ecological cleanup applies to both small and large enterprises.

Social Environment

The small business typically has fewer problems in coping with the social environment than the large corporation. First, the small firm typically has only one community with which to deal. Also, the small firm's manager, being part of the local community, is better able to understand its customs and mores than is the manager of a large corporation. Customers in the community may patronize the business because they know the owners. A small grocery store may find that some of its customers will pay a higher price for their groceries because they know and trust the owner. The small company should enjoy an advantage in this portion of the external environment.

OBJECTIVES

The objectives of a small business are typically no different from those of a large enterprise although the priorities that the owner may place on them may be different. As we discussed in chapter 3, the major objectives that a firm may have are the following:

- survival
- profit
- service
- growth

For a small business, survival of the enterprise is often a most crucial goal. Over 70 percent of all business bankruptcies involve firms with less than $100,000 in liabilities. Over 50 percent of these firms are less than five years old. More numerous are those firms where the owner-manager merely exhausts all personal resources without going through bankruptcy proceedings. A significant percentage of these involve new business ventures of less than one year of existence. It is also estimated that 95 percent of entrepreneurs seeking venture capital never even get the business off the ground.[6] And among those that are actually funded, only one in twenty will survive and prosper.

Earning a profit is absolutely essential to long-term business survival. But, a newly formed small business must be prepared financially and psychologically not to earn a profit during the early phases of operation. The profit objective provides incentive to assume business risks, and without the profit motive, few people would start their own business.

It is apparent that the survival objective constantly haunts the small business. Because of its very nature, the small business is limited, short on capital, subject to competitive destruction, and often operates on a hand-to-mouth existence. As we shall note later, this objective, along with

6. Jeffry A. Timmons, "Guided Entrepreneurship," *Business Horizons* 18 (December 1975): 50.

other situational factors affecting the small business, requires a particular managerial approach. The personalities, orientations, and philosophies appropriate to managing in the more secure environments of a large enterprise will often not fit the requirements of an organization that must constantly fight for its sheer survival.

With respect to the service objective, the typical small business is highly customer oriented. Whereas the large enterprise can manipulate and control products and markets with its vast resources, the small firm must be highly attuned to specific customer wishes and requirements. In this way, a unique market niche can be identified and carved out. On occasions, the small business is forced to provide accompanying services that are not commensurate with the profit generated, such as more frequent deliveries of smaller quantities.

The small business can acquire some of the advantages of specialization by concentrating on a limited number of services. Though real estate agents often concentrate on a particular type of property, such as residential or commercial, one particular agency carved out a niche by concentrating solely on providing faculty housing in a city that contained a major university. A retail supermarket may develop special excellence in providing unusually good meat products. One small pharmaceutical company prospered in competition with larger firms by concentrating on the needs of one type of medical specialty, the ophthalmologic surgeon. A retail clothing store believed that courteous treatment of customers was of equal importance to selling their merchandise. The large enterprise must also adapt to customer requirements, but such adaptations are not usually as specific or as rapid.

Another basic objective of most small businesses is growth. However, there are certain limitations to growth that must be considered. Unlimited growth cannot be an objective of the small business if—

1. the owner-manager seeks to retain direct and personal control of the firm;
2. the firm wishes to remain in certain selected products or services;
3. management wants the firm to remain highly flexible; or
4. if the owner does not value growth.

The personal values and stage in life of the owner of a small business has a significant effect on the goal of growth. This point has been vividly illustrated to one of the authors by his father-in-law on numerous occasions. The father-in-law owns and operates a highly successful photography studio in a large city. The father-in-law's lack of interest in growth of his business has often perplexed the author. Despite the author's "good suggestions" as to how to increase overall revenues and profits, the father-in-law has not shown an interest in growth. The author's father-in-law is sixty, is an excellent and avid golfer, and operates a ranch during his spare time. He values time for these activities and realizes that if the volume of business increases, he will probably have to work longer and harder or hire additional personnel. He chooses to do neither. He prefers to "pioneer the two-day work week" and thus is not interested in, nor does he need, the greater income that could be generated if he pursued a growth strategy. The quality of his studio's work is so exceptional that the firm has continued to do well and he has been able to increase his prices at least enough in recent years to offset the effects of inflation. Thus, in a small business it is virtually impossible to separate the values and objectives of the owner from those of the business.

TECHNOLOGY

technology

Technology exerts a significant impact on the types of products and services provided by small business firms. These products and services tend to possess characteristics that distinguish them from those of larger enterprises. These include the following:

1. The technology needed to create these products and services is characterized by shorter processing cycles. This enables promptness of service and does not require extensive investment in facilities.
2. The demand for products and services of many small businesses tends to show greater seasonal variations.
3. Small businesses are often in a better position to produce higher quality products than larger firms. A $90,000 automobile cannot be produced on the typical mass production line.
4. The technology used to produce the products and services tends to be relatively stable. The small firm does not have the resources to be constantly bringing out new products as markets for old products disappear.

5. Small businesses may have certain advantages over larger firms in offering certain products and services. It is difficult for the large firm to provide unusually short delivery times, or multiple delivery schedules peculiarly adapted to different customer requirements. The large enterprise is also more limited in its ability to provide customized products; for example, the tailor versus the large clothing manufacturer.

Because of these technological characteristics, there will always be a place for small business to provide products and services uniquely adapted to their capabilities. With over 70 percent of small businesses being engaged in retailing, wholesaling, and services, some have suggested that the most commonly needed technology is that of dealing directly with customers. Because customers are not completely controllable, this would demand greater flexibility and freedom.

The small businesses that are not involved in retailing, wholesaling, and services confront other situational factors. Many small businesses were started because of one technological innovation by its owner. As the owner begins to deal with the day-to-day operations of the business there often is not sufficient time to devote to continued research and development. The reason that caused the small business to be created may also be the cause of its failure. Should the competition develop a superior product, the small business may find itself in severe difficulties.

ORGANIZATION STRUCTURE

The major characteristics of small business organization structure are: (1) an emphasis on informality, (2) the critical importance of the owner and/or manager; and (3) the necessity for increased departmentalization with growth. Small firms tend to operate in a somewhat informal manner. The small size permits it; the need for flexibility demands it. High degrees of formalization, in terms of organization charts, job descriptions, and procedures, do not encourage creativity and change. The large organization must formalize in order to effect coordination and control. In addition, the large firm must make special provisions for introducing innovation and adaptability into its formalized structure. On the other hand, the small business operates more informally and flexibly.

Because of the size of the small business, its owner and/or operator is of critical importance. There has been a tendency for operators of successful small firms to remain in the position for long periods of time—sometimes as much as 20 to 40 years. In the large enterprises, a president typically remains for a much shorter period, as few as five to ten years. The head of the small business almost always wears two or more hats—he or she must perform several important functions. Not only does he or she manage the total enterprise, but also a second or third function is almost always performed. Frequently, it is the finance function. In some small manufacturing firms, owners personally handle the big "bread-and-butter" sales, thus placing themselves in competition with subordinate sales personnel. If a labor union is present, the owner/manager often handles the negotiations personally. If the owner has an engineering degree, he or she may be the firm's only machine maintenance person. Management problems will just have to wait until the key machine is back in operation.

As the small business grows larger, the variety, number, and complexity of functions and relationships will increase. Companies with annual sales of less than $100,000 typically are not divided into departments.[7] For sales of between $1 and $3 million there may be two or three departments set up—typically, sales and production. For sales of between $3 and $6 million, there are typically three to five departments; and for those between $6 and $20 million, there may be as many as eight. The typical span of control in the small firm ranges from four to seven subordinates, whereas that in the large company ranges from five to over eleven. Thus, in the small business, communication distances are short and personal contacts frequent.

Not only does the typical small business manager and virtually all personnel wear two or more hats, they are expected to perform many activities that would normally be handled by a staff of experts in a large organization. For example, there may be only six people in a small business. One day all six may be sales personnel, the next day they may spend seeking financing, and the next day they all may be on the production line. The limited amount of different departments and specialization of personnel enables the small business to operate with speed and flexibility.

There also tends to be fewer rigid or formal rules to follow in small firms as compared to large businesses. Employees may leave assigned work places without permission, have more flexible starting and quitting times, and have a more flexible dress code. The climate of the organization is more personalized. Names are more important than time clock numbers. It is likely that there are neither time clocks nor codified rule books. When instances calling for disciplinary action do arise, there is more individualized handling of the case. The less rigid scheduling of tasks permits greater degrees of interaction among employees.

The nature of the job assignment combined with the friendly climate that can be developed in a small business leads to greater employee

---

7. Theodore Cohn and Roy A. Lindberg, *Survival and Growth: Management Strategies for the Small Firm* (New York: AMACON, 1974), p. 95.

identification with the enterprise. There is an excitement in being in on things, of having personal contact with managers and customers. Individual impact upon the total organization is greater and one can see what has been personally accomplished. Absence rates are significantly lower in the small firm. There is considerably less likelihood that an organized labor union will be present.

PERSONNEL

There are many noneconomic reasons for a person to prefer to work in a small business. While work in a large organization is often highly specialized, the typical task assignments in the small firm offer variety, challenge, and greater degree of self-control. This is why many recent graduates are beginning to seek jobs with small businesses. At times, an employee has an opportunity to carry a job through from the original idea to its introduction into the market. Experience is gained at an accelerated pace. Such opportunities provided by a small business are very important to many people.

Although there are exceptions, larger organizations usually pay their employees higher salaries than do most small businesses. Most small firms have a tendency to view salary as an expense rather than the employee as an asset. If the owner of a small business had to choose between a $15,000 accountant and one costing $20,000, the odds are heavily in favor of a quick decision for the former. If the owner were choosing between a $15,000 piece of machinery and one costing $20,000, considerably more deliberation would go into the decision. The owner may be more aware that the more expensive machine might have certain advantages over the other that makes the additional expenditures worthwhile.

nepotism
  A type of employee that is sometimes characteristic of small firms is a member of the owner-manager's family. The practice of hiring one's own relatives is known as **nepotism.** In the past this has been the son or son-in-law of the owner. One writer states that the most lethal of all deadly triangles in small businesses is where all three—father, son, and son-in-law—are key people in the enterprise.[8]

Using family members has some advantages to the concern. Identification with "our business" should be great, thereby leading to increased effort and dedication. In addition, family members may constitute sources for funds to finance the enterprise. Bringing the son into the firm enables

8. Howard J. Klein, *Stop! You're Killing the Business* (New York: Mason & Lipscomb, 1974), p. 2.

retention of control by the family in the years ahead. However, if a firm rigidly follows a policy of nepotism in its hiring or promotion practices, competent nonfamily personnel may leave the firm because they see little opportunity for advancement.

But employing family members can cause a number of interpersonal problems. Family quarrels can and do spill over into the everyday operations of the firm. In one instance, the introduction of the son initially caused few problems in a small hardware business. As the firm prospered, the standard of living of the son's family exceeded that of the daughter and her husband. The daughter brought pressure on the father to bring the son-in-law into the firm. After this was done, head-on competition began to develop between the son and the son-in-law as the daughter used the firm to increase her family's status. Ultimately, the father was forced to dissolve the firm because of the family warfare.

Family-dominated enterprises are sometimes unable to objectively assess problems and take appropriate action. The small firm may be operated to honor family traditions; for example, it is expected that all in the family who wish to join the company will be provided with some type of job. If family members heavily depend on the firm for income, they may object to buying new equipment or making other capital expenditures that may be necessary to meet competition. In father-son combinations, there is a tendency to continue the family relationship into the enterprise. The son or daughter may be excessively dominated and closely supervised by the father.

MANAGERIAL APPROACH

The foremost key individual in most small businesses is the owner. Because of the nature of the factors in establishing small businesses, the small business owner is often referred to as an entrepreneur. In fact, the small business is a natural haven for the entrepreneur. The entrepreneur is a unique type of person whose major characteristic is the ability to create an ongoing enterprise where none existed before. He or she performs the act of bringing ideas, skills, money, equipment, and markets together into a profitable combination. It has been suggested that this type of person strongly feels that security cannot be found in working for others in a well-structured situation; rather, security is found only in working for oneself with minimum external restraints.

The major personality characteristics of the entrepreneur are the following:

- need for achievement
- need for independence

- self-confidence
- high level of activity
- courage, curiosity, innovativeness, and competitiveness

entrepreneur

The **entrepreneur** desires to control his or her own destiny and has a tremendous need for independence. There is a constant drive to remove all restrictions and threatening figures. Should any other person in the small firm appear to aspire for power, he or she will be quickly removed. It is for this reason that some small businesses fail when their owners die or retire; no one has been developed to take their place.

This yearning for security by independence demands a great deal of self-confidence. An entrepreneur finds it exceedingly difficult to accept leadership from others. Thus, he or she often makes a relatively poor member of a large enterprise. In addition, there is little fear of failure. Risks are sought eagerly. Venturesomeness is almost an obsession; the level of activity is steadily high. Entrepreneurs are ardent believers in a truly competitive system and take great joy in winning.

The management style of the entrepreneur is not one that fits well into structured and orderly organizations. The entrepreneur shows great reluctance to formalize structure and processes. Leadership is primarily based on charismatic attraction. The entrepreneur is more concerned with personal expression than with building an organization; they are organization "starters" rather than organization "builders." As a consequence, the level of mobility is great. They move from one "deal" to another, all of which are rationalized in the name of profit. They have few qualms about severing relationships with people or with organizations. They would rather leave intolerable situations than to stay and resolve problems. Entrepreneurs provide a highly dynamic and innovative element in our economic system.

However, not all owners or managers of small businesses are entrepreneurs. Certainly, as the size of the enterprise gradually expands, managerial skills are increasingly necessary. As indicated in Table 15.2, the enterprise, if it survives, will progress through a series of stages in a typical life cycle. The initiation stage requires managerial qualities similar to those of the entrepreneur. The major functional emphasis is upon the idea and the technology necessary to fulfill it. Frequently, the technical inventor does not have the drive and self-confidence to begin the business. He or she either finds a promoter to transform the concept into business reality, or attempts to sell the idea to a large enterprise.

Some large firms have established subsidiaries whose major objective is to search out, purchase, and develop new businesses from inventors unable to develop them on their own. As the business moves into the second stage, it will still be a small business. The primary functional emphasis is upon finance. The critical nature of this function has been

TABLE 15.2
Relationship of Basic Managerial Skill and Capability to the
Stages of the Life Cycle

Life Cycle Stage	Managerial Role	Managerial Qualities	Basic Skill Requirement	Primary Functional Emphasis
1. Initiation	Originator-Inventor	Innovation Independence Self-confidence Risk-taking Vision	Perceptual and Conceptual	Technology
2. Development	Planner-Organizer	Investigation Planning Evaluation Judging Organizing Negotiation Decision making	Analytical, External-Behavioral Interpersonal Relations	Finance
3. Growth	Developer-Implementer	Leadership Delegation Motivation Supervision Achievement Decision making	Budgeting, Scheduling, Controlling, Intergroup Relations	Production Marketing
4. Maturity	Administrator-Operator	Maintenance Coordinating Efficiency Seeker	Internal Intergroup Relations	Marketing
5. Decline	Successor-Reorganizer	Type A—Innovative Change Agent Risk-taking Vision Strategic Planner	Perceptual and Conceptual, External Interpersonal Relations	Technology
		Type B—Efficiency Seeking Change Agent	Budgeting Controlling Internal Intergroup Relations	Finance

From Carroll V. Kroeger, "Managerial Development in the Small Firm." © 1974 by the Regents of the University of California. Reprinted from *California Management Review*, volume XVII, number 1, pg. 43, by permission of the Regents.

previously emphasized in dealing with the small business objective of survival. Now the more typical managerial skills come into prominence, particularly those concerned with planning. In the small business, the formulation of the plan is the most difficult function. Its communication to organization members is comparatively easy. The smallness in size makes individual identification and motivation more readily obtainable.

In the small company being correct in planning is more important than in the large business. There are limited resources and a restricted capacity to recover from mistakes. Almost all of the planning is of a relatively short-term nature. This enables the flexibility that provides the unique strength of the small business.

Decisions in the small enterprise tend to be more subjective, being heavily based on the personal knowledge of the manager. In the large firm, they are more often based on facts, figures, and recommendations of expert staff. Yet, decisions in the small business can be just as accurate given the shorter time period covered and the more limited environments experienced.

In the next three stages of the life cycle of the firm portrayed in Table 15.2, the small business has grown into a larger enterprise. In the third and fourth stages, the manager must develop internal systems, procedures, organization charts, and capital and operating budgets. He or she must become skilled in interpersonal processes involved in communication and motivation. External managerial capabilities are developed in dealing with the community, governmental agencies, and trade associations.

It is suggested that in the final stage of decline, the business can be saved in one of two ways. The Type A stage would take us back to a visionary risk-taking entrepreneur who comes up with the revolutionary innovation that rescues the enterprise from disaster. The Type B savior is the hardnosed and efficiency-seeking manager who slashes expenditures, cuts budgets, and lays off personnel.

PITFALLS TO STARTING A SMALL BUSINESS

A person who desires to start a small business should be aware of the limitations or pitfalls that they may confront. Dun and Bradstreet has prepared a list of potential problems that small businesses often encounter.[9] An awareness and understanding of the possible pitfalls discussed below should be of value to the small business manager.

LACK OF EXPERIENCE IN THE BUSINESS

A good rule of thumb is: "You don't enter a business that you know nothing about." Much more experience is needed than merely a knowledge of the product or service that will be provided. Experience relates also to areas such as purchasing, marketing, and finance. It is because of this lack of balanced experience that many small businesses fail. The old adage that said, "Build a better mousetrap and the world will beat a path to your door" is not necessarily so when discussing small business. For

---

9. *Pitfalls of Starting A Small Business* (New York: Dun and Bradstreet, Inc.).

instance, an engineer who has a tremendous idea for a new product will likely discover that the above statement is correct. Before the product can be manufactured, capital must be available to secure parts required to produce the product. The engineer must determine what quantities and quality levels are needed. Most important, once the item has been manufactured, it must now be marketed. A certain amount of personal selling is necessary. Thus, in order to go into business for oneself, a person should ask if they have the "package" of experience that is necessary to operate the business on a sound basis.

LACK OF CAPITAL

capital

A good idea does not guarantee success of a small business. A person should also evaluate carefully the amount of **capital** that will be required to start and maintain his or her business. Often these calculations are much too low and a person can actually go out of business before the business has opened. One of the authors has observed this situation occur in several instances. An individual decided to take over the operation of a small convenience store. All expenses were carefully calculated: salaries, rent, utilities, and advertising. The only thing that was forgotten was that additional inventory had to be purchased for the successful operation of the business because the previous owner had reduced inventory to a very low level prior to selling the store. The new owner was not aware of this and did not have funds to purchase the inventory required and the store was never opened. In another instance, the owner of a small retail store employed more personnel than necessary to operate the store. At the end of the month, sales had not been sufficient to pay the salaries, and the store was forced to close.

LACK OF A GOOD LOCATION

A large percentage of small businesses are retail store operations. As such, a major factor that should be considered is the selection of the proper location. A major factor for consideration is that low rent in the wrong location may be high; high rent in the right location may be low. Factors that should be considered might be the following:

1. *Population.* What is the traffic volume surrounding the store? Are the type of customers who will potentially purchase the product located within the trading area? For instance, approximately 70 percent of all convenience store customers reside within one mile of the store.

2. *Accessibility.* Do cars have to cross traffic to get to the location? How fast is the traffic generally moving when they pass the location?

3. *Competition.* Are there a large number of similar type businesses in the marketing area? The question that must be answered is, "How will the competition affect the proposed location?"

4. *Economic Stability.* The site must be considered not only from its current location potential but also from future potential considerations. The anticipated move of a large supermarket across the street may have a detrimental effect on some businesses.

LACK OF ADEQUATE INVENTORY MANAGEMENT

inventory
mismanagement

Inventory represents a debt for management; it ties up funds that could be used for other purposes. **Inventory mismanagement** may be thought of as a double-edged sword. If a person attempts to get by on only minimum inventory, customers may begin visiting other locations because all of the items that were wanted are not available. On the other hand, if excessive inventory is carried, funds cannot be used for other purposes. Also, if the items cannot be sold, they represent a complete loss for the business.

Another major factor related to inventory mismanagement is internal theft. The greatest amount of thefts occur from "in-house" personnel. Managers of small businesses often become so closely involved with their personnel that they never believe that they would steal. There have been numerous instances where the employee was making more than the owner because of internal theft. An inventory control system should be established to discover shortages before they become excessive.

EXCESSIVE CAPITAL INVESTMENT IN FIXED ASSETS

Fixed assets such as buildings and equipment cannot be converted into cash easily, if at all. Sales may be increasing so the owner decides to purchase additional equipment. Additional personnel are then hired to use the equipment. If a decline in sales is experienced, payment on the equipment may prove difficult. Because of this the business may be actually forced into bankruptcy even though it had an excellent chance for success. The small business owner must consider this factor much more carefully than large established firms.

POOR CREDIT POLICIES

One sure way to make a sale is to give credit. But, small business owners have discovered that one of the fastest ways to go out of business is to give excessive credit. In many instances, credit is granted based on whether the owner "likes" a person or not. The owner has not determined if the individual is a poor credit risk or not. With this approach, an owner may find that sales are increasing but there is little cash inflow. Because the owner may feel uncomfortable in asking people to pay their debts, the debt owed by the customer may not be collected.

THE OWNER TAKING TOO MUCH CASH OUT OF THE BUSINESS

Money that is spent by the owner cannot be used to make the business grow. When a small business is just starting to develop, it is likely that a major problem relates to securing sufficient capital. If the owner takes too much cash out of the business to maintain a high lifestyle, growth may be stymied. Sacrifices must be made at first to enjoy future success.

UNPLANNED EXPANSIONS

If one store is doing fine, there may be the temptation to add an additional store and do twice as well. This growth by acquisition has often caused major problems for owners of small businesses. When rapid expansions occur, difficulties are often experienced. The manager will likely discover that running two locations is much more difficult than one. He or she may not be accustomed to delegating authority and this must be done if there is more than one location. If the owner has been making all the decisions, efficiency may drop when additional locations are involved.

HAVING THE WRONG ATTITUDE

Let's face it; starting your own business is difficult. There is a good possibility of failure. It is certainly not a nine-to-five job where you can leave the problems of the job behind at quitting time. If a business is to be successful, it will take a lot of hard work. The responsibilities of the business will likely mean that many outside interests will have to be reduced. When an outside activity is considered, the question that must be raised is, "Can I afford it?" The answer is not merely in terms of money. Personal decisions may need to be made in the light of how they will affect the business. If the owner decides to go fishing, this decision could even affect the business. Sacrifices will be necessary, but to see a business survive and grow is worth the effort. The business is yours and you are answerable to no one but yourself.

> **QUALITIES NEEDED FOR SUCCESS
> AS A MANAGER IN YOUR ORGANIZATION**
>
> · Imagination
> · Early responsiveness
> · Ability to identify proper niche for involvement of our small and
> now medium-size company
>
> K. B. WATSON, President & C.E.O., Pioneer Corporation

In addition to understanding the pitfalls discussed above, an individual may find that additional questions must be answered prior to starting a small business. As may be seen in Appendix C, the SBA has developed a comprehensive checklist of questions related to "Going Into Business." These questions are organized under such topics as: "Before You Start," "Getting Started," and "Making It Go." A careful consideration of these questions should prove very beneficial to persons considering starting their own business.

ASSISTANCE PROVIDED BY THE SMALL BUSINESS ADMINISTRATION

As previously mentioned the Small Business Act of 1953 created the Small Business Administration (SBA) to provide assistance to prospective, new, and established small businesses. The SBA provides financial assistance, management training and counseling and helps small firms obtain government contracts. The types of assistance provided by the SBA are discussed below.

FINANCIAL ASSISTANCE

financial assistance

The SBA offers a variety of programs of **financial assistance** for small businesses that need money and cannot borrow it on reasonable terms from conventional lenders. The SBA, individually or working with a local financial institution, may make or guarantee loans for small businesses. The typical practice is for the SBA to guarantee up to 90 percent of a loan which a bank or other lender agrees to make to a small business. The SBA is only permitted to make direct loans to small businesses if local financial institutions are unable or unwilling to provide the funds. SBA loans may be used for these purposes:

- business construction, expansion, or conversion
- purchase of machinery, equipment, facilities, supplies, or materials
- working capital

PROCUREMENT ASSISTANCE

procurement assistance

Each year the U. S. government purchases billions of dollars worth of goods and services from thousands of businesses in the U. S. In recent years, about one-third of the total government purchases have been from small businesses. The SBA provides **procurement assistance** and counseling to small businesses on how to obtain government contracts. Specific services offered by the SBA include: counseling on how to prepare bids and obtain contracts, help in getting the name of the business placed on the bidders' lists, and advice on research and development projects and new technology.

MANAGEMENT ASSISTANCE

management assistance

As we have said earlier in this chapter, most small businesses fail because of a lack of effective management. In fact, more than 90 percent of the business failures each year are due to ineffective management. To prevent business failures, an important service provided by the SBA is management assistance. **Management assistance** takes the form of counseling and management training. The Management and Technical Assistance Program offers extensive and diversified services including the following:

- free individual counseling by retired and active business executives, university students and other professionals
- courses, conferences, workshops, and problem clinics
- wide range of technical and management publications

Small Business Institute

Free counseling is provided by SBA Management Assistance staff and by members of the Service Corps of Retired Executives (SCORE) and the Active Corps of Executives (ACE) and many professional organizations who offer volunteer services to small businesses. Another program that has gained considerable recognition in recent years is the counseling provided through the **Small Business Institute** (SBI) program. The SBI, using senior and graduate students of leading business schools throughout the country, provides on-site management counseling to small businesses. There are more than 450 colleges and universities that have SBI programs. Guided by a faculty member, students provide consultant services to the small business and receive academic credit for their work.

In addition to the above forms of management assistance, the SBA pays for management and technical assistance provided by professional consultants, offers short courses, conferences and workshops for small business operators. Finally, the SBA publishes hundreds of management, technical, and marketing publications that provide valuable information to small businesses. Most of these publications are free and can be obtained from the nearest SBA office.

THE FUTURE OF SMALL BUSINESS: CRITICAL AREAS OF FUTURE CHALLENGE

During the next two decades, numerous challenges will confront small business managers in this country. The most critical areas include the following and are discussed next:

- capital
- raw materials
- energy
- technology
- labor
- management
- markets
- government regulations

CAPITAL

The capital needed to finance small business operations will become more difficult to obtain in the future and, if it will be available, only at a high rate of interest. The shortage of capital has made it extremely difficult to begin new businesses or expand existing ones. Also, another factor with regard to capital is the impact of inflation. Every year it costs more than it did the previous year to acquire land and construct businesses, or acquire equipment and materials. Lack of adequate capital and/or management mistakes will quite likely cause a small business to go bankrupt much faster in the future than in the past. Small businesses with less capital needs will tend to have good chances for success.

RAW MATERIALS

Raw materials will also be more costly and difficult to obtain. This will likely result from expected shortages of these materials due to political, economic, or weather conditions. Small firms must continually stay abreast of these developments. Potential raw materials shortages may cause a small firm to maintain a larger inventory, thereby requiring more working capital than previously needed.

ENERGY

Energy will increasingly be a problem confronting the United States including small businesses. The era of cheap and available energy ended rather dramatically with the shortage created during the Arab oil embargo of 1973. However, the so-called "energy crisis" may well create excellent opportunities for small businesses. There are many new firms involved in the emerging fields of solar heating and cooling and insulation. Also, rising fuel costs will tend to favor the growth of smaller more regional businesses to reduce the costs of transportation.

TECHNOLOGY

Small businesses will continue to benefit from technological advances in the future. Changes and/or advancements in technology in such fields as energy, home construction, small tool manufacturing and numerous service type industries will create profitable opportunities for small businesses. Because of its flexibility, small businesses may be more able to take advantage of technology in these instances than are large firms.

PERSONNEL

A plentiful supply of personnel seems likely in the future of small business. Because of a fairly low level of capital investment in labor-saving machines and equipment, overall labor productivity may stagnate. However, as we have stressed earlier in this chapter, personnel in small businesses tend to be highly motivated and may achieve an improved level of productivity despite the lack of labor-saving capital equipment.

MANAGEMENT

Small business managers of the future most likely will need to be better educated and trained to cope with the challenges discussed above. It is likely that the environment the small firm will be operating in will become more demanding and competitive in view of continually increasing shortages and high costs of materials and energy, customer resistance to higher prices, and the costs of complying with government regulations.

MARKETS

The markets for products and services provided by small businesses in the future are likely to favor those that offer prices that are lower in cost than those charged by big business. As inflation continues its upward climb, the consumer will seek industries that assist him in confronting the "money crunch."

GOVERNMENT REGULATIONS

Although the business people of tomorrow will exert considerable effort to reduce the influence of government regulation, the influx of regulation is likely to continue to increase. The small business person will be faced with an ever expanding number of regulations.

SUMMARY

An American dream for millions of people is to own and manage their own business—"to be my own boss." This dream has been realized by many people in the nearly fourteen million small businesses that exist in the U. S. While the freedom to start and manage one's own business is available to everyone, each year thousands of businesses fail. In fact, statistics reveal that half of all new businesses fail within the first two years of operation and 70 percent fail within five years. Despite the grim statistics, virtually every large, successful business began as a small business. Also, it is important to note that small businesses make significant contributions to the health and vitality of our economy. The U. S. government, in an effort to provide financial and managerial assistance to small businesses, created the U. S. Small Business Administration (SBA) in 1953.

The small business enterprise offers unique challenges and opportunities—and considerable problems—that differ from those encountered by large businesses. The six situational factors that have been discussed in previous chapters may have a greater impact on small businesses than on large companies since the large firm usually has the resources to withstand adverse circumstances. Limited resources may make it difficult for the small business to exert a major influence upon the economic or political legal environment. However, in certain respects, a small business, because of its size, may be more flexible and responsive to changing conditions. For example, a small firm may be able to offer more personalized service, maintain lower operational costs, be less susceptible to some federal regulations, and often is not unionized.

As noted above, the failure rates for small businesses are very high. Why do failures occur? Failures are caused primarily by ineffective management. Some of the major pitfalls or problems that small businesses often encounter include lack of experience in the business, lack of capital, lack of a good location, lack of adequate inventory management, excessive capital investment in fixed assets, poor credit practices, the owner taking too much cash out of the business, unplanned expansions, and having the wrong attitude. To help prospective, new, and established small businesses avoid and/or overcome problems that might cause failure, the Small Business Administration provides financial, procurement, and management assistance.

Review Questions

1. What was the purpose of the Small Business Act of 1953?

2. What is considered to be a small business in the following types of business? Manufacturing, retailing, and wholesaling.

3. What situational factors affect the management of small businesses? Do each of these factors impact small firms more than large companies?

4. What are the failure rates for small businesses? Why? Discuss briefly.

5. What are the basic objectives of the typical small business? Is *growth* always an objective of a small business? Why or why not?

6. Products and services of small businesses tend to possess characteristics that distinguish them from those of larger enterprises. Discuss any three of these characteristics.

7. What are the major characteristics of small business organization structures?

8. What is meant by nepotism? Briefly discuss how the practice can affect a small business.

9. What is an entrepreneur? What are the major personality characteristics of entrepreneurs?

10. List and briefly discuss five of the more important "pitfalls" often encountered in starting a small business.

11. Review Appendix C, "Checklist For Going Into Business." What areas covered in the "Checklist" are most significant?

12. Briefly describe the various types of assistance available to small businesses from the U. S. Small Business Administration.

Exercises

1. Assume that you are considering starting your own restaurant, specializing in steak dinners. What major factors should be evaluated before you begin the business? Before attempting to complete the assignment, visit a local steak house or other restaurant and discuss the problems of owning and/or managing a restaurant.

2. Visit three successful small businesses in your local area. Discuss with the owners/managers of each business the reasons for success of their business. Ask them if they would advise a person to begin his or her own small business.

3. Visit or call the local office of the Small Business Administration (or use library sources if the SBA does not have an office near you) to determine the types of financial and managerial assistance available to small businesses. How does a business qualify for SBA assistance?

REFERENCES

Abdelsamad, M. H. and Others. "Fourteen Financial Pitfalls for Small Businesses." *S.A.M. Advanced Management Journal*, Spring 1977, pp. 15–23.

Apostolidis, P. "Criteria For Success In Small Business." *Journal of Small Business Management*, January 1977, pp. 48–51.

Broom, Halsey N., and Longenecker, Justin G. *Small Business Management*, 4th ed. Cincinnati: Southwestern Publishing Co., 1975.

Buskirk, Richard H., and Vaughn, Percy J., Jr. *Managing New Enterprises.* St. Paul: West Publishing Co., 1976.

Carrington, J. H., and Aurelio, J. M. "Survival Tactics for the Small Business." *Business Horizons*, February 1976, pp. 13–24.

Fruntz, Forrest H. *Successful Small Business Management.* Englewood Cliffs, N.J.: Prentice-Hall, Inc., 1978.

Henderson, C. "What the Future Holds for Small Business." *Nations Business*, March 1976, pp. 25–26 +.

Henry, E. "Ten Businesses Most Likely to Succeed—And to Fail." *Money*, March 1978, p. 50.

Hlavacek, J. D., and others. "Tie Small Business Technology to Marketing Power." *Harvard Business Review*, January 1977, pp. 106–116.

Pickle, Hal B., and Abrahamson, Royce L. *Small Business Management.* New York: Wiley Publishing Co., 1976.

Rossam, C. "Small Is Beautiful." *International Management,* April 1976, pp. 41–44.

Said, K. E., and Hughey, J. K. "Managerial Problems of the Small Firm." *Journal of Small Business Management,* January 1977, pp. 37–42.

"Small Business: The Maddening Struggle to Survive." (Special Report) *Business Week,* June 30, 1975, pp. 96–104.

White, W. L. "What Will Determine the Future of Small Business?" *Journal of Small Business Management,* July 1976, pp. 1–5.

Woodward, H. N. "Management Strategies for Small Companies." *Harvard Business Review,* January 1976, pp. 113–121.

Case Study

MANAGEMENT INCIDENT
OLE MISS INN*

For many years, John Goodson had thought that Oxford, Mississippi, a town of 10,000 population, needed a first-class motel, restaurant, and private club. Although there was limited industry in the city, Oxford was the home of the University of Mississippi. The building of a quality motel, restaurant, and club facility in Oxford had long been a dream of Goodson. He became particularly enthusiastic about the potential success of the motel facility after discussing his plans with local business people and university officials. The business and university leaders pledged their support and encouraged Goodson to continue with plans for the creation of the facility. Goodson, the president of a local bank, was able to interest his brother-in-law, Charles Jones, and two of Jones' business associates, Paul Prince and Bob Johnson, in the venture. Jones was a vice-president with World Book Encyclopedia and Prince and Johnson were highly successful sales managers. All three men lived in Memphis, some eighty miles from Oxford and travelled extensively.

After considerable discussion, the four men—Goodson, Jones, Prince, and Johnson—formed a partnership and began serious preparations for entering the motel business. While none of the partners had any previous experience in the motel, restaurant, or club business, each was considered a successful businessman. The partners hired a nationally known consulting firm, specializing in hotel/motel operations to conduct a study to determine the feasibility of the project. Prior to engaging the consulting firm, the four men agreed on the location and size of the proposed facility. The consulting firm recommended the creation of the proposed motel, restaurant, and club facility on the location specified by the partners. The study was completed in ten days at a cost of $5,000 to the partners. The consultants based their recommendation of the project on the following factors:

---

* This is a condensed version of the Ole Miss Inn, #9-377-710 case written by Robert E. Holmes and R. Dean Lewis and listed in the Intercollegiate Bibliography. Intercollegiate Case Clearing House, 1977.

1. Favorable general business conditions and projected growth of Oxford and the University.
2. Supply of and demand for motel rooms seem to be favorable.
3. There was a lack of "quality" motel and/or restaurant facilities in Oxford.
4. Financial projections appeared excellent—a forecast of $50,000 net income during the first year of operation.
5. The proposed site was excellent because of its location on a major state highway and its proximity to the university.

Much of the consultants' study consisted of interviewing business and university leaders to obtain their estimate of the potential for such a venture.

After reviewing the feasibility study, the partners decided to proceed immediately with plans for the facility which was to be named "Ole Miss Inn." An architectural firm completed plans for the facility and construction began in September, and the motel opened for business the next September, with 60 rooms, a restaurant, and a private club. The total capital invested in the facility was $800,000 with $100,000 being contributed directly by the partners. A $700,000, twenty year loan at 9 percent annual interest provided the remainder of the capital.

Almost immediately on opening, Ole Miss Inn began experiencing operational and financial difficulties. None of the partners were interested in managing the facility, so a professional manager was hired as well as a staff of several full and part-time personnel. During the first two years of operation, Ole Miss Inn had five managers and experienced losses totaling over $200,000. The occupancy rate was much lower than the level predicted by the feasibility study and expenses for food and salaries were far out of line.

When questioned about the lack of success of Ole Miss Inn, Mr. Goodson stated, "Our poor results during the first two years of operation were due to poor management—particularly in the areas of control of salaries and food expenses. Also, we haven't had the business we were promised from the university, particularly the Division of Continuing Education, or from local towns people. We've also had a tough time finding competent managers."

Questions

1. What were the primary problems being experienced by Ole Miss Inn? What were the causes of these problems?
2. Do you think that Goodson and his partners should have entered the business? Discuss.
3. Do you spot any apparent weaknesses in the consultants' feasibility study? If so, what are they?
4. What do you predict in the future for Ole Miss Inn?

Case Study

HARRISON PHOTOGRAPHY STUDIO

The Harrison Photography Studio located in Atlanta, Georgia, has an excellent reputation for high quality photography. The studio specializes in bridal, family, and executive portraits. In addition, the studio is very active in photographing weddings. John Harrison is the owner and manager of the studio. He started the business in his garage thirty years ago, and it has since grown to become one of the leading photography studios in Atlanta with revenues in excess of $150,000 annually and five full-time employees. Mr. Harrison has earned the reputation as a highly creative and innovative photographer.

One example of this is the fact that he was the first portrait photographer to take outdoor garden color portraits some fifteen years ago. Most of his bridal portraits and many of the individual and/or family portraits are taken in his outdoor garden studio. Because of the unique features of the studio's portraits, the studio has as much business as Mr. Harrison believes he wants. He has never advertised in any form—depending on "word-of-mouth" to carry his message of quality photography. Throughout the history of the business, Mr. Harrison's goal has been to be a high quality photographer. In recent years, he has raised prices considerably, but has noticed no overall decrease in revenues.

There are five key employees in the business. Mr. Harrison; his wife Joan who handles customers and manages the office; Mr. Harrison's son, Ken, who is also a professional photographer; Hilda, a professional spotter (touch-up work on negatives and prints), and Cathy, who performs such duties as framing pictures and working with customers. Ken, 32, is one of Harrison's three sons. He is very interested in someday owning the business. Ken has had a history of instability and unpredictability, especially with regard to work. He has either quit or been fired by his father several times and has not always been a very conscientious employee. Recently, however, he seems to have taken a more responsible attitude. Mr. Harrison's other sons have never been interested in the photography business.

In recent years, Mr. Harrison has been spending less and less time in the business. Several years ago, he decided to close the studio on Mondays—which meant that the business was open from 9-5 Tuesday through Friday and from 9-noon on Saturday. Although the studio is currently operating on this schedule, Mr. Harrison, who is 60, and is interested in retiring from the business, has chosen to work a fewer number of days. His typical work week is as follows:

Wednesday: 9-5
Thursday: Plays golf
Friday: 9-5
Saturday: 9-Noon (He actually works every other Saturday)

While not at the studio, Mr. Harrison spends most of his time at his ranch located about ninety miles from Atlanta. Six years ago, he bought 150 acres of land and built a large, beautiful "retirement" home. He has twenty-five head of cattle on the ranch and enjoys having a garden. Mr. Harrison and his son-in-law, Bob Shroeder, have frequent discussions about the future of the Harrison Photography Studio. One of their recent conversations was as follows:

Bob: "John, how are your plans for retirement coming along? Do you think that Ken is ready to take over the business?"

John: "I'm ready to get out now, but I don't believe that Ken can handle the business on his own yet. He is doing a good job, but if Joan and I leave the studio, I'm not sure he could make it. Ken wants to buy the business but I think that he would have a difficult time making the payments. Just the other day I was offered $300,000 for the studio property by a group of investors who want to build condominiums on the land. That's an excellent price, don't you think?"

Bob: "The $300,000 offer sounds good to me, especially when you consider the interest income from that amount of money. However, your annual earnings from the business are more than the interest on the $300,000."

John: "I want out of the big city and the pressures of the business. However, I have been able to work two or three days a week now for two years and still earn almost what I earned when I was spending 5 days in the studio. Our business has declined some during the past year, but not drastically. Besides, I enjoy my golf day on Thursdays with the boys and Joan likes to come in to Atlanta to visit friends—so I'll probably continue the two or three day schedule for a while longer."

Questions

1. What are the present goals of Mr. Harrison as a small business-person? Have they changed over time?

2. Why has the Harrison Photography Studio been successful in the past? Do you believe its current goals ensure continued success in the future?

3. In view of what we discussed in this chapter, evaluate the effectiveness of Mr. Harrison as an owner-manager.

4. Since Mr. Harrison wants to retire, would you advise that he accept the $300,000 offer for the studio property?

5. Why do you think he does not have much confidence in his son Ken's ability to run the studio when he retires?

Chapter 16

KEY TERMS

multinational
company

multinational

multinational management

parent country

host countries

developed countries

less developed
countries

parent country
nationals

host country
nationals

third country
nationals

godfather system

repatriation

Managing the Multinational Enterprise

LEARNING OBJECTIVES

After completing this chapter you should be able to

1. Describe the characteristics of multinational enterprises.
2. Explain the history and development of multinationals.
3. Identify and describe the situational factors to be considered in managing multinationals.
4. Explain the personnel problems encountered by multinationals.

Dan Shelton, a production manager for Axton International Corporation, a multinational organization operating primarily in developing countries, has been on his present assignment in a foreign country for only two months. During these two months, he has learned a great deal about the country's culture and today he is being further educated. Dan has been very dissatisfied with the performance of one of his production foremen (a national of the country where Dan is working). When he told his assistant to terminate the foreman, he was told, "You can't fire that person. The government will not permit the dismissal of an employee unless the company agrees to continue paying his salary."

As the new manager for the Mideast division Office of Dester International, Beth Adams is experiencing a bit of adjustment. Beth is a hard working manager and was selected for her new assignment while working in the corporate headquarters in New York. There is one highly efficient and productive worker in Beth's office. When Beth requested a pay increase for this individual, she was told by her supervisor that merit increases are not permitted in this country. All employees must receive equal salary increases.

Salama Saloma is a foreign national of a developing country who has come to the United States to train as a manager in the firm's Chicago headquarters. After two years of training with Bedford International, Salama will return to his country to work in one of Bedford's offices. Salama is currently experiencing "management shock." He is unaccustomed to the freedom that is given him in accomplishing his job. In the U. S., when a task is assigned, he has the responsibility for completing the project; no one is constantly standing around him to tell him precisely what to do. For Salama, it is quite a new experience.

As the above illustrations indicate, there are problems associated with conducting business in foreign countries. However, few developments have had the overall impact of multinationals. These firms have caused the countries of the world to be more closely related to each other. A firm engaged in business in two or more countries is referred to as a **multinational company** (MNC). These firms typically have sales offices and sometimes manufacturing plants in many different countries. These organizations are not only instrumental in improving the world economy and standards of living of many people but also significantly affect the technology, culture, and customs of the countries in which they operate. The organization with a truly multinational orientation is a social invention of recent decades.

multinational company

Peter Drucker refers to the multinational company as "the outstanding social innovation of the period since World War II."[1]

Many people believe that with resources, technology, food, and trained manpower unevenly distributed throughout the world, the multinational enterprise has the potential for bringing about a more equitable distribution of goods and services and improved living standards. The complexities and challenges of managing in the international environment are illustrated by the following comments from practicing executives of multinational firms.

In general, the fundamental challenge in international management is to understand new sets of economic and business factors, their relationships, their interconnectedness in the world, their impacts on business strategy, and develop responses to these factors consistent with particular business goals.

W. W. HAMILTON
Manager—International Communications
General Electric Company

While many problems have existed in managing in the international environment, one of the more troublesome areas is in establishing the limits of authority for the foreign operation so that the manager at that location has sufficient control and power, that the decision-making process and operation of the business is not delayed by the necessity of frequent consultations through the normal chain of corporate command. Also, in the last few years, the incidence of terrorism in some countries has placed stress on managers, handicapping the normal management function and limiting the effectiveness of the person in the assignment.

D. A. GULLETTE
Director, Administration
International Division
A. E. Staley Manufacturing Company

. . . Development of an effective, talented management cadre; government constraint and intervention; effective financial control; encouragement of entrepreneurship; falling international currencies; inflation.

DAVID W. ORTLIEB
President
Abbott International, LTD

The multinational is the type of enterprise that literally demands a situational approach to management. Effectiveness in managing in an

1. Peter F. Drucker, *Management* (New York: Harper & Row, 1973), p. 729.

DR. ARMAND HAMMER

Chairman of the Board and Chief Executive Officer
Occidental Petroleum Corporation

.

Dr. Armand Hammer is Chairman of the Board and Chief Executive Officer of the Occidental Petroleum Corporation. He took over the company in 1958 when it was almost bankrupt and has since built Oxy into the tenth largest oil company in the U. S. with annual sales of more than $6 billion. Dr. Hammer, who was 80 on May 21, 1978, has continued to work 12–14 hour days and has traveled an average of 250,000 miles per year for many years. Dr. Armand

Hammer, who was born and grew up in New York, became a millionaire while attending medical school at Columbia University.

While Dr. Hammer has never practiced medicine, he has become one of the most successful entrepreneurs and managers in U. S. history. His business accomplishments include building pencil factories in Russia, cattle breeding, drug manufacturing, distilling whiskey, asbestos mining, and the oil business. He currently serves on the board of dozens of organizations and also has one of the most extensive art collections in the world, valued in excess of $30 million. Many people know Dr. Hammer as the "Russian Connection"—the man who developed the first foreign business contacts with Russia. He forged a personal relationship with Lenin and has since negotiated the sale of over twenty billion dollars worth of fertilizer to the Russians.

Dr. Hammer made the following statement in regard to his success as an entrepreneur and manager:

> Well I suppose I have a natural flair for business. It really doesn't make much difference to me what business I'm in; I always seem to find a way to make it pay, to make it profitable. I suppose people say luck plays a big role. But I think to a large extent you make your own luck. Some people have the same opportunities as others and they don't take advantage of them. When you work 14 hours a day, 7 days a week, you get lucky.

Dr. Hammer had the following advice for managers:

- Never lose your enthusiasm. No matter what you do, do it with enthusiasm.
- People should try to do a better job than anyone else has done before and to do it with zest. I suppose my ambition in life is to leave the world a little better than when I found it.

international environment requires that the manager give careful consideration to factors such as the following:

- *external environment*
- *objectives*
- *technology*
- *structure*
- *personnel*
- *management approach*

After a brief discussion of the role of multinationals in today's world, the six situational factors will provide the framework for the remainder of the chapter.

Although there are many difficulties associated with multinational operations, the benefits often outweigh the risks.

WHAT IS A MULTINATIONAL?

multinational

A **multinational** was previously defined as a company conducting business in two or more countries. However, this definition is far too simplistic because it does not give adequate recognition to the size and scope of operations of many such organizations. Some experts in the field of multinational enterprises believe that organizations designated as multinationals should meet the following criteria:

1. Conduct operations in at least six different countries
2. Have at least 20 percent of the firm's assets and/or sales from business in countries other than that where the parent company is located
3. Have and demonstrate an integrated, global managerial orientation
   a. Resources of the enterprise are allocated without regard to national boundaries.
   b. National boundaries are merely a constraint that enters into decision-making process; they are not part of the definition of the company itself.
   c. The firm's organization structure cuts across national boundaries.
   d. Personnel are transferred throughout the world.
   e. Management takes on a broad, global perspective—they view the world as interrelated and interdependent.

A list of the largest fifteen multinational companies is presented in Table 16.1. As may be seen in the exhibit, IBM has subsidiaries in eighty different countries and almost 40 percent of their sales is generated from operations outside the U. S. Eighty-eight percent of the sales of British Petroleum originate in the fifty-two countries outside of Great Britain. To illustrate the impact of the multinational, a Massey-Ferguson executive stated, "We combine French-made transmissions, British-made engines, Mexican-made axles, and United States-made sheet metal parts to produce in Detroit a tractor for sale in Canada.[2]

INSIGHTS TO SUCCESS

Get where the action is. If it's sales—sell. If it's manufacturing—run a production line. Get to know the product and the people and process for producing that product. Learn how to listen to and communicate with people.

BILL HANSON, Vice-President, Digital Equipment Corporation

---

2. Robert W. Stevens, "Scanning the Multinational Firm," *Business Horizons* 14 (June 1971): 53.

TABLE 16.1
The Top 15 Multinational Companies

Country	Company	Foreign Sales As Percentage of Total	Number of Countries in which Subsidiaries Are Located
USA	General Motors	19	21
USA	Exxon	50	25
USA	Ford	26	30
Netherlands	Royal Dutch/Shell	79	43
USA	General Electric	16	32
USA	IBM	39	80
USA	Mobil Oil	45	62
USA	Chrysler	24	26
USA	Texaco	40	30
Britain	Unilever	42	40
USA	ITT	42	40
USA	Gulf Oil	45	61
Britain	British Petroleum	88	52
Netherlands	Philips Gloeilampenfabrieken	n.a.	29
USA	Standard Oil of California	45	26

Source United Nations data.

HISTORY AND DEVELOPMENT OF MULTINATIONALS

The first multinational corporation (MNC) established with a global orientation grew out of a merger in 1929 between Margarine Unie, a Dutch firm, and Lever Brothers, a British company. The company became Unilever and it has since become one of the largest companies in the world with 500 subsidiaries operating in about sixty nations throughout the world. Unilever even has two headquarters units, one located in Rotterdam and the other in London.

Multinationals usually operate through subsidiary companies in countries outside their home nation. Some of the names of the largest multinationals have become household words including such companies as General Motors, Ford, IBM, General Electric, Gulf Oil, and Exxon. The worldwide impact of these companies is very significant. Their operations create interrelationships between countries and cultures, as well as between economic and political systems.

The economic output of MNCs contributes a significant portion of the total economic output of the world. Some economists have estimated that by the year 2000, about 200–300 multinationals will account for one-half of the world's total output of goods and services. In recent years, there has been a rapid growth of direct investment by multinational firms averaging about 10 per cent per year. MNCs based in the U. S. account for more than half of this worldwide investment.

SITUATIONAL FACTORS TO BE CONSIDERED IN MANAGING INTERNATIONAL OPERATIONS

multinational
management

As noted previously in this chapter, **multinational management** requires careful consideration of several situational factors including the external environment, objectives, technology, structure, personnel, and management approaches of multinational corporations. These will be discussed next.

EXTERNAL ENVIRONMENT

parent country

host countries

The external environment that confronts multinational enterprises is diverse and complex. The success or failure of the MNC is determined largely by how they respond to this environment. As portrayed in Figure 16.1, the MNC must deal with the environment not only of the **parent country** but of all **host countries** as well. There are numerous problems associated with this undertaking. Examples of the types of major problems experienced in managing in the international environment are presented in Table 16.2. As may be seen, a diversity of problems exists; the majority of the problems can be summarized under the topics of (1) economics, (2) political-legal, and (3) social. When we add the barriers of distance and national boundaries, we can visualize an external environment characterized by great complexity, variety, and uncertainty. Such a situation requires that managers develop sophisticated skills to deal effectively with this environment.

THE ECONOMIC ENVIRONMENT

The economic environment of the various host countries is of prime importance to the management of multinational companies. A number of crucial questions must be answered.

- What are income levels, growth trends, inflation rates, balance of payments, gross national product, and the number and nature of economic institutions?
- Is there a local banking and financial resource that can be tapped?
- Are there organized labor unions, economic planning agencies, and the necessary service structures for power, water, housing, communication, and the like?
- How politically stable is the country and what about the stability of the currency?

FIGURE 16.1
The Multienvironments of MNCs

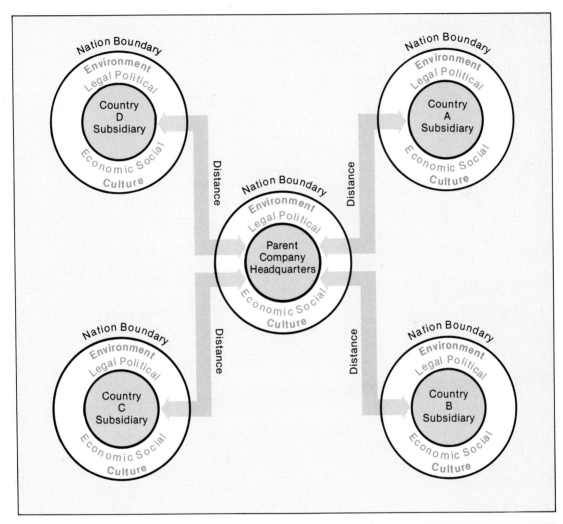

Source Edwin B. Flippo and Gary M. Munsinger, *Management*, 4th ed. (Boston: Allyn and Bacon, Inc., 1978), p. 583.

A major economic problem that affects multinationals is the stability of currency of the host country. The comments of T. P. Townsend, group vice-president of Daniel International, illustrated this point when he said, "A quick change in government directions can cause a fluctuation in currency exchange rate and cause difficulties in repatriating profits." A multinational must be constantly aware of the economic stability as

TABLE 16.2
Examples of the Types of Major Problems Experienced in Managing in the International Environment

Company	Name and Title of Person Responding	Major Problems Experienced
Abbott International, LTD	David W. Ortlieb President	Development of an effective talented management cadre; government constraint and intervention; financial control; encouragement of entrepreneurship; falling international currencies; inflation.
American Hospital Supply Corp.	J. George Harris President International Group	Currency fluctuations. Finding personnel to meet criteria for international managers, then building experience. Learning curve for international job is longer than for domestic. How to stimulate domestic divisions' interest in international operations for which they are not directly responsible.
Champion Spark Plug Company	G. M. Galster International Sales Vice President–Director	The major problem is maintaining two-way communications between the local managers and the home office. Local managers tend to look toward their own markets. They often forget that local expertise developed in one market often can be utilized outside their immediate area of responsibility.
Chrysler	D. H. Lander Group Vice President International	By far effective communications and employee motivation to a common purpose are the most difficult to obtain. Differences in management style produced by culture are most difficult to adapt to our restructure.
Colgate-Palmolive Co.	Roderick L. Turner Vice President Europe	We don't have major management problems and can't generalize here. Problems are business oriented and vary in each country.
Daniel International Corp.	T. P. Townsend, Jr. Group Vice President	Quick change in government direction in developing countries. Foreign governments' inability to recognize their lack of depth in experienced management. Fluctuating currency exchange. Difficulty in repatriating profits.
Fruehauf International	G. F. Malley President	Inability of expatriate managers to adjust to local conditions. Also problems caused by family's inability to adjust.
General Electric Company	W. W. Hamilton Manager International Communications	In general, the fundamental challenge in international management is to understand new sets of economic and business factors, their relationships, their interconnectedness in the world, their impacts on business strategy, and to develop responses to these factors consistent with particular business goals.
Illinois Tool Works	Donald J. Bachner President International Group	Ramifications of local laws and customs.

TABLE 16.2
Examples of the Types of Major Problems Experienced in Managing in the International Environment (Continued)

Company	Name and Title of Person Responding	Major Problems Experienced
McDonnell Douglas Corp.	Gordon M. Graham Corporate Vice President	Language barrier, personnel adjustments to culture and customs, difficulty in securing trained nationals.
Murphy Oil	Robert J. Sweeney President	The fact we are not citizens of the various countries. Time differences affect communications. Superimposing our ethics on a foreign environment.
Raytheon Company	Philip A. Phalon Vice President International Affairs	Maintenance of efficient, effective communications, maintaining the morale of personnel assigned to overseas locations in order to preclude too high a turnover rate.
Rockwell International	A. B. Kight Vice President	Lack of qualified people and interference from U. S. govt.
Signode Corporation	L. R. Flandreau Vice President International	Local laws that restrict imports and/or repatriation of profits or royalties. Inability to locate quality local personnel. U. S. laws on anti-boycott and sensitive payments, and the ever present communications problem due to language differences & customs.
A. E. Staley Mfg. Co.	D. A. Gullette Director, Administration International Division	While many problems have existed in managing in the international environment, one of the more troublesome areas is in establishing the limits of authority for the foreign operation so that the manager at that location has sufficient control and power that the decision-making process and operation of the business is not delayed by the necessity of frequent consultations through the normal chain of corporate command. Also, in the last few years, the incidence of terrorism in some countries has placed stress on managers, handicapping the normal management function and limiting the effectiveness of the person in the assignment.
U.C.C.	T. Kason President	Not understanding fully market opportunities or exposures.
UTC	Gregory W. Jordan Director International Admin.	Difficulty of communications and transportation.

553

INSIGHTS TO SUCCESS

- Patience
- Be opportunistic
- Do not be afraid of changing jobs or taking on new assignments
- Have confidence in the long-term merits of your qualifications

R. E. LINDBLOM, Vice-President—Finance, Bausch & Lomb Incorporated

reflected by the country's rate of inflation and the degree of stability of the host country's currency.

developed countries

less developed countries

On a general basis, the countries of the world are classified as either **developed countries** or **less developed countries** (LDC). An LDC lacks modern industry and the supporting services. The output per person is low. There is often an unequal distribution of income, with a few very rich, a small middle class, and a great number of poor. The MNC provides an opportunity for a fast start in the building of an economy. The objective is to reach a level where the economy can grow on a self-sustaining basis. Approximately 80 percent of the MNC total investment is located in LDCs. Often, the LDC has an identity problem which is shown in strong feelings of nationalism. Though they need the MNC to exploit their national resources, they perceive it as a threat to sovereignty. When they feel that they have effected sufficient transfer of skills in a particular technology, they are likely to expropriate or confiscate the business organization. The MNC must consider this risk in making an investment decision.

The fact that so much of total foreign investment is in LDCs is evidence that possible returns are worth the risk. If the most important resources of a multinational are technological and managerial skills rather than property and goods some companies can reduce the risk of expropriation or host country take-overs by one or more of the following means: (1) licensing agreements, (2) contracts to manage host country-owned installations, and (3) turnkey operations (constructing and developing the unit to the point where the key can be turned over to ownership by nationals of the host country). It is far more difficult to expropriate skills of persons than of property. There are also far fewer conflicts of interests between this type of MNC and the various nation states.

THE POLITICAL-LEGAL ENVIRONMENT

"Local laws that restrict imports and/or repatriation of profits or royalties" constitutes a major political-legal barrier that confronts many multinationals according to L. R. Flandreau, Vice-President—International, for Signode Corporation. The MNC must assess the stability of the existing government through careful analysis of conditions existing within the countries. Such analysis should consider competing political philosophies, how recent was political independence obtained, and the amount of social unrest and violence. The impact that violence has on the operations was highlighted by D. A. Gullette, Director for Administration—International Division, of A. E. Staley Manufacturing Company when he said, "In the last few years, the incidence of terrorism in some countries has placed stress on managers, handicapping the normal management function and limiting the effectiveness of the person in the assignment."

Because there is no comprehensive system of international law or courts, the MNC must become acquainted in detail with the laws of each host country. The United States, England, Canada, Australia, and New Zealand have developed their legal requirements by means of English *common law*. Judges and courts are extremely important, for they are guided by principles declared in previous cases. In most of continental Europe, Asia, and Africa, the approach is one of *civil law*. The judges play a lesser role because the legal requirements are codified. The civil servant or bureaucrat has greater power under the civil law than under the common law.

Management of an MNC must be highly interested in specifics such as:

1. laws governing profit remission to the parent country
2. import and export restrictions and investment controls
3. degree of foreign ownership permitted.

Though the United States is a highly legalistic country and MNCs tend to "carry" American law with them, executives must realize, for example, that the Japanese dislike laws, lawyers, and litigation. In France, lawyers are prohibited from serving on boards of directors by codes of the legal profession. The vastness and sheer complexity of varying legal systems throughout the world demonstrate quite clearly the intricate and demanding environment of the MNCs.

SOCIAL AND CULTURAL ENVIRONMENT

It is apparent that the culture of one nation will differ to some extent from the cultures of all other countries. As Robert J. Sweeney, President of Murphy Oil, said, "A major problem exists because we are not citizens of the various host countries and tend to superimpose our ethics on a foreign environment." Customs, beliefs, values, and habits will vary. If the MNC is to operate in many nations, it will of necessity be required to adapt some of its managerial practices to the specific and unique expectations and situations of each nation. Attitudes will differ concerning such subjects as work, risk taking, change introduction, time, authority, and material gain. It is dangerous to assume that the attitudes within the parent country will be similar in all other countries. These comments were reinforced by G. F. Malley, President of Fruehauf International, when he said a major problem experienced by international managers is the ". . . inability of expatriate managers to adjust to local conditions."

In some nations, authority is viewed as a natural right and is little questioned by subordinates. In other cultures, authority must be earned and is provided to those who have demonstrated their ability. In some cultures, work is good and moral, whereas in others it is to be avoided. Building up wealth in some nations is indicative of good and approved behavior. In others, riches are to be avoided. David McClelland has discovered that the fundamental attitude toward achievement is somewhat correlated with rates of economic development. If a nation's citizens are willing to commit themselves to the accomplishment of tasks deemed worthwhile and difficult, a country will benefit economically. McClelland contends that the achievement motive can be taught.[3] Certainly, cultural beliefs concerning one's ability to influence the future will have impact upon the behavior of a country's work force. If the basic belief is one of fatalism—what will be, will be—then, the importance of planning and organizing for the future is downgraded. Cultures also vary as to interclass mobility and sources of status. If there is little hope of moving up to higher classes in a society, then fatalism and an absence of a drive for achievement are likely.

In many instances, the MNC will have to adapt and conform to the requirements of the local culture. A multinational must introduce new technology and skills into a host nation's culture if economic development is to occur. Some changes proposed are revolutionary. There must be one common language and system of measurements when communicating between subsidiaries and headquarters of the MNC. English and French are the two most commonly chosen MNC languages. Despite the slowness of the United States to adapt, the metric system will be the common method of measurement.

Thus, a review of the bare outlines of differences in the economic, political-legal, and social environments of a variety of nations in the world serves to highlight the enormous complexity of the task of managing an MNC. It is apparent that sophisticated and unique approaches to managing will be necessary for survival and growth.

---

3. David C. McClelland, *The Achieving Society* (Princeton, N.J.: D. Van Nostrand, 1961).

OBJECTIVES OF THE MULTINATIONAL

On first glance, the objectives of multinational companies would not appear to be any different from the objectives of businesses operating exclusively within the United States. The typical goals of survival, profit, and growth are indeed similar to companies operating exclusively in the U. S. An MNC seeks to produce and distribute products and services throughout the world in return for a satisfactory return on their invested capital. It seeks to survive and grow by maintaining its technological advantages and minimizing risks. As may be seen in Figure 16.2, the objectives of Owens-Illinois illustrate the diverse goals and operations of a large multinational company.

However, the MNC differs from the firm that operates only within the U. S. because of the potential clash of its goals with the objectives of the economic and political systems of the various countries within which they operate. Some of the objectives of countries may coincide with the objectives of the MNC and some may not. Most countries want improved standards of living for their people and such goals as: a trained labor force, full employment, reasonable price stability, a favorable balance of payments, and steady economic growth.

In achieving some of these goals, there is an overlapping of interests between the MNC and the host country (see Figure 16.3). For example, a new MNC in a country will usually create new jobs, thereby contributing to a higher level of employment, increased income and economic growth. While the company contributes to the accomplishment of these goals, it may not do so at the rate expected by the host country.

In some areas, there will be conflicts of interest. A multinational may close a plant in one country to streamline its worldwide production facilities. A company may subsidize a beginning assembly operation in Country A by underpricing component parts produced in Country B. Country B's economy in effect is required to make a sacrifice to enable the plant in Country A to get started.

If the MNC is to achieve its return-on-investment objective, some portion of subsidiary earnings must be returned to headquarters in the parent country. This could adversely affect the host country's balance of payments, particularly if the subsidiary unit does no exporting of its products. Funds may be shuffled among various countries so that profits are maximized in countries having the most stable political systems and the lowest tax rates.

Some of the complaints various countries have regarding multinationals are the following:

1. Restrict or allocate markets among subsidiaries and do not allow manufacturing subsidiaries to develop export markets.
2. Are able to extract excessive profits and fees because of their monopolistic advantages.

FIGURE 16.2
International Operations of Owens-Illinois

What In The World Is Owens-Illinois?	A manufacturer and marketer of glass, plastic, paper, and metal packaging materials; Kimble® brand glass and plastic laboratory ware and health-care products. Libbey® glass tableware; Lily® paper and plastic convenience products; television bulbs and faceplates. We are the world's largest manufacturer of glass containers, and among the world's largest manufacturers of corrugated boxes and blow-molded plastic containers. Our consolidated sales are currently in excess of $2.6 billion, and we employ more than 84,000 individuals. We are big, diversified, and growing.
Where In The World Is Owens-Illinois?	Internationally, you'll find O-I operations in Europe, Latin America, the Middle East, South Africa, the Pacific, and the Far East. O-I is involved with more than 124 production facilities in 29 countries, manufacturing most of the items we produce domestically, and a few we don't such as flat glass and glass block. And O-I exports American products to more than 90 foreign countries.
And What Do We Do Internationally?	Owens-Illinois is enthusiastically involved with the global marketplace, and reaches international customers in one of three basic ways. Through partially or wholly owned affiliates, through technical assistance and licensing agreements, and through exports.

Each of our affiliates and licensees is an experienced manufacturer and marketer in its own respective market areas. Through our corporate headquarters in Toledo, Ohio, and our European office in Geneva, Switzerland, we can help coordinate or guide our various operations when needs extend beyond country or even international boundaries. And we can assist customers who may be facing shortages or who may be entering a foreign marketplace for the first time.

Of course, the concept of an international marketplace doesn't mean that individual nations are losing their traditions, their local color or their identity. We recognize that international business is not simply a matter of selling the same products in different foreign locations. The people, the markets, the rules, the regulations must all be carefully considered in any given situation.

From a relatively modest beginning in 1956, O-I International Operations has expanded and diversified to the point where it now accounts for one-fourth of O-I's total sales and earnings, and employs some 32,000 individuals overseas—of whom less than 40 are U.S. citizens.

In management philosophy, O-I International Operations naturally seeks a fair return on investment, but our success is founded on long-term relationships that are mutually beneficial, rather than on short-term policies. National managers are developed not only to operate affiliates in their own countries but also to take an active part in the O-I International management team.

Working abroad carries with it responsibilities and obligations—obligations that touch people at all levels in the host countries: government, customers, the general public, employees, and partners. By meeting those obligations fairly and honestly, by exercising in our operations overseas the same good corporate citizenship which we stress in the U.S., O-I extends the benefits of the free enterprise system in the best economic, political, and social interests of both the U.S. and the host countries.

It is indeed one world, and through its International Operations, Owens-Illinois is very much a part of it.

W. F. Spengler

William F. Spengler
President and Chief Operating Officer
International Operations

FIGURE 16.3
Overlapping Interest of MNC and Host Countries

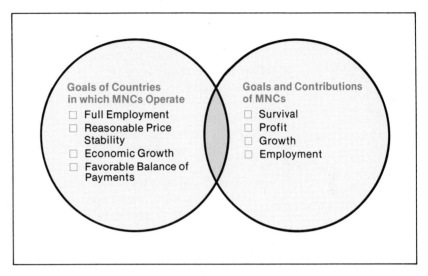

3. Enter the market by taking over existing local firms rather than developing new productive investments.

4. Finance their entry mainly through local debt and maintain a majority or up to 100 percent of the equity with the parent.

5. Divert local savings away from productive investments by nationals, hire away the most talented personnel, exhaust resources, and so on.

6. Restrict access to modern technology by centralizing research facilities in the home country and by licensing subsidiaries to use only existing or even outmoded technologies.

7. Restrict the "learning-by-doing" process by staffing key technical and managerial positions with expatriates.

8. Fail to do enough in the way of training and development of personnel.

9. Affront the country's social customs or frustrate the objectives of the national plan.

10. Contribute to price inflation.

11. Dominate key industrial sectors.

12. Answer to a foreign government.[4]

4. R. Hal Mason, "Conflicts Between Host Countries and Multinational Enterprise." Copyright © 1974 by the Regents of the University of California. Reprinted from *California Management Review*, volume XVII, number 1, pp. 6 and 7, by permission of the Regents.

In response to the type of complaints noted there have been moves toward applying restrictions upon the operations of multinationals. For example, one of the guides in the Andean Common Market (Bolivia, Chile, Colombia, Ecuador, and Peru) is that 51 percent of the stock in manufacturing subsidiaries should be held by nationals of the host country within fifteen to twenty years of start-up. When extremely discontented with the MNC or in response to the rising tide of national-ism, subsidiaries may be expropriated or confiscated by the host country. Recently, France gained control over its telephone system by purchasing a controlling interest from International Telephone & Telegraph Corpora-tion of the United States and Sweden's L. M. Ericsson Group.[5] That country is also striving to obtain control over various high-technology areas such as computers, semiconductors, and electronic switching sys-tems. In other instances, the host country has seized the subsidiary unit without compensation, for example, the Anaconda and Kennecott Copper units in Chile and all subsidiary units in Cuba.

Though the host country has power as a result of national sovereignty, the multinational is not helpless. Its power lies in its ability to grant or withhold needed economic resources and technological knowledge. Other MNCs will observe the nature of treatment accorded by the host country, and this will affect their decision to invest in that country. Should the host country have enterprises with investments in the parent country, retalia-tion can be threatened. If the parent country provides foreign economic aid, this can also be used as leverage in promoting equitable treatment for the MNC subsidiary.

In most instances, the economic power of the MNC and the political power of the host country will lead to accommodations whereby both parties can achieve some of their goals. The intense emotions of national sovereignty do not always coincide with long-term national interests. The MNCs will have to alter objectives to suit minimum requirements of the host countries if operations are to be conducted in that country. If such requirements do excessive damage to global objectives, the MNC may choose to conduct its business elsewhere in the world.

To head off a possible effort by less developed countries to ram through the United Nations a tough set of restrictions upon MNCs, the govern-ments of twenty-four of the most highly developed noncommunist nations have developed a proposed code of ethics. Important aspects of the Code of Ethics are listed as follows:

1. MNCs are not to meddle in the political processes of the countries in which they operate.
2. No bribes are permissible under any conditions.

5. "France Seizing Control of Technical Industries," *Business Week*, May 17, 1976, p. 47.

3. No donations to political parties are proper unless national laws allow them.

4. MNCs should make full disclosure of local sales and profits, number of employees, and expenditures for research and development for major regions of the world.

5. MNCs should refrain from participating in cartels and avoid "predatory behavior toward competitors."

6. The proper amount of taxes in the countries in which they are earned should be paid. One should not seek to avoid taxes by switching money from high-tax to low-tax countries.

7. MNCs should respect the right of their employees to organize into unions.[6]

INSIGHTS TO SUCCESS

I hardly need to point out that it is more difficult and demanding to be a successful business manager today, in our national and international environment, than ever before. Nevertheless, a basic component of management's job is to adapt effectively to a continually shifting business environment.

JAMES E. LEE, President, Gulf Oil Corporation

TECHNOLOGY AND MULTINATIONALS

Technological expertise is the primary advantage of the multinational enterprise. Many of the MNCs operate in such high-technology industries as oil, tires, pharmaceuticals, electronics, and motor vehicles. There are fewer MNCs in such fields as cotton, textiles, and cement. It is this technological gap in other nations that provides the unique opportunity for the MNC to transfer high technology from the parent country. The more simple industries are likely to be developed by each country for itself.

The more important the economies of scale to be derived from a particular technology, the greater the opportunity for an MNC to transfer knowledge to other countries. If the market size of a particular country is not such that it can absorb the output of an advanced economic unit, then many nations must be interlocked. MNCs in the many small European countries started before those in the United States for just this reason. The development of the European Common Market constituted an attempt to develop a wide market area.

6. United Nations information.

The situation existing within a country will dictate the nature of the technology required to accomplish work. There is obviously a wide range of environments, objectives, and technologies which would preclude any significant general statements that would apply to all multinationals. It should be noted, however, that the peculiar strength of most MNCs lies in their ability to operate highly complex technologies.

MULTINATIONAL ORGANIZATION STRUCTURES

The organizational structure of a multinational firm must be designed to meet the needs of the international environment. Normally, the first effort of a firm to become a multinational is the creation of an export unit in the domestic marketing department. At some point in time, the firm may perceive the necessity of locating manufacturing units abroad. After a time, these various foreign units are grouped into an international division. This is the typical structure for the United States multinational.

The international division becomes a centralized profit center with equal status with other major domestic divisions. It is typically headed by a vice-president and operates on a fairly autonomous basis from the domestic operations. The reasons for this approach are: (1) the necessity of obtaining managerial and technical expertise in the diverse environments of many countries, and (2) the reduction of control from the often larger domestic divisions. Of course, this approach to organization has the disadvantage of decreased coordination and cohesion of the international division with the rest of the company.

As the international division grows, it usually becomes organized on either a geographical or product base of specialization. In giant MNCs the international division is often a transitional stage in moving toward a worldwide structure that discounts the importance of national boundaries. As portrayed in Figures 16.4, 16.5, and 16.6, any such global structure requires a careful balance of three types of specialization: functional, geographical, and product. When the primary base is any one of the three, the other two must be present in the form of specialized staff experts or coordinators. A clear-cut decision that is heavily in favor of any one base is usually inappropriate.

Figure 16.4 illustrates a functional organization structure for a multinational. The executive in charge of the production function has a worldwide responsibility. Together with the presidents and executives in charge of sales and finance, a small group of managers enable worldwide centralized control of the MNC to be maintained.

MNCs with widely diversified lines of products requiring a high technology to produce and distribute tend to use the product base in their global structures. This form is portrayed in Figure 16.5. During the 1960s, General Electric moved from the international division form to the global

FIGURE 16.4
MNC: Global-Functional Structure

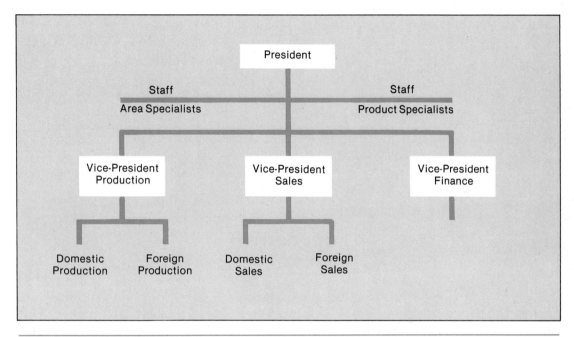

Source Edwin B. Flippo and Gary M. Munsinger, *Management,* 4th ed. (Boston: Allyn and Bacon, Inc., 1978), p. 588.

product structure. Primary responsibility for world-wide operations was assigned to the fifty to sixty general managers in charge of product divisions. International specialists, formerly in the international division, were reassigned to the various product divisions to provide aid in adapting to a multitude of national environments. To ensure that the product orientation did not dominate to the exclusion of area emphasis, four regional managers were established in Europe, Canada, Latin America, and the rest of the world. These executives were General Electric's eyes and ears in the countries assigned. They advised on the most suitable approach in each country for the product executives, identified potential partners, and aided in establishing locally oriented personnel programs. The area executive might be given line authority when a product division had not yet sufficient skill in the region, or when a subsidiary unit reported to many product divisions. Though the basic emphasis is on product, the addition of the geographical concept produced a type of matrix organization structure.

Finally, when the range of products is somewhat limited, or when the product is highly standardized, MNCs tend to use the initial base of geography, as shown in Figure 16.6. Executives with true line authority are placed over major regions throughout the world. This type of structure

FIGURE 16.5
MNC: Global-Area Structure

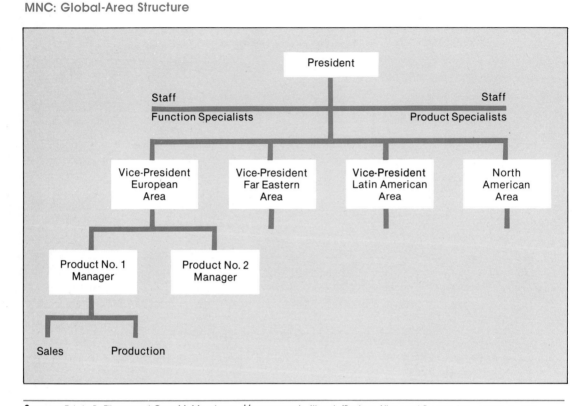

Source Edwin B. Flippo and Gary M. Munsinger, *Management*, 4th ed. (Boston: Allyn and Bacon, Inc., 1978), p. 589.

is utilized by international oil companies (limited variety of products) and soft-drink producers (highly standardized product). As in the other instances, some supporting staff is necessary in the product and functional areas. In all forms of MNC structures, one makes sure (1) that the product is properly managed and coordinated throughout the world, (2) that the functional processes of production, sales, and finance are executed efficiently, and (3) that proper and effective adaptations are made in response to the environments in the host country.

PERSONNEL

Successful management of an MNC requires that the manager understand the needs, values, and problems of personnel in the countries where the company operates. Management must recognize that there is no one style of leadership that will be equally effective in all countries. People in the

FIGURE 16.6
MNC: Global-Product Structure

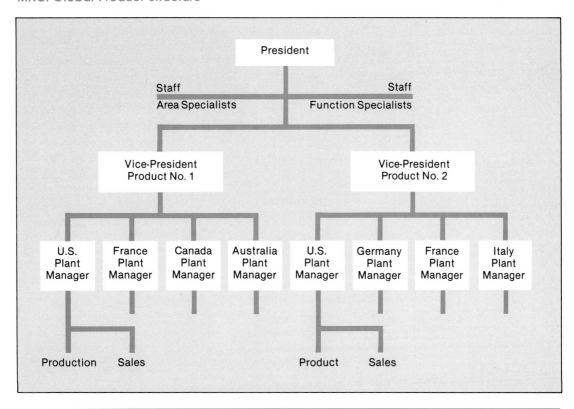

Source Edwin B. Flippo and Gary M. Munsinger, *Management*, 4th ed. (Boston: Allyn and Bacon, Inc., 1978), p. 588.

various countries have widely divergent backgrounds, education, cultures, religions, and live within a variety of social conditions, and economic and political systems. All of these factors must be considered by managers because they have a rather dramatic effect on the working environment. These require that managers adopt a situational approach to managing people.

The requirements for effective leadership of personnel in the U. S., Canada, Great Britain, Australia, or many of the Western European countries would differ significantly from countries such as Turkey, Mexico, Malaysia, Taiwan, Thailand, or certain African, Asian or South American countries. Research has shown that the needs and values of people do vary from nation to nation. This is often the result of differences in economic living standards, cultural or religious influences.

As you may recall from our discussion in chapter 8, unsatisfied needs motivate behavior. In the U. S. and other highly developed countries, people's basic needs—physiological, security, and social—are fairly well satisfied. Research on the application of Maslow's hierarchy of needs theory of human behavior has shown considerable differences between the dominant needs of people in different countries. Thus, in some advanced countries, managers must try to satisfy the needs for esteem and self-actualization, the so-called upper-level needs of man. However, in developing countries with lower standards of living, appeals to man's basic needs may prove to not only be appropriate, but the primary means for motivating desired behavior. The Maslow need hierarchy appears to be very applicable when conducting business in the U. S., Canada, United Kingdom or Australia. We may well have to ignore it in Japan, and be somewhat cautious with it in dealing with employees in other nations.

TYPES OF MNC EMPLOYEES

parent country
nationals
host country nationals
third country nationals

In filling key managerial, technical or professional positions abroad, multinationals can choose among three basic types of personnel: (1) **parent country nationals** (PCN), (2) **host country nationals** (HCN), and (3) **third country nationals** (TCN). Up until the 1950s, it was very common for MNCs to fill their foreign key posts with trusted and experienced personnel from home. Recently, stronger nationalistic feelings have led companies to alter their policies and employ more people from host countries. Still, many companies attempt to keep parent country personnel in at least one-half of the identified key positions, particularly in the financial function.

Using personnel from the parent nation of the multinational ensures a greater degree of consistency and control in the firm's operations around the world. This is not without its costs because these personnel may experience considerable difficulty in understanding cultural differences. In an attitude survey of personnel in forty-nine multinationals, personnel from the host country contended that parent country personnel tended not to question orders from headquarters even when appropriate to do so.[7] This enabled them to advance their own long-term interests in the firm by getting better headquarter evaluations and facilitating repatriation at the end of their tour of duty. In addition, the common practice of frequent rotation of key personnel intensified the problem of understanding and adapting to local cultures. However, employing the PCN does facilitate communications with headquarters because both parties are of the same culture.

Utilizing personnel from the host country in key positions will improve the MNC's relations with the host-country government. It will also enable

7. Yoram Zeira, "Overlooked Personnel Problems of Multinational Corporations," *Columbia Journal of World Business* 10 (Summer 1975): 96–103.

a quicker and more accurate adaptation to requirements of the local culture. Disadvantages would include a lessened degree of central control and increased communication problems with headquarters. In addition, if the HCNs perceive that the opportunity for higher positions is blocked for ethnic reasons, they will use the MNC to gain experience so they may transfer to local national firms at higher positions.

PERSONNEL PROBLEMS IN SENDING PARENT COMPANY NATIONALS ABROAD

One of the most difficult personnel problems for the multinational is that of selecting the appropriate people to be sent on foreign assignments. Careful plans should be made to assure that selectees possess certain basic characteristics. Among these are the following:

1. a very real desire to work in a foreign country
2. spouses and families who have actively encouraged the person to work overseas
3. cultural sensitivity and flexibility
4. high degree of technical competence
5. a sense for politics

Several surveys of overseas managers have revealed that the spouse's opinion and attitude should be considered the number one screening factor. Cultural sensitivity is also essential if we are to avoid antagonizing host-country nationals, unnecessarily.

Table 16.3 presents a summary of comments from top-level executives of multinationals relating to how their company selects managers for international assignments. The comments of these executives would suggest that managers given international assignments possess considerable education concerning the culture, country, politics, language, and business setting of the country where the operations are located.

A second major problem that confronts MNCs is the establishment of equitable compensation systems for personnel given international assignments. Typically, personnel from the parent country receive a salary plus an overseas premium of 10 to 25 percent plus moving expense allowances and certain living allowances. Personnel from the parent country of the MNC receive higher pay than personnel employed from the local country. This tends to create resentment and reduce cooperation. Many Americans have found their standard of living and social class to be considerably improved in foreign countries over what it had been in the United States. This makes for some difficulties when they return to the U. S. As illustrated by the comments included in Table 16.4, international

TABLE 16.3
Illustration of How Multinationals Select Managers

Company	Name and Title of Person Making Comments	Description of How Company Selects Managers for International Operations
Abbott International, LTD	David W. Ortlieb President	. . . demonstrated performance and understanding of what general management is all about including a solid understanding of international finance, of our products and marketing as well as an adequate understanding of manufacturing–processes and technologies. Personal qualities are also critical such as business judgment, intellectual honesty, ambition, restrained aggressiveness and cultural empathy.
American Hospital Supply Corp.	J. George Harris President International Group	We try to find the based managers for the assignments based on general management skills, mature, ability to relate to U. S. management style, language skills plus cultural understanding and not cast-offs. Prefer foreign nationals.
Champion Spark Plug Company	G. M. Galster International Sales Vice-President–Director	Managers are primarily selected from within our local organization, based on careful analysis of academic training, experience, performance and personality traits.
Chrysler	D. H. Lander Group Vice-President International	Carefully examine professional & managerial skills. Attempt possess drive, family compatibility, track record is important. Interviews are held with both O/S and functional staff managers.
Colgate-Palmolive Co.	Roderick L. Turner Vice-President Europe	We train them internally on-the-job in successive positions of increasing responsibility. After that, we select the best men available.
Daniel International Corporation	T. P. Townsend, Jr. Group Vice-President	Train and observe in a domestic position. Because of the high cost and high risk, we use only proven and tried people in our international operations.
Fruehauf International	G. F. Malley President	We select people based on initiative, ability to make decisions alone, ability to adjust to local conditions and willingness to travel. All managers have previous experience within company so that work habits, etc. are previously well defined.
General Electric Company	W. W. Hamilton Manager International Communications	Managers are selected internationally by the same criteria as in the U. S., leadership ability, effectiveness in teaching and developing people, appropriate priority on long and short term goals, understanding of the business, etc. In sending a U. S. national to a foreign country, or a foreign national to the U. S., it is extremely important that the individual be outstanding in his field, because he will be perceived as representative of his country's best qualifications.

TABLE 16.3
Illustration of How Multinationals Select Managers (Continued)

Company	Name and Title of Person Making Comments	Description of How Company Selects Managers for International Operations
Illinois Tool Works	Donald J. Bachner President International Group	We look for young managers with capacity for growth and good capability in their product field preferably from inside the company.
McDonnell Douglas Corp.	Gordon M. Graham Corporate Vice President	Product familiarity, company experience and proved managerial talent, volunteer status (if assigned abroad), future worth and advancement potential.
Raytheon Company	Philip A. Phalon Vice-President International Affairs	Proven domestic performance with a desire to move into the international arena.
Rockwell International	A. B. Kight Vice President	Besides usual management qualities—flexibility—diplomacy and a liking for "foreigners."
Signode Corporation	L. R. Flandreau Vice-President International	Selected mostly from within the company, and local to the operation to be managed if possible. New hires are looked at from standpoint of marketing skills, language skills, desire for international environment, logic, personality (sensitive, flexible yet tough minded).
A. E. Staley Mfg. Co.	D. A. Gullette Director Administration International Division	With the qualities of leadership, mental and physical endurance, and a broad knowledge of parent company operations and products, we would then first screen our International managers for the skills or potential talent for these skills. Our selection process would not be limited to U. S. nationals, but would also include our foreign nationals who had or could develop the necessary skills and were culturally acceptable for the new position.
U.C.C.	T. Kason President	Based on national performance. Flexibility to become international.

TABLE 16.4
Illustration of Types of Incentives Multinationals Offer to Managers

Company	Name and Title of Person Responding	Incentives Offered to Managers
Abbott International, LTD	David W. Ortlieb President	. . . career opportunities to progress within the company. . . Attractive salaries, incentive compensation, prerequisites including company automobile, etc., and for the non-national manager, who we prefer, certain allowances that permit him to live in a fashion similar to that in his home country.
American Hospital Supply Corp.	J. George Harris President International Group	Salary, bonus based on results. Expatriates: salary, bonus, living allowance, school for children, all moving expenses.
Champion Spark Plug Company	G. M. Galster International Sales Vice-President–Director	This varies from country to country. In addition to higher remuneration, including in some cases year end bonus, incentives could include use of a company car, improved office facilities, first class air travel, etc.
Chrysler	D. H. Lander Group Vice President International	A full range of O/S premiums, allowances and income protection, career advancement and job challenge exceed that of domestic operations. Family experiences can be very significant if so oriented.
Colgate-Palmolive Company	Roderick L. Turner Vice-President Europe	Obviously, an overall attractive compensation program including fringe benefits. Most importantly, the opportunity to run their own company.
Daniel International Corp.	T. P. Townsend, Jr. Group Vice-President	Normally a title of importance, i.e., V.P., General Manager, Managing Director, etc. Incentive of 10–15% on base salary plus a C.O.L. allowance. Tax protection. Education Assistance. Foreign Language Lessons. Extra Vacation.
Fruehauf International	G. F. Malley President	We pay a premium over U. S. scales for overseas positions. Also pay a cost of living adjustment covering housing, education, etc. Also "make them whole" on taxes.
General Electric Company	W. W. Hamilton Manager International Communications	There are no special financial incentives as such. Appropriate allowances are made to compensate for personal expense levels from the individual's home country. A primary incentive for taking an assignment outside of an individual's home country is to obtain broader experience as part of an overall career path.

TABLE 16.4
Illustration of Types of Incentives Multinationals Offer to Managers (Continued)

Company	Name and Title of Person Responding	Incentives Offered to Managers
Illinois Tool Works	Donald J. Bachner President International Group	Generally compensation is 15% above equivalent domestic positions and certain expense support and reimbursement tends to be an additional perq.
McDonnell Douglas Corp.	Gordon M. Graham Corporate Vice-President	Cost of living increment, expatriate premium, housing, schooling, etc. An understanding of position in the company and return job expectancy.
Murphy Oil	Robert J. Sweeney President	25% of salary up to $5,000/yr. School fees, vacation travel, living cost equalization, tax equalization.
Raytheon Company	Philip A. Phalon Vice-President International Affairs	Foreign Service Premiums, Cost-of-Living Allowances, Dependent Education Allowance, Housing Allowance and, for some areas of the world, hardship premiums.
Rockwell International	A. B. Kight Vice-President	Premium above base pay plus housing and living allowances, tax protection, education allowances, etc.
Signode Corporation	L. R. Flandreau Vice-President International	Pay is consistent with remuneration for the assignment in the country of residence, usually in upper ⅓ of competitive companies in terms of pay and benefits.
A. E. Staley Mfg. Co.	D. A. Gullette Director, Administration International Division	Depending on the country involved outside the United States, we generally offer a 10–20% bonus for the overseas assignment on top of salary plus the usual fringe benefits provided by the company, and, in addition, those normally offered in the country where the employee is located. Further, there are cost of living adjustments, tax equalization programs, housing and education assistance for dependents where local conditions do not offer conditions equal to or superior than the prior assignment for the individual involved.
U.C.C.	T. Kason President	Based on P & L performance.
UTC	Gregory W. Jordan Director International Admin.	For few expatriates, foreign service allowance, sometimes hardship pay and tax equalization.

assignments typically include many incentives. An important incentive for United States citizens to accept assignments in foreign countries is the opportunity to exclude a portion of their income earned in the foreign country from U. S. income taxes. Internal Revenue regulations allow U. S. citizens to exclude up to $15,000 of foreign earned income provided that the individuals are bona fide residents of a foreign country for eighteen months or longer. Until 1977, an individual could exclude up to $20,000 of earnings from U. S. income taxes. In addition to financial rewards, the assignment often provides excellent career advancement opportunities.

Despite the company's intention to provide career advancement opportunities, there is still some danger that skilled personnel will come to feel that their career progress has suffered by leaving their home company. Some personnel have returned from foreign assignments to find no job available; or they are given jobs that do not utilize skills obtained during the overseas service. To solve this problem, a **godfather system** has been set up in companies such as Control Data Corporation.[8] Before the person leaves on the assignment, a specific executive is appointed his or her godfather. A **repatriation** plan is worked out including how long the assignment is to be, and to what job the appointee will return. Ordinarily, the godfather is the person's future boss upon return to the parent country. During the assignment, the individual is kept informed of major ongoing events occurring in the unit of future assignment. In this way, not only is there a logical career plan worked out, there is no feeling of being lost in the vast international shuffle of the company.

godfather system

repatriation

MANAGEMENT APPROACH

As noted previously in this chapter, managing in an international environment requires careful consideration of significant situational factors. This point is vividly illustrated by the following remarks of a multinational executive in describing the unique qualities necessary for a manager to possess in managing in the international environment.

History:	A knowledge of basic history, particularly in countries of old and varied cultures.
Sociology & Economics:	A sound background in basic economic and sociological concepts which differ from country to country.

8. David M. Noer, "Integrating Foreign Service Employees to Home Organization: The Godfather Approach," *Personnel Journal* 53 (January 1974): 45–50.

Languages:	A working knowledge of languages and willingness to learn and practice a language to a level of perfection needed to carry on business conversations.
Cultural Nuances:	A genuine respect for different philosophical and ethical approaches.

The multinational company by definition is faced with a wide variety of situations—differing cultures, economic and political systems, and religions. Management must capitalize on its unique strength of being able to make world-wide decisions in the selection of markets and allocation of resources. Yet in each market, there are different environmental constraints. Thus, multinational managers must adapt to and work with the varying cultures of a multiplicity of nations throughout the world. See Table 16.5 for a summary of comments from multinational executives concerning the important qualities needed by managers.

The chief executive officer of each foreign subsidiary is confronted by opposing flows of corporate uniformity and cultural fragmentation. If the officer is from the parent country, uniformity is likely to be emphasized. If the manager is from the host country, cultural adaptation may take precedence. Because of growing nationalistic tendencies of many countries, there is an increased chance that the top manager will be from the host country. Yet, even here the MNC may be forced to adapt to local cultural requirements. In Germany, for instance, the chief executive officer must have an engineering degree to be accepted and respected. In France, graduates of the Grandes Ecoles are favored. If third-country nationals are to be used as chief executive officers, varying mobilities must be considered. A married Frenchman living in Paris is almost unmoveable to another country. However, most German managers are quite enthusiastic about working in other countries. The English and Scandinavians are typically willing to relocate, but they require assurance of return to their native lands.

Adaptation is not all one way. Local nationals will have to try to understand and adapt to the culture of the MNC which inevitably requires some understanding of the culture of the parent country of the MNC. This learning, too, will require considerable effort and time. In dealing with headquarters executives of an American MNC, the local national will have to learn to get to the point quickly. Americans are notoriously impatient with lengthy and expanded explanations. Nationals must be basically positive in approach and they must avoid constant criticism. However, they must also learn to argue with the American executive, but know just how far they can go.

Effective managers of multinational operations must develop a style of leadership consistent with the needs of the situation existing in the host

Company	Number of Countries In Which Company Operates	Name and Title of Responding Person	Unique Qualities Required to Be An Effective Manager in International Operations
Abbott International, LTD	160	David W. Ortlieb President	Cultural empathy, solid understanding of international currency and finance, ability to adopt a style of management related to the relative sophistication of the management cadre and market and a certain intellectual scepticism.
A. E. Staley Mfg. Co.	12	D. A. Gullette Director, Administration International Division	Leadership, mental and physical endurance, and a broad knowledge of parent company operations and products.
American Hospital Supply Corporation	18	J. George Harris President International Group	U. S. Based: Very good general management skills—planning, organization, motivation and control, maturity. Foreign-Based: General management skills, mature, ability to relate to U. S. management style, language skills, cultural understanding. Prefer foreign nationals.
Champion Spark Plug Company	16 (Market products in 140)	G. M. Galster Vice-President–Director International Sales	Cognizant of local laws & business practices to maintain high ethics, sensitive to cultural & economic aspects of local market, with particular emphasis on personnel relationships within company & community, understand & implement corporate directives which assure reasonably profitable operations and efficient production. In non-English speaking countries—bilingual with local language primary.
Chrysler	22	D. H. Lander Group Vice-President International	High cultural adaptability, ability to teach & train others, good professional skills, family capacity to operate cohesively & independently, language ability helpful.
Colgate-Palmolive Company	50	Roderick L. Turner Vice-President Europe	Self-starter, initiative, self discipline, good communicator, skills in management of people, integrity.
Daniel International Corporation	10	T. P. Townsend, Jr. Group Vice-President	Ability to empathize with people, good common sense, effectively communicate—question too avoid when communicating in second language, must be willing to travel extensively.
Fruehauf International	16	G. F. Malley President	Ability to innovate & adapt U. S. techniques to local conditions, ability to act alone very important.

TABLE 16.5
Illustration of Multinational Companies—Qualities Needed
for Management (Continued)

Company	Number of Countries In Which Company Operates	Name and Title of Responding Person	Unique Qualities Required to Be An Effective Manager in International Operations
General Electric Company	26	W. W. Hamilton Manager International Communications	In general, same as for U. S.: leadership ability, effectiveness in teaching and developing people, appropriate priority on long and short term goals, understanding of the business. Also, degree of self-sufficiency and willingness to understand though not necessarily adapt to local cultures and problem-solving approaches.
Illinois Tool Works	19	Donald J. Bachner President International Group	Everything it takes to be a domestic manager and more—particularly: self-starter, handles people well, patience, well balanced emotionally, enjoys working hard and late, good health.
McDonnell Douglas Corp.	Worldwide except Iron Curtain Countries & PRC	Gordon M. Graham Corporate Vice-President	Business acumen, integrity, initiative, innovativeness, desire to travel, desire to work with people and be successful at it.
Murphy Oil	15–20	Robert J. Sweeney President	Same as domestic.
Raytheon Company	49	Philip A. Phalon Vice-President International Affairs	Creativity, adaptability, thorough knowledge of company's objectives and policies.
Rockwell International	140	A. B. Kight Vice-President	Besides usual management qualities—flexibility, diplomacy and a liking for "foreigners."
Signode Corporation	101	L. R. Flandreau Vice-President International	After an extensive learning process, since business conditions in each country are varied and complex, must have strong analytical mind and be capable of sorting out priorities. Ability to sort out complicated and frustrating conditions, organize them and start the enterprise in the direction of accomplishment.
U.C.C.	10+	T. Kason President	Management and full understanding of national and international market and business
UTC	Essentially all countries of the world	Gregory W. Jordan Director International Admin.	International operations are largely run by locals for the local market so qualities for success are not unique to international operations.

country. The appropriate managerial style of leadership can be determined only after a careful assessment is made of the external environment of the host country, the type of and personnel to be managed, the level of existing technology, and the specific goals and operational requirements of the company.

SUMMARY

We are now in the age of the multinational corporation (MNC). Few developments have had the overall impact of multinationals. These firms have caused the countries of the world to become more closely related to each other. A multinational corporation is a firm engaged in business in two or more countries. These firms typically have sales offices and sometimes manufacturing plants in many different countries. The MNC's are not only instrumental in improving the world economy and thereby standards of living of many people, but also significantly affect the technology, culture and customs of the countries in which they operate.

The multinational corporation is the type of enterprise that provides a special challenge to managers. Effectiveness in managing in an international environment requires the manager to give careful consideration to such factors as the external environment, objectives, technology, structure, personnel, and the management approach. The external environment that confronts multinational enterprises consists primarily of the economic, political-legal and social cultural system of the various countries in which the MNC operates. This external environment characterized by complexity, variety, and uncertainty, requires that managers develop sophisticated skills to deal effectively with these conditions. Objectives of the MNC would not seem to be any different from the objectives of businesses operating exclusively within the U. S. However, the MNC differs from domestic firms because of the potential clash of its goals with the objectives of the economic and political systems of the various countries within which they operate.

Technological expertise is the primary advantage of the MNC. Many MNCs operate in such high-technology industries as oil, tires, pharmaceuticals, electronics, and motor vehicles. Another major factor to be considered in managing the MNC is the organization of the firm. The organization structure of an MNC must be designed to meet the needs of the international environment. Such a structure may differ significantly from the company's domestic operations.

Successful management of an MNC requires that the manager understand the needs, values, and problems of personnel in the countries where the company operates. Management must recognize that there is no one style of leadership that will be equally effective in all countries. People in the various countries have widely divergent backgrounds, educations, cultures, religions, and live in a variety of social conditions and economic and political systems.

Effective managers of MNCs must develop a style of leadership consistent with the needs of the situation existing in the host country. The appropriate managerial style of leadership can be determined only after a careful assessment is made of the external environment of the host country, the type of and personnel to be managed, the level of existing technology and the specific goals and operational requirements of the company.

Review Questions

1. What is a multinational corporation? List three of the major criteria used to classify multinationals.

2. Name four of the largest multinational corporations (MNC).

3. "The success or failure of the MNC is determined largely by how they respond to the external environment." Comment.

4. List the major situational factors affecting the management of multinationals.

5. Describe two major economic problems that often confront multinationals.

6. Distinguish between developed and less developed countries.

7. How does the political-legal environment affect the MNC?

8. What specific types of laws or local regulations must a multinational corporation be concerned with?

9. How may the objectives of the MNC differ from domestic firms?

10. Identify *five* of the more typical complaints host countries have against MNCs.

11. Is a code of ethics needed for MNCs? Why or why not? Give examples of what might be included.

12. "Technological expertise is the primary advantage of the multinational enterprise." Explain.

13. Describe the types of personnel used by MNCs and any potential problems with these personnel.

Exercises

1. Assume that you have agreed to accept a position in the international division of General Electric, and have been assigned to the Helsinki, Finland office effective in sixty days. You are married and have a six-year-old daughter. What would you do to prepare yourself and your family for this assignment?

2. A. If you were selecting personnel to be sent on international assignments with your company, what qualities, experience, and characteristics would you look for in prospective personnel?

B. Review two current journal articles on the problems multinational companies have in recruiting and placing U. S. managers and/or technical personnel in assignments in foreign countries. Make a list of the *problems* and how the companies are able to overcome them.

REFERENCES

Bauer, D. "Indefinitely Defined Multinational." *The Conference Board Record,* July 1975, pp. 21–24.

Brown, W. B. "Islands of Conscious Power: MNC's in the Theory of the Firm." *Michigan State University Business Topics,* Summer 1976, pp. 137–141.

Capstick, R. "The Perils of Manufacturing Abroad." *International Management,* March 1978, pp. 43–46.

Davis, S. M. "Trends In the Organization of Multinational Corporations." *Columbia Journal of World Business,* Summer 1976, pp. 54–71.

Galbraith, J. K. "The Defense of the Multinational Company." *Harvard Business Review,* March 1978, pp. 83–93.

Galbraith, J. K., and Edstrom, A. "International Transfer of Managers: Some Important Policy Considerations." *Columbia Journal of World Business,* Summer 1976, pp. 100–112.

Ghymn, K. I., and Bates, T. H. "Consequences of MNC Strategic Planning: An Empirical Case Study." *Management International Review,* 1977, pp. 83–91.

May, W. F. "Between Ideology and Interdependence." *California Management Review,* Summer 1977, pp. 88–90.

Mitchell, J., and Shawn, A. "All Multinationals Aren't the Same." *Financial World,* January 1, 1977, p. 36.

"Multinationals Find the Going Rougher." *Business Week,* July 14, 1975, pp. 64–65+.

Pohlman, R. A. "Policies of Multinational Firms: A Survey." *Business Horizons,* December 1976, pp. 14–18.

Prahalad, C. K. "Strategic Choices in Diversified MNC's." *Harvard Business Review,* July 1976, pp. 67–78.

Sparkman, J. "Economic Interdependence and the International Corporation." *California Management Review,* Fall 1977, pp. 88–92.

Vernon, R. "Multinational Enterprises and National Governments: An Uneasy Relationship." *Columbia Journal of World Business,* Summer 1976, pp. 9–16.

Weekly, J. K. "Expropriation of U. S. Multinational Investments." *Michigan State University Business Topics*, Winter 1977, pp. 27–36.

Weinshall, T. D. "Multinational Corporations—Their Development and Universal Role." *Management International Review*, 1975, pp. 17–28.

Zeira, Y., and Harari, E. "Managing Third Country Nationals In Multinational Corporations." *Business Horizons*, October 1977, pp. 83–88.

Zeira, Y. "Management Development in Ethnocentric Multinational Corporations." *California Management Review*, Summer 1976, pp. 34–42.

Case Study

THE CASE OF THE MISSING ADS

When several Americans came to work as department heads at one of the largest Japanese automotive firms in the United States, they had all been reading extensively on Japanese methods. Most of them had come from a major American automotive company, and all had had long experience in the industry. Inevitably, under the pressure of business in this fast-growing organization, they turned instinctively to their accustomed Western management techniques. They looked to the Japanese nationals at the top levels of the organization to give them direction, objectives, and priorities. But nothing was forthcoming; the Japanese were waiting patiently for initiatives from them.

After a time, on the Americans' initiative, an organization chart was drawn up in an effort to settle where the authority and responsibility for decisions rested. It was a thoroughly American document, showing in neat boxes the various departments—parts, service, sales, marketing, planning, and so on—and the vertical relationships, with the Japanese president at the top and the lowest subdepartment on the bottom. The Japanese, who rarely draw up organization charts (and who, if they do, invariably make them read horizontally, like a flow chart), tolerated the American version as a "when in Rome" accommodation. But the chart did not solve the problems; the organization was not functioning well, and decisions were not being made.

For example, there was the simple problem of timing the availability of advertising media for the introduction of new models each year. In the U. S. market this occurs in October; in Japan, new models are introduced in January. From the parent company in Japan, the advertising materials consistently arrived two to three months late for the introduction of new models. Year after year, the U. S. distributors complained about the delay. The American heads of the sales and advertising departments took the problem up the chain of command and requested their Japanese president to contact Japan and straighten the matter out. The president did contact Japan—but the problem remained.

By chance, other developments in the organization provided an opportunity for overcoming the difficulty. Beginning in the early 1970s top

Source Richard Tanner Johnson and William G. Ouchi, "Made In America (under Japanese Management)," *Harvard Business Review* 52 (September–October 1974): 67–68. Copyright © 1974 by President and Fellows of Harvard College. Used with permission.

management began to assign a Japanese "coordinator" to each American department head. The coordinators, usually promising young executives in training for international assignments, were to become acquainted with U. S. business practices. It was not long before they began observing with dismay that the American managers tended to concentrate on their functional roles and to expect coordination between functions to occur at the senior management levels—as is the practice in many U. S. companies. To the Japanese, it appeared, as one put it, "as if the various departments were separate companies, all competing against each other."

As inveterate communicators, some coordinators began to pick up problems that cropped up in one department and share them with their counterparts in other departments. In this roundabout way, the Americans learned what their colleagues were doing. Coordination between departments improved.

Soon the Japanese coordinators became aware of the difficulties typified by the late arrival of the advertising materials. True to their training in U. S. companies, the Americans were sending a report on every problem up the chain of command. Japanese top management in the United States would listen to each complaint, then send the American manager back for "more information." Translated, this meant "Come back with a proposal." Not comprehending, the Americans became increasingly impatient and frustrated. Occasionally, as in the case of the ads, the problems became so serious that the Americans insisted they be reported to Japan. The Japanese president obliged them, but the parent company remained unresponsive. The reason was simple: since Japanese organizations are unaccustomed to dealing with problems from the top down, the Tokyo organization did not know how to handle a letter from the president of the Japanese subsidiary in the United States to the president of the parent company in Japan.

Once the coordinators understood the nature of the difficulty, remedying the advertising materials lag and similar problems was easy. A coordinator would simply pick up the telephone and call somebody at his managerial level in Tokyo. In a few days an answer would come back—and in this manner the matter of the ads was resolved.

The coordinators took some time—and the American department heads a somewhat longer time—to realize that the neat boxes in the organization chart were not interacting. By U. S. standards, the Americans were doing a good job. But without American superiors to make decisions and weave the organization together, they found that their effectiveness was diminished. To bridge the gap in managerial styles, the coordinators created a shadow organization. In this manner they not only solved the coordination problem but also involved the parent organization.

Questions

1. Identify the major situational factors that affected American managers working for a foreign company.

2. Why do you believe the informal organization was so important in the solution of this problem?

Case Study

MARK IS TRANSFERRED OVERSEAS

In college, Mark Hammer majored in industrial management and was considered by his teachers and peers to be one of the best all around students to graduate from Midwest State University. Mark not only took the required courses in business but he also acquired a minor in foreign language. The language that Mark concentrated on the most was French and he became quite fluent in the language.

After graduation, Mark took an entry-level management training position with Tuborg International, a multinational corporation with offices and factories in thirty countries, including the United States. Mark's first assignment was in a plant in New York. His supervisors quickly identified Mark for his ability to get the job done and still maintain excellent rapport with subordinates, peers, and superiors. In only three years, Mark had advanced from a manager trainee to the position of assistant plant superintendent.

After two years in this position, Mark was called into the superintendent's office one day and told that he had been identified as being ready for a foreign assignment. The move would mean a promotion and the location of the plant was in a small industrialized region in France. One of the reasons that Mark has been chosen for France was due to his knowledge of French he had gained in college. Mark was excited and he wasted no time in making the necessary preparations for the new assignment.

Prior to arriving at the plant in France, Mark took considerable time to review his books in the French language. He was surprised at how quickly the use of the language came back to him. He thought that there wouldn't be any major difficulties in making the transition from the United States to France. But, on arriving, Mark rapidly discovered that there were to be problems. The small industrialized community where Mark's plant was located did not speak the "pure" French that he had learned. There were many slang expressions that meant one thing to Mark but had an entirely different meaning to the employees of the plant.

While meeting with several of the employees a week after arriving, one of the workers said something to Mark that he interpreted as very uncomplimentary (in actuality, the employee had greeted him by saying a rather risque expression but in a different tone than he had known before. All of the other employees interpreted the expression to be merely a friendly greeting). Mark's disgust was evident and as time went by, this type instance occurred a few more times and the other employees began to limit their conversation with Mark. In only one month, Mark managed to virtually completely isolate himself from the workers within the plant. He became disillusioned and thought about asking to be relieved from the assignment.

Questions

1. What problems had Mark not anticipated when he took the assignment?
2. How could the company have assisted Mark to reduce the difficulties that he confronted?
3. Do you believe the situation that Mark confronted is typical of an American going to a foreign assignment? Discuss.

MANAGEMENT CONCERNS: PRESENT AND FUTURE

Part 7 concerns additional important considerations managers presently face and are expected to confront in the future. The section is directed toward discussion of the importance of corporate social responsibility and business ethics.

Chapter 17

KEY TERMS

social responsibility

economic function

awareness of changing
social demands

voluntary social action

ethical responsibility

environmental responsibility

human social responsibility

iron law of responsibility

Friedman's view of
social responsibility

social audit

ethics

unethical practices

Kodak's SPICE concept

ethical dilemmas

managerial code of ethics

Corporate Social Responsibility and Business Ethics

LEARNING OBJECTIVES

After completing this chapter you should be able to

1. Define what is meant by the "social responsibility of business."
2. List the various groups in society that affect a business firm.
3. Describe the role of business in society.
4. Explain the arguments "for" and "against" the acceptance of social responsibility by businesses.
5. State the major federal legislation affecting social responsibility.
6. Describe the current practices of some companies with regard to social responsibility.
7. Explain the importance of business ethics and identify the major factors affecting managerial ethics.
8. Define ethics and provide examples of unethical practices.
9. Describe and illustrate typical ethical dilemmas faced by managers.

The management of Centron Corporation is concerned that if they make a decision to implement a more effective pollution control system in their tire manufacturing plants, current profits will be adversely affected. Centron meets the minimum environmental air and water quality standards as specified by the Environmental Protection Agency, but management has just become aware of new and improved pollution control systems that can further reduce air and water pollutants being emitted from Centron's plants. The management of Centron recognizes that their plants are major sources of pollution in the communities in which they operate.

Bill Smith, manager of purchasing with the Allied Wholesale Company, has been offered expensive gifts including an expense paid vacation to Hawaii for him and his wife, by a sales representative of one of his firm's major suppliers. In return for these gifts, Bill realizes he would be expected to show favoritism toward this supplier by purchasing from him.

The Centron Corporation is confronted with a social responsibility dilemma that many of today's organizations constantly face. While striving to earn a satisfactory profit, it recognizes that the socially responsible firm attempts to meet the needs and interests of society. On the other hand, Bill Smith is faced with a decision that involves determining what is ethically right or wrong. Bill's ethics may be severely tested as he decides whether or not to accept the gifts and give the vendor preferential treatment.

In recent years, managers and the corporations they work for have been subjected to increasing criticism and have received low levels of approval from the public. Hardly a week passes without news headlines of corporate bribery, illegal political contributions, or price-fixing practices being alleged about some of America's largest business organizations. If a person reacts just to these headlines, the impression might be that almost all businesspeople engage in illegal and/or unethical conduct. Nothing could be further from the truth! But, nevertheless, there is a certain amount of corruption in businesses and in most other forms of organizations. In today's complex and rapidly changing environment, businesspeople constantly ask themselves how concerned should business be with social responsibility issues and ethical behavior?

Large corporations are being pressured to increase minority hiring, provide safer products for consumers, provide a safer working environment for employees and reduce pollution. In addition, dissident stockholders are demanding that management be more accountable for its actions, that the corporation be more responsive to social responsibility concerns, and that illegal and/or unethical behavior of corporate executives cease. In this chapter we are concerned with examining the basic issues of social responsibility and business ethics.

THE PUBLIC'S VIEW OF BUSINESS

The fact that the public mistrusts business and business executives is exemplified by the findings of numerous recent surveys of public opinion. Surveys have revealed a serious decline in the public's confidence in business. In one such study, over 50 percent of the respondents believed that the "bad" features of our business system either equal or outweigh the "good."[1] One poll indicated that public confidence in the executives who manage major corporations had declined drastically from 55 percent in 1968 to 16 percent in 1978. In another survey, 87 percent of those interviewed agreed that most businesspeople are more interested in profits than in serving the public's needs, and 53 percent felt that many major companies should be dismantled.

Other surveys have revealed that the public's estimate of the profits of business was considerably out of line with reality. For example, the public's estimate of the level of after-tax profits per dollar of sales for the typical business was between 25 and 30 cents; the actual amount was about 5 cents in 1978. Also, surveys have pointed out that the general public has a relatively low opinion of the caliber of the business executive's ethics. While surveys have also found that a substantial majority of the public contend that business firms have an obligation to help society even if it means making less profit, less than half of those surveyed accept the notion that executives have a social conscience. Many people believe that business executives do everything within their power to earn a profit even if it means ignoring the public's needs. Such attitudes held by members of the public could indicate one or a combination of the following:

- Businesses have not been very responsive to the needs of society.
- Businesses have not been able to effectively communicate their concerns and interests to the public.
- Society often questions the ethics of business leaders.
- The news media blow out of proportion the wrongdoings of a few businesses or executives.

INSIGHTS TO SUCCESS

At all costs, *avoid* the *very bright* person who has lower ethical/moral standards—he or she can always find ways to mess up your business operation by embezzling, cheating your customers, etc.

JOHN R. HILL, Jr., Chairman and C.E.O., Gifford-Hill & Co., Incorporated

---

1. Thomas Benham, "The Factual Foundation," in Clarence H. Danhof and James C. Worthy, eds., *Crisis in Confidence II: Corporate America* (Springfield, Ill., Sagamon State University, 1975), pp. 21–53.

MS. KATHARINE GRAHAM

Chairman of the Board
The Washington Post Company

The Washington Post As chairman and the chief executive officer of The Washington Post Company, some feel that Katherine Graham is one of the most powerful executives in the United States. It was through her courage and determination that the reputation of the *Post* was placed on the line when she backed two young reporters, Carl Bernstein and Bob Woodward during the Watergate investigation. It is this same kind of dedication that has taken her from a reporter on the *San Francisco News* after graduation from the University of Chicago in 1938 to her present position as chairman and chief executive officer.

Ms. Graham refers to The Washington Post Company as a media conglomerate, though far from the largest. The company publishes *The Washington Post, Newsweek* magazine, the *Trenton Times* and *Sunday Times-Advertiser, The Everett* (Washington) *Herald,* and operates four television stations. Even so, she says that the company has become conspicuous out of proportion to its size. In part, this is because *Newsweek* and the news services are national and the newspaper base is in the nation's capital. Beyond that, Ms. Graham says, "I like to think—as any manager does—that much of our success results from our high standards and hard work." She believes that the media should not be self-censors or editorialists. "We are transmitters and translators of information," she says. "The ultimate power of judgment, on events and our own performance, rests with the American people."

As a leader, Ms. Graham believes that people, when given the opportunity, can evaluate and make objective decisions. "I can't emphasize that enough," she states. "I don't accept the view that newspaper readers and television viewers are a passive, sponge-like lot who will accept, uncritically, everything served up by the press. The public is much more thoughtful and discerning and cantankerous, than that. If stories are overblown or off the track, they sense it soon enough. And where the information does justify the headlines, they recognize that too. In short, people make their own editorial judgments every day. And, if they get enough information, their judgment is likely to be sound." This philosophy concerning trust and the ability of people to make their own decisions carries over into every phase of operations as chairman of the board for The Washington Post Company.

Whatever the situation, business managers must recognize and be concerned with the social responsibility and ethical issues confronting them, their organizations, and society.

BUSINESS AND SOCIAL RESPONSIBILITY

social responsibility **Social responsibility** is concerned with how organizations deal with the issues and problems confronting society. Although a universally acceptable definition has not been developed, social responsibility can be defined this way: The basic obligation of an organization to ensure that its decisions and operations meet the needs and interests of society.

Socially responsible decision makers within corporations consider both the economic and social impact of their decisions and the firm's operations on the various groups in society. Keith Davis, a leading writer in this area, believes that in meeting its social responsibilities to society, a firm must be concerned with more than the narrow, technical and legal requirements.[2] It should recognize that an obligation exists to protect and enhance the interests and welfare of not only the corporation, but also those of society.

In today's environment, business organizations are being expected to assume broader and more diverse responsibilities to the various groups within society. There is little doubt that there is an increasing amount of attention directed to the social responsibilities in business firms. However, critics argue that there is more "lip service" than action, more public relations programs than concrete social responsibility activities. Nevertheless, social responsibility is an area in which the modern business firm must develop a stance, accompanied by appropriate policies and activities.

The essence of corporate social responsibility is illustrated by Figure 17.1 which depicts the relationship of a business firm to the many groups in society. Businesses have frequent contacts with and are affected by the many diverse groups in the environment in which they operate. How business conducts itself with regard to each of these groups will greatly affect its opportunities for survival, growth, and profitability. The needs and values of each of these diverse groups have significant effects on the firm. Management must continually assess the impacts of their decisions and the operations of the business on each group. This is a most important, but difficult challenge.

Labor unions and governmental units are among the most powerful groups in the external environment in terms of the potential effects on the firm. Consumer groups are gaining increased power as have special

2. Keith Davis, "The Case For and Against Business Assumption of Social Responsibilities," *Academy of Management Journal,* June 1973. Reprinted in Archie B. Carroll, *Managing Corporate Social Responsibility,* Little, Brown, and Company (Boston: 1977, p. 35).

FIGURE 17.1
Relationship of the Firm to Groups in Society

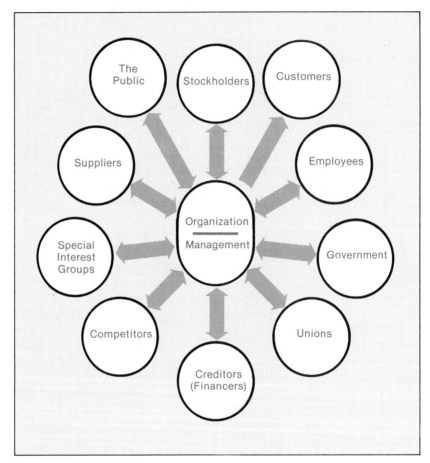

interest groups, such as the Urban League and the National Organization of Women. On occasion, even stockholders have organized to alter or overthrow the existing management of an organization when the firm has not conducted business in a socially responsible manner.

Managers must assess the power of each group and its potential threat to organizational activities. They should pursue what they deem to be the primary goals of the enterprise, but always with an eye out for constraints imposed by forces in the external environment. When managers go too long without responding, or when they fundamentally disagree with actions demanded by various groups, they risk the possibility of boycotts, picketing, new legislation, government hearings, proxy contests, and strikes. However, demands made by groups in society will keep the organization from becoming too selfish and irresponsible. Actions by these groups, rather than profits or conscience, have often led a firm to pursue socially responsible actions.

THE ROLE OF BUSINESS IN SOCIETY

Traditionally, the responsibility of the business firm has been to produce and distribute goods and services in return for a profit. Businesses have performed this function extremely effectively. Largely as the result of our economic system and the important contributions of business firms, the U. S. enjoys the highest overall standard of living in the world. Rising standards of living have enabled a very high percentage of the U. S. population to have their basic needs for food, clothing, shelter, health, and education reasonably well satisfied. Businesses can take pride in these accomplishments because they had a great deal to do with making the higher standards of living possible.

Business has been able to make significant contributions to the rising living standards primarily because of the manner in which the free enterprise economic system operates. The profit motive provides incentive to business to produce products and services as efficiently as is possible. Business firms try to improve the quality of their products and services, reduce costs and prices and thereby attract more customers to buy from the firm. By earning profits, the successful firm pays taxes to the government and makes donations to provide financial support for charitable causes. Because of the efficient operations of business firms, an ever increasing number of people have the means and the leisure time to enjoy the "good life."[3]

But, businesses operate by public consent with the basic purpose of satisfying the needs of society. Despite significant improvements in standards of living in recent years, society has begun expecting—even demanding—more of all of its institutions, particularly large business firms. Goals, values and attitudes in society are changing to reflect a greater concern for improvements in the quality of life. An indication of these concerns would include such goals as the following:[4]

- Elimination of poverty and provision of quality health care
- Preservation of the environment by reducing the level of pollution
- Providing equal employment and educational opportunities regardless of race, color, creed or sex

3. "Social Responsibilities of Business Corporations," Committee for Economic Development, June 1971, pp. 11–40.

4. Adapted from the Committee for Economic Development and from Sandra L. Holmes, "Corporate Social Performance and Present Areas of Commitment," *Academy of Management Journal* 20 (1977): 435.

- Providing a sufficient number of jobs and career opportunities for all members of society
- Improving the quality of working life of employees
- Providing safe, livable communities with good housing and efficient transportation.

economic function

Society's expectations of business have broadened considerably in recent years to encompass more than the traditional economic function. This is illustrated in Figure 17.2. Inner circle I represents the traditional economic functions of business. The **economic function** is the primary responsibility of businesses to society. In performing the economic func-

FIGURE 17.2
Primary Roles of Business

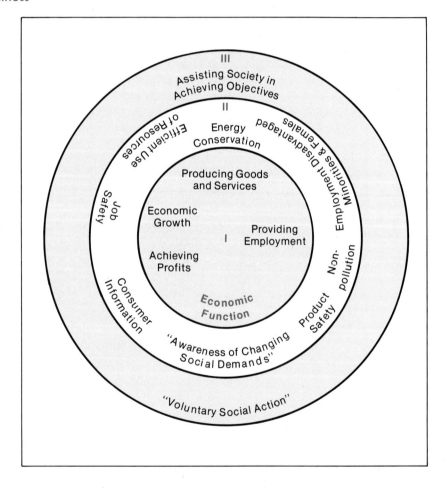

tion, businesses produce needed goods and services, provide employment, contribute to economic growth, and earn a profit. Level II represents the responsibility of business to perform the economic functions with an **awareness of changing social goals,** values, and demands. Management must be aware of such concerns as: the efficient utilization of resources, reducing environmental pollution, employing and developing disadvantaged minorities and females, providing safe products, and providing a safe working environment. In Level III, the outer circle is concerned with the corporation's responsibility for assisting society in achieving such broad goals as the elimination of poverty and urban decay through a partnership between business, government agencies, and other private institutions. While the responsibilities in Level III are not primary obligations of businesses, there is increasing interest by business in **voluntary social action** programs.

awareness of changing social goals

voluntary social action

Mr. Jerry McAfee, Chairman of the Board and Chief Executive Officer of Gulf Oil Corporation, summarized his view of a corporation's responsibilities to society as performing "three simple but important functions":

1. To do the job
2. To do it at a profit
3. To do it in accordance with the limits imposed by society—ethical, environmental and social limits.[5]

The first two functions mentioned by Mr. McAfee are concerned with the traditional economic functions of a business. The third function involves achieving the economic goals of the firm within the "limits" of society. These limits include:

- ethical responsibility
- environmental responsibility
- human social responsibility

ethical responsibility

Mr. McAfee explains his view of **ethical responsibility** by giving an illustration from his own company, Gulf Oil.

Unhappily, the corporation I now represent, because of some serious past errors in judgment, found it necessary to take Draconian actions to ensure a continuation of its traditionally high level of ethical conduct. Tragic as Gulf's ordeal has been, I am convinced that we have gained new strength from the experience. Gulf has learned the hard way that, with a corporation

5. Jerry McAfee, "The Corporation and Society: The Responsibilities of Each to Each," An Address Before the 84th National Meeting of American Institute of Chemical Engineers, Atlanta, Georgia, February 27, 1978.

as with an individual, there is no possession more precious than one's integrity and that corporate integrity, like personal integrity, is a fragile treasure to be nurtured and guarded above all else.

Environmental responsibility is the concern of the corporation for the maintenance of clean air and water and the aesthetic beauty of the physical environment. Mr. McAfee adds:

environmental responsibility

Another limit imposed by society's expectations is **environmental responsibility.** There should be no basic cause for disagreement here; after all, the public's environment is business's environment; the people who make up corporations have to breathe the same air, drink the same water, and gaze at the same scenery as the people they work among. And a deteriorating physical environment will sooner or later result in a deteriorating business atmosphere. Thus, it stands to reason that corporations should use resources with due regard for the effects on society.

human social responsibility

The third limit imposed by society, **human social responsibility,** is the firm's concern for people.

. . . specifically the responsibilities to people . . . in the areas of employee safety and equal employment opportunity. Society today insists that corporations have an intrinsic respect for their many special publics— including but not limited to shareholders, customers, and current and retired employees—as well as for the public in general. And society has every right to expect the business community not only to help support its educational, cultural, health, and welfare institutions financially—but also by active participation.

In summary then, if business organizations make a sincere and dedicated effort to meet these challenges and obligations—to recognize, accept, and adapt to an evolving world; to do their job; to do it in such a way as to merit a just and reasonable return; and to do it within society's bounds—they can hope to keep pace with change and hopefully even help lead it.

Social responsibility is not a one-way street. It can be viewed as a two-sided coin in which society also has an obligation to businesses. McAfee believes that society has five basic obligations to business. These are

1. Set rules that are clear and consistent.
2. Keep the rules within the bounds of technical feasibility.
3. Make sure the rules are economically feasible, and recognize that society itself must be prepared to pay the cost—not only of their implementation by business, but also their administration by government.

4. Make the rules prospective, not retroactive.

5. Make the rules goal-setting, not procedure-prescribing—tell us what to do, not how to do it.

**QUALITIES NEEDED FOR SUCCESS AS
A MANAGER IN YOUR ORGANIZATION**

* Character, integrity, courage, wisdom, and business acumen

* Drive, and a "can-do" attitude

* A dedication to the enterprise, and the concept of making a profit with *decency*

PHILLIP HARTLEY SMITH, Chairman and President, Copperweld Corporation

---

VIEWS FOR AND AGAINST SOCIAL RESPONSIBILITY

As in every controversial area there are always at least two opposing views. This is the case with regard to the acceptance of social responsibility by businesses.

ARGUMENTS FAVORING SOCIAL RESPONSIBILITY

Numerous associations and groups of respected business leaders including the American Management Association and the Committee for Economic Development have encouraged corporations and managers to become involved in socially responsible activities. These groups have stressed such programs as providing: better job and promotion opportunities to minorities and women; financial support for education; financial and managerial support for improving the health and medical care; a safer working environment; leadership and financial support for urban renewal; and means to reduce environmental pollution.

The major arguments for the acceptance of social responsibility by business can be summarized below:

1. People expect businesses and other institutions to be socially responsible.

2. It is in the best interest of the business to pursue socially responsible programs.

3. It improves the image of the firm.

4. Business should be involved in social projects because it has the resources.

5. Corporations must be concerned about society's interests and needs because society, in effect, sanctions business operations.

6. If the business is not responsive to society's needs, the public will press for more government regulation requiring more socially responsible behavior.

7. Socially responsible actions may increase profits in the long run.

iron law of responsibility

Keith Davis summarizes these arguments with what he terms the **iron law of responsibility.** The *law* states that "in the long-run, those who do not use power in a manner in which society considers responsible will tend to lose it." Thus, if business firms are to retain their social power and role, they must be responsive to society's needs.[6]

ARGUMENTS AGAINST SOCIAL RESPONSIBILITY

There are numerous arguments against businesses assuming an active role of social responsibility. A leading opponent of businesses' assumptions of social responsibilities is Dr. Milton Friedman, a Nobel prize-winning economist. **Friedman's view of social responsibility** can be stated as follows:

Friedman's view of social responsibility

> There is one and only one social responsibility of business—to use its resources and engage in activities designed to increase its profits so long as it stays within the rules of the game, which is to say, engages in open and free competition without deception and fraud. . . . Few trends could so thoroughly undermine the very foundations of our free society as the acceptance by corporate officials of a social responsibility other than to make as much money for their stockholders as possible.[7]

Friedman goes on to assert that social responsibility is a "fundamentally subversive doctrine." He argues that managers are agents of the owners of the enterprise and that to engage in any activities not related to earning profits may be illegal. Diverting funds to social projects without stockholders' approval is, in effect, "taxation without representation." He says that business performance is economic not social.

6. See Keith Davis, "The Case for and Against."

7. Milton Friedman, "The Social Responsibility of Business Is to Increase Its Profits," *The New York Times Magazine,* September 1970, pp. 33, 122–126.

Concentrating resources in the social area could lead to less economic efficiency and therefore actually be detrimental to society. Friedman and others who argue against the assumption of social responsibility by business believe that government should deal with the social demands of society.

The major arguments against social responsibility may be summarized as follows:

1. Violates sound economic business decision making that should rightfully concentrate on earning profit.
2. Might be illegal—executives do not have the legal right to use corporate resources to pursue social responsibility.
3. *Costs* are excessive compared to the *benefits* to society and would tend to raise prices to excessive levels.
4. Managers aren't trained nor do they possess the skills or resources to determine which socially desirable projects to support.
5. Concentrates too much power in the hands of business executives.
6. Leads to the deterioration of the free enterprise system.

AN EVALUATION OF THE "PROS" AND "CONS" OF SOCIAL RESPONSIBILITY

Both the positions for and against the assumption of social responsibility by business make logical arguments to support their case. What we often find is that business and executives themselves are very "pro" social responsibility when profits are high or social conditions unfavorable, and "anti" social responsibility when the economy is under great pressure or when the company is in financial difficulty or when social conditions do not warrant a great deal of concern.[8]

Friedman's arguments against the assumption of social responsibility by business firms have been criticized on a number of grounds. First, Friedman implies that business should engage in "open and free competition" as a part of the "rules of the game." However, open and free competition in most sectors of our economy does not exist. A second and more fundamental counterpoint to Friedman's position is that business firms (particularly large ones) cannot ignore their social responsibilities. Almost every major decision made in a corporation impacts various groups in and outside the organization (refer to Figure 17.1). Problems confronting society—employment discrimination, environment pollution, unsafe

8. William F. Glueck, *Management* (Hinsdale, Ill., The Dryden Press, 1977), pp. 569–571.

products, corporate bribery, illegal political contributions, and price-fixing—are all past practices of some companies not in the best interest of society.

Because of the social undesirability of many acts of managers, there has been an increasing amount of governmental regulation. Some managers have concluded that "if it's legal, it's ethical." If it is not in violation of the law, one is free to do as one wishes. This managerial philosophy will tend to invite more and more outside regulatory attempts and may be self-defeating in the long-run. Being socially responsible means more than just following the law. It means considering the *consequences* of one's actions and asking if such actions are morally and ethically responsible. *Social responsibility starts where the law ends.* Keith Davis stresses this point by the following statement:

> A firm is not being socially responsible if it merely complies with the minimum requirements of the law, because this is what any good citizen would do. A profit maximizing firm under the rules of classical economics would do as much. Social responsibility goes one step further. It is a firm's acceptance of a social obligation beyond the requirements of the law.[9]

THE LEGISLATION OF SOCIAL RESPONSIBILITY

There have been numerous laws passed in recent years because business has ignored or not recognized its responsibilities to society. To illustrate the steadily increasing amount of federal legislation in the field of social responsibility, the treatment of organizational employees is a good example. Arranged in chronological order, the following list is a sample of federal legislation decreeing minimum acceptable level of organizational conduct:

1. National Labor Relations Act (Wagner) of 1935 (protects right of employees to form unions and levies bargaining responsibilities upon management).
2. Social Security Act of 1936 (obliges organizations to provide retirement income, medicare, and unemployment compensation for employees).
3. Fair Labor Standards Act of 1938 (requires firms to pay minimum wages and extra compensation for overtime).
4. Equal Pay Act of 1963 (requires that males and females on the same job get equal pay).

9. Keith Davis, "The Case For and Against," p. 36.

5. Civil Rights Act of 1964 (prohibits discrimination in hiring, training, promotion, and pay on basis of race, color, religion, nationality and sex).

6. Executive Order 11246 (requires firms dealing with the federal government to establish affirmative action programs to promote hiring of minorities and females).

7. Age Discrimination Act of 1967 (prohibits discrimination against older employees).

8. Occupational Safety and Health Act of 1970 (sets safety and health standards and enforces them through surprise inspections and fines).

9. Rehabilitation Act of 1973 (requires government contractors to take affirmative action in the hiring of handicapped personnel).

10. Employee Retirement Income Security Act of 1974 (protects employee rights in private pension plans).

Concerning future legislation, it is predicted that the legitimacy of power of the large corporation will come under increasing scrutiny. Ralph Nader's Corporate Accountability Research Group has proposed that the largest corporations be chartered directly by the federal government. In addition, public members are being added to the board of directors with staffs provided to deal with organization activities concerning consumer rights, compliance with legislation, and shareholder rights. They would provide a communications link to public agencies to propose laws and standards, and alert the public to the need for industry-wide solutions to social problems.[10] It has also been proposed that any corporate executive found guilty of violating laws related to corporate activities should be barred from holding an executive job for five years. The corporation would also be prohibited from paying fines or penalties for executives.

It has also been proposed that the corporation be required to disclose vast amounts of information concerning its activities in such areas as: (a) degree of pollution and measures taken; (b) employee statistics by race, sex, income, etc.; (c) lobbying efforts undertaken; (d) income and benefits of the thirty highest paid executives; and (e) names of one hundred largest stockholders. Also, an employee "bill of rights" would: prevent employees from being fired for "whistle blowing"; prevent the use of polygraphs in hiring; and prevent company interference with employee privacy. The fact that such proposals are being made and hearings held in Congress should cause concern for the manager who claims "if it's legal, it's ethical."

---

10. There is precedent for this. One federal court has ordered that two public directors be added to the board of a toy manufacturing company in settlement of a fraud action.

> **QUALITIES NEEDED FOR SUCCESS AS
> A MANAGER IN YOUR ORGANIZATION**
>
> * Basic honesty
> * Loyalty
> * Dedication to the job
> * Eagerness to learn
> * Humility
> * Ability to communicate effectively
>
> CHARLES W. MERRITT, President, Commercial Metals Company

MANAGEMENT'S REACTION TO GOVERNMENT LAWS AND REGULATIONS

Business is regulated by a large number of federal, state, and local laws and agencies. In recent years, there has been considerable discussion on the issue of whether there is excessive and unnecessary regulations of business by government. The sheer volume and complexity of government laws and regulations creates a great deal of frustration for many managers. All levels of government have played an increasingly active role in business operations. The laws and regulations impact managers and organizations because they add a degree of uncertainty into the organization and limit the decision making freedom of managers.

While most managers accept some degree of government regulation of business, many people believe that excessive controls prevent the business from operating efficiently and effectively. They argue that the costs of many government regulations are far greater than the benefits to society. Practicing managers often cite several complaints about laws and regulations such as:

1. Lack of understanding on precisely how to comply with the laws and regulations
2. The excessive reporting load created
3. The difficulties of accurate record keeping
4. Duplication of regulations
5. The costs incurred in implementing laws and regulations
6. Inconsistency in the application of laws and regulations
7. The dilution of managerial decision-making authority brought about by government intervention.

Consumer groups and others insist that government plays an essential role in protecting society from business practices that are not in the best interests of people.

CORPORATE SOCIAL RESPONSIBILITY: CURRENT PRACTICES

Many firms are doing more than just complying with the law. A survey of 232 large corporations revealed that approximately two-thirds have established definite policies regarding social responsibilities, and have created special organizational units to deal with these areas.[11] The most common unit is a social responsibility department headed by a vice-president reporting to the chief executive officer or president. It appears that the larger the number of stockholders for a corporation, the more committed the management to a sense of social responsibility. Allied Chemical, for example, has set up an Environment Service Department concerned with air and water pollution control, occupational health, and product safety. Its manager reports directly to the company's president. Some firms have approached the task through the boards of directors to ensure a greater concern for social responsibility. Koppers Company established two board committees composed of four outside directors each. One committee is concerned with the environment and the other with human resources. At least twice each year, the management of Koppers will account to these two committees concerning their efforts in this regard.

Other companies feel that you cannot segment and compartmentalize the responsibility. When its treatment of migrant field workers was brought rather forcefully to the attention of the Coca-Cola Company, a special project was established at the direction of the president of Coca-Cola's food division. Expenditures on housing, education, and health services for migrant workers have now been integrated into the company's regular activities.

With respect to specific activities by particular companies, in one year Dow Chemical invested $20 million in pollution control equipment. At a 9 percent depreciation rate, the yearly cost came to $1.8 million, to which was added $10.5 million to run the equipment. The environmental clean-up cost came to $12.3 million for the year, but Dow claims to have recovered at least that much in terms of reduced corrosion on cooling towers and the saving of valuable chemicals previously pumped out as

11. Vernon M. Buehler and Y. K. Shetty, "Managerial Response to Social Responsibility Challenge," *Academy of Management Journal* 19 (March 1976): 69.

waste. In three years' time, over $6 million was saved in recovery of these wasted chemicals alone. Although this attempt at a Michigan plant was quite successful, Dow still has serious air and water pollution problems to be solved in other plants owned by the company. But this case indicates that both economic and social values can at times be coaligned in the short run.

In recent years, *Business Week* has given awards for private company efforts in the two major areas of (1) improving the physical environment and (2) developing human resources. The process of selecting companies for these awards has brought to light many examples of specific company actions in these two fields. Among these are

- an educational program to combat drug abuse
- provision of seed money to minority suppliers
- urban rehabilitation
- loans to construct low-cost housing
- providing managerial training to minority groups
- establishing manufacturing plants in ghetto areas

International Business Machines Corporation located a new plant in the Bedford-Stuyvesant neighborhood of Brooklyn in 1968. After a financially disastrous beginning, the facility became profitable in 1970. The plant probably could have been immediately profitable if located elsewhere, but the economic decision to build the plant in Brooklyn was affected by a felt responsibility for providing jobs in an area that probably had the largest concentration of hard-core unemployed in the United States at the time. An example of a systematic effort at improving the quality of worker life is described in Figure 17.3 outlining changes in the quality of worklife at the U.S. Eaton Company.

THE SOCIAL AUDIT

social audit

A **social audit** is defined as a commitment to systematic assessment of and reporting on some meaningful, definable domain of a company's activities that have social impact. Some firms have demonstrated their concern for the area of social responsibility by periodically surveying and assessing their activities. This practice, when formalized, has become known as *social auditing.* Systematic social auditing is only in its infancy and relatively few firms have undertaken a periodic appraisal process.[12] Its uses are to

12. Raymond A. Bauer and Dan H. Fenn, Jr., "What Is a Corporate Social Audit?" *Harvard Business Review* 51 (January-February 1973): 38.

FIGURE 17.3
Changes in the Quality of Life at U.S.: Eaton

Rather than introducing specific programs such as job enrichment and decision participation, the U.S. Eaton Corporation proposed to improve the general climate and quality of work life in all new plants built since 1968. Some thirteen plants involving over 5,000 personnel now work within climates characterized by:

1. Counseling rather than a rule-penalty process in altering undesirable behavior.
2. Hiring as a two-way exchange process. Procedures normally accorded only to managers and white-collar employees are now extended to all.
3. Abolition of probationary periods.
4. Abolition of time clocks and buzzers.
5. The same fringe benefit package for both factory and office personnel.
6. Biweekly departmental meetings to discuss work problems.
7. Periodic plant manager roundtables with chosen representatives from departments.
8. Staff specialists conducting most business at the work site rather than within their offices.
9. More employee participation in a variety of managerial staff meetings.

As a consequence, some employees asked for job enlargement and enrichment, while others did not. The company responds to these initiatives, rather than pushing a standard program for all. Major concrete results thus far are: (1) new plants have an absenteeism rate ranging from .5 to 3 percent, compared to 6 to 12 percent for older installations, (2) new plants have annual turnover rates under 4 percent, as compared to up to 60 percent in other plants, (3) hourly outputs for identical products range up to 35 percent more in the new plants, and (4) scrap and rework range up to 15 percent less for the new installations. The only negative for the new plants is a poorer safety record, presumably caused by personnel striving harder to improve output.

* For greater details, see Donald N. Scobel, "Doing Away With Factory Blues," *Harvard Business Review* (November-December 1975): 132–142.

provide internal information to management which aids in decision making and to provide external information to the public in response to pressures on the enterprise.

Four possible types of audits are currently being utilized: (1) a simple inventory of activities, (2) compilation of socially relevant expenditures, (3) specific program management, and (4) determination of social impact. The inventory is generally the place where one would start. It would consist of a simple listing of activities undertaken by the firm over and above what is required. For example, firms have itemized the following types of social activities: (1) minority employment and training, (2) support of minority enterprises, (3) pollution control, (4) corporate giving, (5) involvement in selected community projects by firm executives, and (6) a hard-core unemployed program. The ideal social audit would involve determination of the true *benefits* to society of any socially oriented business activity.

BUSINESS ETHICS

Our previous discussion has been concerned with the issue of social responsibility as it relates to the decisions made by managers within organizations. Whereas social responsibility is primarily concerned with **ethics** the overall operation of the corporation, **ethics** are contemporary standards or principles of conduct that govern the actions and behavior of

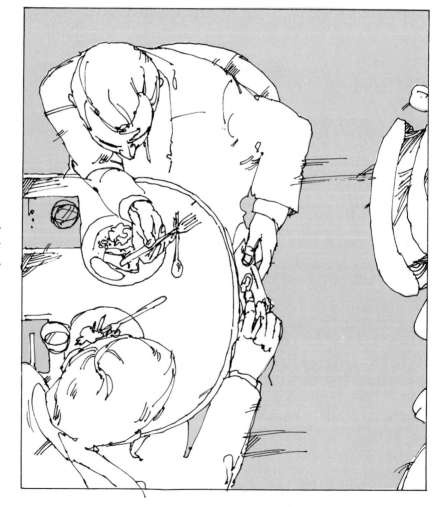

Where ethics are concerned, actions speak louder than words.

individuals within the organization. They provide a basis for determining what is *right* or *wrong* in terms of a given situation. Defining what is ethical or unethical is complicated because societal values, moral concepts, tend to change over time. Different groups within society may have divergent views of acceptable conduct.

A distinction between laws and ethics should be made. While laws provide an overall framework of restrictions, they should not be confused with ethics. What is within a literal interpretation of the law may not be ethical. If a practice is defined by the law as illegal, then it is not a matter of ethical or moral standards, but a legal requirement. Society, through its government representatives, may pass laws to stop harmful practices where the ethical standards of individuals in the industry have been unsuccessful in preventing such practices.

As illustrated in Figure 17.4, ethical norms are established by society and govern the development of ethical standards for an industry, a

FIGURE 17.4
Frames of Reference for Ethical Standards for Managers

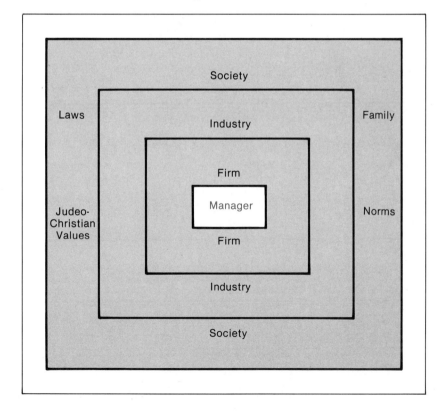

business firm, or an individual manager. Each industry develops its own ethical standards and the firms and individual managers in the industry must adapt to these *codes of behavior.*

The ethical norms provided by society in general are not so specific and long lasting that they always give clearly defined guidelines for everyone to follow. The differences between conduct that is just barely tolerated and that which is clearly indefensible are often difficult to identify. Our elected federal representatives often take lavish foreign trips on taxpayers' money to investigate some phenomena that have low probabilities of affecting future legislation. Highly respected members of society hire professional lawyers to look for loopholes in tax laws.

EXAMPLES OF ILLEGAL AND UNETHICAL PRACTICES

unethical practices

Reading the newspapers or watching the evening news provides ample illustrations of illegal and/or **unethical practices** of individuals within large corporations. While ethics are our primary consideration, there are numerous examples of illegal practices engaged in by managers. How widespread are these illegal activities? An article in the *Wall Street Journal* indicated that the IRS was investigating 111 companies on political gifts. "These 'political gifts' involved most of the top-level executives of the companies." The executives involved allegedly either falsified expenses to obtain reimbursement for "contributions," or brought "laundered money" back from Europe, or stashed money in secret safes in their offices.[13] Executives of such major companies as American Airlines, Ashland Oil, Gulf Oil, Goodyear, Minnesota Mining, Phillips, and Braniff Airways and other companies have admitted making illegal contributions to political candidates.

While there are many practices that are clearly illegal, deciding what is unethical is much more difficult. The following provide examples of unethical behavior or activities of managers:

- Padding expense accounts to obtain reimbursement for "questionable" business expenses (expenses in excess of the "three martini lunch")
- Using company property and/or materials for one's own personal use
- Giving or receiving "gifts"
- Divulging confidential information or trade secrets
- Terminating employment without giving sufficient notice

13. Glueck, *Management,* p. 578.

- Downgrading fellow employees or managers
- Being severely critical of your competitors

FACTORS AFFECTING MANAGERIAL ETHICS

There are at least five factors that help shape managerial ethics. These significantly affect decisions made by managers involving ethical issues. These factors include:

- laws
- government regulation
- industry or company ethical codes of behavior
- social or societal pressures
- conflicts between the manager's personal standards and the needs of the firm.[14]

LAWS

Laws may be viewed as the results of a trend of what society expects in terms of acceptable behavior. A practice can be made illegal if society views it as being excessive or unethical. The law defines and clarifies acceptable standards or practices in a given area. For example, if contributions to political candidates from corporations are illegal, then one either obeys the law or violates it. However, in either case the guidelines or standards are clear and the violator may be punished for engaging in the illegal activity. Laws are often passed as a result of low ethical standards or the failure to recognize social responsibilities.

GOVERNMENT REGULATIONS

These rules or standards define acceptable and unacceptable practices. For example, government regulations in the areas of minimum product safety, acceptable level auto emissions, safe working conditions, and nondiscriminatory employment practices are all supported by federal and state laws. However, the interpretation of the laws by the courts and the development of guidelines by government agencies assist managers in understanding what are acceptable practices.

14. James A. F. Stoner, *Management* (Englewood Cliffs, N. J.: Prentice-Hall, Inc., 1978), pp. 73–74.

INDUSTRY AND/OR COMPANY ETHICAL CODES OF BEHAVIOR

Many industries and individual companies have formal, written codes of ethics that provide specific guidelines for managers and other employees to follow. The key question in this regard is whether or not individuals within organizations are truly governed by the code of ethics or simply give lip service to the guidelines. Another issue is whether or not the company or industry *enforces* the code if individuals or companies violate it. In any event, these *codes of ethics* define or clarify the ethical issues and allow the individual to make the final decision.

As mentioned above, companies have developed specific codes of ethics. Eastman Kodak and Texas Instruments provide excellent examples. **Kodak's SPICE concept** provides guidelines for company practices (see Figure 17.5) and as such is dynamic and flexible. Kodak intends for SPICE to reflect the needs in the marketplace and to anticipate legal changes.

Kodak's SPICE concept

FIGURE 17.5
"SPICE" Concept Guides Kodak Business Practices

Throughout the history of Eastman Kodak Company, the principal factor in its growth has been the conviction that fulfilling customer needs and desires is the only road to corporate success. Such clichés as "share of the market," when used to explain performance, gloss over the fact that the consumer is supreme in a free economy and that all ingredients contributing to corporate success rest ultimately with him.

Kodak recognizes that it has to meet many responsibilities to assure successful operations. Our concern for Shareowners, the Public Interest, Customers, and Employees has come to be known throughout the Kodak organization as the "SPICE" concept.

A review for management of each element in the SPICE concept reveals how its combined approaches to influencing business operations apply to the company's growth and success.

Shareowners

Currently there are more than 222,000 shareowners of Eastman Kodak Company—an increase from 210,000 a year ago and from fewer than 121,000 in 1960. Kodak investors now own more than 161,000,000 common shares. These figures indicate that investors expect continued good performance from Kodak.

Men, women, and institutions have used their savings to invest in Kodak, and the Company has a primary obligation to satisfy their fair interests. Their judgment of Kodak and their confidence in the Company rest on the prospects of dividends and growth from their investments. In response to shareowners' interst in the Company, it is necessary to produce profits and provide an adequate return on investment. Today, the shareowners' judgment also is based increasingly on the ability of Kodak to meet its responsibilities to employees and the public interest.

In this respect, the concern of investors and employees should be parallel, serving each other for mutual benefit.

FIGURE 17.5
"SPICE" Concept Guides Kodak Business Practices (Continued)

Public Interest

Our corporate social responsibility may take diverse forms, but in essence it reflects concern for the well-being of the communities and countries in which Kodak carries on its activities. Examples of Kodak's activities in the public interest can be found in the improvement of communities through special training programs to upgrade the disadvantaged; clean air and water (healthful environment) programs; aid to education; and numerous other projects for civic betterment. This concern also is reflected in Kodak's encouragement of employee participation in civic, community, political, and other similar individual pursuits. It is exhibited, too, in the constant, substantial research and development efforts to produce new and improved products and services. Although often overlooked, corporate profits are essential to finance public interest projects. Kodak's 114,000 people are, of course, members of the public that renders judgement of performance in the public interest. While this judgment of accomplishment obviously varies among Kodakers, collectively it will have a substantial influence on public opinion about the Company.

Customers

Kodak must sell products and services—and continue to sell them in volume. Only satisfied customers will come back again and again. Thus, customer satisfaction is both a short- and a long-term goal. To reach this objective, the Company must produce and offer—at fair prices—high-quality products and services containing the features and capabilities that customers desire. This requires all the inventive genius we can muster in research and development leading to new and improved products and services; better ideas and greater efficiency in production, purchasing, distribution, marketing, and every other area of the Company's activities. This also means continued attention to the informative quality and scope of advertising and promotion; better exercise of personal and collective skills and capabilities; improved training programs for product users and for Kodak people as well as for our intermediate customers, the dealers and distributors.

Employees

Each Kodak man and woman is likely to judge the Company's overall performance in a different way; perhaps in terms of wages and salaries, opportunity for advancement, or direct and indirect benefits such as the Wage Dividend, hospital and medical care benefits, and work environment. There are also intangibles that he may consider, such as pride in the Company, opportunity through his job to make contributions to improving products or services and personal recognition for his accomplishments. The interests of Kodak people, Kodak shareowners, and Kodak customers are not mutually exclusive as one might initially be inclined to believe. During the past 10 years, 31,000 Kodak people have shown their faith in the future of the Company by deferring $146,000,000 in Wage Dividend payments for investment in the Savings and Investment Plan. Their interests merge with those of other shareowners in renewed appreciation for achieving profits and growth.

This, then, is a summary of the SPICE concept. It emphasizes that concern for shareowners, public interest, customers, and employees must motivate any successful business. Companies that are dedicated to satisfying the fair needs of these elements to the exclusion of all others are indispensible for the continued health of our society and the survival of the free enterprise system.

Used with permission from Eastman Kodak Company.

Kodak communicates this concept to its employees in meetings and discussion groups by members of management.

Texas Instruments recently published a handbook entitled "Ethics in the Business of T.I."[15] The company's overall philosophy of business can be summarized as follows:

> It is fundamental to TI's philosophy that good ethics and good business are synonymous when viewed from moral, legal and practical standpoints. The trust and respect of all people—fellow workers, customers, consumers, stockholders, government employees, elected officials, suppliers, competitors, neighbors, friends, the press, and the general public—are assets that cannot be purchased. They must be earned. This is why all of the business of TI must be conducted according to the highest ethical standards.

In the handbook, TI has statements establishing guidelines for ethical decision-making in business. Areas covered include: truthfulness in advertising, gifts and entertainment, improper use of corporate assets, political contributions, payments in connection with business transactions, conflicts of interest trade secrets and proprietary information and other matters.

There are advantages for organizations to form industry associations to develop and promote improved codes of ethics. It is difficult for a single firm to pioneer ethical practices if its competitors undercut it by taking advantage of unethical shortcuts. For example, with respect to abolishing bribes to overseas purchasers, perhaps the best hope would be for the major multinational enterprises to jointly agree to such a prohibition. When codes are not voluntarily followed, a society usually resorts to specific laws and penalties. In the case of international bribes, there is no international law. Should the U. S. declare the practice illegal, its multinational companies may find it difficult to compete with firms based in nations that do not disapprove. In this case, a voluntary code adopted by the leading firms of the world is likely to be the most effective method of handling the situation.

SOCIETAL PRESSURES

Social forces and pressures have considerable impact on ethics or acceptable standards of behavior. Examples of pressure groups seeking to make organizations more responsive to the needs and desires of society are numerous. Groups have demonstrated for more employment of blacks or other minorities, boycotted products, and complained and threatened

15. Texas Instruments, "Ethics in the Business of T.I.," Dallas, 1977.

action to prevent the construction of nuclear power plants. Such actions by pressure groups may, in fact, cause management to alter certain decisions by taking a broader view of the environment and the needs of society.

CONFLICTS BETWEEN A MANAGER'S PERSONAL STANDARDS AND THE NEEDS OF THE FIRM

The needs and goals of the firm may conflict with the values and ethical standards of a manager. This dilemma between organizational goals and personal ethics or values greatly complicates the life of the typical manager. There is often considerable pressure on the managers to increase performance and generate higher profits. At times, this may create pressures to compromise personal ethics for the goals of the company. A study by Archie Carroll found that managers feel a great deal of pressure to compromise their personal ethical standards in order to achieve organizational goals.[16] Carroll's study, representing the response of 258 managers, revealed that 50 percent of top-level managers, 65 percent of middle-level managers and 84 percent of lower-level managers felt "under pressure to compromise personal standards to achieve company goals."

ETHICAL DILEMMAS FACED BY MANAGERS

ethical dilemmas

Today's managers are confronted by many ethical dilemmas. The following are examples of legal but perhaps **ethical dilemmas** faced by managers in business today:

- The vice-president of a California industrial manufacturer "being forced as an officer to sign corporate documents which I knew were not in the best interests of minority stockholders."
- A Missouri manager of manpower planning "employing marginally qualified minorities in order to meet Affirmative Action quotas."
- A manager of product development from a computer company in Massachusetts "trying to act as though the product (computer software) would correspond to what the customer had been led by sales to expect, when, in fact, I knew it wouldn't."
- A manager of corporate planning from California "acquiring a non-U. S. company with two sets of books to evade income taxes—

16. Archie B. Carroll, "Managerial Ethics: A Post Watergate View," *Business Horizons*, April 1975, p. 77. See also, Archie B. Carroll, "A Survey of Managerial Ethics: Is Business Morality Watergate Morality?" *Business and Society Review*, 1976, pp. 58–63.

standard practice for that country. Do we (1) declare income and pay taxes, (2) take the 'black money' out of the country (illegally), or (3) continue tax evasion?"

· The president of a real estate property management firm in Washington "projecting cash flow without substantial evidence in order to obtain a higher loan than the project can realistically amortize."

· A young Texas insurance manager "being asked to make policy changes that produced more premium for the company and commission for an agent but did not appear to be of advantage to the policyholder."[17]

CHANGES IN THE ETHICS OF BUSINESS

As we have discussed, concern over ethical issues is not new. Brenner and Molander[18] compared views of over twelve hundred 1976 *Harvard Business Review* readers with a similar survey done in 1961. The survey was concerned with determining if business ethics had changed since the early 1960s and if so, how and why? Also, the study investigated the relationship between ethical issues and the dilemma of corporate social responsibility. The highlights of this study can be summarized as follows:

1. There is substantial disagreement among respondents as to whether ethical standards in business today have changed from what they were.

2. Respondents are somewhat more cynical about the ethical conduct of their peers than they were.

3. Most respondents favor ethical codes, although they strongly prefer general precept codes to specific practice codes.

4. The dilemmas respondents experience and the factors they feel have the greatest impact on business ethics suggest that ethical codes alone will not substantially improve business conduct.

5. Most respondents have overcome the traditional ideological barriers to the concept of social responsibility and have embraced its practice as a legitimate and achievable goal for business.

6. Most respondents rank their customers well ahead of shareholders and employees as the client group to whom they feel the greatest responsibility.

---

17. Steven N. Brenner and Earl A. Molander, "Is the Ethics of Business Changing?" *Harvard Business Review*, January-February 1977, p. 60.

18. Ibid., pp. 58–73.

According to Raymond C. Baumhart, President of Loyola University and author of a 1961 study on the ethics of businessmen,

> Business behavior is more ethical (in 1976) than it was 15 years ago (1961), but the expectations of a better educated and ethically sensitized public have risen more rapidly than the behavior.[19]

The study also found that respondents thought that they were more ethical than the average manager and that their department and company were more ethical than others. The respondents suggested that a written code of ethics would help to improve business practices.

A MANAGERIAL CODE OF ETHICS

The medical and legal professions have established codes of ethics that provide guidelines and standards for conduct. These "codes" are known to everyone in the profession, but may or may not be practiced to the letter. Managers do not have an established code of ethics but in recent years there have been numerous attempts to develop and promote one. The following list provides an example of such an attempt to formulate a **managerial code of ethics:**

managerial code
of ethics

- I will recognize that management is a call to service with responsibilities to my subordinates, associates, supervisors, employer, community, nation, and world.
- I will be guided in all my activities by truth, accuracy, fair dealings, and good taste.
- I will earn and carefully guard my reputation for good moral character and citizenship.
- I will recognize that, as a leader, my own pattern of work and life will exert more influence on my subordinates than what I say or write.
- I will give the same consideration to the rights and interests of others that I ask for myself.
- I will maintain a broad and balanced outlook and will look for value in the ideas and opinions of others.
- I will regard my role as a manager as an obligation to help subordinates and associates achieve personal and professional fulfillment.
- I will keep informed on the latest developments in the techniques, equipment and processes associated with the practice of management and the industry in which I am employed.

19. Ibid., p. 68.

- I will search for, recommend and initiate methods to increase productivity and efficiency.
- I will respect the professional competence of my colleagues in the ICPM and will work with them to support and promote the goals and programs of the Institute.
- I will support efforts to strengthen professional management through example, education, training, and a lifelong pursuit of excellence.[20]

SUMMARY

In recent years, managers and the corporations they work for have been subjected to increasing criticism and have received low levels of approval from the public. Most people have become well aware via newspaper and television coverage of corporate bribery, illegal political contributions, or price-fixing practices among some of America's largest business organizations. If one reacts only to these headlines, the impression might be that almost all businesspeople engage in illegal and/or unethical conduct. However, this is certainly not the case even though there is some corruption in businesses and in most other forms of organizations. Whatever the situation, managers must recognize and be concerned with the social responsibility and ethical issues confronting them, their organizations and society. But what is socially responsible and ethical behavior?

Although a universally acceptable definition of social responsibility has not been developed, we defined it as the basic obligation of an organization to ensure that its decisions and operations meet the needs and interests of society. While business firms have contributed greatly to the high standards of living enjoyed in the U. S., they are being expected by many people to do more. But, how much responsibility for society's problems should business assume? Those favoring increased corporate social responsibility advance arguments: (1) that it is in the best interest of the firm to pursue socially responsible programs, (2) that they have the resources to do so, (3) that society expects business to be socially responsible, (4) long-run profits for the business may increase, and (5) if business is not responsive to society's needs, the public may press for more government regulation.

There are several arguments against business assuming social responsibility. Dr. Milton Friedman, a leading opponent of business assumption of social responsibility, asserts that there is one and only one social responsibility of business and that is to generate profits so long as it stays within the rules of the game by engaging in open and free competition without deception and fraud. The major arguments against social re-

20. Code of ethics of the Institute of Certified Professional Managers.

sponsibility include these: it misdirects resources and violates sound business making that should concentrate on making profits; costs are excessive relative to benefits and therefore may cause prices to increase; managers do not have the resources or skills to engage in social projects; it concentrates too much power in the hands of business executives; and it may lead to the deterioration of the free enterprise system. What has been the response of business? Many large corporations are engaged in numerous socially responsible programs such as minority employment and training, pollution control, job and product safety programs, energy conservation, quality of life, and the elimination of poverty.

While social responsibility is primarily concerned with the overall operation of the corporation, ethics are contemporary standards or principles of conduct that govern the actions and behavior of individuals within the organization. Ethics provide a basis for determining what is right or wrong. What is ethical or unethical is complicated because societal values and moral concepts tend to change over time. Acceptable practices are established by society and govern the ethical standards for an industry, a business firm, or an individual manager. Laws, government regulations, industry ethical codes, social pressures, and conflicts between the manager's personal standards and the needs of the firm all affect decisions made by managers involving ethical issues.

Review Questions

1. In general, how is American business viewed by the general public? Provide examples. Is the perception accurate? Why or why not?

2. What is meant by social responsibility? Define and describe the relationships a firm has with groups in society.

3. What is the primary role(s) of business in society? Explain. Should the role(s) change? Why?

4. Compare and contrast two opposing views of social responsibility (arguments for and against). Which, in your view, is most correct or appropriate?

5. Can social responsibility be legislated? If so, give examples of laws.

6. What are some examples of current practices of companies engaging in social responsibilities? Be specific. Are there others you are aware of from your own experience or reading?

7. What is meant by the term *ethics*? How ethical are business people and what determines ethical norms for managers?

8. Briefly discuss several examples of unethical practices by business managers. What factors affect managerial ethics?

9. What is Kodak's "SPICE" concept? How does the company use it?

10. What are some examples of ethical dilemmas faced by managers? How can they cope with these dilemmas?

11. Are the ethics of business/managers changing?

Exercises **1.** Visit two local companies that have formal codes of ethics. Compare the codes of ethics with our discussion of ethics in this chapter.

2. Select what you consider to be a local social or environmental problem—such as water or air pollution. Make a list of the groups or businesses within the community who are concerned about the problem. Analyze the impact of the problem on the various segments of the community. Develop a proposal for solving the problem giving consideration to the benefits and costs of your solution.

REFERENCES

Allen, F. T. "Corporate Ethics, A View form the Top." *Industry Week,* April 11, 1977, pp. 52–54.

Attwood, J. A. "ABC's of Responsibility." *Business and Society Review,* Summer 1976, pp. 75–76.

Bluementhal, W. M. "Business Ethics: A Call for a Moral Approach." *Financial Executive,* January 1976, pp. 32–34.

Bowman, J. S. "Managerial Ethics in Business and Government." *Business Horizons,* October 1976, pp. 48–54.

Buchholz, R. A. "Alternative to Social Responsibility." *Michigan State University Business Topics,* Summer 1977, pp. 12–16.

Buehler, V. M. and Y. K. Shetty. "Managerial Response to Social Responsibility Challenge." *Academy of Management Journal,* September 1975, pp. 589–599.

Burgen, C. "How Companies React to the Ethics Crisis." *Business Week,* February 9, 1976, pp. 78–79.

Carroll, A. B., and Beiler, G. W. "Landmarks in the Evolution of the Social Audit. *Academy of Management Journal,"* September 1975, pp. 589–599.

Hills, R. M. "Views On How Corporations Should Behave." *Financial Executive,* November 1976, pp. 32–34.

Holmes, S. L. "Corporate Social Performance: Past, Present, and Areas of Commitment." *Academy of Management Journal,* September 1977, pp. 433–438.

Kramer, O. P. "Ethics Programs Can Help Companies Set Standards of Conduct." *Administrative Management,* January 1977, p. 36.

Lodge, G. C. "Ethics and the New Ideology: Can Business Adjust?" *Management Review,* July 1977, pp. 59–61.

Ostlund, L. E. "Attitudes of Managers Toward Corporate Social Responsibility." *California Management Review,* Summer 1977, pp. 35–49.

Parket, I. R., and Eilbirt, H. "Social Responsibility: The Underlining Factors." *Business Horizons,* August 1975, pp. 5–10.

Simon, W. E. "Great American Challenges: Education and Ethics." *Financial Executive,* April 1977, pp. 143+.

Case Study AN ETHICAL DILEMMA

James Yang is marketing manager for a large heavy equipment manu-facturer. He has a staff of twenty sales representatives who report directly to him. Business has been rather poor lately. Another firm in the industry has developed a product that is slightly lower in price and Mr. Yang's sales force has been having a rather difficult time competing with this new product. James recognizes that production will likely have to be reduced and personnel terminated unless sales improve. This bothers James quite a bit as some of his close friends are employed in the production depart-ment.

One of James' top salesmen is Bobby Trezivant. Bobby has had the reputation for obtaining sales when no one else could. But, James has become extremely concerned of late because of rumors that have come to his attention regarding Bobby. James has heard that Bobby has been giving "kickbacks" to purchasing agents for recommending the com-pany's product. James calls Bobby in to speak with him regarding the kickback rumors and the conversation goes as follows:

> *James:* Bobby, I realize your sales are tops in the firm. We really appre-ciate your efforts. However, a very difficult subject has come to my attention lately. I have heard that you are providing inappropriate payoffs to certain purchasing agents when they helped you out. Is this so?
>
> *Bobby:* You are darn right it is! Our products aren't selling well now. That's the only way to compete with that new, lower-priced product. Some of my best friends are in production. I don't want them to be laid off.
>
> *James:* ?

Questions
1. What should James tell Bobby?
2. Is what Bobby is doing ethical?
3. What controls should be initiated to reduce this practice in the future?

Case Study THE HIRING OF A FRIEND'S DAUGHTER

Marcie Sweeney had recently graduated from college with a degree in general business. Marcie was quite bright although her grades might lead a person to think otherwise. She had thoroughly enjoyed school—dating, tennis, swimming, and similar academic stimulating events. When she graduated from the University she had not found a job. Her dad was extremely upset when he discovered that she did not have a job and he took it on himself to see that Marcie became employed.

Her father, Allen Sweeney, was executive vice-president of a medium-sized manufacturing firm. One of the people he contacted in seeking employment for Marcie was Bill Garbo, the president of another firm in the area. Mr. Sweeney purchased many of his firm's supplies from Garbo's company. On telling Bill his problem, Allen was told to send Marcie to his office for an interview. Marcie did as instructed by her father and was surprised that before she left that day she had a job in the accounting department. Marcie may have been lazy but she certainly was not stupid. She realized that this job was obtained because of the hope of future business from her father's company. Although the work was not challenging it paid better than the other jobs in the accounting department.

It did not take long for the employees in the department to discover the reason she had been hired—Marcie told them. When a difficult job was assigned to Marcie she normally got one of the other employees to do it, inferring that Mr. Garbo would be pleased with them by helping her out. She developed a pattern of coming in late, taking long lunch breaks, and leaving early. When the department manager attempted to reprimand her for these unorthodox activities Marcie would bring up the close relationship that her father had with the president of this firm. The department manager was at his limits when he asked for your help.

Questions

1. From an ethical standpoint, how would you evaluate the merits of Mr. Garbo employing Marcie? Discuss.

2. Now that she is employed how would you suggest that the situation be resolved?

3. Do you feel that a firm should have policies regarding such practices? Discuss.

Appendix A
A Profile of
Chief Executives of
the 500 Largest
U. S. Companies

Although most managers will not attain the level of a president or a chief executive officer of a major corporation, many aspire to such positions. This may be due to the fact that giant corporations have tremendous impact on us as individuals and on society as a whole. Firms such as General Motors, Exxon, Ford, Texaco, General Electric, and other corporations in *Fortune's* 500 survey account for 70 percent of our nation's total Gross National Product and some 25 percent of total employment. For their efforts, the presidents of large corporations often earn a million dollars annually. Despite these facts, very little is known about the executives who manage these large companies. As a student of management, can you identify the chief executives of even five giant corporations? Very few members of the public at large can identify the chairman of the board or presidents of General Motors, Sears, AT&T, Exxon, or almost any other large firm. Yet these chief executives, as managers, exercise considerable power and influence over millions of employees and over the majority of consumers. Who manages today's large corporation, what are their backgrounds—age, education, family—and how much do they earn?

According to a survey made by *Fortune,* the top managers in the largest 500 industrial companies in the U. S. are typically younger, better educated, more apt to come from a middle-class background, and have less predictable political and religious beliefs than previous generations of top-level managers. Another very notable characteristic of chief executives

FIGURE A.1
A Summary Profile of the Chief Executives of the 500 Largest
U. S. Companies

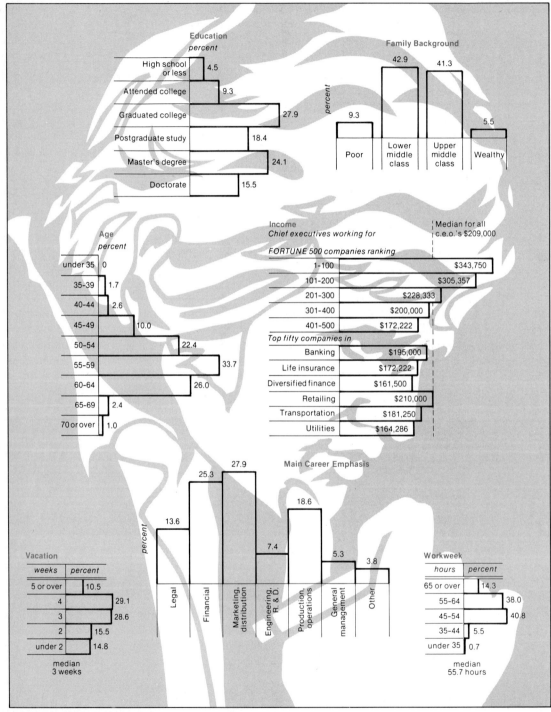

Courtesy of Joe Argenziano for *Fortune* Magazine.

is that they are "professional managers" by training.[1] Over half the chief executives have attended graduate school, with most studying business administration and law. In addition to graduate degrees in business and management, top-level corporate executives have usually been exposed to in-depth managerial training and development programs on their way to upper-level management positions. The career paths to the position of Chairman of the Board or President probably "reflect the shifting priorities and needs of their corporations."[2] A summary profile of the chief executives is illustrated in Figure A.1.

In recent years, the proportion of executives with their primary experience in production, operations, engineering, design and research/development has declined from a third to about 25 percent of all chief executives. There has been a significant trend for the emergence of managers with accounting, finance, or legal backgrounds to become chief executives.

Lawyers and financial managers are the Chief Executive Officers (CEO) of 40 percent of the largest 500 industrial corporations and the trend would appear to continue. The growth in the size and complexity of corporations, their expansion in international business, and increasing government regulations have created an increased need for financial and legal expertise at the top of today's large company. In *Fortune*'s survey, many chief executives said that they would have benefited from additional formal training in business administration, accounting, finance, management, and law. However, the quality of the education, training, and development has significantly benefited today's top-level managers.

1. Charles G. Burck, "A Group Profile of the Fortune 500 Chief Executives," *Fortune,* May 1976, pp. 173–177 and 308–312.
2. Ibid.

Appendix B
Careers in
Management

A person needs to know much more than that he or she desires a career in management. The number and types of managerial positions are many. If a person is to be happy in a chosen career, the best position that meets his or her specific needs must be obtained. This is precisely what this chapter is about—finding the right job that will lead to a career in management.

In order to do this a person should progress through a series of very important steps. This chapter begins by illustrating how to develop an in-depth self-assessment that should provide valuable insight into what a person desires from a career. It is followed by a discussion of how to identify career objectives. Next, the type of careers available in management is presented after which the actual sequence for searching for the right job is discussed. Finally, we present some job realisms. The overall purpose of this chapter is to identify what entry-level management positions are available and how a person can obtain the best match with the firm.

THE SELF-ASSESSMENT[1]

Successful managers come from a wide variety of experiences. Some know immediately that they want to be managers. Others believe that they want to be in management and learn later on that management is not *their cup of tea*. There are individuals who may be extremely successful as a manager in one situation and a dismal failure in another environment.

The number of students who graduate from college without a clear understanding of their career goals is astounding. It is difficult to achieve a goal if you do not know what you want to accomplish. Statements such as "I want to be a manager," or "I want to be in a job where I can work with people," are not sufficient. A person must be willing to go into much

1. The concept of the self-assessment was adapted from the book Personal Selling: Function, Theory and Practice by James R. Young and Robert W. Mondy, The Dryden Press, 1978, pp. 50–56.

greater depth to gain a realistic appreciation of what he or she desires to accomplish in a career.

The *self-assessment* is designed to help a person develop a realistic understanding of himself or herself. Once this has been accomplished, it is likely that an individual will be in a much better position to identify what he or she desires as a career. The following discussion is directed primarily toward the college student who has little or no business experience and is unsure of his or her career goals. Any student may benefit through the use of the self-assessment; it is not restricted to people who are only attempting to pursue a career in management.

Through the self-assessment a person is attempting to gain critical insight into who he or she is and what he or she desires out of life. The self-assessment consists of a strength/weakness balance sheet, a likes/dislikes analysis, talks with business professionals, and the use of the university or college testing services.

STRENGTH/WEAKNESS BALANCE SHEET

Just as no two personalities are exactly alike, each of us has different strengths and weaknesses. A person who is serious about an attempt to gain better insight into his or her career objectives will need to know his or her strengths or weaknesses. It is through the recognition of your strengths that you are encouraged toward a particular career. A knowledge of weaknesses shows a person what cannot be accomplished unless the deficiencies are removed.

A technique developed by one of the authors when he was trying to identify what change in career objectives he should undertake is the *Strength/Weakness Balance Sheet* (SWBS). Many students of management have also found the procedure beneficial in deciding what career objectives to pursue. The procedure involves identifying all of your strengths and weaknesses as *you* perceive them.

The emphasis is placed on *perceived* strengths and weaknesses. If a person believes he or she has a weakness, whether it is a real weakness or not, it may affect a career decision. For instance, if a man thinks he is not liked by many people, it is likely he will make only feeble attempts to gain new friends.

The procedure for preparing a SWBS is simple. A line is drawn down the middle of a sheet of paper; *strengths* are placed on the left side and *weaknesses* are placed on the right side. Then perceived strengths and weaknesses are listed. However, the process is not complete after only one preparation. Several attempts must be made in completing the SWBS. For the majority of people the first attempt most likely will produce many more weaknesses than strengths. It is only after completing the SWBS several times that a perceived weakness may sometimes be seen as a strength. For example, a perceived weakness such as "I cannot stand to merely look busy when there is no work to be done" may also be viewed as a strength if thought of in a different perspective.

The most important consideration in completing the SWBS is that a person must be completely honest. No one else will have access to the SWBS and it should be used strictly as a means of gaining a better understanding of factors that could affect a person's career. Naturally, not all answers will be forthcoming, but the SWBS does provide the beginning for a thorough self-assessment.

LIKES/DISLIKES ANALYSIS

Similar to the SWBS in mechanics, the *likes and dislikes analysis* provides a person with the ability to assess certain situational factors that could have an impact on the successful accomplishment of a job. *Dislikes* should be considered *restrictions* that we place on *ourselves.* For instance, if an individual is unwilling to seek employment outside of a certain region, this item should be listed as a dislike. Likewise, a disdain for a desk job would be placed in the same category. *Likes,* on the other hand, are endeavors that we have discovered to be enjoyable. An example of a likes item would be wanting to work for a large company, a medium-sized company, or a small company. There are advantages and disadvantages associated with any of the choices; which size firm should be placed in the Likes category is a personal preference.

TALK TO PROFESSIONALS

People who have gained success in their jobs are a valuable resource from which to uncover career information. It is likely that you, your parents, or close friends know individuals who would be willing to share career information with you. Most likely these people would be willing to talk to you about the demands of a particular job. However, prior to setting up an interview with such a person, it would be wise to identify some questions you would like answered. To get your mind working, some potential questions are provided below:

1. What type entry-level position would be available to a person with my education and experience?
2. If I didn't start off in a managerial position, typically how long would it take to progress to a first-level managerial position?
3. What type of training does your firm regularly provide management personnel?

4. What is the typical salary range for a person like myself starting with your firm?

5. What would be the typical duties a new employee would be expected to perform?

6. How supportive is your firm when you make a mistake?

7. Whom should I contact if I am interested in a position similar to yours?

8. What's your firm's policy regarding promotion from within?

9. What type of preparation or qualifications does a person need for a career with your firm?

The list could go on and on. The point to be stressed is that you should ask the professionals questions that concern you the most. The benefits are numerous. You are now in a position to discover if a particular job might be interesting or not. The professional is not under the pressure of conducting an interview and will answer questions candidly. Also, if this type of job proves interesting, you have gained valuable information that can be used in future job interviews. Confidence is built up because you can now talk intelligently about the position you are applying for. You are also able to learn the typical salary range for a specific position. This information is important because a recent college graduate can be realistic about salary expectations by not asking for too much or too little.

A final point to remember with regard to speaking with professionals is that they have progressed through the ranks and are proud of their accomplishments. It is surprising how easy it is to obtain an appointment with a person you do not know. The conversation might progress in the following manner:

> *Bobby Halmes:* "Mr. Shudlesworth, I'm Bobby Halmes and I'm currently attending school at the University, majoring in industrial management. I have one more year to go before graduation and I have some unanswered questions that only a professional who is active in the field can answer. I recognize that your time is valuable, but I sure would appreciate your advice and counsel."

Once an affirmative reply is obtained you continue:

> *Bobby Halmes:* "Could we possibly set up a brief appointment to discuss some questions?"

You are now off and running. This approach is used by some professional search firms in the placement of personnel. Since you are not applying for a job, the tension that may be built up in a normal job interview is reduced and the opportunity is available to develop rapport with Mr. Shudlesworth. Once your questions have been answered, a final one such as the following may be appropriate.

> *Bobby Halmes:* "Mr. Shudlesworth, do you know of a company that might have a need for my particular skills?"

If the discussion has progressed satisfactorily, Mr. Shudlesworth might say,

> *Mr. Shudlesworth:* "Why don't you come back and see me when you graduate. One of my employees is retiring next year."

He could also say,

> "Yes, I have several friends whom you might want to speak with."

At the very least you have gained insight into the requirements that are needed to be employed in the firm for which Mr. Shudlesworth works. There is also a potential to develop excellent contacts prior to graduation.

THE UNIVERSITY TESTING CENTER

A resource that often goes unused by most college students is the university testing center. One might say, "Why should I use the testing service? There is nothing wrong with me." Perhaps this myth has been built up because it has been assumed that only people who are really "messed up" should use the university testing service. Nothing could be further from the truth. The unique feature of the testing center is that one can discover many things about himself or herself prior to going for an interview. One can be absolutely honest because only the individual taking the test and his or her counselor will see the results. Since many companies give similar tests to their job applicants, it is likely individuals will discover that they feel much more relaxed when these tests are administered. If a person waits until after graduation to utilize a similar service, it may be quite expensive. Fees up to over $5,000 are sometimes charged for these services.

The purpose of using the testing services is to gain an insight into oneself that may prove beneficial when seeking a job. Some of the topics you may desire to explore in greater detail relate to interests, aptitude, personality, and intelligence. Each will be briefly discussed from the standpoint of how the tests can be beneficial in selecting the best job.

Interest Tests

One would be surprised at the number of college students who do not know what they want to do once they graduate. One of the authors of this book in fact changed majors five times! In the "old days," he did not have the opportunity to use a modern university testing service. *Interest tests* are designed to help a person identify career fields. If the test interpretation supports the person's belief in what is desired in a career, there is a good chance that the situation has been properly assessed. A person is reinforced in the belief that the proper decision has been made. On the other hand, the individual may discover that there are other areas that were not initially recognized. Knowledge of these additional interests can provide a person with the stimulus to evaluate other alternatives.

Aptitude Tests

At times our abilities and our interests do not match up. A person may have an interest in being a brain surgeon but not the aptitude for the career. *Aptitude tests* assist individuals in determining if they have the natural inclination or talent needed for a particular job. These tests are valuable in determining a person's probability for success in a selected job.

Personality Tests

There are jobs for which certain personalities have proven to be more useful. *Personality tests* assist a person in determining if they possess the proper personality for a particular job. Although it is difficult to generalize about which qualities may be beneficial on a particular job, a person should benefit from the interpretation of the test results. Corporations, like individuals, have distinctive personalities. People tend to be attracted to organizations that provide the means for meeting their goals and aspirations. A person may be quite successful in one firm and a failure in another merely because of personality differences.

Intelligence Tests

If a career field requires a certain level of intelligence, it is best to find out if you meet the minimum levels before pursuing this career. Through hard work a person may meet the entry requirements, but what will the results be in the long-run? Instead, a more realistic job, with just as much challenge, may need to be considered. We cannot all be Albert Einsteins! *Intelligence tests* assist in this endeavor.

The testing service should not be expected to provide all the answers. Test results should only be viewed as indicators and should never be thought of as providing the final decision concerning the entry into a profession. However, if the results of the tests suggest an alternate career path would be warranted, it may be beneficial to re-evaluate personal goals. A conference with a respected instructor may provide some assistance. You will do well to remember that we are often *pushed* into careers not of our choosing because of well-intending, but perhaps misinformed, friends.

CAREER OBJECTIVES

Once a thorough self-assessment has been accomplished, a person is in a much better position to develop realistic career objectives. It is at this juncture that a person either enhances or diminishes his or her chances to obtain a position that will lead to a career of his or her choice. Take for instance these two career objectives which were found on resumés of recent college graduates.

I. *Career Objective:* To obtain a position where I can work with people, perhaps in management.

II. *Career Objective:* To obtain an entry-level position in personnel management that provides the opportunities for ultimately progressing into a middle-management position.

The personnel director who showed these career objectives to one of the authors was amazed at how many college seniors are not capable of identifying what they desire in their first job. Two general guidelines are provided:

1. Be as specific as possible in identifying the type of job you would like. This point becomes quite obvious when comparing Career Objective I to Career Objective II. The company needs to know the type of job you are interested in if they are to be capable of evaluating your credentials. The personnel director is also in a position to see whether a person has given serious consideration to the type of job he or she would prefer.

2. In the objective statement provide an indication of your goals during the next five years. Most personnel directors recognize that a person

does not want to stay forever in an entry-level position. But, they also want to know if a prospective employee is realistic in his or her expectations.

Once a person has clearly thought out his or her career objectives, he or she is, for the first time, in a position to evaluate the firms that have the potential for satisfying these goals. It is not a task that is accomplished overnight. Often this is the most agonizing part of the job search, but it is likely one of the most important. But, since a thorough self-assessment has been developed, it should become easier.

ENTRY-LEVEL POSITIONS IN MANAGEMENT

Now that you have decided that you ultimately want to be a manager, the decision must be made as to what avenues are available to accomplish this goal. But, now a problem arises. What type of managerial positions are available? Few first-level managerial positions are available for recent college graduates with minimal work experience. The discussion of possible entry-level positions in management will begin by gaining an appreciation of the risk factor as it applies to determining whether or not a person has an opportunity to secure a particular job. Next, four of the many possible avenues for obtaining entry-level management positions will be discussed. As each type of entry-level position is presented, you should consider the significance of the risk factor.

THE RISK FACTOR

A major factor in determining the type of managerial positions that may be available to recent college graduates relates heavily to the risk factor that a company places on a particular position. *Risk* will be defined as the probability of a particular decision(s) having an adverse effect on the company. A low risk managerial job is one in which if a mistake is made, there is a minimal potential loss for the firm. On the other hand, a high risk managerial job is one in which a mistake by the manager may have a major impact on the organization. The type of managerial positions that are available may be viewed as a continuum that goes from low risk to high risk.

Typically, the lower the risk, the greater the opportunities available for a recent graduate with minimal work experience. A person who desires to enter management after graduation must usually search for these low risk positions. It will do little good to set your sights on a job that is associated with high risk; these positions are likely reserved for individuals who have already proven themselves in lower risk jobs.

The risk continuum might be viewed as a thermometer. The better the impression a person makes on the individual(s) doing the hiring in a firm, the higher the temperature rises. For many management positions you may want, however, there will be no movement on the thermometer. This means that there is no chance for that particular job. But, if an individual has done his or her *homework*, it is likely that the *temperature* will rise at least enough to permit you to get an entry-level position. It may not mean that a person will go immediately into management.

However, the concept of risk as it applies to different firms is often not consistent. There are organizations that rapidly place inexperienced new employees in positions of responsibility. One manufacturing firm may hire recent industrial management graduates and place them immediately into first-level supervisory positions. Another firm that manufactures a similar product may have a policy of placing only experienced individuals into first-line managerial positions. It is necessary for the graduate to study the risk factor as it applies to specific firms.

Risk should also be considered from the standpoint of how much security a person desires from their job. There is a common myth currently circulating among some college seniors that their risk of failure will be less in a major corporation as opposed to a smaller one. They reason that a large firm will take the time to train a person on a job prior to placing them in a position of responsibility. Job security is therefore enhanced. This myth should be dispelled. A firm, no matter what size, is in business to make money. If economic conditions do not warrant keeping an employee, the large firms as well as the small ones must reduce the number of personnel. This fact was vividly illustrated to one of the authors when he began his business career. One of his first jobs was with General Electric in computer sales. G.E. decided to get out of the computer business and terminated a vast number of personnel. His next position was with a "big eight" CPA firm as a systems analyst. The recession of 1969 reduced the staff from fifty consultants to ten within one month. Risk is associated with any position, whether the company is large or small.

ENTRY-LEVEL MANAGEMENT

As was discussed in the section concerning risk, there are instances where a person with limited work experience can progress immediately into management. The risk factor will have to be low but there are entry-level management positions. Many of these positions carry the title of assistant manager. Decisions typically are made under the supervision of a manager with experience. These jobs offer young graduates the opportunity to *get their feet wet* without fear of making that one wrong decision that could be detrimental to a career. Many of these positions are in retail management with titles such as an assistant manager of a department or grocery store.

MANAGEMENT TRAINING PROGRAMS

A smaller number of the entry-level management positions involve a formal *management training program* (MTP). In an MTP, a college graduate is provided formal training for from three months to two years in the job that he or she will ultimately be filling. The trainee is often exposed to both classroom and experiental training so as to get the overall "big picture" of operations within the firm. Along with the formal classroom training an individual may work in production one month, marketing the next, and find themselves in accounting the following month. A person is exposed to the many different aspects of the firm that could affect performance. Once the training program is completed the individual is placed in a managerial position.

A point that should be remembered is that formal management training programs are often quite expensive for a firm. The firm does not receive any benefits from the employee until the training is complete. Thus, it is likely that a highly competitive screening process will be used. The company must feel that the individual will become a productive long-term employee before the employee is permitted to enter the training program. If a MTP is desired, a young graduate must thoroughly convince the company representatives of his or her potential and that the risk factor is not excessive.

PROFESSIONAL TO MANAGEMENT

There are many people who graduate in a technical field such as accounting, computer science, and engineering. Perhaps management was not their initial goal but they later see their future in management. It is likely that a person must first prove ability in the technical aspect of the job before being considered for a managerial position.

There are times when this path to a managerial position can be a delicate transition. A person who has always been associated with the technical aspect of a job has been known to have difficulty in moving into a managerial position. A good engineer or accountant will not always become an effective manager. But, since many firms believe that their first level supervisors must have the technical ability, managers must come from the ranks of technical and professional staff members.

Jerry Wayne Box, currently Manager for the Rocky Mountain District of Sunmark Exploration Company, is a person who has progressed from a technical job to a managerial position. On receiving his M. S. in geology in 1967, Jerry went to work for Sunmark. After being with the firm four years, Jerry was identified as a *high potential* individual, meaning that he had impressed his supervisors as possessing certain managerial qualities. In preparation for moving Jerry into management, he was placed in assignments outside the geology department and moved to other locations in the firm for training. He worked for several months in the human resources department, supervising a task force of three people in developing a management by objectives program. Jerry was then moved to the organization and systems development department where he again directed a task force in reorganizing a geology department. Finally, after approximately eighteen months, Jerry was transferred back into geology as a manager. Sunmark views the additional corporate exposure as vital in the career progression of a manager.

SALES TO MANAGEMENT

An avenue that is being used increasingly by college graduates is to progress to a management position through an entry-level sales job. A person who is in sales is in a position to learn the operations of the entire company. Thus, many college graduates have found that the quickest path to a managerial position is through sales. It is likely this situation has occurred because approximately 50 percent of all entry-level positions open to college graduates are in sales.

There are some firms that make it mandatory to progress through sales before any of their employees can enter management. For instance, one large insurance company has initiated a program to attract bright college graduates into their management ranks. In this program a new employee spends three months at the home office working in various departments and another three months observing in the field. He or she is then required to produce as a salesperson for one year. At this point he or she has the option of going into management or remaining in sales.

The point that should be clearly understood is that a sales position can lead to managerial positions other than in sales management. Many people have been able to go from sales to many other departments such as production. Because salespeople have been dealing with the customer who purchases the product, it is reasoned that they provide valuable input if placed in the production area of the business.

THE SEARCH FOR THE RIGHT INDUSTRY

Many college graduates begin their search for a career by first evaluating the type of job(s) available within particular firm(s). The authors believe that this is not the most advisable starting point. This became clear to one of the authors when he was a college senior interviewing a number of companies through the university placement center. After several interviews, it became somewhat obvious that companies in certain industries had considerably more potential for growth than did firms in other industries. It then began to be evident that a good starting point after a person has identified his or her career and personal goals was to identify the growth industries. Industries that are projected to grow rapidly in the future would be the target for further analysis to identify several of the *best* companies operating within the industry.

Examples of *fast*-growth industries might include: health-care products and services, electronics, energy-related, banking and financial services, various leisure time industries, and various types of service industries. Slow-growth industries might include education, transportation (particularly railroads), and aerospace.

Thus, an individual should follow this recommended procedure:

1. Identify growth industries.
2. Pinpoint or select for further study and analysis the industries that would seem to fit his or her goals, needs or interests.
3. Determine the three or four "leading" firms in the industry—these firms may not be the largest—but they may be growing or predicted to grow at a rapid rate over the next several years.
4. Seek interviews with the companies you select from your analysis as described above. The procedure to be followed will be discussed in the following section entitled "The Search for the Right Company."
5. Finally, be concerned about the specific entry-level position, fully recognizing that if you perform well, you won't be in this position long—probably not more than one–two years.

Naturally, there are excellent opportunities available in some industries that are identified as slow growth. This discussion should not be taken to mean that a person should not apply to firms in the slow-growth industries. The authors merely suggest that considerable thought should be given to the selection of which industry should be pursued.

THE SEARCH FOR THE RIGHT COMPANY

You have now accomplished a thorough self-assessment, developed an appreciation of your career goals, have determined companies in growth industries, and have obtained an overview of the type jobs that are available to begin a career in management. But a person cannot start his or her career until a job offer is obtained (a truism if there has ever been one). Thus, this section will concentrate on the remaining sequence of events that should be accomplished in order to obtain the management position of a person's choice. The importance of preparing a resumé will first be presented. This will be followed by the steps necessary to match yourself with the right company.

THE RESUMÉ

In many instances the first contact that a prospective employee has with the person in charge of hiring is through a resumé. As such, the resumé becomes an extension of an individual's personality. The resumé *sells* in a person's absence. It should be designed to present an individual in the best possible perspective.

The importance of proper attention to resumé preparation was vividly illustrated to one of the authors immediately after receiving his doctoral degree. He had been divorced for seven years and thought nothing of placing *divorced* in the marital status category. However, he discovered that many colleges and universities still remain quite conservative and the placing of *divorced* in a conspicuous place often meant that the resumé was not read. In addition, the author had received three degrees from one university (not extremely acceptable to many employers) and this item was placed directly following career objectives. The author had ten years of business experience with major corporations and had published numerous articles but this fact would not be known unless the entire resumé was read.

It did not take long to realize that a problem existed. The fact that the telephone did not ring and numerous letters of rejection were received contributed to this realization. This prompted a few modifications to be made which presented the qualifications of the author in a different perspective. The ten years of business and consulting experience were highlighted immediately following career objectives. Biographical data was moved to the back of the resumé and *divorced* was changed to *Dependents: one, Alyson Lynn.* The author was amazed at the change in responses. Invitations to visit campuses were received immediately and the author was able to obtain a position of his choice.

The above illustration provides an excellent example of the importance of a clearly thought out resumé. The same intensive evaluation must be made for college seniors preparing themselves to enter the job market. It must be remembered that the resumé must be developed to present *you* in the best possible image. Any deficiencies can be explained during the interview; but, it is difficult to accomplish this task if the opportunity to participate in the interview is not available.

Through experience and through contacts with numerous personnel directors some guidelines have been developed that may prove to be beneficial in the preparation of a resumé. They are as follows:

1. Present your most significant accomplishments and attributes. If it is the truth, it is not bragging.
2. The order of the presentation of items on a resumé is dictated by your strengths. If you have high grades, stress your grades; if you

have a significant amount of work experience, it is possible that this item should receive top priority.

3. Companies are beginning to place additional emphasis upon activities outside the classroom such as membership and offices held in social and business organizations. If you have been particularly active in various campus organizations, it would be wise to highlight these endeavors.

4. The amount of college expenses that you personally paid is also receiving additional attention. A statement such as "Paid 50 percent of college expenses" is often quite helpful.

5. If you are willing to be mobile, this should be stressed. For a company that is located in cities throughout the United States a statement of geographical preference of "None" would likely receive higher attention than one that said "Butte, Montana." Naturally, if geographical preference is truly a restriction, it should be stated as such.

6. A person who has had work experience while in college should stress this fact. A firm recognizes that individuals who are working to finance their way through college will not likely have fancy titles. They are interested in determining how you performed while employed. It is highly satisfying for a recruiter to call one of your past employers and receive statements such as "He is a hard worker," or "She did not constantly watch the clock."

7. A person who has work experience should describe the functions that were performed while working. Merely listing the position titles does not give the recruiter significant insight into what type work was actually performed. Action phrases such as "was responsible for," "coordinated the activities of," and "in charge of" are much more descriptive.

8. If references are to be placed on a resumé, permission should be requested even though the reference is a good friend. A reference can assist you by tailoring his or her comments to meet the requirements of the job that you are seeking.

MATCHING YOURSELF WITH THE RIGHT COMPANY

The next step in searching for the right company is to identify the firms that can afford a person the greatest opportunity to achieve career objectives. However, remember what the old philosopher said, "You can never turn down a job until an offer has been made." Identification of these firms is a task that often proves quite difficult for students seeking their first job. But, it is one that must be done. Here you will be attempting to identify firms that might meet your specific needs.

There are numerous sources from which to obtain the names of the firms which will match your specific needs. A great deal of information can be found in *trade journals* that apply to the particular firm in which you are interested. Also, a large amount of useful data may be found in *Standard and Poors, Fortune, Forbes,* and *The Wall Street Journal.* A person should select only the firms that have the potential for fulfilling specific needs. For instance, if an individual's goal was to be employed by a medium-sized firm headquartered in the Southwest, he would likely not place Coca-Cola on the list (headquartered in Atlanta). Dr. Pepper (head-quartered in Texas) and much smaller might meet the requirements. The authors have found it beneficial to select a maximum of twenty-five companies representing several industries from which to continue the job search.

Once a list of prospective companies has been developed a person is still not in a position to send out a resumé. A certain amount of research remains. Data concerning each company should be obtained so as to send a personal cover letter to each firm. This also includes obtaining the name of a person to be addressed. In the cover letter the reason for wanting a job with this company should be stated. Remember that the *only* reason a firm will consider a person for employment is that they expect the services rendered will make money for the company.

The job search does not stop here. The waiting process begins. This also is quite difficult. But, because a person has done his or her homework it will now be assumed that an invitation has been received to visit a company. Before leaving on a trip additional research, or at least a review of your previous research, may be necessary. Much more information than last year's sales is necessary. In addition, it may be wise to develop a list of questions that you as a perspective employee would like to know about the company. The interview is a two-way street; the interviewee is attempting to determine if this particular company is a good place to work and the firm is evaluating the individual for potential to fit into the organization.

If the interview goes well and you believe that the company has the potential to satisfy your career objectives, it is customary to write a letter expressing your sincere interest. In this letter you should also tell them precisely why you feel qualified to take a position with their company. A comment such as, "The work that a quality control inspector with your firm performs appears extremely interesting and challenging. I am confident that I possess the type personality to be capable of working with the people on the line, my supervisor, and top management." On the other hand, if you discover after your visit that the position is not what you expected, a courteous letter should be written thanking them for their interest, but telling the company representative that you do not believe a proper match exists.

A technique that has been used quite successfully in further enhancing the chances of obtaining the desired position is the follow-up phone call. Approximately one day after the follow-up letter has been received by the company, a phone call should be placed to the person who interviewed you. During this call, you should ask intelligent, searching questions as well as again express interest in the firm. Once the call has been completed you have had the opportunity to visit with the company representatives four times: by resumé, in person, by letter, and by phone.

Once an offer has been tendered, the decision must be made as to whether it should be accepted or rejected. This usually poses no problem unless several offers are received. Hopefully, since your homework has been done, this will be the case. In making a decision as to which job to take, a major point should be remembered. The job with the greatest long-run potential should be selected. As R. H. Scharz, Vice-President of Kaiser Aluminum and Chemical Corporation said, "Try to pick a company you can be comfortable with, including their head office location." This job is not necessarily the one with the highest starting salary. It is often tempting to take the highest salary offer without considering all factors. But, success on the first job after graduation can have a tremendous impact upon an entire career. It should be chosen with care. Congratulations on your successful entry into management!

INITIAL JOB THREATS

A recent college graduate has conquered a major hurdle in his or her life. The world's problems are now going to be solved. But, from a realistic viewpoint certain cautions should be observed. This section is not inserted to frighten or disillusion a person, but it is felt that it is needed so that the first job will be approached from a realistic appreciation of the work environment. Although a job has been secured, there are numerous initial *job threats* that a person should be aware of if long-term success is to be achieved.

THE YOUNG BRAT SYNDROME

All employees of a firm will not always welcome with open arms a new college graduate. Although top management may realize that it is important to bring bright, young, college educated people into the firm, this enthusiasm may not be shared by all. Graduates may find themselves working either with or for people without a college degree. The starting salary of college graduates may be more than that of employees who have been with the firm for a long time. Some may even perceive a new college graduate as a threat. Graduates have found that out of necessity their college degree may need to be *played down*. In time people will discover that you have your degree and will likely respect you more for not bringing it to their attention.

MAKING CHANGES

After graduation, a college graduate's mind is filled with new ideas or approaches that have been learned in the classroom. But, the company may have been successful accomplishing a task in a certain manner for many years. To the graduate it may be obvious that changes need to be made, and it may come as quite a shock when his or her ideas are not immediately accepted. Although a person's first inclination may be to start making changes, it may be best to first establish a good working relationship with members of the department and gradually bring forth new ideas.

POLITICS

The hardest lesson a young person must learn is that hard work and long hours do not guarantee advancement. In school, most likely students were told that salary increases and promotions were a direct result of productivity. In reality, obtaining a promotion or raise may depend on whom one knows and with whom a person plays golf or tennis. While this policy is certainly not advocated, it does at times occur and an individual should be alert to the different power groups at work within the organization.

THE FREE SPIRIT

Just as each of us have different personalities, companies are also different in their attitudes toward what is an acceptable standard of appearance. If a graduate goes to work for a firm in which all of the company's managerial personnel wear suits, conformity will likely be the order of the day. Resistance to this image can only result in difficulties. If a person wants to be this *free spirit* there are firms that totally accept this attitude.

THE BOSS

Some graduates often feel that their superior is not as intellectually enlightened or supportive as they believe a person in that position should be. Assuming that a person desires to maintain that position (a reasonable alternative might be to quit or request a transfer), he or she must realize that the supervisor is still the boss. If an individual desires to progress in that firm, an overt effort must be made to support the activities of the department. Expressing doubt concerning the superior's abilities to other employees can only hurt the chances for advancement. If a person wishes to make changes, they must be accomplished within the system.

Appendix C
Checklist for Going into Business

BEFORE YOU START

How About YOU?

- Are you the kind of person who can get a business started and make it go?
- Think about why you want to own your own business. Do you want badly enough to keep working long hours without knowing how much money you'll end up with?
- Have you worked in a business like the one you want to start?
- Have you worked for someone else as a foreman or manager?
- Have you had any business training in school?
- Have you saved any money?

How About the Money?

- Do you know how much money you will need to get your business started?
- Have you counted up how much money of your own you can put into the business?
- Do you know how much credit you can get from your suppliers—the people you will buy from?
- Do you know where you can borrow the rest of the money you need to start your business?
- Have you figured out what net income per year you expect to get from the business? Count your salary and your profit on the money you put into the business.

- Can you live on less than this so that you can use some of it to help your business grow?
- Have you talked to a banker about your plans?

How About A Partner?

- If you need a partner with money or know-how that you don't have, do you know someone who will fit—someone you can get along with?
- Do you know the good and bad points about going it alone, having a partner, and incorporating your business?
- Have you talked to a lawyer about it?

How About Your Customers?

- Do most businesses in your community seem to be doing well?
- Have you tried to find out whether stores like the one you want to open are doing well in your community and in the rest of the country?
- Do you know what kind of people will want to buy what you plan to sell?
- Do people like that live in the area where you want to open your store?
- Do they need a store like yours?
- If not, have you thought about opening a different kind of store or going to another neighborhood?

GETTING STARTED

Your Building

- Have you found a good building for your store?
- Will you have enough room when your business gets bigger?
- Can you fix the building the way you want it without spending too much money?
- Can people get to it easily from parking spaces, bus stops, or their homes?
- Have you had a lawyer check the lease and zoning?

Equipment and Supplies

- Do you know just what equipment and supplies you need and how much they will cost?
- Can you save some money by buying secondhand equipment?

Your Merchandise

- Have you decided what things you will sell?
- Do you know how much or how many of each you will buy to open your store with?
- Have you found suppliers who will sell you what you need at a good price?
- Have you compared the prices and credit terms of different suppliers?

Your Records

- Have you planned a system of records that will keep track of your income and expenses, what you owe other people, and what other people owe you?
- Have you worked out a way to keep track of your inventory so that you will always have enough on hand for your customers but not more than you can sell?
- Have you figured out how to keep your payroll records and take care of tax reports and payments?
- Do you know what financial statements you should prepare?
- Do you know how to use these financial statements?
- Do you know an accountant who will help you with your records and financial statements?

Your Store and the Law

- Do you know what licenses and permits you need?
- Do you know what business laws you have to obey?
- Do you know a lawyer you can go to for advice and for help with legal papers?

Protecting Your Store

- Have you made plans for protecting your store against thefts of all kinds—shoplifting, robbery, burglary, employee stealing?
- Have you talked with an insurance agent about what kinds of insurance you need?

Buying A Business Someone Else Has Started

- Have you made a list of what you like and don't like about buying a business someone else has started?
- Are you sure you know the real reason why the owner wants to sell his business?
- Have you compared the cost of buying the business with the cost of starting a new business?
- Is the stock up to date and in good condition?
- Is the building in good condition?
- Will the owner of the building transfer the lease to you?
- Have you talked with other businessmen in the area to see what they think of the business?
- Have you talked with the company's suppliers?
- Have you talked with a lawyer about it?

MAKING IT GO

Advertising

- Have you decided how you will advertise? (Newspapers—posters—handbills—radio—by mail?)
- Do you know where to get help with your ads?
- Have you watched what other stores do to get people to buy?

The Prices You Charge

- Do you know how to figure what you should charge for each item you sell?
- Do you know what other stores like yours charge?

Buying

- Do you have a plan for finding out what your customers want?
- Will your plan for keeping track of your inventory tell you when it is time to order more and how much to order?
- Do you plan to buy most of your stock from a few suppliers rather than a little from many, so that those you buy from will want to help you succeed?

Selling

- Have you decided whether you will have salesclerks or self-service?
- Do you know how to get customers to buy?
- Have you thought about why you like to buy from some salesmen while others turn you off?

Your Employees

- If you need to hire someone to help you, do you know where to look?
- Do you know what kind of person you need?
- Do you know how much to pay?
- Do you have a plan for training your employees?

Credit for Your Customers

- Have you decided whether to let your customers buy on credit?
- Do you know the good and bad points about joining a credit-card plan?
- Can you tell a deadbeat from a good credit customer?

A FEW EXTRA QUESTIONS

- Have you figured out whether you could make more money working for someone else?
- Does your family go along with your plan to start a business of your own?
- Do you know where to find out about new ideas and new products?

- Do you have a work plan for yourself and your employees?
- Have you gone to the nearest Small Business Administration office for help with your plans?

If you have answered all these questions carefully, you've done some hard work and serious thinking. That's good. But you have probably found some things you still need to know more about or do something about.

Do all you can for yourself, but don't hesitate to ask for help from people who can tell you what you need to know. Remember, running a business takes guts! You've got to be able to decide what you need and then go after it.

Good luck!

Source SMA 71, Small Marketers Aids, U. S. Small Business Administration, September 1977 Revision.

Glossary

ABC method: An inventory technique in which inventory is classified into groups according to cost.

Accountability: Final responsibility for results that a manager cannot delegate to someone else.

Action planning: Establishment of performance objectives and standards for individuals. Requires that challenging, but attainable standards be developed for the purpose of improving individual or group performance.

Activity: In PERT it is the time-consuming element of a network.

Adult: The ego state of Transactional Analysis that identifies the person who tends to evaluate the situation and attempts to make decisions based on information and facts.

Analytical skill: The ability of the manager to use logical and scientific approaches or techniques in the analysis of problems and business opportunities.

Arbitration: Calls for outside neutral parties to enter the situation to assist in resolving the conflict. The arbitrator is given the authority to act as a judge in making a decision.

Aptitude tests: Determine a person's probability for success in a selected job.

Attribute sampling: Sampling plan in which there are no degrees of conformity to consider. The product is either good or bad.

Authority: The right to decide, to direct others to take action, or to perform certain duties in achieving organizational goals.

Awareness of changing social demands: Management's awareness of such concerns as the efficient utilization of resources, reducing environmental pollution, employing and developing disadvantaged minorities and females, providing safe products, and a safe working environment.

Bankruptcy: The financial failure of a firm.

Barriers to communication: Factors that can reduce the communication effectiveness between the sender and the receiver.

Behavior: Goal-oriented actions of individuals.

Behavior modification: Shaping, changing, or controlling behavior by reinforcing or rewarding desired behavior.

Behavioral theories of leadership: Leadership theories that focus attention on the actual behavior and actions of leaders.

Body language: Unintentional signals that are transmitted, such as a frown, a smile, or a blank stare.

Breakeven analysis: Approach used to determine the amount of a particular product that must be sold if the firm is to generate enough revenue to cover costs. The point at which revenues and costs are equal.

Budget: Formal statement of financial resources—planned expenditures of money for personnel, time, space, or equipment.

Budgetary standard: Concerned with the comparison of actual to planned expenditures.

Capital: Money used to finance business operations. Primary sources of capital are from owners or creditors or funds generated internally within the business.

Capital budget: Indicates planned capital acquisition usually for the purpose of purchasing additional facilities or equipment.

Career objectives: A determination of the specific type of career that an individual desires to pursue.

Carrying costs: Expenses that would be associated with maintaining the product in inventory before it is sold or used.

Cash budget: Summarizes planned cash receipts and disbursements.

Centralization: The type of situation in which decision-making authority is concentrated at the upper levels of the organization.

Chain of command: Means by which authority flows from top to bottom in the organization.

Change sequence: The sequence of events that is needed to bring about change in an organization.

Child: The ego state of Transactional Analysis that identifies the person who bases decisions primarily on personal satisfaction.

Coercive power: The leader's ability to administer and control punishments (such as the power to fire, demote, or reprimand) to others for not following the leader's requests.

Cohesiveness: The degree of attraction that the group has for each of its members.

Comparison controls: These are used to determine whether deviations from plans have taken place, and, if necessary, to bring them to the attention of the responsible managers.

Communication: The achievement of meaning and understanding between people through verbal and nonverbal means in order to affect behavior and achieve desired end results.

Communication overload: State that exists when the sender attempts to present too much information to the receiver at one time.

Communication skill: The ability to provide information orally and in written form to others in the organization for the purpose of achieving desired results.

Conceptual skill: Ability of the manager to understand the complexities of the overall organization and how each department or unit fits into the organization.

Conflict management: A facilitator to communication. Has the ability to resolve disagreements between individuals within the organization that could have an adverse effect on attainment of organizational goals.

Consideration: The extent to which leaders have relationships with subordinates characterized by mutual trust, respect, and consideration of employees' ideas and feelings.

Contact chart: Identifies the connections that an individual has with other members of the organization.

Control: The process of comparing actual performance with established standards for the purpose of taking action to correct deviations.

Control charts: Procedure which measures the process against actual performance during operations.

Control process: Involves establishment of standards, comparison of performance to standard, and taking corrective action.

Critical path: In PERT and CPM it is the longest path from start to finish of a project.

Critical Path Method: A network technique developed by industry. Only one time estimate is used thereby making the network a deterministic model.

Cultural differences: Can cause breakdowns in communication as a result of differences in culture and/or countries.

Cyclical: Variations in demand that fluctuate around the long-run trend line. A cycle typically consists of two to three years in duration.

Decentralization: The type of situation in which decision-making authority has been delegated to lower levels in the organization.

Decision maker: The person who has the responsibility for choosing the course of action that will solve the problem within the area for which he or she is accountable.

Decision making: The process by which we evaluate alternatives and make a choice among them.

Decision-making ability: The manager's skill in selecting a course of action designed to solve a specific problem or set of problems.

Delegation: The process of assigning responsibility and the granting of authority to personnel to accomplish work.

Demand forecasting: An attempt to estimate the demand for a firm's products.

Departmentation: Involves the grouping of related functions or major work activities into manageable units to achieve more effective and efficient overall coordination of organization resources.

Developed countries: Country with modern industry, technology, and supporting services—and a fairly high standard of living.

Directing: Motivating and leading personnel.

Discounted cash flow: A procedure of analyzing economic alternatives which takes into consideration the time value of money.

Dissatisfiers: According to Frederick Herzberg, the factors also known as "hygiene" factors include such items as pay, status, working conditions, etc. Also referred to as hygiene factors.

Economic function: Businesses' production of needed goods and services, provision of employment, contribution to economic growth, and earning of profit.

Economic objectives: Goals of the firm that are associated with survival, profit, and growth.

Empathy: The ability to identify with the various feelings and thoughts of another person.

Employment application: Form that collects objective, biographical information about an applicant, such as education, work experience, special skills, general background, marital status, references, etc.

Entrepreneur: The owner and/or founder of a business.

Environmental responsibility: Concern of the business firm for the maintenance of clean air and water and the aesthetic beauty of the physical environment.

Equity: Involves an individual comparing his or her performance and the rewards received with the performance and rewards others receive for doing similar work.

Ethical dilemmas: Situations that confront managers that are often difficult to resolve or avoid.

Ethical responsibility: Concern for personal and corporate integrity and honesty.

Ethics: Contemporary standards or principles of conduct that govern the actions and behavior of individuals within the organization.

Event: In PERT it is a meaningful specified accomplishment (physical or intellectual) in the program plan, recognizable at a particular instance of time.

Expatriate: A person who is out of his or her native country.

Expectancy: An individual's perception of the chances or probability that a particular outcome will occur as a result of certain behavior.

Expected time: In PERT it is calculated by using a formula consisting of three time estimates—optimistic, most likely, and pessimistic.

Expert power: Based on the special knowledge, expertise, skill, or experience possessed by the leader.

Exponential smoothing: Technique using the forecast from the previous period, the actual demand that resulted from this forecasted period, and a smoothing constant.

External environment: Anything outside the organization (legal, sociological, political, and economic) that can affect the firm.

Fiedler's contingency model: Suggests that there is no one most effective style that is appropriate to every situation.

Filtering: Attempts to alter and color information to present a more favorable image.

Financial assistance: Refers to programs offered by the Small Business Administration designed to provide aid for small businesses that need money and cannot borrow it on reasonable terms from conventional lenders.

Financial budget: Indicate the amount of capital the organization will need and where it will obtain the capital.

Fixed costs: Costs that do not change with the level of output.

Flow process chart: A production method using symbols to depict the flow of a job.

Forecasting: An attempt to project what will occur in the future.

Formal power: Derived from authority or legitimate position in the firm.

Friedman's view of social responsibility: There is one and only one social responsibility of business—to earn maximum profits so long as it stays within the rules of the game.

Functional authority: Direct-line authority over specialized functions or activities.

Functional organizations: Structure in which specialists are given authority to issue orders in their own names in designated areas of the work.

Functions: Work that can be identified and distinguished from other work—such as production, marketing, and finance.

Godfather system: A program in which an experienced executive is assigned to assist a manager in his or her development when on an international assignment.

Group: Two or more people who join together to accomplish a desired goal.

Hersey/Blanchard's situational leadership theory: Theory based on the notion that the most effective leadership style varies according to the level of maturity of the followers and the demands of the situation.

Hierarchy of needs: Maslow's theory that human needs such as psychological, safety, social, esteem, and self-actualization are arranged in a hierarchy.

Host country: Place where the multinational company is operating.

Host country nationals: Personnel from the host country.

Human resources: All personnel, both managerial and operating who perform work of the organization.

Human resources system: A comprehensive approach to recruiting, selecting, evaluating, training, and compensating personnel.

Human skill: The ability of a manager to understand, work with, and get along with other people.

Human social responsibility: A firm's concern for people.

Hygiene factors: See definition for dissatisfier.

Hypothesis: A tentative statement of the nature of the relationships that exist.

Inappropriate controls: Controls that do not conform to the need of the situation.

Informal relationships: Relationships that are created, not by officially designated managers, but by any and all organizational members.

informal work group: A group of people who join together to accomplish mutually satisfying goals.

Initial controls: Attempt to monitor the resources—material, human, and capital—that come into the organization for the purpose of ensuring that they can be used effectively to achieve organizational objectives.

Initiating structure: The extent to which the leader establishes goals and defines and structures their roles and the roles of subordinates toward the attainment of the goals.

Innovative objectives: Concerned with unique or special accomplishments, such as the development of new methods or procedures.

Inputs: Human (employees to run the plant) or nonhuman (fuel for the factory) energies, supplies, and information. Processed within the organization to create desired outputs.

Interactions: The interpersonal contacts and relations that one has with others.

Interest tests: Assists a person in identifying career fields.

Interview: Method of assessing the qualifications of job applicants.

Intuition: Acquired through experience and accomplishment rather than through a formal decision making process.

Inventory control: A quantitative approach that assists in determining the optimum amount of inventory to maintain.

Iron law of responsibility: States that if business firms are to retain their social power and role, they must be responsive to society's needs.

Job analysis: Process of determining the responsibilities and operations of a job leading to the development of a job description.

Job description: Summarizes the purpose, principal duties, and responsibilities of a job.

Job enlargement: Provides a horizontal expansion of duties. An approach that involves an increase in the number of tasks employees are required to perform.

Job enrichment: Increasing the level of autonomy, skill, variety, task significance, and feedback that leads to better job performance and more satisfied employees. Provides a vertical expansion of responsibility and authority.

Job specification: Statement of the minimum acceptable human qualities necessary to perform the job.

Job threats: Encounters that a new employee should be aware of when entering the job market for the first time.

Leader-member relations: The degree to which the leader feels accepted by the subordinates.

Leadership: The process of influencing the behavior and actions of others toward the accomplishment of goals.

Leadership continuum: As developed by Tannenbaum and Schmidt, suggests that choosing an effective leadership style depends on the demands of the situation. The continuum ranges from boss-centered, autocratic management to subordinate-centered, participative management.

Less developed countries: A country lacking modern industry and the supporting services.

Likert's system of management: Universal theory of leadership consisting of a continuum of styles ranging from autocratic to participative.

Likes/dislikes analysis: Provides a person with the ability to assess certain situational factors that could have an impact on successful accomplishment of a job.

Line and staff organization: Type of structure that makes provision for the use of staff specialists who provide advice to line managers.

Line organization: Structure that shows the direct, vertical relationships between different levels within the firm.

Linear programming: Method used in attempting to allocate limited resources among competing demands in an optimum way.

Listening: One of the most effective tools to facilitate communication. Entails actively participating in hearing what type communication the sender is attempting to transmit.

Lower-level managers: Usually referred to as supervisors or foremen. Responsible for managing employees in the performance of the daily operations.

Make/buy decisions: Process through which a manager evaluates the benefits of making a product in-house or going outside to another manufacturer.

Management: The process of planning, organizing, directing, and controlling to accomplish organizational goals through the coordinated use of human and material resources.

Management assistance: Service provided by the Small Business Administration that offers counseling and management training in an attempt to prevent business failures.

Management by objectives: A systematic and organized approach that allows management to attain maximum results from available resources by focusing on achievable goals.

Management development programs: Technique used to assure that managers are capable of learning more effective approaches to management.

Management information system: A means that facilitates managers in obtaining timely, accurate, and useful information.

Management training program: Through this program, a college graduate is provided formal training regarding the job that he or she will ultimately be filling for from three months to two years.

Managerial code of ethics: Provides guidelines and standards for conduct of managers.

Managerial grid: Leadership theory developed by Blake and Mouton that depicts five primary styles of leadership described according to the leader's concern for people and production.

Manpower planning: Assures that the organization will have the right numbers and kinds of people available when and where they are needed to perform useful work.

Mathematical models: An equation or set of equations that defines and represents the relationship among elements of a system.

Mediation: Calls for outside neutral parties to enter the situation to assist in resolving the conflict. Suggestions and recommendations are given in the hope that the two parties in conflict will reach a solution.

Middle managers: Concerned primarily with the coordination of programs and activities which are necessary to achieve the overall goals of the organization as identified by top management.

Model: An abstraction of a real-world situation.

Most likely time: In PERT, it is the most realistic completion time for the activity.

Motivation: The process of influencing or stimulating a person to take action that will accomplish a desired goal.

Motivators: According to Frederick Herzberg, these factors make up a continuum leading from no job satisfaction to satisfaction. They consist of factors intrinsic to the job, such as recognition, responsibility, achievement, and opportunities for growth and advancement.

Motives: Explain why people engage in certain behavior. They are the drives or impulses within an individual that cause behavior.

Moving averages: Technique for smoothing the effects of random variation.

Multinational company: A firm engaged in business in two or more countries.

Multinational management: Individuals that manage companies engaged in international operations.

Need for achievement: According to David McClelland, the need for achievement is concerned with an individual's desire for excellence.

Need for affiliation: According to David McClelland, this need is concerned with the desire for affection and establishing friendly relationships.

Need for power: According to David McClelland, this need is concerned with an individual's desire for influence and control over others.

Nepotism: The practice of hiring one's own relatives.

Network: An approach through which the various interdependencies of a project may be studied.

Nonroutine decisions: Those decisions that are designed to deal with unique problems or situations.

Norms: Standard of behavior that is expected from group members.

Objectives: Describes the end result that a firm desires to accomplish.

Ohio state leadership studies: Indepth studies of the behavior of leaders in a wide variety of organizations.

Operating budget: Indicates the revenues and expenses the business expects from producing goods and services during a given year.

Operating planning: Plans that specify specific means by which a goal is to be accomplished. Primarily accomplished lower in the managerial hierarchy.

Operations chart: Used to analyze the movement of the right and left hand in a production operation.

Optimistic time: In PERT, it is the time that if everything goes right and nothing goes wrong, the project can be completed in this amount of time.

Ordering costs: Relate to the expenses associated with preparing an inventory order.

Organization: Two or more people working together in a coordinated manner to achieve group results.

Organization development: A planned and calculated attempt to move the organization as a unit from one state to another, typically to a more behavioral environment.

Organization structure: Framework for providing a pattern for organizing the formal relationships of responsibility, authority, and accountability.

Organizational climate: The psychological environment of the firm.

Organizing: Allocation of resources and establishment of the means to accomplish plans.

Outputs: The products and/or services that are the end result of the conversion process.

Overseeing controls: Monitor the actual creation of products or services. Accomplished largely by observation and by conference between supervisor and subordinate while the actual work activities are being performed.

Parent: The ego state in Transactional Analysis that identifies the person who bases decisions primarily on what the individual has heard or learned in the past.

Parent country: Home base or headquarters for multinational firms.

Parent country nationals: Personnel from the parent country.

Participative climate: An open type of climate characterized by trust in subordinates, openness in communication, considerate and supportive leadership, group problem solving, worker autonomy, information sharing and establishment of high output goals.

Patterned interview: Method of interviewing in which the interviewer follows a predetermined series of questions in interviewing applicants.

Perception sets: Differences in individuals' background and experience which may result in different meanings and interpretations being associated with various words or phrases.

Performance results standards: Standards used when it is relatively simple to specify what end results are desired.

Personal development objectives: Provide the opportunity for each individual to state their personal goals and action plans for self-improvement and personal growth and development.

Personal objectives: Goals of individuals who are employed by the firm. Hopefully, the goals of the employees and the firm will be relatively close.

Personality tests: Assist in determining if a person possesses the proper personality for a particular job.

Pessimistic time: In PERT it is the time that if everything goes wrong and nothing goes right, the project will be completed in this amount of time.

Physical models: Models that look like the system they represent.

Physical resources: Materials, equipment, and money required to accomplish the objectives of the organization.

Planning: The determination of what is to be achieved in the accomplishment of objectives.

Planning-programming budgeting system: Aids management in identifying and eliminating costly programs that were duplicates of other programs

and to provide a means for the careful analysis of the benefits and costs of each program or activity.

Policies: A predetermined, general course or guide established to provide direction in decision making.

Politics: A network of interaction by which power is acquired, transferred, and exercised when dealing with others.

Position number of the leader: The degree of influence over rewards and punishments as well as by his or her official authority.

Power: The ability of one person to influence the behavior of another person.

Preliminary screening interview: Used to eliminate the obviously unqualified applicants for reasons such as excessive salary requirements, inadequate education, inability to speak coherently, lack of job-related experience or other reasons.

Problem solving objectives: Are goals that are established to deal with special projects or situations that need management attention.

Procedures: A series of steps or functions established for the accomplishment of some specific project or endeavor.

Process layout: A type of plant layout in which pieces of equipment that perform virtually the same function are grouped together.

Process standards: Standards used when attempting to evaluate a function for which specific standards are difficult or impossible to formulate.

Procurement assistance: Program sponsored by the Small Business Administration designed to provide assistance and counseling to small businesses on how to obtain government contracts.

Product layout: A type of plant layout in which equipment is sequenced to permit a product to go from start to finish through the use of automated equipment and assembly lines.

Professional decision maker: A person who uses the best features of both the intuitive and research approach in the decision-making process.

Professional decisions: Encompass the best features of both the intuitive and research approach to decision making.

Program Evaluation and Review Technique (PERT): A network technique developed by the Navy that is used to think through a project in its entirety. Three time estimates are used which permits the user to develop probabilities of occurrences.

Project organization: Temporary organization structure designed to achieve specific results by using a team of specialists from different functional areas within the organization.

Purchase/lease decisions: Process through which a manager decides whether to purchase the product outright or lease the use of the product.

Quality control: Measures the degree of conformity according to form, dimension, composition, and color.

Quantity control: Established standard in terms of volume or numbers.

Queuing theory: A quantitative technique that involves determining the optimum number of stations or queues to operate. It is a balancing approach. Also referred to as Waiting Line Theory.

Random: No pattern. Occurs for reasons that the manager cannot anticipate.

Reactive planning: Flexibility of the planner to be able to respond to changing external and internal conditions.

Receiver: Interprets the signals from the sender through means such as listening, observing, and reading.

Recruitment: Process of searching for prospective employees and stimulating them to apply for available jobs.

Reddin's leadership theory: Theory that suggests four basic styles of leadership that can be effective depending on the situation.

Referent power: Based on the leader's possession of personal characteristics that make him or her "attractive" to other people.

Regression analysis: A quantitative technique that is used to predict one item through knowledge of other variables.

Reinforcers: Rewards used in organizational behavior modification.

Relationship behavior: Consideration of people, level of socio-emotional support.

Reliability: Concerned with the degree of consistency of test results.

Resources: Manpower, machines, material, and capital necessary to produce outputs.

Responsibility: An obligation of personnel to perform certain work activities.

Resumé: A written description that a job applicant provides to a prospective employer with information such as career objectives, education, work experience, and other type biographical data.

Reward power: Based on the leader's ability to administer and control rewards (such as pay, promotions, and praise) to others for complying with the leader's directions.

Risk: The probability of a particular decision having an adverse effect on the company.

Role: The total pattern of expected behavior, interactions, and sentiments of an individual.

Routine decisions: Daily decisions made by managers that are governed by policies, procedures, and rules of the organization, as well as the personal habits of the manager.

Routine objectives: Represent recurring day-to-day activities that are expected to be performed. They represent standards of performance.

Rule: A very specific and detailed guide to action that is set up to direct or restrict action in a fairly narrow manner.

Satisfiers: Another name for motivators. (See motivators)

Schematic models: Line drawings, flow charts, graphs, maps, organization charts, and similar items that represent the major features of a particular system.

Scientific approach: Based on a systematic formal approach to decision making.

Seasonal: Evaluates demand patterns in a shorter time frame than cyclical. Forecasted period is typically twelve months.

Self-assessment: Assists a person in developing a realistic understanding of themselves. The individual attempts to gain critical insight into who they are and what they desire out of life.

Self-fulfilling prophecy: What one expects to happen actually occurs. A manager's expectations often determine employee performance.

Semantics: Breakdowns in communication resulting from language barriers and different meanings being applied to the same word.

Sender: The person who transmits the message to the receiver.

Sensitivity training: Technique used to develop awareness of sensitivity to oneself and others.

Sentiments: The emotional reactions that we have to other people, the organization, and the physical factors.

Service objectives: The reason that a firm is in business as viewed by society.

Short-circuiting: An attempt by one person to reduce effective communication by another individual.

Signal: Medium by which the message is transmitted from sender to receiver.

Simulation: Process of representing a real life situation through mathematical logic in an attempt to predict what will occur in an actual situation.

Single accountability: Each person should be answerable to only one immediate supervisor—one boss to each employee.

Situational approach: The ability to adapt to meet particular circumstances and constraints that a firm may encounter.

Situational theories of leadership: An approach to the study of leadership that suggests that there is *no one* most effective style of leadership that is appropriate to small situations.

Small business: A business that is independently owned and operated and that is not dominant in its field.

Small business administration (SBA): An agency empowered to set more specific criteria for defining a small business in conjunction with the number of employees and the dollar volume of business.

Small business institute (SBI): Program using senior and graduate students of leading business schools throughout the country to provide on-site management counseling to small businesses.

Social audit: A commitment to systematic assessment of and reporting on some meaningful, definable domain of a company's activities that have social impact.

Social responsibility: Basic obligation of an organization to ensure that its decisions and operations meet the needs and interests of society.

Span of control: The number of employees a manager can effectively supervise.

Specialization of labor: Division of functions into smaller work activities.

Standard: Basic guidelines of performance desired.

Standing plans: Guidelines to assist in the implementation of plans.

State of doubt: The probability that a particular state of nature will occur.

Statistical quality control: Technique that allows for a portion of the total number of items to be inspected.

Status: A person's rank or position in a group.

Status symbol: A visible, external sign of one's social position.

Stopwatch method: Method using a stopwatch to estimate the time it will take to complete a task.

Strategic control points: Critical areas that must be monitored if accomplishment of the organization's major objectives are to be achieved.

Strategic planning: The determination of how the organizational objectives will be achieved. Primarily accomplished by top-level management.

Strength/weakness balance sheet: Technique to identify what change in career objectives should be undertaken. Involves identifying all strengths and weaknesses.

Synergistic effect: Sum of the parts is greater than the whole ($2 + 2 > 4$ idea)

System: An arrangement of interrelated parts designed to achieve objectives.

Systems approach: Approach through which the functions of management are interrelated to achieve the goals of the organization.

Task behavior: Behavior of the manager designed to provide direction and emphasis on getting the job done.

Task-relevant maturity: Defined in terms of the follower's desire for achievement, level of education, and skills, and his or her willingness and ability to accept responsibility.

Team development: Approach in which a type of sensitivity session is conducted for the members of an operating unit, away from the job site.

Team objectives: Established in group meetings to provide overall direction and coordination of action of a group or division.

Technical skill: Ability to use specific knowledge, methods, or techniques in performing work.

Technology: All the skills, knowledge, methods, and equipment required to convert resources into desired products and/or services.

Testing: Process of screening job applicants in terms of skills, abilities, aptitudes, interest, personality, and attitudes.

Theory X: Traditional philosophy of human nature. Suggests that motivation of employees requires managers to coerce, control, or threaten employees in order to achieve maximum results.

Theory Y: A theory of human nature that provides an alternative to Theory X. Theory Y suggests that people are capable of being responsible and mature.

Third country nationals: Personnel from countries other than the parent of host countries.

Time series analysis: Mathematical approach in which the independent variable is expressed in units of time.

Time standard: Monitor the time required to complete the project.

Timing: Selecting the most appropriate time to transmit a message.

Top management: Referred to by such titles as president, chief executive officer, vice-president or executive director. Responsible for providing the overall direction of the firm.

Trade journals: Publications that are written primarily for individuals who are associated with a particular type industry or business.

Trait approach: Study of leadership that focuses on leader's physical, intellectual, and personal characteristics.

Transactional Analysis (TA): A method that assists individuals in understanding both themselves and the people with whom they must work daily. TA consists of three ego states that are constantly present and at work within each individual—the Parent, the Adult, and the Child.

Trend: Projects the long run estimate of the demand for the product being evaluated.

Unethical practices: Practices that, although legal, are questionable in terms of ethical standards, honesty, or personal integrity.

Upward channels: Means through which information is transmitted upwardly through the organization.

Valence: How much value an individual places on a specific goal or result he or she is seeking.

Validity: Concerned with the relationship between the score on the test and performance on the job. Questions whether the test measures what it was intended to measure.

Variable costs: Costs that are directly related to changes in output.

Variable sampling: A sampling plan developed to determine how closely an item conforms to an established standard. Degrees of goodness and badness are permitted.

Voluntary social action: Achieving the economic goals of the firm within the limits of society.

Waiting line theory: See Queuing Theory.

Work sampling: Method in which workers are observed at random times to determine the proportion of time being spent on different tasks.

Work simplification: Organizes jobs into small, highly specialized components.

Worker machine charts: Used to determine if there is excessive idle time associated with either the worker or the machine.

Workforce analysis: Process of identifying the skills of current personnel to determine if workloads can be accomplished by these employees.

Workload analysis: Process of estimating the type and volume of work that needs to be performed if the organization is to achieve its objectives.

Zero base budgeting: Requires management to take a fresh look at all programs and activities each year rather than merely building on last year's budget.

Index

657